AF361562

READING ARISTOTLE WITH

THOMAS AQUINAS

READING ARISTOTLE WITH THOMAS AQUINAS

His Commentaries on Aristotle's Major Works

Leo J. Elders

Edited by Jörgen Vijgen

THE CATHOLIC UNIVERSITY OF AMERICA PRESS

Washington, D.C.

Originally published as *Aristote et Thomas d'Aquin:*
Les commentaires sur les oeuvres majeures d'Aristote
© Les Presses universitaires de l'IPC, 2018
English translation copyright © 2023

The Catholic University of America Press
All rights reserved
The paper used in this publication meets the minimum requirements
of American National Standards for Information Science—Permanence
of Paper for Printed Library Materials, ANSI Z39.48-1984.
∞

Cataloging-in-Publication Data is available
from the Library of Congress
ISBN 978-0-8132-3579-0

CONTENTS

Editor's Preface — vii
Author's Preface — ix
Abbreviations — xi

Introduction — 1

1. The Commentary on the *Peri hermeneias* — 14

2. The Commentary on the *Posterior Analytics* — 59

3. The Commentary on the *Physics* — 85

4. The Commentary on the *De caelo* — 152

5. The Commentary on the *De generatione et corruptione* — 191

6. The Commentary on the *Meteorologica* — 205

7. The Commentary on the *De anima* — 233

8. The Commentary on the *De sensu et sensato* — 279

9. The Commentary on the *De memoria et reminiscentia* — 302

10. The Commentary on the *Metaphysics* — 311

11. The Commentary on the *Nicomachean Ethics* — 401

12. The Commentary on the *Politics* — 473

Select Bibliography — 511
Index Nominum — 527
Index Rerum — 533

EDITOR'S PREFACE

As visiting professor at the Center for Thomistic Studies at the University of St. Thomas in Houston, Texas in the 1980s, Leo Elders, S.V.D. (1926–2019), gave a series of graduate courses on some of Thomas Aquinas's commentaries on Aristotle. At least since that time (but probably earlier), he envisaged a book-length monograph on all of these commentaries with the goal of evaluating, by way of a close reading of the text, Aquinas's reception of these foundational texts. His many teaching, lecturing, and writing assignments in subsequent years did not allow him to undertake this task, although he would occasionally return to the project in smaller articles. A crucial factor assisting in the completion of the project was the invitation by the then-director of the *Revue Thomiste*, Father Marie-Vincent Leroy, O.P. (1917–94), to write an annual review essay of publications on Aristotle and the Aristotelian tradition. These review essays, published as *Bulletin aristotélicien* in 1984–2001, allowed him to acquaint himself with the latest research in this area. In doing so, he continued his earliest research which had resulted in three monographs on Aristotle published in the 1960s and 1970s.

During the last years of his life, freed from many of these obligations after his retirement in 2016, he was able to devote his time almost entirely to what he regarded as his *magnum opus*. While originally written in English, a French translation appeared already in 2018 as *Aristote et Thomas d'Aquin* (Paris: Les Presses universitaires de l'IPC). The review process of the English manuscript brought to light a number of interesting suggestions, both formal and material. Although these suggestions did not touch on the essence of the arguments put forward, by the summer of 2019 it became evident that Fr. Elders was no longer in a position to undertake these revisions all by himself, given also that he was working on what would be his final book on Dionysius and Aquinas. As I had been assisting him in various ways in preparing and editing his publications for the last twenty years, he asked me to see to it that the English manuscript would turn into a book, trusting that any revision would stay true to the initial text. We were, however, able to go through many of these revisions in the course of the final weeks of his life.

A brief word about the method and structure of the book will be helpful. Between 1969 and 1989 seven of the twelve works of Aristotle upon which Thomas commented appeared in a critical edition published by the Leonine Commission. For the remaining five works, which include among others the *Metaphysics* and the *Physics*, the so-called Marietti edition remains the standard edition. The Leonine edition, which is also more difficult to access than the standard Marietti edition, divides Thomas's commentary into much larger sections than does the Marietti edition, so that the historical-critical advantages have to be weighed against the pedagogically useful numbering of the Marietti editions. While using the best editions available, Fr. Elders has chosen to consistently use the Marietti numbers throughout his text.

Each chapter has an identical threefold structure. In the introduction the content of Aristotle's work under review is discussed, including its reception up until Aquinas, indicating the Latin translations and main sources of the commentary. The second and largest section contains a review of Aquinas's reading of the work. Each chapter ends with some concluding remarks. As such, each chapter stands on its own and can be read separately.

At the end of this preface, I would like to thank my good friend and colleague Jacco Verburgt for his assistance in editing this book as well as John Martino for his excellent guidance throughout the entire process.

Jörgen Vijgen

AUTHOR'S PREFACE

Over the years, the interest that scholars and philosophers have taken in the thought of St. Thomas Aquinas has increased considerably. In recent decennia we have witnessed the publication of numerous studies on his biblical commentaries as well as on the role and importance he has allotted to the Church Fathers. His expositions of the major works of Aristotle have also attracted the attention of several scholars, and some of these commentaries became the subject of lively discussions. In particular, the question was raised if they contained Thomas's own philosophy and if they were a reliable presentation of Aristotle's thought, or, on the contrary, if they deformed it in some places by introducing some of Thomas's Christian faith and theology.

To create some clarity on this question I have examined the text of these twelve commentaries, analyzed and summarized their contents, and drawn attention to all the places where Thomas intervenes and makes special observations. In this way the reader can study Aristotle's treatises guided by Thomas. The conclusion reached is that the commentaries are a masterful and faithful presentation of Aristotle's thought and of that of Thomas himself. Thomas's Christian faith does not falsify or adulterate the text, but gives occasionally an outlook at what lies behind philosophical thought.

The book is also the reflection of the author's lifelong interest in Aristotle's main works and the philosophy of Thomas Aquinas. There exists an immense literature on the subject of this study and I thank my friend and colleague Dr. J. Vijgen for having collected many of the books and articles I needed to consult. The existing English translations of the commentaries by Thomas on the main treatises of Aristotle have also been helpful and will be mentioned in the different chapters. Dr. Vijgen compiled the bibliography and helped improve the computerized presentation of the text.

Finally, a word of thanks to the publishers of this very voluminous and difficult book for accepting it among their publications as well as for their understanding and collaboration.

Leo J. Elders, S.V.D.

ABBREVIATIONS

CAG	Commentaria in Aristotelem Graeca et Byzantina
NE	*Nicomachean Ethics* (Aristotle)
PG	Patrologia Graeca (ed. Migne)
SCG	*Summa contra gentiles* (Aquinas)
SLE	*Sentencia libri Ethicorum* (Aquinas)
ST	*Summa theologiae* (Aquinas)

READING ARISTOTLE WITH

THOMAS AQUINAS

INTRODUCTION

The commentaries of St. Thomas Aquinas on a dozen major works of Aristotle invite us to study at close quarters Aquinas's position with regard to Aristotle's philosophy. These commentaries occupy more than five thousand pages in small print, the fruit of immense labor and much research during the last six or seven years of his life. Thomas's method of commenting was considered highly original in his day because of the clarity of his exposition, the depth of his understanding of the text, his command of the entire thought of the Stagirite, his knowledge of the positions of the different philosophers, his efforts to secure the best translations of the Greek text, his use of the available Greek commentaries on Aristotle's writings as well as those of Averroes, and, above all, his meticulous explanations of every single sentence of the text. But what is the reason for the extraordinary importance given to the philosophy of Aristotle in the thirteenth century at the University of Paris and also in England and in the many schools of translators, in particular in Spain and in Italy?

The enormous cultural revival and the growing interest in the study of nature and cosmic phenomena made the intellectual elite turn to Aristotle, who by his works on formal logic had dominated studies in the liberal arts during the *aetas boethiana,* while in theological studies the masters followed Augustine. As a consequence of the encounter of this revival and interest in philosophy with the established venerable theological tradition, two opposite doctrinal tendencies clashed at the University of Paris during the thirteenth century: a Platonizing trend of the Augustinian tradition, on the one hand, and Aristotle's realism and scientific explanation of nature and the world, on the other. To the partisans of the tradition, Aristotle's philosophy enhanced the value of creation so much that God's glory was diminished. But those who followed Aristotle felt that their adversaries did not use a correct scientific method, could not explain nature, and got lost in unreal speculations. In the teaching at the faculty of theology in Paris, the writings of Augustine and

Dionysius were dominant, but studies at the Faculty of Arts stood under the sign of Aristotle's philosophy.

At first sight, the growing admiration of the thirteenth-century philosophers for Aristotle is surprising. In fact, the attitude of the Church Fathers with regard to Aristotle had been quite negative.[1] Certain tenets taught by or attributed to Aristotle made them suspicious. In particular, his theory of the eternity of the world (which excluded the central dogma of creation), an unclear idea of God, and the denial of divine Providence with regard to the sublunar world, as well as of the immortality of the human soul, had been vigorously rejected by the apologists and Fathers of the Church.[2] A further reason for this lack of enthusiasm for Aristotle was the highly scientific level of his school writings, which seemed free from any religious inspiration. The fact that some heretics, in particular the Arians, used Aristotle's logic to attack the orthodox expression of the mysteries of Christ and the Trinity—although this was totally unjustified—was not conducive to removing this lingering suspicion.[3]

Even so, in the course of time the Christian authors began to use certain terms and categories of Aristotle's philosophy and became more positive toward his thought.[4] The Neo-Platonists of the fourth and fifth centuries used the school writings of Aristotle in their teaching. In this way, Aristotle became the leading authority in all philosophical disciplines except philosophical theology, where Plato was preferred. This explains why from the sixth to the eighth century Aristotle was studied in Syria and Mesopotamia in the schools directed by Christians. With the help of Christian teachers, the Arab conquerors learned this scientific and philosophical culture, so that Aristotelian studies flourished in several of the countries ruled by Muslims.[5] In the twelfth century, the Christian West became acquainted with those schools writing of

1. See Leo Elders, "The Greek Christian Authors and Aristotle," in *Aristotle in Late Antiquity*, ed. Lawrence P. Schrenk (Washington, D.C.: The Catholic University of America Press, 1994), 111–42.

2. Their knowledge of Aristotle's school-writings was often rudimentary, based on collections of the teachings of the great philosophers; or they quoted from the dialogues of Aristotle, not from his school-writings.

3. See Joseph de Ghellinck, "Quelques appréciations de la dialectique et d'Aristote durant les conflits trinitaires du IVe siècle," *Revue d'Histoire Ecclésiastique* 36 (1930): 5–42.

4. See for example the Christian historian Socrates, *Historia ecclesiastica* II.35, in vol. 67 of the Patrologia Graeca series, ed. J.-P. Migne (Paris, 1857–66) [hereafter PG], 300AB.

5. See De Lacy O'Leary, *How Greek Science Passed to the Arabs* (London: Routledge, 1957); Franz Rosenthal, *Das Fortleben der Antike im Islam* (Zürich: Artemis, 1965); F. E. Peters, *Aristotle and the Arabs: The Aristotelian Tradition in Islam* (New York: New York University Press, 1968); Fernand Van Steenberghen, *Aristotle in the West: The Origins of Latin Aristotelianism*, 2nd ed. (Leuven: Nauwelaerts, 1970), *Arabic Philosophy, East and West: Continuity and Interaction*, ed. Th.-A. Druart (Washington, D.C.: The Catholic University of America Press, 1988); *The Cambridge Companion to Arabic Philosophy*, ed. P. Adamson and R. C. Taylor (Cambridge: Cambridge University Press, 2005). For detailed studies see *Wissen über Grenzen: Arabisches Wissen und lateinisches Mittelalter*, ed. Andreas Speer (Berlin: De Gruyter, 2006).

Aristotle, which until then had not been known very well in the West. Parallel to this getting acquainted with Aristotle through Arab scholars as intermediaries, more intense contacts with the Eastern Roman Empire brought manuscripts of some of the Church Fathers and also of Aristotle to the West. James of Venice made the first complete translation of several works of Aristotle, the so-called *Vetus,* while in Toledo and other Spanish towns, in Sicily and in Naples, intercultural exchanges took place and Latin translations of the Arabic versions of Aristotle's works were made. The first disciplines that experienced a renaissance were the study of nature and medicine; logic and epistemology followed; finally, ethics and metaphysics began to flourish.

The writings of Aristotle and the commentaries by Averroes not only brought a treasure of new knowledge to Europe—where it made an overwhelming impression—but the learned were also attracted by Aristotle's objective and scientific way of proceeding.[6] Aristotle's philosophy is realistic: it is concerned with the world of perceptible things and relies on observation and the power of our reason, which proceeds in full autonomy in order to reach certain knowledge by means of analysis and deduction. Aristotle's texts provide the basic concepts, principles, definitions, and ways of arguing by means of which we come to know the world and man.[7] At first this wealth of new knowledge was gratefully accepted by almost everyone.[8] Aristotle's authority in philosophy became about as great as that of the Bible in theology. However, difficulties arose when certain doctrines of Aristotle were placed side by side with the dogmas of the faith. The result was that the use of the *Libri naturales* at the Faculty of Arts in Paris was forbidden by the Church. A council held in Paris (1210) decreed that the works of Aristotle on the philosophy of nature as well as commentaries on these works were not to be used in public and private teaching.[9] In 1215, the papal legate Cardinal Robert of Courçon issued the statutes of the Faculty of Arts. He reiterated the prohibition of 1210 and included the teaching of Aristotle's *Metaphysics* as well.[10] The adversaries

6. Edward Grant, *God and Reason in the Middle Ages* (Cambridge: Cambridge University Press, 2001), 83–114.

7. John Henry Newman expressed this exceptional importance of Aristotle as follows: "While the world lasts, will Aristotle's doctrine on these matters last, for the great Master does but analyze the thoughts and feelings, views and opinions of humankind. He has told us the meaning of our words and ideas before we were born. In many subject matters, to think correctly, is to think like Aristotle, and we are his disciples whether we will or no, though we may not know it." John Henry Newman, *Idea of a University* (London: Longmans, Green, and Co., 1901), 109–10.

8. See Roger Bacon, *Opus maius* 2.13, ed. John Henry Bridges (Oxford: Clarendon, 1897), 1:55: "Et licet alia logicalia et quaedam alia translata fuerunt per Boetium de Graeco, tamen tempore Michael Scoti, qui annis Domini 1230 transactis apparuit deferens librorum Aristotelis partes aliquas de Naturalibus et Metaphysicis cum expositoribus authenticis, magnificata est s philosophia Aristoteli apud Latinos."

9. *Chartularium Universitatis Parisiensis,* vol. 1, ed. H. Denifle and É. Châtelain (Paris: Delalain), no. 11.

10. *Chartularium,* no. 12: "non legantur libri Aristotelis de methafisico et de naturali philosphia, nec

argued that Aristotle only knows an endless cycle of succeeding generations and denies the creation of the world, divine Providence, and the immortality of the soul. Moreover, in the moral life he wants to make man independent. Instead of praising humility, he extols magnanimity and pride; his theory of the virtue of magnificence is at odds with evangelical poverty.[11] But Aristotle's contribution to scientific knowledge was considered so valuable that the objections were set aside and his texts came into general use about the middle of the thirteenth century.[12] Even Bonaventure, who fifteen or twenty years later would react so sharply during the debate with the Averroists in his *Collationes*, used Aristotle's philosophy freely and extensively in his *Commentary* on the *Sentences,* although he never fully assimilated certain fundamental Aristotelian tenets.[13]

Together with the texts of Aristotle, translations of numerous works of Muslim scholars became known in the West, in particular the Aristotelian commentaries of Averroes. Certain points of doctrine that Aristotle had left unclear, as for instance the status of the agent intellect, were now presented by some Parisian masters in an unacceptable form. Some upheld the theory of a dual truth: as philosophers they sided with Aristotle and Averroes, but as Christians, so they claimed, they took a different position.[14] Soon a reaction set in and warning voices were heard. Robert Grosseteste informs the sympathizers of Aristotelianism that they should not cheat themselves and labor in vain by using all the resources of their minds to make Aristotle a Catholic, while in fact they were turning themselves into heretics.[15] While

---

summe de eisdem." This prohibition was not universal as is shown by a letter from the University of Toulouse from 1229–30: "libros naturales, qui fuerant Parisius prohibiti, poterunt illic audire qui volunt nature sinum medullitus perscrutari" (*Chartularium*, no. 72).

11. See William of Auvergne, *De universo* II, p. 1, c. 2, in *Opera omnia* (Paris, 1674; reprinted in Frankfurt am Main: Minerva, 1963), 1:808.

12. In 1231, Pope Gregory XI's bull *Parens scientiarum* granted university masters the right to decide on the content of their courses and in 1255 the statutes of the Faculty of Arts stipulated a program of studies in which all of Aristotle's translated works were included (*Chartularium*, nos. 79 and 246). For an analysis of these texts see Fernand Van Steenberghen, *La philosophie au XIIIe siècle. Deuxième édition, mise à jour* (Louvain: Peeters, 1991), 81–93.

13. See Leo Elders, "Les citations d'Aristote dans le Commentaire des *Sentences* de saint Bonaventure," in *San Bonaventura, maestro di vita francescana e di sapienza Cristiana* (Rome: Pontificia Facolta Téologica San Bonaventure, 1974), 831–42; J. F. Quin, *The Historical Constitution of St. Bonaventure's Philosophy* (Toronto: Pontifical Institute of Mediaeval Studies, 1973), 854–78.

14. Nowadays some historians say that the theory of the uniqueness of the intellect of all men was not taught by Averroes himself; see Salvador Gomez Nogales, "Saint Thomas, Averroes et l'averroisme," in *Aquinas and the Problems of His Time*, ed. Gérard Verbeke and D. Verhelst (Leuven: Leuven University Press, 1976), 161–77. However, some affirm the opposite; see B. C. Bazan, "Le commentaire de S. Thomas d'Aquin sur le Traité de l'âme," *Revue des sciences philosophiques et théologiques* 69 (1985): 521–47.

15. Robert Grosseteste, *Hexaëmeron*, ed. R. C. Dales and S. Gieben (Oxford, 1982), I, viii, 4: "Non igitur se decipiant et frustra desudent ut Aristotilem faciant catholicum, ne inutiliter tempus suum et vires ingenii sui consumant, et Aristotilem catholicum constituendo, se ipsos haereticos faciant."

Grosseteste himself borrowed a great deal from Aristotle's writings and Albert the Great, as we shall see, considered it his task to make the contents of the works of Aristotle accessible for students, others launched sharp attacks, as did Bonaventure in his *Collationes* addressed to the students of the University of Paris between 1267 and 1273.

The struggle of the theologians against alleged aberrations and dangers to the faith became fiercer because of these unacceptable theories of Averroes. After his return to Paris in 1268, Thomas became involved in the fight against heterodox theories. While writing his commentary on the *De anima*, when still in Rome, he had already mentioned and refuted the Averroist theory of the oneness of the intellect and the rational soul of all men.

Soon a reaction set in and there was a threat of condemnation of all of Aristotle's philosophical writings. The result would have been that medieval learning would have remained enclosed in Platonism, no adequate explanation of the physical world would have been provided, and no scientific method would have been available for the study of nature, and also the exposition of the doctrine of the faith would have suffered. Some historians believe that the condemnation of Averroistic tenets by the bishop of Paris three years after the death of Thomas dealt in fact a terrible blow to medieval Aristotelianism from which it never fully recovered. On the other hand, the condemnation would also have been instrumental in preparing the downfall of the ancient philosophy of nature and have made possible the rise of mathematical physics.[16]

The conflict between the masters of the faculty of theology and those of the liberal arts faculty was also partly that between Platonists and Aristotelians. Thomas was aware that the Church Fathers were not Aristotelians[17] and on several occasions wrote that, in philosophical matters, Augustine mentions the views of Plato without (however) subscribing to them.[18] Thomas was not unaware of the difficulties certain positions of Aristotle could cause to the study of theology, but he nevertheless accepted the substance of Aristotle's philosophy, as we shall see in my analysis of his commentaries of Aristotle's major works. The reason for his choice was that he was certain that many of these positions expressed the truth, and that Aristotle's method was adequate for the study of nature and human life. Aristotle offered a greater clarity.

---

16. These condemnations have received extensive attention. For a good summary see the introduction to *Nach der Verurteilung von 1277: Philosophie und Theologie an der Universität von Paris im letzten Viertel des 13. Jahrhunderts*, ed. Jan Aertsen, Kent Emery Jr., and A. Speer (Berlin: de Gruyter, 2001).

17. See *In II Sent.*, d. 14, q. 1, a. 2: "Basilius et Augustinus et plures sanctorum sequuntur in philosophicis, quae ad fidem non spectant, opiniones Platonis."

18. *Summa theologiae* [hereafter *ST*] I, q. 77, a. 5, ad 3: "In multis autem quae ad philosophiam pertinent Augustinus utitur opinionibus Platonis, non asserendo sed recitando." In doctrinal questions he follows the opinions of Plato, insofar as the faith allows; see *De veritate*, q. 21, a. 4, ad 3.

Modern students of these commentaries have raised the question as to whether they contain Aquinas's own philosophy or, rather, are to be considered a more or less faithful rendering of Aristotle's thought.[19] A first general answer is found in the role of similar commentaries in the age of Aquinas. Francesco Del Punta has shown that the medieval notion of a commentary does not entail that the text necessarily differs from the commentator's own position; it can very well be an expression of the commentator's own views too.[20] To this one may add that in the tradition of the school of Thomists, the commentaries have generally been considered as expositions of the thought of Thomas himself.[21]

Some moderns argue that the commentaries are to such a degree infected by Thomas's own philosophy and theology that they are useless for a historico-critical exegesis of Aristotle's works.[22] They argue that Thomas warps the latter's doctrine and even adulterates it on some occasions so as to render it more acceptable to Christians. Joseph Owens suggests that Aquinas's allegiance to the Christian faith repeatedly vitiates the scientific objectivity of his commentaries and that his explanations are infected by his own different philosophical views.[23] In his study of the commentary on the *Nicomachean Ethics*, Harry V. Jaffa argues that Thomas does not give a reliable presentation of Aristotle's thought.[24] Mark D. Jordan speaks of "Thomas Aquinas' disclaimers in the Aristotelian Commentaries," so that "Aquinas cannot be burdened with the views expressed in the commentaries."[25] Most scholars, however, praise the light that the commentaries shed on Aristotle's often difficult texts

19. For a cursory overview see Rolf Schönberger, "Aristoteleskommentare," in *Thomas Handbuch*, ed. Volker Leppin (Tübingen: Mohr Siebeck, 2016), 216–38.

20. Francesco del Punta, "The Genre of Commentaries in the Middle Ages and its Relation to the Nature and the Originality of Medieval Thought," in *Was ist Philosophie im Mittelalter?*, ed. Andreas Speer and Jan A. Aertsen (Berlin: De Gruyter, 1998), 138–51.

21. Contrary to the view of Joseph Owens, Christopher Kaczor refers to the fact that in the thirteenth century, both those friendly to Aquinas as well as those who opposed him considered his commentary on the *Nicomachean Ethics* as presenting Thomas's own views. Henricus Bate considers the commentary on the *Metaphysics* as expressing Thomas's own doctrine of the question of whether knowledge of the separate substances is possible: see "Reading Aquinas's Commentary of Aristotle's *Nicomachean Ethics*: A Reply to Mark D. Jordan," in *Theology Needs Philosophy: Acting Against Reason is Contrary to the Nature of God*, ed. Matthew Lamb (Washington, D.C.: The Catholic University of America Press, 2016), 279–92.

22. See the introduction by Francis Cheneval and Ruedi Imbach in *Thomas von Aquin: Prologe zu den Aristoteleskommentaren*, ed. Francis Cheneval and Ruedi Imbach (Frankfurt am Main: Klostermann, 1993), xiii.

23. Joseph Owens, "Aquinas as an Aristotelian Commentator," in *St. Thomas Aquinas on the Existence of God: Collected Papers of Joseph Owens C.Ss.R.*, ed. John R. Catan (Albany: State University of New York Press, 1980), 18.

24. Harry V. Jaffa, *Thomism and Aristotelianism: A Study of the Commentary by St. Thomas Aquinas on the "Nicomachean Ethics"* (Chicago: University of Chicago Press, 1952).

25. Mark D. Jordan, "Thomas Aquinas' Disclaimers in the Aristotelian Commentaries," in *Philosophy and the God of Abraham: Essays in Memory of James A. Weisheipl, OP* (Toronto: Pontifical Institute of Mediaeval Studies, 1991), 99–112, esp. 109–10; see also his *The Alleged Aristotelianism of Thomas Aquinas* (Toronto: Pontifical Institute of Mediaeval Studies, 1992).

and are convinced that they substantially express Aquinas's own philosophical doctrine.

This means that in a study of all the Aristotelian commentaries we should attempt to show to what extent Thomas accepted what Aristotle writes, and what were his reasons for undertaking the enormous task of writing these commentaries during the seven last years of his life. Was it his desire just to provide material to students for an exercise in analysis and dialectic?[26] Raising this question is answering it: as a *Magister in Sacra Pagina*, Thomas had other concerns than composing texts for dialectical practice, concerns such as his daily lectures on scripture, the organization of academic disputes, the writing of his *Summa theologiae*, and other shorter treatises. In addition, it is meaningful that the composition of some of the commentaries coincided with the redaction of parts of *Summa theologiae* and provided Thomas with Aristotle's often excellent analyses of a particular subject, such as that of the sense faculties of the human soul. Besides the commentary on the *De anima*, apparently written in Rome while Thomas was also composing the First Part of the *Summa theologiae*, one may think here of his commentary on the *Nicomachean Ethics*, which seems to date from the time that Thomas worked on the redaction of the Second Part of the *Summa* on man's moral life. This is a clear indication that St. Thomas considered these Aristotelian treatises to be valuable and helpful for his own theological work. But did he also have other purposes in mind, such as confirming Aristotelianism as basically true and providing the tools for the interpretation and scientific analysis of creation?

Why did Aquinas undertake the task of writing commentaries on Aristotle's main works? It stands to reason that in undertaking this enormous task Thomas had some very good motives. As I have indicated, some of these treatises of Aristotle provided Thomas with useful material for composing his own works.[27] But let us tentatively mention some other reasons why Thomas made his choice in favor of Aristotle's philosophy and devoted so much of his time to writing these commentaries. He was convinced that most of the basic positions of Aristotle were right, as they were immediately taken from the observation and analysis of nature: in addition to the doctrine of the categories of being and the place assigned to substance, Aristotle analyzes causality in

26. As J. Jenkins suggests in "Expositions of the Text: Aquinas's Aristotelian Commentaries," *Medieval Philosophy and Theology* 5 (1996): 39–62.

27. The fact that his commentaries on Aristotle were written relatively late in life and *de facto* accompanied the composition of *ST* should not lead to the conclusion that Thomas did not already have a first-hand, detailed, and unique knowledge of Aristotle as has been shown by Marta Borgo. See her "La 'Métaphysique' d'Aristote dans le 'Commentaire' de Thomas d'Aquin au I livre de 'Sentences' de Pierre Lombard: quelques exemples significatifs," *Revue des sciences philosophiques et théologiques* 91 (2007): 651–92.

the four genera of causes and assigns a fundamental role to the first principles of being. The object of the sciences is the universal and the necessary, which is abstracted from concrete reality. Real things, not *a priori* concepts of the human mind (such as the Ideas in Platonism), are the basis of our knowledge. In addition to this realism, Aristotle proposed a division of the sciences and assigns the first place to the theoretical sciences. This allowed Thomas to determine the nature of theology, while Aristotle's logic provided him with the tools for scientific work.

Aristotle's philosophy gives priority to knowledge rather than to the appetite or feelings. The happiness of man lies essentially in knowledge. Aristotle is optimistic with regard to man's capacity to acquire a real knowledge of things: there is finality in all natural processes, and beings are intelligible, at least to a certain extent. The main task of philosophy is the study of the causes of becoming. The gradual discovery of these causes by the Pre-Socratic philosophers provided Aristotle with a method to organize the history of ancient philosophy. The discovery of primary matter, hylomorphism, the analyses of movement, place, and time, and of generation and corruption, are some of his accomplishments. His doctrine of act and potency became the key to deciphering the universe. We may add to this that he took the first steps toward a scientific cosmology and the study of living beings, as well as the soul and its faculties.

Aristotle also developed a theory of the first principles, although he failed to apply it to the moral order. Opposing himself to Plato and the Academy, he taught the primacy of being over the Good and the One; he explained what knowledge is, distinguished the different sciences, and defined metaphysics as the study of being *qua* being, laying the foundation for the theory of transcendental concepts, which, however, he did not elaborate. While Plato attempted to reduce all things to two contrary principles, the One and the Indeterminate Dyad, Aristotle elaborated the theory of the categories of being and their mutual irreducibility, a doctrine that opened the way for the theory of the different meanings of *being* and *analogy*. Substance is the heart and center of reality. The other predicaments are beings of being or beings in being. He demonstrated that all movements in the universe derive from an unmoved first mover who is pure reality and subsistent thinking, and who finds its beatitude in self-contemplation. Aristotle's contributions to the development of biology, ethics, politics, and aesthetics are no less important. When we try to indicate more precisely the reasons why Thomas undertook to comment on the main works of Aristotle, the following may be mentioned.

First, it was certainly the intention of Thomas to make the books of

Aristotle more accessible by analyzing and stating their contents in clear language and by showing their structure and composition, as well as the wealth of sound doctrine contained in them. At the beginning of his exposition of the *Physics*, St. Albert said that his purpose was to help students understand correctly the books of Aristotle and to hand down an elaborated natural science as the groundwork for the foundation of a Christian philosophy.[28] The medieval Latin translations of Aristotle's text were often difficult to decipher, and Aristotle's text in itself also was (and remains to this day) in some passages not easy to understand. For that reason, a clear restatement of what Aristotle taught must have been extremely welcome. Thomas purports to place the students in direct contact with Aristotle's text, while providing guidance. He himself stays in the background.[29] It was also a challenge to any master to make the books of the great philosopher easier to use in the schools.

Second, Thomas also intended to set forth the doctrine contained in Aristotle's text and to test the strength of the arguments. The division of the text was the method practiced at medieval universities and was the foremost means to get an overview of the doctrine contained in the different chapters of a treatise. To a modern reader these numerous divisions and subdivisions seem tedious, but in reality they presuppose that the commentator understood the contents of the entire treatise, had an overview of them, and was able to indicate the logical order of the themes dealt with by the author (or its absence). Thomas is aware of the fact that the unity of some of these treatises, such as the *Physics* or *Metaphysics*, each consisting of several "books," is far from perfect. But it is perhaps less known that Thomas very carefully weighs the arguments advanced by the Stagirite and certainly does not consider the text as consisting of uniform pages with a content of equal certitude. Sometimes, he says, Aristotle proceeds from the presumptions of others. Thomas is aware of the fact that before stating his own view, Aristotle argues occasionally from what people have commonly held or proceeds *disputatively* and does not yet determine the truth in the text under discussion.

Third, a further purpose of the commentaries is to reject any interpretation in disagreement with the text or the intention of Aristotle. In this connection, Thomas often uses such expressions as *secundum intentionem Aristotelis*. By *intentio* Thomas means in the first place Aristotle's doctrine as one can reconstruct it by reading a text attentively and by comparing it to his philosophical doctrine as such, but sometimes the word carries the more profound sense

---

28. Albertus Magnus, *Physica* I, tr. 1, c. 1, ed. Paul Hossfeld (Aschendorff: Münster, 1987), 1.

29. See J. Isaac, O.P., "Saint Thomas, interprète des oeuvres d'Aristote," in *Scholastica ratione historico-critica instauranda* (Rome: Pontificium Athenaeum Antonianum, 1951), 360–61.

of the text which becomes manifest when one carefully studies a passage in its context, as in a remark like *patet igitur praedicta verba Philosophi diligenter consideranti quod non est intentio eius*. In the third place, *secundum intentionem Aristotelis* may also mean a sense which is not contained in a particular text, but which is found elsewhere in the *corpus* or which may be concluded from what Aristotle says at some other place or from certain of his principles. To give an example, in *Metaphysics* XII.9, Aristotle denies that God has knowledge of the world and of what happens in human life, because this would make God depend on what is outside him. Thomas writes that there is no such dependence if God knows things in himself, as he actually does. Aristotle himself points to this solution, Thomas says, when he writes that heaven and earth depend on the first mover.

Fourth, Thomas also notes the agreement or disagreement of some particular teachings of Aristotle with the doctrine of the faith. On several occasions he writes that a certain passage, when interpreted carefully, does not contradict the Christian faith, even if it seems to do so at first sight. Aquinas's purpose is to show that basically and in its main doctrines Aristotle's philosophy is not opposed to the faith. He admits, however, that certain statements are in disagreement with Catholic doctrine, as will be shown in my subsequent analysis of the different commentaries.

Fifth, I am convinced that in composing his commentaries it was also Thomas's intention, as it had been that of Albert the Great, to make the study of the philosophy of nature, metaphysics, and ethics more easily accessible and to present them as leading to a true grasp of reality. This does not mean that Thomas substantially completes the text of Aristotle where it shows lacunae. He respects the text—the principle is *reverenter exponere*—and is convinced that such a completion is not the task of a commentator. He consistently interprets passages in light of Aristotle's own philosophy and principles, as he himself understands their implications. Christopher Kaczor, referring to M.-D. Chenu, observes that the medieval commentator accepts the doctrine of the author he is explaining, unless he states that the truth according to his view is different.[30] This has been very well expressed by Francesco del Punta:

> In the medieval commentary a rigidly formalized structure coexists with various degrees of speculative originality. This coexistence, the first essential characteristic of the medieval commentary, manifests itself as a polarity between, on the one hand, a strictly codified and relatively standardized

---

30. "Aquinas's Commentary on the *Ethics*: Merely an Interpretation of Aristotle?," *American Catholic Philosophical Quarterly* 78, no. 3 (2004), 353–78; M.-D. Chenu, *Introduction à l'étude de saint Thomas d'Aquin* (Paris: Vrin, 1950), 177.

form, and, on the other, a remarkable capability to adapt itself to the commentator's expression of his own personal views. . . . When properly viewed in its historical context, therefore, the medieval notion of "commentary" is not antithetical to the notion of originality, but rather complementary to it. The medieval commentary is *a way of receiving knowledge* that leads to the development of such knowledge.[31]

However, some modern readers of the commentaries have seen a real distance between what Aristotle writes and Thomas's own thought. Perhaps inspired by Gilson's theory of Thomas's metaphysics, based on the revelation that God is being of being, Joseph Owens held that Aquinas's philosophy is fundamentally different from that of Aristotle. Inspired by James Weisheipl's essay "Albert's Disclaimers in the Aristotelian Paraphrases,"[32] Mark Jordan has argued that the commentaries are not so important, given that they occupy only a small part (13 percent) of Thomas's works: Thomas had some definite aim when starting to write them, and when this had been reached he left them unfinished.[33] Jordan lists several ways in which Thomas expressed his disagreement: by negating what Aristotle writes; by additions; by noting that the text is presented elsewhere by Aristotle in a more complete form; or that in some passages Aristotle proceeds disputatively. To the question of whether the commentaries contain the core of Aquinas's own philosophy, Jordan answers by doubting that Thomas even has a philosophy independent from theology. Kaczor replied to these remarks by saying that the commentaries should be read as Aquinas's own work rather than as a presentation of the philosophical doctrines of Aristotle.[34] Our careful reading of the individual commentaries will provide the answer that the commentaries also contain and propose Thomas's own philosophy, which—however—for the most part coincides with that of Aristotle.

Sixth, in those places where Aristotle's statements or explanations are insufficient or partly wrong Thomas makes a remark at the end of a passage or of a lesson. These remarks begin with phrases like *sciendum est autem, advertendum est autem, considerandum est autem*, etc. As an example of such corrections, of which there are hundreds in the commentaries, I refer to *Metaphysics* VI, the text of the well-known tripartition of the theoretical sciences. Contradicting Aristotle on this point in a *sciendum est autem*, Thomas writes that metaphysics considers *also* material beings. These corrections of

---

31. Del Punta, "The Genre of Commentaries in the Middle Ages," 139 and 151 (emphasis added).

32. James Weisheipl, "Albert's Disclaimers in the Aristotelian Paraphrases," *Proceedings of the PMR Conference* 5 (1980): 1–27.

33. Jordan, "Thomas Aquinas' Disclaimers in the Aristotelian Commentaries," 101.

34. Kaczor, "Reading Aquinas's Commentary on Aristotle's *Nicomachean Ethics*," 279–92.

particular theories and short additions show that the doctrine of the remaining part of the chapter is accepted.

Seventh, the overarching goal of Aquinas's commentaries is to replace a Neo-Platonic interpretation of Aristotle's doctrines, as Avicenna and Albert frequently present them, with a rigorous exegesis based on the texts and principles of Aristotle himself. Moreover, he frequently rejects interpretations proposed by Averroes, in particular in his commentaries on the *Physics* and the *De Anima*, in order to show that the "Commentator," as Averroes was called, is not above all suspicion as to the correctness of his views.[35] Notwithstanding his severe criticism of several positions of Averroes (or of those attributed to him, such as the theory of the one intellect for all men), Thomas nevertheless occasionally uses some valuable insights of the philosopher of Cordova.

Eighth, in order to determine to what extent Aquinas shares the theories of the Stagirite one must notice what he has to say about the proofs advanced by Aristotle. Quite often he will observe that Aristotle uses probable arguments and only begins to determine the truth further on.[36] Elsewhere Thomas writes that after first investigating disputatiously whether place is real, Aristotle now considers what place is.[37] In another place, Thomas notes that thus far Aristotle has discussed the Pre-Socratics and Plato at the level of a dispute and so his arguments are partially true but not entirely.[38] Thomas also distinguishes between probable and better proofs.[39]

On several occasions Aquinas draws attention to Aristotle's custom of proceeding from the assumptions of others or from common opinions, before stating his own view.[40] He even writes that sometimes Aristotle uses a sophistic argument.[41] Elsewhere an argument is said to be *ad hominem, non ad veritatem*.[42] An important source of arguments is what Thomas calls *induction*. The term often has the meaning of an inference one makes on the basis of observation. The fact that natural things move, either all or part of them, is evident by induction. Likewise we observe that nature proceeds in an orderly

---

35. See my "The Commentary of St. Thomas Aquinas on the *Physics* of Aristotle," in Leo Elders, *Autour de saint Thomas d'Aquin* (Paris / Bruges: FAC-éditions / Tabor, 1987), 1:23–53, esp. 28–33. On the place assigned to Averroes in Aquinas's works, see C. Vansteenkiste, "San Tommaso d'Aquino ed Averroè," *Rivista degli Studi Orientali* 32 (1957): 585–623. Vansteenkiste mentions some five hundred references. See also Leo Elders, "Averroès et saint Thomas d'Aquin," *Doctor communis* 44 (1992): 46–56.

36. *In I Phys.*, lesson 12, no. 98.

37. *In IV Phys.*, lesson 3, no. 422.

38. *In I Phys.*, lesson 13, no. 114.

39. *In VII Phys.*, lesson 2.

40. *In III Phys.*, lesson 8, no. 353: "Semper antequam probet id quod est suae opinionis procedit ex suppositione opinionis aliorum communis."

41. *In IV Phys.*, lesson 1, no. 407.

42. *In VI Phys.*, lesson 4, no. 779.

way in its activities. One must also draw attention to the verb *supponere*, which has the sense of "to assume" or "to suppose," but the verb can also denote a false assumption, for example, Parmenides supposed that being is unmovable. On countless occasions Thomas comments on the arguments of Aristotle, clarifies, and sometimes corrects them.

As evident from the texts referenced above, and also from numerous others, we can see a certain reservation about what Aristotle writes in particular passages. Apparently, we must read the commentaries with the utmost attention in order to be able to distinguish between sections which express mere opinions and other passages where, according to Aquinas, definitively true doctrine is set forth. I am convinced that Thomas adopts the bulk of Aristotle's doctrines, but there are some particular theories of the Stagirite where he appears to disagree, as we shall see when we consider the expositions on the different treatises.

In order to trace the relatively few texts where Thomas disagrees with certain doctrines of Aristotle or completes certain statements, my method is to go through each chapter of the different commentaries and to note where Thomas makes observations and advances a different explanation. In order to do so, it seemed best to present a summary of the contents of the different chapters of each treatise, noting those places where Thomas makes corrections and additions, or brings in sentences expressing truths of the Christian faith. In going through the entire text of each commentary, the reader will hopefully discover the answers to questions raised by some modern critics, and will also discern the basic agreement between Aristotle's principles and the philosophical truth as defended by Thomas.

1 ❧ THE COMMENTARY ON THE PERI HERMENEIAS

The *Peri hermeneias*, the second book of the *Organon*, is a relatively short treatise. In a concise style, Aristotle deals with the nature of our language, focusing on the logical form of affirmative and negative sentences and their parts, such as nouns and verbs.[1] The title, *On Interpretation*, must not be understood as an investigation of how to interpret texts. It is best to follow the suggestions of the Greek commentator Ammonius, who interprets the title to mean a study of how to manifest what one has in mind, by affirming or denying something.[2] The title is probably not from Aristotle himself, but the authenticity of the treatise, at least of the first thirteen chapters, is generally acknowledged. While Andronicus of Rhodes denied it, Alexander of Aphrodisias, Ammonius, and others in antiquity defended it. It is accepted nowadays by most students of Aristotle. A strong argument in favor of its authenticity is the terse writing, its depth in meaning, and the fact that, so far as one can judge from the remaining fragments of Theophrastus's works on affirmations and negations, Aristotle's successor at the Lyceum treated certain questions relative to the contents of the *Peri hermeneias* not dealt with in detail by his master, a procedure he followed also in regard to some other works of Aristotle.

In this treatise, Aristotle studies certain subjects dealt with by Plato in his *Cratylus*, *Theaetetus*, and *Sophist*. He rejects Plato's theory according to which words have a basis in the nature of the things they designate. In this view, a wrong statement is hardly possible. According to Plato, when a sentence is wrong, its words also are, but Aristotle argues that words as such are neither false nor true, as they are conventional signs for what is in our mind. A sen-

---

1. In his *Institutiones divinarum et humanorum litterarum* II, 3, 11, Cassiodorus writes that Aristotle dipped his pen *in mente*: "Sequitur liber Perihermenias, suptilissimus nimis et per uarias formas iterationesque cautissimus, de quo dictum est: 'Aristoteles, quando Perihermenias scriptitabat, calamum in mente tingebat.'" In Patrologia Latina, ed. J.-P. Migne (Paris, 1841–55), 70:1170D.

2. Ammonius, *In Aristotelis De Interpretatione* 5, 20–21: "ὡς ἑρμηνεῦον τῶν γνῶσιν τές ψυχῆς" (Commentaria in Aristotelem Graeca et Byzantina [hereafter CAG] 4.5).

tence connects the contents signified by the words or it denies such a connection or identity.

The date of composition of the *Peri hermeneias* is a matter of discussion. Some consider it a late work because of its unfinished character (assuming that chapter XIV is not by Aristotle himself) and its literary qualities. J. M. Bochenski, however, and others pointed out that from the point of view of formal logic, the *Analytics* are more refined and therefore probably written later, but some disagree.[3] It is perhaps best to assume that the *Peri hermeneias* is not one of the earliest works, nor very late.[4]

The *Peri hermeneias* has attracted much attention. The Greek commentaries by Aspasius (100–150), Herminus, Alexander of Aphrodisias (second century A.D.), Porphyry (234–ca. 305), and Iamblichus have all been lost. A whole series of Greek commentaries written from the sixth to eleventh centuries survives in texts by John Philoponus (ca. 490–570s), Olympiodorus (495/505–after 565), Stephen of Alexandria (seventh century), John Damascene (eighth century), and others. The commentary by Ammonius (ca. 435/445–517/526) deserves special mention because of his extensive use and knowledge of his predecessors.[5] Within the Arabic tradition, apart from the discussion of Aristotle's *Peri hermeneias* in philosophical encyclopedias and logical textbooks, the detailed commentary by Al-Farabi (d. 950/51) as well as Averroes's commentary, translated from the Arabic into Latin in the thirteenth century, need to be mentioned.[6]

The medieval Latin tradition of the *Peri hermeneias*, however, begins with Boethius. He made the translation which would become the standard throughout the Middle Ages and wrote two influential commentaries, an *editio minor* for beginners, and an *editio maior* for advanced students.[7] Especially from the late tenth century onward, the *Peri hermeneias* become frequently

---

3. Joseph Bochenski, *Formale Logik* (Freiburg im Breisgau: Alber, 1978), 50.

4. Hermann Weidemann, *Aristoteles: Peri Hermeneias* (Berlin: Akademie-Verlag, 1994), 47–57. Heidemann's richly annotated German translation as well as the English translation by J. L. Ackrill deserve special mention: *Aristoteles Peri Hermeneias: Aristotle's "Categories" and "De Interpretatione,"* trans. J. L. Ackrill (Oxford: Clarendon, 1963).

5. The Greek original is published in CAG 4.5; an English translation can be found in the series Ancient Commentators on Aristotle. Published in *Aristotelem Commentaria Graeca*. Moerbeke made a Latin translation, which became an important source for Thomas Aquinas.

6. In her careful study "Aristotle's *Peri Hermeneias* in Medieval Latin and Arabic Philosophy," in *Aristotle and His Medieval Interpreters*, ed. Richard Bosley and Martin Tweedale (Calgary: University of Calgary Press, 1992), 3–36, Deborah Black notes that, as to the understanding of the *Peri Hermeneias*, there is no direct influence of Arabic philosophers upon their Latin counterparts.

7. For the reception history, see J. Isaac, *Le « Peri Hermeneias » en Occident de Boèce à saint Thomas: histoire littéraire d'un traité d'Aristote* (Paris: Vrin, 1953). Isaac's study remains the only book-length treatment of the *Peri hermeneias* commentary tradition. In addition, there is *Aristotle's "Peri hermeneias" in the Latin Middle Ages: Essays on the Commentary Tradition*, ed. H. A. G. Braakhuis and C. H. Kneepkens (Groningen: Ingenium, 2003), in particular the lengthy introduction.

read and studied as well as used in theological writings. In his *De divina omnip-otentia* Peter Damian made use of the treatise, as did Anselm in his *Cur Deus homo* when trying to reconcile divine prescience and predestination with man's free will. From that moment onward all Christian authors who tried to solve this problem refer to the *Peri hermeneias*. In the first half of the twelfth century, the *Peri hermeneias* enjoyed a remarkable interest from logicians such as Peter Abelard whose glosses set the stage for the development of various branches of logic in the Middle Ages.[8] In the second half of the thirteenth century, the *Peri hermeneias* is a standard text at the Faculties of Arts.[9]

As Gauthier has shown, the Latin translation in use in the thirteenth century—and also the one used by Thomas—is not the pure text as written by Boethius but a somewhat corrupted edition of it.[10] William of Moerbeke also translated the text of the *Peri hermeneias,* placing each time a passage of it ahead of the relevant section of the commentary. Thomas, however, comments on the text of Boethius, probably because this was the text used at the university, but he occasionally compares it with that of Moerbeke.[11]

Several thirteenth-century masters commented on the treatise, either by way of a literal commentary or, toward the end of the century, by way of formulating *quaestiones*. Among them there are Robert Kilwardby, Peter of Ireland, Peter of Saint-Amour, Hervaeus Brito, and Albert the Great, who wrote his commentary in 1257–58 or 1264–67.[12]

The study of Aquinas's commentary on the *Peri hermeneias* has now been greatly facilitated by a number of excellent editions of Aristotle's text itself, of the Greek commentary by Ammonius and its Latin version by G. Verbeke[13] and of the Latin commentaries of Boethius by L. Minio-Paluello. Apart from the standard study on the reception of the *Peri hermeneias* in the Middle Ages by J. Isaac, mentioned above, there is also the new Leonine edition of the *Expositio* of Thomas with a historical introduction by R. A. Gauthier, a critical edition beyond praise because of all the references to the sources that Thomas

8. Petrus Abelardus, *Glossae super Peri hermeneias I*, ed. K. Jacobi and C. Strub (Turnhout: Brepols, 2010). For an extensive survey of the treatise in this period see J. Marenbon, *Aristotelian Logic, Platonism, and the Context of Early Medieval Philosophy in the West* (Aldershot: Variorum, 2000), 77–140.

9. See Braakhuis and Kneepkens, *Aristotle's "Peri Hermeneias" in the Latin Middle Ages*, xxvi.

10. *Expositio Libri Peryermeneias*, vol. 1*/1 in *Opera omnia iussu Leonis XIII P. M. Edita*, introduction by René Antoine Gauthier (Rome / Paris: Leonine Commission / Vrin, 1989), 48*. He calls it *translationis Boethii textus deterior.*

11. See the Leonine ed., 1*/1: 89, 101ff., where Thomas quotes, besides *secundum consequenciam*, the translation of κατὰ τὸ στοιχοῦν by Moerbeke.

12. For a first impression see A. Wilder, "St. Albert and St. Thomas on Aristotle's *De interpretatione*: a Comparative Study," *Angelicum* 57 (1980): 496–532.

13. Ammonius, *Commentaire sur le « Peri Hermeneias » d'Aristote: Traduction de Guillaume de Moerbeke,* ed. G. Verbeke (Leuven: Leuven University Press, 1961). See also G. Verbeke, "Ammonius et Saint Thomas. Deux commentaires sur le *Peri Hermeneias' d'Aristote,"* *Revue philosophique de Louvain* 54 (1956): 228–53.

used and the publication of the critical text of these real or possible sources.[14]

Thomas's commentary abruptly breaks off at 10.19b26, but several completions or continuations by fellow Dominicans Thomas of Sutton, Robert of Vulgarbia, William Arnaldo, and Gratiadeo of Ascoli are known today and often formed part of early printed editions.[15] Thomas's commentary itself was highly regarded. Gauthier quotes several masters who referred to it, such as Martin of Dacia and Peter of Saint-Amour. The continuation by Thomas de Vio Cajetan, written in 1496, has been printed in the first version of the first volume of the Leonine edition.[16]

In his commentaries on Aristotle, Thomas Aquinas is inclined to ascribe a certain order to the different books of the *Corpus aristotelicum*. With regard to the *Organon*, he proposes the following explanation of the order of its parts. The first is a treatise on words and concepts, the *Categories*; the second deals with sentences, the *Peri hermeneias*; and the third examines the syllogisms, the *Analytics*. Aquinas assumes that there is a rational order in which the works of Aristotle are arranged in the *Corpus aristotelicum*. He is obviously correct insofar as, in the first century B.C., the editors arranged the treatises they found in what they thought was the best order. Aristotle himself, however, may not have planned his logical writings in such a systematic way.

Deborah Black draws attention to a dispute, in the first part of the thirteenth century, as to whether the subject matter of the *Peri hermeneias* belongs to the liberal art of grammar studies or to logic. But the grammarian does not study the logically relevant properties of nouns and verbs.[17] There is no doubt as to Aquinas's position: the study of the subject matter of the treatise is subservient to the forming of correct statement and arguments.

Thomas quotes almost exclusively the ancient commentators, to whom, as Gauthier notes, even his *aliqui* and *quidam* usually refer, with two possible exceptions.[18] His sources are Ammonius, as translated by William of Moerbeke, and Boethius's second commentary. Boethius appears to have been inspired

---

14. *Expositio Libri Peryermeneias* (Leonine ed.), esp. 45*–84*. See also the very useful survey by María Regla Fernández Garrido, "Los commentarios griegos y latinos al *De interpretatione* aristotélico hasta Tomás de Aquino," in *Boletín de Lingüística y Filología clásica* 64 (1996): 307–23.

15. O. Lewry, "Two Continuators of Aquinas: Robertus de Vulgarbia and Thomas Sutton on the *Periher-meneias* of Aristotle," *Mediaeval Studies* 43 (1981): 58–130.

16. *In Aristotelis libros Peri hermeneias et Posteriorum analyticorum, Editio prima* (Rome: Ex Typographia Polyglotta S. C. de Propaganda Fide, 1882), 88–128. See also *Aristotle: "On Interpretation": Commentary by St. Thomas and Cajetan ("Peri Hermeneias")*, trans. Jean T. Oesterle (Milwaukee, Wis.: Marquette University Press, 1962).

17. "Aristotle's Peri Hermeneias in Medieval Latin and Arabic Philosophy," *Canadian Journal of Philosophy* 21 (1991): 25–83.

18. In Book I, lesson 14, the *quidam moderni* are unknown masters (Leonine ed., 1*/1:254) and the *aliqui magistri* might be those who defended some of the errors condemned in 1270 (Leonine ed., 1*/1:464).

by a Greek manuscript that contained comments by various authors such as Aspasius, Syrianus, Herminus, and Alexander, and presented the common doctrine of the School of Athens and/or of Alexandria.[19] The precise relation between the *Expositio* of Aquinas and the commentary of Ammonius has been studied by G. Verbeke, in his edition of the text of this Greek commentator referred to earlier. Thomas knew of some of Ammonius's views through the commentary of Boethius, who mentions Ammonius several times, but above all through a direct acquaintance with the work of this great Greek commentator. Ammonius is mentioned by name ten times.[20] Verbeke has shown that in all these passages, Thomas used the text of the Greek commentator.[21] But the influence of Ammonius goes much beyond these passages and Aquinas used his commentary continuously throughout the *Expositio,* often without even mentioning the author, much in the way the Greek commentator himself had used his predecessors. Nevertheless, Verbeke adds, the originality of Thomas is not affected by this persistent recourse to the commentary. He shows a remarkable mastery of the contents and an unsurpassed penetration of the often difficult doctrine.[22]

Noticing that Thomas interrupted his comments at exactly the same place as an incomplete codex of Moerbeke's translation, the *Basilicanus* H 6, Verbeke suspected that Thomas would have brought the not-yet-completed translation with him from Italy. However, Gauthier rightly rejects this hypothesis. It is better to assume that Thomas received the entire translation of the commentary in Paris, but that he did not complete his *Expositio* for other reasons, such as the departure of the addressee for Louvain, or the greater urgency of other tasks.

The dependence of the *Expositio* in respect to Boethius is more difficult to determine. Moreover, both Boethius and Ammonius probably used the same sources. Gauthier draws attention to the fact that the influence of such Greek commentators as Andronicus, Aspasius, and Alexander is much greater than the occasional critique of their views seems to warrant. Commenting on texts in late antiquity, one did not quote the authors by name when one agreed with what they said, but only when there was disagreement. And even so, the disagreement of the Greek commentators led Aquinas to formulate his own solutions. Deviations from the views of others are politely mentioned by him. Thomas most likely did not have and did not use the commentary by St. Albert. Likewise he does not refer to Averroes.

19. See James Shiel, "Boethius' Commentaries on Aristotle," *Medieval and Renaissance Studies* 4 (1958): 217–44.

20. Or even eleven times, if one also counts the *ipse* in Book II, lesson 2, 204 (Leonine ed., 1*/1:204).

21. Ammonius, *Commentaire sur le « Peri Hermeneias »*, xi–lxvi.

22. Ibid., xxxi.

Thomas's Intention in Writing the *Expositio*

As Thomas himself writes in his dedication, he composed his commentary at the request of a student, who had just been appointed provost of the Church of St. Peter in Louvain. This person, who is not further named by Thomas, has been identified by Gerard Verbeke as William Berthout, who was nominated provost of the Church toward the end of 1269 or in 1270, a fact which helps to date the composition of the *Expositio*. On the other hand, in his *Expositio*, Thomas refers to Book Lambda of the *Metaphysics* as Book XI, which shows that he did not yet have the new translation made by William of Moerbeke, who had now inserted Book Kappa (lacking in the *Media* translation), which became Book XI. Thomas began to use it after the middle of 1271, calling Book XII from now on Book Lambda. Moreover, William Berthout's departure from Paris to Leuven on October 15, 1270, might explain the fact that the *Expositio* ends abruptly. This yields a *terminus ante quem* for the redaction of the *Expositio*.

The fact that Thomas wrote the commentary at the request of Berthout might also explain why he based his commentary on Boethius's translation of Aristotle's work and not on that of William of Moerbeke, which accompanied Moerbeke's translation of Ammonius's commentary. As a student in Paris, Berthout was accustomed to use Boethius's translation and commentary, and thus a commentary based on a different translation would only have confused Berthout and his fellow students all the more. It may seem extraordinary that Thomas who, as he writes himself in his dedication of the treatise, was beset with a crushing amount of work, composed a commentary on a treatise of Aristotle at the request of a student who experienced some difficulties with it.[23]

As a matter of fact, the treatise contained important material for the study of logic and philosophy. Together with the *Categories* and other works, the *Peri hermeneias* was obligatory reading during the first year at the Faculty of Arts in Paris. Thomas may have had his reasons to accede to this request of the son of an influential family. The book deserves special attention: its text presents many difficulties and so commenting on it was a challenge, considering its importance in the scholarly tradition of the West.[24]

Moreover, as Isaac suggests, Thomas most likely also had an apologetic intention.[25] In his fourteenth lesson, as we will see, he refutes several errors taught by some Averroists about necessity and man's free will, some of which

---

23. Thomas himself writes "inter multiplices occupationum mearum sollicitudines."
24. As Thomas writes: "multis obscuritatibus involuto."
25. Isaac, *Le « Peri Hermeneias » en Occident de Boèce à saint Thomas*, 121.

were condemned by Bishop Étienne Tempier in December 1270. Giles of Rome listed many incorrect theories on the matter in his *Errores philosophorum* (written ca. 1270). Most errors concerned determinism as taught by some Averroists. About fifteen of the condemned errors are refuted directly or indirectly in lesson 14 of the *Expositio*. On March 18, 1277, Archbishop Robert Kilwardby condemned thirty theses, some seven of which have to do with the contents of the *Peri hermeneias,* such as "every proposition concerning the future is necessary."[26] Aquinas's interest in exposing defective interpretations of Aristotle's doctrine and in exposing false theories had been growing ever since he had composed the *Summa contra gentiles,* defended the mendicants against attacks, and argued against the theory of a single intellect for all men.

One may add also the following consideration. The idea had been forming in Thomas's mind to write commentaries on the major works of Aristotle in order to give an account of Aristotle's main doctrines, to defend his philosophy against the critique of those masters who felt that it was at variance with the doctrine of the faith, to secure their use in theology, to discard false interpretations, and to construct a coherent philosophy. In this context, the *Expositio* of the *Peri hermeneias* was to take its place among the other Aristotelian commentaries. Thomas could subscribe to the substance of the book not because Aristotle had written it, but simply because he was convinced that its contents were true.

An additional reason why, despite a very heavy load of work, Thomas undertook writing his *Expositio* at this particular moment of his life might well be that he had just received a copy of Moerbeke's translation of the commentary by Ammonius (finished in September 1268), about the time that he, Thomas, left Italy for Paris. This commentary provided him with a wealth of observations not just by Ammonius, but also by earlier Greek commentators quoted by Ammonius.

As Thomas says in his dedication, he wants to explain the deeper and more difficult contents (*altiora*) in such a way that the *Expositio* would be useful for those advanced in understanding and learning, but nevertheless would be of help to younger students. Clarity and simplicity of style, and the courage and insight with which he tackled the most difficult and obscure sentences, have made not only this *Expositio* but also his other Aristotelian commentaries famous. In fact, the method he uses is that of explaining the *littera, sensus,*

---

26. The condemned propositions can be found in *Chartularium Universitatis Parisiensis,* ed. H. Denifle and E. Chatelain (Paris, 1889), 1:558–60. These condemnations by Tempier and Kilwardby have been the topic of much research recently. For an excellent *status quaestionis* see the introduction to *Nach der Verurteilung von 1277* (ed. Aertsen et al.).

and *sententia* of the text, establishing as far as possible its *veritas*, setting forth its doctrine, placing it in the context of the whole treatise and of Aristotle's philosophy in general. Finally, he also tries to solve difficult questions. The *Expositio* is extremely detailed as it comments on every sentence, even on almost every word. Yet it is not pedantic. In his introduction to the Marietti edition of the *Expositio*, Fr. Raymund Spiazzi writes that Thomas explained the text in such a marvelous way (*mirifice amplificando et illustrando*) that his commentary seems more learned than the original. The reader discovers much more in the text than he had ever thought possible, yet it is still Aristotle's doctrine that Thomas is commenting on. He makes us see the astounding wealth of intelligibility hidden in the terse phrases of Aristotle. Besides explaining the doctrine contained in the *Peri hermeneias* up to its smallest details, Aquinas also develops the plan of the entire work and the principles on which it is based.[27]

The Commentary of Thomas Aquinas

Several of the Aristotelian commentaries of Aquinas are preceded by a preface or proem, in which he places the treatise in question in the context of Aristotle's other works and of the latter's whole philosophy, but these introductions are lacking in the commentary on the *Physics* and that on the *De anima*. The first chapter of the *Physics* is already such an introduction and this also applies to the *De anima,* where part of the first chapter, commented on in the first lesson, functions precisely as such a proem. For Thomas, the task of a proem is to present the subject matter of a treatise, setting it off against other disciplines and dividing it into its main subdivisions. Then, the proem should try to gain the favor of the readers of the treatise, invite them to open their minds to its contents, and warn them of the difficulties of the subject.[28] Likewise, in the *Expositio* of the *Peri Hermeneias*, a proem in the strict sense of the term is lacking, but Thomas adds an introduction that runs from lines 1 to 64 in the Leonine edition.[29]

He first sets the treatise in the ensemble of the *Organon*. As logic is the art of ordering the work of the intellect, it deals with its operations, which are two according to Aristotle: the apprehension of the intelligible content of

---

27. Isaac, *Le « Peri Hermeneias » en Occident de Boèce à saint Thomas*, 139.

28. See K. White, "St. Thomas Aquinas on Prologues," *Archivum franciscanum historicum* 98 (2005): 803–13.

29. In what follows, I use the English translation published as *Commentary on Aristotle's "On Interpretation,"* trans. J. Oesterle (Notre Dame, Ind.: Dumb Ox Books, 2004).

things, namely their essences, and the combination or separation of these in a second operation of the mind. But a third operation is usually added, he says; namely, the reasoning by which the mind proceeds to investigate what is as yet unknown to it.[30] The first operation is presupposed by the second, and this in turn is ordered to the third. Aristotle himself speaks of *two* operations of the mind,[31] clearly stating an essential difference between the simple apprehension and the second operation, while the third is at the same level as the second. Thomas considers these operations as intimately connected: they are all directed "having certitude about something not yet known" (*ad certitudinem accipiendam de aliquibus ignotis*). The distinction provides a way to divide the logical works of Aristotle into three groups: the *Categories*, the *Peri hermeneias*, and the *Analytics* (and related treatises).

In the following lines, Thomas explains the meaning of the title. According to Boethius, he says, the term *interpretatio* may be used to indicate words which signify something (but not natural sounds uttered by animals who do not intend to express anything): a person "who interprets something, wants to expose and set forth." In this understanding, verbs and nouns are "interpretations" but, according to Aquinas, names and verbs are *principles* of interpretation rather than interpretations themselves. Only the enunciation in which there is truth or falsehood can be called an interpretation. Such sentences and wishes, requests and commands express affections.[32] In a closing remark of this introductory section, Thomas notes that the treatise deals with names and verbs insofar as they are parts of an enunciation. This prepares the transition to the exposition of the doctrine of the treatise.

Book I

In lesson 1 (nos. 5–8; 1.16a1–2), Thomas notes that when dealing with enunciations one must first consider their parts, that is, names and verbs. These are not considered absolutely taken, but insofar as they belong to sentences. Compared to the long-drawn-out explanations of Ammonius (18–19), Aquinas is very concise. Two difficulties are raised:

(a) Why does Aristotle not speak of other terms besides the name and the verb, such as pronouns, particles, etc.? The answer is that names and verbs are necessary, and these other words are not. Moreover, the other words can be reduced to names or verbs. Thomas uses Ammonius's explanation: the other

---

30. The words *additur autem et tertia* express a certain reservation.

31. *De anima* III.6.430a10ff.

32. Thomas is quite close to the original sense of the term ἑρμενεία in *Poetics* 1450b14. Ammonius has the same explanation.

words may be compared to the nails that hold the boards of a boat together, which is made of wooden boards, that is, nouns and verbs.[33]

(b) Aristotle deals with negations and affirmations, but there are also hypothetical propositions. Thomas appears to accept the current division into categorical and hypothetical propositions.[34] Thomas states that one might say that a hypothetical proposition consists of some categorical ones, but then adds a better explanation, which was also proposed by Ammonius: in this treatise, Aristotle wants to show how to reach absolute truth, and hypothetical sentences do not lead to it.

In the first sentence of his text, after mentioning the name and the verb, Aristotle continues as follows: after dealing with names and verbs we must determine "what a negation, an affirmation, a statement and a sentence are." The difference between the last two terms is not clear at first sight. The term *statement* (ἀπόφανσις) indicates a complex of words that may comprise one or more sentences; if it consists of one, it can be either a negation or an affirmation. *Sentence* (λόγος) is a generic term that may mean a statement but also other types of sentences.

One might find fault with this enumeration insofar as the affirmation is prior to the negation and the statement (as their genus) prior to both, and, again, the sentence as encompassing statements is also prior. But, Thomas says, the answer to this difficulty is that Aristotle proceeds from the parts to the whole. In this way, a negation that divides and separates the parts of a proposition is prior to the affirmation. Thomas mentions a second explanation that, however, he is reluctant to make his own: in the realm of the contingent, not-being precedes being. Now, a negation signifies not-being. Aquinas closes the first lesson with an explanation proposed by Porphyry, as mentioned by Ammonius and Boethius: if we take affirmations and negations to be a species dividing a genus on an equal footing, it does not matter which one is mentioned first. In fact, after dealing with names and verbs in chapters 2 and 3, Aristotle discusses sentences in chapter 4, statements in chapter 5, and affirmations and negations in chapter 6.

The text of the first chapter, after the few introductory lines, is only about a half-page long, but in St. Thomas's commentary it covers lessons 2 and 3. In lesson 2 (nos. 9–13; 1.16a3–9), Aristotle briefly explains the function of speech and recalls that words such as names and verbs by themselves are neither true

---

33. Ammonius, *Commentaire sur le « Peri Hermeneias »*, 23, 65.

34. Did Aristotle exclude hypothetical propositions and was Theophrastus the first to discuss them? See J. Barnes, "Theophrastus and Hypothetical Syllogisms," in *Theophrastus of Eresus: On His Life and Work*, ed. W. W. Fortenbaugh (Oxford: Clarendon, 1985), 125–41.

nor false. St. Thomas first mentions the function of speech: spoken sounds are symbols of affections of the soul and these, in turn, originate from our perception of things. Written marks are symbols of spoken words. Thomas adds a short but fine survey of the function of speech. As a political and social animal, man needs to communicate with others.[35] He does so through the spoken word. If he had sense cognition only, uttering sounds like animals do would be sufficient to signify certain concrete things, but because he is gifted with intellectual knowledge, which abstracts from the here and now, there also results in him a preoccupation with the future. Thus, to manifest his thoughts to those far away or to a future generation, man needed to resort to the written word. Logic being ordered to the acquisition of knowledge from things, the study of the meaning of words, which is immediately dependent on the concepts in the mind, is part of its main subject matter. The study of the individual letters, on the other hand, belongs to the subject matter of grammar.

Spoken words express what is in the mind and can be represented in writing. Aristotle speaks of "affections" of the mind. This term also signifies the passions in the sensitive appetite, which, at the level of animal life, are expressed by certain sounds.[36] But in this context, the term means the concepts of the mind signified by names, verbs, and sentences. The term "affections" is convenient insofar as it recalls that people often communicate with others, moved by passions, and also because concepts result from one's being affected by impressions coming mostly from the outside. The affections are likenesses of things. Things, Thomas says, are not known by us except by means of some likeness of them present in the senses or in the intellect.[37]

Aristotle points out that these inner affections of the soul—concepts—are the same for all men, as are the things of which they are concepts, but that the words by means of which we express them and the written symbols are not the same for all. This shows, says Thomas, that names and verbs do not come to us by natural determination, for in that case they would be the same for all.

According to some authors people do not always have the same opinions about a number of things and that then their concepts must also be different. Completing an explanation by Boethius, Aquinas answers that the concepts produced in the simple apprehension of things are the same: if people really

---

35. Thomas stresses man's social nature, which was implicitly contained in the Greek idea of being a citizen of a *polis*, but that was no longer so obvious in the days of the Roman Empire or the Middle Ages. Gauthier sees Stoic influences at work (Leonine ed., 1*/1:9).

36. In lesson 4 (Leonine ed., 1*/1:22, 175–80), Thomas distinguishes between *sonus* and *vox*. Certain animals that do not have lungs nevertheless utter their inner affections by means of sounds (*sonus*). The remark was made by Boethius.

37. In his *Cratylus*, Plato writes that in sense knowledge the soul goes toward things in which it comes to rest (ἵστησιν).

grasp what "man" is, they have the same concept. A different concept is no longer that of man. Our words signify in the first place these simple concepts. With regard to the difficulty of equivocal words (to which more than one concept corresponds) Thomas answers that Aristotle does not say that everywhere the same word must correspond to a concept, but he holds that, with regard to the same thing, people have the same concept.[38]

Lesson 3 (nos. 14–18; 1.16a9–18) comments on the last section of Aristotle's first chapter, where he goes beyond the statement of the identity between the spoken words and the concepts of the mind, and deals with the different significations that spoken words may have: that some are true, and others are not. This is explained by the fact that the mind is related to these words as a cause to its effects, which imitate their cause. The mind has a dual operation, in one of which there is no truth or falsehood, but in the other there is. When the mind grasps the quiddity of a thing, for example, of man or of colors, there is no truth or falsehood, but when it combines or separates two concepts, it is true or false. To the objection that when the simple concepts are not true or false, their combination will not be so either, Thomas answers that we must compare the understanding reached by the intellect to reality. If the intellect combines what is combined in reality, or separates what is separated in reality, it is true.

But one might object that the simple apprehension also seems to have its truth: for instance, we perceive an object made of true gold. In keeping with this, Aristotle says that the perception of its proper object by a sense is always true. Moreover, in God's intellect there is no composition or division, but the simple grasp of the truth. Similar objections were raised also in other commentaries on the *Peri hermeneias,* as Gauthier points out. In his answer, Aquinas recalls the distinction between the truth in things and the truth in the one who knows and expresses the truth. But in both cases the truth is compared to the intellect. However, a thing can be compared to the intellect in two ways: first, as its measure and, second, as being measured by it. Things are the measure of man's speculative intellect. The intellect is said to be true when it is conformed to what is, false when it is not. Of natural things we do not say that they are true or false in respect to the intellect, except insofar as they may produce a right or wrong concept. A yellow piece of metal may make us believe wrongly that it is made of gold. In the second way, the intellect is the measure of things, as is evident in the case of the practical intellect, which

---

38. See Ana María Mora-Márquez, "*Peri hermeneias* 16a3–8: Histoire d'une rupture de la tradition interprétative dans le bas Moyen-Âge," *Revue Philosophique de la France et de l'Étranger* 136 (2011): 67–84. She concludes that Thomas's account is "structurellement très semblable" to that of Boethius and traces the "drastic change" that occurs in later medieval authors regarding the relation between word and concept.

designs and makes things. An artifact is true when it corresponds to the design of its maker, but erroneous, bad, or a failure when is does not. As all things are compared to the divine intellect as artifacts to an art, each thing *can* be said to be true inasmuch as it has its form that imitates the divine art.

The senses when perceiving their proper objects are true, yet do not know that they are. The intellect, however, can know its conformity to things, and in this way truth (as known) is only in the intellect, as when the intellect judges that a thing is such as it perceives it, for instance, that "the wind is cold." It means that this known conformity is present in us when our intellect combines (wind with cold) or divides (wind, not warm). God knows the truth differently from the way man does, that is to say, without combining or separating a subject and a predicate.

Aristotle concludes that names or verbs, taken individually, do not express the truth, but can become true or false when "is" or "is not" is added. Ammonius mentions some apparent exceptions. Sometimes a single word can be a statement, as an answer to a question, for example: "What swims in the sea? Fishes," where the verb *do* is understood in the answer. The same applies to verbs.

In lesson 4 (nos. 1–24; 2.16a19–b5), Thomas begins by proposing an original division of the contents of the chapter and of the section he first comments upon: as Aristotle intends to deal with statements (enunciations), he first considers the *principles* of a statement before turning to the statement itself. With regard to these principles, he discusses first the material parts of statements—the names and verbs—and then the sentence (of which the statement is a species).[39] A sound uttered by a living being can be articulated or not articulated (such as a whistling not produced to warn or to call someone's attention). A name is a spoken sound with a meaning. Every sound (uttered by living beings) is something natural, whereas a name is established by man. An opponent may argue that if it is man who gives names, their genus is that of signs, and not that of their material substrate. But Thomas answers that a wooden dish is said to be a piece of wood that has been given a certain form. In artifacts, the form is accidental to the substrate, which is its matter. Therefore, if a name signifies a form *in concreto*, we may indicate its matter in its definition, that is, a spoken sound, adding the further, accidental determination "with a meaning." For abstract names this is different. In their case the accidental determination becomes the genus and the material substrate the added determination; for example, a snub nose is a curvature of the nose.

The meaning of a name is established by man, that is, by convention. Thus

---

39. As was pointed out, the word sentence signifies statements, wishes, commands, and prayers.

a name differs from meaningful sounds emitted by animals. Aristotle adds that a name has a meaning without indicating the time factor, whereas a verb signifies action or being affected by something, and therefore has to do with movement, which is primarily measured by time. On the other hand, a substance as such, insofar as it is signified by a name or a pronoun, has nothing in itself that is measured by time. It does so only if it is subject to movement, and is signified by the participle—for example, playing.

A further characteristic of a name is that none of its parts by itself signifies something. This distinguishes it from a sentence that sometimes signifies without reference to time, for example, when one says "a just man," where each of the parts has its own meaning. This raises the problem of composite names such as Calippus (composed of "beautiful" and "horse").[40] According to Aristotle, the parts of such a name do not signify anything by themselves, although they may give the impression of doing so.

Aristotle adds (16a27) as the third part of his definition of names that names signify by convention, and not naturally, but only after a name has been accepted as a symbol. Sounds with a certain signification, uttered by animals, are not names. Repeating what Ammonius says, Thomas notes that according to some authors, names have no natural signification whatsoever, whereas others assert that names signify by their very nature, as if they were likenesses of things. But Aristotle's view is that their signification is not by nature, but may be called "by nature" insofar as it allegedly corresponds to the nature of things, as Plato believed. For certain things several names are used. Because of different properties things may have, they can be given several names.

In the following section (16a30–b5), negative names and the inflected cases of names are excluded from use in statements. Negative names such as "not-man" have no definite signification, but can mean anything from chimeras to physical bodies, plants and animals. Aristotle calls them "indefinite names." They are excluded from use in affirmations and negations. Likewise, the inflected cases of names, such as the genitive and dative, are excluded from statements with the verb "to be"; a sentence like "mother's is" is neither true nor false.

In lesson 5 (nos. 25–31; 3.16b6–25), Aristotle now turns to a discussion of the verb and defines it as he already defined the name, adding that a verb additionally signifies *time*. Thomas recounts that Ammonius wondered why Aristotle also added "of which no part signifies separately," a characteristic that the verb has in common with names (while he omits to mention the other

---

40. Thomas, who follows Boethius's translation, reads *equiferus*.

property it has in common with names, namely that it is "a spoken word which signifies by convention"). Ammonius believes he did so in order to distinguish it from a sentence like "walking is moving." But Thomas suggests that here the addition is more necessary than in the case of names, because the verb is the more formal part of a sentence, as it brings about the composition.

The verb is "a sign of things which are said of something else, as it is always on the side of the predicate." When one objects that sometimes a verb functions as a name (e.g., in "to walk is to move"), Thomas solves the difficulty as follows: names signify things as existing by themselves, while verbs signify actions. But "action" can have a triple meaning: (1) when it is taken abstractly by itself, then it signifies as a name (e.g., an activity, a walk); (2) as emanating from a substance, in which it is inherent to the subject and signified by verbs in other modes (e.g., Peter will speak; John underwent surgery); but (3) because this emanation from or inherence in a subject can be apprehended by the intellect as a certain thing, the infinitive form of verbs can be taken either as a name (insofar as they signify certain things) or as verbs insofar as they form a concrete compound.

From 16b8 onward, Aristotle explains his definition of verbs. A verb such as "he runs" signifies an action but also time. Movement is measured by time, and actions are known to us as taking place in time. Aristotle's sentence "a verb *additionally* (προσσημαίνει) signifies time" means that a movement signified by it is measured by time. On the other hand, to signify time as the main sense of the term (e.g., a day or week) may be done by names. However, to signify time as an added sense cannot be done by names, but only by verbs.

Aristotle adds that a verb signifies what actually is (πάρχεῖν) and is always a sign of what belongs to or applies to a subject. Thomas gives a remarkable explanation: a verb signifies an action as being performed. It is characteristic of an action to be inherent in a subject. Therefore, it always has the role of a predicate and brings about the composition of the predicate with the subject, so that in every statement there must be a verb.

Differently from the Oxford text as established by Minio-Paluello, the Greek manuscript on which the translation of Boethius is based reads: a verb "is always a sign of what is predicated of a subject or is in a subject" (16b10).[41] This distinction seems superfluous. Boethius himself says that it does not make a difference because an accident is predicated of a subject and is in a subject. Thomas explains the disjunction as follows: a verb is always a sign that something is predicated (as every predication comes about by a verb that

---

41. The Oxford text omits the last part: ἡ ἐν ὑποκειμένῳ.

establishes the composition), whether essentially (Socrates is a living being) or accidentally (Socrates is white).[42]

In the next lines (16b11–b18), Aristotle excludes certain forms from qualifying as verbs in statements. He does not consider "does not recover" and "is not sick" to be verbs in the strict sense of the term, although they co-signify time and are always in a subject or said of someone, but they are different from ordinary verbs and should be considered indefinite verbs because they can apply to what is and to what is not. Thomas comments that they eliminate rather than state action or passion. However, they do agree with verbs insofar as they co-signify time and function always as a predicate. "Is not sick" expresses something passive, but undergoing, as a privation of action, is also measured by time, as is rest. In short, according to Thomas, these indefinite verbs fall short of the perfect definition of verbs. There is but one way, Thomas says, in which indefinite verbs signify, which is by the exclusion of one precise action or passion. Verbs in a negative clause negate a certain action (or passion), excluding it from the subject.[43]

In the following lines, Aristotle considers the different tenses of verbs and argues that the tenses of verbs other than the present are not true verbs because they do not signify the present time. Thomas observes that one should not understand Aristotle as meaning "the present moment," because the present exists in an indivisible now, whereas action and movement do not take place in an instant. The words "co-signifies time" refer to time as the measure of an action that begins but is not yet finished. Indeed, a true verb signifies an action or passion as taking place. The past and the future tenses may be called inflected cases of a verb, but conjugated forms in the singular and plural and according to the persons must not be referred to in this way (here the difference lies in the subject, not in the action), notwithstanding that conjugation according to moods and tenses are like cases of verbs.

When uttered just by itself a verb is a name, that is, a spoken word which signifies a thing (according to Thomas). Because even action and passion are certain realities, the verbs that signify them fall under the common denominator of names. But insofar as names are distinguished from verbs, they signify things that can be conceived as existing by themselves. This is the reason that names can be subjects and things can be predicated of them. A verb used by itself calls up a concept in the mind of the hearer at the level of the first

---

42. For an extensive study of this passage, emphasizing the originality of Thomas's position, see J. A. García Cuadrado, "La consignificatio verbal (Per hermeneias 16b 8–10): Ammonio, Boecio y Tomás de Aquino," *Revista Española de Filosofía Medieval* 19 (2012): 87–100.

43. Thomas writes that they are used *in vi duarum distinctionum* (Leonine ed., 1*/1:5, 185–86).

operation of the mind, that is, simple apprehension. It does not yet say whether the thing expressed by this concept exists or not. Not even "to be" or "not to be" by themselves indicate actual existence. This statement recalls the distinction between the first and the second operation of the intellect.

There are slight differences in the ways that Alexander, Porphyry, and Ammonius explain Aristotle's remark that not even "to be" is a sign of an actually existing thing. Alexander thinks it is not because it is analogically said of the different categories. But Thomas observes that this cannot be the reason, for it is said primarily of the substance, and so it has a primary meaning. Porphyry understood Aristotle's words as saying that "to be" does not signify the nature of a thing, but only the conjunction of the subject and the predicate. Thomas replies that if this explanation were correct, "to be" would be neither a name nor a verb. Ammonius understands the expression as meaning that "to be" as such does not signify what is true or false, but does so together with something added to it. But, says Aquinas, this is common to all names and verbs, and is therefore not sufficient. At this point Thomas introduces his own understanding of being. Being (*ens,* τὸ ὄν) signifies "that what is" and thus a certain composition, but it does not signify this composition primarily but rather secondarily, inasmuch as it signifies a thing that has being. But this composition ("that which is") is not yet enough to make a statement about what is true or false.

Availing himself of the Latin text in the codex of Boethius's translation at that time in use in Paris, Thomas now makes a most important doctrinal statement. This Latin text reads *nec ipsum est* instead of *ipsum quidem nichil est.* It means that without the parts of the statement being expressed, there is no perfect understanding of a composition and so there is neither truth nor falsehood. Aristotle writes that "the verb 'to be'" signifies in addition a composition. Thomas explains that this "signifies in addition" means that "to be" does not signify the composition principally, but consecutively. The somewhat unclear expression of Aristotle enables Thomas to add his own doctrine of being. "To be" signifies in the first place that which enters the mind as actuality (actual existence) in an absolute way.[44] For "is," stated without anything additional, signifies "to be actually" and therefore its signification is by way of a verb. This *actualitas* (actualization, reality) is the primary meaning of "to be." Because the actuality that this verb "to be" signifies is the actuality of every form or act, as common to all, whether substances or accidents, we use it of whatever form to indicate that it is inherent in a subject, whether simply in the present tense, or according to other tenses. From this results its signifying a composition.

Verbeke refers to Ammonius as the background of this doctrine but that is

---

44. "Significat enim quod primo cadit in intellectu per modum actualitatis absolute."

not quite correct. Ammonius only says that the verb mainly signifies participation in being and, secondarily, the connection of a subject and a predicate, but he does not mention at all the fact that its primary sense is absolute actuality.[45]

As announced in the introduction, we now pass, in lesson 6 (nos. 32–35; 4.16b26–17a2), to an examination of sentences of which names and verbs are the material parts. The sentence (λόγος) is the genus of which the statement (ἀπόφανσις) is a subdivision. First, Aristotle states what the sentence has in common with the name and the verb, namely "spoken sounds," and then points out the difference by adding the phrase "of which some part has a meaning when used separately," that is to say, "as an expression, not as an affirmation" (ὡς φάσις, ἀλλ'οὐχ ὡς κατάφασις). According to Thomas, Aristotle, who expresses himself very tersely,[46] means a reference to the parts of a sentence, some of which at least have a meaning of their own,[47] but are not statements. The ancient commentators, as quoted by Boethius, saw a difficulty in this definition of sentences. There are, Aspasius says, complex sentences such as conditional clauses, of which a part can be a statement. Alexander defends Aristotle, noting that we first deal with incomposite sentences, or that Aristotle discusses what is common to both simple and composite sentences. Against Philoponus, Thomas argues that the definition applies to both perfect and imperfect sentences.

Aristotle explains his definition in the following lines. The word "man" as part of a sentence signifies something, but it does not say that a man exists, except potentially: only when a verb is added can the name "man" do so. However, a single syllable signifies nothing. When one objects that sometimes a syllable as part of a name does have a meaning (as "re" in real or "par" in party), Thomas answers that when a syllable is part of a word in a sentence, there is only one signification, although such a part of a word may, in a different context, be a name in its own right. Aristotle therefore says that in double words a part has a meaning, but not in its own right. By "double words" Thomas is referring to composite terms like "breakfast."

Every sentence signifies something. It does so not as a natural tool but by convention. Aristotle wants to say that speech is not a natural instrument. The lungs and the throat are natural tools by which the spoken sound is formed and which becomes articulate by the tongue, lips, and teeth.[48] They are used

---

45. See A. Zimmermann, "'Ipsum enim ("est") nihil est' (Aristoteles, Periherm. I, c.3). Thomas von Aquin über die Bedeutung der Kopula," in *Der Begriff der Repraesentatio im Mittelalter*, ed. A. Zimmermann (Berlin: De Gruyter, 1971), 282–95.

46. Suggesting that he wants to avoid repetitions *studens brevitati* (Leonine ed., 1*/1:25, 12).

47. The "some" refers to particles or to terms such as "no."

48. See Ammonius, *In de interpretatione* 120.9.

by the interpretative power,[49] which produces the sentence and its parts as effects of its art. The meaning of sentences depends therefore on convention. This interpretative power belongs to human reason and so it is not a natural power, but stands above all corporeal things.

The short lesson 7 (nos. 36–38; 4.17a2–b7) comments on the last five lines of Aristotle's fourth chapter. Because sentences that are statements are distinguished from those that express a wish (and are neither true nor false), Thomas sees this passage as an introduction to the rest of Book I, which, he writes, deals with statements in general, while Book II considers the different types of statements according to the additions made.[50] With astonishing concision, Aristotle mentions in one brief sentence both the definition and the division of statements. A statement is a sentence in which there is truth or falsity.

Thomas explains this as follows: there is truth or falsehood in a sentence insofar as it is a sign of truth or falsehood in the intellect. Truth or falsehood are in the intellect as in their subject, and in things outside the mind insofar as they are the cause of truth or falsehood in the human mind: according to whether something is or is not, the statement that asserts it is true or false.[51]

In addition to imperfect or incomplete sentences, which do not state truth or falsehood because they do not express a judgment of the mind, there are five kinds of sentences of which only the first is a statement, expressing truth or falsehood. The four remaining kinds, which Aquinas mentions after Boethius and the Peripatetics, are prayers/requests, orders, questions, and evocations. Those of the last group must consist of more than one word and call someone to attention, like calling someone "illustrious professor."

Thomas gives a fine explanation of these four types of sentences that does not appear in his sources. The human mind does not only conceive the truth, but it must also direct others according to its understanding. Now people are directed by someone (a) to pay attention, (b) to answer questions, or (c) to perform a task. Prayers or requests are addressed to one's superiors. One can reduce wishes to this last group. With regard to our superiors we have no other way to bring them to do something than by expressing our wishes to them. As these four kinds of sentences do not express the truth or falsehood present in the mind, but rather a certain relation to it, there is no truth or falsehood in them. Dubitative sentences are reduced to the group of questions. These four types of sentences belong more properly to the subjects studied in rhetoric

---

49. The expression *virtus interpretativa* occurs in this chapter of the commentary and in *In II Sent.*, d. 3, q. 1, a. 6, in the sense of *virtus loquendi*.

50. In his *Expositio*, Thomas has Book II begin at chap. 10.

51. Thomas refers to *Metaphysics* VI.4.1027b25ff. and *Categories* 4b8–10.

or in poetics, but not to that of the present research. In line with Ammonius, Thomas indicates the reason for this: the doctrine stated in the *Peri hermeneias* is meant to serve demonstrations that can help us assent to the truth, arguing from what is proper to things, so that demonstrations use statements only; on the other hand, rhetoric and poetics attempt to bring people to agree to something also by reasoning from the subjective dispositions of the public. In a final remark, Thomas adds that it is the task of grammar—one of the liberal arts—to see to the correct use of words and the construction of the sentence.[52]

Having defined statements in the previous section, in lesson 8 (nos. 39–45; 5.17a8–26) Aristotle gives (very succinctly, says Thomas) a twofold division of statements: affirmations and negations, on the one hand, and single statements and statements that are one in virtue of a connective, on the other. Thomas sees the basis for the latter group of statements in the fact that certain things are one because they are indivisible or form a continuum, others by being connected, compounded, or by being ordered to each other. Because each being is one, each statement must be so too. This conclusion is based on the theory that language expresses our thinking, which, in turn, reflects reality.

Statements that are one must be either affirmations or negations. An affirmation is prior to a negation for three reasons, according to the spoken word being the expression of thought and thought that of reality. Consisting, as it does, of words, an affirmation—being simpler—is prior to a negation, which adds the particle "not." Considered from the point of view of the intellect, an affirmation is also prior because it denotes composition, which precedes division: one can only divide that which is composed. Finally, when considered from the point of view of reality, an affirmative statement is also prior because it signifies being, while a negation signifies not-being. Now, a being or a *habitus* is prior by nature to a negation or privation. Here, Aquinas does not tell us how to reconcile this conclusion with the fact that the first principle, namely the principle of contradiction, has the form of a negation. The answer is that despite its negative formulation ("being is not nonbeing"), the principle expresses the otherness of whatever is not a particular thing. In this way it expresses a positive structure of reality. One may add that the question of the priority of affirmations over negations applies to statements with the same subject and predicate.

Ammonius notes that Alexander of Aphrodisias objected to affirmations and negations being considered species of the same genus, as affirmations are

---

52. As Gauthier indicates in his invaluable edition of the text, what Thomas says was the standard theory of the twelfth- and thirteenth-century Latin authors. See also Q. *de malo*, q. 3, a. 6; *ST* I-II, q. 94, a. 1: *per habitum grammaticæ (aliquis) agit orationem congruam.*

prior and more basic, just as substance is prior to the being of the accidents. However, Thomas writes that the natural priority of affirmations in respect to negations does not take away their common generic nature of being sentences that state the truth or express what is not.

Aristotle continues by saying that every sentence that qualifies as a statement must contain a verb or an inflexion of a verb (πτώσεως). Without the addition of "is" or "will be" or "was" or something of the kind, even the definition of man is not yet a statement. And Aristotle adds that the mere fact that words are placed together does not make them one, while explaining why the notion "two-footed land animal," which is one and not many, is to be investigated in a different discipline.[53] A first remark by Thomas concerns the question why only the verb is mentioned and not also the name. Thomas gives three reasons in the order of increasing likelihood, which had been put forward by Peter of Spain, Porphyry, and Ammonius, respectively: (1) no statements are without a verb, but in some there is no name; (2) the verb, being the predicate, is the most formal part of a statement; and (3) from what Aristotle had said before about some statements being one or simple (while others are one by a connective) someone might conclude that those of the first group are not composed at all. Now, this is excluded by the remark that in every statement there must be a verb, which always implies some composition, whereas a name does not imply composition. Thomas adds that in this way Aristotle makes plain that the absolute unity of a statement is not impaired by the composition that is implied by the verb nor by the number of names of which the definition consists. The predicate is to the subject what form is to matter. This holds also for the specific difference and the genus.

In 17a17–20, Aristotle says that a single statement is either one because it manifests something that is one, or because it is one in virtue of a connective. We have more than one statement if more things are manifested or if there are no connectives. Thomas extensively comments on this sentence, apparently borrowing little from other commentators. First, he refers to a suggestion by Boethius according to whom unity and plurality, said of sentences, refer to their signification, but that "simple" and "composite" refer to the words beings used. "A man is white" is one statement, but it is composed of more words. Some conditional sentences are composed of more statements, which nevertheless signify one thing. When two sentences such as "Socrates walks,

---

53. Thomas adds "in metaphysics." The specific difference becomes a unity with the genus, in the way matter is determined by the substantial form, so that "man" signifies one essence. The mere fact that "two-footed" and "land-animal" are pronounced the one after the other without interval is not sufficient to constitute this oneness; the specific difference must be integrated in the generic subject.

Plato debates" are juxtaposed, they do not form a single sentence. But this interpretation is not quite satisfactory, because Aristotle seems to distinguish between sentences that signify one thing and sentences that are one because of a connective. Moreover, Aristotle states that "two-footed land animal" is one thing and not many, but what is one in virtue of a connective is one proceeding from many. Therefore, Aristotle is likely to indicate in the text that a statement is one if it signifies one thing, even if it uses several words, and that if one statement signifies more things, it will not be one without more, but one by conjunction.

Statements are more than one if they signify more than one thing,[54] or when they not only signify more than one thing, but also when these more than one are not connected at all. This yields three types of statements: (1) statements that are simply one due to signifying one thing; (2) statements that are more than one insofar as they signify more things, but are one secondarily insofar as they are one in virtue of a connective; and finally, (3) statements that are simply more than one, as they do not signify one thing nor are one by being connected.

In 17a17–20, Aristotle says that names and verbs may be called just expressions (φάσις) which reveal nothing in the way of a statement whether in answering a question or saying something spontaneously. As Ammonius had observed before him, Thomas notes that when sometimes a single name or verb is used to state an answer to a question, this name or this verb is always understood as connected to something else that was said in that question.

The last section of lesson 8 concerns the final lines of 5.17a20–25. Aristotle summarizes what he said before: a statement can be one by signifying just what is one, or because it is one when compounded, but it always affirms or denies something of something (a name or a verb is one but does not affirm or deny something of something).

Against the interpretation of Alexander to which Boethius refers, Thomas maintains that Aristotle uses the term "statement" in a generic way, comprising both affirmations and negations. According to Boethius, Aristotle would have melted together in one short sentence both the definition and the division of statements, but Thomas says that one may well understand the phrase "a simple statement affirming or denying something of something" as the definition of statements, or, perhaps better, one may say with Ammonius that the sentence only gives a division of statements. The reason is that in the definition of a genus, the species and their properties should not be mentioned.

---

54. A statement such as "an animal is endowed with sense cognition" contains much information, yet is one.

So we should retain the definition given above: "a statement is a sentence in which there is truth or falsehood." The definition of an affirmation is "a sentence stating something of something" and a negation is "a sentence denying something of something."

Thomas ends his comments on this chapter with a note of admiration for Aristotle, who divides statements as a genus in its specific differences (stating what is or what is not) and formulates, with the help of these differences, the definitions: an affirmation is a sentence stating something of something, a negation is a sentence denying something of something.

The introductory lines of lesson 9 (nos. 46–48; 6.17a26–37) let us see at what point of the investigation we have arrived by contrasting affirmative and negative statements: for every affirmation there is an opposite negation and vice versa. The former affirms that something is, the latter that something is not. One can also compare the statements to reality: if the statement, whether affirmative or negative, is in agreement with reality, it is true; if not, it is false.

Aristotle, Thomas says, proceeds from what is less to what is more, and so he goes from negative to affirmative statements and from false to true sentences. The statements need not refer to the existence of things, but may also concern the presence of a predicate in a subject. For example, the statement "a crow is white" is a false statement, not because the bird does not exist, but simply because the attribution of "white" is wrong.

Aristotle adds that, in addition to the present tense, this holds also for the past and future tenses, which in a sense lie outside the present moment. It follows from the above that every affirmative statement can be denied, and every negation affirmed. For one can affirm only what is real in the world (*in rerum natura*) in one of the three tenses (or what is not), and all of this can be denied and *vice versa*. It follows that for every affirmation there is a negation, and for every negation an affirmation. The opposite would only be the case if one could affirm something in a statement that could not be denied. An affirmation and a negation that are opposite are called a contradiction (ἀντίφασις).

Aristotle calls statements contradictory when they affirm and deny the same thing of the same thing (the terms not being used in an equivocal sense). Thomas comments that the statements must have the same subject and predicate, such as "Plato walks" and "Plato does not walk." Not only must the terms be the same, but they must also have the same meaning. There are four ways, Thomas continues, in which diversity might occur, so that there is no contradiction: (a) if statements concern different parts of something, for example, if someone says that an Ethiopian is black (according to the color of his skin) and a second person that he is white (referring to the color of his teeth), there is no contradiction; (b) if the predicate is qualified, for example, "Peter is jogging (in the morning)" and "Peter is not jogging (at noon)"; (c) if place or time are different, for example, "it rains (in Italy)" and "it does not rain (in France)"; (d) if there is a reference to something extrinsic, for example, "ten people are a crowd (in this room)" and "ten people aren't a crowd (in a public square or a theater hall)." The same examples are used by the commentators. Aristotle explains these distinctions in his *De sophisticis elenchis,* 165b23–168b16, as Thomas notes (following Ammonius), in order to counter the objections of certain sophists.

At this point, in lesson 10 (nos. 49–56; 7.17a38–b16), Aristotle proceeds by distinguishing the various ways in which affirmative and negative statements can be opposed to each other. There is, in the first place, the difference of the subjects of the sentence, which is a name (or something which takes its place). Now, a name is a spoken word that expresses the concept of the intellect in its simple apprehension, which is a likeness with some being. Aristotle distinguishes the subject of a statement according to the way reality is divided, where certain things are universal (essences) and others are singulars. The universal is of such a nature that it can be predicated of many, while the singular can only be said of one individual thing, for example, "man" (universal) and "Plato" (singular). But is there a real difference between both, insofar as the universal "man" is found in the individual "Plato" and does not exist by itself?

In agreement with other commentators, Thomas solves the problem by saying that words represent things in the way these are conceived by the intellect, which can separate what in reality is united, and so distinguish between the individual and the universal present in it. When a thing is named after what belongs to it insofar as it is this particular thing, this name signifies an individual something. However, when a thing is named after what is common to it and to many other things, such a name signifies a universal (concept), as it denotes an essence or some determination that is common to many. Thomas continues his extremely clear explanation (not found, it seems, in his sources) saying that Aristotle presents this division not according to the way things exist outside the mind, but insofar as they are referred to the mind. He defines the universal in relation to the human intellect.

Thomas observes that the addition "of such a nature" to the phrase "that it can be predicated of many" is necessary to cover those cases in which an essence that as such can be a universal predicated of many individuals, is in fact not predicated in this way, because of some impediment; for example, if there were only one human being left, "man" would no longer be predicated of many individuals. Every form that by its nature is apt to be received in matter is communicable, but it happens that a form is not communicable: namely, when it is entirely determined by this matter (e.g., the names Socrates or Plato), or when a form is not apt to be received in matter (e.g., the abstract form "whiteness"). In a final remark on this section, Aquinas points out that Aristotle does not divide names in universal and particular names but reality. A universal is that which is of such a nature that it can be in many. Once more, Aquinas stresses that reality is the basis of the way in which we make statements.

In 17b1–3, Aristotle concludes from what he said above—that some things are universals, others particulars—that our statements affirm or deny something of a universal or of a particular thing. Thomas adds the following doctrinal development that takes up what he said in the *De ente et essentia* 3, drawing perhaps on Arab sources. One can state something of a universal in four ways.

First, by considering a universal as existing by itself, either by way of Plato's Ideas or as Aristotle conceived the existence of universal concepts in the intellect. If one does so, one may consider the universal as a species or genus, attributing these qualifications to the universal in that the intellect compares them to things outside the mind. Second, one may attribute to the universal, considered in this way, something that does not belong to the act of the intellect, but to things as they are outside the mind. For example, in the statement "man is the noblest of all creatures,"[55] we have a qualification that applies even to individual persons, who are not one being, but the intellect brings them together as if they were one. Third, one may also attribute something to a universal insofar as it is in individual things, in a twofold way: by attributing something to a universal that belongs to its very essence or is consecutive on its essential contents (e.g., when we say "man is an animal" or "man is a being that can laugh"). Fourth and finally, one may attribute something to a universal even by predicating something of a universal that is just an accident of individual things, as, for example, one does in the sentence "man walks."

Of particular things, by contrast, something can be predicated in three ways: in the manner the thing is in our perception, as when we say "Socrates is a particular being" or "(the name) Socrates can be predicated only of one being"; as something common also to others, as when I say "Socrates is an animal"; and as something that holds only of this individual, as when I say "Socrates is walking." These divisions have their corresponding negations.

---

55. As Gauthier explains (Leonine ed., 1*/1:54*), the sentence was a typical example used in the schools. Several logicians distinguished between a *suppositio simplex* (which concerns the essential nature) and a *suppositio personalis* of the terms *omnis homo*. In the latter supposition, it is not true that every particular person is the worthiest being. Thomas quietly contradicts this position in that he says: "Hoc enim convenit naturæ humanæ secundum quod est in singularibus, nam quilibet homo singularis est dignior omnibus irrationalibus creaturis." Thomas keeps his distance from the technique of the logicians and writes in terms understandable to all.

Thomas concludes his commentary on this short section of the text by noting that here we have a third division of statements, namely, according to a difference in the subject, which can be predicated of more things or of only one.

The comments of Thomas on 17b3–6 are quite extensive. According to the differences occurring in the subjects of statements, as outlined above, different ways of opposition result in statements and he examines how these different types of opposition relate to truth and falsehood. With regard to universals outside the human mind, Plato used some additional words to indicate that he had universals in mind, such as "man *per se*" or "man *himself.*" As for universals predicated of particulars, sometimes "every" is added to make clear that the term is used in its universal meaning (as in "*every* man is mortal") and holds of all particulars contained in it, and for negative statements "no" or "not any" are added in order to indicate that the universal is to be denied of the particulars contained in it. However, it happens that something is attributed to a universal or denied of it with regard to a limited number of particulars. In these cases, adjectives or pronouns like "someone" or "some" are used. In negations there are no set terms to indicate this situation, but one may use "not every."

Summing up, Thomas concludes that there are three sorts of affirmative statements in which something is predicated of a universal: (a) when something is predicated of a universal universally, as when we say "every man is an animal"; (b) when something is predicated of a universal with some limitation, as when we say "some men are white"; (c) when something is predicated of it without further determining whether it is universal or particular. Thomas does not give an example, but Apuleius has "an animal breathes" (not all animals are doing so).[56] Then, there are the corresponding opposed negations. Contrary to what happens when the subject of a statement is a universal, when it is particular, even if predicates may be said of it in different ways, we always presuppose that it is a particular thing. When we say "Socrates is an animal," we mean the individual man. If we add this way of predication of a particular subject to the three sorts of predication mentioned, we have a fourth type of predication.

Passing to the following lines of the text, 17b6–12, Thomas points out that in this section Aristotle examines the different ways in which opposed statements relate to each other. First, he mentions universal propositions opposed to one another, such as "every man is white" and "no man is white." These statements are contrary, where this signifies "what is furthest removed (in the same genus)." The sentence "no man is white" totally denies the first statement

---

56. See Leonine ed., 53 and 273.

and is a contradictory sentence. With regard to indefinite sentences the text says that, when something is affirmed or denied of a universal subject, but not universally, the statements are not contrary, although the things one is speaking about may be so. Examples are: "a man is white" and "a man is not white."

In the first proposition "man" is a universal, but "white" is not predicated universally. Thomas sees a difficulty in what is added: "although the statements are not contrary, what is signified by them may be contrary" (17b8). The Latin text reads: *quae autem significantur est esse contraria.* This addition is understood differently by the commentators. Some take it to refer to the opposition between truth and falsehood, but this does not seem to apply, as Aristotle has not yet begun with his treatment of truth and falsehood. Moreover, that could be said also of statements about particular things, and not just about universal sentences, with which we are dealing now. Porphyry understood the words as referring to the predicate: "not white" can be denied of a person because its contrary, black, is present. But this might not be what Aristotle intended to say, as he is not speaking about a contrariety of things, but of statements. Thomas makes Alexander's explanation his own: indefinite statements do not make clear whether the predicate is predicated universally of the subject (which would make the statements contrary) or particularly (which would not). However, one may have a statement that is *de facto* universal ("man is an animal") although this is not expressed, so that its opposite ("man is not an animal") is also a universal statement.[57]

The last section of the text commented upon in this lesson (17b12–16) says that it is not correct to predicate a universal universally of a subject ("every man is every animal"). Thomas has the following explanation, probably not found in his sources. One reason, he says, why this is wrong is that it goes against the nature of the predicate, which must be the formal part of a sentence. But, when a universal is said universally, it is used in the sense of its relation to the things that come in under it. And so both the subject and the predicate are the material part of the statement. For this reason it is better to add the words that signify universality or particularity to the subject than to the predicate, namely, to say "some people are white" instead of "people are some white thing" and "no man is a donkey" instead of "every man is not some donkey." A second reason is derived from the question of the truth of a statement, above all of affirmations that would be false if the predicate would be said universally of the subject: as an example, "every man is every animal" is evidently false. The reason is that the predicate together with everything contained in it must apply

---

57. Alexander's explanation is mentioned by Ammonius and Boethius, both of whom prefer the explanation of Porphyry.

to the subject with everything contained in it. The statement would amount to saying that even one single man would be all the animals. However, a word that signifies a negation universally or an affirmation particularly may nevertheless be true in certain cases if connected with the predicate, although it is better to connect them with the subject. "All human beings are not stones" is true, while "all human beings are all animals" is false.

The text commented upon in lesson 11 (nos. 57–60; 7.17b16–37) may be divided into two sections, 17b16–26 and 17b26–37. In the first section, Aristotle calls an affirmation and a negation contradictory when what is signified universally by one of them is not universally denied by the other (or vice versa). On the other hand, a universal affirmation and a universal negation are contrary. Thomas observes that a particular affirmation and a particular negation are not opposed to each other in the strict sense, because the subject (e.g., "some people are white" and "some people are not white") is not the same. However, a sentence that has a universal signification is contradictory to one that signifies in particular. "Every man is white" is contradicted by "not every man is white." Likewise "no human being is white" is contradicted by "some human beings are white." Thomas explains it as follows: contradicting means that an affirmation is replaced by a negation. A universal affirmation is contradicted by denying some particular instance of it, while a particular affirmation cannot be neutralized except by a negative universal statement.

"Every man is just" and "no one is just" are contrary: the negative statement denies the positive one and is also furthest removed from it by denying all that can be denied of it. Because an affirmative universal statement and a negative universal statement are contrary to each other, both cannot be true at the same time, as contraries exclude each other. But contrary particular statements that contradict their universal opposite can both be true with regard to the same subject ("some people are white" and "some people are not white").

In 17b26, Aristotle discusses contradictory statements, both those about a universal, taken universally, and contradictory particular statements, where one is necessarily true, the other false. Thomas explains this obvious necessity by means of the principle of contradiction and refers to the well-known text of Aristotle in *Metaphysics* V.1017a30–35, about truth being the agreement of what one says with reality. Sometimes two universal statements seem to be contradictory but are not, if the universal is not taken universally. For example, "man is white" and "man is not white" are both true if the universal is not taken universally.

Agreeing with Ammonius, Thomas writes that some authors did not accept this. They felt that a negative sentence such as "man is not white," of which the subject is indefinite, should be understood as universal, as the subject stands on the side of matter and matter always goes for the worse. They did not apply this argument to affirmative indefinite sentences. Even Aristotle himself would have sometimes used a negative statement as having a universal meaning. But Thomas comments that the idea that matter tends to the worse is a Platonic theory. Matter as such cannot be called evil. Moreover, even if it would be true that an indefinite statement should be taken in a pejorative sense, this would not mean that it should be understood as holding universally, as a negative universal statement is stronger but not worse than a particular negative statement.

In the closing lines of this passage, Aristotle points to a somewhat surprising situation. At first sight "people are dishonest" seems to mean that "people are not honest." Nevertheless both statements may be true: for example, "a man is handsome" and "a man is not handsome." One may also have an opposition based on less or more perfection. Thus the statements "man is dark skinned" and "man is not dark skinned," meaning that someone is becoming dark skinned, can be true at the same time, although this is not necessarily the case.

Lesson 12 (nos. 61–64; 7–8.17b37–18a26) points out that a single affirmation corresponds to a single negation. What has been argued in the previous section might make us think that a single affirmation such as "every man is white" has two opposites, namely, "no one is white" and "some are not white." However, on close inspection, only "not everyone is white" or its equivalent "someone is not white" appear to be the denial of the affirmation, as these formally deny the universality of the statement. "Nobody is white," Thomas says, also denies this universality, but it does more, for it denies each part that is contained in the affirmative statement. The negation must deny precisely the predicate that the affirmation stated and it must do so with regard to the same subject, that is to say, universally if it is taken in a universal sense and in particular if it is taken in a particular sense. Now this happens only in one way: when the negation denies what the affirmation stated and nothing else. Thomas mentions several examples that illustrate what Aristotle means. The negation of "Socrates is a musician" is the statement that he is not. The negation of "every human being is white" is "not every human being is white." The negation of "some people are white" is "no one is white." The negation of "man is white" is "man is not white."

In the next passage, which is the first part of chapter 8 in the original text, Aristotle explains what a single affirmation or negation is, namely, a statement that signifies one thing about one thing. This one thing, however, can also be a universal in its universal meaning. The plurality of individuals contained in the universal is no impediment to the unity of a statement, Thomas says, provided that the predicate means *one thing*. If that is not the case, if one name signifies two different things, the statement is not one. This condition of signifying "one thing" is not meant to exclude generic unity, such as "man" and "horse" being animals, but to exclude that a plurality of parts is taken as a unity, such as integral parts or logical parts. To illustrate what he means by this oneness, Aristotle gives the following example, reproduced by Aquinas: if one uses the word "cloak" to signify both "man" and "horse," the statement "a cloak is white" would mean two statements, one about a man and another about a horse. If one objects that by "a cloak is white" he means one thing, he affirms nothing, as a combination of man and horse in one being does not exist. It follows from the above that in those affirmations and negations that use an equivocal term as the subject of the statement, one of them need not always be true and the other false.

In lesson 13 (nos. 65–69; 9.18a28–b25), Aristotle deals with the question of the truth of particular statements about the future. Thomas comments on it in lessons 13, 14, and 15. He recalls the triple division of statements, that is, from the point of view of the unity of the statement (single sentences and sentences that are one by means of a connective), from the point of view of their quality (affirmative and negative statements), and from the point of view of quantity (universal, particular, indefinite, and singular sentences). In this chapter, Aristotle gives a fourth principle of division, according to the tense of the verb, a division that had been intimated before in lesson 8 (17a10), where he said that every sentence stating something must have a verb or an *inflective form* of a verb, that is, a form of the verb which signifies the past or the future.

Thomas adds a fifth division of statements according to the subject matter of the sentence: if the predicate belongs *per se* to the subject, the logicians speak of a statement concerning a necessary matter; if the predicate excludes the subject, the statement is about something impossible (e.g., "mass is a donkey"), if the statement lies between these two (i.e., concerns something that is neither necessary nor impossible), it concerns a possible or contingent matter. Gauthier mentions that in his sources, Thomas found two ways of dividing the matter of statements: (a) the division proposed by the Greek and Latin commentators of Aristotle, that is, in necessary, impossible, and contingent matter; (b) a second division is that of the logicians of the twelfth and thirteenth century in natural, removed, and contingent matter ("removed" in the sense of "denied").

Thomas combined both, by writing "necessary or natural" matter. Statements about the present or past must be true or false: of universal statements and those about singular things either the negative or the affirmative must be true, but in statements in which something is said about universals but not universally applied, it is not necessary that one is always true and its opposite false, but both can be true at the same time, as was shown before. This is also the case with propositions about the past and the present. But the situation is different with regard to statements about the future: it is true that in a necessary matter, affirmative statements in the future tense, whether universally or not universally taken, are always true, and in an impossible matter false, and that concerning an indefinite matter both the affirmation and the negation are true, exactly as is the case with regard to statements about the present and the past.

However, with regard to singular contingent events that may happen in the future, there is a difference. For in statements about the present or the past, one of two opposite sentences must be true and one false, regardless of whether they concern a necessary or a contingent matter. But in statements about a singular future fact concerning a contingent matter, it is not necessary that one of two opposite statements be definitely true and the other false.[58] A first reason why one cannot always determine which statement is true and which false is that, if one could, everything would necessarily be so or not be so. If a statement is true, reality is such as it says; if it is false, reality is not so. If either the affirmation or the negation of a future contingent event is definitely true, the event is as stated. But then there is no longer any contingency, neither that of things happening in a few cases, nor that of things happening more often but not always, nor that of events that may or may not happen. Thomas says that in that case the *ad utrumlibet* (the possibility that either one of the members of the alternative may happen) no longer applies and adds that, according to Aristotle, this holds also for what happens in most cases (*ut in pluribus*).

A second reason is indicated by Aristotle in 18b9ff.: if being true or false of propositions would be the same in the case of statements about the present and about the future, it would follow that whatever is true at this moment was true before with regard to what then was still to come and that before it was always true. But in that case one can no longer say that such an event is going to happen or not going to happen. Therefore, it is necessary. The result is that nothing happens by chance.

As he does elsewhere in his commentary, Thomas indicates in a doctrinal development the ontological foundation of Aristotle's argument. "True" means that one states what is, so that something is true in the way it has being.[59] What

---

58. Aristotle does not explicitly say that he is speaking about a contingent matter, but this is understood because we are dealing with singular facts or events.

59. "Hoc modo aliquid est verum quo habet esse."

exists at the present moment has being in itself, but when something lies in the future, it has not yet any being in itself, but somehow in its cause. This can happen (a) in such a way that it lies in its cause, from which it must come forth necessarily, so that one can say that it is definitely going to be. In the second place, (b) the future event can be in its cause in such a way that the cause tends to produce it, if it is not impeded. This event lies in its cause, but so that a change may occur. One can affirm that it will happen, but not with absolute certitude. Finally, (c) something can be present in its cause in such a way that the cause is no more determined to produce it, than not to produce it.[60]

In 18b17ff., Aristotle argues that, nevertheless, in the latter group of statements, truth is not wholly absent.[61] As one cannot say that one of the statements is definitely true, one cannot say either that neither of the two is true by asserting that the event will not take place, nor that it will take place. The reason is that when an affirmation is true, its negation is false and *vice versa*. But according to those who say that none of them is true, both the affirmative statement "this will be" and its negation are false.

A further argument by Aristotle runs as follows: if it were correct that neither of the two statements of the alternative is true, it would follow that the event will neither come about, nor not come about, but this contradicts the fact that both ways are possible, as happens in the case of a sea battle. It would necessarily neither happen nor not happen.

In the passage Thomas comments upon in lesson 14 (nos. 70–79; 9.18b26–19a22), more absurd consequences are pointed out regarding the position that holds there is no truth whatsoever in either of two opposite statements about a future contingent event. A first consequence is that there would no longer be any need to deliberate about what will or may happen in the future. In the second place, all activity in view of some end, such as a business deal that aims at making some money,[62] would be superfluous: if everything comes about necessarily, whether we work for it or not, what we have in mind will be. But this is contrary to what people do, as they deliberate and engage themselves in work, knowing that when they do this, a particular goal will be reached, but a different one will be reached if they do something else. It would also follow that if a

---

60. As Gauthier indicates in a note, this triple distinction is standard teaching of Aquinas. See *In Isaiam*, chap. 3; *In I Sent.*, d. 38, q. 1, a. 5; *In II Sent.* d. 7, q. 2, a. 2; *Q. de veritate*, q. 8, a. 12; *ST* I, q. 57, a. 3; I, q. 86, a. 4; II-II, q. 95, a. 1; *Comp. Theol.* I, 134; *Q. de malo*, q. 16, a. 7. Similar explanations in Boethius, Ammonius, and Aristotle: *Prior Analytics* I.13, *Topics* II.6, *Physics* II.8, and *Metaphysics* V.30 and VI.2.

61. Thomas explains: "Veritas non omnino deest" (lesson 13, no. 174).

62. The Latin text has *negotiari*, which Thomas understands as "doing business," whereas the Greek πραγματεύεσθαι has the broader sense of "busying oneself." But in *NE* 1176b29, the verb does have the sense of "doing business."

thousand[63] years ago someone said that a particular city would be devastated and a second person that this would not happen, one of the statements would necessarily be true and the other false. Everything would happen necessarily. Aristotle adds that it would not make any difference whether people actually made these statements or not, for things do not come about because people make statements about them. Thomas adds that the truth of our statements is not the cause of the existence of things, but that the opposite is the case. Likewise it does not make any difference for what happens now, if it has been affirmed or denied a thousand years ago. In fact, if we assume that someone tells the truth when affirming that this event will happen, it cannot not happen.

In 19a7–22, Aristotle indicates some further impossible consequences of the theory that holds that everything occurs of necessity. If that position were true, man would no longer be free to act and not to act, human society as well as all the principles of moral philosophy would be demolished. There would no longer be any room for advice, threats, punishments, or rewards by which people are drawn to what is good and moved to refrain from what is bad. This theme, which Thomas considers important, has been treated by Aristotle, Epicurus, Boethius, and Ammonius. It is also found in the *De fato* of Alexander of Aphrodisias, which was translated by William of Moerbeke.[64]

Thomas takes *videmus enim esse principium futurorum* to express Aristotle's position with regard to man's free will, but the correct translation of the Greek is "for we see that future events have their origin both in deliberation and in action," which comes down to the same and concerns human deliberation and work. Aristotle continues by saying that it holds true also of natural things, which are not always actualized and which can be or not be. If something that can be white does not become white, it remains something not white. In the things that can be and not be, there is also becoming and not becoming. These do not happen necessarily, but there is a possibility in them to become and not to become, to be and not to be. Aristotle illustrates what he says with the help of some examples. A cloak can be cut up, but can also be worn out first. So it can be cut up and not be cut up. The same can be said of all other events where this kind of possibility exists.

Excursus

Having arrived at this point, Thomas recalls the opinions of some of the ancients about this question and gives his own evaluation, drawing much of

---

63. The Greek text has "ten thousand."

64. See Leonine ed., 1*/1:74. Gauthier also refers to St. Augustine and to some other texts in the works of Aquinas.

his information from Boethius.[65] At the end of the excursus,[66] he explains why he added this explanation, which seems to go beyond what logic requires in order to secure contingency.[67] On the possible and the necessary with regard to future events, Diodorus Cronos, one of the masters of the dialectic of the Megarians (fl. 300 B.C.), subscribed to the arguments of Zeno against motion, and accepted only actual existence: impossible for him is what will never be, necessary is what will always be, and possible is what sometimes is and sometimes is not. The Stoics, who professed a strong determinism, distinguished between the three states according to external impediments: necessary is what cannot be hindered from being true, impossible is what is always impeded from being true, and possible is what may or may not be obstructed.

But Thomas considers both approaches inadequate and not *ad rem*. With regard to the opinion of Diodorus, he observes that something is not necessary because it exists always, but because it is necessary, it will always be. The second opinion of the Stoics rests on causal influences coming from the outside and describes the *per accidens*. What is necessary, however, cannot be frustrated by an impediment. For that reason, other authors argued that being necessary depends on the nature of things: necessary is what in its nature is determined only to be; impossible is what is determined only not to be; and possible is what is not entirely determined to either of these two, regardless of whether it is closer to one of the two alternatives or at an equal distance from both. It is called "contingent with regard to either of them." Boethius ascribes this opinion to Philo the Dialectician of the School of Megara,[68] who attempted to soften the determinism of his master Diodorus. Thomas thinks that this opinion, insufficiently described by Boethius, is also Aristotle's view. The reason for the possibility (to be or not to be) would be, for human beings, the fact that we deliberate and, for the rest of possible things, the fact that matter is potentially each of the two opposites.

Thomas considers this explanation insufficient. For in the incorruptible celestial bodies there is a certain potentiality to be in different places, but no contingency whatsoever.[69] For this reason, the potentiality of matter, open to the two members of an alternative, generally speaking, is not a sufficient ground of

---

65. As is often the case, these sections are introduced by a formula similar to the one here: "Est autem hic considerandum quod" (Leonine ed., 1*/1:73, 160).

66. See Leonine ed., 1*/1:79 and 520–22.

67. As Boethius observed already, the discussion of necessity, contingency, and fate seems to belong to a higher discipline, while Ammonius considered it part of logic, but said that it also had importance for other philosophical disciplines.

68. See Leonine ed., 1*/1:73 and 190n.

69. This is Aristotle's position in *Metaphysics* XII.2.1069b25f.

contingency, if one does not take into account an active potency that is not fully determined by one of the members of the alternative. If the active potency (of the agent) is to such an extent determined by one of them such that it cannot be impeded, it will necessarily reduce the passive potency into actuality and that (always) in the same way. Importantly, according to Aquinas, contingency does not only depend on the passive potency of matter but also on the active potency of an agent. The point has its weight, as it opens the way for the contingency of our free choices and also intimates the doctrine of the first cause as being the ultimate source of the contingency of certain beings and events.[70]

At this point in his commentary, St. Thomas gives an extensive evaluation of philosophical opinions regarding necessity, fate, and contingency. As mere passive potency is not sufficient to explain why certain things happen necessarily and others happen contingently, Stoic philosophers introduced the idea of a series of causes that together determine the course of events. However, Aristotle had destroyed this argument beforehand:[71] what happens *per accidens* does not have a cause and is closer to not-being. Moreover, it is not correct to say that if there is a sufficient cause, the effect follows, because some causes cannot prevent their effect from being impeded: heat is a sufficient cause to ignite timber, but if the timber is wet, it may not be able to do so.

If both statements are true, namely, "every effect has a cause" and "when there is a cause, the effect results necessarily," everything would happen necessarily. An example illustrates what this opinion implies: someone eats a salty meal and gets thirsty; when thirsty, he will leave his house to find some drinking water; if he leaves his house, he will be killed by robbers. The example would mean that one who eats a salty meal will necessarily be killed. To exclude this conclusion, Aristotle shows that each of the above propositions is false. Now, some authors object that whatever is *per accidens* must be reduced to causality *per se*. But this objection does not hold. If a musician kills someone, the causality is patently *per se*, that is, the man who happens to be also a musician is the murderer, but an effect that results because of what is inherent *per accidens* to the cause is not reduced to a cause *per se*. For instance, that a thirsty person went to drink from a streamlet on this particular afternoon and got killed by some robbers who chanced to be there, is not reducible to a cause *per se*. Thomas quotes the principle that effects must be referred to their causes proportionally, that is, if the effect is *per accidens*, the cause also is.[72]

70. *ST* I, q. 19, a. 8.

71. Thomas has his chronology wrong, assuming as some other medieval masters had done that the Stoics flourished before Aristotle. But when Aristotle introduced causality *per accidens* in *Metaphysics* VI.3.1027a29ff. to secure contingency in the world, he was arguing, it seems, against the school of Megara.

72. See *In VI Metaph.*, lesson 2. See also G. Verbeke, in Ammonius, *Commentaire sur le « Peri Hermeneias »*, xlviii, "Contingence et vérité."

Next, Thomas turns to those authors who, while ignoring the difference between these different types of causality, resorted to the theory that the celestial bodies exercise a determining influence on processes in the physical world and on the human will. To them fate is nothing else but the position of the stars and their ensuing causality.[73] But this cannot be the cause of necessity in whatever happens in the world. In our world much happens through the intervention of the intellect and the will, of which the acts are not something bodily. No corporeal power can act directly on what is immaterial. Our sense faculties, on the other hand, may be exposed *per accidens* to the influence of the celestial bodies. However, representations and passions at the level of the senses cannot impose necessity on the intellect and will. Thomas quotes from Aristotle to stress this point.[74] This applies also to many other events happening in the world, where much occurs *per accidens.* What happens in this way cannot be reduced to a cause *per se,* because it has no unity:[75] more than one causal process is involved. Now, the natural causality of things is always ordered to one sort of effect. This explains why many effects announced by the atmospheric conditions, such as rain or storms, do not actually take place because of certain impediments. Although such impediments are to be reduced to cosmic causes, their coming together cannot be reduced to a natural cause.

Thomas adds another observation: our mind can overlook what happens by chance and consider it as a certain unity. The intellect can even order such a coming together of unrelated actions. A good example is that of a master sending two servants on errands, and knowing beforehand that they will meet each other in town, although the encounter is neither intended nor foreseen by the servants themselves.[76] Keeping this in mind, some devotees of astrology[77] believed that everything that happens in the world, even fortuitous events, is arranged by (the necessity of) a divine mind.

Before he explains in which sense this view is right, Thomas rejects the opinion of those who deny this on the ground that God would not know the singular things in the universe. Augustine criticizes Cicero on this point, but Thomas may have in mind a text of Averroes[78] and refutes this view: the divine intellect and will are God's very being. Because God is the cause of all beings,

---

73. As Gauthier points out, Thomas quotes (without naming him) St. Augustine, *De civitate Dei* V.1: "Quid dixerit fatum? Nam id homines quando audiunt usitata loquendi consuetudine, non intelligunt nisi vim positionis siderum, qualis est quando quis nascitur sive concipitur." See *Summa contra gentiles* [hereafter *SCG*] III.93.

74. *Topics* IV.5.125b24. Thomas also refers to *NE* IV.

75. Take the case of a thirsty person looking for drinking water and being murdered.

76. *ST* I, q. 116, has the same example.

77. The *quidam* of the text probably refers to astrologists. See *De civitate Dei* V.1.

78. See *In I Sent.*, d. 36, q. 1, a. 1, and *Q. de veritate*, q. 2, a. 5: "Quidam, ut Commentator dicit . . . negaverunt Deum singularia cognoscere, nisi forte in universali." According to Augustine, Cicero held this theory.

he knows them and his will comprehends whatever striving one can think of. Because things are knowable, they are the object of God's intellect; because they are good and desirable, they are the object of God's will. However, if divine Providence is the proper and direct cause of what happens in the world, at least of what is good, everything would seem to happen by necessity, for his science does not fall short, and so it seems that what he knows will also come about. Likewise, God's will cannot be impeded, so that what he wills must necessarily happen.

These objections, which are also mentioned by Augustine, Boethius, Peter Abelard, and Peter of Spain, result from conceiving God's intellect and will in the way human beings proceed, although their way of knowing and willing is very different from that of God. Divine knowledge stands outside the order of temporal things. Thomas illustrates this with an example he also used in *Summa theologiae*:[79] travelers climbing a winding path will not see those who come behind them, but an observer on a high point, overlooking the whole road, will see all the travelers at the same time.[80] Thomas gives some details of the way human knowledge is inserted in the process of time: man knows the now-existing things, which to a certain point can be perceived by the senses; he knows what was in the past when remembering it; and he knows future things not in themselves (as they do not yet exist), but in their causes, and that with certitude if they are entirely determined in their causes from which they will come forth necessarily, but with some probability if they are not determined to such a point that they cannot be impeded—if so, man knows what happens in most cases. But he does not know future events at all if they are entirely undetermined in their causes. One only knows what is in some way actualized.

However, God is completely outside the order of time and in his eternal being everything is simultaneous. Therefore, he sees whatever happens in the course of time, in one vision, as things exist in themselves, exactly like the human eyes see things present. (He also sees the chain of causes leading to the existence of the effects.) When we see before us someone sitting, this does not take away that the fact that this man is sitting there is contingent, although we are certain that he is sitting there. Likewise God knows with total certitude whatever happens in time, without things becoming necessary.[81] God's will must also be conceived as being outside the order of time, as a cause that extends to all beings and their differences, that is, comprising necessary and contingent beings. Therefore, necessity and contingency in beings are derived

79. *ST* I, q. 14, a. 13, ad 3. The comparison is found in Boethius's commentary.

80. Gauthier (Leonine ed., 1*/1:77n) quotes examples from classical authors about such observation posts in mountainous areas.

81. Gauthier points to a parallel text in Boethius, *De consolatione philosophiae* V, prose 6.

from God's will, as is their difference with regard to their proximate causes. God gave necessary causes to the effects he wanted to be necessary, and contingent causes to those he decided would come about in a contingent way. God's will never fails and it transcends the level of necessary and contingent beings. This is not the case with the human will or with other (created) causes, which all fall under the order of necessity or contingency.

Thomas now turns to the second ground of contingency and free choice mentioned by Aristotle, that is, as what is implied by the fact that we deliberate about what to do. Some rejected this argument: in our choices we would be moved necessarily by the object presented. The will cannot deflect from what appears to it as good, nor can reason refrain from assenting to what appears true. It would seem, then, that a choice resulting from a deliberation is always made necessarily, so that all the actions that proceed from our deliberation and choice are necessary.[82] Thomas's answer is most interesting. Drawing a parallel between the good and the true, he says that some of the insights that are true are so because they are evident by themselves, such as the first principles of being.

Other propositions are not known by themselves but by other things. This can be in a twofold way: certain conclusions follow necessarily from the principles, so that they cannot be false, if the principles are true. The intellect assents necessarily to them after it has understood their connection with the principles. But with regard to conclusions that do not follow necessarily from principles and that may be false, as certain opinions are, the intellect may be attracted more to some of them than to others. In analogy with what is the case with the truth seen by the intellect, there is also a good that is desired necessarily because of itself, such as happiness, which has the nature of a last end, while other goods are desired because of their relation with the end and may be compared to the end as conclusions are to the first principles of being. If there are goods without which we cannot be happy, these goods are desired necessarily, above all by those who are aware of this relation with the end. To exist, to be alive, and to think, and other things of this sort qualify as such goods. But the particular goods that human acts are concerned with are not of this kind and are not perceived as things the possession of which is necessary in order to be happy. Thomas quotes as an example eating delicious food. Therefore, Aristotle was right in considering deliberation the root of the contingency of our choices, as deliberation concerns the things that are ordered to the end and that are not beforehand determined.

---

82. The "some" (*quidam*) might be masters of the Faculty of Arts in Paris. Their position was condemned by Bishop Étienne Tempier in 1270 and in the condemnation of 219 articles in 1277. However, as Gauthier writes, the theologians may have misunderstood the position of the masters of the Faculty.

It must be noted that, in this lesson, Aquinas uses Aristotle's proper name as the person holding an opinion. I suppose that he does so when a statement does not seem totally correct to him or when it seems insufficient. Elsewhere, when he agrees with Aristotle and considers a particular doctrine of the Stagirite definitely true, he uses *Philosophus*, as he does here, at the end of this lesson, in no. 79.

After this long digression on fate, chance, and contingency, Thomas excuses himself for adding these observations. He did so to safeguard the basis of contingency, although he acknowledges that the theme of the appendix seems to go beyond what should be treated in logic. Several of the earlier commentators had done the same, although according to Albert the Great, it is a mistake to deal with these questions at this point because they should not be treated on the basis of logical principles.[83]

Continuation of Book I

In lesson 15 (nos. 80–82; 9.19a23–b4), which addresses the well-known passage at the end of chapter 9, Aristotle points out the difference between "something being necessary, when it is" and "being necessary unconditionally." He illustrates what he is saying by the example of a sea battle to be fought. One of the two propositions, "a sea battle will take place tomorrow" and "there will not be a sea battle tomorrow" will become absolutely true; which one of them depends on whether a sea battle will be fought tomorrow. Aristotle passes from the truth about things and events to that of propositions and argues that although one of the two propositions must come true, neither of them is definitely true at this moment, but the outcome will be as chance has it.

The passage about the sea battle has given rise to numerous commentaries.[84] Thomas points out that the propositions "whatever is, is necessary when it is" and "whatever is not, is necessarily not, when it is not" follow from the principle of contradiction, namely: "It is impossible for the same thing to be

---

83. *In I Peryermeneias*, tract. V (ed. Borgnet), 1:423a–b: "Sed de his hic quarere stultum est: quia quaestiones istae ex istius scientiae principiis (cum logica procedat ex communibus quae in pluribus vel in omnibus inveniuntur) non possunt determinari: ista autem determinari volunt ex propriis."

84. See V. Celluprica, *Il capitulo 9 del "De interpretatione" di Aristotele. Rassegna di studi 1930–1973* (Bologna: Il Mulino, 1977); D. Frede, "The Sea Battle Reconsidered. A Defence of the Traditional Interpretation," *Oxford Studies in Ancient Philosophy* 3 (1985): 31–87; A. Bäck, "Sailing through the Sea Battle," *Ancient Philosophy* 12 (1992): 133–51; C. Whitaker, *Aristotle's "De interpretatione": Contradiction and Dialectic* (Oxford: Clarendon Press, 1996), esp. 109–31. For a study of the medieval debate see William Lane Craig, *The Problem of Divine Foreknowledge and Future Contingents from Aristotle to Suarez* (Leiden: Brill, 1988); J. Marenbon, *Le temps, la prescience et les futurs contingents de Boèce à Thomas d'Aquin* (Paris: Vrin, 2005), and more succinctly S. Knuuttila, "Medieval Commentators on Future Contingents in De Interpretatione 9," *Vivarium* 48 (2010): 75–95.

and not to be at the same time." Now this necessity is not absolute but based on an assumption,[85] for example, that Socrates is sitting now. Therefore, one cannot say just that "everything that is, is necessarily" and that "every being exists necessarily." One cannot set apart one of the statements about a sea battle taking place or not taking place tomorrow and consider it absolutely true,[86] but one can say that it is necessary that either a sea battle will take place tomorrow or that it will not take place. Thomas speaks of a *necessitas sub disiunctione*, meaning that one of the two ways or possibilities suggested must be true.[87]

Starting with 19a32, Aristotle passes from what he said about things and real events to what is the case with statements, arguing that their truth follows the being of things. A statement is true or false, according as the thing it speaks about is or is not. It follows necessarily that what applies to all things that act or happen in either of two ways[88] and to things that are such that their contraries can happen in one way or another, whether these possibilities are equal or one of them happens in most cases, also holds of contradictory statements about them. Aristotle explains which are these things, the contrary of which may happen; that is, things that are not always in this way or are not always not so. One of the two contradictory statements about them must be true, not however this one or that one. In the final lines, the difference is stressed between statements about the present or past and statements about the future. Gauthier mentions a note by Cardinal Zigliara, the editor of the first Leonine edition of the *De interpretatione,* in which he rejects a claim that Aristotle's solution jeopardizes the principle that a medium between being and not-being is excluded.

Book II

The text of the *Peri hermeneias* has been divided in several ways.[89] Thomas follows a division customary in the Latin West since the eleventh century, going back to the first and shorter commentary of Boethius on the *Peri hermeneias.* Thomas explains that in the second book, Aristotle deals with

---

85. Thomas writes *ex suppositione*, which renders the Greek ἐξ ὑποθέσεως; see *Physics* 199b34. In some places, Thomas uses a different terminology to indicate this condition.

86. Thomas puts it this way (81, 67): "Non tamen si divisim alterum accipiatur necesse est illud esse absolute verum."

87. See *Q. de potentia*, q. 6, a. 6, ad 11, and *Q. de malo*, q. 16, a. 7.

88. Thomas writes (after the Latin translation): "ut sint ad utrumlibet."

89. See Weidemann, *Aristoteles: Peri Hermeneias*, 57: "Die verschiedenen Einteilungen der Schrift *Peri Hermeneias*." The three Greek commentaries that have come down to us divide the text into five main sections. This division may go back to Proclus or Ammonius. In his first and shorter commentary, Boethius divides the treatise into two books—chaps. 1–9 and 10–14—whereas in his second commentary he divides the text in six books. The division into two books prevailed and was generally accepted in the Latin West from the end of the eleventh century. See Lorenzo Minio-Paluello, preface in *Aristoteles Latinus*, 2:1–2, vii–lxix.

statements to which something is added.[90] One may think, first, of additions to the parts of a statement, that is to say, to names and to verbs; second, there are additions to the very composition in affirmative and negative statements; thirdly, one can consider additions to the opposition of one statement to another. Accordingly, Thomas divides the remaining part of the treatise in three sections, the second beginning at 21a34, and the third at 23a27. Unfortunately, his commentary ends at 19b26.

Lesson 1 (nos. 83–86; 10.19a23–b4) has some interesting observations on the difference between names and verbs under certain conditions. If a negation is added to a verb standing alone, it denies the form expressed by the verb (as it does when added to a name), but when the negation is added to a verb functioning within a sentence, it removes the verb from the subject,[91] and so it constitutes a negative statement. One can make a statement with an indefinite name, but not with an indefinite verb. It is not possible to make a statement with the negation bearing on the formal content of the verb, for in that case there is no longer a verb, nor a predicate, and so there is no statement at all. If one would say that a statement with a negative name as its subject is invalid, because the subject is not one, the answer is that such a negative name has a sort of unity *secundum quid,* inasmuch as the many things coming in under it form a group. Thus we have two kinds of affirmative statements, a first consisting of a name and a verb, a second consisting of an infinite name and a verb. The same division applies to negative statements.

As Boethius said previously, one can add a negation to a verb when this stands alone. In this case, it is not a predicate and has the same value as a negative name. "Not walking" comprises all activities (or passive states) except walking. Moreover, Aquinas adds, whether one attaches the negative particle to the verb so as to render its meaning infinite or to the sentence, the truth of the statement does not change and therefore we take it in its more obvious sense, namely, as the negation of the statement. One must furthermore keep in mind that in addition to the difference between finite and infinite names and verbs, there is also that between non-inflected and inflected forms. With inflected names, one does not get a sentence stating what is true or false. The reason is that the non-inflected form of a name is not included in its inflected form. But this is different with verbs, as past and future tenses are verbs (co-signifying time) because they are said in respect of the present tense. "This will be" is a statement about what will become real. It is noteworthy that

---

90. Gauthier points out that Peter of Ireland made the same observation.
91. Thomas writes "removet verbum ab aliquo."

Aquinas adds that the relation of the conjugated forms of verbs to the present must bear on reality in order for the statement to be true.

In conclusion, Thomas says, one can conceive[92] a triple division of statements: (a) a first division is that in affirmative and negative statements; (b) a second division is that of statements with a finite subject or with an infinite subject ("not-man"); and (c) a third division is that of sentences universally or not universally taken ("every man is"). Aristotle does not mention a division according to the inflected forms of verbs, because, says Thomas, the past and future tenses refer to the present.

Thus far Aristotle dealt with statements consisting of a name as their subject, and a predicate such as "man is." Now, in lesson 2 (nos. 87–92; 19b19–26), he considers the statements from a somewhat different point of view, namely, as consisting of three elements, for example, "man is mortal." The logicians speak of statements *de tertio adiacente,* such as "Socrates is wise." This usual form of most statements led them to consider the composition of a subject and a predicate by means of the copula as the typical form of all judgments. A sentence like "Peter runs" was analyzed as expressing the underlying form "Peter is running." In doing so, they reduced the verb *est* to the function of a copula. Now, Thomas had argued before, in his comments on Book I, lesson 5, that the first and principal meaning of "to be" is that of reality (*actualitas*) absolutely, that is, the actuality of all forms and that, in the second place, "to be" or "is" signifies the composition of the subject and the predicate. Here he stresses this point again and expands on what he had written before. When we say "Socrates is," we want to say that he exists, but when we say "Socrates is white," we do not so much want to draw attention to the reality of Socrates, but to that of the form of whiteness in him. In these cases, "is" is used as connected with the main predicate (hence the qualification of such statements as *de tertio adiacente*). But Thomas points out again that the "is" and the predicate together form one predicate. A statement consists of two parts, not of three.[93]

Thomas goes on explaining a difficult sentence of Aristotle in 19b20ff., namely: "Because of this there will here be four cases, two of which will be related, as to the order of sequence, to the affirmation and negation in the way privations are, while two will not."[94] Aristotle means such statements

---

92. The wording of the phrase (*intellegi potest*) intimates that one should not attach too much importance to these divisions.

93. As Gauthier comments (Leonine ed., 1*/1:87n), Thomas avoids the term *copula* to signify the "is," although he does use it on a few other occasions. The reason is that he wants to underline that the copula and the predicate are together the predicate.

94. He writes: "Quod quidem breviter et obscure dictum est, diversimodo est a diversis expositum."

as "a man is just," "a man is not just," "a man is not-just," and "a man is not not-just."[95] Thomas points out that in these types of sentences the predicate has a certain duality, so that one may let the negation bear on the "is" or on the name functioning as predicate. Speaking of the "is" as a component of the statement, Aristotle says "whether you call it a name or a verb." Thomas explains: as for its contents one may call "is" a name, but according to our customary way of speaking, it is considered a verb. The words "as to the order of sequence" were translated by Boethius as *secundum consequentiam*, but differently by Van Moerbeke. Thomas follows Boethius's translation: the two sentences with an "infinite" predicate ("a man is not-just" and "a man is not not-just") follow on the two corresponding statements with a finite predicate ("a man is not just" and "a man is just").

With regard to the final words "two (statements) will not," Thomas first discards an explanation recorded but rejected by Ammonius, and then formulates in his own words Ammonius's interpretation, that is, comparing the scope of application of the various figures of statements. A simple negative statement ("a man is not just") is applicable more extensively than the corresponding affirmative infinite statement ("a man is not-just"). For the same reason a simple negative statement is applicable more extensively than a privative affirmation ("a man is unjust") and an affirmative infinite ("a man is not-just") more than an affirmative privative statement ("a man is unjust"). Thomas illustrates the last example by saying that a child that does not have the virtue of justice is not-just, but that it is not unjust. A negative privative statement ("is not a not-just man") has a wider extension than a negative infinite one ("is not a not just man").

The upshot is, Thomas says, that the two infinite statements are related to the simple affirmation and negation as two privative statements: as a simple affirmation is followed by a negative infinite statement (which has a greater extension), so a simple affirmation is also followed by a negative privative statement (which has a larger extension); as a simple negation follows upon an infinite affirmative statement (of less extension), so a simple negative statement follows upon a privative affirmation (of less extension). Nevertheless, Thomas says, this interpretation (of Ammonius) is somewhat artificial, and so he prefers to return to the much simpler explanation of Porphyry as presented by Boethius. The "order of sequence" of Aristotle's text means that the negative statements follow upon affirmative ones and not the opposite, but in such a way that a simple affirmative is followed by the negation of an infinite one,

---

95. On these statements see Allan Bäck, "Aquinas on Predication," in Braakhuis and Kneepkens, *Aristotle's "Peri Hermeneias" in the Latin Middle Ages*, 321–38.

and an affirmative infinite one is followed by a simple negation. Therefore, "a man is just" is followed by the negation of "a man is not not-just" and "a man is not-just" is followed by "man is not just." In affirmative statements with an infinite predicate, the negation does not bear on the verb "is" but on the predicate, so we have two affirmative statements to which two negative ones correspond.

At this point the commentary of St. Thomas abruptly ends, although in his introduction to the first lesson of Book II he divides the contents of the last five chapters, confirming his intention to comment on the entire treatise. Unfortunately, his commentary concerns only about fifty-eight percent of the text of the *Peri hermeneias*. As with several of his other Aristotelian commentaries, the *Expositio* remained unfinished. In his edition of the Latin translation of Ammonius's commentary, G. Verbeke suggested that the text of this translation, which Thomas had at his disposition, may have stopped at this particular point, so that Thomas would have interrupted his work, waiting for the last part of Moerbeke's translation.[96] However, the departure for Louvain of William Berthout (at whose request he undertook to write his commentary) to defend his interests as the recently nominated provost of the Church of St. Peter's, together with a mountain of other urgent tasks, are more likely to have made Aquinas decide to interrupt the redaction of the commentary, perhaps the more so because he had finished the important excursus on necessity and contingency, and felt that he had achieved at least partially the purpose of his undertaking: the refutation of some errors about human free will, divine foreknowledge, the contingency of many events, and the influence of the celestial bodies on what happens in the sublunar part of the universe.

Concluding Remarks

Thomas's *Expositio* contains his most detailed treatment of the semantics of terms, verbs, and propositions, and their truth or falsehood. Although drawing heavily on the sources available to him, Boethius and Ammonius in particular, from whom he borrows many explanations and digressions, there are cases where Thomas departs from their interpretations. This is particularly the case with regard to his argument, developed in lesson 5 of Book I, to the effect that the verb "to be" signifies in the first place "to be actually." Compared to these sources, his commentary excels by its unparal-

---

96. Verbeke, introduction in Ammonius, *Commentaire sur le « Peri Hermeneias »*, xxxiii.

leled grasp of the contents of the *Peri hermeneias,* its clarity and concision. Avoiding useless explanations and using the method of dividing a text to be studied, he sheds light on certain obscure passages of Aristotle's treatise. His purpose is to arrive at a commentary which is "at the same time, philologically accurate and doctrinally reliable."[97] When one familiarizes oneself with Thomas's explanations, one can easily understand why the commentary met with so much acclaim. It is in fact very pedagogical in his approach to Aristotle's text and rich in doctrinal contents. In view of the extreme terseness of Aristotle's text, it is no wonder that many masters and students looked for a clear explanation of its more difficult passages and sentences. While Amerini, following Gauthier, is correct in his assessment that Thomas was "not interested in exploring and discussing" logical matters as such and as a result left many questions undiscussed, one should keep in mind that Thomas was fundamentally interested in offering an aid to William Berthout and his fellow students in understanding Aristotle's text.[98] This pedagogical aim also might explain why he interjects a long discussion, in lesson 14, on chapter 9 of the *Peri hermeneias,* regarding fate, chance, and contingency and their compatibility with divine Providence. Against this background, Thomas was able to give a correct and profound explanation of the text, not least because of his connaturality with Aristotle's thought. He could make the contents of the *Peri hermeneias* his own without any reservations. In the second place, his perfect mastery of such disciplines as the philosophy of nature, ethics, political philosophy, and metaphysics allowed him to highlight the doctrinal background of Aristotle's text and to show the lasting truth and actuality of what the Philosopher wrote on the subject.

97. F. Amerini, "Aquinas's Philosophy of Language in His Commentary on *De Interpretatione,*" *Divus Thomas* 118 (2015): 80–113, at 88.

98. Ibid., 107.

2 ✌ THE COMMENTARY ON THE POSTERIOR ANALYTICS

Aristotle's *Prior* and *Posterior Analytics* belong to the group of logical works called the *Organon*. As there are no references in the *Analytics* to Aristotle's main works—such as the *Physics, Metaphysics, On the Soul,* etc.—but rather only to the *Topics,* one may assume that it dates to an earlier period of Aristotle's life. W. D. Ross suggests the years 350 to 344 B.C. as the most likely period of their composition.[1] As is to be expected, there are many uncertainties as to the dating of the two *Analytics,* their relationship, and the contents of the treatises, in particular that of the *Prior Analytics,* which has been criticized by some modern authors.[2]

At the start of *Posterior Analytics* II.19, the final chapter of the treatise, Aristotle summarizes what he takes himself to have accomplished thus far: "As regards syllogism and demonstration, the definition of, and the conditions required to produce each of them, are now clear, and with that also the definition of, and the conditions required to produce, demonstrative scientific knowledge [ἐπιστήμης ἀποδεικτικῆς], as it is the same as demonstration" (99b15–17). For Aristotle, scientific knowledge is concerned with the identification of a universal nature as immanent in a particular thing. In order for there to be a true demonstration, Aristotle argues in II.4.73a26ff., three requirements are needed: (1) an attribute should be predicable of all instances; (2) it should belong to the subject in virtue of the subject's proper nature; and finally, (3) an attribute should belong to the subject in virtue of

---

1. See his *Aristotle's "Prior and Posterior Analytics"* (Oxford: Clarendon, 1949), 23. Ross rejects Friedrich Solmsen's view that the *Posterior Analytics* subscribes to Platonic theories and must be dated early (6–23). See Solmsen, *Die Entwicklung der aristotelischen Logik und Rhetorik* (Berlin: Weidmann, 1929); See also Solmen's review of Ross's work in "Aristotle's Syllogism and its Platonic Background," *Philosophical Review* 60 (1951): 563–71. Robin Smith thinks that *Posterior Analytics* I does not at all presuppose the development of the theory of syllogisms as given in *Prior Analytics* I. See his "The Relationship of Aristotle's Two Analytics," *Classical Quarterly* 32 (1982): 327–35.

2. Aristotle, *"Posterior Analytics,"* trans. J. Barnes (Oxford: Clarendon Press, 1993): xi–xii. G. E. M. Anscombe for instance considers *Analytica Posteriora* I Aristotle's worst book in *Three Philosophers* (Oxford: Blackwell, 1961), 6.

the subject's entire nature. Definition is of central importance in this process (II.8.93a16–33). The aim of the process is not merely, however, to investigate whether the categorization by way of definition obtains in reality, but it should also reveal why a state of affairs is the case (II.10.93b38–94a7). The connection between subject and attribute should be necessary (I.6.75a28ff.) and the conclusion of a demonstration should be eternal (I.8). Hence, strictly speaking, there cannot be demonstrative knowledge of something that is corruptible.

Not all knowledge is demonstrative. In fact, Aristotle begins his treatise with the opposite: "All instruction given or received by way of argument proceeds from preexistent knowledge" (I.1.71a1–2). Such knowledge is the starting point of scientific knowledge (ἀρχὴ ἐπιστήμης, I.3.72b24) and concerns first principles. This is the type of knowledge that is the subject of the famous final chapter (II.19) of the *Posterior Analytics*. Here Aristotle describes how we apprehend the first principles as a result of sense perception through the intermediate stages of memory and experience. Because the perceived particulars already have some universality in them, one can start a process of arriving at higher universals and ultimately at the starting points for knowledge. While the passage from particulars to universals is called induction (ἐπαγωγή), it is the intellect (νοῦς) which is the cognitive disposition that enables one to grasp the principles which are truer (ἀληθέρος) and more accurate (ἀκριβέτερος) than scientific knowledge (100b5–17). A variety of interpretations have been put forward regarding Aristotle's claim in this chapter, which Myles Burnyeat, for example, has characterized as "perfunctory in the extreme."[3] One view argues that, while induction is necessary, it is not sufficient for reaching knowledge of the first principles but must receive the help from the intuitive activity of the νοῦς and in particular the agent νοῦς of *De anima* III.5.[4] An alternative view suggests that induction is sufficient for reaching first principles and that νοῦς plays no role in the result of induction.[5] In any case, one has to be careful in anachronistically labeling these positions with typically modern notions such as "empiricism" and "rationalism."[6]

3. M. Burnyeat, "Aristotle on Understanding Knowledge," in *Aristotle on Science: The Posterior Analytics*, ed. E. Berti (Padua: Editrice Antenore, 1981), 97–139, at 133.

4. See C. Kahn, "The Role of Nous in the Cognition of First Principles in Posterior Analytics II 19," in *Aristotle on Science: The Posterior Analytics*, 385–414; T. Irwin, *Aristotle's First Principles* (Oxford: Clarendon Press, 1988), 134–37, 531–32; G. Bayer, "Coming to Know Principles in Posterior Analytics II 19," *Apeiron* 30 (1997): 109–42.

5. Barnes, *Aristotle: "Posterior Analytics,"* 267–70. For a mitigated defense of Barnes see D. Bronstein, "The Origin and Aim of Posterior Analytics II.19," *Phronesis* 57 (2012): 29–62.

6. See M. Ferejohn, "Empiricism and the First Principles of Aristotelian Science," in *A Companion to Aristotle*, ed. George Anagnostopoulos (Malden, Mass.: Wiley-Blackwell, 2009): 66–80. See also S. Herzberg, *Wahrnemung und Wissen bei Aristoteles* (Berlin: De Gruyter, 2011), esp. 218–21.

The *Posterior Analytics* has been received by a number of important ancient Greek commentators.[7] Fragments of a commentary by Alexander of Aphrodisias, working in the late second and early third century A.D., have survived.[8] In the fourth century A.D., Themistius wrote a paraphrase of the work.[9] Among the Neo-Platonic authors, the influential commentary on the first book of *Posterior Analytics* by Philoponus and other fragments stand out, not least because they were quite early on received in the Middle Ages due to their Latin translation by James of Venice. An influential role in the reception of the *Posterior Analytics* in the Middle Ages concerns a commentary on the second book sometimes ascribed to Philoponus or another writer from the school of Ammonius.[10] Some of these Neo-Platonic commentators connected Aristotle's νοῦς of II.19 with Plato's theory of innate Ideas, thus that it becomes the capacity to obtain knowledge of the divine—a reading which will prove influential in medieval Augustinianism.

The *Posterior Analytics* became known in the West mainly due to James of Venice's translation between 1125 and 1150, together with a commentary, possibly by Alexander or Philoponus. Additionally, there is an anonymous translation by a certain "Ioannes" and Gerard of Cremona's translation from the Arabic. By the middle of the thirteenth century, *Posterior Analytics* had become an integral part of the curriculum of the Faculty of Arts in Paris. Nevertheless, it took almost a century until the treatise was commented upon as a whole by the later bishop of Lincoln, Robert Grosseteste, in the 1220s in Oxford, followed by the paraphrase of Albert the Great, composed between 1245 and 1260.[11]

Thomas comments on the first book of *Posterior Analytics* in forty lessons and on the second book in twenty lessons. He bases his exposition of the first twenty-six lessons of Book I on the translation by James of Venice. Once he became acquainted with the new translation, completed by William of Moerbeke toward the middle of 1271, he used this text from lesson 27 of the first book onward.[12] Thomas began the commentary in Paris sometime

---

7. *Interpreting Aristotle's "Posterior Analytics" in Late Antiquity and Beyond*, ed. F. A. J. De Haas, M. Leunissen, and M. Martijn (Leiden: Brill, 2009).

8. *Le commentaire d'Alexandre d'Aphrodise aux 'Seconds analytiques' d'Aristote*, ed. P. Moraux (Berlin: De Gruyter, 1979).

9. CAG 5.1: *Themistii Analyticorum posteriorum paraphrasis*. See also J. R. O'Donnell, "Themistius' Paraphrasis of the Posterior Analytics in Gerard of Cremona's Translation," *Medieval Studies* 20 (1958): 239–315.

10. See the introduction to Philoponus (?), *On Aristotle "Posterior Analytics" 2*, trans. O. Goldin (London: Bloomsbury, 2009). See also CAG 13.3: *Ioannis Philoponi in Aristotelis Analytica posteriora commentaria cum Anonymo in librum II*.

11. Robert Grosseteste, *Commentarius in Posteriorum analyticorum libros*, ed. P. Rossi (Florence: Olschki, 1981). Grosseteste provides a useful list of thirty-two conclusions for each book. See D. Bloch, "Robert Grosseteste's *Conclusiones* and the Commentary on the Posterior Analytics," *Vivarium* 47 (2009): 1–23.

12. For these texts see the edition in the *Aristoteles Latinus* series: *Analytica posteriora. Translationes Iacobi*,

before April 1272 but completed it in Naples toward the end of the same year. From Naples it was sent to Paris where the exemplar was made and published in 1275.[13] R. A. Gauthier surmises that, similar to the commentary on the *Peri hermeneias*, Thomas wrote his exposition on the *Posterior Analytics* at the request of the masters of the Faculty of Arts in Paris. Gauthier has established that, while Thomas probably had knowledge of Grosseteste's commentary, it is Albert's paraphrase that serves as his principal source. Gauthier did not detect any influence from Averroes's commentary. He also indicates the use of Thomas's exposition by authors during the final decades of the thirteenth century such as Gilles of Rome.[14]

The division in lessons does not correspond exactly to the chapters of the text of Aristotle. Sometimes two chapters are studied in one lesson, or a somewhat longer chapter in two lessons. It also happens that the first lines of the next chapter are discussed at the end of the previous lesson. Thomas does not give a division of the entire treatise (*divisio textus*) in either the proem or the beginning of the first lesson, as he usually does, but at the beginning of lesson 4, commenting on chapter 2 (71b9–72b8). In Book I, he writes, Aristotle examines the demonstrative syllogism, and in Book II the medium from which the demonstration proceeds. As appears from the text of the first chapter of Book I, this entails clarifying the fact that something exists (*quia*), why it is, if it is, and what it is. Book I, Thomas says, is divided into a section on the demonstrative syllogism as such and a second section comparing the different demonstrative syllogisms (lesson 37). The section on the demonstrative syllogism as such explains its matter, that is, the terms of which it consists, and its form, that is, the figure in which it is formulated (nos. 28–30). Other philosophical authorities are not quoted, contrary to what he does in most of his other commentaries on Aristotle. In what follows, I summarize Thomas's exposition and examine the interesting and important additional observations of Thomas and their relation to Aristotle's text.[15]

Anonymi sive 'Ioannis,' Gerardi et Recensio Guillelmi de Moerbeka, ed. L. Minio-Paluello and B. G. Dod (Paris: Desclée De Brouwer, 1968).

13. See *Expositio Libri Posteriorum*, vol. 1*/2 in *Opera omnia iussu Leonis XIII P. M. Edita*, preface by René Antoine Gauthier (Rome / Paris: Leonine Commission / Vrin, 1989), 46*; See also C. Marabelli, "Note preliminari allo studio del commentario sulla *Analytica posterior*," *Divus Thomas* 88 (1985): 77–88.

14. Gauthier, preface in ibid., 59*–66*.

15. I have consulted Richard Berquist's excellent translation and commentary: *St. Thomas Aquinas: Commentary on Aristotle's "Posterior Analytics"* (Notre Dame, Ind.: Dumb Ox Books, 2007).

The Commentary of Thomas Aquinas

As he does in several other commentaries, Thomas begins with a proem in which, in a masterly way, he situates the book among the other treatises of the *Organon*, the group of Aristotle's works concerning logic. Logic is the art that directs the acts of our intellect and, Thomas says, the different treatises of logic must correspond to the three operations of the intellect. The first of these is the simple apprehension of universal concepts. The *Categories* deals with the predicates used in propositions—the concepts of indivisible things that are known by a simple apprehension. The *Peri hermeneias* considers propositions as the elements of which arguments are built up: in this so-called second operation, the intellect composes or divides things, an act called judgment, in which truth or falsehood is found. Both operations are ordered to a third one, reasoning, by which we proceed from what is known to what is unknown.

To explain why Aristotle studies this third operation in all the remaining books of the *Organon*, Thomas compares the activity of the intellect with the actions of nature. In some of these, nature acts with necessity; in others it mostly attains its purpose; and in yet other cases it fails to achieve its end. This threefold distinction is likewise found between the acts of the intellect. To the first correspond the acts of our reason that lead to certitude and truth; they are treated in the *Analytics*: the certitude of a judgment results from the very form of the argument, which is a syllogism. It also results from the matter of the propositions of the syllogism, because to attain certitude we use necessary propositions. To the second correspond those acts by which we reach truth for the most part, but in which our conclusion lacks necessity. But in a third set of acts our reason fails to attain the truth.

The first set of acts is treated in the *Prior* and *Posterior Analytics*. In the first treatise, the correct form of reasoning is determined, while the second examines the material from which *per se* and evident propositions are taken. The second group of acts, called *inventio* (inquiry), lead to a greater or lesser degree of probability, depending on the degree in which the arguments leading to opinion, or even to belief, approach certitude. Aristotle deals with these types of acts in the *Topics*. Thomas mentions a process of reasoning somewhat akin to Aristotle, where one does not fully accept one of two contradictory statements, although one may feel attracted more to the one than to the other, a situation treated by Aristotle in his *Art of Rhetoric*. The third group of acts by which our reason fails to attain the truth is treated in the *Sophistic Refutations*.

Book I

In the first lesson, Thomas comments on the opening lines of the first chapter (I.1.71a1–11). In Book I of the *Posterior Analytics*, Aristotle shows the need for demonstrative syllogisms, and in Book II he examines the demonstrative syllogisms as such (*de ipso*). Going beyond the text, Thomas recalls that according to Plato, scientific knowledge is not caused in us by syllogisms but by the action of the Ideas: the forms of material things do not act on our mind. Aristotle holds the opposite view. Forms present in the material things are abstracted and brought to actuality in our mind. Furthermore, he holds that science becomes science in us in act by (a form of) science preexisting in us. Thomas notes that this means that science results from a syllogism or from some form of argument. Moreover, Aristotle does not say that all knowledge comes from previous knowledge, but limits what he says to doctrine and organized learning. The knowledge of the senses and imagination are excluded. In dialectic reasoning we use things already known, and an orator attempts to convince the audience with the help of examples.

In lesson 2 (I.2.71a12–24), Thomas explains how according to Aristotle previous knowledge is sometimes necessary with regard to the subject (of a proposition) where we must know what it is and that it is (no. 15); with regard to the passion or the predicate we must know what it is, but we do not yet know that it is in the subject; with regard to the principles we must know that they are (*quia sunt*). In the philosophy of nature and in metaphysics the subject is substance, but in propositions belonging to mathematics, for instance, it can be an accident, such as a figure. And while principles or propositions are known in and through a judgment, the subject and the predicate are known by the first operation of the intellect, that is, simple apprehension. The subject is known and defined absolutely, while the predicate is known and defined insofar as it depends on the subject. The major premise of a syllogism is known earlier than the minor (the middle proposition), both by natural priority and in time. If that which is stated by the minor is not yet known to be contained explicitly in the major, there is no conclusion. Individual beings are not predicated of any subject.

Lesson 3 (II.2.21a24–b8) notes that, in a certain way, we know already what we are going to demonstrate. Thomas explains that before formulating a demonstration we must know the principles on which it is based. These principles, he says, are like the causes active in the world of natural things. Before an effect is produced, it exists in the power (*virtus*) of the active cause, and likewise the conclusion preexists in its principles, which we know already. What one learns is not totally unknown, nor totally known, but potentially known (no. 22). In this way, Aristotle explains Plato's theory that learning is a form of remembering (no. 27).

Passing to lesson 4 (II.2.71b9–72b8), the commentary gives a summary in the form of a division of the entire *Posterior Analytics*, as mentioned in my introduction above. Thomas explains that we can know a thing just in itself, or know it up to a point, for instance, if we know it in something else, as part of a whole, or as the effect of a cause, etc. In these cases we know things in a secondary way. That of which we have a scientific knowledge must be necessary and not capable of becoming different. There are other ways of knowing, such as knowing a thing through its effects, or knowing the first principles that have no cause.

To really know something we must proceed from true, first, and immediately known propositions (i.e., known by themselves). Aristotle writes that the things that are first and better known are those close to the senses, that is, the individual things, as opposed to the universal concepts. But in *Physics* I.1, the universals are said to be prior to us, although they are later according to their nature. The difference between the texts can be explained, Thomas says, if we understand the latter as comparing the less universal with the more universal, while in the *Posterior Analytics* sensitive and intellectual knowledge are meant. In a final passage of this lesson, Thomas notes that, in this chapter, "first" also means "from its proper principles" (no. 43).

In lesson 5 (I.2.72a9–25), Aristotle further determines the terminology he is using: immediate proposition, premise proposition, thesis, axiom, and definition. Thomas explains that a definition is called a part of a proposition, but not a proposition (in the full or proper sense), because it does not state whether the thing defined is or is not. One may call it a virtual proposition.

In lesson 6 (I.3.72a26–b4), Thomas comments on Aristotle's statement that the premises are known before the conclusion and are better known than it. The reason is that they are the cause of its being known. In lesson 7, the opinion is refuted that the first principles must also be demonstrated. Thomas stresses that there must necessarily be certain knowledge of some things without demonstration (no. 62). If not, there would be an infinite series of intermediates. The knowledge of the (first) principles results from an immediate intuition of the terms of which they are composed. Resorting to a so-called circular demonstration is rejected in lesson 8 (I.3.72b25–73a20) as it demonstrates the same by the same (no. 69). Thomas presents a detailed discussion of Aristotle's arguments (nos. 71–74).

In lesson 9 (I.4.73a21–34), Aristotle points out that the conclusions reached in a science are necessary because its premises are necessary, for in them something is predicated of all (i.e., universally) *per se* (it is contained in the subject itself), and also first in relation to the things prior to the subject (no. 78). Subsequently, Aristotle explains the predication of all instances and of all temporal modalities (nos. 79–80).

The predication "per se" is explained in lesson 10 (I.4.73a34–b24). The preposition "per," Thomas writes, signifies a material, formal, or efficient cause. "Per se" signifies the subject itself or something that is its cause. Belonging "per se" to something can mean that it belongs to its form, or it may express its relation to the material cause. It can also signify something which exists by itself as an individual being and, finally, a predicate that is caused by its efficient cause. For example, whatever is in a thing because of the thing itself belongs "per se" to it (no. 83). Thomas gives the following example of "per" signifying efficient causality: "What was killed died," meaning that it died because it was killed. But "per se" can also signify a being that exists by itself, as Socrates or Plato. A "per se" attribute belongs necessarily to its subject (no. 87).

In the short lesson 11 (I.4.73b25–74a3), Aristotle first explains what the universal is. Thomas notes that "universal" is not used here in the sense of something that is said of several things, but in the sense of the predicate being on equal footing with the subject and as the predicate that is not found outside the subject, while the subject is not without a predicate (no. 91). This universal is what belongs *per se* to the subject, as the fact that the angles of a triangle are equal to two rectangles (no. 96). In lesson 12 (I.5.74a4–b5), the mistakes are mentioned that may occur when one resorts to universals. An attribute belongs to a subject universally when it belongs *per se* and primarily to any instance of it. Three mistakes may occur when we apply an attribute universally to a subject: (1) when it belongs in the first place to another subject; (2) when we assign it to only one species while it also belongs to other species; or (3) when an attribute is assigned universally but does not apply to all the species of the genus (nos. 100–102).[16] In lesson 13 (I.6.74b5–75a17), Aristotle shows from which pre-known things a demonstration proceeds, that is, from what is true of the genus to which they belong and what cannot be otherwise. A conclusion will only be necessary when the premises are necessary. If the middle term is not necessary, the conclusion becomes problematic. The person who formulates a demonstration does not just take any first

---

16. Berquist notes that Thomas thinks that the error as mentioned in Aristotle's example of the third case (they "do not meet") applies to straight lines rather than to perpendicular lines versus a horizontal one (*Commentary on "Posterior Analytics,"* 360).

predicate, but the first that is proper to the genus he is dealing with (no. 114).

In lesson 14 (I.6.75a18–37), Aristotle explains that demonstrations proceed from proper principles, not from extrinsic and common ones. Therefore, accidents that are not *per se* are excluded from scientific demonstrations and the middle term must belong to the same genus as the extremes of the syllogism. Thomas explains that an attribute belongs necessarily to a subject when this subject is its cause. It follows that no science demonstrates anything about the subject of another science; a science demonstrates only attributes belonging to the genus of its own subject (nos. 125–26).

In lesson 15 (I.7.75a38–b21), a warning is issued: while demonstrating something we must not pass to another genus, for example, from geometry to arithmetic (nos. 129–30). In a *sciendum est* ("one has to consider"), Thomas notes that we have the same genus when we deal with the subject as such, and no factor is added foreign to the nature of the genus; for example, "visible" is foreign to the genus "line" (no. 131). Three factors are to be observed in a demonstration: (1) it must concern an essential attribute that needs to be proved; (2) we must know the axioms on which the demonstration rests; and (3) we must also know the proper passions and the *per se* accidents of the genus that our demonstration is concerned with. Thomas notices that, for instance, arithmetic and geometry are not simply one genus. No science demonstrates anything about the subject of another science (no. 133); it demonstrates only those accidents that are accidents of the genus it is dealing with (no. 134).

Lesson 16 (I.8.75b21–36) notes that from the viewpoint of strictly scientific demonstrations, there is no demonstration of corruptible things (nos. 136–37), and neither can there be definitions (no. 138). Thomas explains that according to the causes from which we take the definitions, the latter will be different: the causes are mutually related, as form and matter; the efficient cause depends on the end, and so the definition taken from the final cause must be the reason and ground of the definitions taken from the other causes. Thomas illustrates this with the example of the building of a house, where we must understand the final cause before we can meaningfully discuss the material cause (no. 139). Corruptible things are at one time this, then something else. Thomas recalls that this position makes us think of Plato's theory of the Ideas (no. 140), but writes that demonstrations about corruptible things are possible insofar as what is universal in them is considered (no. 141). In the final passage of this lesson, Aristotle considers the question of whether strict demonstrations are possible for things that happen frequently. In some cases there is a regular pattern which can be discerned, even if it is sometimes obstructed. Thomas makes a further distinction: some of these things always exist when their causes are active, but in other cases the causes can be impeded (no. 142).

In lesson 17 (I.9.75b37–76a25), Aristotle argues that scientific demonstrations are formulated with the help of the principles that are proper to a particular genus. By means of an example, he shows why and how it is improper to use common principles outside the particular genus (nos. 143–46). Thomas, who is apparently thinking of the first principles and their indispensable role, notes that the principles proper to the different sciences have something common prior to them (no. 145). These are the first principles studied in metaphysics. They cannot, however, be demonstrated (no. 147).

We are certain to have acquired scientific knowledge when we draw inferences that are conformed to the primary truth of the particular science we are concerned with, as is explained in lesson 18 (I.9–10.76a22–b23). Aristotle calls principles in each genus those principles that cannot be proved. We just accept their meaning and truth. There are also common principles. (An example of such a common principle is the following: when equals are taken from equals, the remaining things are equal.) Every demonstrative science is concerned with three things: the subject (the genus studied), the common axioms, and the attributes. Sometimes one of these is disregarded (e.g., a principle when it is well known), but all three are supposed to be present in every science.

In lesson 19 (I.10–11.76b24–77a9), Aristotle first describes what a hypothesis is, namely a probable assertion assumed without demonstrating it. When it is not accepted by the respondent, we speak of a postulate. Definitions are not statements because they do not assert that something is. In the last lines of the lesson—a passage that belongs to chapter 11—we read that the existence of Forms or Ideas is not needed for valid demonstrations because demonstrations are about universals and, therefore, about eternal truths. But to have a valid demonstration, there must be one thing which is present in many: the middle term must be universal.

In lesson 20 (I.11.77a10–35), Aristotle argues that all the sciences share in the use of the common principles, such as the principle of contradiction. He first explains how the demonstrative sciences relate to the common principles, and in I.12, which is discussed in lesson 21, he expounds what relation to the principles is proper to these sciences. The principle that either the assertion or the negation of a predicate must be true is shown by a reduction to the impossible. The sciences use the common principles, as does dialectics, but dialectics is not concerned with a particular class of things and leaves the alternative open. *Se habet ad utramque partem contradictionis* (it is open to each of two contradictory terms), Thomas says (no. 172). But contraries belong to the same subject: love and hate are found in man's concupiscence. In lesson 21 (I.12.77a36–b15), the different sciences are said to relate to specific premises proper to them, from which the conclusion, proper to that science, is drawn (no. 174). When one argues and reasons, one must always remain within the field belonging to a particular science, as every science has its own questions and answers (nos. 176–78).

One should not go outside the field of the subject one is discussing. As each science has its own questions, it has also its invalid answers and inferences (no. 181). In lesson 22 (I.12.77b15–78a22), the sophistical paralogisms are briefly mentioned (no. 184). In demonstrative sciences, what we define relates to the intellect, as visible things relate to the senses. Because we proceed from definitions, fallacy is excluded, but our reasoning may nevertheless go wrong in several ways, as when we argue from false premises or from premises belonging to a different genus: for instance, questions concerning music lie outside the field of geometry. Premises must hold for all cases within a genus. When demonstrating something, we do not use several middle propositions (*media*) to prove one conclusion. Thomas notes that this applies to demonstrations *propter quid*. But middle propositions can be multiplied by assuming one middle term under another. By adding and multiplying medium sentences—while subordinating them to the previous medium—the demonstration is also multiplied (nos. 188–91).

Lesson 23 (I.13.78a22–b12) deals with the difference between a demonstration *propter quid* and a demonstration *quia* within the same science: the knowledge of facts and the knowledge of their causes differ. By means of some examples, Aristotle shows that these types of knowledge differ: a star that does not twinkle is near; the planets do not twinkle, so they are near. But this argument does not show the reason why they do not twinkle. It argues from an effect, but one can also show certain things indirectly, when the middle term belongs to a different genus (nos. 194–200, lesson 24; I.13.78b12–34) and is not interchangeable with the major. An example explains what is meant here: this wall does not breathe because it is not an animal. But not being an animal is not the cause why it does not breathe because not all animals breathe (nos. 202–6).

In lesson 25 (I.14.78b34–79a16), the difference is examined between arguments *quia* and *propter quid* in subordinated and not-subordinated sciences. Aristotle distinguishes between sciences that consist in the collection of facts and those explaining why things are this way. He gives an interesting example: why do circular wounds heal more slowly? Medicine knows the fact, geometry indicates the reason. In a *sciendum est,* Thomas notes that the sciences that are subordinate to mathematics apply the principles of mathematics to sensible things. To know "that something is" (*scire quia*) is proper to lower sciences, which use mathematical principles and apply them to a subject matter (e.g., astronomy), while mathematics itself does not consider matter (nos. 210–12).

In lesson 26 (I.14–15.79a17–b22), we are told that, in syllogistic reasoning, demonstrations in the so-called first figure of the syllogism are superior, being the most scientific ones. They are also the most widely used, for they indicate the cause of the conclusion. Thomas presents Aristotle's reasons for this preeminence: (1) the middle term is contained in the last term of the major, which is the predicate of the conclusion; (2) in the first figure, the definition of what a thing is (which is so prominent in the sciences) has the most important role; and (3) in demonstrations, the other figures need the first which supplements them (nos. 214–16). The last part of the lesson (on the first section of chapter 15) deals with immediate, negative propositions. Thomas concludes his commentary by observing that the meaning of this passage is obvious (no. 220).

Lesson 27 (I.16.79b23–80a5) deals with false statements and arguments— that is, defective syllogisms—and with ignorance. Ignorance can either be simply negative—a simple error—or the result of an inference (no. 222). Sometimes one premise of the syllogism is false, and sometimes both premises are. Thomas reminds the reader that we cannot rationally deny the principles, but that we can do so in our words (no. 223). Next, he resolves certain difficulties a reader may come across in the text. And he explains how ignorance may be caused by a syllogism and also, in lesson 30 (see below), when there is no syllogism. In most cases, ignorance is caused by the failing of reason (*ex defectu rationis*) (no. 226). A syllogism can be wrong due to a defect in its form (then, in fact, it is no syllogism at all) or by wrong propositions (nos. 227–29).

In lesson 28 (I.16.80a6–b17), Aristotle explains that error in the first figure is possible when one premise is false or both are (nos. 234–39). Lesson 29 (I.17.80b17–81a37) deals with deceptive syllogisms, namely, if the major proposition in this false syllogism has been changed to enunciate the opposite of what it was in a true syllogism (no. 241). These false syllogisms originate when a false or improper medium is introduced or when the medium is taken from a different context. Thomas explains and comments on the oft-cryptic text explaining admirably the several ways in which true syllogisms can become false (no. 247).

Lesson 30 (I.18.81a38–b9) deals with forms of ignorance not forthcoming from defective syllogisms but from other factors, as for instance error or abuse of one of the senses. Thomas reminds us that we must in fact draw our knowledge from particular things through the senses. If the use of a sense is defective, we cannot have a precise knowledge of its object (e.g., knowledge of colors, if our vision does not function). Thomas adds the following: this statement is a rejection of Plato's theory according to which we know things by means of concepts we receive from the Ideas.[17] Another rejected theory is the opinion that we can know the separate substances through the medium of their essences (nos. 250–54).

Is it possible to proceed indefinitely in demonstrations (I.19.81b10–82a20)? This larger question is examined in the next five lessons (lessons 31–35). Can one ascend from one predicate to the next in order to arrive at a predicate that is said universally of others, but of which nothing else is predicated (no. 261)? A second question runs as follows: if one starts at this most universal predicate, which is said of others like a whole of its parts, can one descend *ad infinitum* (no. 262)? These two questions come down to the question as to whether one can go on indefinitely in a series of proofs, an opinion Aristotle has already discarded (nos. 263–67). In lesson 32 (I.20–21.82a21–b35), Thomas addresses the following question: can the intermediate terms in a demonstration be infinite? The answer is negative, as there are limits to the upward movement of the universal concept and also in its downward movement to the particulars. The answer applies also to negative statements (nos. 272–77). In lesson 33 (I.22.82b36–83a35), we read that when a term is said of another, what we say is either part of its essence or an accident. Thomas says that we cannot give a definition of a thing unless we come to a last term going downward. In affirmative predicates, one does not proceed *ad infinitum*, neither when one uses a circular argument (nos. 292–93) nor when one follows a straight path going up and down (nos. 294–96), as lesson 34 (I.22.83a36–b8) indicates. In lesson 35 (83b8–84b2), Thomas observes that Aristotle first proves his thesis logically and, second, by the fact that we would not be able to know premises in an endless succession: when we would go through an infinite series, we would know nothing by demonstration, but only by supposition.

In lesson 36 (I.23.84b3–85a12), we see that things with common attributes need not always have the same middle propositions. Thomas notes that Aristotle does not want to say that when one thing is said of several things that are not predicated of each other, it is not said of them because they have something in common (no. 312). In fact, Thomas affirms that this thing must

---

17. One may also mention Avicenna's theory of the *dator formarum* as the origin of our concepts.

be in them, although it may not have a name. And this is true for every term predicated as a property. Finally, Aristotle shows how to use those first principles, which are different in the different genera (nos. 312–22). Thomas explains this difficult text in an admirable way.

Lesson 37 (I.24.85a13–b22) presents the different classes of demonstrations, such as universal and particular demonstrations. Particular demonstrations tell us more about the subject in question and seem to be superior to universal demonstrations. However, using the triangle as an example, Aristotle points out that when we have shown that a particular attribute belongs to it, we also have a more profound and universal knowledge. The universal is not some entity apart from the particular. And the one who knows a thing in a universal way knows it better than the one who knows it as a particular thing.

In lesson 38 (I.24.85b23–86a30), Aristotle advances seven arguments, analyzing first the reasons in favor of particular demonstrations (nos. 327–28) in order to show why general (universal) demonstrations are more powerful than particular demonstrations: a universal one has more of the nature of a cause, as in human actions the final cause provides the ultimate explanation. The one who knows the universal also knows the particular contained under it. And ultimately, the particular demonstration ends at the level of sense knowledge, whereas the universal demonstration approaches the first principles (nos. 329–31), so that Aristotle closes this section (and also begins the next chapter) by stating that a demonstration based on the universal is superior to one which remains at the level of the particular (nos. 334–39).

In lesson 39 (I.25.86a30–b38), Aristotle argues that an affirmative demonstration is superior to a negative one, as it uses fewer premises. When both premises are negative, there is no demonstration at all. There can only be one negative premise in a syllogism. A demonstration that uses fewer medium terms is more effective (*potior*, Thomas says, in no. 340) than one using more. An affirmative demonstration proceeds from fewer medium terms than a negative one (nos. 341–44). Further reasons for the preeminence of affirmative propositions are given in the last part of the lesson (nos. 345–48). In lesson 40 (I.26.87a1–30), Aristotle shows that negative demonstrations are superior to reductions to the impossible. Such a reduction is more complex and involves more intermediates, while the negative demonstration proceeds from better known and prior premises.

In lesson 41 (I.27–29.87a31–b18), Aquinas's commentary is exceptionally long compared to that found in the other lessons. Aristotle argues that a science is prior and more precise when it concerns the *quid*, the "what a thing is" and its causes. He adds a comparison of things that are forms without a substrate with those that are in a substrate, also by assuming the notion that forms give a greater certitude. Now, there are two ways of inhering in a substrate. The first way is that of sensible things, all of which have a substrate; the second way is by addition, as a point adds to a unit (the unit as such abstracts from any matter or subject, while a point is an individual thing with a position in a continuum). Thomas adds that because the form is the principle, it lets us know the matter and gives us a greater certitude (no. 360).

Passing to the next theme (I.28), Aristotle compares sciences from the point of view of their unity. Sciences differ if their principles belong to different genera. The unity of a science depends on the unity of the genus it is studying, as the nature of a movement depends on the end toward which the thing in motion is moving. For a science this end is the knowledge of its object (nos. 360–62). One science may have a wider range than others, as metaphysics has with regard to natural philosophy. If things have no other things prior to them, a demonstrative science is not possible. The essential unity of a science is given with the fact that the genus it examines is one (no. 365), but the reason for the difference between the sciences lies in the diversity of their principles. If certain things are of the same nature, but must be studied according to different principles, they obviously belong to different sciences (no. 366). Thomas says that here Aristotle means the diversity of their first principles. To have different sciences, these principles must be different (nos. 363–70).

In lesson 42 (I.30–31.87b19–88a18), Aristotle affirms that there is no demonstration of things that happen by chance, for every syllogism argues according to what is necessary or happens in the majority of cases (nos. 372–74). In I.31, we read that science is not of what is known at the level of the senses, for sense knowledge, Thomas writes, has as its object the qualities of particular things at a given place or time, while the universal does not come in under what the senses perceive (no. 376). Aristotle writes that the universal is not a particular thing, nor does it exist at a particular time, for it is always and everywhere. Thomas says that this sentence must be understood in the way of a negation or abstraction, because the universal abstracts from every local and temporal determination (no. 377). The senses are concerned with the particular and cannot perceive the universal. But as we have already seen, Thomas nevertheless speaks of a certain awareness of the universal when the senses perceive individual material things (no. 376). After his strong rejection of the view that the senses can give us scientific knowledge, Aristotle concedes that they may lead us to a demonstration. Thomas comments that a demonstration may result when, by way of experimental knowledge, we discover the universal (no. 381).

In lesson 43 (I.32.88a18–b29), we learn that not all syllogisms have the same principles, as Aristotle shows by means of a dialectical argument (no. 383). Moreover, their principles sometimes belong to different genera (nos. 385–89). It is not possible, Thomas observes, to construct a syllogism exclusively from such principles (no. 387). But when the premises vary, the conclusions also vary. The conclusions are often more numerous than the premises, because the same premises can be used to draw a variety of conclusions (no. 388). Certain of the premises are necessary, others contingent. But one cannot use just any premise to demonstrate anything whatever. In a later section, Aristotle deals with an objection: some divide the first principles into absolutely first and not absolutely first, such as "man is an animal." But Aristotle replies that nevertheless there must be in each genus a first principle proper to it, although this is not first absolutely speaking. Different sciences have different principles, as they are in different genera. The common principles, Thomas says, must be applied to the principles common to each genus (nos. 390–94).

In lesson 44 (I.33–34.88b30–89b20), Aristotle reaffirms that scientific knowledge is about the universal and about what cannot be otherwise, while opinion is concerned with what is true or false with regard to contingent events and things, whether universal or particular, and its premises do not result from an asserted principle and are not necessary. But how is it possible to explain that sometimes one person has an opinion about a particular point, while another has a scientific knowledge of it? The explanation is that the latter knows that the conclusion results from the essence, while the reasoning of the former, the one who has merely an opinion about it, proceeds from contingent attributes. The same person cannot have an opinion and knowledge about the same object. As for the nature of our conclusions or assents, Aristotle distinguishes other degrees or types of knowledge than that of necessary knowledge, such as διάνοια (having something in mind, *cogitatio*), grasping its object directly (νοῦς), practical intelligence, and wisdom.

Thomas comments that Aristotle first explains how true scientific knowledge and opinion differ, and then explains certain terms such as νοῦς, a term that in this context signifies certain knowledge without demonstration (and not having the intellect as a faculty). He writes that opinion is the acceptance of a proposition without the mediation of a demonstration, which is not necessary even when the proposition by itself might be necessary, or when the proposition is contingent (no. 399). Thomas notes that a contingent proposition may be mediated, but the proposition "a person does not walk" presupposes that this person does not move, so that even mediated contingent propositions can be opinions. By contrast, νοῦς is a type of knowledge without previous demonstration; it is the apprehension of an immediate proposition. Its object is the indemonstrable and known *per se*. Science is not about contingent things that are the object of opinion. Thomas also adds that one can think that all mediated propositions that are the object of scientific knowledge could be otherwise, but that this does not apply to the first principles (no. 402). Is it possible, then, to have both science (scientific knowledge) and an opinion about the same thing? While Aristotle strongly denies this, Thomas says that in a less precise sense it is possible. For instance, when one talks about a diagonal as being commensurate with the side of a square, while someone else thinks it is incommensurate; when considering a diagonal, both opinions can be held (no. 377).

Thomas correctly takes the last lines of chapter 43 as belonging to chapter 44 (and thus belonging to the same lesson). This text explains how the different forms of knowledge—wisdom, science, and prudence—are present in the arts. He refers to *Nicomachean Ethics* VI.3, where five cognitive *habitus* (habits) are mentioned as being ordered to the knowledge of truth, namely art, science, wisdom, prudence, and *intellectus* (i.e., understanding and insight). Two of these habits concern what is both true and erroneous, suspicion and opinion. Thomas explains that science, wisdom, and intellect concern the necessary (i.e., the conclusions, the principles, and the highest causes); prudence has the field of human actions as its object; and art directs man's activity in the field of work to be done. Thomas adds reason (*ratio*), which leads us from principles to conclusions. The study of reason, science, and understanding (*intellectus*) comes in under the subject of first philosophy, but prudence falls under ethics, and *sollertia* (quick-mindedness) falls under the philosophy of nature (nos. 405–6).

Book II

While in Book I of the *Posterior Analytics*, Aristotle studies the demonstrative syllogism, in Book II he examines its basic principles: the middle term, how we must define it, and which the first indemonstrable principles are.[18] In lesson 1, Thomas comments on II.1–2 and the first part of II.3 in a very clear and detailed exposition. The central argument is that in all demonstrations by means of syllogisms their demonstrative force lies in the middle term, that is, the middle proposition, and the first principles. Aristotle begins II.1 by listing the four questions we ask about the middle term, namely, whether it is, why it is so, if it is, and what it is.[19] A seemingly different

18. These first principles are studied in the last chapter of Book II.
19. "Quattuor autem sunt quae quaeruntur, scilicet, *quia propter quid, si est et quid est*" (no. 408). The *si est* is the question of existence, the *quia* is the question of fact, e.g., whether the sun suffers eclipses.

enumeration of these questions in *Topics* I.3 is reduced by Thomas to the first of these four questions (no. 408). Statements (*enunciationes*) express the truth. Science is concerned with the truth, and statements are the subject of our inquiry (no. 408). The first thing therefore that we investigate is whether a thing is this or that. Next we ask why it is and what it is, but these questions are reducible to the first one (nos. 409–17). The question of whether something exists or whether this is this something implies, as all four questions do, that we are looking for a middle term that helps us to obtain the answer. By means of the example of the eclipse of the moon, Aristotle shows that in this case knowing something is the same as knowing why it is; for example, the moon moving into the zone where the earth intercepts the light of the sun. So we see that the middle term, the moon moving into the shadow of the earth, expresses what an eclipse is and why it happens. Thus, to the questions whether something is, what it is, and why it is, the middle term gives the answer. In certain cases the medium is what is perceived by the senses, but sometimes we grasp the universal in what the senses perceive, so that the universal becomes the medium.

In lesson 2 (II.3.90a34–91a12), Aristotle says that in all our inquiries we must try to find a middle term and examine how we come to know it.[20] Aristotle first investigates whether it is possible to know something, and to know it under the same respect, by a definition and by a demonstration, and he concludes that it is impossible to know the same thing both by a definition and a demonstration. Defining an attribute does not make us know it. The definition lets us know what a thing is, the demonstration that it is (no. 421).

Thomas divides the remaining part of the second book as follows: how are the what (*quod quid*) and the why (*propter quid*) related to demonstration (lessons 2–12)?; and in II.13 (lesson 13), Aristotle shows how we should investigate the what and the why (in eight lessons), that is, how to hunt for "the what things are." In the second lesson at hand, Aristotle explains how we come to know what a thing is and how what we observe about it is reduced or reducible to it. The definition says what a thing is and what can be affirmed of it universally, but not all syllogisms do this, for some are negative. Furthermore, we know certain things through their definition and not through a demonstration. Definitions, however, do not confer knowledge of the accidents and of things that are *per se* in the particular subject which we have defined. Definitions concern the substance, demonstrations the accidents that are present in things (no. 424).

---

20. This sentence is read by Thomas as the closing text of the previous lesson.

In the following section, the question is raised whether there are demonstrations of things of which we have definitions. Because definitions are the principles of demonstrations, they are as such beyond proof, so that we cannot have proof of all things of which we have definitions. Are there some things of which there are both a demonstration and a definition? The answer is negative, as definitions show what a thing is (i.e., its essence), but this is presupposed in demonstrations. Moreover, in the conclusion of a demonstration, something is predicated of a subject, but this is not the case in a definition. Definitions show what things are, demonstrations that they are or that they are not.

In lesson 3 (II.4.91a13–b11), Aristotle examines whether the essence can be demonstrated by syllogisms or by some other proofs. By "essence" is meant here the middle term, so that the question is how we come to know the middle term. Aristotle's investigation—which Thomas calls the disputative part of this particular topic—extends up to line 93a1, that is, up to the end of lesson 7. Thomas gives a fine explanation of the not always easy or clear text. The conclusion is that there is no demonstration of the middle term (nos. 432–42).

Lesson 4 (II.5.91b12–92a5) shows that divisions do not prove what a thing is. The method of division was practiced in the Academy to classify the Forms (i.e., the Ideas).[21] Aristotle points out that a division must show that there is no other member, for example, no third party in the divisions leading to that of man as a two-footed animal. A further objection is mentioned: if with the mere help of divisions we define man as a two-footed animal, we overlook whether this indicates the essence of man. The answer is that if one uses the method of division, even avoiding all its defects, the method is not syllogistic, but gives an understanding in a different way, without answering the question of why something is. Aquinas comments on a certain resemblance between the method of division and induction (no. 446; see nos. 443–48).

In lesson 5 (II.6–7.92a6–b3), Aristotle argues that it is impossible to prove by supposition what a thing is, that is, on the basis of certain characteristics that belong exclusively to it. In a supposition, one assumes that a statement about a genus and the specific differences tells us what a thing is, but in doing so one assumes that the genus and the specific differences express what a thing is. However, the "what-a-thing-is" must remain outside the premises

---

21. See A. E. Taylor, *Plato: The Man and His Work* (London: Methuen, 1952), 374. An example of Plato's method of division in *Statesman* 262a–264b is the following: nonliving and living beings; living beings are divided into those living in the sea and land animals; land animals are divided into those that fly and those that march on the land; those animals that march on the land into horned animals and those without horns; land animals without horns into those mixing with other species and those that do not; and those without horns that do not mix with other species into four-footed and two-footed animals.

of a syllogism. Aristotle gives another example of a wrong conclusion from a supposition. Assuming that the One (which is indivisible) is the same as the Idea of the Good,[22] we cannot argue that "bad" is divisible (no. 455; see nos. 452–59).

In lesson 6 (II.7.92b4–34), with the help of three further arguments, Aristotle shows that what a thing is cannot be demonstrated. What a man is and the fact that he exists are different, for existence is not the essence of things. Those who define things do not demonstrate their existence, but presuppose it. In his commentary, Aquinas repeats Aristotle's statement that the existence of a thing and its essence differ, but notes that they are the same only with regard to the first principle of being, which is being by its very essence; in all other things, which are beings by participation, their being is necessarily different from their essence (no. 462). A few lines further on (no. 463), he comments on Aristotle's saying that being is not a genus, adding that God, who is his own existence, is not in a genus (nos. 461–69).

In lesson 7 (II.8.93a1–b21), Thomas notes that while the previous chapters were written in the form of disputations, Aristotle now engages in establishing the truth. We cannot know what a thing is when we do not know whether it exists, but when we know that it is, we understand at least something of what it is. When we know some accidental property of a thing, or one of its accidents, we know that the thing exists and what it is although we do not know it perfectly. Thomas illustrates Aristotle's arguments with some examples: every *habitus* that leads to happiness makes us act according to right reason; virtue is such a *habitus* that leads to happiness; therefore, it makes us act according to right reason (no. 472). Thomas also draws attention to a situation in which the "what it is" is the cause of a thing in one or more of the different species of causality. Another example explains this: what a house is can be considered according to its material cause, but also according to the other causes; one aspect can show itself, while other aspects are implicitly understood (no. 472). But this way of demonstrating shows that a predicate belongs to a subject through something other than the thing itself, for instance through one of its causes. Sometimes we know that a thing exists when we know some of its accidents or properties. Because of the speed with which a small animal moves in a field, we know that it is a hare (nos. 473–78).

Lesson 8 (II.8–9.93b21–28) points out that certain things have a cause that is different from what they are themselves, and others have not. The things that do not have a cause are immediate and are principles. Thomas comments

---

22. As taught by the Platonists.

that this statement may be understood as referring to the first cause, which has no cause of its existence but is the cause of the being of all things. He then adds that God is the cause even of necessary things, but he admits that Aristotle's sentence need not be understood as referring to the first cause; it could also mean a prior cause in the order of causes, as for instance the final cause. And it might refer to things the cause of which lies outside the genus of a particular science under which the thing in question comes in. Thomas notes that the last sentences he has commented on are not found in the Greek manuscripts (nos. 480–81).[23] In the following passage, Aristotle shows how definitions are related to demonstrations, namely that there are definitions that signify what a thing is, but do not tell us if it exists. Other definitions signify why a thing is. Of things that have no cause, the definitions must be accepted as we accept first principles. If a thing has a cause distinct from it, demonstration is either possible or impossible. It has now become clear in which way a demonstration of "what a thing is" is possible and in which way it is not (nos. 488–89).

In lesson 9 (II.10.93b29–94a19), Aristotle discusses demonstrations by means of the four causes and shows how the different causes are taken up as middle terms and the way they function in demonstrations (no. 492). Aristotle illustrates this with an example taken from mathematics. Thomas adds a note to explain that this text is not in conflict with *Metaphysics* III, where Aristotle says that mathematics does not resort to the material cause. The example in this chapter is based on the fact that what mathematics studies is not abstracted from intelligible matter (no. 494). In the following lines we read how formal causes, the moving cause and the final cause are engaged in demonstrations. In the last sentence, Thomas quotes Aristotle's saying that nothing which happens fortuitously is for the sake of something else (no. 503).

Lesson 10 (II.11.94a10–95a9) examines the simultaneity or non-simultaneity of cause and effect. If the cause and the effect are simultaneous, they will be so in all the stages of the process of coming to be, of being in an actual state and of coming to be in the future (nos. 504–7). When there is no simultaneity, one may ask if the time lapse between the action and the effect is continuous with the cause or not (no. 508). At this point, Thomas adds a *considerandum est* re-

---

23. The passage reads as follows: "Et secundum hunc sensum in quibusdam libris interponitur quod: 'diffinitiones secundum speciem facte nullum habent medium quo demonstrentur: diffinitiones autem secundum materiam facte possunt habere medium' . . . Predicta tamen verba non habentur in libris Grecis; unde magis videtur esse glossa, que per errorem scriptorum introducta est loco textus." As Gauthier has established, the sentence beginning with "diffinitiones secundum" is a gloss added by James of Venice whereas the sentence beginning with "Predicta tamen" is most likely a note by William of Moerbeke. See the introduction to the Leonine edition of the *Sentencia libri De Anima* at 204*–5*.

ferring to a line and a point in the process of becoming or moving. Is the now of the cause, at the time of causing, continuous with the now of the effect? (no. 510). One cannot say so because the effect can be impeded (nos. 511–12). Becoming or moving is a certain continuous; a point is indivisible.

Next, Aristotle studies the case when the cause produces its effect always or frequently. But here we pass to the next part of the second book, from lesson 11 (II.11.95a10–b37) onward. In his edition of the Greek text, Sir David Ross calls chapter 11 one of the most difficult chapters in the whole of Aristotle; similarly, Jonathan Barnes calls this section opaque and unsatisfactory.[24] In the first section of the text, as commented upon by Thomas, Aristotle shows that a continuum, when it has come to be, is indivisible. Having become is the effect of becoming; however, coming-to-be and what-has-come-be are not contiguous but related, such as a line and a point. In the following section of the text, Aristotle examines how an effect can be related to a cause. An example makes clear what is meant here: a sick person has gotten well since he took his medicine. In reality taking medicine is earlier and the cause of getting better, but in terms of the argument it comes after we have noticed that the sick person has recovered. The present now is the first point from where we start our argument. Another example: a house has been built; we conclude that before it had been built, stones had to be baked or cut and a foundation has been laid (nos. 514–20).

Lesson 12 (II.12–13.95b38–96a22) deals with things that come into being in a circular process. The issue had some actuality, because in Aristotle's view the circular motions of the heavens are the cause of the becoming of things in the sublunar region of the universe. The process of the generation of the elements is marked by circularity, but when an element, for instance water, is formed, it is not numerically the same as the water earlier in the process, which evaporated to return as rain. Thomas notes that this circularity is not found in the order of *per se* causes, where there is a first cause in each genus of causes: when the elements change into each other, it is a process *per accidens*, as here beings *per se* are generated from beings *per accidens* (nos. 522–23). In a final section, Aristotle writes that in order to demonstrate something that is true for the most part, we must use a middle term of the same nature. In such cases the conclusions are true for the most part (nos. 524–26).

In lesson 13 (II.13.96a22–b14), Aristotle considers predicates that are elements in definitions. We can examine what a thing is by analyzing its predicates that signify it. Such predicates belong to this thing always and universal-

---

24. Ross, *Aristotle's "Prior and Posterior Analytics,"* 78; Barnes, *Aristotle: "Posterior Analytics,"* 236.

ly, but they may extend beyond it and apply also to other species within the genus, Thomas explains (no. 533). The ultimate specific differences, however, do not extend beyond the particular species. We should only use those predicates that do not extend beyond the particular genus to which the thing to be defined belongs (nos. 527–35).

In lesson 14 (II.13.96b15–97a6), Aristotle explains that in order to define a genus we should first divide it into its primary parts, which are indivisible with regard to their specific nature. It is essential to find the common genus of these parts. In order to find the definition of a genus, we may divide it according to the specific differences of the species that it contains. And it makes a difference in which order we place the terms, for example whether we say that man is a two-footed tame animal, or that he is a tame two-footed animal. In the first definition, "tame animal" is taken as a genus (no. 540; see also nos. 536–41).

In lesson 15 (II.13.97a6–b6), Thomas discusses Aristotle's observations on the use of the method of division to obtain definitions. It is not necessary to know all the differences of things within a species to define this species. Within a species individual things show many differences. Without knowing them all we can nevertheless give a definition of the species. Likewise, we do not need to know all the species of irrational animals in order to define man as a rational being (nos. 545–46). Next, Thomas discusses the three rules concerning the predicates that are said of a thing in defining it (no. 548), namely: (1) they must signify the thing; (2) they must be placed in the proper order; and (3) we must be certain that we have stated the basic difference, for instance, when defining man, that he is a rational animal. When we observe these three rules, our definitions will not lack anything, nor have any superfluous predicates. As always, the commentary of Thomas is very clear (nos. 542–51).

In lesson 16 (II.13.97b7–37), another way of formulating definitions is described, namely, by examining what it is that persons who are said to have certain characteristics actually have in common. Aristotle notes that every definition is universal. When defining a thing, one should proceed from the particular to the universal. At the end of the lesson, Thomas repeats Aristotle's warning that we should not use metaphors in definitions (nos. 552–59). In short, Aristotle advises us to look for common characteristics when trying to define things.

In lesson 17 (II.14–15.98a1–34), Aristotle tells us to look for the reason why in a particular genus things have certain characteristics by noting the characteristics that are proper to all animals and by considering those characteristics that are typical of a group or species within this genus. When we attempt to define a thing by what is characteristic of it, we must also examine which properties of things within a particular genus entail these characteristics (nos. 560–63). At the end of the lesson, in regard to II.15.98a24–34, Thomas quotes Aristotle as writing that many problems are the same because they have the same middle term, that is, the reason why they come to be. An example: why does an echo or a reflection appear? The answer is that these different things come to be by repercussion or reflection (nos. 564–65).

Lesson 18 (II.16.98a35–b38) asks about the coexistence of cause and effect. If the cause and the effect are demonstrated through each other, they will be simultaneous. Yet cause and effect are not always simultaneous, for the effect may have several causes. When the effect exists, one of its causes must be acting or active, but not necessarily all of them (nos. 567–74). In lesson 19 (II.17–18.99b1–16), Aristotle shows how cause and effect go together, as he is writing in the context of the study of syllogisms. The unity of the effect shows that of its cause: if it is the *per se* cause, the cause can only be one, but if we are speaking of an accidental aspect there can be more causes; for instance, blameworthy conduct may be caused by cowardice, but also by rashness. In the *Prior* and *Posterior Analytics*, according to Thomas, Aristotle has made clear what a syllogism is, what a demonstration is, and how to construct them, and in this way he has shown us how to obtain a demonstrative science (no. 581). We formulate a scientific demonstration by stating the middle proposition of a syllogism, that is, by knowing "what it is" (the *quid*) and "why it is." If there are more middle propositions, we must always take those that are closer to the subject and proceed to what is immediately connected with the conclusion (nos. 575–81).

Lesson 20 (II.19.99b17–100b17) studies the first principles that are presupposed and present in all scientific demonstrations, as their basis, and how we apprehend these principles. The commentary of Aquinas is more detailed than the relatively short text of Aristotle, who also lists the difficulties that beset the knowledge and use of these principles. The chapter contains three questions: (1) is the knowledge of all immediate principles the same?; (2) is there a science of all immediate principles?; and (3) does "the habitual knowledge of those principles comes to exist in us after previously not existing, or have they always been in us but escaped our notice." Clearly the last question is for both Aristotle and Thomas the most important one and is treated first.[25] The second possibility, namely that such knowledge would have gone unno-

---

25. See H. Seidl, "Über die Erkenntnis erster, allgemeiner Prinzipien nach Thomas von Aquin," in *Thomas von Aquin. Werk und Wirkung im Licht neuerer Forschungen*, ed. A. Zimmermann (Berlin: De Gruyter, 1988), 103–16.

ticed, is absurd because, as was already established in I.1, knowledge through demonstration means knowledge of the necessary connection between subject and attributes, whereas knowledge of the principles is even more certain.

The first possibility of somehow acquiring the principles seems impossible as well because the knowledge of them is precisely the "cause of certitude of the things which are made known through it." On the basis of this negative outcome, Thomas writes that Aristotle posits (*necesse est in nobis*) the existence of "a certain cognitive power" existing prior to the knowledge of principles, but one that is not more certain (*potior quantum ad certitudinem*) than the knowledge of principles. Following Aristotle, Thomas elucidates the "three grades" of a preexisting cognitive principle by way of sense-perception, memory, and experience. Inspired by Aristotle's remark in 100a2 about reason's "power of systematizing" (*fiat ratiocinatio*, γίνεσθαι λόγον) sense-impressions, Thomas emphasizes reason's power over experience: reason takes "one common item which is consolidated in the mind and considers it without considering any of the singulars."[26] He gives an example from Themistius's commentary to the effect that, when a doctor comes to know, on the basis of experience, that a particular species of herbs cures an illness absolutely (*simpliciter*), such knowledge forms a rule for the art of medicine.[27] Aristotle's claim in 100a13 that "the soul is so constituted to be capable of this process" (in Latin: *anima autem existit talis ens qualis possit pati hoc*) leads Thomas to write that Aristotle wants to answer to those ancient philosophers who did not distinguish between sense and intellect—a topic which Aristotle indeed develops at length in his *De Anima* III.3.427a16–b26. Thomas interprets *possit pati* as referring to the need to have, alongside sense and memory, a soul which is susceptible of universal knowledge (*intellectus possibilis*), as well as a soul which "makes things intelligible in act by abstraction of universals from singulars." Starting at 100a14, Aristotle gives a clearer explanation of what it means when a universal is taken from experience. With our senses (αἴσθησις) we come to know the individual, but the act of perceiving the individual involves the universal: we see Callias, but also a "man." If the senses alone perceived what makes up the individual and did not know at all the universal nature in the particular being, the knowledge of the universal would not be caused in us by what the senses perceive.

The final paragraph, beginning at 100b5, gives a response to the first two

---

26. Gauthier refers to a passage at the beginning of his exposition where Thomas describes what is proper to reason, namely, "to advance from one thing to another in such a way that through that which is known a man comes to a knowledge of the unknown." See *Expositio Libri Posteriorium* I, 1, and in particular the extensive note on pages 4–5 (commenting on lines 45–47).

27. See *Expositio Libri Posteriorium* II.20, the note on page 245 (commenting on lines 163–69).

questions mentioned above, namely whether the knowledge of all immediate principles is the same and whether there is a science of all immediate principles. While holding firmly to the claim that all our knowledge comes from the senses, Thomas stresses that there is a capacity in our soul to grasp the universal and the underlying principles of the various fields of the sciences and the arts (that is, the immediate premises on which the demonstrations depend). The habitual knowledge of these principles is the same insofar as they are all concerned with what is true and hence exclude false or erroneous habits. The principles about which the text is speaking are only in a more remote sense the first principles of being. There is no science of these principles, as science results from a demonstration, but there is understanding (*intellectus*) and wisdom (*sapientia*). They both amount to the something similar insofar as wisdom is the chief of the sciences (*caput scientiarum*) and understanding the principle of science (*principium scientiae*) because it "is cognoscitive of the principles from which science proceeds" (nos. 582–96). Thomas concludes in a customary fashion by saying that this chapter completes Aristotle's *Posterior Analytics*, "to the honor of Christ, who is God, blessed forever."

Concluding Remarks

My summary of Thomas's exposition has shown to what extent he discusses the text of Aristotle, explaining the arguments and clarifying difficult sentences. The agreement with what Aristotle writes is so far-reaching that Thomas's commentary is a faithful exposition of the text with only a small number of clarifications or additions. Other philosophical authorities are not quoted, contrary to what he does in most of his Aristotelian commentaries. Regarding the difficulties of II.19, Thomas claims, contrary to many of the present-day commentators, that Aristotle did indeed offer a solution to the questions Aristotle himself raised. Thomas's very helpful division of the chapter certainly is of use to contemporary readers. And while his invocation of the agent intellect goes beyond the text at such, it is not contrary to Aristotle's thought.

3   THE COMMENTARY ON THE *PHYSICS*

The *Physics* is a critical study of the ancient Greek philosophers' theories on nature and an attempt to show what is true in them. It is also and primarily an exposition of Aristotle's own thought on material being, that is, on motion, time, space, and the void. It ends with a demonstration that there is a perpetual continuous circular motion in the world and a first unmoved mover. Aristotle observes that, in the question of natural principles, we are inclined to accept a principle that is better than others, and one principle is better than many. Hence, to cause perpetual motion, one immobile principle is sufficient. Aristotle's exposition of the nature of the physical world unfolds in the *Physics* within the framework of the image of the world as it was conceived in his time: the earth in the center of the world surrounded by the concentric spheres of the moon, the sun, the planets, and finally of the fixed stars, while the four elements with their natural movements have their natural places in the sublunar region. Aristotle's *Physics* is a most remarkable work, which exercised a profound influence on the Arab and Western world and marked practically all studies of physical nature until the time of Galileo. But for many moderns it is only a historical document, without value for our knowledge of the world.[1]

How about the composition of the whole treatise and the mutual relationship of the eight books of the *Physics*? Simplicius writes that Aristotle and his disciples describe the first five books as dealing with the principles of physical nature, while the last three books are treatises about movement.[2] However, this division of *Physics* into five and three books, respectively, is not without its difficulties. Porphyry and Philoponus reckoned Book V as belonging to

---

1. See Jonathan Barnes, "An Aristotelian Way with Scepticism," in *Aristotle Today: Essays on Aristotle's Ideal of Science,* ed. Mohan Matthen (Edmonton: Academic, 1987), 75. Francis Cheneval and Ruedi Imbach consider the commentary of Thomas without value for a historical and critical analysis of the text in *Thomas von Aquin. Prologe zu den Aristoteleskommentaren* (Frankfurt am Main: Vittorio Klostermann, 1993), xiii.

2. *Simplicii Aristotelis Physicorum in libros posteriores Commentaria* 801.13–16 (CAG 9).

the series VI, VII, and VIII on movement. As Sir David Ross writes, the title τὰ περὶ τῆς φύσεως had three meanings: a narrower, an intermediate, and a wider meaning depending on whether the title refers to a part or multiple parts of the *Physics* or to other treatises such as the *De Caelo* as well.[3] One may consider Books I and II a block. Books III and IV also form a group, but Book V makes a fresh start. Books VI and VIII appear to be connected, while the beginning of VII does not perfectly fit in with Book VI, nor its end with Book VIII. Some say that it interrupts the unity of V, VI, and VIII. Books I and II are commonly thought to date to an early period of Aristotle's scholarly activity, along with Book VII.

After the publication of Werner Jaeger's *Studien zur Entstehungsgeschichte der Metaphysik des Aristoteles* in 1912, attempts flourished to date the works of Aristotle or parts of them as belonging either to the period of his stay at the Academy, to his years at Assos, or finally to the period of the Lyceum. But at present such dating is no longer the first concern of Aristotelian scholars.[4] As Jaeger himself once told me, we must be satisfied with the *Corpus aristotelicum* as its editors bequeathed it to us. The real Aristotle—he meant the philological precision of the texts rather than their doctrinal contents—is hidden behind the text that was handed down to us. The *Physics*, as we received it, deals with the following subjects: Book I has a short introduction to the philosophy of nature, discusses the positions of the Pre-Socratic philosophers regarding the principles, and lays down Aristotle's doctrine of matter, form, and privation. Book II examines the "principles" of natural science, that is, it studies nature as the source of movement and process and the four causes, as well as chance and finality in nature. Book III examines what movement is and, because the continuous movement is infinitely divisible, it also discusses the infinite. Book IV considers place, the void, and time as measures of movement. Book V presents a division of movement in its species. Book VI deals with the quantitative parts of movements, in particular the indivisibles. Book VII has some considerations about the principles of movement: what is moving is moved by another; one cannot proceed indefinitely in a series of movers; it examines whether there is movement in such categories as *habitus*, figure, relation, action, and receptivity and compares movements with one another. In Book VIII, Aristotle determines that there is a first, perpetual movement and a first unmoved mover. The reasoning in the successive chapters runs as follows: he presupposes that whatever is moved is moved by something else and that

---

3. *Aristotle's "Physics": A Revised Text with Introduction and Commentary* (*Commentaria in Aristotelem Graeca*, vol. 10), ed. William D. Ross (Oxford: Clarendon, 1936), 2.

4. Georgios Anagnostopoulos, "Aristotle's Works and the Development of His Thought," in *A Companion to Aristotle* (ed. Anagnostopoulos).

an endless series of movers is not possible. If there would be a self-moving mover, part of it would be immobile, part moved. Local movement is the first movement. Circular movement is the only movement which can really be continuous. The first mover must be indivisible and incorporeal, as its power must be infinite, and nothing that has magnitude is infinite. The first mover must be one, as a plurality of movers would jeopardize the continuity and unity of the movement.

Aristotle's *Physics* has been the object of numerous commentaries. Unfortunately, many Greek commentaries by Eudemus, Aspasius, Alexander of Aphrodisias, and others have been lost entirely or only preserved in fragments. Three commentaries by Themistius, Philoponus, and Simplicius have been preserved.[5] In particular the commentary by Simplicius contains a wealth of information on earlier commentaries which have now been lost. None of these commentaries were translated into Latin during the Middle Ages although a significant portion of their content has come to us through translations into Arabic of Aristotle's text as well as the Greek commentators Themistius, Philoponus, and in particular Alexander of Aphrodisias. In the late twelfth and early thirteenth century, the *Physics* received at least five translations, almost simultaneously from both the Arabic and the Greek into Latin. Of particular importance is the early thirteenth century Arabic-Latin translation and Averroes's *Long Commentary* by Michael Scotus. Averroes's commentary will constitute an important indirect source for our knowledge about the earlier Greek commentators. Among the Greek-Latin translation one should mention the earliest translation by James of Venice (before 1187), the *translatio vetus*. Between 1260 and 1270 William of Moerbeke revised this translation into what is now known as the *translatio nova*.[6]

The Latin commentary literature on the *Physics* saw an important increase in the second half of the thirteenth century both at the University of Paris and of Oxford, the result of which has only partially been identified, much less edited.[7] Apart from the numerous anonymous commentaries, one can men-

5. These texts can be found in CAG and are in the process of being translated into English in the Ancient Commentators on Aristotle series.

6. Gerard Verbeke, "Saint Thomas et les commentaires grecs sur la Physique d'Aristote," in *La philosophie de la nature de Saint Thomas d'Aquin*, ed. Leo Elders (Vatican City: Libreria Editrice Vaticana, 1982), 134–54. For the critical edition of the *translatio vetus* see *Physica. Translatio Vetus*, ed. F. Bossier and J. Brams; *Translatio Vaticana*, ed. A. Mansion (Leiden: Brill, 1990). On the still-unedited *translatio nova*, see J. Brams, "La Recensio Matritensis de la Physique," in *Guillaume de Moerbeke. Recueil d'études à l'occasion du 700e anniversaire de sa mort*, ed. J. Brams and W. Vanhamel (Leuven: Leuven University Press, 1989), 193–220.

7. See S. Donati, "Commenti parigini alla Fisica degli anni 1270–1300 ca.," in *Die Bibliotheca Amploniana im Spannungsfeld von Aristotelismus, Nominalismus und Humanismus*, ed. Andreas Speer (Berlin: De Gruyter, 1995), 136–256; S. Donati, F. Del Punta, C. Trifogli, "Commentaries on Aristotle's Physics in Britain, ca. 1250–1270," in *Aristotle in Britain during the Middle Ages*, ed. John Marenbon (Turnhout: Brepols, 1996), 265–83.

tion the commentaries by Albert the Great (1252), Boethius of Dacia (1271), Siger of Brabant (1270–71), and Gilles of Rome (1274–75). The first chapter of Albert's commentary on *Physics*, composed in Cologne and the first in a long list of commentaries on Aristotle's works, contains the famous phrase announcing his project to, at the request of his Dominican brothers, "render intelligible" the entire "natural science" of Aristotle into Latin.[8] Gilles of Rome will soon after receive the title *Novus Expositor*, compared to Thomas Aquinas who will be known as the *Antiquus Expositor*.[9]

The interest in Aristotle's *Physics*, especially in the second half of the thirteenth century, is directly related to two events. First, in 1255, the University of Paris decided that Aristotle's works on natural philosophy, ethics, and metaphysics would serve as the basic texts for instruction in the Paris arts faculty. Practically speaking this meant a reading of Aristotle alongside Averroes's commentaries.[10] Moreover, second, it is well known that a "radical" or "Averroistic" reading of Aristotle, in particular of topics touched upon in the *Physics* such as the eternity of the world, determinism, etc., resulted in a series of condemnations by ecclesial authorities in the final decades of the thirteenth century.[11]

The *Expositio* and Its Time of Composition

Thomas wrote a most detailed commentary, belying the words of Étienne Gilson and Josef Pieper that he would not have had a connatural sympathy for this subject matter.[12] For us, the important question is whether Thomas is in substantial agreement with Aristotle's philosophy of nature, accepts theories that seem outdated and false, and invites us to consider his commentary as containing his own philosophy of nature.[13]

8. "Intentio nostra in scientia naturali est satisfacere pro nostra possibilitate fratribus ordinis nostri nos rogantibus ex pluribus iam praecedentibus annis, ut talem librum de physicis eis componeremus. . . . nostra intentio est omnes dictas partes facere Latinis intelligibiles." *Physica* I, tr. 1, ch. 1, ed. Paul Hossfeld (Münster: Aschendorff, 1987), 1.

9. A more detailed and complete investigation into Thomas's sources and relation to the commentaries of his contemporaries will have to wait until the new Leonine edition of the text is published, which will hopefully show the same excellence as Gauthier's editions of the commentaries on the *De anima* and *Ethica*.

10. See C. Lohr, "The New Aristotle and 'Science' in the Paris Arts Faculty (1255)," in *L'enseignement des disciplines à la Faculté des arts (Paris et Oxford, XIIIe–XVe siècles)*, ed. Olga Wijers and Louis Holtz (Turnhout: Brepols, 1997), 251–70.

11. As noted above, see the introduction to *Nach der Verurteilung von 1277* (ed. Aertsen et al.) for a helpful *status quaestionis* on this topic.

12. Josef Pieper, *Hinführung zu Thomas von Aquin* (Münich: Kösel-Verlag, 1963), 36. Pieper refers to Gilson's *Le Thomisme*. Thomas's real interest in the study of the physical nature of things is also evident in his commentaries on the *De generatione et corruptione* and *Meteorologica*. Hence Thierry-Dominique Humbrecht concludes: "Thomas s'intéresse à la Physique plus que Gilson ne l'a dit, au moins au vu de ses œuvres, puisqu'il s'attache à étudier les derniers retranchements." In his "Thomas d'Aquin s'intéresse-t-il à la physique?," in *Lire Aristote au Moyen Âge et à la Renaissance*, ed. Joëlle Ducos and Violaine Giacomotto-Charra (Paris: Honoré Champion, 2011), 94.

13. James Weisheipl, *Friar Thomas D'Aquino: His Life and Work*, 2nd ed. (Washington, D.C.: The Catholic

The commentary is a voluminous work and differs from the commentaries on the *De caelo*, *De generatione et corruptione*, and *Meteorologica* in that it covers the entire text, practically line for line. Thomas seems to have composed it in Paris, during his second stay in the city. Gauthier suggests 1268–70 as the date of composition.[14] He points to a quotation in *Physics* VI, lesson 5, from the *De sensu et sensato* in the translation of the *Nova*, which had been completed shortly before that date. William of Moerbeke's revision, the *translatio nova*, of James of Venice's translation formed the basis of Thomas's *Expositio*.[15] During the redaction of his commentary, Thomas did not have a Latin translation of the commentaries by Simplicius and Philoponus, but relied for his information on Averroes.[16] Alexander of Aphrodisias is mentioned four times, as well as Themistius, but these references are also borrowed from Averroes.

The Structure of the *Physics*

How did Thomas see the division of the *Physics* and the relationship between its individual books? The beginning of Book I, he says, presents a general introduction to the division of the sciences and the place of the philosophy of nature (called *scientia naturalis*) among them.[17] The remaining part of Book I is devoted to the analysis of what he calls the principles of movable things, and Book II to the study of the principles of this science. The study of the concept of nature as the source of moveable things and the study of the causes are meant. Thus Thomas sees a strict relationship between Books I and II. At the beginning of Book III, he presents an overview of the contents of Books III–VII, which deal with the subject matter of natural science (*de naturalibus*). It is divided into two parts: Books III and IV study movement itself and what is consequent on it; Books V and VI study the parts of movement; and VII examines movements in relation to movers and bodies moved.

Surprisingly, Book VIII is not mentioned in this overview. Some assume

---

University of America Press, 1983), and Benedict Ashley, *The Way Toward Wisdom* (Notre Dame, Ind.: University of Notre Dame Press, 2006), 152ff., concur in stating that the answer is overwhelmingly positive with regard to the core elements of the *Physics*, which are far from being so outdated as some want to make us believe.

14. Introduction to the Leonine edition, vol. 45/1, *Sentencia libri De anima*, 270*. Gauthier refers to a study by Auguste Mansion on the date of the commentary, published in *Revue néoscolastique de philosophie* (1934): 304–5.

15. Verbeke, "Saint Thomas et les commentaires grecs sur la *Physique* d'Aristote," 141. See also Gauthier in the introduction to *Sentencia libri De anima*, 205*. See *In VII Phys.*, lesson 3, no. 905, where Thomas, while using the *Nova*, refers to an *alia littera*.

16. In my study of the commentary, the frequent references by Thomas to Averroes will be mentioned.

17. Thomas did not add a proem as he does in most of his commentaries. The first chapter of the text functions as such. See his *In I Phys.*, lesson 1, no. 5: "Huic autem libro praemittit Philosophus premium"; no. 12: "Posito proemio."

that Thomas sees it as the continuation of VII. But this is not quite correct, for in lesson 2, no. 972, he sets Book VIII a part[18] and writes that Aristotle, after having studied movement in general in the previous books, begins to apply, in Book VIII, the conclusions he reached to things (*res*), probably meaning that the study of the first and basic cosmic movements leads us to the first mover and so Thomas would no longer consider the last book as part of natural science in the strict sense of the term. In lesson 23, no. 1172, we read "Et sic terminat Philosophus considerationem communem de rebus naturalibus in primo principio totius naturae, qui est super omnia Deus benedictus in saecula. Amen." My interpretation, namely that Thomas wanted to separate Book VIII somewhat from the other books, is confirmed by a text in II.7 (lesson 11, no. 243): "Whichever beings which move (other things) so that they are moved (themselves), are part of the subject matter studied in the philosophy of nature; but those which move, without being moved themselves, do not belong to the subject matter of the philosophy of nature" (see also no. 245).[19]

An Analysis of Aristotle's Arguments

Thomas pays careful attention to the arguments used by Aristotle. If one wants to determine to what extent he shares the views of the Stagirite, it is imperative to check what he has to say about the proofs advanced by the Philosopher. But the commentary contains also more general remarks on Aristotle's ways of arguing. Thomas first states that when dealing with opponents who deny the principles, no direct refutation is possible, but that in this case one must proceed from what the opponent supposes.[20] Somewhat later he writes that the correct form of arguing against Melissus would be to proceed from the destruction of the conclusion (*destructio consequentis*) to that of the antecedent.[21] Concerning the way in which Aristotle refutes the opinions about the first principles of some of his predecessors, Thomas notes that one cannot put forward a strict demonstration against them, *ex magis notis simpliciter* ("from the things which are simply better known"), but only a refutation of what is presupposed by the opponent.[22] In his discussion of the theories of first principles of the Pre-Socratics in Book I, Aristotle proceeds *disputatively*, Thomas says, using probable arguments. However, these

---

18. *In VIII Phys.*, lesson 2, no. 972: "praecedentes libri habent quandam distinctionem ad hunc librum octavum in quo iam incipit motum ad res applicare."

19. "Quaecumque moventia movent, ita quod moveantur, pertinent ad considerationem naturalis philosophiae. Quae vero movent sed non moventur non sunt de consideratione naturalis philosophiae."

20. *In I Phys.*, lesson 3, no. 24.

21. Bk. I, lesson 5, no. 32.

22. Bk. I, lesson 3, no. 24.

arguments are not decisive and are not sufficient to explain generation: Aristotle first shows that the principles are contrary, and next that contrary principles alone are not enough to explain generation. From two partial arguments he concludes the truth.[23] Up to I.6, Aristotle proceeds *disputatively,* according to Aquinas, but in I.7 he begins to determine the truth.[24]

A similar observation is made regarding a passage from Book IV in which Aristotle determines what place is: he first investigates disputatiously whether place is real, and then he considers what place is.[25] Passing to the study of the infinite, he first mentions some different opinions on its nature but he proceeds by showing that there is no infinite body.[26] Aquinas repeats his warning about the nature of some of Aristotle's arguments: it becomes clear that in the earlier texts, Aristotle argued with the Pre-Socratics and Plato at the level of a dispute, and so his arguments were partially true, but not entirely.[27] This might be a polite way of saying that he himself does not subscribe fully to this discussion, but considers the section that now follows—on matter, form, and privation—to be a truly philosophical exposition. In the last chapter of Book I, Aristotle compares matter (first matter, to be precise) to a mother. Matter is a cause of becoming and, like a mother, it desires form. Avicenna objected against this way of explaining the causality of matter: matter does not have such a nature as to make it tend to something. Thomas provides an elegant defense of the comparison: it is just an extrinsic example, not an analogy.[28] We must use examples taken from sensible substances to explain the inner structure of things: the natural appetite of things is nothing else but their being ordered to their end according to their nature. That matter desires a form means that it is ordered to the form, as potency to act.

A distinction similar to that between disputative arguing and philosophical proofs is the one we make between proper reasons and common or logical arguments. The latter start from what is common to things in general, while the former argue from what is proper to particular things. An example of a logical argument is to declare it fitting that a circular movement is perpetual.[29] What is somewhat surprising in the commentary on Book I is that, according to Thomas, it is up to metaphysics to demonstrate that in all natural processes of becoming there must always be some subject, something which in the phi-

23. Bk. I, lesson 11, nos. 88 and 93: "ex utrisque rationibus unam veritatem concludit."

24. Bk. I, lesson 12, no. 98.

25. Bk. IV, lesson 3, no. 422.

26. Bk. III, lesson 10, no. 370.

27. Bk. I, lesson 13, no. 114: "Sic igitur patet quod priores sermones disputati ad utramque partem fuerunt secundum aliquid veri, sed non totaliter."

28. Bk. I, lesson 15, no. 138: "Nec etiam utitur hic figurata locutione sed exemplari."

29. Bk. VIII, lesson 18, no. 1123.

losophy of nature becomes clear by induction,[30] for in all modes of becoming, things always become out of a subject.[31]

Thomas is open to the fact that certain arguments in the text have little value and that Aristotle may say again or state with better arguments what he had discussed before without reaching certitude. An example is the statement that in a series of movers one cannot go on indefinitely, affirmed in VII.1 (lesson 2). Thomas says that a better proof is found in VIII.5 (lesson 9). In Book IV, Aristotle argues that if the void were real, one could not explain the greater or lesser speed at which the different celestial bodies move. Thomas thinks that this argument leads to an inconvenient conclusion. Thomas notes, however, that in the *Physics*, Aristotle does not consider bodies in their proper nature, but according to what is common to them.[32] Aquinas rejects the argument that the medium through which bodies move is decisive for their speed.[33]

On several occasions, Aquinas draws attention to Aristotle's custom to mention and analyze the assumptions of others or common opinions before stating his own view.[34] To show that according to common opinion whatever exists is in a place, Aristotle uses a sophistic argument.[35] With regard to an explanation of why local movement is the cause of alteration and augmentation, he says that Aristotle is speaking according to what was probable from the viewpoint of the other philosophers who did not fully acknowledge the specificity of alteration.[36] Aristotle may argue provisionally along the lines of what is generally held; for example, that there is a self-moving mover as the source of movement. As far as the argument goes, it does not show that the first mover itself is moved rather than unmoved.[37] Thomas even offers an explanation of why Aristotle resorts to common opinion: man's intellect may sometimes tend to the truth by its natural inclination, although it may not understand the causes involved.[38] To show that there is no infinite, Aristotle first gives two arguments, based on what people commonly say. Thomas qualifies them as only probable.[39] In connection with his study of place, Aristotle uses arguments

---

30. See *In VII Metaph.*, Bk. I, lesson 6, no. 1388.

31. Bk. I, lesson 12, no. 108: "Unde manifestum est quod omne quod fit, fit ex subiecto."

32. Bk. IV, lesson 12, nos. 534 and 538.

33. Bk. IV, lesson 12, no. 539.

34. Bk. III, lesson 8, no. 353: "Semper antequam probet id quod est suae opinionis, procedit ex suppositione opinionis aliorum communis."

35. Bk. IV, lesson 1, no. 407.

36. Bk. VIII, lesson 14, no. 1089.

37. Bk. VIII, lesson 9, no. 1040. Thomas even refers to a Platonic principle to explain this theory of a self-moving first mover: "Semper enim causa quae est per se est prior ea quae est per alterum" (ibid., no. 1049).

38. Bk. I, lesson 10, no. 79: "Ita interdum intellectus hominis quadam naturali inclinatione tendit in veritatem, licet rationem veritatis non percipiat."

39. Bk. III, lesson 8, no. 352.

based on what people commonly hold, namely, that there are four elements, and does not take into account his doctrine of the fifth element, which is mentioned in the *De caelo*.[40] In his study of time, Aristotle proceeds by debating first with his predecessors, to determine next the truth in IV.11.

Thomas is fully alert to apparent (or real) contradictions in the text. When Aristotle refutes Anaxagoras's theory of the infinite divisibility of bodies in I.4, Thomas observes that this contradicts the division of the continuous *ad infinitum*, but he solves the difficulty by noting that natural bodies are not infinitely divisible.[41] He also singles out a wrong argument in the chapter on place, a *sophisma consequentis*, as it proceeds in the second figure of two affirmative premises.[42] Another defective argument, pointed out by Aquinas, runs as follows: what is not, is nowhere, so what is, is in a place.[43] Contrary to what the text says, Thomas writes that the medium through which a body passes cannot be the decisive factor for the speed it travels at.[44] In the commentary on Book VI (lessons 4 and 11), where Aristotle is arguing against Zeno, Thomas has some harsh words. One argument is said to be *ad hominem, non ad veritatem*.[45]

In his comments on Book VIII (lesson 6, no. 926), Thomas says that the argument as to how science is acquired is Platonic rather than being in line with Aristotle's own doctrine of abstraction, as exposed in *De anima* III. It is Aristotle's custom, Thomas notes, to use first the arguments of others. This may mean that in Aquinas's view we have to do with a historical survey, but the modem reader will resort to the hypothesis of a doctrinal development. The argument by which Aristotle in Book VIII shows the perpetuity of the first movement is not conclusive: God may cease moving the world.[46] In this connection, Aquinas points out another flaw: earlier Aristotle had demonstrated the immobility of the first mover from the perpetuity of movement in the world. Here he deduces the perpetuity of movement from the immobility of the first mover. One can solve the difficulty, Thomas says, if we assume that Aristotle first spoke of movement in the world as a whole and later of the movement of the first.[47] The *Expositio* also gives a fine analysis of the difficult argumentation of Book VIII, distinguishing the following steps: there is always movement; all movements originate from some mover; in a series of movers one cannot proceed *ad infinitum*, so that there must be some first

40. Bk. III, lesson 8, no. 353.
41. Bk. I, lesson 9, no. 66.
42. Bk. IV, lesson 3, no. 424.
43. Bk. IV, lesson 1, no. 407.
44. Bk. IV, lesson 12, no. 539.
45. Bk. VI, lesson 4, nos. 779 and 863: "quae quidem solutio est magis ad interrogantem."
46. Bk. VIII, lesson 13, no. 1084.
47. Bk. VIII, lesson 13, no. 1083.

mover, either one or many; the first mover is unmoved, even if one of its parts would move another part; however, a being which moves itself is not divided in two;[48] movement in the cosmos being eternal, the first mover must be eternal; there is one such mover rather than many.[49] At this point, Thomas reminds the reader that Plato posited several souls as movers, while Aristotle holds that only the intellect is incorruptible and unmoved, the other parts of material things are moveable.

The analysis is continued in lesson 21: the first mover is indivisible and incorporeal; an infinite movement requires an infinite moving power; an infinite power cannot exist in a finite magnitude; the first mover who causes a continuous and perpetual movement must be one. In lesson 22, Aristotle demonstrates the unity of the first mover: if there are more movers, the movement (of the first heaven) would have no unity and continuity; there must always be movement; a continuous movement is one.[50] An unmoved mover is able to move always, and will never become worn out; no mover that itself is moved can cause continuous movement; it is impossible that a mover of finite power moves something during an infinite time. And so, Thomas concludes, Aristotle finishes his general considerations about physical things arriving at the first cause of the entire nature.

Repeatedly, Aquinas uses the expressions *secundum intentionem Aristotelis, contra intentionem Aristotelis,* or *repugnat veritati et intentioni Aristotelis.* We can best understand these expressions as a reference to the overall philosophical thought of Aristotle, or at least to its principles, which allow Thomas to advance an interpretation that goes further than the text he is commenting on. He may even advance a different interpretation under the cover of *secundum intentionem Aristotelis.* An example of this regards a sentence from Book VIII (lesson 21, no. 1153), where Aquinas goes beyond the incorruptibility of the celestial bodies, claimed by Aristotle, shifting the argument to *substantiae simplices* in order to argue against Averroes that according to the *intention* of Aristotle there is no potency for not-being in the simple substances, a statement that goes beyond what Aristotle says in the text. This applies also to a passage in Book VIII (lesson 2, no. 974): the fact that a particular agent needs matter to work with does not mean that according to the intention of Aristotle the first universal cause would also presuppose something. To demonstrate his position Thomas refers, as he does repeatedly, to *Metaphysics* II.1.993b26,

---

48. Bk. VIII, lesson 10, no. 1060; lesson 11, no. 1068.
49. Bk. VIII, lesson 12, no. 1069.
50. Bk. VIII, lesson 12; Bk. V, lesson 7.

where we read that what is the most true and the most being is the cause of the being of all things.[51]

Sometimes the expression ("according to the intention of Aristotle") is used to discard the commentary of Averroes. An example: according to Averroes the qualities finite/infinite do not apply to power, but this is against the intention of Aristotle and against truth, says Thomas, thinking here of infinite divine power.[52] While Aristotle's proofs of the first mover are totally tied to his cosmology of the spheres, Aquinas attempts to disengage them from their less valid assumptions and so to present a coherent, well-argued philosophy of nature, as being in some way that of Aristotle.[53]

We sometimes notice in Thomas's text a certain reservation with regard to some particular theories of Aristotle or to the validity of the arguments used. In such cases, as well as when he comments on Aristotle's account of the theories of other philosophers, Aquinas may use the name "Aristotle," while he speaks of "the Philosopher" when espousing what he considers secure and definite philosophical doctrine. I would like to point out that in Book VIII, with its theory of the perpetual revolution of the first heaven, the name "Aristotle" comes up some sixty-five times, over against eighty-nine times in the seven other books together, while Aristotle passes as "the Philosopher" only some twenty times in Book VIII. I understand this to be an indication that Aquinas does not consider all the theories displayed by Aristotle in the last book of the *Physics* as definitely established doctrines. But typical of his way of commenting is that he tries to establish everywhere the coherence of the arguments and the subjects discussed, smoothing over irregularities that modern students of Aristotle would be inclined to attribute to different times of composition and to an adherence to Plato's thought.

Induction and Supposition

An important source of Aristotle's arguments is what Thomas calls induction. In the *Expositio*, the expression usually has the meaning of an inference one makes on the basis of observation. For instance, that natural things move, either all or part of them, is evident by induction.[54] The principle that nature is ordered becomes evident from what we see: nature pro-

---

51. Bk. VIII, lesson 2, no. 974.

52. Bk. VIII, lesson 21, no. 1149; see no. 1153: "contra intentionem Aristotelis et contra veritatem."

53. One must keep in mind that the term *intentio* as used in the *Expositio* may also mean simply what Aristotle intends to say, or also one's application to a task or to a particular subject.

54. Bk. I, lesson 2, no. 18: "Quod naturalia moventur vel omnia vel quaedam manifestum est ex inductione."

ceeds in an orderly way in its activities and goes from one task to the next.[55] It is also by induction that we know that there must be a subject in all natural processes of becoming.[56] In Book IV (lesson 4, no. 440), Aristotle argues that something cannot be primarily and *per se* in itself. One can verify this by considering all instances (i.e., by induction) and by argument. Also in Book V (lesson 8, no. 723), contrariety in movements is studied both by induction and by (logical or syllogistic) argument. Book VIII (lesson 3, no. 994), has a proof resulting from an induction, namely, by examining individual cases in order to determine whether there is always movement, while another proof consists in a reasoned exposition.

In his comments on Book VII, lesson 2, Thomas writes that Aristotle is considering local movement and *supposes* that the mover and the moved are contiguous or continuous, but that his argument is weak. It is a simple supposition. All through the commentary the verb *supponere* occurs more than a hundred times. Its meaning is "to assume," "to suppose," yet this original meaning develops in various directions. The verb is used to signify what must be accepted as fundamental, for instance, the principle of contradiction.[57] One must suppose in natural science that natural things are moved, either all or certain of them.[58] A further fundamental presupposition of the sciences is that contradictory qualifications cannot be predicated of the same thing.[59] The verb "to suppose," however, often denotes a not-proven or even a false starting point. Parmenides and Melissus "suppose" that being is unmovable.[60] Parmenides "assumes" that the only meaning of being is being one.[61] Anaxagoras "supposes" that contraries come into being out of each other, which is partly true insofar as what is cold is potentially hot.[62] The verb can also be used in mathematics: let us assume, for instance, that we inscribe lines inside a circle. Thomas draws attention to the fact that, quite frequently, in a later section of the *Physics*, Aristotle demonstrates what he had supposed earlier, for example that nature acts in view of an end.[63] Thomas observes that frequently a starting point is probable or true but is not demonstrated in a particular passage, but only later on; for example: "let us assume that the forms of artifacts are accidents" or "let us suppose that the philosophy of nature studies

<hr>

55. Bk. VIII, lesson 3, no. 993.
56. Bk. I, lesson 12, no. 107.
57. Bk. I, lesson 6, no. 42.
58. Bk. I, lesson 2, no. 18.
59. Bk. I, lesson 6, no. 42.
60. Bk. I, lesson 2, no. 18.
61. Bk. I, lesson 6, no. 42.
62. Bk. I, lesson 9, no. 61.
63. Bk. II, lesson 12, no. 250. See Bk. III, lesson 3, no. 295.

both form and matter."[64] In such cases, Thomas may use the formula *probat quod supposuerat* ("he proves what he had presupposed").[65] On several occasions Aristotle simply "supposes," meaning that he starts from what he had demonstrated earlier. We find a good example of this in Book IV (lesson 14, no. 553), where Aristotle supposes that there are four principles, something he had shown to be true in I.7.190a8ff.: (1) contraries have the same matter; (2) whatever is in act, becomes out of what is in potency; (3) matter cannot be separated from the contraries, so that it would be without them, although it is distinguished from them by reason; and (4) while matter is now under this contrary, then under another, it is numerically the same matter. With regard to the theory of the eternity of movement, Thomas observes that Aristotle *supposes* that it has been demonstrated, while of course Thomas does not accept this position.[66]

Corrections and Additions

On countless occasions in the course of his *Expositio*, Thomas comments on the arguments and explanations of Aristotle, clarifies and sometimes corrects them. Here are some examples. The first four numbers of the commentary on I.1 are a general introduction of amazing clarity, added by Aquinas. It deals with the division of the sciences as based on the theory of abstraction. Second, it also explains the place of the philosophy of nature among the sciences. We must determine, Thomas writes, the subject matter of the natural sciences and the place of the philosophy of nature among the philosophical disciplines. But in order that something may be the subject matter of a science, it must be intelligible. While the objects of mathematics abstract from sensible matter, physics is concerned with things that depend on matter, but it abstracts from individual matter. Now whatever has matter is moveable and so moveable things are the subject matter of natural science.[67]

In the following part of this first lesson, Thomas explains a number of terms used by Aristotle whose meanings are not immediately clear: by *intelligere* (νοεῖν) is meant the knowledge of definitions, by *scire* (ἐπιστάσθαι), knowledge resulting from demonstration. When Aristotle says that we must come to know the principles, the causes, and the elements, Thomas provides a systematic explanation covering the different genera of causality: the term *principles* seems to signify the causes of movement; the word *causes* would

---

64. Bk. II, lesson 2, no. 141; lesson 4, no. 167.

65. Bk. V, lesson 9, no. 735; Bk. VII, lesson 2, no. 892.

66. Bk. VII, lesson 2, no. 386: "manifestum est quod supponit hoc tanquam probatum."

67. Bk. I, lesson 1, nos. 1–4.

signify formal and final causes upon which things depend most for becoming and being; the term *elements* denotes material causes (matter is known last).[68] In no. 6, the tenet that our knowledge begins with what is better known to us and then proceeds to what is more knowable in itself is a reminder of Plato's philosophy, added by Aquinas. What is better known to us is indistinct, as are the universals. In this connection, they are the things that have potentiality in themselves. Thomas adds that one may consider that which is better known to us on two levels, namely, the level of the senses, where the sensible individual things are better known, and the level of the intellect, where the wider universal concepts are known first. From there we must pass to a more detailed knowledge and come to know the species of the genera.[69] Thomas avoids the word *singularia* in his text and speaks instead of species, to maintain the inner coherence of the account: we are dealing with scientific knowledge, which does not in the first place consider individuals. The upshot of the first chapter and the first lesson is that the science of physical nature must examine the principles and causes of things. After this lengthy introduction, it is now time to turn to the study of Thomas's *Expositio* itself.[70]

The Commentary of Thomas Aquinas

Book I

In lesson 1 (I.1.184a9–b14), Thomas begins his *exposition* by defining as the subject matter of natural philosophy those things in whose definition sensible matter is present, things that depend on matter both for their definition and for being. Whatever has matter is subject to movement.[71] With great

---

68. Bk. I, lesson 1, no. 5.

69. Bk. I, lesson 1, no. 7. Thomas understands ἐκ τῶν καθόλου ἐπὶ τὰ καθ'ἕκαστα δεῖ προιέναι as referring to the fact that we proceed from the study of the genus to that of its species.

70. For a good English translation of Thomas's commentary, see *Commentary on Aristotle's "Physics,"* rev. ed., trans. Richard J. Blackwell, Richard J. Spath, and W. Edmund Thirlkel (Notre Dame, Ind.: Dumb Ox Books, 1999).

71. In explicitly saying that the subject matter is *ens mobile* and not *corpus mobile*, Thomas refutes the position of Albert. The latter's position creates the difficulty of integrating *De Anima* because the soul is not the species of a body. See Book I, lesson 1, no. 4: "Hic autem est liber physicorum, qui etiam dicitur de physico sive naturali auditu, quia per modum doctrinae ad audientes traditus fuit: cuius subiectum est ens mobile simpliciter. Non dico autem corpus mobile, quia omne mobile esse corpus probatur in isto libro; nulla autem scientia probat suum subiectum: et ideo statim in principio libri de caelo, qui sequitur ad istum, incipitur a notificatione corporis. Sequuntur autem ad hunc librum alii libri scientiae naturalis, in quibus tractatur de speciebus mobilium: puta in libro de caelo de mobili secundum motum localem, qui est prima species motus; in libro autem de generatione, de motu ad formam et primis mobilibus, scilicet elementis, quantum ad transmutationes eorum in communi; quantum vero ad speciales eorum transmutationes, in libro Meteororum; de mobilibus vero mixtis inanimatis, in libro de mineralibus; de animatis vero, in libro de anima et consequentibus ad ipsum." For Albert's text, see *Physica* I, tr. 1, c. 1 (ed. P. Hossfeld), 1.

precision, Thomas explains such terms as principle, cause, and element. It is a natural way to proceed from what is better known to us to what is better known in itself, that is, to what is more in being, more in act, and thus more knowable.[72] The Commentator (Averroes) thinks that Aristotle in this passage is speaking of the way demonstrations are formulated in physics, that is, going from the effects to what comes naturally earlier and is more simple, and from the universal to the less universal.

In lesson 2 (I.2.184b15–185a20), Thomas says that we must now study the universal principles of things subject to motion—the study of mobile being.[73] All Pre-Socratic philosophers dealt with the material principles of natural things, with the exception of Parmenides and Melissus (nos. 14–15). Their views must not be examined in physics, but in another science. The theory of Parmenides does away with the notion of principle, as it excludes all motion (no. 16). What Parmenides and Melissus assume, namely that being is immobile, is against what is presupposed in natural science, so that the refutation of their theory is not a subject treated in natural science.

In lesson 3 (I.3.185a20–b24), Aristotle criticizes the theory of the Eleatic School by introducing the distinction between substance and accidents. What is composed of substance and accidents is not strictly one (nos. 21–22). Moreover, what is indivisible cannot have magnitude, while Melissus, on the contrary, attributes infinity to the One; but in order to have infinity there must be quantity, and substance with quantity is no longer one. In a second argument, Aristotle says that the word "one" is used in several senses: as *continuous* and as a *point*. But the continuous is divisible in many parts; if it is *indivisible,* it does not have parts and cannot be infinite; if "one by definition" is meant, "good" will be "bad," as Heraclitus said. In short, Thomas points out the absurdity of the theory (no. 24): being and nonbeing would be the same. At the end of the lesson, Thomas observes that this is a type of demonstration that proceeds from what the adversary accepts.

In lesson 4 (I.2.185b25–186a3), we read that some of the ancients tried to solve the difficulties that result from the theory of oneness by way of a linguistic device, for instance, by not using the copula "is," to avoid implying that things are many. Thomas notes that the previous arguments show that it is impossible that all things are one (nos. 25–28). Lesson 5 (I.3.186a4–a22) is a refutation of Melissus, whose argument is a *fallacia consequentis*: what is made has a beginning, therefore what is not made has no beginning, and no end, so that it is infinite and hence immobile. This conclusion, however, does not follow.

---

72. See also my introduction (above) on the place of Book I in the whole of Aristotle's treatise on nature.

73. Thomas singles out Book II, in which the *principles* of the doctrine of natural sciences are examined.

Likewise, it is wrong to say that what has no beginning is infinite (nos. 29–35).

In lesson 6 (I.3.186a22–187b35), Thomas comments on the final part of chapter 3, except for the last ten lines. He gives a very clear survey of the terse arguments of Aristotle against Parmenides, who did not understand that the concept of being is analogous and can signify both substance and accidents. His assertion that being is one is only true when applied to substance (no. 42). If one assumes that there is only one being, this being cannot have quantitative parts (no. 45). Averroes understood the text as formulating a second argument against Parmenides: when the One of which he claims the existence is conceived as a body, one could split it into two halves, and being can be predicated of each half, and one could continue dividing it. But Thomas says that this explanation is *extorta*, it has been dragged in and is against what Aristotle is saying (no. 46).

In lesson 7 (I.3.187a1–a11), the argument is refuted that being, which is one, excludes all other things and all plurality. Plato accepted part of the arguments of Parmenides. For instance, he admitted that accidents are nonbeings (i.e., they are not substances). Thomas writes that for Plato, what is outside the substance, the accidental, is nonbeing, but Plato would not say that it is nothing (no. 49). Being itself is just a particular substance.

In lesson 8 (I.4.187a12–a26), the opinion of the natural philosophers on the principles is examined. Some of them accepted only one material principle (e.g., air, water, or fire) from which all other things were generated, while others argued that things and contraries proceed from one initial reality, namely, Empedocles and Anaxagoras who, however, differed on the way this happens (nos. 53–57).

The theory of Anaxagoras is discussed in lesson 9 (I.4.187a26–188a18): nothing comes into being from nonbeing (no. 59), and so contraries must proceed from each other. Aristotle would say that this is right but not in the sense that from a contrary in act, like what is cold, comes forth warmth, but from the contrary insofar as it is in potency to the opposite contrary (no. 61). Anaxagoras developed his famous theory of the infinitesimally small particles to explain change: bread, as our food, contains already the particles of our flesh (no. 62). Aristotle advances five arguments against this theory (no. 64ff.): if particles are infinite in kind and in number they cannot be known; if they are infinitesimally small, the being consisting of them, as for instance an animal, would not have a certain size, for how can there be infinite particles in a body of limited size; if the particles, say, of flesh are too small, they are no longer flesh; we would have an infinite number of particles of all the different things in one body (nos. 65–73).

Lesson 10 (I.5.188a19–189a11) deals with the contrariety of principles according to the ancient philosophers. In this and the following chapter, Aristotle examines the theories of the ancient philosophers on the principles of nature. In chapters 5 and 6 he does so disputatively, Thomas says, using probable arguments, and subsequently he determines the truth by demonstration. The expression *disputative procedit* returns several times in Thomas's writings.[74] It means that Aristotle gives a critical survey of different opinions concerning a certain theme, which prepares the determination of the truth about the question. Although in this chapter Aristotle lays down his own view, he first mentions other probable views. The first point to be discussed is whether the first principles are contrary, as the ancient philosophers thought they were. Even Parmenides placed hot and cold among the principles perceived by the senses, while others spoke of the rare and the dense, and Democritus of the solid and the porous (no. 76). Thomas notes that in this chapter Aristotle does not mention Anaxagoras and Empedocles, whose views were referred to earlier, although they also teach a certain contrariety, namely, that of concentrating and separating. Aristotle mentions three properties of the first contraries: they are not derived from others; they are not derived from each other; and all other contraries proceed from them (no. 77).

A next point is that action and passion do not happen at random: "white" does not come from "musician," but a musician from a nonmusician. All things that become, come forth from their contraries (no. 78). Some philosophers spoke of contrarieties as they appeared to the senses: warm and cold, moist and dry, and the like. Others took contraries as they appeared to reason: even and odd, concord and discord; but Aristotle sees a certain agreement between the different opinions, insofar as the contrary principles accepted by them have the same function—that one is in act, the other passive, one is better, the other worse (nos. 79–81). All these philosophers assume that the principles are better known either to the senses or to the intellect. At the end of the lesson, Thomas says that the conclusion of this long survey is that the theory that was uppermost in Aristotle's mind is confirmed: the principles are contraries (no. 81).

In lesson 11 (I.6.189a11–b29), the *number* of principles is examined. There is not just one principle, nor are they infinite in number. Aristotle presents four arguments to show that the principles are not infinite in number. Next, according to Thomas, Aristotle proceeds disputatively (no. 88): he assumes as true what is the opinion of many of these authors. Thomas insists that

---

74. See *SCG* I.6; *In Phys.* I, lesson 11; III, lesson 10; IV, lessons 1, 3, 4. The expression is also found in the commentaries on the *Metaphysics, Posterior Analytics,* and *Sententia De anima.*

Aristotle accepts three principles, not just two (no. 89). The third principle is conceived of as underlying the contraries, but has nothing of them. So some philosophers suggested that air is this subject, as the contrary qualities in it are less pronounced (no. 93). But Thomas writes that it is not clear which position is true, whether there is no contrariety in substances, or that in substance there is one first contrariety (no. 96): the exposition *habet multam dubitationem* ("raises many questions") (no. 97).

In lesson 12 (I.7.189b30–190b17), Aristotle begins to determine the truth about change in nature. In all things that become there must always be a subject of which we say that it is becoming (no. 104). In this subject there is something that remains and something that does not. Here again, Aristotle insists on our way of speaking as an indication of how to discover reality: in every activity, when something is made, there must be a subject (no. 106). This is evident by induction from what we observe in activities that concern accidents, but a subject is required in substantial changes too (nos. 107–8).

In lesson 13 (I.7.190b17–191a22), we learn that whatever becomes, becomes out of a subject and a form, but Aristotle adds that privation is also a principle *per accidens* (nos. 111–18). In lesson 14 (I.8.191a23–191b34), he refutes some errors resulting from the ignorance of the above three principles. In the monism of Parmenides nothing comes forth from being and nonbeing. The solution of the difficulty he wanted to explain lies in the distinction of the *per se* and the *per accidens* and in the concept of matter as nonbeing (nos. 121–28).

In lesson 15 (I.9.191b35–192b4), Aristotle explains why and how matter differs from a privation. A privation is nonbeing *per se,* whereas matter as such is potency to being, and is a nonbeing *per accidens.* Matter is ordained to form, and when it has one form it is in potency to other forms. In a sense Plato also accepted a material principle, but Aristotle clarifies how we must understand this principle. Next, Aristotle refutes errors about the concept of privation. Some philosophers failed to distinguish between matter and privation and attributed to matter what is proper to a privation, considering matter as nonbeing. Thomas presents Aristotle's doctrine of primary matter as follows: when a new being comes into existence it is always from something preexistent. He draws attention to the fact that the potency of matter to become things differs in each subject: a potency to a different length is not a potency to a color, but within the same genus one can distinguish (by means of reason) in such a potency several potencies, in accordance with the different forms that may become out of it (nos. 130–40). In no. 131, Thomas lists two differences between matter and privation: (1) matter is nonbeing *per accidens,* insofar as it does not, when it is under one form, have another form but is essentially this thing, while privation is essentially nonbeing; (2) matter is close to the being (*prope rem*) and is being in a certain sense, as it is in some way the substance of a thing, entering as it does into its composition.

Potency is found in the different categories and differs accordingly, but is restricted each time to the genus of the category (no. 131). Matter and privation are one in a subject, but differ by what they are or represent (*ratione differunt*). Matter is nonbeing when considered without a form, but a privation is nonbeing by itself. The Platonists deserve praise for their insight that there must be a single nature at the basis of all natural forms, although they held on to the duality of what he called the Great and the Small and ignored privation.

In no. 135, the true concept of matter is put forward. Matter together with form is the cause of the things which become. Privation belongs to the category of evil, being deprived of form. Form is something divine, excellent, and desirable. The reason is, Thomas says, that it is a participation in and a likeness with God's being, which is pure act. Things are in act insofar as they have a form. Form is the best reality (*optimum*) because, as act, it is the perfection of a potency and its good. Because of this it is desirable, for all things desire their perfection. A privation, on the other hand, is opposed to form, of which it is the removal and, therefore belongs to the class of evil.

In no. 136, Thomas explains the meaning of the phrase "matter seeks a form," insofar as it is in potency to a different form, that is, different from the one under which it is now. A privation as such does not seek a form. Answering an objection of Avicenna, Thomas further explains that matter under a certain form is in potency to other forms; in itself, it is not generated and incorruptible. Whatever desires something either knows it or is directed to it by a cause that does know it. A natural appetite is just being ordained to a certain thing in accordance with its own nature. When primary matter is under a certain form, it retains this potency to other forms. Aristotle uses a metaphor while explaining what primary matter is, because he is arguing against Plato who also used metaphorical language (no. 138). Examining the formal principle as such and the question whether it is one or many is the subject of first philosophy, but the forms of physical things are studied in the following books of the *Physics* (no. 140).

Book II

In Book I, Aristotle examined the principles of natural *things*; in lesson 1, he now investigates those of natural *science* (II.1.192b8–193a8), namely, what belongs to the subject of natural science and must be employed in a demonstration, that is, which causes must be examined. Natural things have a principle of motion in themselves, as do the elements, but artifacts only have it insofar as they are made of natural things (no. 142). But the elements seem to undergo motion rather than having an active principle of movement within themselves. Thomas explains that they may be moved by external movers but they have a potency proper to their type of natural motion. Heavy and light bodies have a passive potency to movements downward and upward. Thomas explains that the thesis that *nature is a principle of motion and rest* must be understood in a general way (namely, as that from which something else proceeds), but not as an active force (no. 145). Moreover, not all things have a principle of rest in their nature; for instance, it is not present in the celestial bodies. Thomas ends his comments by criticizing Avicenna who, contrary to Aristotle, thought that nature could be demonstrated to exist (no. 148).

In lesson 2 (II.1.193a9–b21), we read that matter and form are the nature of things, but form more so than matter. However, what is composed out of these two—for example, man—is not nature but something from nature. Form is more nature than matter; it returns and appears in the process of generation, while the forms of artifacts do not (nos. 149–56). In lesson 3 (II.2.193b22–194a15), natural science is considered insofar as it differs from mathematics, which studies lines, surfaces, and points in abstraction from natural bodies, and not insofar as they are the boundaries of them. Things that in reality are joined together, while their conceptual contents are different, can be considered separately from each other. Things that are earlier (*priora*) can be considered without what comes after, for example, animals without man. Quantity can be conceived without matter subject to motion, but not without a substance, for we do not say that the objects of mathematics (points, lines, etc.) can exist without a body. The Platonists posited the existence of forms or ideas because they did not see that the intellect is able to abstract from what in reality is not separate (nos. 158–65).

In lesson 4 (II.2.194a12–b15), Aristotle argues that physics considers what is composed of both matter and form: (1) art imitates nature, but in art both are considered, for example, in architecture. Thomas explains why art imitates nature: the starting point of art is reason, and reason draws its knowledge from sensible things. The latter have been ordered to their end by an intelligent principle (nos. 170–71); (2) the same science studies the end and the things ordered to the end. Because form is the end of matter, physics studies both. Form is the cause of matter, as for its sake matter is in movement; and (3) things ordered to something else come in under the same science as the one to which they are ordered. Hence, matter comes in under the study of nature. Does the study of forms not come in under the subject studied in first philosophy? Thomas adds that such forms as the human soul exist in matter, but are nevertheless somehow separate insofar as their faculty of thought is concerned. Nevertheless they are studied in natural science (no. 175). Thomas goes beyond Aristotle, who raises the question of how far the physicist goes in his study of forms: it studies forms separable from matter, but they do not exist apart from matter. It is the task of first philosophy to consider those forms that by their essence are separate from matter.[75]

In lesson 5 (II.3.194b16–195a27), having determined the subject matter of natural philosophy, Aristotle passes to the examination of the question regarding which causes are studied in this science. The study of causes as such belongs to first philosophy. In natural philosophy, causes are studied insofar as they are factors involved in natural changes. In fact, all four genera of causes are involved in these processes, as is shown in this part of chapter 3. The efficient cause is the cause of movement and rest but, as Thomas explains, it also prepares or disposes the subject in which changes occur, and it helps and assists in the process (no. 180). Aristotle shows the reality of the causality of the final cause, which is less patent to the eye, being the last of what is attained in the generation of things (no. 181). More than one genus of causality may intervene in the coming-into-being or making of something, as the material and the efficient cause. Causes may also be causes of each other (no. 182). Thomas explains that propositions can be said to be the matter of the conclusions, insofar as the terms, which are their matter, are also those of the conclusion. Seed, active in generation, is also a cause, as a medical doctor is of health. The end is the most powerful cause, for the agent acts in view of an end (nos. 183–86).

In lesson 6 (I.3.195a27–b30), the different *modes* in which causes exercise their causality are examined. A first mode is that of priority. A prior cause is more universal. A second mode is that of the distinction of the cause *per accidens* and the cause *per se*. Polycletus is the cause *per accidens* of the statue, as he is not part of its essence. A third distinction mentioned by Aristotle is that of being able to operate as a cause and actually operating as a cause. But Thomas speaks in this case of a difference in the effects, which are more immediate or remote, for instance: a special dish is good for our health but, *per accidens*, it is also tasty. In no. 195, Thomas adds an important observation: when a cause is actually operating and producing its effect, both are simultaneous as long

---

75. See Jakob Hans Josef Schneider, "Physik und Natur im Kommentar des Thomas von Aquin zur aristotelischen Ethik," in *Mensch und Natur im Mittelalter*, ed. Albert Zimmermann and Andreas Speer (Berlin: De Gruyter, 1991), 161–92.

as the effect is becoming. The divine agent who is the cause of the being of things is simultaneous with their existence. We must look for the main and highest cause: this man is building, because he is a builder. The cause must be proportional to the effect: this statue is made by this sculptor (nos. 187–97).

In lesson 7 (I.4.195b31–196b9), we begin the study of fortune and chance, in other words of those cases where it is less clear which type of causality is involved. Are fortune and chance the same, and what are they? Aristotle recalls the lack of clarity in what the ancient philosophers taught about fortune and chance, but what is said to happen by chance has a cause. Even when the ancients felt that chance is not a real cause, they nevertheless spoke sometimes about it (no. 202). According to Democritus, the combination of atoms is by chance. But if plants and animals do not come about by chance, how could the celestial bodies owe their existence to chance? Some call fortune a cause but, because of the fact that the cause of what happens is sometimes not manifest to us, some said it was due to some kind of divine causality. As to this point, Thomas observes that the view that ascribes it to divine causality has some truth. All events are ordained by divine Providence, but we do not call this fortune. Aristotle is not to be blamed for not mentioning it. The theme of divine Providence belongs to first philosophy (no. 206).

In lesson 8 (II.5.196a10–197a8), Aristotle determines what fortune is. In events that happen only in a few cases or exceptionally, we speak of fortune or chance. Avicenna says that in all things that are open to several different ends (i.e., things that are indeterminate; in Latin, *ad utrumlibet*), there is some influence of fortune. But Thomas comments that in those sorts of things there is always something else that determines, for example man's appetite. This explains why Aristotle does not speak of the indeterminate in this chapter (no. 209). In the following section, Thomas says that according to some authors, that which is necessary is not hampered by impediments, whereas the contingent is that which can be impeded; but he also observes that impediments do not refer to what is necessary. Is that necessary which by its nature cannot not be? Is that contingent which can not be? (no. 210). What does Aristotle mean when he says that some things do not happen for an end, but that every agent acts for an end? Aristotle may mean actions carried out because of themselves because they give pleasure or are honorable, or he means actions done without a deliberate purpose such as rubbing one's hands (no. 211). Things that happen by decision or by nature happen in view of an end, and what happens in view of an end happens always or in most cases (nos. 212–13). In the last sections of lesson 8, Aristotle explains how in daily language we speak of fortune or chance. Fortune is a cause *per accidens*, showing up in a small number of those actions that aim at an end, but only then when done by those agents which pursue something (no. 216).

In the previous lesson, Aristotle mentioned some views about fortune, for example the theory that chance would be the cause of what happens in the world. He now discusses, in lesson 9 (197a8–35), the opinion according to which fortune is a cause that is concealed from man, and shows in which sense the view is true that nothing happens by chance. The number of causes *per accidens* is infinite and fortune is a cause *per accidens,* so that when we speak of fortune or chance an infinite number of possible causes may have intervened. But what is *per accidens* does not exist without more, so that fortune as such is not the cause of anything. Thomas relates what Aristotle says without adding further comments (nos. 217–25).

In lesson 10 (II.6–7.197a36–198a21), Aristotle explains the different senses of chance and fortune. Fortune is good luck in things that could have turned out differently for an acting person. The meaning of good fortune is close to that of happiness, especially for those who put their well-being in external goods. We speak of good fortune only for those who act voluntarily, but not for a child or animals, although a human person may treat such beings well (nos. 227–31). We speak of chance in those things that happen to someone because of some outside factor not willed by the person in question (no. 233). "In vain" is said of that which does not attain what it was intended to attain, but we speak of chance when something different from that which was intended is attained (no. 234). Both fortune and chance are reduced to the moving cause. Chance is a cause *per accidens* and is not prior to a cause *per se.* The superior cause of the world cannot be said to be fortune (no. 238). Next, Aristotle shows that there are four causes (no. 240).

In lesson 11 (II.7.198a22–b9), the four genera of causes are discussed in the context of the philosophy of nature. Thomas notes that in natural processes the final cause, the form, and the moving cause work together or are even the same, especially in univocal generation when the form of the engendering cause is the same as the one produced (no. 242). Causes that do not change themselves when they move other things are studied in first philosophy (no. 243). The last lines of the chapter explain that the final cause must also be studied in natural philosophy and, in his commentary, Thomas elucidates a cryptic text (no. 248).

In lesson 12 (II.8.198b10–32), Aristotle states that nature acts in view of an end. Thomas writes that this consideration is helpful in the study of divine Providence. Things that do not know the end nevertheless tend to it, moved by a cause which does know it. Therefore, if nature acts in view of an end, it must be directed by an intelligent being, an observation that is fitting to the orientation of the text of Aristotle (no. 250).

To which species of causality does the necessary in natural processes belong? The importance of the question is evident when one is aware that all processes in nature result necessarily. Even Empedocles and Anaxagoras, who introduced other factors besides necessity, limited the influence of these factors to the formation of the world, but not to particular processes (no. 252). Thomas explains the arguments of those who deny finality in nature, for example, that of rain: according to them, rain is produced by natural causes and sometimes happens to be beneficial. The same way of arguing is used in other fields of natural activity. Certain things just happen to be useful.[76] Thomas rejects this way of arguing: rain has physical, necessary causes and has a general usefulness to keep living beings alive. Moreover, the growth and preservation of things is in most cases also due to rain. The few exceptions where rain is harmful do not devalue the argument (nos. 253–54).

In lesson 13 (II.8.198b34–199a32), Aristotle rejects the denial of finality in nature by means of five arguments: (1) things that happen by nature always happen in the same way, or frequently so, while nothing happening by chance happens always, or in most cases, in the same way; (2) we assume that things are disposed by their nature to act in the way they act. Now, things that happen by nature happen in such a way as to reach their end. This is what is meant when we say that natural things tend to an end; (3) with regard to things that can be made by nature and art, art imitates nature, for example returning a sick person to health; (4) that nature acts for an end is very visible in the behavior of such animals as ants, spiders, and bees; but also in the case of plants we see that certain activities serve a purpose, such as the way they grow, shed their leaves in fall, etc.; and (5) in natural beings many activities are done for the sake of the form; the form is the end of generation (nos. 256–60).

In lesson 14 (II.8.199a33–b33), Aristotle shows that nature acts for an end by refuting the arguments to the contrary: (1) sometimes monsters result in the process of natural generation, but that shows that ordinarily nature works for an end like art does; (2) where there is a determinate order in which nature proceeds, there is an end for the sake of which things happen in this particular way, as we see in the generation of animals; (3) even in plants we see this order toward an end, although it is sometimes less clearly visible; and (4) seeds of a particular species produce effects that correspond to them. Some critics object that nature does not deliberate about what it produces, so that it cannot

---

76. A similar view is that of Darwin who also thought that of the different forms of living beings produced by chance, those that happen to be best adapted to their environment will survive.

be said to work in view of an end. Thomas replies that even an artist does not deliberate, as long as he knows his art. Nature is an intrinsic, art an extrinsic principle (no. 267). Nature is nothing else but a certain art placed in things by which they move toward a determinate end, as a shipbuilder joins the different materials so that they constitute a ship (no. 268).

With lesson 15 (II.9.199b34–200b8), we approach the end of Book II. As to the question about necessity in natural processes we must first distinguish between what is absolutely necessary and that which is conditionally necessary. The absolutely necessary is so because of its causes, such as where matter and form determine the species: that man is rational is absolutely necessary; day and night are necessary because of the rotation of the sun, their efficient cause (no. 270). As for the final cause, Thomas refers to the example of a house, the parts of which are so disposed as to serve the end (no. 272). In natural beings as well as in artificial things, there is also what is necessary because of a presupposition. The matter must be such because of the end to be reached. In things that come to be in view of an end, the end has the same function as the premise in a demonstration (no. 273).

Book III

In lesson 1 (III.1.200b13–201a9), after having examined the principles of natural things and also the principles of natural science, Aristotle determines the subject matter of this science, that is, mobile being. At this point Thomas divides the subject matter into two parts: Books III–VI deal with motion as such, whereas Book VII considers movement in its relation to movers and moveable things. More specifically: Books III and IV deal with movement itself, Book V with its species, and Book VI contains the division of motion according to its quantitative parts. To bring out the importance of these investigations, Thomas notes in no. 276 that the one who does not know what motion is, ignores what nature is.

Place, the void, and time are extrinsic to motion, while infinitude is intrinsic to motion. After the usual divisions that explain the text passage dealt with in this lesson, Thomas gives a splendid explanation of a short sentence, in which Aristotle says that motion is not outside the different predicaments (substance, quantity, etc.): one must take into account that motion as an imperfect act is in the same genus as the perfect act is, not as one of its species, but by reduction, as primary matter is in the genus of substance (no. 281). The concept of motion is analogous: there are as many modes of motion as there are of being (no. 282).

In lesson 2 (III.1.201a9–b5), an incorrect definition of movement is rejected, namely that of a not sudden passing from potency to act. Then the correct definition is explained: motion is the act of what exists in potency, insofar as it is still in potency (which is determined further as the motion proceeds). In the remaining part of this lesson, Thomas follows the text of Aristotle very closely, as he does in lesson 3 (that is, the last part of III.1–2.201b5–202a2). We mention here the refutation of the view which places motion in the category of nonbeing, alterity, and inequality. Those who hold this view maintain that it must be this way because motion is something indeterminate and must be placed in the second series of opposites (no. 295).

In lesson 4 (III.2–3.202a3–a21), we read the explanation of why and how the mover is also moved when moving, that is, when moving by contact. The celestial bodies, however, exercise causality by touch (*tangunt*) but do not undergo any influence themselves (*non tanguntur*). The (substantial) form of the movers is the moving factor or principle (*principium movens*) (nos. 298–307).

Lesson 5 (III.3.202a21–b29) is a very detailed explanation of the question as to whether action and passion are the same movement. Thomas answers it by pointing to the doctrine of the predicaments. In a note he observes that the last predicament—*habitus*—is also said of animals other than man (no. 322). When a change in terms of efficient causality is said of the subject in which it takes place, it is called a passion, but if the efficient cause is meant insofar as it produces an effect, this has to do with the predicament of action. In this way, two predicaments are involved in motion (no. 323). In this matter, the point of view of our reason is determining. Thomas comes back to it in no. 324: the concept (or the essence) of motion comprises not only what makes up movement in the physical world, but also that which reason apprehends in it. Motion is conceived as an imperfect act, but our reason first grasps the situation as the medium between the state of potency and that of act, and next as the act of what was in potency. In this lesson, Thomas does not consider the question of how an agent can cause an effect outside itself (no. 325).

In lesson 6 (III.4.202b30–203b15), the question of the infinite is studied. It falls under the subject of natural philosophy, which deals with magnitude, time, and movement (no. 327), but some say that it belongs to first philosophy because of its proximity to the concept of being. In ancient Greek philosophy, an important question was how the opposites could come forth from a single element, for example from water. The atomists asserted that the number of atoms is infinite, as are their shapes. All natural philosophers mention the infinite (no. 328). The Pythagoreans and the Platonists considered the infinite as a being existing by itself, as they taught that numbers and quantities are the substance of things (no. 330). Thomas comments on the Pythagorean theory of numbers, which asserted that by an ordered addition of odd numbers we obtain squares, namely, by adding the odd numbers three, five, seven to one, four, nine. But when we add two to one we get three, the figure of a triangle; adding two to five, the heptagon results, and so on; the form of geometric figures changes by the addition of even numbers. And so, according to the Pythagoreans, uniformity comes with odd numbers, variety and the infinite with even numbers (no. 332).

Plato attributed the infinite to the Great and the Small, which are also called matter. In no. 333, Thomas mentions the theories of some natural philosophers about the infinite. None of them said that the infinite is a subsistent reality; it was considered something of an accidental nature, an accident of some reality, for example that of air or water. Others ascribed it to number. According to Anaxagoras, there is an infinite number of small things, namely, particles. All Pre-Socratics considered the infinite a principle, as it does not have a determinate place among things. It did not begin to exist, for the things that begin to exist also have an end. But Aristotle's text is equivocal, Thomas says; the infinite in the quantitative order does not have a beginning nor an end in this order (no. 335). The Pre-Socratics also attributed to the infinite, as they conceived it, that it contains and governs all things. Those who said so did not accept other causes besides matter. A fourth property several natural philosophers and Anaximander ascribed to the infinite is that it is something divine, as it is immortal and incorruptible (no. 335).

In lesson 7 (III.4–5.203b15–204b4), Aristotle determines the truth about the infinite. He first indicates why those philosophers accepted the infinite: (1) most ancient philosophers—except Plato—assumed that time is eternal; (2) magnitude can be divided indefinitely; (3) generation and corruption seem to be eternal, as most authors believe. If there is no infinite, generation and corruption will not last forever but will cease at a certain moment, yet that is contrary to what most authors think; (4) what is finite is always contained and enclosed in something else; and (5) our reason can always add something to any given finite thing; likewise, we can always imagine something larger than any given magnitude (nos. 337–41). Thomas adds that in this way we can imagine that in the universe infinite space unfolds and that there is an infinite body, but if we conceive space to be infinite, all of reality will be uniform and there would not be empty space anywhere. The body of the world would also be infinite. Thomas explains this section of the text with great clarity. Aristotle writes that the arguments of those who posit the infinite are of dubious value (no. 342). Both regarding the hypothesis that there is no infinite and that which affirms its existence, difficulties arise. We must, therefore, first consider what the infinite is, and whether it is a substance or an accident (no. 343). The infinite is described by some as that which cannot be traversed, or which cannot be traversed by us, or which cannot be passed through to the end, as if one is moving along a line which has no terminus. At the end of the lesson, Aristotle rejects with several arguments the concept of the infinite as something separate from sensible things, as the Platonists accepted it. The question of the infinite in mathematical magnitudes and in intelligible things is not considered here (nos. 345–48).

He then discusses arguments that exclude the existence of the infinite as a separate being of its own and exclude the infinite of sensible things. If we posit the infinite as a substance without accidents, it is not divisible, and hence it cannot be traversed. Those who accept its existence consider it something through which we can move, although it cannot be passed through. But if we consider it as an accident of a subject, for example as a magnitude, then its substance itself will not be infinite. However, this is not what those philosophers thought who assumed the existence of the infinite. The infinite is considered by them a passion of magnitude or number, but these cannot exist by themselves (no. 346). If, on the other hand, the infinite is conceived as an infinite substance, it is either indivisible or it has an infinite number of parts, which in turn will also be infinite. But that is impossible: out of many infinite parts we cannot put together something that is the same. Therefore, a part of the infinite cannot be infinite, and the infinite is indivisible. But what is infinite in act has magnitude, and whatever has magnitude is divisible. Hence the Pythagoreans were wrong in considering the infinite a divisible substance (no. 347).

Lesson 8 (III.5.204b4–205a7) affirms that there is no infinite body among natural things. Aristotle argues that an infinite body has no determinate limits and no surface, so a body cannot be infinite. An infinite number is also impossible, for a number can be counted. Thomas writes (no. 350–52) that these arguments are based on the common way of speaking of people and have no more than a certain probability. Those who say that there exists an infinite body will not admit that it must be delimited by a surface. The notion of number belongs to quantity insofar as it is a measure, but the notion of multitude can be infinite, as it belongs to the transcendentals. In no. 353, Aristotle puts forward philosophical arguments to show that, actually, there is no infinite body. Thomas observes that in the *Physics*, Aristotle has not yet shown, as he will do in *De caelo* I.2, that the nature of the first heaven differs in being from the sublunar elements. Here he proceeds from what was generally accepted.

In the *De caelo* he argues that no sensible body is infinite. In the *Physics* he assumes that the elements are finite in number and shows that no sensible body is infinite, for if one of the elements were infinite, it would totally dominate the other elements. If one of the elements in a *corpus mixtum* would be infinite, it would have infinite dimensions in all directions and so the *corpus mixtum*, that is the body as consisting of several elements, would be impossible (no. 355). Therefore, a composite body cannot be infinite, but neither a simple body nor one of the elements can be infinite: the elements are contrary to each other; if one of them would be infinite, it would corrupt the other elements; and there is no other body besides the four elements, for such a body has never been discovered (no. 356). If one of the elements were infinite, the entire universe would be this one element and all the rest would be converted into it (no. 357).

In lesson 9 (III.5.205a7–206a7), we read that it is entirely impossible that an infinite body could be perceived by the senses, as all sensible things are somewhere and in some place, and an infinite body cannot be in a place (no. 358). None of the ancient philosophers said that earth or fire would be infinite, but rather air or water (no. 362). A further difficulty is that the infinite was said by Anaxagoras to rest in itself, but no good reason was given for this (no. 365). Even an infinite body would have an above and below, but it is impossible that such a body contains above and below in itself (no. 367).

In lesson 10 (III.5–6.206a7–b33), Thomas writes that in the previous lessons, the discussion about the infinite unfolded at the level of a disputation, but that now (lessons 10–13) Aristotle undertakes to determine the truth. If there simply is no infinite, we face some difficulties: (a) time would have a beginning and an end, a supposition which, Thomas says, is simply impossible for those who accept the eternity of the world; (b) magnitude would no longer be entirely divisible. But if according to what has been said, the infinite is no longer a being in act, it simply does not exist as such. Therefore we say that in a way the infinite is, but that in another way it is not (no. 371). Aristotle shows that it is a being in potency (e.g., the infinite divisibility of a magnitude or the infinite addition of numbers) (no. 372), but it is not in such a way in potency that all of it can be reduced to act at once; it can only be realized successively (no. 373).

Aristotle further considers the infinite of time and the infinite in the series of generations, on the one hand, and the infinite by addition or by division of a magnitude, on the other. And he finally shows what these forms of the infinite have in common (no. 374). What is common to all types of the infinite is that the infinite is found in what is always other and other again, in the sense of a certain succession, but in such a way that what we take as the being in act of the infinite, is always finite. We cannot conceive the infinite as something that exists like a man or a house, but as a successive reality (like a day), the being of which is not that of a substance existing in act. In the (endless) series of generations, that which comes about and actually exists is finite. The same happens in the process of the corruption of things. In the course of time new beings come about through generation, and generation never ceases (no. 375). But in magnitudes the situation is different. Quantitative finite beings (such as a point) are permanent, while in the process of generation the finite parts (such as a day or a man) perish. In the following section, we find a description of what happens if we keep adding or subtracting indefinitely. Both processes are possible (no. 376). In the so-called infinite division, the infinite exists only in potency. Plato distinguished between these two infinites. He considered numbers the substance of all things. In the case of numbers, he claims, we do not find the infinite by division, as there is a smallest number, the one. Also, according to him, we do not reach the infinite by addition, as ten is the largest number (no. 381).

In lesson 11 (III.6.206b33–207a32), we read that some of the ancients defined the infinite as that outside which there is nothing, but that they were wrong: this is rather the definition of what is perfect, for we call perfect the being that lacks nothing. No being that has not reached its end is perfect, because the end is the termination of the being of which it is the end. It follows that nothing, which is infinite and unterminated, is perfect. One cannot define the infinite as that which is perfect (no. 385). The infinite is instead comparable to matter, it is in potency—for example, insofar as in the case of numbers one can always keep adding—and a magnitude is in potency to further division. Matter does not contain things; rather, it is contained by the things in which it is present. As it is in potency, it is unknown. It has the nature of a part rather than of the whole, for it is compared to the whole being, as a part of it. It follows that Plato's theory of the Great and the Small, which would contain the *intelligibilia*, is impossible (nos. 386–89).

Lesson 12 (III.7.207a33–208a4) points out that by adding magnitudes one never obtains more than a determinate magnitude. By division one always gets smaller quantities. Because by division one goes from the whole to its parts and so to matter, it is reasonable that we incur a terminus that is not transcended by infinite division. In addition, we are concerned with the whole, which functions as a containing form. It is to be expected that there is a determined quantity that is not further enlarged by infinite adding (no. 391). Thomas explains that in counting numbers there is a limit or terminus beyond which we cannot go into further division, for the number "one" is indivisible, and so the division of numbers comes to end (no. 392). As there is nowhere an infinite continuum we do not accept that by adding to it a thing can grow indefinitely, for that would yield a body larger than heaven (no. 395). In primary matter there is only a potency to a determinate quantity (nos. 396–98). Averroes proposes another explanation: the potency for the addition of magnitude remains within the same magnitude, but the potency for the addition of numbers concerns different numbers insofar as numbers can be added to any number (no. 396). The remark has little weight, Thomas says (*sed haec ratio parum valet*): by adding a number we get another species of numbers but, in a similar way, by adding magnitudes we also get different species of measure, such as two cubits and three cubits. Infinitude is characteristic of the material cause, insofar as we consider matter as being a state of privation. Magnitude as a physical reality cannot be separated from sensible things (nos. 397–99). Lesson 13 (III.8.208a5–23) gives a survey of popular views about the infinite followed by a refutation (nos. 400–405).

Book IV

In this book of the *Physics*, Aristotle deals with place, the void, and time as measures of mobile beings. In lesson 1 (IV.1.208a24–209a1) he examines place, namely, whether it is real or not, how it is, and what it is. All things are somewhere; what is not is nowhere. Aristotle points out that it is proper to things to be in a place. Thomas observes that here Aristotle argues from the position of those philosophers who said that all things are sensible and did not go beyond the representations of their imagination (no. 407). Besides the examination of this position, Aristotle shows that we must study place in natural philosophy because we study motion, and local motion is foremost among movements (nos. 407–8). He first discusses the views of some other authors, as Thomas reaffirms, before determining the truth (in IV.3). Where at first was body A, we now have body B. This shows that place differs from the bodies that are in a place. But place is something, a sort of receptacle, distinct from the bodies that are successively in it. It is the point from where local movements start and toward which they are moving (nos. 410–11). A second argument shows that such elementary bodies as earth and fire move toward their proper place, if not impeded. What is heavy goes downward, what is light upward. From this we may conclude that place has a certain power to conserve the body that belongs to it. But Aristotle does not speak of a power of attraction. For him, natural places figure as final causes (no. 412). Those philosophers who accepted the void also accepted the existence of place, as the void is nothing but place deprived of a body (no. 413). Hesiod said that before all other things, chaos was made as the receptacle of bodies. So place would have an astonishing power, as the first of all things, and could also be without a body (no. 414).

Is place the mass (bulk) of a body or is it of a different nature (lesson 2; IV.1.209a2–30)? It does not seem to have the three dimensions (length, width, depth) characteristic of each body. A next argument points out that place does not extend beyond the body that is in it. Not being a body, place does not consist of one of the four elements. Hence it is not corporeal (nos. 417–18). Whatever exists is in some way the cause of something. But place is wholly foreign to the four genera of causality (no. 419). If it were a body, it would be in a place, and this place would in turn be in another place, and so on (no. 420). Each body is in a place. Therefore, the place of a body is neither larger nor smaller than the body in it. If the body gets larger, its place must also grow (nos. 415–21). Thomas just reproduces the arguments without making special observations.

Lesson 3 (IV.2.209a21–210a13) notes that according to Plato, place would be matter, as it is indeterminate. He called it the receptacle, and matter is the substrate that receives forms. But one can easily see that place is neither matter nor form, because matter and form are in and with the thing that they compose, while place is frequently separated from the body that at a certain moment is in it (nos. 425–28). Things are said to be *in* a place, so that place is neither matter nor form, as things already have matter and form (no. 429). According to Plato, the ideas and the numbers are not in a place, but how is this possible if what is participated is in the participant? (no. 431). Now, according to Plato, the ideas and numbers are participated by matter (or by the Great and the Small). So they are in a place, if matter is. If a thing is corrupted, this affects its form and matter, and if place is matter, it would be corrupted (no. 433).

In lesson 4 (IV.3.210a14–b31), Aristotle determines the truth about place and to this effect he first examines the different ways in which things are in a place, notably (a) as water in a vase, which is the most proper way of being in a place, and (b) as part in a whole. The other ways of being in a place are derived from these two (no. 436). It is impossible that something is in itself, for if so, it would contain and be contained at the same time (nos. 438–42). He then refutes an argument of Zeno who denied the reality of place, because if place exists, it would have to be in something else (no. 443).

In lesson 5 (IV.4.210b32–211a30), four suppositions are made: place contains what is in it, but is not part of it; a place is equal to the body in it, and not larger or smaller; each body has a place, and if it moves away from it, it will have another place. In each place there is an above and a below (no. 446).

The proper place of natural bodies is upward and below, but Aristotle does not speak of the heavenly bodies, which are neither heavy nor light. Thomas suggests that the account is incomplete and provisional. Aristotle is speaking according to the view of those authors who did not accept any other physical body besides the four elements. He will introduce the fifth element in *De caelo* I (no. 446). He supposes that the body in a place and the place it is in are complementary. Aristotle distinguishes between that which is contained in something, so that it is not divided from it, and bodies that are distinguished and separated from their place, such as water in a vase (nos. 447–53).

It is evident that place must be one of the four following things (lesson 6; IV.4.211b5–212a30): matter or form or the space between the extremities or finally the extremities of the containing body. Three of these are excluded (no. 457ff.). In fact, space is not place (nos. 461–63). Thomas indicates the solution: place does not change as a part of the heaven does. Place is immovable, as it is in relation to the entire celestial sphere of the first heaven, which has a certain immobility with regard to the center of the world and its poles. So place is the immobile terminus of the body that it contains primarily (no. 470). Aristotle says "primarily" to indicate that the proper place of a body is meant, not place in a vague, comprising sense, such as the place where one was born.

In lesson 7 (IV.5.212a31–b22), Aristotle determines how the four elements are in a place. He notices that the body that has some other body adjacent to it and which contains it, as the element air contains the hydrosphere, is in the true sense of the term (and *per se*) in a place. There is one body in the world that does not have another body surrounding and containing it, that is, the ultimate sphere of the universe, whatever it may be. Thomas suggests that the nature of the sphere of the fixed stars is not determined here (*quaecumque sit illa*) and will be discussed in another treatise (no. 473). But if we assume that the ultimate sphere is not in a place, impossible consequences follow, as it moves (daily rotation) and whatever moves is in a place (no. 474). Thomas mentions the opinion of Alexander of Aphrodisias who writes that the last sphere is not in a place and that being in a place does not enter into the definition of a body. But this position creates a new difficulty, as every movement must be in a definite genus (quantity, quality, or place).

Avicenna, therefore, said that the motion of the first heaven is motion *in situ,* adding this species to Aristotle's enumeration, but Thomas declares this impossible for a site is indivisible; if one adds something to it or takes something away from it, it no longer is the same site (no. 475). Avempace proposed a shrewd solution: a body that moves in a circle finds its perfection in this circle and does not need a body that delimits it from the outside—it is in a place if there is a place around which it revolves. But Thomas notes that this solution contradicts what was said before, namely that a place contains what is in it (no. 476). Averroes says that the last sphere is *per accidens* in a place insofar as the center around which it moves is in a place. But Aristotle has another view of being in a place *per accidens*, namely, when something external to the body moves with it, like a nail moving with a ship (no. 477). Thomas himself inclines to the position of Themistius (*ego magis approbo sententiam Themistii*): the first heaven is in a place through its parts that succeed each other in a place (no. 478). In the following numbers, the discussion is continued: the first heaven is in place by reason of its parts (no. 484). Outside the heavens there is perhaps nothing. Aristotle uses the word "perhaps," Thomas says, because the point has not yet been proven. It would seem, then, that the place of the heavens is its ultimate surface turned to us. Averroes observes that, in the text, "heaven" is used in two meanings: the whole world and the ultimate sphere of the universe. The latter is accidentally in a place. Thomas does not further discuss this question.

In lesson 8 (IV.5.212b22–213a11), Aristotle explains why the elements move to their natural places. Thomas comments that, when we accept that the place of a body is the terminus of what is containing it, we have a good reason why each body moves to its proper place: the containing body is next to it (*proximum*) according to its nature, so that movements of the simple bodies to their natural places are not enforced motions. The proximity in nature between the containing body and the contained are the cause for a body moving to its natural place. The order in the gradation of natural places corresponds to the rank and hierarchy of natural bodies. Thomas observes that if one considers place to be just space, the reason for the distinction between the natural bodies and their places disappears. On this issue the commentary of Thomas is more detailed than Aristotle's text (no. 492). Another question is why bodies naturally rest in their respective natural places. Air is like the whole in respect to water, and water is like matter in respect to air as to its form, because water is potentially air, but Thomas notes that air is also in some way water in potency. At this point the question is not further discussed, and Thomas notes that what Aristotle wrote was not considered by him to be certain. The question will be determined in the *De generatione et corruptione*, Thomas says (no. 493). In a final remark, Thomas observes that, in this context, Aristotle is speaking of the bodies according to their substantial forms, which they have due to the causal influence of the body of the heavenly sphere, which is the primary place and gives locating power to all other bodies. But according to their active and passive qualities there is contrariety between the elements and the one is corruptive of the other.

In lesson 9 (IV.6.213a12–b29), the notion of the void is discussed. Aristotle gives an overview of different opinions about the void, namely from Anaxagoras and Democritus, and of their negation by Melissus, and finally mentions the Pythagoreans, who posited an infinite void outside the heavens. According to them, by entering into the world, the void brings about a separation between things. The void exists in the first place in numbers: by the void, one unit is distinguished from another unit. But what they said was ambiguous, says Aristotle, when they called the distinction between things the void (no. 505).

The exposition about the void is continued in lesson 10 (IV.7.213b30–214b11). The void can be understood as the place in which there is no body at all, or as a place in which there is nothing or, finally, the place in which there is neither a heavy nor a light body. The void is space that can receive a tangible body (nos. 506–12). Next, we read that the void is a place without a body, and place is not space, so that the void is neither space separated from bodies nor space within bodies (as place also is not separate from bodies). As place is not space without a body, likewise the void cannot be space without bodies (no. 513). In no. 515, the reasons alleged by some for the existence of the void are given, but Aristotle argues that there is no separate void, and that the void is not necessary for local motion (no. 516). Nor does absorption prove the existence of the void. But how to explain an increase in volume? Aristotle suggests that it may happen by alteration or by filling empty (void) spots in the body that is increasing in size. But Thomas writes that the real reason for growth and increase is indicated in the *De generatione et corruptione*, namely, by the conversion of food into the body that grows (no. 518).

Chapter 8 extends over three lessons (lessons 11–13). Aristotle attempts to determine the truth about the void. In lesson 11 (IV.8.214b12–215a24), Thomas insists on the fact that the void is not something apart (i.e., separated from beings). It was assumed to exist to explain local motion. But the simple bodies just move to their natural places: their very nature is the cause of their motion and not the void (no. 521). Natural bodies move to their natural places because they have some affinity with them. But the void has nothing to attract them, so that no natural body would be drawn to the void. Those who identify place and space have difficulty explaining why a body changes its place or rests in it. Place is separate from the body, but that is not the case if the void is the place (no. 522). If a body were in the void, we could not give a reason why it moves to one part of it rather than to another. In the void there is no difference between above and below; there is no natural motion, nor other motions derived from natural motions (no. 524). If place is a void, one cannot explain why projectiles continue to move after leaving the arc. If motion takes place in the void, there is no reason why it stops in a certain place, for there is no difference between the parts of the void (nos. 525–26).

In lesson 12 (IV.8.215a23–a26), Aristotle explains that there is no subsistent void because of the speeding and slowing down of motions. Bodies move faster or slower because of the medium through which they move or also because of the difference between the bodies that are moving, whereas the void cannot cause a difference. There is no proportion between motions through the void and through filled space (nos. 529–32). Thomas says that Aristotle's explanation leads to several difficulties with regard to the fact that different media may retard (or not) the velocity of a body moving through it. The movement of the celestial bodies is not obstructed, but their speed is nevertheless determined. Furthermore, there are also other impediments besides the medium through which a body moves. Thomas does not say who raised these difficulties, but he writes that Averroes tried to answer them (no. 535).

Other authors accepted the view that in a void the movement of simple bodies would not be obstructed. If the medium, which is filled, impedes the motion of bodies traversing it, there is no unimpeded natural movement. Averroes suggested that in fact the natural movement of heavy and light bodies requires that there is a hindrance from the side of the medium, so that there is some resistance to the mover (at least with the help of the medium). But Thomas stresses the role of the natural places. It is possible that a factor such as the medium renders the natural motions more difficult, but the bodies are freed from this when they get close to their natural places (no. 537). In respect of the arguments of Aristotle, Thomas writes that in the *Physics* Aristotle examines the moving bodies in common and uses certain arguments "which are wrong when one considers the determined natures of these bodies, but possible when one considers the nature of the bodies in general" (no. 538). The void would not make much difference if the moving body has a greater bulk or a broad shape. If the void exists, the contrary would happen of what the supporters of the theory think, that is, there would not be motion (no. 540).

In lesson 13 (IV.8.216a26–b21), the void as such is considered without reference to motion and moving bodies. If one considers the void as such, independently from moving bodies, it simply does not exist. The word "void" already indicates that it is nothing. If one would conceive a body as coexisting with the void, it would be together with part of the void, something that is impossible. One could no longer indicate the difference between the two, for the portion of the void occupied would be the same as the occupying body. If one says that the void is empty space, bodies do not need to be in a place, for each body has its own dimensions (space). A final argument is that the void simply has never been observed in the world.

After having shown that there is no separately existing void, Aristotle argues in lesson 14 (IV.9.216b22–217b28) that there is no void in bodies, as some authors claimed there is in order to explain rarefaction and condensation. But these do not occur because more or less of the void is occupied but because of more or less quantity (no. 552). It is clear that there is no void in the sense of a separated volume of space; there is no void existing outside the physical bodies. Likewise, there is no void existing as hollow space or holes in some bodies. The commentary of Thomas is a clear reproduction of Aristotle's arguments, which he does not question (nos. 553–57).

Lessons 15–23 (IV.10–14) are devoted to the study of time. Lesson 15 (IV.10.217b29–218a31) asks the question: does time exist? It seems not, as the past is no more and the future is not yet (no. 559). Certain parts of time are not yet; other parts belong to the past. But the *now* that actually exists is not a part of time, because a part either measures the whole or is that out of which the whole is composed. But time is not composed of *nows* (no. 560). Is the *now*, which distinguishes between the parts of time, real? The *now* that was real passed away. Two *nows* are never together, so the *now* that perishes, cannot perish in the subsequent *now*. The last *now* cannot be the same as the first succeeding *now*; if they were the same, past things would be the same as future ones (nos. 561–64).

In lesson 16 (IV.10–11.218a31–219a1), Aristotle proceeds by calling into question different views on time and examining the relation of time to motion. Thomas writes that the text is an inquisition in the form of a dispute. Aristotle argues against the theory that the circular motion of the heavens would be time. There are many other circular motions. But time is not movement (no. 566). Others thought that the spherical body of the heavens is time, because things exist in time and are surrounded by this spherical body. But that is not the same, Aristotle objects, as being in a place is different from being in time; moreover, all the parts of the heavenly sphere exist simultaneously, while the parts of time do not (no. 567). Time is not motion, for motion is found only in certain bodies, whereas time is everywhere; moreover, motions are slow or fast, but time is uniform (nos. 568–69). Yet time is not without motion, for we perceive time when we perceive change. When we do not perceive any change, we think that no time has passed. In fact, in lesson 17 (IV.11.219a2–b8), we read that time has to do with motion. When we experience some motion, we perceive time (no. 572). But if this motion is outside us, those who do not sense it have no sense of time. According to some, time is only something of the human mind. Furthermore, if time accompanies motion, are there as many kinds of time as there are of motion (no. 573)? Thomas resolves the difficulty by pointing to the fact that there is one primary motion in which all other motions participate (*unus primus motus*). When we perceive a motion, we perceive change and therefore also the first movement, that is, the cause of all motions (no. 574). So the definition of time is a counted motion in respect of before and after. Time is consequent on motion insofar as there is an earlier and later in it (nos. 576–79). An objection against this definition is that earlier and later are already time and should not enter the definition. The answer is that here the earlier and later are taken as points or marks of a magnitude, but not yet of time. Time is a numbered number (*numerus numeratus*), but not a number by which we count (*numerus numerans*).

In lesson 18 (IV.11.219b9–220a26), Aristotle further examines the *now*. Is the *now* the same in the course of time? No, in the succession of time it is different, but considered as the reality of a certain being, it is the same in its subject (*idem subiecto*). This means that the same subject is carried through time, from one *now* to the next. Thomas adds that the succession of the *nows* helps us to understand what is meant by eternity. When we leave out that the *now* is moving and see it as stationary, and if its mobile being remains the same, we are left with a substance that is always in the same state (nos. 585–86). The thing that is moving is better known than its motion, for it is always this particular thing. The *now* is related to the body in local motion. Aristotle compares a line and a point to a local motion and to a *now*. A point divides the line as the *now* does motion, but the *now* is not at rest. We express our counting of a motion by time, when one *now* is taken as the beginning and another *now* as the end of it. The *now* is not part of time, it is a terminus.

Numerically, there is no smallest time, which like a line can always be further divided (lesson 19; IV.11–12.220a24–b30). Time is the same with regard to all things in motion everywhere. The past and the future are different times, just as a hundred sheep are different from the same number of horses (nos. 594–99). Lesson 20 (IV.12.220b33–222a9) compares time as a measure with regard to things in time, for example, one hour of a day with the whole day. Things can be in time in different ways. The *nows*, earlier and later, are in time, but not all things are in time; for example, things that always exist are not in time (no. 603). Thomas adds an observation: celestial bodies are not in time with regard to their being, but they are with regard to their motions (no. 605). According to our way of speaking, time corrupts things, that is, they are removed from their initial disposition in the course of time. Time is also a measure of things at rest, as time itself is not motion but the numbering of motion. Things at rest are apt to be moved, and so time is a measure *per accidens* (nos. 606–8).

In lesson 21 (IV.13.222a10–b15), Aristotle writes that as a point divides a line, the *now* divides the time, but one can take the *now* as the end of one part of time or as the starting-point of the future, and so it is different. Thomas notes that the *now* can also indicate the present moment (no. 614). According to Aristotle's view (*secundum opinionem eius*), movement will never cease, as it never began. The question will be further examined in Book VIII, but Thomas writes that if motion had a beginning, there is a *now* that is not the end of a movement. Likewise, when motion will come to an end, the last *now* will not be the beginning of another motion (no. 617). Thomas is clearly thinking of the creation of the world and of the end of time.

In lesson 22 (IV.13–14.222b16–223a15), the question is raised whether time is subject to corruption. All motions are taking place in time. When in the process of the corruption of things the moving cause does not clearly appear, we attribute corruption to time. In generation there is always the generating cause. All changes take place in time, for we see that there are slower and faster changes, so they take place in time. We also attribute a "before and after" to motion, and so motion takes place in time (nos. 622–24).

In lesson 23 (IV.14.223a16–224b16), Aristotle examines how time is related to our soul. Only the intellect can number motion, so that without an intellect there is no time. There may be motions of which the speed differs, but time is for all things the same. The circular movement of the first heaven is the most regular movement and the measure of all other movements. Thomas repeats what he had said in lesson 17, no. 574, namely that a person who perceives any movement senses time because of the fact that all movements depend from the first movement of the heavens (no. 636).

Book V

In the first lesson (V.1.224a21–b35) of the fifth book of the *Physics*, Aristotle discusses the division of movements in motions *per se* and motions *per accidens*, that is, the division of motions according to their species; in Book VI, he considers movements as divided in quantitative parts. Movements *per accidens* are excluded from consideration, as they are indeterminate (no. 647). Five things are required for a movement: a first mover, a mobile being, times in which a movement unrolls, a point of departure, and an end terminus. A movement differs from both termini (nos. 641–42). A movement is unrolling from an intermediary to either of the extremes. The intermediary has some correspondence with both extremes (no. 648). In lesson 2 (V.1.225a2–b5), Aristotle explains which changes are motions. Generation, for instance, is a change but not a motion (no. 659).

In lesson 3 (V.2.225b3–226a23), the species of movements are distinguished according to their predicaments. In predicaments other than quantity, quality, and place, there are no motions. There are no motions in substance either, as there is no contrariety except the contrariety between excellence and defect (no. 662), but changes do occur. Averroes thinks that the argument from the absence of contrarieties is only probable, but Thomas accepts it as valid. In all genera we can speak of excess and deficiency, and when there is a continuous passage between these, we have contraries (no. 664). The text of the chapter is difficult, but Thomas explains in an admirable way what Aristotle says about mutations (nos. 666–68). There are no motions in the predicament of the relations, nor in those of actions and passion. In the remaining part of the lesson, Aristotle presents several arguments to show that there cannot be a mutation of mutation, except *per accidens* (nos. 669–77). In his detailed commentary, Thomas explains the text and even removes misunderstandings, as in no. 673, when he points out that the subject of generation is not that which is generated, but matter.

In lesson 4 (V.2.226a23–b17), motion is said to occur only in quantity, quality, and place. The reason is that it is only in these predicaments that contrariety is found. Motion in respect of quality is called alteration; motions in respect of quantity are increase and decrease. Motions in respect of place do not have a name. There is no real contrariety, except insofar as the two termini are far removed (nos. 679–81). The chapter ends with a trifold explanation of the term "immovable": (1) something that cannot be moved at all (Thomas gives the example of God); (2) that which is difficult to move; and (3) a thing that can be moved but which is at rest (no. 683).

In lesson 5 (V.3.226b18–227b2), Aristotle explains certain concepts such as touching, being in contact, and being together in a place. Things are in contact when their extremities are together. Before a changing thing reaches its terminus, it arrives first at what is *between* the point of departure and the final terminus. There can be more than one medium (no. 686). In order that a motion is continuous there must not be an interruption, and there must be succession. To be continuous there must be contact between the several sections the moving thing is passing through (nos. 687–93).

In lesson 6 (V.4.227b3–228a20), Aristotle discusses the generic, specific, and numerical unity of motions. If motions are in the same predicament, they also are in the same genus. They are in the same species when they take place in a species that cannot be further subdivided. In his commentary, Thomas limits himself to a careful explanation of the text (nos. 696–702). In lesson 7 (V.4.228a22–229a6), Aristotle intends to show what is required for the numerical unity of a motion: unity of time, unity of the being in which the motion takes place, and unity of the object in motion (nos. 703–6). An irregular motion (because of irregularities in the medium or in the motion itself) is nevertheless one if it is continuous (no. 713).

In lesson 8 (V.5.229a7–b22), Aristotle determines which motions are contrary to each other. The examination of the theme is continued in lessons 9 and 10. He distinguishes the following modes of contrariety: (1) approaching and leaving the same terminus; (2) motions from contrary termini, for example, from health to illness and from illness to health; (3) motions to different termini, for example, to health and to a disease; (4) a motion from one contrary to the opposite contrary; (5) motions from one contrary to its opposite, such as from health to sickness, and from sickness to health. But Aristotle eliminates (2) and (4). The contrariety of the termini toward which the motion goes is more determining than that of the terminus from where the motion begins (nos. 719–20). Contrary motions have two clearly determined contrary termini. Motions to the right and to the left, as well as motions forward and backward, are found only in movements caused by the soul (nos. 722–23).

In lesson 9 (V.6.229b23–230a18), the contrariety of different states of rest are examined. Rest also appears to be contrary to motion, as its privation is, but not every type of rest is opposed to motion; rest in health, for instance, is opposed to rest in illness (nos. 728–36). The Latin text of lesson 10 (V.6.230a18–231a10) used by Thomas has about four lines at the end of the chapter not found in the Greek. Generation and corruption are neither according to nor against nature, except in a remote sense (no. 738). But Thomas refers to *De caelo* II, lesson 9, where we read that aging and defects are against nature, but not, he says, if we consider nature in a universal way (no. 738). Generation can be contrary to generation. Section 231a5–17 is missing in certain manuscripts and, according to Averroes, also in certain Arab translations. He thinks that the difficulty mentioned above, whether we can speak of a violent state of rest due to generation, is answered here. But Thomas gives a somewhat different answer: we can speak of a violent state of rest when the power of the mover is violently impeded. Thomas very meticulously analyzes the arguments of Aristotle with all their distinctions (nos. 738–49). As to the section added, Simplicius considered it a repetition, but Alexander commented on it.[77]

Book VI

While in Book VIII Aristotle investigates which is the first motion and what is the nature of the first mover, in Book VI he considers the division of motion into quantitative parts. In lesson 1 (VI.1.231a21–b18), we read that the continuum in which the extremities (of its parts) are one, and which is, therefore, infinitely divisible, is not composed of indivisible parts, for in that case it would not be infinitely divisible. One cannot obtain a continuum out of indivisible parts. For example, a line cannot be composed of points. The middle between points is a line that between two *nows* is time (nos. 751–56). In lesson 2 (VI.1.231b18–232a17), the exposition about the continuum is pursued in the sense that the argument about the divisibility of the continuum is shown to apply to time and motion as well as to magnitudes. As a line cannot be composed of points, a motion cannot consist of small impulses (nos. 759–65).

In lesson 3 (VI.1–2.232a18–233a17), Thomas comments on the last lines of VI.1 and the first part of VI.2. Both magnitude and time are composed of indivisibles. What moves faster covers a certain distance in less time than a body moving slower (no. 770). Every motion is in time.[78] Aristotle says that in any species of moving things, we may find something that moves faster or slower. Thomas objects that this statement does not seem to be true—for the motion of the first heaven is the fastest motion—but then solves the difficulty: Aristotle is speaking of what is common to things in general, not of what may happen in particular circumstances (no. 774). By means of an example, namely, of bodies that are moving during the same time, one faster, the other slower, Aristotle shows that time is divisible: when the faster body has reached the terminus, the other body is still underway. The faster one covered the distance in less time, so time is divisible (nos. 766–76).

In lesson 4 (VI.2.233a17–b37), we read that the finite and the infinite are found both in magnitudes and in time, which as continuous realities are both divisible. Time has no end and is like a magnitude, such as a line which we conceive as being infinite. The division of time follows that of magnitudes and, like a magnitude, time can be divided infinitely, and there is no end to the

---

77. Ross, Aristotle's "Physics," 638. The expression "quae tamen in exemplaribus graecis dicuntur non haberi" is an instance of the influence of Moerbeke's revision of the *translatio vetus*.

78. This was demonstrated in Book IV, lesson 20.

series of *nows*. The infinite number of points are crossed by an infinite number of *nows*. Aristotle used this as an argument against Zeno, who asserted that a body cannot move from A to B, as it would have to traverse an infinite number of points. But, Thomas says, Aristotle's solution is merely *ad hominem* and does not correspond to the truth, as Aristotle writes and Thomas will show in Book VIII, lesson 17 (no. 779). A body cannot cross an infinite distance in a finite time, nor vice versa (no. 780). Thomas carefully mentions the various arguments of Aristotle, although he is aware that some aspects of them are open to criticism. In no. 783, he writes that one might also object to the first argument (*cavillando dicere*). The upshot of the chapter is that no continuum is indivisible (no. 786).

Lesson 5 (VI.3–4.233b33–234b20) is one of the longest lessons of Aquinas's commentary on the *Physics*. In the preceding chapter, Aristotle has shown that magnitude and time are divisible in the same way. In this lesson, he proves that the *now* of time is indivisible. There is no motion or rest in an indivisible point of time: as there is no line stretching further than the point that is the end of it, there is no time (past or future) beyond the *now* that is the end of what is past and the *now* that is the beginning of the future. Nothing is naturally moved in a *now*. Because rest is the privation of motion, nothing is at rest in the now, as it cannot move in it (nos. 794–95). Aristotle shows that everything that moves (i.e., changes) is divisible: for instance, while something is changing from black to white, it is partly in one terminus (e.g., black) and partly in the new one. Averroes objected that this might be valid for changes in quantity, quality, and place, but that generation and corruption of substances are indivisible (nos. 797–99). But Thomas explains that Aristotle proceeds from the divisibility of the mobile body: before it is in motion, it is still entirely in terminus A; when it has changed it is in terminus B. When it changes, it must be partly in one terminus, partly in the other, insofar as the dispositions to the new form are present in it. This is, Aquinas thinks, what Averroes wants to say when he writes that some mutations are *per accidens* and not in time (no. 800). Thomas formulates another difficulty: in alterations there seems to be a gradual change, so that what is changing, such as temperature, is not partly in one terminus and partly in another. Thomas answers that Aristotle has a continuous motion in mind, which is primarily found in local motions, while there is a difference in alterations, as Aristotle writes in his *De sensu et sensato* (nos. 800–801). And Thomas also refers to an explanation that applies what Aristotle writes on alterations, but this is forced (no. 804).

Lesson 6 (VI.4.234b21–235b5) deals directly with the division of motion. The discussions of the previous lessons were necessary before we could actually examine the division of motion, a theme that is the subject matter of the next five lessons (lessons 6–10). Lesson 10 gives the division of the different forms of rest, while lesson 11 presents the refutation of Zeno's denial of all motion. In no. 807, Aristotle argues that motion can be divided in two ways: (1) according to time, as motion is not in a *now*, but in time; every motion is divided according to the time of its duration; and (2) according to the parts of that which is moving. Each part moves according to its own position in the moving thing, and not according to that of another part. The motion of the entire moving body is divided according to the movement of its parts (no. 807). Motions in place, quality, and quantity are in time. Movement as such is proper to quantitative things, but is found *per accidens* in the predicament of quality, where it is called alteration (no. 812). If a body moves over a whole magnitude, such as a distance in space in a certain time, it will cover half this magnitude in half the time. If we divide the motion, we divide also the time of its duration (no. 813). The distance covered by a body moving in a place can be divided according to the time used (nos. 814–17).

In lesson 7 (VI.5.235b6–236b18), Aristotle explains that when things move from one terminus to another and the change has ended, they are in the terminus to which they were moving. This also applies to contradictory changes from not-being to being, as in the case of generation and corruption. The thing that has changed or has been transformed is now that into which it has been changed. This is also the case in all types of changes (no. 819). This is illustrated by the example of local motion. What has changed, its place, is in the place toward which it has moved (no. 820). Whatever has been generated or corrupted has been so in an indivisible moment (no. 821). As time is infinitely divisible (just as the body that is moving), there is no part of it that was changed first (because of its infinite divisibility, there will always be another part that changed earlier) (no. 824). Thomas limits his commentary to a detailed explanation of the text (no. 825).

The argument is continued in lesson 8 (VI.6.236b20–237b22). Aristotle examines the way in which a thing that moves at a uniform speed has already changed when it arrives at a point between the point of departure and the terminus. It changes, he says, in each part of the total time that is to be traversed. That which is moving (changing) has already changed at any point of the trajectory. But if the motion is not actually interrupted at such a point, the change (*mutatum esse*) is only potential (no. 829). The motion ends at the last *now*. Prior to each "having changed" is the actual changing (no. 832) and this change occurs in time, with a before and after. But does this also apply to generation and corruption, which are instantaneous? Thomas explains that if one considers generation as the beginning of a thing together with the preceding moment of which it is the terminus, it is not instantaneous (no. 834). What has been said is more evident in motions according to magnitude and also applies to alteration (nos. 836–37). In each part of a motion we must assume a "having changed," although we do not find it yet in the very first indivisible part of it (no. 838). With regard to continuous and divisible things, Aristotle adds that the thing that has become must have been before in the process of becoming and previously has become. Aristotle adds this remark, Averroes writes, to exclude things that become without a continuous motion (such as thought), or, says Thomas, to allow us to consider generation together with the preceding continuous motion (no. 839). Things come into being in different ways: certain elements are generated all at once, but living beings are generated part after part (no. 840).

In lesson 9 (VI.7.237b22–238b22), Aristotle treats of finite and infinite motions, as both are related to what the continuum is (*ratio continui*). When time is finite, magnitude also is. An infinite distance cannot be covered in a finite time (no. 845). As motion is not in an indivisible instant, rest is not either. There is no infinite motion in a finite time (nos. 846–50). In lesson 10 (VI.8.238b23–239b4), the notion of rest is further examined. The cessation of motion produces rest. Whatever ceases moving does so in time, for whatever moves, moves in time (no. 856). Just as motion is not in an indivisible instant, rest also is not (no. 858). In the *now* there is neither motion nor rest.

The theory of Zeno is refuted in lesson 11 (VI.9.239b5–240a7). Zeno taught that nothing is moved, not even a flying arrow. It is not moved in an indivisible *now*, so it is not in the total time too. But this is contradicted by the fact that time is not composed of indivisible *nows*, so that it does not follow that if there is no motion in a *now*, there is no motion either in time (no. 861). In the following numbers, the four arguments of Zeno to deny motion are refuted. (1) If a body moves through a certain space, it must first cross half of it and, before that, half of this half and so on infinitely. The answer is that these parts exist only in potency, not in act. (2) The second argument is that of Achilles, competing in a race with a slow-moving opponent, the tortoise, who is given a head start. Achilles can never catch up, because when he reaches the point where the tortoise had arrived just before, the animal has progressed meanwhile somewhat further and so on. The argument supposes the infinite divisibility of space. (3) The arrow that one shoots at a target never arrives, because of the fact of the infinite divisibility of this distance. (4) The fourth argument supposes two bodies of equal magnitude moving into opposite directions, B and C, with equal velocity, one starting from the end of a race course, the other from the middle (no. 867), while passing a body of equal size, at rest in the middle of the race course.[79] The argument of Zeno is not clear.

In his commentary, Thomas points out a first error in the text as he read it: when a body is in motion next to another body at rest, there is only one motion (no. 868). Moreover, Zeno concluded from the speed of B and C passing A that half the time needed to pass A is equal to the full time. Thomas rejects the argument: it is false to say that C crosses B and A in the same time (no. 869). Zeno also excludes change between contradictories, for when one of them is changing into the other, it would be neither the one nor the other. Thomas answers that there is no difficulty provided we accept the divisibility of the contradictories, for example of a quality. However, the answer does not apply, Thomas says, to cases when the whole thing is changed at once. But this will be explained in Book VIII (no. 870). Finally, Zeno argued against the possibility of circular motion: the supposedly moving body remains in the same place. Thomas quotes the answer of Aristotle: the argument is not true with regard to the proper place of each part. The whole circle also changes its place insofar as its parts are at each time in a different place (no. 871).

Lesson 12 (VI.10.240b8–241a26) deals with the theory of Democritus, who holds that the indivisible particles (atoms) of which material bodies are composed move through space. Aristotle shows that these atoms cannot move because they have no parts. If they would move, part of them would be in the initial position, part in the new position (no. 876). He refers to the indivisible points, which cannot move (no. 877). In the last lesson (VI.10.241a26–b20), Heraclitus's theory that all things are always in motion is discussed: Aristotle points out that everywhere there are limits to movements. For instance, contraries pose limits to the changes taking place between them, as contradictory termini also do, where the affirmation and the negation constitute these limits. The same applies to increase and decrease, where the nature of the subject sets a limit (no. 880). Locomotion seems to be an exception. But Aristotle notices that there is a maximum distance in the motions of the heavy and the light. In violent motions the maximum distance is determined by the purpose or the degree of violence used by the mover (no. 881). As for local motion, Aristotle reminds us that nothing tends to the impossible. The infinite cannot

---

79. Thomas speaks of a magnitude, but in the original Greek one reads about sets of bodies or masses (239b34). The argument is not clear, at least as we find it in Aristotle's text (see Ross, *Aristotle's "Physics,"* 660–65). The upshot of Zeno's argument seems to be that series A remains at rest, and series B and C move in the opposite direction passing A. Zeno wants to show that half the time of passing would be equal to the whole of the time, an impossible result that would destroy the reality of motion. I only discuss how Thomas saw the argument. For Aristotle's argument, see P. J. Bicknell, "The Fourth Paradox of Zeno: An Interpretation of Aristotle Physics 239 B33–240 A18," *Acta Classica* 4 (1961): 39–45.

be crossed. Hence no local motion is infinite. Another question is whether a motion can continue during an infinite time, or whether a succession of motions can, such as local motion, alteration, increase, generation, etc. Thomas points out the cautious way in which Aristotle expresses himself in respect of this question. It would seem that there is nothing to prevent it. If so, motion can go on during an infinite time. A circular motion can also continue during an infinite time, as will be shown in Book VIII (no. 883).

Book VII

In Book VII, Aristotle examines motion as compared to movers and moveable objects, while in Book VIII he deals with the question of the first motion and the nature of the first mover. In the first three chapters, he demonstrates the existence of a first motion. In chapters 4 and 5, he gives indications for comparing motions. The relation of Books VII and VIII is not very clear, as much of VII is taken up again in VIII. W.D. Ross suggests that Book VII is not an integral part of the *Physics* because the book does not fit in very well with Books V and VI.[80] Ross also reminds us that there are two Greek versions of the text, generally referred to as α and β, of which he prefers the first. More recently, G. Verbeke has argued that Book VII leads to an impasse to be taken up again in Book VIII, whereas R. Wardy has argued for the continuity between Books VII and VIII. Wardy's position has been severely criticized by Olshewsky, who defends Ross's thesis.[81] However, as Olshewsky has pointed out, the medieval commentators and translators, contrary to the ancient commentators, had no awareness of the differences and "almost universally followed the β version."[82] There is indeed no indication that Thomas, or Averroes for that matter, knew of the existence of another version.

In lesson 1 (VII.1.241b34–242a48) of his commentary on Book VII, Thomas mentions some differences compared to Book VIII: in Book VII, Aristotle determines that there is a first motion and moving body and a first mover; while in Book VIII, he determines the nature of this motion and of the first mover (no. 884). Aristotle formulates the principle that whatever is moved is moved by another, which is obvious in things that do not have the

---

80. Ross, *Aristotle's "Physics,"* 15.

81. See Gerard Verbeke, "L'argument du livre VII de la Physique. Une impasse philosophique," in *Naturphilosophie bei Aristoteles und Theophrast. Verhandlungen des 4. Symposium Aristotelicum veranstaltet in Göteborg, August 1966*, ed. I. Düring (Heidelberg: Stiehm, 1969), 250–67; Robert Wardy, *The Chain of Change: A Study of Aristotle's "Physics" VII* (Cambridge: Cambridge University Press, 1990); Thomas Olshewsky, "Self-moved Movers and Unmoved Movers in Aristotle's Physics VII," *The Classical Quarterly* 45 (1995): 398–406.

82. Thomas Olshewsky, "The Bastard Book of The Physics," *The Classical Quarterly* 64 (2014): 58–74, at 59.

principle of motion in themselves. He shows that even those things that seem to move themselves are moved by an outside mover (no. 885). Because everything that is moved is divisible, Aristotle argues that when a part of it is at rest, the whole also is, and if a part is moved, the whole also is (no. 899). There is no mobile object whose motion does not depend on its parts. Galenus and Avicenna objected to the validity of this argument (no. 887). Avicenna thinks that Aristotle gives a demonstration that it is so (*quia*), but not why it is (*propter quid*), but Thomas says that it is a proof why it is, because Aristotle indicates why a mobile body cannot move itself: in divisible things there is no first, neither in motion, nor in time, nor in magnitude, because of their divisibility. For the movement of the whole depends on that of its parts (no. 889). Thomas sees a confirmation in Plato's philosophy: the Platonists hold that certain beings move themselves, but these are immaterial. Thomas adds that to move oneself is reserved to a spiritual substance that knows and loves itself, making here an opening for philosophical theology (no. 890).[83]

The conclusion of the previous section is applied in lesson 2 (VII.1.242a19–b67). In a series of movers we cannot proceed to infinity. Therefore, there must be a first mover, which is the first cause of motion. This first mover does not move itself, it moves others (no. 891). But one might object to the theory of a unique mover that it is impossible that the elements are continuous with each other and with the celestial bodies (no. 896). In his answer, Thomas explains that Aristotle is speaking about movers and mobile things in general, and does not apply his conclusion to particular moving bodies. It is not yet necessary to show that all mobile things are continuous, something that also seems impossible if one considers them in their specific natures, such as air and water (no. 896).

In lesson 3 (VII.2.243a32–244b2), Aristotle shows that in local motions the mover and the moved must be together, as the efficient cause with its effect. They must not be separated by something else (no. 898). This applies to the three species of motion: alteration (no. 899); local motion in its different kinds, such as pushing and pulling (no. 900); and augmentation (no. 901). Other kinds of motion, such as striking, can be reduced to these (no. 905). Thomas carefully mentions the different form local motion can take and concludes that the mover and the moved are together and that there is no intermediate (no. 908).

Lesson 4 (VII.2.244b2–245b2) notes that this applies also to alteration, increase, and decrease. There is no intermediate between the mover and the

---

83. *In VII Phys.*, lesson 1, no. 890: "movere seipsum est tantummodo substantiae spiritualis, quae intelligit seipsam et amat seipsam."

moved. In this connection, Thomas also mentions the predicament "passion," which is placed under the category of quality, that is, the so-called *patibiles qualitates* (no. 909). Thomas notes that action and passion in respect of the senses concern in the first place the organ of the different senses. As it is proper to the senses to operate in and with an organ (i.e., with the body), passion and alteration are more properly said of the senses than of the intellect (no. 910). In the perception of the senses the active factor and that which is altered are together without an intermediate (no. 911).

In lesson 5 (VII.3.245b3–246a9), Aristotle argues that there is no alteration in the first and in the fourth species of qualities. Here we can recall that the division of the genus "quality" into its species happens according to four measures or differences. The first species of quality (habits and dispositions) happens according to nature as its measure; the second (capacity and incapacity) according to action; the third (passion and sensible qualities) according to passion; and the fourth (form and figure) according to quantity.[84] The fact that there is no alteration with regard to figures, that is, the termination of dimensive quantity, is obvious, but also in the group of faculties (*potentia operativa*) there is no alteration (no. 915). Alteration is in respect of sensible things, and occurs only secondarily in the accidents of the first and fourth species, subsequent to alterations of the more primary qualities. The figure of a thing may change if the thing expands because of heat. This applies also to the second species of qualities, namely, the faculties (*potentia*) (no. 914). In order to show that in figures there is no alteration, Aristotle argues that we associate figures with the thing itself; they reveal the species of things, something that is especially visible in plants and in animals (no. 917). Thomas mentions an explanation by Averroes, but offers a better one of his own (no. 918).

There is no alteration, primarily and *per se*, in qualities of the first species, that is, the *habitus* of the soul (lesson 6; VII.3.246a10–248a9).[85] This demonstration is subsequent to that of the previous lesson where alterations with respect to processes affecting some dispositions of the body were excluded. Here, Aristotle is considering virtues and vices. Now, a virtue is a certain perfection following upon the form. If the form has its virtue(s), it is perfect. Averroes excluded alteration from virtues because these are simple and indivisible. But because this does not apply to vice, Thomas prefers to use the same argument as in the previous lesson:[86] there is no alteration in respect

---

84. See *ST* I-II, q. 49, a. 2.

85. The Latin text is shorter than the Greek text of Ross.

86. In the *ST* I-II, q. 52, Thomas examines the question of the growth of the virtues. His answer is that according to that by which virtues acquire their specific nature, they must be fixed and stable, but considered from the side of the subject participating in a virtue, there can be a more or less.

of figures and virtues (no. 920). But it is obvious that some change must occur so that a virtue or a vice can become present or disappear. Aristotle confirms this: when a virtue enters, there occurs a modification in the passions. Passions are located in the sensitive part of our soul, where alterations may occur (no. 921). In a second argument, Aristotle says that virtues are accompanied by some pleasure or sadness, emotions located in the sensitive appetite, in which there are alterations (no. 922), but then he shows that there is no alteration in the immaterial part of the soul. Thought results from an active principle and not from alteration, whereas in seeing, hearing, etc., changes occur in the senses caused by the object (no. 924).

Aristotle also argues that speculative thinking takes place when the soul is at rest, and not through a process such as generation. What Aristotle calls "rest," Thomas comments, concerns the disturbances in the body that have quieted down. This explains why for children and the young it is difficult to judge about what they have learned (no. 925). Thomas adds the following comments. Aristotle's argument is in line with Plato's theory of knowledge as a participation in the Ideas, which is facilitated by tranquility in the body. Aristotle's own doctrine is that our concepts result from the abstraction of forms by the agent intellect, as discussed in *De anima* III, yet he is not inconsistent by mentioning Plato's view, as he usually mentions the theories of other authors before formulating his own opinion (no. 926). In a final paragraph, Thomas says that Plato's argument is also valid, against the background of Aristotle's own doctrine, namely: if there is no obstacle in the person who acquires new knowledge, he will immediately receive it, but if some disposition obstructs the process, alteration is required (no. 927).

In lesson 7 (VII.4.248a10–249a8), Aristotle takes up again the study of motion, investigating when motions are comparable with each other. Thomas very carefully analyzes the steps in the arguments by making numerous divisions and subdivisions. Not all motions are comparable (no. 929). Circular motion is not equal to motion along a straight line with regard to its speed. At the end of the lesson, he summarizes the conditions required for motions to be comparable: (1) motions must not be equivocal; (2) they must not be different with regard to the subject in which they are received, for example, a quality received in an animal must not be compared to that received in a stone; and (3) they must be comparable with regard to their form, which must be of the same species (no. 938).

These conclusions are applied in lesson 8 (VII.4.249a8–b26). A change of place is not comparable to an alteration. A motion along a straight line and a circular motion are also not comparable (no. 944). Thomas understands

Aristotle as intending to say that the motions differ in species because of the figures of the path they follow (no. 945) and draws attention to a further point, namely that a genus is not simply one, whereas a species is (no. 947), although, according to the Platonists, the genus is also a simply one. In the following section of the lesson, the question of the comparison of alterations is dealt with. We must ascertain that the species of the compared alterations are the same, and also the subject and the parts of it in which they occur are the same. In the last part of the lesson, Thomas discusses Plato's theory of the One as well as the Great and the Small, which are principles that can make the substance, which as such is one, more, and less.

How to compare motions? This is the question of lesson 9 (VII.5.249b27–250b7). Aristotle first deals with the comparison of local motions before turning to that of the other motions. What moves locally always moves in a certain time and passes through some space. Aristotle adds that that which causes motion also moves itself. Thomas understands this as meaning that the mover also moves in time and covers some distance, but he is quick to add that not every mover is subject to quantity. He is thinking here of the first unmoved mover of Book VIII (no. 956). Aristotle gives some rules for a comparison: if some mover moves a body over a certain distance in time x, half that body will be moved by the same mover twice that distance in the same time x. The smaller the moved object is, the faster the same mover will move it (no. 957). Half the power will move half the object over the same distance in the same time. Thomas observes that power is a reality of a different kind and not affected by division in the same way (no. 958). Zeno argued that when a whole sack of grains of millet dropping to the ground makes a sound, one grain would also do so. But Aristotle says that when we separate a small part from a large whole, it does not follow that it will move as the whole did. One man will not be able to move a ship one-hundredth of the distance a hundred haulers do (no. 960). In the last part of the chapter, Aristotle notes that it is not necessary that half the power will move an object half as much as the full power did (no. 964).

Book VIII

Thomas introduces his commentary on Book VIII as follows: after having shown in the previous book that we must assume a first moving body, a first movement, and a first mover, Aristotle now examines how this first mover is and what the first motion and the first moving object are. A necessary presupposition is that motion is eternal. Averroes thought that at this point Aristotle is only examining the question of the first circular motion of the heaven, but Thomas says that when one carefully considers what Aristotle says, Averroes is totally wrong, because in his text Aristotle speaks of motion in general, not of the circular motion of the sphere of the celestial bodies. Moreover, if the existence of the eternal first motion would already have been demonstrated elsewhere, it would be ridiculous to repeat the demonstration and the argumentation in the remainder of the text. Another argument by which Thomas aims to show that Averroes is mistaken reads that it is Aristotle's custom always to start arguing from what properly belongs to the subject, as can be seen in the fact that in this context he nowhere else brings in the motion of the first heaven. What Averroes says is superficial (*frivola*) (no. 966).

All authors who treated of nature affirmed that motion exists. Even generation and corruption do not happen without motion (no. 967). Some of them say that there is always motion, others reject that. Democritus holds that the atoms are always forming new worlds, while Anaxagoras and Empedocles assert that there is sometimes motion, sometimes not (no. 969). The question is important: if the world and its motion are eternal, there must obviously be an eternal principle of this motion. And if there has been a beginning of motion, a cause is needed even more (no. 970). In lesson 2 (VIII.1.251a8–254a4), Aristotle shows that there is always motion and writes that he takes up what was determined about motion in the previous books of the *Physics*. Thomas avails of this remark to notice that there is something special about Book VIII, in which Aristotle begins to apply motion to things.[87] In order to have motion, there must be a subject in which this motion is, and this subject is prior to what comes to be in it (no. 972). Averroes used this statement to argue that there must be a subject to receive motion and so to reject the Christian doctrine of creation out of nothing.

Thomas mentions two more arguments of Averroes against this doctrine: whatever becomes, becomes out of a subject, and *per accidens* out of its contrary. But "nothing" is nonbeing and the world cannot come out of nonbeing, Thomas objects. Averroes finally alleges that all ancient philosophers were convinced that being does not come forth from nonbeing. He suggests that the origin of this view might be that when primitive people do not see what sorts of material things come into being, they assumed that nonbeing was their origin. He also suggests that when the agent has less power, he needs matter to carry out his work. But Thomas comments that the need of a subject results from the very nature of motion, not from a lack of power of the

---

87. *In VIII Phys.*, lesson 2, no. 972: "praecedentes libri habent quondam distinctionem ad hunc librum octavum in quo iam incipit motum ad res applicare."

agent (no. 973). From the fact that every agent needs matter to work on, we must not draw the conclusion that the universal agent also needs a subject to work on. Not even Aristotle made this inference. Thomas refers again to *Metaphysics* II.1.993b26, where we read that the principles of eternal things are the cause of the being of other things; and the cause of why true things are true is most true.[88] Because every motion needs a subject, the universal cause of beings, God, not only produced motion, but also produced a being that is its subject. Therefore, we should not suppose that he needs a subject when creating motions. Given the supposition that the production of the world is from all eternity, as Aristotle and some Platonists hold, we no longer need to postulate the existence of a subject to receive this motion. This is also the case when we assume, in accordance with the Christian faith, that the creation of the world is not from all eternity. Aristotle's statements that motions need a subject is not in conflict with the faith (no. 975). Likewise, when he writes that becoming is either *per se* or *per accidens* (from a contrary), this is true in the processes within the universe, but not universally. It does not apply to creation. Individual things become from what they were not, but when a being *qua* being is produced, it becomes out of what was nonbeing. As for the production of things, Thomas distinguishes three groups of philosophers: (1) those who only accept accidental changes; (2) those who also accept substantial changes; and (3) others, such as Plato and Aristotle, who arrived at the knowledge of the cause of all reality.[89]

When a mover begins to move, there must be an earlier motion in this mover, so as to explain the removal of the state of rest (no. 976). Some argue that movers who move through their intellect do not need a cause to remove their state of rest, as the intellect comprises and knows contraries. But Thomas observes that this knowledge is not equally related to the two contraries, but mainly to one of them. There is always a mutation prior to the mutation that is thought to have been the first (nos. 977–78). The same can also be shown when one argues from the point of view of time. When one speaks of a "before," one presupposes time. Moreover, in order that time may be, motion is

---

88. The text of *Metaphysics* II (*a*) is close to Platonism. On this text see Vincent de Couesnongle, "La causalité du maximum: L'utilisation par Saint Thomas d'un passage d'Aristote," in *Revue des Sciences philosophiques et théologiques* 38 (1954): 433–44.

89. In *ST* I, q. 44, a. 2, Thomas lists a similar tripartition of views with this difference: Plato's and Aristotle's doctrines are placed in the second group, while some other thinkers looked further and discerned the cause of the being of things. I would suggest that when Thomas is writing for a broader public, at the Faculty of Arts in Paris, he attempts to present Aristotle's doctrine as being as close to the Christian faith as possible. A similar text in the *Quaestio disputata de potentia*, q. 3, a. 5, appears to suggest how to understand this statement: those who followed Plato and Aristotle, that is, who used the principles they formulated, acknowledged the existence of the first cause.

required (no. 979). If time exists always, motion must also be perpetual (no. 980). But time does exist always: all philosophers affirm that time has no beginning except Plato. Plato thought that time came into being together with the world, but he did hold that time cannot be without motion (no. 981).

From the existence of the *now* follows that there is a before and after, that there is time. When time is always, motion also is, because time as the number of motion is a property of motion. But Aristotle's proof is invalid, Thomas says, for a *now* can be just a beginning. Averroes, on the other hand, tries to save Aristotle's argument by arguing that a *now* is in flux, but for Thomas the flowing character of time does not make a *now* to be the case, meaning that in a continuum a point is not a flowing reality (no. 983); when Aristotle says that every *now* is both a beginning and an end, he presupposes that there is time (no. 984). By the same argument, Aristotle shows that motion will always be: there is always a change after the one we take to be the last one, that is to say: after the corruption of the mobile thing, motion will cease (no. 985).

Aristotle argues that there has always been motion but that is contrary to the Christian faith. However, when he says that motion will never totally cease, he is not in full contradiction with faith. Aristotle is speaking of motion in general, not of that of the first heaven. According to faith, the substance of the world has come into being and will never end, but Thomas prudently does not speak of the heavens—we do not know what it will be in the end—but there will always be some motions in man (no. 986). God, remaining the same and without undergoing any change, made the world by a decision of his will (no. 988). The world and time are simultaneously produced. He made things so that a likeness of his goodness would come into being. That is about all our human reason can say about the beginning of the world (no. 989). Coming back once more to Aristotle's arguments, Thomas says that we must accept a first indivisible instant in motion, before which there was no motion. Before time there is the eternity of God (no. 990). In an admirable way Thomas reproduces the arguments of Aristotle and shows what they do not prove. He formulates what follows from the dogma of creation about the beginning of the world.

Lesson 3 (VIII.1.252a4–b6) contains a refutation of the theories of Anaxagoras and Empedocles, who thought that motion has not always been. Aristotle considers this assertion a sort of fantasy (*figmentum*), put forward without any demonstration. But cannot the same be said of the doctrine of creation, namely, that it is an assertion without proof? Thomas writes that the authority of God prevails over human reason. This authority at the basis of what is revealed to us is attested by miracles, that is, by actions and works that only God can perform. The theory of Anaxagoras and Empedocles that sometimes there is motion, and sometimes not, must be rejected (no. 992). Thomas writes that these theories—an infinite time is succeeded by another infinite— do not provide an orderly organization, whereas nature always proceeds in an orderly fashion (no. 993). At the end of the lesson, Thomas reiterates what he had written in the previous lesson: although Aristotle taught the eternity of the world, he nevertheless accepted, as indicated with reference to *Metaphysics* I, that it has a cause of its being (no. 996).

In lesson 4 (VIII.2.252b7–253a21), Aristotle refutes the arguments of some other authors who said that motion began after previously not existing: no mutation is perpetual, so it would seem that there can be a time in which there is no motion; in certain mobile things, motions occur that first were not, so that the same might happen in the whole universe (no. 998); some animals that first had no motions later were moving—and if in animals, why not in the whole universe? (no. 999). Aristotle replies that there is no evident reason why a circular motion that has no contrary cannot be perpetual. If some inanimate things begin to move, there is no difficulty as long as there is an outside mover. The same applies to the third argument: there is no problem, as long as there is an outside mover. Thomas adds an important note at the end of the lesson: Aristotle refers to how the celestial bodies may act on us, not directly on our souls but on our bodies, and some of the motions in the latter may influence the intellect and the will (no. 1003).

Lesson 5 (VIII.3.253a22–254a3) presents some more arguments about the first mover and the first motion. In lessons 5–13, Aristotle shows that the first motion is eternal and that the first mover is entirely immobile; in lessons 14–21, he determines the nature of the first motion and of the first mover. As to the first part, he examines how we must explain that certain things are sometimes moving and sometimes at rest. When we have determined this, we shall have arrived at the first eternal motion and the first immobile mover (no. 1005). Aristotle excludes certain situations: not all things are always at rest, nor are all things always moved. He also excludes that all the things that are in motion are always in motion. To affirm that all things are at rest is the sign of a sick mind, and is in conflict with the sciences that affirm the thesis that there is motion. One can even say that mathematics assumes motion in an imaginary way, insofar as a point is said to make a line. Heraclitus says that all things are always moving and this view is less wrong than the view which argued that everything is always at rest (no. 1007). Aristotle says that certain motions, such as an increase or the erosion of a stone, seem to be interrupted at some moments, so that it is necessary that every motion is continuous (no. 1008). Alteration, for instance, does not need to occur in all the sections in which time is divided (no. 1010). It is unreasonable to affirm that all things are always subject to alteration. Concluding these arguments, Aristotle recalls that natural bodies are at rest when they are in their natural places (no. 1013).

In lesson 6 (VIII.3.254a3–b6), Aristotle discusses a related theory and argues against it. According to this theory, certain things would always be at rest but other things always in motion. A first observation he makes is that we do see that certain things are at rest, but that later they are moving. In the theory mentioned, violent motion—increase as well as generation and corruption— would no longer occur (no. 1015).

In lesson 7 (VIII.4.254b7–255a18), Aristotle, after having shown (Thomas says) that there is a totally immobile being while there are other things that are always moving, recalls the principle mentioned at the beginning of VII.1, namely that whatever is moving is moved by another. He then considers the animals that move themselves. After carefully distinguishing the ways in which living beings move (no. 1024), he shows that light and heavy bodies, moving to their natural places, do not move themselves: they have no control over their motions; if they would move by themselves, it would be strange if they had only one motion. Thomas notes that these arguments are probable insofar as our experience goes. So Aristotle does not say that the objection is impossible, but that it is irrational. A last argument against this opinion says that no continuum moves itself, but the heavy and light are continuous realities: if a continuum would move itself, there should be a distinction between the moving part and the one that is being moved, but in a continuous reality there is no such distinction (nos. 1026–28).

Thus, heavy and light bodies do not move themselves. Aristotle shows in lesson 8 (VIII.4.255a18–256a2) how they are moved. They can be moved with no relation to their natural potency, such as a stone that is thrown upward. But we now consider a natural potency. A light element, such as air, has a natural aptitude to be up, so that the light as such is compared to its natural place as potency to act, and its act is to be up (nos. 1030–33). So the cause of their motion is that they have a natural aptitude to be in their natural places. If they are impeded by some obstruction—a column that sustains a stone—they follow their natural inclination when the impediment disappears. Their motion is natural, but they do not move themselves. It is against Aristotle's exposé to make the nature of the elements an active principle (nos. 1034–35).

In lesson 9 (VIII.5.256a4–257a33), Aristotle now argues that there must be a first mover that must either be immobile or must move itself. The first mover can move a body through one medium, or through several media (a man moves his hand, the hand moves a stick, and the stick a stone). But he can also directly move the stone himself. We must always arrive at a first mover, not moved by another, as one cannot proceed infinitely in a series of movers. In that case, no motion would arrive at the last moving object. The first mover is either unmoved or it moves itself, as Plato supposed it does (no. 1040). From the fact that a series of movers cannot proceed infinitely, it follows that there must be a mover that is not moved by another. Aristotle refers to Anaxagoras, who was right in that he said that there is an intellect which is not subject to change and unmixed with other things (no. 1045).

In lesson 10 (VIII.5.257a33–258a5), Aristotle examines Plato's theory that the first mover (also) moves itself, but shows that even if one assumes the existence of a self-moving mover, one must finally arrive at a first mover that is unmoved. The reason is that for a mover which moves itself, one part moves another part, because it cannot move all by itself. The motion by which it moves part of itself is different from the motion of the moving part (nos. 1051–53). Aristotle excludes that the part that moves is also moved itself. The conclusion is that the mover that moves itself is composed of a part that moves and another that is moved.

In lesson 11 (VIII.5.258a5–b9), Thomas points to an ambiguity in the text. A thing that moves itself is composed of two parts, one of which moves while being immobile, while the other part is moved in such a way that it does not move anything else. This sentence could be understood in an absolute way, or it could mean that the moved part does not move something external to the mover (which, however, it could move) (no. 1062). The upshot of the argument is that the self-mover has two parts: one part is the immobile mover, a second part cannot move anything (no. 1063). These two parts must be joined by contact, because what moves and that which is moved cannot be continuous (no. 1064). The conclusion is that there is a first immobile mover. At this point, Thomas says, Aristotle still leaves open the question of whether this immobile mover also moves itself (no. 1068).

Lesson 12 (VIII.6.258b10–259a 21) begins with a summary of the conclusions reached thus far: the first mover is incorruptible and it is not moved by itself, nor by other movers. With regard to the self-movers, Aristotle has shown that one part of them must be immobile. Among the self-movers, the living beings are corruptible, so there must be an incorruptible mover, but Thomas notes that it has not yet been shown that this mover is one and incorruptible. There will always be motion, and motions are always caused by a mover. In a series of movers, one cannot proceed to infinity, so that there must be a first (no. 1069–72). The first mover, however, must be perpetually moving because it cannot do so at one time and not at the next. Even if there are many things that move themselves, there must be a mover above all that contains the others by its power and is the cause of their activities (no. 1074). The cause of the eternal generation of certain self-movers (organism and their souls) cannot be not-eternal movers, for what is not eternal cannot be the cause of what is eternal. There must be an eternal cause of the generation and corruption that are continued eternally. An effect that lasts forever can only proceed from a perpetual cause. The cause must be eternal and contain in its power whatever is generated and corrupted (no. 1074).

In lesson 13 (VIII.6.259a21–260a19), Aristotle argues that, assuming that natural things are ordered in the best way, we may conclude that one principle is better than many. It follows that there is a first mover that is one and eternal (nos. 1080–81). Thomas mentions an objection: the mover-souls of the planets move *per accidens*, as the planets to which they are attached are subject to other cosmic motions, such as the rotation of the first heaven. But Aristotle rejects this being moved *per accidens* by another and distinguishes it from being moved *per accidens* by oneself (no. 1082). Thomas observes that earlier Aristotle deduced the immobility of the first mover from the eternity of motion, but that here he proves the eternity of motion through the immobility of the first mover. Thomas solves the difficulty by saying that, in his earlier proof, Aristotle argued from motion in general and not from that of the first heaven. In passing, Thomas rejects the opinion of Averroes who wrote that already at the beginning of Book VIII Aristotle demonstrated that the first moved being (*motum*) is perpetual (no. 1083). A further proof of the perpetuity of the first motion is the perpetuity of generation and corruption. When sometimes generation and corruption happen with intervals, this cannot be the effect of the first mover, which always causes one and the same motion. Thomas concludes his observations with the remark that the arguments put forward to show that the first motion is eternal do not yield a necessary conclusion, as it is possible that the first heaven ceases to move without any change in the first mover (no. 1084). The things moved by an unmoved perpetual mover will as such be always moving (no. 1085). In an admirable way, Thomas explains the often difficult arguments of the chapter.

In lesson 14 (VIII.7.260a20–261a27), Aristotle shows what the first moved being is, and determines the nature of the first mover. The first motion[90] is necessarily perpetual, as there must always be motion. It is continuous and eternal, caused by the first mover. But no local motion can be continuous and

---

90. Apparently the first heaven is meant.

eternal except circular motion. Before any alteration takes places there is local motion; the reason is that there must be some outside cause of alterations. When this is present, alteration begins; when it goes away, alteration ceases. If there is always mutation, there is always local movement too (no. 1088). Rarefaction and a changing density also presuppose local motion. Thomas observes that rarefaction and density seem to be the concentration or dilution of matter and imply local motion, but he calls attention to the fact that the concentration of the same matter or its expansion is not a question of local movement but of alteration. Local motion is also required for increase (no. 1089). Local motion is the first of motions. It can also occur without alteration or increase. It alone can be eternal. It is also prior in time, and some local motions precede generation. It is first in perfection, as is shown by the fact that it is found in the more perfect living beings. It is the first among motions and does not affect in any way the moving thing (nos. 1090–95).

In lesson 15 (VIII.7.261a27–b26), Aristotle shows that no motion, except local motion, can be continuous and perpetual, as can be seen by an analysis of alteration. In alteration, a thing moves to a contrary and was first in what was the opposite of this contrary, and so the motion is not continuous (no. 1098). This applies also to generation and corruption: no mutation is continuous. Thomas carefully renders the objections raised and the answers given by Aristotle. Lesson 16 (VIII.8.261b27–262b8) presents Aristotle's arguments by showing that no local motion can be continuous and perpetual without the existence of an infinite magnitude, the impossibility of which was demonstrated previously. Circular motion, however, is the exception. It is also impossible to conceive an eternal rectilinear motion, which would become contrary when reaching its terminal. But in this case we no longer have a continuous motion (no. 1106), and even less so because at its turning point it would be at rest (no. 1108). This turning point would comprise two instants: one as the end, the other as the beginning, Thomas says (no. 1110).

In the first part of lesson 17 (VIII.8.262b8–264a8), some difficulties relative to reflex motions are resolved. Thomas gives a fine analysis of this difficult text passage and notes that Aristotle uses the letters "D" and "I" in a different signification from that in a previous text. Aristotle emphasizes, again, that a continuous rectilinear motion cannot be infinite if it is not reflected (no. 1114). In *Physics* VI, lesson 4 (no. 779), he had refuted a paradox of Zeno (a moving object would pass through an infinite number of points, of *nows*) but Thomas called this a refutation *ad hominem*, not an argument determining the truth. In this lesson, Aristotle puts forward a better argument (no. 1118): if a continuum is actually divided, it is no longer continuous. But if it remains a continuum, for example, as a motion or as time, it contains in potency an infinite number of intermediate points. Therefore, one can traverse the infinite (in time or magnitude) as it is in potency. Another difficulty was that in the process of a corruption the last instant a thing exists is also the first instant it no longer is. The same *now* is common to the previous and to the new substance. But in thought it is double. From the above it has become clear that time must not be divided in indivisible instants of time (no. 1122). Aristotle's concern is to show that a reflex motion is not continuous.

In lesson 18 (VIII.8.264a8–b9), we read that it can also be shown by plain arguments that a reflex motion is not continuous: this motion returns to its starting point and appears to consist of two contrary motions. The second one is first at rest (no. 1126) and activated later; the two motions are not continuous with one another. Thomas calls it a logical argument because it uses certain common principles (no. 1128).

In lesson 19 (VIII.8–9.264b9–265a27), Aristotle argues that a circular motion can be continuous, as the same order of parts is preserved in it, while in a reflex motion this order is reversed. A circular motion goes from the same point to the same, while in a reflex motion the end is not the same as the beginning. Against several of his predecessors, Aristotle concludes that no motion is continuous, except circular motion. Likewise, no mutation can be infinite and continuous (no. 1132). Circular motion is prior to, and more perfect than, straight local motion. A straight rectilinear motion cannot continue infinitely. As circular motion is more perfect, it is also prior (no. 1134).

In lesson 20 (VIII.9.265a27–266a9), Aristotle presents some other common reasons to show that a circular motion is continuous and prior: what moves in a circle is in a sense always in the point of departure and in the terminus. The center of the circle is outside the circular motion. What is moving with a circular motion is in a sense always at rest. There is no reason for intensification or relaxation and so the circular motion is more one and naturally prior (no. 1138). Aristotle also quotes several of the ancient philosophers to corroborate that local motion is the first of motions (no. 1139). There has always been and there will always be motion (no. 1140).

In lesson 21 (VIII.10.266a10–b27), one of the longest chapters of the *Physics,* Aristotle deals with the first mover, while in the previous chapters he had examined the first motion. It has already been demonstrated that this mover is immobile, but it must also be shown that it is indivisible, without magnitude, and incorporeal. To do so, Aristotle first mentions some prerequisites. To cause an infinite motion, an infinite power is required, and such an infinite power cannot be in a body of finite magnitude. Besides, this first mover must be one and move continuously and forever. A finite mover cannot move others over an infinite time (no. 1142). Avicenna had some doubts about the value of the demonstration, as it is not universal. He thinks of a celestial body from which we cannot subtract anything, meaning that we cannot divide it. But Thomas gives an explanation: the dissolution of a continuum by removing parts of it can mean that we assign a point (e.g., in thought) and so separate a part, and thus a part of the first heaven can be said to have less power to move (no. 1143). Another difficulty is the question of why a finite mover would not be able to move during an infinite time. Thomas solves it as follows: given that the proportion or ratio of the part of the mover to the moving body is the same as that of the whole mover to the whole moving body, in an equal amount of time a part of the moving body will cover part of the total distance, as the moving body covers the entire distance. So a finite moving object cannot move during an infinite time. An infinite motion is the motion of an infinitely moving body by an infinite mover (no. 1144).

In a finite magnitude, on the other hand, there cannot be an infinite power (no. 1146). At this point Thomas mentions several objections against the demonstration of Aristotle (no. 1147), which are discussed and rejected in the following part of the lesson. Thomas is quite critical in his analysis and even writes that an argument put forward by Aristotle has no value whatsoever (*nullo modo concludit*). Motion and time go together so that when there is an infinite moving power, it does not follow that the resulting motion is not taking place in time. But, he writes, we must understand the argument as a demonstration that the opposite view leads to what is impossible. The conclusion is that there is no infinite moving power that has magnitude (no. 1148). Averroes gives the following objection: a moving power that has no magnitude is neither finite nor infinite. But Thomas replies that this objection is both against what Aristotle says and against the truth: the magnitude of the first mover is the immaterial power of the form, and is not limited by matter. Averroes, Thomas continues, gave a different answer in his commentary on *Metaphysics* XI,[91] but also his second answer here is not satisfactory. Thomas states that the first mover moves by the intellect and that the effect caused is according to the thought and intention of this mover. The argument is founded upon a distinction between "acting through a material agent" and "acting through intellect." In the former case the action is proportioned to the nature of the agent, whereas in the latter case the action is proportioned to the apprehended form. For instance, a builder builds "as much as the notion of the

---

91. See Thomas's commentary on *Metaphysics* XII, lesson 7.

proof, Thomas refers to the authority of divine revelation attested by miracles (no. 991). Aristotle's arguments in support of showing that the first motion is eternal do not yield a necessary conclusion: the first heaven can stop moving without a change in the mover (no. 1084). Thomas argues against Averroes that the celestial bodies have a potency for the act of being and that God is the cause of the act of being of things. He writes that Aristotle's demonstration of the existence of the first principle by the analysis of movement is most effective. In this connection, he quotes a text from *Metaphysics* II.1.993a26, arguing that God is the cause of being and so the text becomes a stepping stone to natural theology. He notes that the arguments for the perpetuity of movement are not conclusive. At the most they show that movement did not have a natural beginning. By his intellect and will, God can produce non-eternal effects (nos. 1151–53).[93]

Concluding Remarks

Convinced that many of Aristotle's analyses express the true nature of the physical world, Thomas wrote a most impressive commentary, covering the entire text as well as every single statement of the treatise. Only on a few occasions does he refer to the *De caelo* and the *De generatione et corruptione*. Thomas extensively discusses Aristotle's doctrine of matter, form, and privation (Book I) as well as the four causes, chance, and finality (Book II). These books also contain Thomas's foundational reflections on the subject matter of natural philosophy, the division and principles of the sciences, the concept of nature, and the different kinds of causality. In particular in the books on motion (III–IV) and its parts (V–VI), Thomas often clarifies Aristotle's argument and sometimes even corrects him. Thomas regards Book VII as a stepping stone toward Book VIII, which in itself he regards as a somewhat separate treatise insofar as it leads to metaphysics.

In the school of St. Thomas, the commentary on the *Physics*, as well as the other commentaries, have been considered as being entirely faithful to the thought of Aristotle. Sylvester Maurus states that Aquinas explains the text in such a way that not someone else, but Aristotle himself seems to be doing the explaining.[94] It is indeed a cause for marvel to see how faithfully Thomas

93. For more on Thomas's critique of Averroes, see Leo Elders, "St. Thomas Aquinas's Commentary on Aristotle's *Physics*," *The Review of Metaphysics* 66 (2013): 713–48, esp. 735–41.

94. See the introduction to the first Leonine edition of the text: *Commentaria in octo libros Physicorum Aristotelis,* Léonine edition, vol. 2 (Rome: Ex Typographia Polyglotta S. C. de Propaganda Fide, 1884), vi: "Item Sylvester Maurus de commentariis D. Thomae in libros Aristotelis sequens encomium protulmit: 'op-

comments upon the text. He places Aristotle's affirmations in the context of the whole of his philosophy and tries to solve difficulties by arguing along the lines of Aristotle's own principles. His *Expositio* is complete, yet sober. The only liberty he allowed himself is a number of very short remarks to put the theory in line with a more encompassing philosophy as well as Christian faith.

Behind the text of the commentary we can find a coherent philosophy of nature, which expresses the *veritas rerum,* the philosophy to which Thomas himself fully subscribes. This philosophy is not quite identical with the text of Aristotle: the numerous occasions on which Thomas criticizes the arguments of Aristotle, as well as the large sections which he considers to be merely disputative and not strictly scientific, do not belong to this basic and underlying philosophy. Instead of writing a philosophy of nature himself, he preferred to do it this way: conforming himself to the university program where only *libri magistrales* of acknowledged authorities could be used. He made Aristotle easily readable and showed that Averroes was an unreliable, although useful, commentator and had not always caught the sense of the text. Thomas established the general conformity of the principles of Aristotle's thought with tenets of the Christian faith, except for the creation of the world at the beginning of time and divine Providence. It is a debated question whether Aquinas really thought that Aristotle taught that the world receives its being from God. Some texts of the commentary on Book VIII, as well as from the *Summa theologiae,* make us doubt it but Thomas quotes texts, especially from *Metaphysics* II, to show that the being of the cosmos does depend on God. With regard to this question, we must realize that it was Thomas's intention to defend Aristotle and to show the conformity of his philosophy with Christian doctrine. In the *Summa theologiae,* where he was writing for a limited audience of students of his own Order, he did not need to draw conclusions from principles Aristotle himself did not draw conclusions from.

As regards the question of whether Thomas subscribed to the theory of the four elements and the celestial spheres, there are few references to them in the text, except insofar as he insists on the unity of the cosmos and a primary causality from the first heaven (he does not say what this heavenly body precisely is) on the other bodies in the universe. We also see that in *Summa theologiae* I, q. 2, a. 3, he does not use Aristotle's cosmology in his demonstration of the first unmoved mover. Furthermore, in his commentary on the *De caelo,* Thomas explicitly says that although the theory of the celestial spheres seems

---

timos quoque ex interpretibus secuti (sumus), et praesertim sanetum Thomam, qui quia ingenio fuit Aristoteli simillimus, ita Aristotelem explicat, ut non alius Aristotelem, sed Aristoteles seipsum exphcare videatur' (Arist. opera. Tom. I, prooem. totius operis, n. 10.-Rom. 1668).''

to save the appearances, we must not say that it is true, because it may well be that these appearances can be explained in another way, not yet discovered by man.[95] This means that Thomas did not consider many of Aristotle's theories to be the definite truth, but a valuable attempt to explain what we observe.

Thomas's enterprise encountered several difficulties. A contemporary student of the text knows of double redactions of certain passages and may prudently resort to the hypothesis of a certain doctrinal development from Platonic theories to a more independent stand, and may qualify certain chapters as early, others as late. The lasting greatness and the unsurpassed quality of the *Expositio in libros Physicorum* lies in its unparalleled penetration of the basic principles of Aristotle's philosophy of nature. I also hope to have shown that occasionally, Aquinas delves deeper into the intelligibility of physical nature than Aristotle himself had done and provides a more coherent treatment. The numerous phrases like *sciendum est autem, advertendum, est, considerandum est*, bring forward the truth which is contained in the text in a less perfect form with the help of Aristotle's own categories of thought and philosophical principles. And the surprising capacity of Aristotle's text to lend itself to this rethinking must be attributed to the high degree of truth it possesses.

I once compared this penetrating examination and explanation of the Aristotelian text with the systematic rebuilding of a historical monument: the old bricks, slates, and beams are cleaned and used again, and a stronger, more coherent whole is produced; the windows are enlarged; there is more light in the building, which becomes more habitable, and a new clarity envelops the whole monument. In a somewhat similar way, Aristotle's *Physics*, nowadays often considered totally outdated, becomes livable for philosophers of our day. All clarifications proceed according to Aristotle's own principles, *secundum intentionem Aristotelis*. Here and there, Aquinas stresses the principles behind the text.[96] Nowhere have I seen an indication that Thomas violates the scientific objectivity of his comments because of his allegiance to the Christian faith. What he did was adapt the natural philosophy of Aristotle for use at the medieval universities. The condemnations of 1277 show how necessary and difficult an enterprise this was. However, while he subscribes to the established doctrine of Books I to VII, Thomas to a certain extent separates himself

---

95. *In II De caelo*, lesson 17, no. 451: "licet talibus suppositionibus factis apparentia salvarentur, non tamen oportet dicere has suppositiones esse vera; quia forte secundum aliquem alium modum, nondum ab hominibus apprehensum, apparentia circa stellas salvantur." See also *In I De caelo*, lesson 3, no. 28; *ST* I, q. 32, a. 1, ad 2.

96. See, e.g.: "contradictoria non praedicantur de seipsis"; "causa per se est prior causa per accidens"; "quae casualiter accidunt reducuntur in aliquam causam superiorem ordinantem ipsa"; "natura facit quod melius est secundum quod competit substantiae uniuscuiusque"; "in perpetuis non differt contingere et esse; "participatum est in participante"; "appetitus autem omnisest propter indigentiam quia est non habiti."

from many of the arguments in Book VIII. He accepts the existence of the first mover, but casts doubts on Aristotle's proof from the infinite divisibility of movement and of time, and he opens a new dimension in bringing out the dependence of the being of the world on God.

We may consider the *Expositio* a sort of reconstruction of Aristotle's physics. While he subscribes to most of Aristotle's views, Aquinas opens the text up on a panoramic view of the first cause. It is a highly ingenious attempt to evaluate and streamline the arguments of the *Physics,* explaining the connections between the books and their chapters, referring forward and backward, with an ease which makes us believe that Aquinas had the entire text stored in his memory.[97]

97. See, e.g., Book VIII, lesson 6, no. 1020: "This chapter prepares what he intends to show"; and Book IV, lesson 7, no. 488: "to understand a passage we must consider what is said in a next section."

4   THE COMMENTARY ON THE *DE CAELO*

The commentary on Aristotle's *De caelo et mundo* is one of the last writings of Thomas, which, at his death in 1274, he left unfinished. His explanations end with the exposition of III.3.302b9. During these last years of his life in Naples, Thomas composed the third part of the *Summa theologiae* as well as the commentaries on the Psalms and perhaps on some of the Pauline epistles, as well as some minor works, so that one wonders what brought him to study Aristotle's cosmology. As I have explained in the general introduction, with his Aristotelian commentaries Thomas apparently wanted to provide the elements for a true philosophy, promote the search for truth and the knowledge of the physical world, and present the tools for the analysis and better understanding of the doctrine of the faith. In his proem to Aristotle's treatise, Thomas says that after studying the whole—meaning nature in general—we must turn to the consideration of its parts, so that after investigating mobile being in general, which he has done in the *Physics*, Aristotle now considers the bodies subject to motion. In the first place, he considers the entire corporeal universe and, in the second place, the simple bodies it consists of. Of these simple bodies, first the body of the heaven, which is the basis of all other material beings, is studied in Books I and II, and next the other simple bodies (fire, air, water, and earth), which he deals with in Books III and IV of the treatise. This tells us how Thomas sees the order of Aristotle's writings on the philosophy of nature and cosmology.

Aristotle's *De caelo*

Turning now to Aristotle's treatise, a first question concerns the latter's conception of the nature and composition of the world.[1] When he wrote the

---

1. There is no need to think that the Greek title περὶ οὐρανόῦ was used by Aristotle himself but it reflects his own description of "heaven" (singular) as the subject matter. At 278b11 he distinguishes three senses of the word οὐρανός: (1) the substance of the extreme circumference of the whole "which we take to be the seat of

De caelo, Aristotle faced the cosmological theories of the first philosophers. Anaximander of Milete, the assistant of Thales, conceived the world as a sphere, while he thought that the earth was cylindrical in shape.[2] He took a special interest in the substance surrounding and containing the world, believed by many to be everlasting, infinite, and of the nature of breath.[3] The Pythagoreans ascribed orderliness and most likely a spherical form to the universe. Parmenides distinguished between different regions in the world: an outer envelope; a band of fire; a mixed band in which the stars, the sun, and the moon are set; and a band of fire at the inner side of which is the atmosphere of the earth and the earth itself.[4] Anaxagoras professed the theory of an evolving universe: its parts were separated off from an original mixture.[5]

The cosmology of the atomists is rather primitive. Democritus thought that the earth had a disc-like shape. For him, there was no basic difference between the stars and the earth. The only real beings were indivisible atoms, which move at random in an infinite space and collide to form "bodies," which later disintegrate again. He did not accept the four elements as distinguished by Empedocles, nor their natural movements. Averse to arguments based upon reasons of proportion, he adhered to immediate sense evidence in the question of the shape of the earth.[6] Plato's contemporary Archytas developed a scientific cosmology and had a profound influence on both Plato and Aristotle. The Italian Pythagoreans conceived of the universe as a perfect sphere: the celestial bodies describe circular movements governed by mathematical laws. Plato's theory differed from that of the Italian Pythagoreans insofar as he did not consider the center of the universe, occupied by fire, to be the worthiest place.[7] The Pythagoreans asserted that the whole universe must share in the rotation of the celestial sphere; hence, in their view, the celestial bodies, with the exception of the outer heaven, have at least two movements: one proper to each of them and a second derived from the rotation of the first heaven.[8]

Plato took over the main points of the Pythagorean cosmology but, con-

----

all that is divine"; (2) the body continuous with the extreme circumference and in this sense it is used in the plural; and (3) the whole world or cosmos and also in this sense the plural is used. In what follows I adhere to the singular or plural as used by Aristotle and Thomas.

2. Hippolytus, *Refutatio haeresum* I, 63, in *Hippolyte contre les hérésies*, ed. Pierre Nautin (Paris: Cerf, 1949).

3. W. K. C. Guthrie, "The Presocratic World Picture," *Harvard Theological Review* 45 (1952): 87–104.

4. Thomas Heath, *Aristarchus of Samos: The Ancient Copernicus* (Oxford: Clarendon, 1913), 67.

5. G. S. Kirk and J. E. Raven, *The Presocratic Philosophers* (Cambridge: Cambridge University Press, 1957), 390.

6. Diels-Kranz I, 68A40.

7. Heath, *Aristarchus of Samos*, 97. Hilda Richardson suggests that originally the Pythagoreans may have placed the central fire inside the earth; see "The Myth of Er (Plato, Republic, 616b)," *Classical Quarterly* 20 (1926): 119.

8. Francis Cornford, *Plato's Cosmology: The "Timaeus" of Plato* (London: Routledge and Kegan Paul, 1952), 120ff.

trary to the latter, he placed the earth at the center of the universe, probably for reasons of symmetry. The world is ensouled and well ordered, ruled as it is by mathematical laws. He stressed the distinction between the stars, more beautiful than anything else, and the central region.[9] Plato is likely to have upheld a division of the cosmos in spheres.[10] There are four elementary bodies, the shapes of which are related in some definite proportions; they are determined by certain qualities. The motion of the celestial bodies is a compound of two factors, the Same and the Different. The universe is saturated with Mind, and this mind or soul is the moving force of the celestial bodies, which consist of a material much superior to that the four elements.[11] By reason of the Mind being present in them, the heavenly bodies are divine beings.[12] But Plato did not resolve the question of how a soul moves the stars. Although he held that the celestial bodies describe circular orbits, he did not admit that there are revolving spherical, material rings to which the planets would be attached. The planets, permeated as they are with mind, have a voluntary, unenforced movement. The stars of the first heaven also move with a voluntary motion, but keep their relative positions.

Eudoxus, a member of Plato's Academy, had a considerable influence on Aristotle's cosmology. Perhaps encouraged by Plato, this great mathematician developed a system by which he thought he could explain the seemingly irregular wanderings of the planets. To this effect, he resorted to the device of assuming a number of revolving spheres with a common center. The poles of one sphere are fixed at the enveloping greater sphere and move with it. The planets are assumed to be located in these spheres. If the number of revolving spheres was sufficiently great, one could explain any observed movement of these celestial bodies.[13] Eudoxus never considered these spheres to be physical substances.[14] In order to explain the cause of their eternal movement, he may have placed (the Platonic) Ideas in the stars.[15]

Heraclides of Pontus, who lived from 387 to 315 B.C., was well known for his cosmological theories. According to him, the universe is infinite and divine.[16] Each star is a world by itself, comprising an earth, an atmosphere, and an

9. *Republic* 529c–530; see James Adam, *The Republic of Plato* (Cambridge: Cambridge University Press, 1938), 2:128–31.

10. Cornford, *Plato's Cosmology*, 246.

11. *Phaedrus* 246a–b.

12. *Timaeus* 34b–c.

13. See Simplicius, *In De caelo* 448–506.

14. *Metaphysics* 991a9 and 1079b21.

15. In a context where he speaks about Eudoxus, Aristotle denies that the Ideas could contribute anything to the movement of the stars: *Metaphysics* 991a9 and 1079b12ff.

16. *Doxographi Graeci* 343a7–13 and fragment 111 in Fritz Wehrli, *Die Schule des Aristoteles. Volume VII: Herakleides Pontikos* (Basel: Schwabe Verlag, 1953).

ether.[17] The lower planets, Mercury and Venus, circle around the sun, not around the earth. The sun would rest in the center of the universe, and the earth would circulate around it, an explanation mentioned twice by Thomas. Calippus, perhaps the most capable astronomer of his time, corrected with Aristotle the astronomical system of Eudoxus.[18] He added a number of spheres to those already assigned to Mars, the sun, and the moon, and succeeded in giving a better account of the complicated movements of these celestial bodies.

Aristotle's Cosmological System

Aristotle's theory of the universe does not appear to have been conceived at once, because in the *De caelo* we find cosmological theories that seem at variance with each other. In II.3, he follows Plato's theory of two revolutions (that of the Same and that of the Different), but elsewhere he holds to his own theory of homocentric spheres. But rather than assigning a role to souls, he stresses the dependence of material beings on mathematical entities. We read in *De caelo* II.1 that a soul could not possibly live under those conditions that prevail in the primary body: it would be devoid of all rational satisfaction. Apart from the theory of natural places and natural movements of the primary bodies, one of Aristotle's most important contributions to cosmology was that he assigned physical reality to the homocentric spheres of Eudoxus. The reason behind this innovation apparently was that from the point of view of physics, isolated and scattered planets moving through a void (or a thin substance) do not make much sense (see II.8). But if the cosmos is conceived as a compact mass, consisting of revolving spheres, reacting spheres are necessary to allow the planets, the sun, and the moon to execute their own movements, while undergoing the influence of the revolution of the first heaven. In this way, substance and place regain their importance in Aristotle's cosmology.

In the universe, the circumference and the center are the two most important places. According to Aristotle, the being of the world depends on them, for both determine the elementary body that belongs to them. Thus, the earth has its natural place at the center and is closest to potency, while fire belongs to the region near the limit of the world. The earth is at rest at the center and is spherical in shape, because of the fact that every portion of it seeks the center. Stars and planets do not rotate or spin, but are carried by their own

17. *Doxographi Graeci* 343a7–13.
18. Simplicius, *In De caelo* 493.5–8.

sphere. Aristotle does not give an estimate of the size of the universe, but suggests that the perimeter of the earth is 9,987 geographical miles.

Elements, Natural Movements, Places, the Fifth Body, and the Moving Force

The subject matter of the *De caelo* is the universe and its main parts insofar as they are moving locally. Aristotle does not always clearly separate mathematics and physics. In I.1, he argues along the lines of mathematical considerations and passes from mathematical facts to conclusions about physical bodies. This fading of the frontiers between physics and mathematics may well be of Platonic origin. Aristotle analyzes the movements and nature of the four elements and introduces a fifth elementary body. The theory of four distinct elements, first posited by Empedocles, was taken over by Plato, who made geometrical shapes their real form and also intimated that there is another element.[19] Yet Aristotle is the first philosopher who introduced the notion of "ether" as a fifth element.[20] Mathematical considerations also led to this theory: a body that moves by circular movement must be different from those that move by rectilinear movements.

Religious thinking may also have had some influence on the formulation of the doctrine of the ether.[21] The criticism that philosophers and playwrights alike directed against the traditional gods, as well as the increasing instability of the social and political world, were instrumental in promoting what is called cosmic religion. Aristotle's entire thought is the opposite of materialism and atheism. To him the order of nature is the work of "mind." That is to say: formal and final causality reign everywhere. All things must have a rational explanation for mind saturates everything. His conviction of the predominance of mind is shown by the frequent use of the words "nature and god provide." These words indicate the source of order and probably the mind that rules the world. One can find some confirmation in I.9.279a17–21: "It is clear that there is neither place, nor void, nor time outside the heaven. [...] Hence the things there [τἀκεῖ] are of such a nature as not to occupy any place nor does time age them [...]." Ross suggests identifying the first mover with τἀκεῖ, others think that the Ideas or mathematical entities are meant, or rather ontological prin-

---

19. *Timaeus* 55c. On intimations of the fifth element see W. K. C. Guthrie, *History of Greek Philosophy*, rev. ed. (Cambridge: Cambridge University Press, 1979), 1:272.

20. Cicero, *Tusculanae Disputationes* I, 26, 65 ("ab Aristotele inducta primum").

21. See his *De Philosophia*, fr. 12 (Ross): "When people suddenly freed from their prison, saw the earth, sea and sky . . . and the sun, the stars and their courses settled to all eternity, they would have judged, both that there are gods and that these great beings are the works of gods."

ciples, separately existing.[22] The last section of Book I (I.9.279a20–22) speaks of things beyond the heaven which "continue throughout their entire duration unalterable and unmodified, living the best and most self-sufficient of lives." In addition, II.12.292b18–22 supposes that there are ensouled celestial bodies which imitate the first mover.[23]

The Structure of the Treatise

The *De caelo* can be divided into three main parts: the first two books deal with the primary body and the relation of the elementary bodies to the whole; the third book gives a general theory of the other simple bodies; and the fourth book is a treatise on weight and lightness considered as the causes of the movements up and down. It is not evident who brought these books together so as to form a single treatise.[24] Alexander thought that Aristotle's purpose in writing the *De caelo* was to study the universe and that the five elements fall naturally within the subject matter of such a study.[25] But Iamblichus felt that the principal object of the treatise is the heaven and that the study of the other elements is only justified insofar as they depend on the heaven. The treatise gives the impression of some loosely connected πραγματεῖαι. In Book I and the first six chapters of Book II, the existence of the primary body is proved and its essential attributes, with an emphasis on motion, are explained (I.2–3). Next, its size is considered (I.5–9), as well as its incorruptibility (I.10–12). Its movement is dealt with in II.1–6. In the remaining chapters of Book II, the nature and the essential movements of the stars as well as their arrangement and shape are studied. Book III treats of the four elementary bodies, their number and movements. Book IV and the *De generatione et corruptione* complete this treatment.[26] Several authors consider Books III and IV to be written earlier than Books I and II, although their arguments are not quite convincing.[27]

---

22. See Leo Elders, *Aristotle's Cosmology: A Commentary on the "De Caelo"* (Assen: Van Gorcum, 1966): 144–45. For a recent survey of the various positions see F. Baghdassarian, "Aristote, De Caelo, I 9: L'identité des 'etres de là-bas,'" *Philosophie antique* 11 (2011): 175–203. She argues that these beings are to be located beyond the highest heavenly sphere although Aristotle remains unclear whether they are to be associated with the prime mover.

23. Ingemar Düring speaks of "transcendent entities." See I. Düring, "Aristotle on Ultimate Principles from 'Nature and Reality': Protrepticus fr. 13," in *Aristotle and Plato in the Mid-Fourth Century*, ed. I. Düring and G. E. L. Owen (Gothenburg: Almquist and Wiksell, 1960), 48.

24. See Paul Moraux, "Recherches sur le 'De caelo' d'Aristote," *Revue Thomiste* 51 (1951): 113–36.

25. Simplicius, *In De caelo* 1.1–2; 10ff.

26. Moraux, "Recherches sur le 'De caelo' d'Aristote."

27. See Friedrich Solmsen, *Aristotle's System of the Physical World* (Ithaca, N.Y.: Cornell University Press, 1960), 293ff.; G. A. Seeck, Über *die Elemente in der Kosmologie des Aristoteles,* Zetemata 34 (Münich: Beck, 1964), 93. Seeck points out that in the first book the primary body is the central theme, while in Books III and IV it is not considered.

The Reception of the Treatise

Aristotle's text received little attention from the Greek commentators. We know of a lost commentary by Themistius. Simplicius's commentary is the only surviving commentary in ancient Greek on Aristotle's *De caelo*. William of Moerbeke's translation of Simplicius's commentary, completed at Viterbo on June 15, 1271, will provide Thomas with one of his basic sources.[28] The ninth-century Arab philosopher Al-Kindi, heavily inspired by Aristotle, wrote several treatises in which he gave his explanation of the system of the world and maintained that the sphere of the first heaven differs from the four elements.[29] Avicenna, whose conception of the world was strongly influenced by the Neo-Platonist doctrine of emanation from a first principle, asserted that a first intelligence emanates from God, and from it the soul and the matter of the first heaven. The intelligences of the different cosmic spheres are active, but there is no question of the celestial spheres having a natural movement by themselves.[30]

Next to Simplicius, however, it was Averroes's long commentary on the *De Caelo*, translated from Arabic into Latin by Michael Scotus around 1220, which became an important source for Thomas.[31] It was the intention of Averroes to stay close to the text and thought of Aristotle himself and to reject Neo-Platonist explanations. Thomas carefully considers the commentary, explains the arguments of Aristotle as Averroes read them, but frequently advances other explanations. The Latin translation of Aristotle's treatise used by Thomas is the translation from the Greek by William of Moerbeke, the *translatio nova*, of which the first recension was made around 1260. While in his commentary on the *Metaphysics* Thomas disposed of at least four translations, in his exposition of the *De caelo* he refers only once to another translation, probably the *translatio vetus* from the Arabic by Gerard of Cremona, which originates from before 1187.[32] This was the version commonly used before the Moerbeke translation, as exemplified by Albert's commentary on the *De Caelo*.[33]

---

28. Simplicius, *Commentaire sur le traité du ciel d'Aristote. Traduction de Guillaume de Moerbeke*, ed. F. Bossier, C. Vande Veire, and G. Guldentops (Turnhout: Brepols, 2004). An English translation from the original Greek has been published in the series Ancient Commentators on Aristotle.

29. See Abdel-Rahman Badawi, *Histoire de la philosophie en Islam* (Paris: Vrin, 1972), 2:418–27; Peter Adamson, "Al-Kindi and the Reception of Greek Philosophy," in *The Cambridge Companion to Arabic Philosophy* (ed. Adamson and Taylor), 2–51.

30. See Cristina Cerami, "The De Caelo et Mundo of Avicenna's 'Šifā': An Overview of Its Goal, Its Structure and Its Polemical Background," *Documenti e Studi sulla Tradizione Filosofica Medievale* 28 (2017): 273–329.

31. See *Averrois Cordubensis commentum magnum super libro De Celo et mundo Aristotelis*, ed. R. Arnzen (Leuven: Peeters, 2003).

32. *In I De caelo*, lesson 24, 4: "Et hoc est quod dicitur in alia translatione."

33. See the critical edition *De caelo et mundo*, ed. Paulus Hossfeld (Münster: Aschendorff, 1971).

Partly because of the Parisian condemnations of 1277 a vast number of commentaries were produced in the century after Aquinas, the most popular form of which was the *Quaestiones*, written questions on Aristotle's books on natural philosophy.[34] Peter of Auvergne, who wrote an exposition of Books III and IV (of the *De caelo*) as a continuation of Thomas's unfinished commentary, also wrote three sets of *Quaestiones* of his own, both before and after the condemnations of 1277. The differences in the way Peter treats the condemned opinions regarding the eternity of the world and the animation of the heavens in these different sets of questions make him "an interesting witness of the way in which the Masters of Arts of Paris changed their teachings" as a result of the condemnations of 1277.[35]

The Commentary of Thomas Aquinas

In the following pages, I attempt to give a summary of how Thomas read the treatise, explain the contents of the different chapters, and elucidate how he placed it in the whole of Aristotle's philosophy.[36]

Book I

In his proem, Thomas notes that there are different ways to study the physical nature of beings and divergent views of the order to be observed in this discipline. In the *Physics*, the mobile bodies, insofar as they are mobile, are the subject matter. When we begin to examine its details, the first body to be considered is the universe in its entirety, before we turn to the study of its parts. After that, the simple bodies are studied, before we turn to those that are composed. Thomas mentions that there are different views as regards the proper subject of the book: according to Alexander, it is the world;

---

34. See Fernand Bossier, "Traductions latines et influences du commentaire In de caelo en occident (XIIIe–XIVe s.)," in *Simplicius, sa vie, son oeuvre, sa survie: actes du Colloque International de Paris (26 Sept.–1er Oct. 1985)*, ed. Ilsetraut Hadot (Berlin: De Gruyter, 1987), 288–325.

35. Griet Galle, "The Relation Between the Condemnations of 1277 and Peter of Auvergne's Questions on *De caelo*," *Ephemerides Theologicae Lovanienses* 91 (2015): 223–38. See also her edition of one of these sets: *Peter of Auvergne Questions on Aristotle's "De caelo": A Critical Edition with an Interpretative Essay* (Leuven: Leuven University Press, 2003).

36. The following English translation has been consulted: Fabian Larcher and Pierre H. Conway, trans. *Exposition of Aristotle's Treatise "On the Heavens,"* 2 vols. (Columbus, Ohio: College of St. Mary of the Springs, 1964), as well as Leo Elders, *Aristotle's Cosmology: A Commentary on the "De Caelo"* (Assen: Van Gorcum, 1966). In the introduction of my commentary, the following themes are discussed successively: the image of the world, the heritage of the past, the elementary bodies, the *De caelo* and the religion of its day, science and scientific method in the *De caelo*, the structure, text, and time of composition of the treatise, as well as its importance. For recent studies of selected passages of the *De caelo* see *New Perspectives on Aristotle's "De caelo,"* ed. A. Bowen and C. Wildberg (Leiden: Brill, 2009).

others think that the main subject is the body of the first heaven, which moves in a circle, and that other bodies are considered insofar as they are contained by the first and undergo its influence. Simplicius's opinion is that Aristotle studies the simple bodies insofar as they are simple; as the first heaven is the most important of them, it gave its name to the book; if the subject matter were the universe, he would have also treated plants and animals. Thomas prefers the view of Alexander: Aristotle studies the universe, called the heaven, and the simple bodies as parts of it, which are all characterized by local movements (no. 5).[37]

All physical bodies move with local movements (lessons 1–3; I.1–2.268a1–269a2), and natural bodies have a natural local movement. But is their motion not caused by an intellect, as Aristotle says in *Physics* VIII and *Metaphysics* XII? Thomas answers by distinguishing a twofold principle of movement, namely an acting principle—the mover—and a passive one, being the nature of these bodies (no. 22). From the fact that there are two magnitudes, rectilinear and circular, it follows that there will be two basic movements. Mathematics, however, is a different genus of science than physics. Do we have the right to conclude from figures to physical motions? Thomas explains that a science that is based on another science (e.g., geometry on arithmetic), uses the principles of the first. As a perceptible body adds perceptible matter to geometrical figures, it uses the principles of geometry (nos. 23–24).

In lesson 4 (I.2.269a2–b17), we read that besides the four elements there must be another simple body with a simple movement. This follows from the consideration of mathematical bodies and the fact that simple bodies must correspond to reason. Circular motion and rectilinear motion are of a different nature: the first is complete with regard to the moving body, whereas the rectilinear motion upward or downward is that of a body that has not yet found its completion proper to its species. Because motion is proportionate to a mobile body as its act, circular motion is due to a body that exists outside the realm of generation and corruption and that cannot be removed from its place (no. 37). The body that is carried around the circumference of the world with a circular movement cannot be the element "fire," because the natural movement of fire is upward, so that this body of the heavenly sphere is not one of the elements. Thomas observes that this conclusion seems to contradict a theory of Plato, who said that the body carried around in circular movement consists of fire, but he suggests that Plato only wanted to say that it looks like

---

37. The main positions of Alexander on the *De caelo* were known to Aquinas by way of Simplicius's commentary. Simplicius himself thinks that the heaven is the main theme of the book. If the theme was the whole world, animals and plants should also have been treated.

fire because it radiates light (no. 38). In the following section, Thomas solves an apparent contradiction of the text with *Meteorologica* I, where Aristotle says that fire and the higher air are carried with a circular motion. Thomas notes that this circular movement is not natural but superimposed; we find similar superimposed motions in the water of the oceans, namely, the tides (no. 39).

When the perfection of the body moving with a natural circular motion is affirmed, the reader notices the importance and prevalence of mathematical considerations, such as the value attached to the circle. In lesson 4, as well in lesson 5, Thomas proceeds, as he does in a "disputed question," by advancing objections and answering them, and we admire the way in which he analyzes the arguments of the text. Plato said that because of the special form of the world, up and down are only descriptions from our point of view, but do not apply to the body of the world. Aristotle, however, argues that up and down are given with the place of the light and the heavy bodies, which occupy the main parts of the world (no. 53). The body that performs a circular movement is neither heavy nor light, for it does not move toward the middle of the universe, nor does it go upward (nos. 55–58).

Lesson 6 (I.3.270a12–22) notes that the fifth body is ingenerate and incorruptible. Thomas says that when Plato calls the heaven generated—what Aristotle appears to deny here—he does not mean that it is a product of a process of generation, but that it has a higher cause of being (no. 61). When the power of the heaven is called finite by Aristotle, he means, Averroes says, that the power causing its movement is not the power of its being, which is neither finite nor infinite. But this position of Averroes, Thomas notes, is clearly against Aristotle, who attributes to eternal things the power to be always (see lesson 26). The power to be belongs to the form, so that not only the celestial bodies but also the separate substances have the power to exist always, although their being is finite (no. 62). The matter of the celestial bodies is not in potency to other forms because their form fills its entire capacity (no. 63). Thomas adds a note: according to the Catholic faith, we do not say that the heaven has always existed, although it will exist forever. Nevertheless, there is no conflict with the doctrine of Aristotle: we do not say that it came into being through generation, but that it came forth from the first principle, which causes the being of all things. Some philosophers defend the same view (the Neo-Platonists?), although we, Christians, say that it was produced at the beginning of time (no. 64).

Simplicius objected to the Christian doctrine of creation by arguing that God produces the world according to his being, that is, as immutable and existing always. Moreover, it would not have been in conformity with God's goodness if the world he made would not exist always (no. 65). Thomas says that these arguments are not necessarily conclusive and he presents an admirable refutation: God's being does not differ from his thought and will, and so it is not necessary that the world be coeternal with God: when something is produced by the intellect (and not by an emanation from the being of its cause), it is produced the way it is conceived and thought. And so it is not necessary that the world be coeternal with God. Thomas quotes 270a20: "nature rightly kept the heaven free from the class of opposites [ὀρθῶς ἔοικεν ἡ φύσις τὸ μέλλον ἔσεσθαι . . . ἐξελέσθαι ἐκ τῶν ἐναντίων] so that it would be ingenerate and incorruptible." Another difficulty raised is that God's goodness would not have had an object when at first there were no creatures, but Thomas replies that God's goodness is not for the sake of the creatures. Another difficulty says that one would expect that what is made by God corresponds to the maker and to the time in which he works. The implication is that the world accompanies God's eternity. Thomas answers that God made time simultaneously with the things existing in it. So we should not ask "why not earlier?," as there was no time prior to the existence of the world. But we can raise the question as to why God has not wanted time and the world to exist always. Thomas answers that this depends on God's decision (no. 67).

Philoponus raised another objection to what Aristotle says, namely that all becoming is out of contraries and that because figures and relations have no contraries they cannot be involved in generation. Simplicius answered that we must understand "contrary" in a broad sense, for instance, as the "opposition" between different species. And Thomas corrects this answer: one can say that there was an opposition to the *dispositions* that accompanied the previous substance (no. 67). Moreover, it does not necessarily follow that a figure like a circle has no contrary: fire in the higher regions has a circular motion, although it is generally characterized by a movement upward (no. 69). Thomas also answers the objection that the contrariety of movements does not necessarily imply the contrariety of mobile bodies, namely by saying that Aristotle argues the other way around: if motions are not contrary, mobile bodies are neither (no. 70).

The fifth body is not subject to increase or decrease (lesson 7; I.3.270a22–b25). If it were, it would somehow be subject to generation and corruption: wherever there is increase, there must be some generation and corruption, for instance of parts of the body and of the food that is consumed (no. 71). Likewise, it is not subject to alteration because increase always involves some alteration (no. 72). But besides the alteration of warm and cold there is a perfective alteration, for example, in the sense powers. This form of alteration might be present in the power of the celestial bodies (no. 73). In this context, Aristotle uses the term "increase" for all movements to a larger quantity. With regard to this discussion about increase, Thomas also notes that it is Aristotle's custom to use and mention the opinions of other authors before presenting the true solution. Here he speaks of physical bodies only, because in mathematical bodies increase is possible without alteration (no. 74). The exceptional place of the fifth body is confirmed by the fact that most people accept many divine beings, or one supreme god to whom the other separate substances are subservient; all assign the highest place to this god or these gods. A further application of this conception is that God is thought to be dwelling in the heaven (no. 75). The perpetuity of the first heaven is confirmed by the fact that during a long period of observation, no change has ever been noticed. But Thomas says that this argument is not decisive: the more lasting a thing is, the more time is needed for changes to become manifest (no. 76). The ancients thought that the heaven is of a different nature, so it was called ether.

In lesson 8 (I.3–4.270b26–271a35), Thomas discusses Aristotle's argument that there are no more simple movements than those mentioned (namely two rectilinear movements, one upward and one downward, and a circular movement) and that a simple body must have one simple movement, and that there are no more than five simple bodies (no. 78). A circular movement has no contrary, as is shown successively in the following sections of the text. Rectilinear motions are not contrary to a circular motion, except insofar as one considers them as different in species (no. 82). Nor is there contrariety between the parts of a circular motion. A long discussion follows about the question of contrariety in the different movements of the celestial bodies, namely that the planets move in circles contrary to the circular motion of the first heaven. Thomas defends Aristotle's theory against the criticism of Philoponus: the planets move from west to east, and the first heaven moves from east to west. Thomas concludes: movements that go to the same terminal, while following different trajectories, are not contrary, as is the case with the motions of the planets. The trajectory of the first heaven is nobler (nos. 83–93).

The question of whether the world is infinite is studied in lessons 9–15 (I.5–7.271b1–276a18). Those who assumed the existence of the infinite thought that the bodies of the beings in the world are formed through separation from the infinite (no. 96). Aristotle advances several arguments against this conception: an infinite body cannot have a circular movement, for the straight lines radiating from the center (of its supposedly circular path) will be infinite, as will be the intervening space, but the infinite cannot be traversed. What moves in a circle is not infinite. An infinite distance cannot be traversed in a finite time (nos. 98–100). In lesson 11 (272b17–273a6), three more reasons are given for why a body with a circular movement cannot be infinite, such as the following: when the time during which the heaven describes its circular course is finite, this implies that the circle itself is finite (no. 109). In lesson 12 (273a7–274a18), Aristotle argues that there is no infinite body that would move along a straight line to the center or away from it. Also, in this section, there is a mathematical approach to the argument: the center of the world is fixed but an infinite motion never ends. The heavy and light bodies move with natural movements, which would be in vain if they went on eternally. Thomas patiently explains these arguments without further comments. In lesson 13 (I.6–7.274a19–b32), Aristotle argues that natural bodies cannot be infinite because of their local movement: the center of the world is determined, as is the upper limit. No perceptible body can be infinite, regardless of it being heterogeneous or homogenous (lesson 14; I.7.274b33–275b11), and there is no body outside the first heaven (no. 144). In lesson 15 (I.7.275b12–276a17), Aristotle shows with logical arguments that not one body is infinite.

There is only one world (lesson 16; I.8.276a18–b25). If there were another world, there would be some movement in it, and all the bodies of such a world would move toward the center or the circumference of our world (no. 161). In lesson 17 (I.8.276b26–277a3), we find another proof that the world is one based on the behavior of the bodies of lower rank, which all move with their natural movements to determinate places. Elements in another world would move to the center or the circumference (of our world), which would be their natural place (no. 168). This shows the unity of the world. Aristotle stresses that, contrary to what Democritus said of the random motion of the atoms, natural movements are not by chance and not without their proper logic; they do not move to what is indeterminate (no. 171). But does circular motion have an opposite terminus? The answer is "yes," if we consider the parts of the revolving body (no. 172). The closer that moving natural bodies come to their destination, the faster they move (no. 173).

The natural bodies are not moved by outside movers (lesson 18; I.8.277a33–b26). This appears from the fact that a larger piece of earth moves faster to the center than a smaller one; if their movements were caused by an outside mover, this would be different. A second argument reads: we see that these bodies (when pushed) move slower when farther away from their starting point, while with natural movements the opposite happens (no. 177). The circular motion of the heaven is eternal, and so the power that moves it must be infinite and not quantitatively determined (see *Physics* VIII.8). This power is immaterial and, consequently, one. Here Thomas formulates an objection:

in *Metaphysics* XII.7, Aristotle writes that the first mover moves as desired. But there is no reason why it could not be desired by several worlds. Thomas answers that several beings can desire a first mover in a certain order and that their coordination would establish the unity of the world (no. 180).

Another argument in favor of the oneness of the world is the following. There are the elements of heaven and earth, and the elementary bodies between them. The place at the center is that of the earth, the circumference is occupied by the heaven, which, Thomas says, Aristotle treats here as an element, as one of the parts of the whole universe (nos. 180–81). Now, each body must be in a place so that a heavy or light body must have its place between heaven and earth. For another world to exist the impossible would have to be true, that is, a light body existing above the heaven (no. 182). In lesson 19 (I.9.277b27–278b8), we read that there cannot be several worlds. The heaven must be a singular reality, as it is sensible and all perceptible things have their being in matter (no. 188). Although forms imprinted in matter can be more than one individual (e.g., the animals of a species), things which are identical with their forms, such as the separate substances, can only be one in a species (nos. 189–90), whereas things of which the essence is in matter, individualized by quantity (*materia signata quantitate*), can be indefinitely numerous within one species (no. 191). But if all matter is taken and engaged by a form, there will only be one being, something which is the case with the heaven (nos. 195–96). In an objection, proceeding from a Christian background and mentioned by Thomas, we read that God's power is infinite and not limited to this world; God might well have created other worlds.[38] Answering this objection Thomas says that if these other heavens were the same, their number would be quite useless and not in conformity with God's wisdom. If they were all different, none of them would have a full perfection but together they would make a perfect world. However, it is a sign of greater power to make one thing, which is perfect, than many which are imperfect (no. 197).

The world consists of the totality of natural bodies, which are its matter (lesson 20; I.9.278b8–279a11). The different meanings of the word "heaven" are listed as follows: (1) the substance that is the most outer and last sphere of the world or, in other words, the natural body that has its place at the circumference of the universe, and which is most high and the place of all divine things; (2) the bodies that are contained by the extreme circumference of the world; and (3) the entire body contained by the highest cosmic sphere (no. 199). These descriptions show that the first and main sense of the term is that

---

38. In traditional Greek atomism, the worlds were believed to be infinite in number. The theory is a deduction from the infinity of the universe. See Epicurus's *Letter to Herodotus* 45.

of the highest cosmic sphere. Outside the heaven there is not any other body (nos. 200–201). Our world contains all matter (nos. 204–5).

Lesson 21 (I.9.279a11–b3) continues on this point. If it is true that outside the heaven there is no simple body, this applies also to composite bodies, nor is there anything of what results from perceptible bodies or accompanies them, such as place or the void (which the Stoics placed in the outer world) (nos. 209–10). As there is not a body outside the heaven, there is no matter, no time, no motion (no. 211), and no aging. Thomas writes that this is best understood with regard to God and the separate substances (no. 213), who are far away from any magnitude and motion; they are unchangeable, impassible, totally self-sufficient (no. 214), and eternal. God exists all at once (*totum simul existens*) (no. 215). From what is most perfect proceeds what is less so (no. 216). In the writings of the ancients the divine is said to be immutable, first, and higher than all other things, and able to escape from all evil (no. 219). Thomas notes that it is not necessary that the motion of the first heaven last forever: the will of the mover can bring it to a halt (no. 220).

In lesson 22 (I.10.279b4–31), the question is examined whether the world has come into being or is eternal. After a first section, in which different views on the issue are examined, the opinions of previous philosophers are mentioned. All philosophers before Aristotle said that the world came into being (*quod mundus sit generatus*), but in different ways: (1) the world began to exist, but will last forever (Plato); (2) the world is the result of a concourse of atoms and is corruptible, as is everything else (Democritus); (3) the world is alternatively generated and perishing (Heraclitus, Empedocles) (nos. 226–27). Some authors say that Plato's actual view was different and hidden under the images he used and that Aristotle did not object to this more profound understanding of what Plato wanted to say. But according to Alexander, the poetical terms of Plato's text did express his real view, so that Aristotle criticized not only the words, but also the way they were understood. At this point Thomas makes a renowned observation: "The study of philosophy has not as its aim to know what people thought, but how reality is in truth [*veritas rerum*]" (no. 228). Because we see that whatever is generated is also corruptible, it follows that the world, which is incorruptible according to Aristotle's theory, cannot be generated. A second conclusion says: if the world had been made of components different from what it is made of now, it would not always remain the same (no. 229).

In lesson 23 (I.10.279b32–280a34), some theories of the Platonists, in particular of Xenocrates, are rejected. Some of these philosophers said that the world was incorruptible, but that it nevertheless was made: God put the elements together and reduced a disorderly collection of things to order (no. 232). Some go so far as to assert that the initial disorder has always continued. Even Aristotle teaches that matter is always accompanied by privation. Others say that the elements as such would be defective if God had not put them into their present order (no. 233). According to Empedocles, the world is eternal insofar as its substance is concerned. This implies that only its dispositions would be changing (no. 234). Finally, the opinion of Democritus is mentioned and refuted (no. 235).

Lesson 24 (I.11.280b1–281a1) lists the different ways in which certain things are said to be generable and ingenerate, corruptible and incorruptible, and explains the meaning of the terms. Lesson 25 (I.11.281a1–27) examines the different meanings of "possible" and "impossible" from the point of view of the agent. In lesson 26 (I.12.281a28–282a4), the question is considered whether something could have been generated and yet be incorruptible. Incorruptible and ingenerate are coincident. What exists during an infinite time cannot be corruptible, for it has the potency to be always and this implies necessity—what exists during an infinite time must be ingenerate. In lesson 27 (I.12.282a4–b1), we read that nothing that is eternal is generated; if something is ingenerate, it must be eternal. Whatever is ingenerate and incorruptible is eternal. In lesson 28 (I.12.282b1–283a4), Aristotle shows that generated and corruptible go together. In lesson 29 (I.12.283a4–b22), he raises the question whether anything that is ingenerate can be corruptible, and vice versa, as some say. By natural reason it can be shown that it is metaphysically impossible that a thing that has always been will later be corrupted, or that a thing which first was not will always exist (no. 278). The argument is that all corruptible or generated things are alterable. But alteration is from contrary to contrary, so that things that began to exist will later pass away (no. 286).

At this point (no. 287), Thomas refers to the Christian doctrine of creation: things came into existence not by generation, but by proceeding from the first principle, God, who made them exist when he wanted, after they had not been before. But things were made by God to be forever and have the potency to be forever once they exist. They have no potency for not to be.

Book II

In lesson 1 (II.1.283b26–284b5), we read that the heaven is eternal and that its circular movement, which has neither beginning nor end, is the final cause of all other movements. Thomas sees the contents of this second book as a more detailed study of what Book I said about the part of the world that moves with a circular motion, the body that performs this motion, and the center about which it moves. Aristotle says that the world did not have a beginning. Thomas explains these words as meaning that the world did not begin to exist in the way some authors said it did (no. 289).

Aristotle notes that the ancients taught the same, so that we should be willing to accept their words, that there is something divine and immortal, which applies also to the celestial bodies which they venerated (no. 290). A circular movement is perfect because it contains the other movements. Thomas adds again a reference to God's power: God is the cause of the being of things, but he is thus also by using the corruption of certain things for the generation of other beings (no. 291). The heaven is eternal as the ancient philosophers said; it has no contrary and its movement is effortless (nos. 292–94). According to Plato, its movement is caused by a soul, but that is not reasonable, for the life of such a soul would be drudgery (nos. 297–98).

Lesson 2 (II.2.284b6–285a27) deals with the different parts of the world, especially with the question whether, by analogy with the human body, we can assign a left and right, above and below, and front and back to the sphere of the heaven. The Pythagoreans spoke only of right and left, but did not mention the other dimensional differences in connection with the heavenly bodies, as these differences are only visible in living bodies (no. 305). In inanimate things we do not see a principle from where motion begins, but in analogy with living beings we speak of right and left (no. 306). It was a mistake of the Pythagoreans to leave out the other four dimensional features. Thomas explains this omission as having been influenced by the table of ten contraries in which these four do not figure (nos. 311–12). Yet they are important, as we see in animals where the above (*sursum*) is more perfect and has a leading function, as motion starts from the head of animals, while local movement goes from right to left.

How do the parts of the heaven correspond to these four dimensional differences (lesson 3; II.2.285a7–286a2)? The heaven is ensouled (*Physics* VIII.5), but not in the sense, Thomas says, that it has a rational soul. Rather, it has a formal principle of life adapted to its body. The soul in the celestial bodies, according to some, would be nothing else but the nature of these bodies. But, Thomas says, this is wrong, as Aristotle writes in *Physics* VIII that these souls move by desiring the first mover (no. 314). It seems better to hold that the substance that moves the heaven is a being separate from matter (no. 315).[39] Does the fact that the heavenly body has the shape of a sphere not render superfluous such qualifications as left and right, up and below? The answer is that in

---

39. Thomas means God, the first mover.

the heavenly body they have different functions (no. 318). Aristotle indicates where the up and below, and the right and left, are in the heavenly body (nos. 321–23). Right is from where the motion of the heaven starts, namely, from the east (no. 324).

In lesson 4 (II.3.286a3–b9), the question is examined why the planets, the sun, and the moon have circular motions that differ in direction from the movement of the first heaven. We do not know much about the accidental characteristics of the celestial bodies, so it is difficult to make judgments about them. An *a priori* argument says that if the heaven is a divine body, its motion must be eternal and circular. But then the earth must also be eternal (as the center of the world), and also fire, and some intermediate bodies subject to generation and corruption. And if so, there must be several (types of) motions (no. 333). The argument is explained later on in the lesson. But Thomas gives first a summary of Plato's cosmology. In the *De caelo*, Aristotle shows the eternity of the motion of the heaven by the eternity of its body, a proof he did not present in *Physics* VIII. Thomas makes a concession to Aristotle's theory: considering things from the side of the heaven, one can show that it can always be in movement, but it depends on God's will that, in fact, it always remains so (no. 334).

Returning to the arguments of Aristotle, we read that a circular movement needs a center that is at rest, and this center must be a body (no. 335). If there is one of a pair of contraries, the other contrary must also exist, and fire is the contrary of earth (no. 336), so it exists. Fire is prior to earth, which has neither movement nor levity (no. 337). Two intermediate elements, air and water, occupy the space between earth and fire (no. 338). These elements perform rectilinear motions, which cannot be eternal. Hence there are generation and corruption in this section of the world (no. 341). This last point will be shown in greater detail in *De generatione et corruptione* II. Thomas mentions a question raised by Alexander: will there still be contrary elements if the movement of the heaven ceases? While Alexander thinks so, Thomas sides with Simplicius and thinks that in that case all other movements would also come to a standstill (no. 342). It is now clear why there must be different bodies with circular motions, namely, to make generation possible (no. 343).

The sphericity of the heaven is demonstrated in lesson 5 (II.4.286b10–287a11). The sphere is the first figure. It is finite and limited on all sides (no. 346), while to a rectilinear line one can always add something (no. 347). As the first of the figures of solids (no. 348), the circle properly belongs to the first body (no. 351). The bodies inferior to the first heaven are also spherical (no. 352). In lesson 6 (II.4.287a11–b21), we read that the heaven has a spherical form, as is most fitting to it, for its parts always successively fill its place (no. 355). The movement of the heaven is continuous, most regular and eternal. It is also faster than other cosmic motions, so that we can use it as the measure of all other movements (no. 356). Because it differs in shape from the lower bodies, the heaven must be spherical (no. 357). Because the first heaven is spherical and contains all the other bodies, the world itself is spherical (no. 360).

In lesson 7 (II.5.287b22–288a12), the question is raised as to why the heaven revolves in one direction, rather than in another. In the foregoing lessons, Aristotle discussed the parts of heaven and its figure. Now, says Thomas, he discusses its movement by arguing that heaven moves in one direction, from east to west, toward what is highest and most noble. Thomas does not consider this argument convincing. We must say that nature always does what is best. But what is the cause of its movement? If the heaven is not this cause—as everything that moves has a cause, distinguished from itself, which imparts this movement (no. 363)—Thomas writes that it is directed by the first principle, which constitutes the very essence of goodness (no. 365). In lesson 8 (II.6.288a13–b7), the reason is given why the movement of the heaven is uniform: it must be regular because it is the measure of all other movements. The irregularity of the movements of the planets is only apparent. It is explained by the concourse of many movements (no. 368). Motions in a direction contrary to the nature of something tend to lose strength, while those according to its nature become more intense (no. 370).

In no. 371, the movement of projectiles is mentioned: when a projectile is no longer in contact with the propellant it still keeps moving. Aristotle thought that the displaced air through which the projectile passes flows around it and pushes it forward from behind. Philoponus rejected this view and introduced the impetus theory.[40] But Thomas does not accept it here, nor in Book III, no. 592, nor in *Q. de potentia*, q. 3, a. 2, ad 5. As to motions which vary in speed, we read that the highest speed of irregular motions can be at the beginning of the trajectory, in the middle of it, or at the end.

In lesson 9 (II.6.288b7–289a10), more proofs are given of the absence of irregularities in the motion of the heaven. The bodies of animals consist of the four elements, which are outside their natural places. Animal bodies will finally disintegrate, but this cannot happen in the celestial bodies, which consist of the fifth element. Their motion knows no remission (no. 375). It is unreasonable to suppose that it will become faster or will slow down (no. 377). An indefinite intensification or remission is also impossible, as every movement

---

40. Richard Sorabji thinks that Philoponus's explanation was dependent on his Christian faith in creation. See his *Matter, Space, and Motion* (Ithaca, N.Y.: Cornell University Press, 1988), 232ff.

must be determinate, proceeding from one point to another (no. 378). One cannot say either that in an imaginary shortest fraction of time the heaven would not move, as movements are always accompanied by their own time, which is consequent on it (nos. 379–80).

The nature of the stars is examined in lesson 10 (II.7.289a11–35). It seems reasonable to assume that the stars in the sphere of the heaven are of the same nature as this sphere itself, as they have a circular movement and are separate from the four elements. Against this conclusion one might allege that the light they emit becomes stronger or fainter, so that the stars themselves might be different, but Thomas says that a difference in their luminosity does not have the character of a contrary quality (no. 383). Some say that there seems to be some difference between the stars and their sphere, but it seems more reasonable to assume that they are of the same matter as their sphere (nos. 384–86). From where do the stars have the power to warm and to illuminate (nos. 390–91)? In this context, Aristotle only speaks of warmth as the effect of their movement. Alexander comments that in *De anima* II.7, light is not considered the proper effect of fire. But Thomas says that, according to Aristotle, the radiation issuing from the stars warms the lower bodies by friction, so that they also emit light. Local motion gives an impulsion that is the primary cause of alteration and calefaction. Averroes argues that heat is produced by the movement of the entire heaven, including all its spheres, as if it were one big animal.

He compares the movements of the planets to those of the members of the animal body. The entire heaven warms the lower regions by one activity. According to Simplicius, this explanation is deficient: if the warming of the air—when the sun is present—would be caused by the compression of the air resulting from the movement of the sphere of the heaven, the higher regions of the earth, such as mountains, being closer to this sphere, would become warmer than the plains, but we see the opposite happen. What really happens, according to him, is that the sun emits rays consisting of matter that pass through the air and cause warmth by friction. But by referring to *De anima* II.7, Thomas rejects this explanation: the rays of the sun are neither bodies nor effluences (no. 392). But he adds that all these explanations have some truth (*aliqualiter vera sunt*). The warmth we receive on earth has a dual cause, namely the movement of the celestial bodies, and the light they emit (no. 393). Alexander says that if the celestial bodies cause friction in the air, they are tangible, and so they are themselves cold or warm. But Thomas, who apparently has stored Aristotle's main works in his memory, refers to *De generatione et corruptione* I.6, where it says that the celestial bodies act but do not undergo changes. In them the tangible qualities are present in a different way (no. 394).

In lesson 11 (II.8.289b1–290a7), the motion of the stars is examined. The stars do not move by themselves. The daily movement is either real or apparent, caused by the rotation of the earth as Heraclides of Pontus and Aristarchus say. As for now (*ad praesens*), Aristotle supposes, Thomas says, that the stars move and the earth is at rest. He will prove this in lesson 26 (no. 396). Aristotle rejects the view that the carrying sphere and the stars in it would move with distinct motions. This would mean that both have to move with the same speed, as both revolve and return to the same starting point (no. 397). But why assume two motions if one suffices?

Given the supposition that the stars have their own movement, besides the motion of their carrying sphere, it is not reasonable to assume that the speed of the stars is proportionate to the length of their circular trajectory, but the speed of circular trajectories will be proportional to their magnitude, because we observe that the larger the circle it describes will be, the faster a natural body moves. It would seem that the stars do not have their own velocity, but are moved or carried by their respective circles or spheres. If one would object that it is by chance that the greater the speed at which a star is moving, the greater its sphere, Aristotle answers that in things that act according to their nature, chance has no place (no. 398). And it is not reasonable to suppose that the stars move while their spheres are at rest; if this were the case, the speed of the stars should still be proportional to the size of the sphere (no. 399). It is best to assume that the stars are at rest while the sphere moves, but the stars are not like a foreign element in their sphere. The closer a sphere is to the center of the universe, the shorter the distance covered and the slower its velocity (no. 400). That the stars revolve together with their sphere signifies that the world is not torn apart. Stars moving by themselves in immobile spheres would endanger the unity of the cosmos (no. 401).

Stars do not move by themselves, this is the topic of lesson 12 (II.8.290a7–29). Spherical bodies have two motions: rotation (*circumgyratio*) and rolling (*volutatio*). Both must be excluded from the stars. What we see is circular movement (nos. 402–5). Why do stars scintillate whereas planets do not? Apparently, because stars are farther away (nos. 406–7). Aristotle did not explicitly ascribe rotation to the stars, as in our world we do not observe any effect of such a rotation (no. 408). The moon always shows the same side to us: as the celestial bodies are of the same nature and do not move by themselves, the moon does not turn around (no. 409). Some attempts were made to show the figures and the unevenness that are visible on our side of the moon. Thomas shows some interest and lists several explanations, but does not present new solutions. Because of the disposition of the celestial bodies, namely as a cause of the elements, there remains something of the elements, in particular of earth, present in the celestial bodies and in the moon (no. 410).

The stars do not move by themselves and have no sense faculties is the topic of lesson 13 (II.8.290a29–b11). It was shown in the previous lesson that the stars do not move by themselves. If they would have to move by themselves, nature would have given them convenient instruments to move, but there is no diversity in their parts (no. 411). A spherical body like the heaven can move faster, but is not outfitted for progression (no. 412). While Alexander denies the presence of sense powers in the stars, Simplicius attributes three senses to them—vision, hearing, and touch (nos. 413–14)—but according to Aristotle, there is only an intellectual soul in them. Thomas quotes two texts from *De anima* II and III, the first of which seems to say that there is sensation in the stars while the second text seems to exclude it. They do not have the sense of touch, because their body is simple (no. 415).

Thomas refers to Themistius and Averroes, who understand the text of Aristotle as excluding sensation from the stars. He says that in order to establish the absence of sensation, it is sufficient to show that sensation would bring the stars no advantage. Finally, he notes that the text of *De anima* III.12.434b3 could refer to those airy animals that Apuleus is speaking about in his *De Deo Socratis*. These animals are not stationary but move and so need sense powers (no. 416). In no. 417, another argument in favor of the absence of sensation is brought forward: the celestial bodies are active, and do not receive sense impressions passively. But Thomas raises a doubt as to whether they are ensouled (*si sint animata*). These bodies are uniform and spherical, while beings with a sensitive soul must have a diversity of sense organs. As they are the universal causes of effects at a lower level than they are themselves, the cognitive species should be in them in a universal way. Thomas adds again: *si sint animata* ("if they are ensouled"), they would know the particular things in universal concepts. Avicenna's theory that the souls of these bodies have the interior sense of imagination must be rejected (no. 418). Simplicius, however, writes that our sense knowledge is a sign of our nobility and should therefore also be found in the stars. Thomas corrects this view: the soul is not there for the sake of the body; the lower bodies do in fact know the sensible things, but in an imperfect way; the celestial bodies know them in a higher way, through the intellectual soul united to them (no. 419).

In lesson 14 (II.9.290b12–291a28), the question is raised if the stars produce some sound, as movements often do. Pythagoras believed that because large bodies moving fast produce sound, the sun, the moon, and the stars also do. The different spheres, while circling around, would produce a harmonious music in relation to the speed of their movements (nos. 421–22). When some people objected by saying that we do not hear this melody, he replied that ever since our birth this music has surrounded us, and so we no longer notice it (no. 423). But it is strange that we do not hear anything and that stones are not shaken or shattered by the shocks this heavenly music must produce. The sound would be much greater than any other sound on earth because of the size of the celestial bodies (no. 424). The argument of having become used to it does not hold, but Simplicius defends the Pythagorean theory. Thomas, however, notes that excessive sound harms us and corrupts our hearing, as does excessive light to our eyes. However, in principle, the senses perceive all sensible objects (no. 426).

While Alexander seems to admit the presence of colors and other accidents in the celestial bodies as coming to them from the outside, Simplicius denies the presence of all accidents in them, insisting that they are substances. But this is criticized by Thomas: the light they emit is of the same nature as that on earth; if the light on earth is an accident, it will also be so in the celestial bodies, namely a determination of the transparent (*diaphanum*) here and in the stars. Figures and shapes are accidents, so they are also accidents in the stars. Finally, how could an imperfect reality—which movement is—be the substance of the celestial bodies (no. 427)? As the stars do not produce any sound while revolving and do not clash with other bodies, we must conclude that they do not move by themselves (nos. 428–29). If they did, nothing here below (*in his inferioribus*) would be the same, as if nature foresaw what would happen in that case. These words intimate, as Alexander says, that God exercises Providence over the beings here below. But Thomas observes that one cannot attribute Providence to nature, as if it were some power in nature, but it rather is the action of the intellect that established nature (no. 430).

In lesson 15 (II.10.291a29–b10), Aristotle examines the velocity of the motion of the planets, which depends on their distance from the first sphere and from the earth. The revolution of the first heaven is a simple, not composite, and very fast movement, as it covers an enormous distance in one day going from the east to the west. The planets, however, revolve from west to east at different speeds. Saturn, which is close to the outer sphere and has a greater distance to cover, needs thirty years to accomplish its circle, Jupiter twelve, and Mars two. Venus, Mercury, and the sun accomplish their trajectory in about one year, while the moon does so in a month (no. 432). The planets that are further away from the first heaven suffer less from the contrary effect of its revolution (no. 433). But do the higher planets, being larger, move faster? Some say that there is only one movement by which the entire heaven moves.

Higher placed bodies move faster, those in lower regions slower (nos. 434–35). Several theories have been proposed to explain the observed movements (nos. 436–37) but Thomas, who in an admirable way weighs the different theories, sees two poles that influence and codetermine the movements of the bodies in the universe and concludes this section with the phrase "apparently we must propose a different solution" (*aliter dicendum videtur*).

We must keep in mind the dual nature of the bodies of the universe: certain things are by their nature permanent—a permanence as we find it in the separate (immaterial) substances and in which the celestial bodies share to a certain extent—while other bodies are subject to generation and corruption. They share in some measure in the *natura difformitatis,* the more so when further removed from the first heaven (no. 438). But Thomas warns that the speeds of the different revolutions are not precisely proportional to their distances from the first sphere, as these movements are also voluntary and directed to an end. The planets Venus and Mercury have a velocity adapted to that of the sun to assist it in its task (no. 439). Thomas warns that we should not speak of a compulsion imposed upon the planets but of a natural order. In this way, we can uphold Aristotle's principles (no. 440).

In lesson 16 (II.11.291b11–23), the shape of the stars is studied. To show that they are spherical bodies, the argument insists on their form, which must make them less apt to move locally. Nature does not do anything in vain; the entire activity of the heavenly bodies has been ordained by an intellect that pursued its end. Therefore, it has given the stars, which do not move by themselves, a spherical shape that is less apt for locally progressive motion but suitable for circular movement (no. 442). Aristotle says here that the stars do not move themselves because they have a spherical shape. He argues that they are spherical because they are immobile, so he seems to argue in a circle. Alexander does not see any inconvenience in the argument, as Aristotle shows in other ways that the stars do not move by themselves (no. 443). Supposing that all the stars have the same shape, he then points to the form of the moon. Its different quarters depend on the position of the sun (nos. 445–46). Its surface must be spherical, for if it were a plane, its parts would not be illuminated successively. Its spherical form is also shown during the eclipse of the sun. But if one celestial body is spherical, the other bodies must be so too (no. 448). Averroes says that all the stars are like individuals of the same species, a statement that Thomas brands as clearly wrong: if they were, they would have the same operations, which is not the case; all their movements would be the same. Moreover, the perfection of the universe demands a plurality of different species.

The reason Averroes puts forward is patently ridiculous, namely, that if these celestial bodies would be of different species, they would be material. Thomas replies that this would much more be the case if they were individuals of the same species. Nevertheless, Thomas says, we should not totally exclude matter from them, for if they have matter, it does not follow that they are subject to generation and corruption. All the stars belong to the same genus, but their species are different. Their spherical shape is subsequent to their generic nature, as is their circular motion (no. 449).

Some difficulties about the nature of the stars are examined in lesson 17 (II.12.291b24–292a18). Thomas recalls that Ptolemy corrected the order of the planets. He placed the sun after Mars and just before Venus, while Aristotle said that it comes after the moon. A second anomaly is the apparently disorderly motions of the planets. Already, Plato had asked the help of Eudoxus to bring these motions to some regular order (*ad rectum ordinem reducere*). He introduced a number of revolving spheres for each planet to explain their only apparently irregular movements. This astronomical hypothesis saves the appearances, but need not necessarily be true, says Thomas. Perhaps another way will be discovered to account for them, although Aristotle used such hypotheses as being true with regard to these movements. Eudoxus assigned four spheres to the planets, attempting to explain their movements, but only three to the sun and the moon (no. 451). According to Aristotle, it is surprising that the sun and the moon, which are furthest away from the fixed stars, revolve with several motions, while the other planets revolve with only few and the fixed stars with only one: the planets nearest to the fixed stars should move with few motions, say with two instead of four (no. 452).

As not all apparent movements could be explained by the hypothesis of Eudoxus, Aristotle invited Calippus to correct and complete the system (no. 453). But even so some difficulties remained. It is indeed surprising that so many spheres were needed to explain the orbits of the planets. Hipparchus and Ptolemy discovered that the planets in their movements do not revolve around the earth but have different centers. The sun does not move in an epicycle but in an eccentric sphere, yet the question raised by Aristotle remains: Mercury and the moon have several motions, while the sun which we place between them has only two (no. 454). The lowest planets—Mercury and the moon—have the most movements. The text has an allusion to personal observations by Aristotle as well as to those by the Egyptians and Babylonians (no. 455). One may also wonder why there are innumerable stars in the first sphere. Thomas notes that at the time of Aristotle, scientists had not yet examined the movement of the fixed stars, as Ptolemy would do. In this connection, he refers to Alexander, Simplicius, and Averroes, saying that, although we know little about the causes of the movements of the celestial bodies, it will become evident that it is not unreasonable to investigate them (no. 457).

In lesson 18 (II.12.292a18–b25), two more difficulties are resolved concerning the apparently irregular motions of the planets. The difficulties we encounter in our investigation are understandable, says Thomas, as we study these stars and planets as if they were just bodies, while they have a rational soul and act in view of an end. The variety of movements must be explained from the point of view of their soul. They do not act just impulsively, but by reason. The variety of movements should be considered by reference to the final end. At this point, Thomas observes that for our problem it does not make a difference whether the stars have a soul or whether these souls are separate entities. Aristotle only says (292a20) that we must think of them as partaking of life and the activity that is proper to beings having a rational soul (no. 458). It is reasonable that the being in the best state possesses the good without having to act, and that beings on the second level attain it by some action, and that those further away need to do more. This applies also to our own body and health (nos. 459–60).

In a somewhat surprising remark Aristotle goes on to say that we must assume that the actions of the stars, whether many or few, resemble those of plants and animals (292b1–3). These are few: plants have only one operation (nutrition) and those of animals are determined by their nature (e.g., a swallow always builds its nest the same way). Thomas observes that we see that a man who has perfect virtue has many different operations, for he can acquire different goods and strive to attain the things ordered to the one end. But God does not need to do something to acquire his good and that of all other things (no. 461). He then distinguishes the following degrees: (1) possessing one's highest good without action (God); (2) acquiring one's perfect good by one or by a few acts; (3) beings that need to perform many activities; and (4) things that cannot reach the perfect good, but strive to attain something, pursuing it by one or more acts (no. 462).

What is highest has (*habet*), and partakes in, the best without any movement. Thomas observes that Aristotle uses the singular while thinking of the supreme cause, God, who is the essence of goodness (*quae est essentia bonitatis*). Lower things attempt to attain some share in what is most divine (292b22–23, τυχεῖν τῆς θειοτάτης ἀρχῆς) (nos. 463–64). The earth has no activity and no movements (no. 465). The best in things is permanence. The sun and the moon, which are the lower planets, can bring about changes in bodies on earth, as, for instance, by generation and corruption (no. 468).

Simplicius thinks that the nobility of the heavenly bodies does not depend on the site of things, but Thomas replies that what has been exposed above seems more true, agreeing as it does with the principles of nature. The first heavenly sphere, which is closest to the supreme substance, is by its daily movement the cause of the eternal duration and permanence of things. The superior planets are more the causes of duration than the lower ones.

Quoting apparently from the *Quadripartitio* of Ptolemy, Thomas writes that Saturn is responsible for immobile things (*res fixae*) and the universal order of time, Jupiter for the yearly order of things, etc. According to the astronomers, the lower planets, such as the sun and the moon, are most efficacious in causing transmutations in the lower bodies. By their successive passing away and coming into being, the lower bodies obtain the perpetuity of their species (nos. 468–69). As Aristotle says in *Metaphysics* XII.6, there must be something in the movements of the celestial bodies that is the cause of the duration and perpetuity of things, and something that has to do with the transmutations of the latter (no. 470). According to Aristotle, the earth is not ensouled but Simplicius, following the error of the gentiles, says Thomas, holds the contrary view. But Aristotle reminds us that no simple body has a soul (*De anima* III.13). Simplicius notes that the fact that the earth does not move proves nothing: also plants do not move. The operation of the earth is to remain in its place but, says Thomas, to stay in one's place is not an operation, it's a privation. The earth cannot be ensouled as it has no vital operation (no. 471).[41]

Lesson 19 (II.12.292b25–293a14) asks: why are there innumerable stars in the first sphere, and just one in the lower spheres? Thomas indicates a reason but expresses himself with reservation: the first sphere is most excellent, has a more noble life, and is a universal cause. It is immediately subordinated to the first mover and contains and moves all other spheres; it has the most simple motion. Because it has these privileges, it must also have a great number of stars, which are the most noble and active bodies, as is shown by their luminosity (no. 473). Thomas notes that the movement of the fixed stars is not entirely simple, as Aristotle thinks, but is composed of two motions (no. 474).

The planets are like the instruments of the supreme sphere (no. 475). A planet has several spheres, in keeping with its complex movement. If its superior sphere had to organize the movements of several spheres, its task would be very heavy (no. 476). But the weight of the planets does not interfere. This does not apply, Thomas writes, to the separate substance and mover, which

---

41. At the background is the theory that the celestial bodies exercise some influence on beings on the earth and their activities. One may refer to *ST* I, q. 110, a. 1: particular powers are administered by universal powers.

has an infinite superiority due to existing outside the order of the world (no. 477). In closing, Thomas notes that modern astronomers do not assign many spheres to each planet, one of which would move the others.

In lesson 20 (II.13.292a15–b16), Aristotle considers the earth as the center of the universe and not as one of the elements. The examination is continued up to II.24 and has as its object the place, the shape, and the immobility of the earth. Those authors who held the universe to be infinite did not assign a definite place to the earth. Philosophers of the Pythagorean school claimed that there is fire at the center of the universe. They believed that the earth itself rotates and causes day and night. They also accepted the existence of a so-called counter-earth. The heat emitted by the stars collects in the center of the world and becomes a fire. But they applied a preconceived theory, Thomas comments, whereas in the study of nature we should discover the plan and reason of what things are and do by observation (nos. 481–82). According to the Pythagoreans, the center and the circumference of the world are its most noble parts, and fire is worthier than the earth (no. 483). But Aristotle reminds us that the center of the universe is not its best and most important part. We should not so much look for the local center of the world, but turn our attention to that which surrounds and determines all other bodies. The bodies that contain others are nearer to the form, while those contained are closer to matter. The center is surrounded by all other bodies and the earth is the most ignoble of all.

In lesson 21 (II.13.293b16–294a11), more opinions about the supposed movement, shape, and position of rest of the earth are discussed. The Pythagoreans accepted what they called the counter-earth in order to obtain ten bodies: the sphere with the fixed stars, the seven planets, the earth, and the counter-earth. The earth revolves like a planet around the center (no. 487). But several observed facts cannot be saved if the earth were in movement at the center of the world (no. 489). Thomas mentions again the theory of Heraclides of Pontus, namely that of a rotating earth and immobile heaven (no. 490). There are different theories about the shape of the earth: that of a sphere or a drum (no. 491). Thomas summarizes the views and explains surprisingly well the thoughts behind them (no. 493).

Doubts on why the earth is at rest are examined in lesson 22 (II.13.284a11–b13). The earth is not at rest because of its supposed infinity. Some say that the infinite is underneath the earth or that its lower part is infinite, so that it does not sink (no. 497), but this view was refuted by Empedocles. Thales thought that the earth rests on water (no. 499), but then it would sink because water is lighter. Aristotle observes that we should not limit ourselves to reviewing the opinions of others, but study the subject ourselves (no. 503).

In lesson 23 (II.13.294b13–295a14), we read that Anaximenes, Anaxagoras, and Democritus considered the flatness of the earth to be the reason that it does not sink. The earth was thought to float on the air, which was compressed under it and not able to escape. Others who said that the earth is located in the center of the world considered the revolution of the heaven the cause that pushed the earth down, as heavier things move toward the middle of a vortex. All authors who believed that the world had a beginning say that the earth moved toward the middle (no. 507). The elements have a natural movement, which is the topic of lesson 24 (II.13.295a14–b10), and the celestial sphere is not the cause of the rest of the earth: as all other natural bodies, the earth also has a natural movement (no. 509). Empedocles considered strife and friendship the causes of the separation of the elements and of their drawing together (no. 510).

In lesson 25 (II.13.295b10–296a13), the reason given by some as to why the earth is at the center amounts to the notion that it is at an equal distance to every part of the universe. But if that is the reason, fire when placed at the center will not move up but remain there. We must say that because of its nature the earth moves toward the center (no. 516) where it rests, while fire rests at the extreme other end of the world (no. 517), where it occupies a much greater space because of rarefaction (no. 520).

Lesson 26 (II.14.296a24–297a8) also deals with the place and rest of the earth at the center. Circular motion is not natural to the earth. If it were, all pieces of earth would move in circles, while in reality they fall downward (no. 522). Further arguments are proposed in nos. 523–24. Heavy bodies move by their nature to the center of the world (no. 527). The cause of the earth's rest in the center is that the center is its natural place. Ptolemy and further astronomical observations confirm it. If this would be denied, one would have to assign another location to it; for example, outside the axis of the world or, if on the axis, a position different from the middle. Thomas carefully quotes Ptolemy's argumentation against these suppositions (no. 530).

In lesson 27 (II.14.297a8–b18), the spherical shape of the earth is demonstrated by the movements of its parts. All its parts, pushed by gravity, move from all directions to the center (no. 533). Another opinion holds that the movement toward the center is caused by the violent turning around of the heaven in a circle. According to this view, the parts of the earth were dispersed and then pushed together (no. 534). But if all the parts are carried to the center, the mass of the earth will form an equalized spherical shape. The heavier parts will push the lighter ones away from the center (no. 536). Whatever is heavy has an inclination toward the center. Whether the earth is generated or not, this scenario will always happen, as the terminus of generation is the nature of the body generated. So this body will move to the center in the same way as when it would not be a product of generation (nos. 537–38).

The spherical form of the earth is demonstrated by the path its moving parts follow, as well as by astronomical arguments, which are discussed in lesson 28 (II.14.297b18–298a20). Heavy objects fall to the surface in perpendicular movements, and not in equidistant parallel lines. This shows the spherical form of the earth. In response to the objection that the existence of mountains seems to contradict this description, Thomas answers that in the formation of the mountains some accidental causes intervened (no. 540). Astronomical arguments also confirm that the earth has a spherical form, for example, during the eclipse of the moon, when a circular line separates light and dark and some stars are not visible in the Northern Hemisphere; if the earth were flat, however, all stars would be visible from everywhere. But the sphere of the earth cannot be too large, as otherwise its rotundity would not have this effect, Finally, the size of its spherical shape can even be calculated by the observation of the heaven from different points on earth (no. 541).

Book III

In the first lesson (III.1.298a24–b12), Thomas writes that after the Philosopher has dealt with the bodies that move along circular trajectories in Books I and II, he continues by studying the bodies that follow a rectilinear path (no. 545). Natural science studies natural substances, that is, bodies (no. 546). Among them the simple bodies come first. Therefore, Aristotle first examines fire and earth, then air and water and the mixed bodies (*corpora mixta*) composed of them, and finally living beings, namely animals and plants as well as their operations, such as local motion, alteration, and transmutation. Thomas also explains the famous sentence: "The study of nature is *for the greater part* concerned with bodies." These words are either a sign of restraint and modesty becoming to a philosopher, or they suggest that in natural philosophy there is also the question of the first mover and of the intellectual soul (no. 547). All natural substances in movement are bodies (no. 548).

Different opinions on generation are examined in lesson 2 (III.1.298b12–299a1). Those who, like Parmenides and Melissus, deny generation, discerned something that is partly true, as there must be some ingenerate and incorruptible entities. If there were no unchangeable things, science would not be possible. However, they admitted only the existence of sensible things (no. 552). Simplicius, quoted by Thomas, completes and confirms this view by saying: being itself (*ipsum ens*), which is being by its essence, is ingenerate, incorruptible, and entirely immobile. They thought that the sensible things, in which generation and corruption are found, are not real beings (no. 553). Aristotle mentions the opinion of those who hold that nothing is ingenerate but that all things come into being, while some things last, others pass away again. Hesiod and the early natural philosophers thought that everything is in a state of becoming and flux, but that there is one substance that is permanent. Thomas goes beyond these statements by saying that there is some first cause, an intellect and divine being, from which all things proceed (no. 554). According to others, all things are generated and exist in a continuous flux, so that nothing is permanent except the principle that underlies all becoming and perishing. This was the view of Thales, Anaximenes, and Anaximander. Heraclitus also accepted this view, but he was the author who most strongly asserted that all things are in a continuous flux (no. 555). Plato thought that all bodies are generable, as they are composed of surfaces into which they are resolved again (no. 556).

This theory of Plato is further examined in lesson 3 (III.1.299a1–b23). A body cannot be generated out of surfaces or planes, Aristotle argues, because this on several points is in contradiction with mathematical science. Aristotle deals with Plato's theory because of Plato's renown and the special generation of bodies it proposes. He refutes it with two arguments (no. 557): (a) for mathematical reasons it is impossible, as points are indivisible and from a series of points we never get a line, nor from lines a plane, nor from planes a body (no. 558); (b) in Plato's theory, bodies consist of planes, planes of lines, and lines of points, but this line of argument has already been refuted in *Physics* VI.1 by indicating that a line is divisible and is not composed of indivisibles. At this point, Thomas adds an important statement: results that are impossible with regard to mathematical bodies are also impossible with regard to physical bodies. The reason is that mathematical figures are abstracted from natural bodies, which add to mathematical figures a sensible body and movement. For this reason, what holds for mathematical figures also applies to natural things (no. 560).

Aristotle shows that accidents, such as passions, may be considered indivisible with regard to their species, but that they are divisible when present in different subjects (no. 561). Physical bodies, such as earth and water, have weight, but points and lines do not. Thomas argues that this is valid for quantitative parts, but not for components of the essence of things. These are beyond gravity (no. 562). Thomas observes that it is not necessary that things of which we say that they are heavier or lighter be heavy or light in an absolute sense. Earth, however, is absolutely heavy (no. 563). No heavy body can be composed out of two or more components none of which is heavy (no. 566).

Lesson 4 (III.1.299b23–300a19) brings more arguments against Plato's theory of the elements. Plato did not distinguish between the number "one" as the principle of numbers, on the one hand, and "one" as a transcendental property of being, on the other. According to Plato, the notion of one, the principle of numbers, constitutes the substance of things. By contrast, Aristotle shows that from points, lines, and planes, which have no weight, we cannot obtain bodies that have some weight. The Pythagoreans, who believed that the world is composed of numbers, run into the same difficulties (nos. 568–74).

In lesson 5 (III.2.300a20–b16), Aristotle argues that natural bodies have a natural movement. The theories of Leucippus and Democritus are insufficient to explain process in our world. The natural movement of the bodies differs from a violent motion (no. 575). As the nature of a body is determinate, it has one movement according to its nature, including one contrary motion, but deviations from this one natural movement are possible (no. 576). If a body is naturally at rest in a certain place, the movement that carried it to this place was also natural. If it rests there against its nature, it was brought there violently (no. 577).

Plato's theory of the inordinate movement of the elements before the formation of the world is studied in lesson 6 (III.2.300b16–301a22). Among the natural movers there is a first mover, according to Plato. But if this mover moves naturally, the effect will also be natural, so that we cannot speak of an inordinate movement. Another objection against Plato's theory reads: if originally these motions in the world were inordinate, how could very well-organized beings result? Against the atomism of Democritus, Aristotle raises the following difficulty: when all atoms are moved by one mover (e.g., gravity) there will not be inordinate movement but one movement will result, for instance upward. But when they are moved by an infinite number of infinite movers (in keeping with the infinite number of atoms) nothing well-ordered could ever result. Some say that Aristotle misunderstood Plato: the inordinate movement was there before the world was made and that all order in the world comes from the first principle (nos. 583–84). In this context, Thomas quotes a remark of Aristotle: we must keep two things in mind about the bodies that, in Plato's theory as well as in that of the atomists, existed before the world was made: they were in motion and they were separate.[42]

---

42. Aristotle probably meant that they did not come together to form larger bodies.

And Anaxagoras was right when he said that there were no bodies in motion before the world was made. The reason is that motion lies between potency and full actualization. In things that become, their beginning is a state of total potentiality (no. 585).

In lesson 7 (III.2.301a22–b31), Aristotle shows that bodies that describe rectilinear movements have weight. Bodies that are weightless will not move with natural movements, nor by enforced movements. The bodies in the sublunar world owe their impulse to weight. Because of their weight their movements are rectilinear. Aristotle shows with an example that we run into difficulties if we suppose that weightless bodies would move in the same way as the elements, namely by a natural and also by an imposed movement (nos. 588–89). Clearly, there are both natural and enforced motions. In the latter, there is no principle of movement in the moving thing itself (no. 590). The power behind violent movements uses the air as an instrument to push a body farther up or away. But Thomas excludes that in the violent movement of a projectile an impetus is conferred to it (no. 591).[43] The air is at the service of both violent and natural motions (no. 592). Averroes proposes a different explanation of why the air intervenes and moves in both types of motions (no. 593). But Thomas says that both these explanations proceed from the same error, namely that, according to Averroes, the form of light and heavy bodies would be the active principles. The (substantial) forms, however, are not agents, but they are that for the sake of which the mover moves (no. 594). Natural movements are in conformity with the nature of the moving bodies.

In lesson 8 (III.2–3.301b31–302b9), the last section of chapter 2 and the first part of chapter 3 are discussed. There is generation but not all things are generated, for the generation of bodies is impossible unless, before, there were a void without any body in it (no. 596). In III.3, the question of what is meant by the term "element" and the number of elements are discussed. According to Aristotle, not all things are the result of generation, but some are. And it remains to be decided which bodies are and which are not. Thomas notes that this theory of Aristotle's is not against the doctrine of the faith, which affirms the simultaneous beginning of things (no. 598). In order to discover which bodies can be generated and why they can be generated, we must know from which elements they are composed. The study of this question is begun here, but will be continued in the *De generatione et corruptione*.

What is the nature of an element and how many elements are there (no. 599)? An element of natural bodies is that into which these bodies can be ana-

---

43. See also no. 371.

lyzed or be dissolved. In this sense, matter and form are the universal elements of all bodies. In a second sense of the term, an element is that which exists either in act or in potency in the composite bodies. If generation takes place by assembling or dissolving, the elements will be in act in the compound, but if it takes place by alteration, the elements will be in potency in it. An element is not divided into specifically different components, so that fire, air, water, and earth are not further resolved into different things (no. 600). Some elements must be present in physical bodies: if we take wood or flesh we discover that they are composed of earth and fire, into which they are resolved. The theory of Empedocles is to be preferred to that of Anaxagoras, who assumed bodies to be composed of a great number of small particles of specifically different things (no. 602). As there are simple movements, there are simple bodies, so that the theory of Empedocles must be preferred (no. 603). At this point, the exposition of St. Thomas ends abruptly.

Concluding Remarks

This commentary presents the reader with several difficulties.[44] Does Thomas fully accept the theory that the world is composed of the unchangeable celestial spheres, the four elements located in the central part of the universe, and the description of the sun and moon as planets? Considering the fact that from the point of view of modern science a large part of the treatise proposes false theories, we can raise the question of the value of the commentary. In order to determine it, we must consider its main doctrinal statements.

First, when Aristotle does not express his thought with the desired precision, Thomas explains this by saying that, as long as he has not yet made a full analysis, Aristotle follows the general view about the theme under discussion.[45] Throughout his commentary, he summarizes the contents of the treatise in a respectful way. We find a beautiful example of this respectful way of proceeding in II.1, where Thomas says that Aristotle's "demonstration" of the eternity of the heaven does not show absolutely that the world does not have a beginning, but that it did not begin to exist the way other philosophers said it did. Aristotle adds, in addition to the arguments for the eternity of the world

---

44. See James Weisheipl, "The Commentary of St. Thomas on the *De caelo* of Aristotle," *Sapientia* 29 (1974): 11–34, and Leo Elders, "Le Commentaire de saint Thomas d'Aquin sur le De caelo d'Aristote," in *Proceedings of the World Congress on Aristotle*, ed. Ioannes N. Theodorakopoulos (Athens: Publication of the Ministry of Culture and Sciences, 1981), 2:173–87.

45. *In I De caelo*, lesson 7, no. 74. See *In III De caelo*, lesson 1, no. 563, where he writes that it is not Aristotle's custom to abuse the terms in use.

he had presented in Book I, the fact that the ancients have always affirmed this eternity and that the contrary opinion forces us to attribute impossible properties to the world.

Sometimes Thomas corrects a theory proposed in the text by saying that Aristotle expresses himself as the Platonists do, for instance about the nature of the heaven.[46] On several occasions, when the text mentions what nature does, Thomas adds that it does so directed by the first principle. In his commentary, Thomas repeatedly mentions the opinions of Alexander and Simplicius to approve or to reject them. He himself formulates objections against certain theories with phrases such as *potest autem aliquis obiicere contra hoc quod dicitur* ("someone might object against what is said") or *videtur falsum esse quod dicitur* ("what is said seems to be wrong").[47] And if a passage is not immediately followed by a criticism or a rejection, it does not mean that Thomas fully agrees with what Aristotle is saying. I have already drawn attention to texts about the theory that the world did not begin to exist. Thomas also writes that, in agreement with his doctrine of the first mover who moves by being desired, Aristotle supposes (*supponit*) that the heaven is ensouled.

With regard to certain particular doctrines, a first question concerns Aristotle's theory that the division of geometrical figures into circle and straight line implies that natural local movements must describe a circle or a straight line. As we have seen, Thomas admits this theory, as geometrical figures do not form a totally different genus: physical bodies add sensible matter to these figures.[48] Thomas accepts the theory of the natural movements of the simple bodies, but does not attribute the same importance to these movements: they manifest only one aspect of the being of the elements.[49] The celestial bodies are not (identical with) their actions, but they have actions; they are beings that have a certain potentiality, although not with regard to place.

According to Thomas, the world is finite and one. In lesson 4 of Book II, he summarizes the arguments in favor of Aristotle's cosmological system: the heaven is a divine body, its motion is circular and eternal; at the center of the world, the immobile earth is placed and, separate from it, fire too; between earth and fire there are the two intermediary elements, water and air, and hence generation and corruption.[50] He considers the theory of the four elements as an established fact. The spherical shape of the world is admitted by Thomas, but he considers Aristotle's cosmological system of homocentric

---

46. *In II De caelo*, lesson 1, no. 114.
47. *In I De caelo*, lesson 22, no. 228.
48. *In I De caelo*, lesson 3, no. 24.
49. *In I De caelo*, lesson 4, no. 24.
50. *In II De caelo*, lesson 4, no. 333.

spheres a hypothesis that is superseded by later discoveries, such as the precession of the stars. Moreover, the construction of Eudoxus, Aristotle, and Calippus does not explain all the (apparent) movements of the planets.[51] Thomas seems to prefer the system of Ptolemy with regard to the order of the planets and their movements.[52] Generally, he considered these theories as hypotheses; other theories might explain the observed phenomena better.[53]

In II.10.291a29–b10, Aristotle considers the order of celestial bodies and mentions that there is a contrast between the motion of the heaven and the movements of the planets that move in a contrary direction. This raises the question if the planets are exposed to coercion by the first heaven. Thomas presents an explanation that is in agreement with the general principles of Aristotle, rather than with the latter's theory in *De caelo* II. There are, says Thomas, two fundamentally different ways in which things can exist. On the one hand, there are beings characterized by an eternal existence and, on the other, there are the corruptible beings. The celestial bodies that exist between the two participate by their movements in these two ways of being; the first heaven has only a circular motion, which is the cause of the permanent duration of things. By their circular motion the planets also express this permanence, but through the other motions performed by them they express the corruptibility of things.[54] Elsewhere in his commentary, Thomas presents his theory of the different degrees of perfection. Above all beings, there is God, who possesses his good without needing any action. Next, there are those beings that possess their good by a unique activity (with some supplementary actions).[55] Man, however, must acquire his good by numerous actions. Finally, at a lower level, there are the plants and animals, which can in no way acquire a perfect good, and the bodies that acquire no good whatsoever.[56]

Thomas also touches upon other subjects of cosmology. First, the question of the eternity of the world is connected with that of its incorruptibility. Aristotle thinks that this is demonstrated by the fact that over a long period no changes have been observed in the stars (230b33), but for Thomas this argument has only a certain probability because of the inherent limitations of

---

51. *In II De caelo*, lesson 17, no. 454: "Nec secundum hanc positionem poterant omnia apparentia solvere."

52. Ibid.

53. *In II De caelo*, lesson 17, no. 451: 'Non oportet dicere has suppositiones esse veras, quia forte secundum aliquem alium modum nondum ab hominibus apprehensum apparentia circa stellas salvantur." See Pierre Duhem, *Essai sur la notion de théorie physique de Platon à Galilée* (Paris: Hermann, 1908), 46.

54. *In II De caelo*, lesson 15, no. 438.

55. Thomas has in mind the immaterial spirits which have one fundamental action, but perform some secondary actions in their ministry.

56. *In II De caelo*, lesson 18, no. 462.

human memory.[57] As mentioned, he underlines that the arguments in favor of the eternity of the world do not show that the world has no beginning, but that it has not begun to exist in the way some have said.[58] Yet Thomas writes that the opinion that the world is incorruptible is probable.[59] In his commentary, Simplicius refers to the arguments of the Christian author Philoponus against the eternity of the world. Thomas writes that these arguments do not oblige us to accept his position.[60] The Christian faith does not profess the eternity of the world, but there is no contradiction between what faith teaches us and what the arguments of Aristotle show, namely that the world is not the product of generation and that it will not fall victim to corruption.

As for the arguments of Simplicius against the dogma of the creation of the world, Thomas says that they are neither conclusive nor reasonable.[61] Generally, the position of Thomas himself on these issues is the following: if the observed facts and considerations regarding the order and structure of things invite us to consider the incorruptibility of the celestial bodies as probable, we must explain this incorruptibility by their substantial forms, which determine their matter to the point of excluding substantial or accidental changes, except local movement. Being (*esse*) follows the form and so the duration of these bodies is not limited. But these forms do not exclude that the stars have begun to exist as the Christian faith teaches.[62] The first principle is free to let the world begin to exist when it wills.

In certain passages of the treatise, Aristotle writes that the heaven has a soul; he also calls it divine.[63] With regard to those texts in which the heaven is called divine, Thomas notes twice that Aristotle merely formulates the common convictions of people and expresses himself as Plato and the pagans, who called God and also other things first causes.[64] Because of its incorruptibility, the heaven was called divine by the ancients. In I.9.279a18, Aristotle speaks of beings outside the heaven. Alexander thought that authentic Aristotelianism could not admit any realities outside our world and suggested that by this expression Aristotle meant the heaven itself.[65] But Thomas rejects this interpretation and writes that we must identify the beings outside the heaven with

<hr>

57. *In I De caelo*, lesson 7, no. 76: "Nec tamen hoc est necessarium, sed probabile."
58. *In II De caelo*, lesson 1, no. 289.
59. *In I De caelo*, lesson 7, no. 77.
60. *In I De caelo*, lesson 6, nos. 61–63: "haec necessitatem non habent."
61. *In I De caelo*, lesson 6, no. 66: "necessitatem non habet . . .; non habet rationem . . .; locum non habet."
62. *In I De caelo*, lesson 29, no. 286; lesson 6, nos. 62–63.
63. *De caelo* 285a29; see 275a23 and 286a11.
64. *In I De caelo*, lesson 7, no. 75; *In II De caelo*, lesson 4, no. 334.
65. Simplicius, *In I De caelo* 287.19ff., 290.4ff.

God and the separate substances.[66] The heaven itself is, even for Aristotle, just one of the elements.[67]

A second question, connected with the theme of the divinity of the stars, is that of whether the heaven is ensouled, as Aristotle appears to confirm in certain texts of the *De caelo*. If the heaven is moved by a final cause, it must be ensouled. From within the hypothesis of a moving soul of the heaven, it is more conform to its dignity if this soul is a substantial principle, according to the doctrine of Aristotle, than when it would be outside the celestial bodies, as Plato thought it was. But, says Thomas, it is better to admit an outside mover whose power is not restricted to the motion of the heaven. In fact, Thomas drops the hypothesis of the ensoulment of the heavenly bodies. This also appears from his comments on the text passage, where Aristotle attributes up and down and left and right to the heaven, which is qualified as a personal opinion of his (*secundum opinionem suam*).[68]

In addition, Thomas rejects the theory of Simplicius who says that the world is a living being and that the absence of the sense faculties would contradict its divine nature.[69] In *Metaphysics* XII, Aristotle attributes an intellectual soul to the heaven. Intellectual knowledge presupposes sense cognition, but this applies only to man. Thomas adds several more reasons why there cannot be sense knowledge in the stars: (1) sense organs would not confer any advantage to them; (2) the celestial bodies are fully active, while in sense cognition a certain passivity is required; (3) the stars do not have the differentiation of the organs needed; and (4) the celestial bodies are universal causes, while the sense powers are concerned with the individual. It follows that, if the celestial bodies are ensouled, they will have an intellect but no sensitive cognition.[70] Thomas also rejects Simplicius's theory of the ensoulment of the earth.[71]

Thomas uses the texts and principles of Aristotle in order to show that one or the other particular theory does not contradict the Christian faith, but he also recurs to the principles of his own metaphysics: the act of being (of the heaven) is adapted to its form and so the heaven can exist forever.[72] Thomas recalls the principle that God and nature do nothing in vain, so as to conclude that God is the cause that made the celestial bodies.[73] The rotation of the

---

66. *In I De caelo,* lesson 21, no. 213.

67. *In I De caelo,* lesson 18, no. 181: "etiam caelum inter elementa computat."

68. *In II De caelo,* lesson 3, no. 313.

69. Simplicius, *In II De caelo* 463.1–12 and 423.21; Aquinas, *In II De caelo,* lesson 8, no. 371.

70. *In II De caelo,* lesson 13, nos. 417–18.

71. *In II De caelo,* lesson 18, no. 471.

72. *In I De caelo,* lesson 6, nos. 60–64.

73. *In I De caelo,* lesson 8, no. 91; see *De caelo* I.4.271a33.

heaven is a fundamental fact for Aristotle, who writes that its necessary being is either the first principle of, or depends itself on, a cause.[74] When Aristotle writes that nature always does what is best, Thomas adds that nature does so precisely insofar as it is directed by the first principle, which is the very essence of goodness.[75] In lesson 14, Thomas notes that the expression "nature foresaw" (291a21: ὥσπερ τὸ μέλλον ἔσεσθαι προνοούσης τῆς φύσεως) means that divine Providence watches over the world.[76]

With regard to the question of Thomas's relationship to the commentary of Simplicius, we notice that, all through his exposition, he uses the commentary as an indispensable source of information and borrows many observations from it about the views of the Pre-Socratics, Plato, Alexander, Philoponus, as well as on Greek astronomy; but frequently Thomas does not follow the doctrinal explanations of Simplicius. As mentioned, he rejects the theory that the world is a living being. He also abridges long explanations. When Thomas borrows from Simplicius he does not always mention his source, except when the text quoted expresses a personal opinion of Simplicius.

In five of the (many) lessons of the exposition, Averroes's interpretations of the text are mentioned but, as we have seen, Thomas is never in full agreement with the Arab commentator and is often severe in his judgment. The erroneous positions with regard to man's intellect attributed to Averroes, and defended by some Parisian masters, may have made Thomas reject more vigorously certain interpretations of the text of the *De caelo*.

In general, Thomas appears to accept the cosmological theories of Aristotle, at least insofar as they affirm a certain hierarchical structure of the universe. With regard to the theory of the numerous heavenly spheres, he considers it a rational hypothesis that could be replaced by other theories that would result from better observations. The admirable order in the world is by Thomas often attributed to divine Providence.

74. *De caelo* II.5.287b27.
75. *In II De caelo*, lesson 7, no. 365.
76. *In II De caelo*, lesson 14, no. 430.

5   THE COMMENTARY ON THE *DE GENERATIONE ET CORRUPTIONE*

In his exposition on the *De caelo*, Thomas refers several times to the *De generatione et corruptione*, which in the editions of the works of Aristotle has been placed after the four books on the heaven and the earth. In view of its subject matter—the coming-to-be and passing-away of things, growth, and the role of the elements in the process of becoming—some authors consider it early and date it to the years Aristotle spent at Assos, on Lesbos, or in Macedonia, before his return to Athens in 335. The text we have was edited by Andronicus and was placed by him after the *Physics* and the *De caelo*, but before the *Meteorologica*.[1] The importance attached to the treatise is evidenced by the large number of medieval and Renaissance authors writing a commentary, such as Albert the Great, Thomas Aquinas, John Buridan, Nicole Oresme, Franciscus Toletus, Jacobo Zabarella, the Coimbra scholars, and Galileo Galilei.[2]

The treatise consists of two books of ten and eleven chapters, respectively. The main subject of Book I is mixture, coming-to-be, and passing-away, as well as alteration and growth as different from generation and corruption. Book II deals with the so-called elements of the physical world. Aristotle begins his investigation with a survey of the views of some of the earlier natural philosophers.

In I.1 he notes that generation and corruption were considered by many natural philosophers to be the same as alteration. Empedocles attempted to give an explanation of coming-to-be by introducing the four elements, but according to him these elements themselves are not the product of generation. In I.2, we are told that many of these authors considered association to be the cause of coming-to-be and dissociation that of passing-away. With regard to

---

1. Paul Moraux, *Der Aristotelismus bei den Griechen* (Berlin: De Gruyter, 1973), 1:45–96.

2. Johannes Thijssen, "The Commentary Tradition on Aristotle's *De generatione et corruptione*: An Introductory Survey," in *The Commentary Tradition on Aristotle's "De generatione et corruptione" Ancient, Medieval, and Early Modern*, ed. J. Thijssen and H. Braakhuis (Turnhout: Brepols, 1999), 9–20, and *Lire Aristote au Moyen Âge* (ed. Ducos and Giacomotto-Charra).

William of Moerbeke, and is called the *Nova*.[5] According to Joanna Judycka, Thomas used the *Nova,* but sometimes consulted the *Vetus*.[6] The exposition of Thomas, which has remained unfinished and ends at I.5.322a34, is likely to date to the last years of his life, as does the commentary on the *De caelo*.[7]

The Commentary of Thomas Aquinas

In the proem to his commentary, Thomas observes that the different parts of the science of nature are distinguished according to different movements. After examining movements and mobile bodies in general in the *Physics,* the first part of natural philosophy, Aristotle studies bodies in their local movements in the *De caelo,* which is the second part of this science. Next he turns to other movements, among which generation and corruption occupy the first place. Alteration is ordained to generation and corruption, while growth (increase) follows upon generation. In our study of the subject, we must first consider it in general before dealing with its different parts. Furthermore, when there is a first within a genus that is also the cause of the other members of the genus, this cause should be studied first. In the genus of generable and corruptible things, the elements are some first principles, so that Aristotle studies these elements in this treatise. Thomas considers this division of the treatise's contents to be the plan Aristotle had in composing it (*intentio Aristotelis*).

In lesson 1 (I.1.314a1–b1), Thomas describes Aristotle's intention: to investigate the generation and corruption of natural things and other movements related to them, such as alteration and increase. In Book I, Aristotle investigates these matters in general, while Book II deals with the generation and corruption of the elements. Certain authors said that simple generation is the same as alteration, because they accepted one material substance underlying all processes. According to others, however, there are several material principles that when coming together cause generation, but that cause corruption when breaking up their combination. Alteration would be a change of some of

5. See Pieter de Leemans, "*Alia translatio planior.* Les traductions latines du *De generatione et corruptione* et les commentaires médiévaux," in *Lire Aristote au Moyen Âge* (ed. Ducos and Giacomotto-Charra), 27–53.

6. *De Generatione et Corruptione (Translatio vetus),* ed. Joanna Judycka, *Aristoteles Latinus* IX, 1, (Leiden: Brill, 1986). On the attribution of the *Nova* to Van Moerbeke, see Judycka, "L'attribution de la *Translatio nova* du *De generations et corruptione* à Guillaume de Moerbeke," in J. Brams and W. Vanhamel, *Guillaume de Moerbeke. Recueil d'Études à l'occasion du 700e anniversaire de sa mort* (Leuven: Leuven University Press, 1989), 247–52.

7. My analysis has profited from the English translation by Pierre Conway and R. F. Larcher, Bk. I, cc. 1–5.

their parts. Anaxagoras is mentioned especially for positing many elementary particles in an original mixture, from which not only the elements are separated—by a process called generation—but also the accidents—by a process called alteration. In this theory, alteration does not differ from generation.

Empedocles introduced several material principles (*materias*), namely, the four elements and two moving powers, friendship and strife. Unlike the theories of Anaxagoras and Democritus, the principles he accepted were finite (nos. 7–8). According to Anaxagoras, things are composed of a collection of small particles of different things, so that there is a portion of everything in everything. Democritus and Leucippus, on the other hand, said that sensible bodies are composed of indivisible bodies, the atoms, which are all of the same specific nature (nos. 9–10) and infinite in number. Thomas points out the difference between the theories of Anaxagoras and Empedocles: the latter's four elements—the seeds of all bodies—are more simple than the homoeomeries (or "things with like parts") of Anaxagoras, who said that things become when similar particles drawn from material beings come together (no. 12).[8]

The reason that some of the Pre-Socratics taught the difference between alteration and generation is indicated in lesson 2 (I.1.314b1–315a25). For those philosophers who thought that all things come forth from one material principle, there can only be alteration but, Thomas says, we accept a primary subject of all those things that come to be and pass away, which, however, is not a being in act but in potency. According to Empedocles, material bodies are a mixture composed of several of the elements. When the elements come together, generation results; when they are separated, corruption occurs. A change in the arrangement of these parts is alteration. But, just as the subject remains the same under increase (growth), alteration, which is a change of qualities, leaves the substance unaltered too. For those who hold this theory of the elements, there is no conversion of one element into another, and consequently no change of qualities, as these are attached to the elements, like black to earth, cold to water, etc. (no. 14). Furthermore, as contraries are in a subject of the same nature, this is also the case in alteration. When a common subject of the different qualities is denied, there will not be alteration. In the next passage, Thomas mentions the contradictions in the system of Empedocles, as pointed out by Aristotle (nos. 15–17).

---

8. On the history and meaning of the term *homoeomery*, see G. S. Kirk and J. E. Raven, *The Presocratic Philosophers* (Cambridge: Cambridge University Press, 1957), 386–88, and G. B. Kerferd, "Anaxagoras and the Concept of Matter before Aristotle," in *The Presocratics: A Collection of Critical Essays*, ed. A. P. D. Mourelatos (Princeton, N.J.: Princeton University Press, 1974), 489–503.

In lesson 3 (I.2.315a26–316a14), the theory of generation and alteration of Democritus and Leucippus is examined. Previous philosophers, Plato included, did not sufficiently explain generation and corruption, nor growth (increase) and mixture (no. 19). Democritus and Leucippus make generation and alteration result from minor changes in the arrangement and position of the figures of things (composed of collections of atoms), like a change of words, and their order can make a text into a comedy or a tragedy (nos. 20–21). The arguments in favor of the theory of Democritus—a body is composed of indivisible small bodies or atoms—are further examined in lesson 4 (I.2.316a14–b18) (no. 28). A body cannot be totally divided because it is not clear what remains after all those divisions (no. 29). It cannot be a body, nor something incorporeal (nos. 30–31). A magnitude cannot be divided into points (no. 32), nor be composed of points (no. 33). In lesson 5 (I.2.316b18–317a31), we read Aristotle's answer to the arguments of Democritus: one can maintain that every perceptible body is divisible at any point whatsoever, but also that it is not divisible. The first statement concerns the state of potency; the second speaks about points in act (no. 35). Democritus argues that the division of a perceptible being may proceed up to a certain terminus: there is a certain magnitude that is indivisible (no. 36). Aristotle also mentions another argument used by Democritus: if generation takes place by association and corruption by dissociation, there must be indivisible bodies. Democritus must say so because for him the forms and natures of things are dependent on their place and mutual order, like the parts of a house. As one cannot proceed forever in the quest of principles, there must be some first indivisible magnitudes from which the bodies are constituted and in which they disintegrate (no. 37).

Democritus believes that when a perceptible body is potentially divisible, it is also actually divided. But this does not hold, for there are things that, according to what they are, are in potency, such as is the case in successive beings: in the first part of a day, the following hours are present in potency. It also happens in nonsuccessive things: the substance of air is in potency to all the forms, but we cannot say that all these forms are actually present, for then there would not be air anymore. This applies also to a line: that it is divisible in parts does not mean that is actually divided (no. 38). Democritus uses a paralogism: a line cannot consist of points in act that would be contiguous with one another, as he conceives it; if so, a magnitude would consist of points. All the points, being indivisible, would so be joined as to be not more than one. Association and dissociation of bodies are possible, Aquinas comments, but do not yield indivisible magnitudes (no. 39). In things whose essence does not consist in a certain order of parts (like in the case of a house), generation and corruption do not happen by association or dissociation of parts, but the first whole (*totum*) is transformed into the next (no. 40).

Generation as such is dealt with in lesson 6 (I.3.317a32–b33), where Aristotle exposes his own theory. We must first consider if there is generation and if what is generated is always coming forth from something. We speak of generation in a secondary sense (*secundum quid*) when there is a limited change, as in the size of something or in its condition (sick/healthy) (no. 42). It is not right to say that something is generated from absolute nonbeing for, if so, nonbeing would be being (nos. 45–47). A thing is generated from nonbeing in a restricted sense, and in another way from being (no. 48). But even after this distinction there remains a difficulty (*mirabilis dubitatio*) (no. 49). Is generation proper to substance or also to such accidents as quantity and quality? Generation in its true sense is only of substance (no. 50). Yet the question remains in which sense we can speak of the generation of such accidents as quantity and quality, while that out of which a substance is generated must be this particular thing (no. 51).

The discussion is continued in lesson 7 (I.3.317b33–318a27), in which Aristotle raises a question and in resolving it he also makes clear what generation really is. Thomas observes that when one accepts the eternity of the world and of motion, one must also make generation perpetual (no. 52). Under the assumption of perpetual generation one can consider the cause of motion, as Aristotle did in his *Physics* and *Metaphysics* XII insofar as the first mover was concerned, but here we are dealing with generation from the viewpoint of the material cause, as it is taking place in the succession of beings (no. 53). But a question arises about generation: if that which is corrupted becomes nonbeing, do we mean total nonbeing? If so, in the course of time many things would disappear into nonbeing and the world, being limited, would turn into the void (no. 54). The ancient natural philosophers, in order to safeguard eternal generation, attributed infinity to their first principle (e.g., air, space, homoeomeries), but Aristotle rejected this: nothing in the world is actually infinite (no. 55). If one objects that a finite magnitude can be infinite in potency, so that without end some part can be detached from it, Aristotle replies that it would become smaller each time. But this is not what we see happening, as what is generated has always more or less the same size (no. 56). The matter out of which a new being is produced is potentially the new form, although as yet it is the subject of another form. Thomas adds a note: Aristotle develops his theory on the supposition that motion and generation are eternal, something the Catholic faith does not teach (*fides Catholica non supponit*, no. 57).

In lesson 8 (I.3.318a27–319a3), the question is examined regarding why we say that some things are generated *simpliciter*, while we say that others are generated in a restricted sense. Parmenides would not speak of simple generation, as when fire turns into earth it changes into nonbeing (no. 59). In fact, nonbeing can mean total nonbeing or, in the case of generation, matter deprived of a form. This form can be a perfect form, but there are also intermediate forms, as for instance between a human fetus and a baby (no. 60). Aristotle also mentions the fact that certain qualities or elements co-signify a privation, such as earth, which is cold by nature compared to fire (no. 61). Thomas adds an explanation of the type of privation we are speaking about. "Coldness" is cold as a privation of warmth, yet it is not a pure privation, but has something of the contrary quality. The case of fire and cold is not simply that of a *habitus* and its privation, for cold has something of itself, so that we are dealing with a deficient quality. Warm and cold as accidents are not substantial forms. The differences between substantial forms are often hidden to us, but we qualify the differences of substances by their accidental properties (no. 62). Some have explained the difference between generation *per se* and generation in a secondary sense (*secundum quid*) as that between what is more perceptible and what is less so, but Aristotle rejects this view because it implies that the most important thing is to be perceptible, whereas the truth lies in the being of things (no. 63). To those who defend this view, the transformation of a thing into air would be a lower sort of generation, while in reality air is more being (no. 65).

In lesson 9 (I.3.319a3–b5), the difference is explained between generation as such and qualified generation in those beings that are not generated out of each other. Certain things are said to be generated *per se*, while other beings are generated in a limited sense. Every generation is the corruption of another thing, and every corruption is the generation of a new being, but one kind of generation is generation in an absolute sense, and another is generation in a limited sense. A question that needs to be answered is why in things that are not changing into one another, one is said to be simply generated (*simpliciter*) and the other is said to be generated in a limited sense (*secundum quid*). For instance: why do we not say that one who is learning and acquires knowledge is generated absolutely, but only in limited sense, whereas a man or an animal when they are born are generated? Clearly, the one who is born and the one who is learned are not generated from one another (no. 67).

Aristotle explains that the difference is that, in the first case, generation is at the level of substance and, in the second, at that of the accidents. What already exists can only become something new or other at the accidental level. Yet within both types of generation, there are differences inasmuch as the change can go from being to nonbeing, from perfect being to imperfect being, or from sensible being to what is deprived of sensation. When something positive comes forth, at the substantial level as well as the accidental level, we speak of generation absolutely, but if the outcome is something imperfect, such as the element earth or a state of ignorance, we do not speak of generation without qualification (no. 68). Matter is the subject that changes in the process of generation; it is never without a form (no. 69). A next question is why something is generated out of the corruption of the other: corruption is directed to nonbeing, generation to being; the terminus of corruption is the beginning of what is generated (no. 70). The nonbeing in the process of corruption is matter (no. 71). The matter, which receives another form in the process of generation, is common to the initial subject and to what is generated, although in some way (*aliqualiter*) it is different (no. 72).

The difference between generation and alteration is examined in lesson 10 (I.4.319b6–320a7) with regard to the type of transmutation and the subject underlying them. We speak of alteration when the perceptible subject remains the same, while transmutation concerns the passions of the subject. In the strict sense of the term, alteration is of a change of the qualities of the third species (no. 74). When there is a transmutation not only of the passions but of the entire substance in that its primary matter receives another substantial form and nothing perceptible of the previous substance remains, we speak of generation (no. 75); and particularly so when the previous being was scarcely perceptible (no. 76). In those bodies that are changed into one another, like air and water, a certain property may seem to remain, like the transparency of water and air (no. 77). Sometimes such a property seems to be the same, but it is nevertheless numerically different (no. 78). According to the class of accidents that are changing, we speak of increase and diminution when the change concerns quantity, of transfer (*latio*) or local motion when there is a change of place, and of alteration when the change concerns a passible quality (no. 79). At the end of this lesson, Thomas mentions a theory of Avicebron who placed a series of successive forms in things—such as that of substance, corporeity, animal being, etc. These later forms, in addition to that of substance, would result from alteration (no. 80). In a final passage of the lesson, Aristotle notes that first matter is the proper subject of generation and corruption (no. 81).

In lesson 11 (I.5.320a8–27), increase (growth) is dealt with as different from generation and alteration. Aristotle also explains how growth takes place. While generation is the transmutation of a substance, and alteration that of a quality, growth concerns magnitude. Growth is a motion from potency to act (no. 83) and involves a local movement, something that does not necessarily happen in the case of generation or alteration, although sometimes it does, as when fire or earth are formed (no. 84). In increase and growth, the parts of the body will change in regard to their place, even if the body itself remains where it was (no. 85). The parts of the body which increase their size do not move with a circular motion, whereas the parts of the heaven that move in a circle remain at the same place, as determined by the circumference of the heavenly sphere (no. 86).

In lesson 12 (I.5.320a27–b14), we learn that the subject that increases in size is not something incorporeal without magnitude. The question is raised whether something that is incorporeal can grow in size and be the subject of increase, for instance, matter by itself without magnitude (no. 87). But Aristotle excludes that matter without magnitude can exist by itself. He also says that matter, if it existed separately by itself, would have to occupy some place (no. 88). Aristotle also refutes the theory that there would be "more matters," for example, in water, so that when air is formed out of water, the matter of the water itself would remain. In this way, an infinite number of things could be generated from water. But experience shows that this is not the case (no. 89).

Lesson 13 (I.5.320b14–34) states that nothing that lacks magnitude can be the subject of increase (growth). Corporeal matter is the subject of increase. Points and lines are not the matter of bodies, as the Platonists thought (no. 91). According to the Platonists, mathematical figures are separated from natural forms and from the passions, which are the objects of the senses, but Aristotle denies the possibility that matter can be separated from natural forms, for it cannot be without a form and without qualities (no. 93). What is generated must be so by an agent of the same species or genus. There are, however, exceptions in an accidental way. A musician may heal someone, but in reality, he does so insofar as he has medical knowledge too. When an agent works with an instrument, the form of the effect is not that of the instrument but of the main cause. It can also happen that the matter of a patient is not proportional to the form of a more perfect agent and, consequently, the effect is not assimilated to the agent (no. 94). Finally, Aristotle observes that matter is always the matter of an individual body, which necessarily has some passions (no. 95).

Lesson 14 (I.5.320b34–321b10) addresses the following question: what is the nature of that by which something increases? When a body is moving, every part of it is also moving. The same seems to be the case in augmentation (growth) (no. 98). If what is added is corporeal, two bodies would be in the same place. If one objects that augmentation can take place without addition, the answer is that this is not a real augmentation, but the generation of a body. As said before, in real augmentation the same subject remains but becomes larger. Some give as an example of augmentation without addition, namely the transformation of water into air. But augmentation means precisely that the same body becomes larger while it remains itself (no. 100). Others object that in rarefaction the same body augments without any addition. Such a transmutation, however, is an alteration rather than an augmentation (no. 101). But the question remains: what is added in a real augmentation? When by food the animal body grows, its substance remains the same, its quantity increases, while the food is dissolved. The body that grows has the power to change the food by using it for its own growth (nos. 102–3).

In lesson 15 (I.5.321b10–34), Aristotle comes back to the main difficulty of augmentation, that is, what precisely happens in augmentation (growth). He points out three conditions that must be observed: (1) the thing that grows must remain itself; (2) augmentation takes place by something that is added; and (3) the visible parts of the growing body must become perceptibly greater (no. 104). Different members of the body consist nevertheless of the same parts (e.g., flesh, bone, sinew). Some authors tried to explain growth in living beings by the addition of these parts in a humid form, as a first humid flesh-matter, which would have spread through the body. But this explanation of Alexander (as Averroes quotes him) does not agree with Aristotle, who considers the growth of living bodies analogous to that of such inanimate things as gold and silver, so that the flesh that grows is the same as that which is considered as flesh-matter (no. 105). Every part of a body grows insofar as the body is considered in its species, but not when considered as matter (no. 106): the species of the body remains, not the matter in which this species is received. Thomas compares it with a river, which remains the same river, while the water is each time different. Materially, what is added to a body may be different and somewhat contrary. What pertains to the specific form of flesh remains, while the matter in which such a form is grounded (*fundatur*) is slowly worn by the action of heat, and new matter enters by nutrition. When what is added by nutrition is more than the original matter, the natural power of growth makes that the body develops to a greater quantity, so that it occupies a larger place. But the species always remains such that the parts of the body grow proportionally.

Alexander suggested that flesh as a species results from humid seed, while flesh as matter is the product of humid food. On this account, Aristotle's words that flesh as matter flows away and comes in are just a way of speaking, not a necessary conclusion (no. 107). In those parts of the body that consist of dissimilar parts, such as a hand, this proportional growth is more evident than in parts of a body with similar pieces and members. The reason is that in such dissimilar parts the distinction between species and matter is more evident (no. 108).

In lesson 16 (I.5.321b35–322a16), Aristotle explains on which points growth and generation are the same, and on which points they differ. It is obvious that in the process of augmentation the whole body grows. What is added may at first be different and contrary in regard to a passion, but it may later turn into the same species, for example, what at first was humid may become dry. In this sense, the like is augmented by its like (no. 110). What should be the form of the things (e.g., food) by which the increase takes place? Obviously, it must be in potency to the form of that which grows, although at first it may be of a different form. It must become the other thing by corruption, so that it loses its initial form (no. 111). Although in growth there is a certain formation of flesh, this is not a generation in its own right of a separate being, but a production of flesh in the flesh. The power of growth (augmentation) makes what was potentially flesh become flesh in and together with the already existing body. A similar augmentation may happen with fire, which subjects adjacent inflammable things to itself by imposing its form (no. 112).

Augmentation is compared to nourishment in lesson 17 (I.5.321b35–322a16). What augments, grows in magnitude, not magnitude as such universally, but rather the magnitude of this particular being. What comes into the growing being must be of a particular magnitude, but not the magnitude of the recipient being. It is the latter in potency (nos. 113–14). It can receive the form of the recipient (flesh), thus making it acquire a greater quantity. Because what comes into the subject (nourishment) is flesh in potency, it nourishes it; insofar as the body acquires a larger quantity through it, it augments it (no. 115). Nourishment continues all through the life of an animal, although the animal does not always grow. Although the food that is taken in has the capacity of both nourishment and growth, both processes are different (nos. 116–17).

Finally, Aristotle explains what decrease is. To this effect, he stresses the difference between living beings and inanimate things. Living bodies can move themselves, not only locally but also by alteration, growth, and generation, particularly insofar as nutrition is a form of generation. But whatever moves itself is divided into a part that moves and another part that is moved. Therefore, there is within living beings a power of their respective species that does not determine, that is, attach to itself as its own, a certain determinate matter (*materia signata*), as one part of its matter flows away and another is added. But one does not find this at all in lifeless beings. Because the power of flesh, and similar things, does not have an individually determined matter (*materia signata*) but determines itself now to this, then to that matter, it is as an immaterial species. However, it is always in a certain matter. When the power of a certain species can no longer convert nourishment into itself in the amount needed, we have to do with a decrease of the quantity, while the species is still preserved, even if it goes on to exist in a smaller quantity. At last even the species ceases to be, just as water added to wine in always greater quantities finally makes the wine become water. At this point, the commentary of Thomas ends.

Concluding Remarks

In his study of Thomas's commentary, Bertrand Souchard lists some differences between the text of Aristotle and the exposition of Thomas.[9] He sometimes uses different examples from those of Aristotle. For instance, in I.5.320b9, Aristotle asks if air can be contained in the water "as in a vessel," whereas Thomas (no. 89) comments by way of the image of wine flowing out of a jar. Souchard suggests that this image directs the thought of the reader to the miracle of Cana, as well as to the conversion of bread and wine in the Eucharist. In lesson 6, no. 47, Thomas introduces the concept of generation out of nothing, while this concept, as Thomas himself admits, is "contrary to natural generation and against the way of thinking of all natural philosophers who dealt with natural generation." As we have seen in lesson 7, no. 57, where Aristotle argued that there would always be generation, Thomas observes that the Catholic faith does not accept the perpetuity of the world and of movement. Yet, Thomas's few references to God, as the cause of things, are not wholly out of tune with the text. In II.10.336b32, Aristotle himself writes that God perfected the world by making coming-to-be perpetual, so that things might come as close as possible to his eternal being. Souchard also emphasizes that Thomas pays greater attention to the relation between substance and accidents, as well as to the theory of Anaxagoras, in order to implicitly argue for the necessity of an exterior cause in order to explain the dynamism of a living organism.

Regarding the relation of Thomas's commentary to that of Albert the Great, written around 1250, Bertrand Carroy sees few common elements be-

---

9. Bertrand Souchard, "Le commentaire de Thomas d'Aquin du *De generatione et corruptione* d'Aristote: de la critique aristotélicienne des matérialistes à la critique thomasienne des spiritualistes," in *Lire Aristote au Moyen Âge* (ed. Ducos and Giacomotto-Charra), 55–83, esp. 68–73.

tween the two.[10] Not only did Albert and Thomas use different translations: the *Vetus* in the case of Albert and mainly the *Nova*, in the case of Thomas. Also, whereas Albert often digresses into related topics, Thomas stays closer to Aristotle's text. Hence, Carroy thinks that Thomas may not have read Albert's text. In the commentaries dated to after the time of Thomas, epistemological questions tend to dominate, such as whether a science of generable and corruptible things is possible.[11] While Albert's commentary is part of his general undertaking to make the works of Aristotle easily accessible for students, so that they could better understand the thought of the great master, it is more difficult to explain why Thomas, at the end of his life and burdened by seemingly more important tasks, began to compose his *expositio* of the *De generatione et corruptione.*

10. Bertrand Carroy, "Héritage et différences: Thomas d'Aquin et Albert le Grand: Commentateurs du *De generatione et corruptione*," in ibid., 95–117.

11. See Joël Biard, "Les commentaires sur le *De generatione et corruptione* comme lieu de réflexion épistémologique dans quelques textes du XIVe siècle," in ibid., 119–34.

6 ❧ THE COMMENTARY ON
THE *METEOROLOGICA*

In the four books of this treatise, Aristotle discusses a great number of somewhat unusual cosmic and natural processes, such as comets, earthquakes, rainbows, the formation of winds, the saltiness of the sea, etc., and shows how they find their explanation in the context of his cosmological vision worked out in the *De caelo* and the *De generatione et corruptione*. The general theory of the four elements developed in these works is now applied to these and other phenomena and some precise details are given about the material of which the sphere of fire consists.[1] On the basis of a most careful observation, partly by himself, Aristotle develops rational theories that explain the observed phenomena.[2] Throughout the treatise observation occupies a central place. Later scientists have admired Aristotle for his unusual and extraordinary talent for observing and analyzing cosmic phenomena, although contrary to the scientists of modern times, he did not confirm his observations and deductions by experiments. What is new in the *Meteorologica* is the fundamental importance attached to what he calls the dry and moist exhalations for the explanation of many observed phenomena in our part of the world. In arguing that these phenomena all have a common origin in one of the two fundamental materials, the dry and the moist exhalations, Aristotle is able to present the treatise as an integrated unity.

There is no certitude with regard to the place and time Aristotle composed this work. The years after the death of Plato, when he lived and worked in Assos, Mytilene, and Macedonia, have been suggested. For at that time and in that region he was also engaged in the careful observation and study of the animal world. On the other hand, the *De caelo* with its theory of the elements

---

1. From antiquity onward the role of the fourth book of the *Meteorologica*, which deals with the transformation of various homeomerous bodies, has been disputed. See C. Viano, *La matière des choses. Le livre IV des Météorologiques d'Aristote et son interprétation par Olympiodore* (Paris: Vrin, 2006): 17–23, for the issue of the continuities and discontinuities between Books 1–3 and 4.

2. See I. Düring, *Aristoteles: Darstellung und Interpretation seines Denkens* (Heidelberg: Winter, 1966), 392.

is likely to be earlier. In *Meteorologica* I.3, the text refers to what had already been determined by him, apparently, in the *De caelo* and the *De generatione et corruptione* about the elements.[3] Aristotle now maintains that the four elements are transmutable into one another because a common substratum, matter, is underlying them. Some investigators think that the work was composed after the *De caelo*, that is, in the years at the Lyceum in Athens. Its contents deviate somewhat from the very regular cosmic zones assigned to water, air, and fire. We read that the cosmic region upward from the moon is neither fire nor earth, but is impure and has something of both. Efforts have been made to date the work on the basis of astronomical observations mentioned in the treatise.[4]

The treatise shows a respectful putting aside of ancient mythological explanations of unusual meteorological phenomena and witnesses to Aristotle's incredible gift of observation coupled with an insatiable curiosity about the causes of cosmic phenomena, though there is no verification by experiments. Throughout his book Aristotle is convinced of the permanence of his cosmological system and of the world, the central part of which is subject to changes. He also shows a remarkable geographical knowledge, although he himself does not seem to have traveled beyond the borders of what at that time was Greece.

Malcolm Wilson has argued that from a contemporary perspective the treatise contains four major surprises. First, whereas the contemporary world values complexity and often equates it with order, for Aristotle, it is the simpler order that is the better order. Second, there is the already mentioned reduction of the observed phenomena to dry and moist exhalations which gives the treatise a unity of cause, whereas contemporary science tends to invoke a variety of causes to explain the phenomena mentioned in the treatise. Third, Aristotle's empiricism, that is to say, his use of observational evidence, does not stand on its own but has to be viewed against the background of the more general philosophical foundations established in the *Physics*, the *De caelo*, and elsewhere. Finally, Wilson argues that the contemporary reader, who is acquainted with ancient teleology, will find it surprising that the *Meteorologica* does not contain references to teleology or a final cause.[5]

The reception of the *Meteorologica* has been somewhat limited. The partial Greek commentaries by Olympiodorus and Philoponus have survived as

---

3. References in a particular treatise to other works, however, do not necessarily show that the treatise is later than the books referred to.

4. See, e.g., S. M. Cohen and P. Burke, "New Evidence for the Dating of Aristotle *Meteorologica* 1–3," in *Classical Philology* 85 (1990): 126–29.

5. M. Wilson, *Structure and Method in Aristotle's "Meteorologica": A More Disorderly Nature* (Cambridge: Cambridge University Press, 2013): 4–6, and chap. 5 (93–116) on teleology.

well as the complete commentary by Alexander of Aphrodisias, which was translated from the Greek into Latin by William of Moerbeke in 1260.[6] An Arabic compendium of the treatise appeared and was translated by Gerard of Cremona, who also offered the first translation of Books I–III of the treatise, the so-called *translatio vetus*. On the basis of these and other sources, Albertus Magnus composed *Meteora*.[7] Aristotle's treatise was the first non-Jewish work of science or philosophy translated into Hebrew in the Middle Ages. Samuel Ibn Tibbon (ca. 1165–1232), who composed the translation on the basis of an Arabic translation made by Yahya of Antioch (ca. 975–1066), chose this text because of its relevance for biblical exegesis, in particular for a rational understanding of the biblical account of creation.[8]

The precise date of Thomas's composition of the commentary is not known. At any rate, the commentary is later than 1260, the date when William of Moerbeke finished his translation at Nicaea of the Greek text of Alexander of Aphrodisias's commentary on the *Meteorologica*. In a detailed study, A. J. Smet has shown that, in his commentary, Thomas relies heavily on Alexander of Aphrodisias's commentary. Smet compares twenty-three passages of the translation by Moerbeke with the corresponding ones in the commentary of Thomas and finds a surprising, sometimes even literal use of Alexander.[9] Martin Grabmann's suggestion that Thomas wrote his commentary in Paris between 1269 and 1272 because of a reference in the text, indicating that the horizon is different for Parisians from what it is for people living in Rome, is mistakenly based upon an inauthentic passage in the commentary.[10] Another *terminus ante quem* relies on the use of Thomas's commentary in an early French paraphrasing translation of Aristotle's treatise by Mahieu le Vilain which is dated between 1260 and 1270. However, the arguments for the dating of Mathieu's version are tenuous.[11] It is perhaps best to assume that the

6. See Alexander of Aphrodisias, *Commentaire sur les Météores d'Aristote*, ed. A. J. Smet (Louvain: Publications Universitaires de Louvain, 1968).

7. Albertus Magnus, *Meteora*, ed. P. Hossfeld (Münster: Aschendorff, 2003), and in particular P. Hossfeld, "Der Gebrauch der aristotelischen Übersetzung in den *Meteora* des Albertus Magnus," *Mediaeval Studies* 42 (1980): 395–406.

8. See R. Fontaine, "The Reception of Aristotle's Meteorology in Hebrew Scientific Writings of the Thirteenth Century," in *Aleph: Historical Studies in Science and Judaism* 1 (2001): 101–39, and A. Ravitzky, "Aristotle's 'Meteorology' and the Maimonidean Modes of Interpreting the Account of Creation," in *Aleph: Historical Studies in Science and Judaism* 8 (2008): 361–400.

9. A. J. Smet, "Alexander van Aphrodisias en S. Thomas van Aquino: Bijdrage tot de bronnenstudie van de commentaar van S. Thomas op de *Meteorologica* van Aristoteles," in *Tijdschrift voor Philosophie* 21 (1959): 108–41.

10. Martin Grabmann, *Mittelalterliches Geistesleben: Abhandlungen zur Geschichte der Scholastik und Mystik* (Münich: Max Hueber, 1926), 1:273.

11. K. White, "Three Previously Unpublished Chapters from St. Thomas Aquinas's Commentary on Aristotle's Meteora: Sentencia super Meteora 2.13–15," *Mediaeval Studies* 54 (1992): 49–93, at 67.

commentary dates to the last period of the life of Thomas, when he also wrote on the *De caelo* and the *De generatione et corruptione*. Torrell concurs and even suggests that most likely the treatise was composed in Naples in 1273.[12] Thomas's commentary seems to be the first to use the new translation (*translatio nova*) of Aristotle's treatise by William of Moerbeke, composed around 1260. It has been established that the Aristotelian text used by Aquinas originated at the University of Paris.[13]

In many printed editions, Thomas's unfinished commentary has been supplemented with inauthentic commentaries on the remainders of Books II–IV, although it has long been established that Thomas's commentary ends at II.5.363a20. Already in 1966, A. Dondaine and L. J. Bataillon pointed out that a number of manuscripts include an authentic commentary on two more chapters of Aristotle's text, namely II.7–8. This text, denoted by the numbered chapters or lessons 13–15 and hence referred to as *Sententia super Meteora* 2.13–15, has been edited by Kevin White, so that the authentic commentary now extends to 369a7.[14]

To conclude this introduction, I will provide a brief survey of the contents of Book I (all fourteen chapters) and Book II (chapters 1–8), covering 338a20–369a7, because this is the part that Thomas commented upon. In I.1, Aristotle recalls what he had written about the stars and their ordered movement as well as about the four elements. Still to be investigated are certain phenomena that happen less regularly, such as shooting stars and comets, rivers and rain, the winds, earthquakes, and the tides. In chapter 2, which specifically deals with the elements, Aristotle wonders whether what fills the space between the sphere of the stars and the central part of the world is one substance, called ether by the ancients and considered divine.[15] At 339b28, we read that in the course of time, theories about the world return in cycles, some of them even quite frequently. Another notion is that the celestial bodies are composed of fire. But in I.3 we are told that the intervals between the celestial bodies cannot be filled by fire—it would destroy them—but neither are they full of air, as that would make the mass of air disproportionately large compared to the three other elements. At 340b4ff., Aristotle puts forward a theory absent from the *De caelo*: the region of the stars, in particular where it borders on the zone

<hr>

12. J.-P. Torrell, *Initiation à Saint Thomas d'Aquin. Sa personne et son œuvre* (Paris: Cerf, 2015), 303.

13. See the critical edition in the *Aristoteles Latinus* series: *Meteorologica*, ed. G. Vuillemin-Diem (Turnhout: Brepols, 2008).

14. White, "Three Previously Unpublished Chapters," 49–93. White suggests that Thomas may have taken over certain suggestions of Adam of Bockfeld on how to divide the text and also the double explanation of the phrase *eclipses lunae*, which he seems to owe to Albert the Great (66).

15. On the theory that people generally consider the heaven divine, see *De caelo* 277b16.

of fire and air, is filled by a body that differs from air and fire, a kind of matter that is potentially hot, wet, and dry, and not uniform. He also states that the sun produces warmth through its rapid movement by which the earth is heated.

In I.4, we read that the earth gives off a dry exhalation of inflammable material, which, when ignited by the motion of the heaven, produces shooting stars. But also rising from the earth is a second exhalation, which is cool and moist. In I.5, Aristotle points out that when the air gets thicker, different colors result in it. In I.6, he warns us that comets are not planets (the wandering stars), as some have thought. He rejects the theories of Anaxagoras, Democritus, and Hippocrates, and he confirms on the basis of his own observations (343b10) that sometimes comets have tails and gradually fade away. In I.7, Aristotle advances his own theory: when the dry exhalation of the earth is carried around by the motion of the heavenly sphere and catches fire, shooting stars are seen. When it collides with an exhalation from below having a sufficient mass, a comet is produced.

In I.8, we read about the formation and the composition of the Milky Way. Putting aside some illusory theories and mythological explanations, Aristotle points out that its constitution remains the same and is not subject to change. He also observes that a moving star produces an exhalation in the fiery material around, and its movement causes a halo. I.9 discusses the region below the sphere of the sun but above the earth, consisting of water and air, which is the place where the heat leads to vapor that, when cooling off, becomes rain. Moisture rises by heat and, when cooled off, returns in the form of rain. I.10 points out that dew and frost are also due to vapor. I.11 notes that snow corresponds to frost at ground level. I.12 observes that some facts about hail are difficult to explain, for although hail is ice, hailstorms occur in spring and autumn. In I.13, Aristotle discusses the winds, the rivers, and the sea, while first rejecting some primitive theories. Mountains and higher regions absorb the water from the rain and become a sort of reservoir feeding the rivers. The largest rivers flow from the highest mountainous regions. In I.14, we hear about a cycle of changes, with certain regions becoming barren but later moist again. Cold and heat are the cause of this very slow process that escapes observation. Egypt is now drying up, but these changes are not due to causes in the higher regions of the universe. He also asserts that the earth is an insignificant part of the whole universe.

In II.1, Aristotle considers why the water of the sea is salty, and rejects the traditional idea that the sea has hidden sources. Ebb and high tide are not so noticeable in the large open sea. Some seas have no connection with the oceans. In II.2, Aristotle notes that the water of the sea evaporates, so that what remains is salty. What we now call the sea occupies a great part of the cosmic region of water. It is also the deepest place on the surface of the earth and because it is the natural place for water, all the rivers flow to it. Much water disappears but nevertheless the sea level remains the same. II.3 addresses the saltiness of the sea, which is due to the admixture of some substance of the earth that remains behind in the process of evaporation. II.4 describes the cause of the winds. The sun in its circular course draws up two kinds of exhalations, one moist, the other dry. The first is the origin of rain, the dry exhalation is the origin of winds. The air consists of two components, vapor (moist and cold) and smoke (hot and dry). These two exhalations can interact. When it rains the wind often dies. The winds blow horizontally, although the air surrounding the earth follows the movement of the heavenly sphere. In II.5, Aristotle claims that the considerable heat caused by the sun can reduce the exhalations. Both hot and cold weather can lower the winds. The greatest heat occurs after the sun has passed its solstice. The zones of the earth beyond the tropics both in the northern and in the Southern Hemisphere are inhabitable. II.6 describes the different winds. II.7–8 deal with earthquakes, the cause of which is related to the wind. He first rejects the theories of Anaxagoras, Democritus, and Anaximenes, before giving his own explanation, namely that earthquakes result from the dry and moist exhalations: when the moisture that the earth contains is heated by the sun and the earth's own fire, wind is generated that circulates beneath the surface of the earth and shakes it up, causing severe shocks. Wind has indeed a considerable moving power. In one of the longest chapters of the book, II.8, Aristotle also explains in which regions earthquakes are more frequent and when they are likely to occur.

Thomas's main *divisio textus* consists of three parts: (1) an introduction in which Aristotle explains his intention (338a20–339a10), (2) a restatement of the relation between the four elements and the ether as established in other works (339a11–32) and (3) the remaining bulk (339a32–369a7) of the treatise, dealing with particular transmutations of the elements, first those which occur "from on high" in Book I and subsequently those which occur "below" from Book II onward (no. 15). Book IV intends to deal with these transmutations insofar as they form a mixture.

The Commentary of Thomas Aquinas

Book I

In lesson 1 (I.1), Thomas explains that in order to make our scientific knowledge complete we must go from what is general in the subject we are studying to its subdivisions and specific differences.[16] In his *De generatione et corruptione*, Aristotle treated the transmutations of the elements in general, so that he must now go into details and study the changes that affect the elements. In fact, Thomas discerns a logical order in the opening lines of Aristotle's text, going from the most universal in the *Physics* to the heaven and the stars in the *De caelo*, and to the generation and corruption of the elements in the *De generatione et corruptione*. He also believes that the subject of the present treatise is wider than the term *meteora*, meaning "on high" or "elevated," indicates (no. 4). Thomas divides its contents in four sections: (1) certain phenomena happen above the earth, close to the heaven. Although the heaven itself is most regular, in the region underneath and closest to the path of the stars (*locum maxime propinquum lationi astrorum*) some unusual or exceptional effects may appear (no. 5); (2) the conjoined effects of air and water; (3) phenomena happening in the lowest region; and (4) the effects descending to the lowest region, such as lightning and typhoons. To these effects belongs what happens to the air and to the water and the exhalations (no. 6), as well as what takes place in the different regions of the earth, such as winds, earthquakes, etc. But Thomas remarks, exceptionally writing in the first person here, that we cannot fully explain all these phenomena and must leave the explanation of many things as being still subject to doubts. This is a modest, most interesting sentence in which he makes himself somehow responsible for the imperfect or wrong explanations of Aristotle but also shows that he does not always fully underwrite all Aristotle's theories (no. 7).[17] In addition, according to Thomas, we must be able to explain lightning and typhoons and the like. Also, we must investigate the causes active in the life of plants and animals and examine their different species. Only then we may have reached the end of the study of natural science, such as is it was planned from the very beginning (no. 9). This sentence, in turn, witnesses to the idea Thomas had of the study of the physical nature of things and its comprehensive character.

16. The individual, however, does not come in under the object of the sciences. In writing the following overview and analysis of Thomas's text, the English translation of *On Meteorology* by Conway and Larcher.

17. "In quibus non omnia perfecte et secundum certitudinem tradere possumus, sed quaedam sub dubitatione reliquemus, ad utramque partem rationem inducentes; in quibusdam vero veritatem attingemus aliquo modo."

Passing to lesson 2 (I.1–2), Thomas says that Aristotle first lays down what we need to know about the causes of the transmutations to be discussed in this treatise before we can undertake their study (no. 10). He begins by noting that the body of the sphere of the first heaven is the *quinta essentia*, the fifth element, also known as the ether. The other bodies consist of the four elements—namely earth, water, air, and fire—which result from the four possible pairs of tangible contrary qualities (hot and cold, dry and moist). These four elements are characterized by two movements: one upward (proper to air and fire) and the other one downward (characteristic of water and earth). Air is closer to fire, water to the earth (no. 11). The zones of these elements are contiguous but subject to the influence of the revolutions of the heavenly bodies (no. 12). The lower regions of the world receive their movement from the heaven, which is the first cause of natural things because of its incorruptibility and nobility (no. 13): its circular movement has no locally determined end. The inferior bodies perform rectilinear and therefore finite motions (no. 14).

In lesson 3 (I.3), we are informed about the transmutations of the four elements into one another; transmutations that are rendered possible because they share in matter, which is common to them (no. 16). Some observations on the individual elements follow. For instance that the size of the earth is very small; compared to the heavenly sphere, it is like a point. As for the element water, Aristotle points out that it has no natural place by itself but is collected in the sea and rivers (no. 17). But we must also inquire whether there is yet another body, or even if there are more bodies, in between the four elements and the fixed stars (no. 18). The ancients sometimes called this body, which they assumed to be there, the ether and considered it something divine and always in motion. Aristotle has taken up again this idea, which shows that the same opinions return in the course of history. Thomas notes that it is the view of Aristotle that the world is eternal and that scientific theories and arts may disappear but come back again in the course of time (no. 19). A body that moves with a circular motion is not one of the four elementary bodies. Some thought that the stars consist of fire and that the space between them would be filled by something like air, as Anaxagoras said. Others thought that upward from the sphere of the moon everything is fire and that the stars are small in size. As we know now, the heavenly bodies enormously exceed our earth in size. Another notion is that if there had been fire everywhere, the elements would have been annihilated (no. 20). In addition, the space between our part of the world and the spheres of the celestial bodies cannot be filled by air, as then the quantity of air would be enormous and totally out of proportion with that of water and the earth (no. 21). In that case, the proportion between the earth and water, on the one hand, and fire and air, on the other, would be totally unsettled (no. 22).

Three questions are raised in lesson 4 (I.3), one of which is answered in this lesson. In a celestial body, there is neither fire nor air, and so it is not hot. If this is the case, how then is heat produced in the lower bodies (no. 25)? Another question relates to the element air, which is the milieu where many of the phenomena that need to be explained take place, namely: why are there no clouds in the higher regions of the air? Heat can impede their formation, but the heat proceeding from the reflection of warmth by the air is much less in this higher region, and this region does not receive warmth from the stars either. And contrary to what is present in the air close to the earth, there is no water in this higher part (no. 26). The type of body that fills the space from the moon upward differs from fire and earth. In this zone, there is not only something pure but also something less pure, that is, less noble, which is found above all in the lower part of it close to the zone of the air (no. 27).[18] The bodies in the lower regions quite naturally receive heat and movement from above. As matter is reduced in act by the agent, particularly by the first agent, material things are determined by the first agent. What is coldest is furthest removed from the movement of the heaven. This is the case with the earth and water placed at the center of the world. Thomas also signals that the proper name of the fourth element should not be "fire," as fire is just the excess of heat (but because we have no other name we call it fire), while "air" is actually the common name of two elements, namely air and fire. A final remark in this lesson explains the difference between vapor and exhalation: vapor is humid and warm, while an exhalation is dry and warm (nos. 28–28bis).

In lesson 5 (I.3), we find an explanation of why in the higher part of the air there are no clouds: this region consists of fire more than of earth. A second reason for their absence is the circular flow of the air in the higher regions: winds occur in those parts where the air stagnates. There is a continuous interchange between fire and air, which pass into one another (no. 30). A further question reads: why do the celestial bodies that are not warm themselves produce heat? The answer: because what is carried around is warmed by this circular motion (no. 33). But here we must distinguish between the daily rotation and the motion proper to the planets (no. 34). The sun, which is not warm itself, causes most heat because of its vicinity to the earth and the speed of its movement as well as its mass. It is also white and not colored. And the warm-

---

18. This explanation, which seems to downgrade the idealistic construction of the layers of the elements and the sphere of the fixed stars of the *De caelo*, prepares the field for the explanation of unusual cosmic phenomena.

ing of remote celestial bodies is hardly noticeable: they are not hot and do not show deviations from their course, as is the case with falling stars (nos. 35–37).

Having thus laid the groundwork for further phenomena to be discussed, Aristotle explains the phenomenon of the falling stars and related observations in lesson 6 (I.4). Besides the appearance of falling stars, one can also sometimes observe flames and stars that move in different directions (*discurrunt*). When the earth is warmed by the movement of the sun, it releases two types of exhalation, one more like fumes (*vaporosa*) and moist, the other foamy and dry. From the watery surface of the earth, the moist and fumy evaporation is set free, but from the earth itself a dry and foamlike one is released. This foamlike evaporation, being warmer, rises above the other one, as in the cosmos we see that the hot and dry element is located below the sphere of the stars. This hot and dry element is commonly called fire (no. 39). This foamlike and dry evaporation is like combustible material and easily bursts into flames when stimulated by the motion of the body above it (no. 40), that is, when it is heated by the circular motion of the heaven. Such fiery phenomena as flames vary according to the different positions and quantities of the matter of this evaporation (no. 41). This is further explained: the burning exhalation when scintillating may take the form of torches or of a goat. When the exhalation is not continuous but scattered, stars appear that seem to fly and for which less material is needed (no. 42). Sometimes the exhalation provoked by the movement of the sun may appear as shooting stars, and when the thickened mass of the exhalation is forced downward, it takes the form of a falling star (no. 43).

Passing to lesson 7 (I.4), we read that it is a question whether shooting stars result when a smoke-like exhalation is set afire by the flame of a higher light and travels downward, or whether they are the projection downward of the same falling body (no. 44). On clear days and nights the path of a shooting star is visible both on land and on the sea. They fall downward because they are expelled by something cold. If they were hot, they would move up (no. 45). The trajectories of the stars resulting from the two sources are different, namely, those from the moist exhalation move downward, pushing with them some of the hot element, while those that are generated in a lower area become dense and cool (no. 46). Aristotle explains that the path of the falling star will be different depending on the position of the exhalation. When, for instance, material from it comes together above the falling star it will move downward. But sometimes the ejected material moves with two motions (no. 47). All these phenomena are produced below the moon; they seem to move very fast for being close to us, although the stars, the sun, and the moon are moving much faster (no. 48).

Lesson 8 (I.5) informs us about the causes of certain phenomena one observes at night in the sky, such as crevices and gashes (no. 49): the upper air is easily ignited, so that flames and other varieties of ignition may appear. When light shines through vapor of thick air different colors may appear: purple, reddish, black, and white. When vapors are condensed they obscure the light of rising or setting stars. The mixture of colors can also be caused by refraction (no. 50). The cause of crevices is that light is hindered by thicker vapors than usual (no. 51). During daytime the colors produced by the mixing of black and white are hardly visible because of the sun's brightness (no. 52).

Aristotle mentions several opinions about comets in lesson 9 (I.6). Anaxagoras and Democritus said that comets are the conjunction (σύμφασις) of the planets that appear to touch each other when coming close so that one comet is like flowing hair (κόμη). Thomas adds a note regarding the number of planets: they are five in number—Saturn, Jupiter, Mars, Venus, and Mercury (no. 54). Another view is that of the Italian Pythagoreans, who said that a comet is one of the planets. It is seldom visible because it does not depart much from the sun (no. 55). Hippocrates and his disciple Aeschylus had another opinion: they thought that a wandering star (a planet) may acquire a tail when in a certain position it draws up moisture (no. 56). When it gets away from the sun it appears to us (nos. 57–58). According to this view, our vision occurs by beams of light emitted by the eye and reflected by the object seen.

In lesson 10 (I.6), these opinions are rejected: not all comets are wandering stars (planets) for some move outside the Zodiac, whereas the planets remain in this Zodiac circle. Several comets have been seen together, something that does not happen to planets (no. 60). If the tail of comets is the effect of the reflection of rays issuing from the eye, as Hippocrates says, sometimes the comets must appear without a tail when moving within the tropics. But no star is seen wandering without a tail except the planets (the wandering stars), which are seen without tails and are all visible above the horizon, while a comet appears as separate from its position (no. 61). It is not true to say that comets appear only north of the tropics (no. 62). According to the theory of the eye emitting beams, the observation of a comet in December, when the sun is near the winter solstice, would seem impossible because of the great distance (no. 63). On the basis of his personal observation, Aristotle writes that nonwandering stars may also have tails (no. 64). Moreover, some disappear without approaching the sun, but they do so by receding from it (no. 65). Contrary to what Democritus said, Aristotle saw Jupiter conjoin with a star in "The Twins" and make it invisible; yet, instead of what was to follow from the opinion of Anaxagoras and Democritus, no comet appeared (no. 66). In a final argument, Aristotle says that according to their appearance to us, the stars are like indivisible points, so that when they are in conjunction they should not appear larger and no tail should be visible (no. 67).

In lesson 11 (I.7), Thomas mentions Aristotle's view of the cause as well as the place and time of the appearance of comets: in this issue no certitude can be reached and we should be satisfied with solving the question in such a way that nothing impossible results (no. 68). To determine the cause of the appearance of comets, Aristotle recalls his theory of the hot-dry exhalations, which are continuous with the fire in the region below the spheres of the stars. These exhalations are drawn into motion by the revolving heavenly spheres. Such an exhalation is frequently ignited (no. 70). When, on the one hand, this fire is not so large as to burn up all the material right away and, on the other, a new exhalation comes up from below to keep it burning for a long time, a comet is formed. The rest of this exhalation appears as a tail. If the exhalation surrounds the star, a circle of hair, called "coma," is formed (no. 71). A comet does not have the movement of falling stars, but it revolves along with the heaven (no. 72). But there are other ways in which comets may appear. For instance, when an exhalation comes together under a star, then this star, because of its motion, becomes a comet, but its *coma* is located in the air under the area of the course of the sun and the moon (no. 73). When a comet is connected with a star, it will appear to move with the movement of this star, but when the comet is an independent fiery material by itself—as is frequently the case—it will seem to lag behind (no. 74). Several comets announce winds and droughts, which are also the result of the dry exhalation drawn from the earth. When many comets appear, the year will often be dry and windy. What has been said is illustrated by some examples (nos. 75–76).

In lesson 12 (I.8), Aristotle examines the Milky Way and, as usual, he tells us first what some of his predecessors said about it. According to some Pythagoreans, it would be like a path either of a certain star that abandoned its own course or of the sun itself, which would have traveled along the Milky Way. The produced heat affected the material to such an extent that the path became white (no. 78). But if this were the reason, the Zodiac should also be white, as the sun and all the wandering stars pass through it (no. 79). A second opinion held that the shadow of the earth covers the brightness of the stars up to the Milky Way but does not reach any further (no. 80). If this were true, the motion of the earth's shadow would successively blot out other stars, but this is not the case (no. 81). Another argument is the following: the sun is much larger than the earth, so that the shadow of the earth is not projected very far, and does not reach as far as the fixed stars (no. 82). Some said these stars act as a sort of mirror for the sun's brilliance (no. 83). But Aristotle writes that, if the mirror moves and also the object seen by the mirror, it is impossible for the same appearance to occur in the same part of the mirror. The stars of the Milky Way are in motion, just as the sun is in relation to us, but they remain in the same place in relation to one another, something that would not happen if their appearance were caused by a reflection (no. 84). The conclusion is that the Milky Way is not the path of any of the planets, nor the brightness of stars that are not reached by the rays of the sun, nor the reverberation of our vision from the stars to the sun.

Aristotle's own opinion about the Milky Way is put forward in lesson 13 (I.8). He first recalls his theory of the exhalation that is drawn up from the earth to the higher part of the air (which is called fire, although strictly speaking it is not fire) and that by the movement of the heaven becomes more dense. In this way comets are formed (no. 86). In the Milky Way, something similar takes place, namely that a comet as a lifted-up exhalation may accompany the course of a star (no. 87). If the motion of one star can drag along an exhalation, then that of all the stars can do it too (no. 88). In the Zodiac, the mass of the exhalation is dissolved because the sun and the other planets move through it and separate it, so that no fringes appear, but in the Milky Way there are so many stars and their stellar virtue is so powerful that they attract exhalation. While there are no causes to impede this accumulation of exhalation (as happens in the Zodiac), the stars of the Milky Way are scattered like seeds, because they do not form certain configurations (nos. 89–91). If we accept the plausibility of this explanation of how comets are formed, it also explains how the stars of the Milky Way have these fringes. The stars use up so much of the exhalations that no surplus is left for the formation of comets (no. 92).

In lesson 14 (II.9–10), Aristotle examines the causes of the moist exhalation present in the lower part of the air and that present in the phenomena of rain, dew, and frost. This lower region is common to water and air. The primary moving cause and the first principle of whatever happens in this part of the air is the sun as it moves in the Zodiac circle. The sun separates the vapors by detaching them from the earth, and when it is absent and it gets colder, clouds are condensed into water. By staying close to us (in the summer) and by going away (in the winter), the sun is the cause of generation and corruption (no. 96). The material cause of these phenomena is this humid layer of water that surrounds the earth at rest in the center (no. 97). When these vapors rise and the warmer part of them rises even higher, what is left behind gets cool, thickens into a cloud, and falls back on the earth (no. 98). What is left in the cloud and is not condensed into water becomes fog (no. 99). This circular transmutation (from water to vapor, to clouds, and to water again, which falls on the earth) imitates the circular movement of the sun. The flow of ascending and descending vapors should be seen as a circular stream common to water and air. When the sun is near, this stream flows upward, but when it goes away it flows downward (no. 100).

When the vapor is condensed into water, it falls down in small drops or in larger drops called rain (no. 102). During daytime some small quantity of the watery mass evaporates but it does not rise very high, and when the air is cooled off at night, it comes down as dew or frost. So the daily motion of the sun has a similar effect to that of its movement in summer and winter in regard to the production of rain (no. 103). When the vapor freezes before it is condensed into water, it becomes frost (*pruina*). But when the vapor is condensed into water and there is not so much heat that it dries out, nor so much cold that it freezes, dew occurs. It must be colder for vapor to freeze than for water (no. 104). For dew and frost to occur the air must be clear, without clouds and winds (no. 105). As the moderate heat that produces the exhalations cannot raise them to a great height, there is no frost on high mountains. Moreover, the upper air above the mountains dissolves the concentrations of vapor (no. 106). Dew forms when southerly winds are blowing, but not when the north wind does (no. 107). The south wind brings mild temperatures, and so dew can form, but it cannot be formed in winter or when it is cold, because then the exhalation cannot rise sufficiently for dew to be formed (no. 108). Because of the cold in Pontus,[19] the south wind is unable to produce sufficient mildness for vapors to arise, so that no dew can form (no. 109).

In lesson 15 (I.11–12), Aristotle instructs us about the place where hail and snow are formed. In the zone of the clouds, rain, snow, and hail develop by cold. Snow and frost are proportionally the same, as are rain and dew. For the formation of rain, a great amount of vapor must be cooled, but for that of frost only a small amount is required, while snow results when an entire cloud is frozen. Rain and snow are generated in the higher regions, dew and frost in the lower (no. 110). The formation of hail is somewhat complex. Hail is a sort of crystal, namely, frozen water. Although water freezes, especially in winter, hailstorms occur in spring and autumn, but less often in winter (no. 111). Besides this phenomenon there is a second difficulty: water freezes on high, but when it is formed there (out of vapors) it falls down immediately,

---

19. The region south of the Black Sea.

so that there is no time for it to properly freeze (no. 112). The answer to this difficulty suggested by some is that small particles of water that remain in the air may congregate and form drops which freeze (no. 113). But Aristotle rejects this solution.

The case of hail is different. Bits of ice do not unite as moist things do (no. 114). He mentions some other opinions about the formation of hail: a cloud would be pushed up high to where it is very cold, so that the water in it freezes. Particularly during the warmer season, clouds are pushed up very high. This explains the formation of hailstorms during that period of the year (no. 115). But contrary to what this theory implies, hail does not occur on higher mountains, while snow does (no. 116). Sometimes clouds are seen near the earth and a hailstorm happens with stones of an incredibly large shape, but which are not round. The reason is that the freezing happened close to the earth and the fall of the hail is of short duration—otherwise the stones, while falling down, would have become round (no. 117). The size of the hail is in proportion to the cause that makes the water freeze (no. 118). Recalling that on hot days the water of fountains is cool, while it is warm in wintertime, Aristotle writes that when the weather is warm, the cold in the air is shut in with greater force, so that on warm days larger drops of water are formed and rains become more violent. The water is frozen by the cold, shut up, and then hail is formed. This explains water can be congealed into hail in warm weather (no. 119). According to a difficulty mentioned above, there would not be enough time for the water high up to freeze and to turn into hail, because the big drops would already fall down. However, the real answer is that because of the intense cold, the freezing is more rapid than it takes the water to fall down (no. 120). Hail falls less in summer than in spring or autumn because the air is drier during the summer. In winter, there is not enough heat to concentrate the cold that generates hail (no. 121). The cold can penetrate better in water that has been heated and rarified before (no. 122).

Lesson 16 (I.13) discusses the way in which rivers are formed. Some philosophers said that as the air is one, the winds are one too. But that is like saying that all rivers are one river and all water is one. On this subject uneducated people may have a better opinion (no. 124). For some authors the water ascending up by evaporation re-descends and is collected under the earth and flows from there to form springs and rivers, as if it emerges from a "great womb." If the reservoir is small and the source of the river runs dry, the river itself will also fall dry, until water falls again from the sky (no. 125). But this opinion does not hold, for in view of the enormous number of rivers and the huge quantities of water that they carry, the underground reservoir would have to be as large as the earth. Although there may be certain reservoirs of water inside the earth, the earth itself is not hollow (no. 126). Aristotle also rejects the theory that water would be continually generated in the earth, as evaporated air is condensed into water in the air (no. 127). Things take place in the same way within the earth, as above the earth. Above the earth vapor is condensed, so that drops form and rain falls down in a certain quantity. The same takes place within the earth: small drops become the sources of springs and rivers (no. 128). The flow of the rivers seems to be originating from the mountains and the larger the mountain, the larger the river will be. Springs are also located close to mountains that collect great quantities of rainwater. Although the mountains are convex, they can receive large amounts of water. They also produce water insofar as the vapor drawn out of the earth is clotted within the earth because of its coldness. To prove what he is saying Aristotle mentions several high mountain ranges, such as the Parnassus,[20] the Caucasus, and the Pyrenees, from which large rivers flow (no. 129). Believing that the water from supposed lakes under the earth would account for all the water that flows through the rivers amounts to saying that springs contain all the water of the rivers. We must nevertheless admit that there are reservoirs of water under the earth, as many streams are absorbed by the earth (no. 130).

The duration and change of rivers are discussed in lesson 17 (I.14). Changes occur that affect the earth: what is now dry may become a sea, and vice versa. But this happens in a certain order (no. 131). The cause of these phenomena is that the earth itself may also become old, but it does so part by part, according to the degree of heat or cold, as its energy comes to a stop, depending on the sun and other heavenly bodies. Some parts of the earth will continue being moist—still in their youth—but later dry out. One part increases in heat or coldness while other parts decrease. These changes affect the rivers, so that in some regions of the earth they dry out but elsewhere new rivers appear (no. 132). These changes take place over a long period of time and so escape our notice. The same people do not always remain in the same area; wars and epidemics as well as migrations bring about changes of the population. Aristotle mentions Egypt and other lands that gradually became habitable or vice versa (no. 133). He rejects the explanation that some have given, namely that the whole world is changing: from transmutations in small areas one cannot draw conclusions about the whole (no. 134). He explains the transmutations by assuming the existence of a great cycle marked by times of excessive drought, storms, and rains, and he refers to the deluge in Greece

---

20. Mountains in central Greece north of the Corinthian Gulf. Thomas mistakenly writes that they are located in Asia.

in the time of Deucalion (no. 135).[21] The fact that rivers continue to flow is explained by the great mountains, which allow them to keep vast stores of water. Where the land is not able to receive much water the flow of the rivers will diminish until there will again be an abundance of rain. This cycle affects the whole earth (no. 136). Aristotle illustrates what he says by some examples, such as Egypt, the Sea of Azov, and the Bosphorus, which is becoming narrower (no. 137). Because there is no end to time and the universe is eternal, the flow of rivers such as the Don and the Nile is subject to changes and the place of sea and dry land may be reversed.

Here, Thomas adds an important note: the theory that the world and time are eternal is erroneous and contrary to the faith (*alienum a fide*). The arguments Aristotle advances do not demonstrate his theory "as was shown elsewhere" (no. 138). Indeed, on several occasions in his commentaries on Aristotle, Thomas rejects the conclusiveness of Aristotle's arguments in favor of the eternity of the world.[22]

Book II

In the first three chapters of Book II, Aristotle examines the sea and its nature. In the next three chapters he studies the winds. In II.7–8, he turns to earthquakes; and in the final chapter, II.9, thunder and lightning. In Book III, he considers what accompanies these principal "passions," such as lightning, thunder, rainbows, etc. Thomas notes that this division of the text is quite fitting (*conveniens*) insofar as the treatise starts from phenomena in the "upper region" and subsequently proceeds to phenomena in the "lower region" (no. 140).

In lesson 1 (I.1), Thomas says the Philosopher came to a conclusion about dry exhalation from the earth, which is at the origin of things generated in the upper region of the air (e.g., falling stars, comets, etc.), after which he treated phenomena related to moist exhalation (e.g., rains and rivers). He now examines the question of the sea, into which all rivers flow. He first recounts the explanation of "ancient theologians" (οἱ ἀρχαῖοι καὶδιατρίβοντες περὶτὰς θεολογίας, 353a34–35), who said that the sea has its own springs in order to avoid resorting to a nonterrestrial cause. For them, the earth and the sea were "most worthy of our reverence," Thomas notes (no. 141). Regarding the expression "ancient theologians," Thomas adds that "before the times of the philosophers there were men called theologizing poets, such as Orpheus,

---

21. When Zeus flooded the earth in wrath at the sins committed in the Bronze Age, Deucalion and his wife Pyrrha built an ark and floated around until the waters subsided.

22. See for instance *In VIII Phys.* l. 2, no. 986, and *In XII Meta.* l. 5, nos. 2496–97.

Hesiod, and Homer, because under the guise of fables they declared divine things to men" (no. 141).[23] Next, Aristotle mentions the opinion of natural philosophers, who used rational arguments only. A first opinion about the generation of the sea held that the surface of the entire earth was full of water but dried out by evaporation. From this evaporation the air and the winds were formed and also the movement of the sun, the moon, and the stars. What was left was the sea, but this will one day dry up. Such was the view of Anaxagoras and Diogenes. Empedocles, however, said that when warmed by the sun, the earth exudes the water of the sea, which is salty like the sweat of animals. Anaxagoras thought that the sea became salty because earth was admixed with the water (no. 142). Of the waters on the surface of the earth some are stationary, some flow. Of those that are stationary, some have their own sources, such as wells. All the water from fountains and rivers flows according to the inclination of nature, while waters that are stationary are made so artificially. Such a quantity of water, as that of the sea, cannot explain itself as if it comes from springs (no. 143).

There are also several seas that are nowhere in contact with one another. The Red Sea has a narrow connection with the ocean that lies outside the Columns of Hercules, from which the Hyrcanian[24] and the Caspian Sea are far removed. People are living all around these seas, so that if they had springs these would have been discovered (no. 144). Thomas underlines that we must not suppose that the sea can flow as if it proceeds from springs as was said in one of the previous arguments. Aristotle indicates three causes of the flow of the sea. A first one is that a flow occurs when a sea is narrowed by the adjacent land and stirred by the movement of the moon. This commotion goes unnoticed in the open sea, but becomes visible in narrow areas. A second cause is that the sea contained within the Columns of Hercules, for instance, flows because it receives its water from many rivers. A third reason is that because seas are of unequal depth, the water of the shallower ones always flows to the deeper ones. The sea beyond the Columns of Hercules is not deep, and the flow is from higher to lower places (no. 145). Aristotle thinks that the earth is higher toward the north, as was suggested by some of the ancients who thought that the sun, turning around the earth, would become invisible at night, obscured by northern mountain ranges (no. 146).

In lesson 2 (I.2), Aristotle shows that the sea is the natural place of all water. The ancients thought that the sea is the source of all the water, its total

23. Wilson agrees that Aristotle most likely had Hesiod in mind. See his *Structure and Method in Aristotle's "Meteorologica,"* 182–83.
24. This might refer to the Aral Sea.

mass. Just as the main body of fire exists in the upper region, its natural place, while the earth is in the center, so that it seems reasonable to assume that there is a place where the mass of water assembles. For every element there must be a continuous and stable place, so the many rivers with flowing water cannot be the natural place of water. The ancients therefore thought that the rivers also flow from the sea. Wherever there was water outside its proper place, it would flow to it. That the water of the rivers is not salty was explained by the filtering of the earth (no. 148). But if the sea is the source of all water, why then is its water salty? When an element is in its natural place it should not be transformed; saltiness is not a natural property of water (no. 149). Because the movement of the sun is the cause of generation and corruption and of all permutations in the lower regions of the world, what is most subtle and sweet in purified water must be evaporated, that is, rise to a higher region, be condensed by the cold, and come down to the earth (no. 150).

Aristotle rejects the somewhat ridiculous opinion that the sun is fed by the moisture and has to move because there is not enough moisture in one place (no. 151). This view is wrong as the vapor does not ascend as far as where the sun is. If the sun were fed, it would be renewed continuously, like a flame which continuously devours other material. He also mentions the following argument: the rising of moist vapor is similar to the steam of boiling water. But the fire under the boiling pan is not fed by steam. It is unreasonable to say that the sun needs food and the other stars do not, although they are also of a fiery nature. Another opinion holds that originally the earth was covered by water, which evaporated by the heat of the sun and became air, which is the cause of winds. But this view is refuted by the fact that what is lifted up returns to the earth. The higher bodies are not fed by vapors from the earth (no. 152). The solution Aristotle advances is that sweet water is lighter and so carried up, while what is salty remains in its place. The sea occupies the natural place of the element water: all water moves to the sea as to its proper place, for the place of the sea is more concave. What is sweet in the water is borne aloft, while what is salty remains (no. 153).

In lesson 3 (I.2), we learn why the volume of the sea does not increase. The total amount of water carried to the sea by the rivers is spread out over an enormously wide area and, without our being able to notice it, evaporates continuously (no. 155). What Plato says in *Phaedo* about the sea and the rivers cannot be true, namely that all the seas and rivers would meet at a subterranean source, the Tartarus, and that this source is always in motion and flows in all directions and that the flowing water acquires its color and taste from the earth through which it flows (no. 156). Aristotle rejects this position with five arguments. If the overflow of the Tartarus is in every direction and if the rivers return there, rivers would have to be higher than their springs. A second reason against Plato's position is that it implies that an equal amount of water is always preserved, for the same quantity that flows from the Tartarus returns. But this would exclude the generation of water in the air by vaporization. A next argument is that rivers end at the sea and do not go down underground (except some but these emerge again). If the rivers flowed out of the Tartarus they would have a full quantity of water from the start, something we do not observe. Finally, Aristotle argues that it would not be fitting that the sea has the Tartarus as its source, as the natural place of the water is where the sea is now located (no. 157). The last passage of this lesson summarizes what has been said: the sea is the natural place of water and not just of the sea, that is, of salt water. The water becomes salty after evaporation and because of residues. Water is generated outside the sea, both in the air (the generation of rain) and within the earth. Water always flows to the sea (no. 158).

The question discussed in lesson 4 (I.3) is whether the sea has always existed and will always be. Aristotle rejects some theories of former philosophers who said that the sea did not always exist, nor did the entire world. Because the world was generated, the sea also was. And if the world is perpetual, the sea also is. Thomas states that Aristotle refers to what he had shown in the *Physics* and in the *De caelo*, but that his theory about the eternity of the world is wrong and contrary to the faith, and he also points to his identical statement at the end of Book I (no. 160). Next, Aristotle rejects what the ancients said about the disappearance of the sea by comparing some views to fables. He mentions in particular the sixth-century fabulist Aesop who said that eventually all the waters will disappear. Both Aristotle and Thomas discard this fable as an unfit explanation for someone seeking the truth (no. 161). But whatever the cause, the water that surrounds the earth will remain forever: the weight of water makes it stay beneath the air, but above the earth. Evaporated water must return to the earth. If the water is all the time carried aloft, it also returns all the time. The sea will never dry out. As the motion of the sun is forever the same, the evaporation of water and its falling down as rain will also continue always (no. 162). The theory that the sea will become dry and came into existence at some past time was suggested by the appearance of dried-out places. But this change between excessive drought and abundance of rain happens in periodical cycles in our part of the world, and is not proper to the entire world (no. 163).

In lesson 5 (I.3), the saltiness of the sea according to the opinion of others is discussed. Those who say that the sea has been generated cannot give an explanation of its saltiness. According to them, in the beginning water surrounded the earth but after the sun had drawn up a good part of the water a considerable area of the earth was left dry. The water that was left behind became the sea. The earth mixed with water, which in this way became salty, but it could not render salty the much larger quantity of water in the sea. (no. 65). However, mixing with earth cannot explain why the sea is salty. Likewise, the water which the rivers carry to the sea gives no explanation, for if the sea becomes salty by mixing the water with earth, the water of the rivers should also become salty. The sea is a collection of the water of all the rivers, which themselves are not salty (no. 166). Aristotle also rejects a third opinion, namely that, according to Empedocles, the sea is salty because it is the sweat of the earth. But this metaphor does not explain why what a person drinks is sweet, but his sweat is salty. We know that water becomes bitter when filtered through ashes and that urine leaves a salty deposit as does sweat, when exuded from the body, but Empedocles did not explain what makes the sea salty (no. 167). In spite of a huge quantity of water having been taken from the sea (by being warmed), the earth does not sweat. How could the huge mass of water of the sea remain salty if the amount of water raised from the earth is only a small portion compared to the water left on the earth; and in the same vein, the sweat and urine that become salty are of a much lesser volume than the humidity that remains behind in the body (no. 168). A third argument against the theory of Empedocles is the following: why does the earth not sweat a salty moistness if it did so at the beginning? At present, when certain areas are drying out, they do not "sweat." Those who say that the sea consists of the water left behind after part of the surface of the earth dried out are closer to the truth (no. 169).

In lesson 6 (I.3), Aristotle gives his own explanation for why the seas are salty. By way of introduction he recalls that there is a dual exhalation, a moist one and a dry one, and that this should be considered the cause of the saltiness of the sea. A related question is whether the parts of the sea remain numerically the same. The parts of a flowing river become different, and something similar happens in the air. The parts of the sea also seem to become other (no. 170). Returning to the problem of the saltiness of the sea, Aristotle says that it is caused by the admixture of something. What is not digested of the food is salty and bitter, especially in sweat and urine. There is also a residue of burnt things (no. 171). Something similar happens to the earth by the action of heat: a dry exhalation mixes with a humid exhalation. Both descend in the form of rain (no. 172).

Because of this mixing the first rains in autumn are brackish and on the salty side. The southern wind moves to us through hot and dry regions and is hot itself. It collects much of the dry exhalation and contributes to the falling of rain. The north wind, as it comes from cold regions, is cold but brings clear weather. The cause of the saltiness of the sea is the dry exhalation, which carries dried-out earth with it (no. 173). But because of the continuous evaporation, the cause of the saltiness seems to be evaporation; it is less the salty water than the sweet water which evaporates. But by being mixed with the dry exhalation the sweet exhalation becomes salty, so that the sea remains constant in the quantity of water and the percentage of salt (no. 174). How, then, can sweet water be generated from the vapors rising from the sea? What evaporates from the sea becomes drinkable when condensed; it is not converted into salt water. For things are resolved into their principles, so that what is produced is just water (no. 175). Some portion of the water of the sea is being raised by evaporation and becomes drinkable when condensed. Together with the falling water of the rain, something of the earth that was taken up high also comes down, but sinks below the drinkable portion of the water, so that the finer portion evaporates more. Thus the parts of earth at the surface change place with those that descend.

At this point of the lesson, Thomas adds a somewhat critical observation, typically introduced by the phrase *considerandum est autem*. Aristotle said that the saltiness is caused by the evaporation of what is sweet, but this would not be a cause if nothing were mixed in the seawater because otherwise the remaining water would be drinkable. This is why Aristotle says that something foreign like burnt earth must be mixed into the water, which sinks and makes the water of the sea salty (no. 176). Several signs point to the fact that the salty taste is caused by the admixture of earth: water seeping through wax is purified and becomes sweet; sea water is heavier than sweet water; it is also more dense than the water of the rivers, so that ships sink deeper when on rivers than when on the sea; eggs float in water to which salt has been added; if anyone would immerse himself in the lake of Palestine,[25] he would not sink; in the province of Chaonia (the northwestern part of Epirus) a spring with salty water flows into a river, in which salt is found instead of fish; in certain regions where reeds are burned, the water becomes salty. So that it follows that both in sweet waters as well as in the sea, combustion takes place that causes saltiness (no. 177).

Lesson 7 (I.4) discusses the cause of winds, which, as Thomas notes, is the same as the mixing of the warm exhalation of the earth with the sea. With regard to the material cause of the birth of winds, the warm exhalation is combined with moist exhalation, called vapor. According to which of them dom-

---

25. Apparently the Dead Sea is meant.

inates, it is called warm or moist. The warm exhalation is sometimes like the smoke of a burning fire (no. 179). The efficient cause is the motion of the sun: when it approaches, the warmth it radiates makes the moist exhalation mount, but when it goes away the vapor is condensed into water because of the cold. For this reason, it rains more in the winter than in the summer and more during the night than at daytime. The sun draws up the water on the surface of the earth and also what was absorbed by it. The latter exhalation—drying out the earth—is called smoke (no. 180). Dry exhalation is the source of the winds (no. 181). Some have said that wind and rain are of the same nature, but this is wrong as their exhalations differ (no. 182).

As was stated in the *De generatione et corruptione*,[26] air has something of vapor and smoke: it is cold and moist; but smoke is warm and dry. The upper air is both hot and moist (no. 183). Aristotle rejects the view that wind is nothing more than air in motion. It is wrong to suppose that every movement of the air around us is wind, as it is wrong to call a river any water around us that flows. The moving air is a wind when it has as its source a dry exhalation (no. 184). As the exhalations take place all the time, clouds, the products of rain and winds, are forever generated in tune with the seasons: some years are more rainy and wet, other years rather dry and windy. Places close to one another are likely to have the same relation to the sun and to have the same kind of weather, although there are exceptions (no. 185). In the places where it has rained, a wind often arises after it has rained and stops when it rains again. When the warm vapor is carried up to a higher place, where it is condensed by the cold, rain is being formed, so that rains may occur after winds, and make them disappear (no. 186). The fact that the winds blow mostly from the north is a sign that they are generated from dry exhalation. As the sun approaches, a moist exhalation arises because of the heat; when it recedes, rain and wintry cold come. Depending on whether the sun is approaching the tropics (Cancer and Capricorn), summer and winter are arriving (no. 187). At the end of the lesson, Thomas observes with a *considerandum est autem* that here, in this lesson, Aristotle says that the southerly wind flows from the South Pole, while later on, in lesson 10, Aristotle will express a contrary opinion, his own contrary opinion. In doing so, Thomas gives us a proof of his masterly grip on the entire treatise.

In lesson 8 (I.4), we are instructed about the direction the winds are blowing. While the exhalation goes upward, the winds blow from one side to the other, from east to west and vice versa. The air of the higher regions is carried in a circular movement. The air in the lower regions participates to a certain extent in this circular movement, so that the exhalations do not push the air

---

26. *De generatione et corruptione* II.3.

up and down, but sideways. Yet the wind's course need not be always westward—as is the movement of the heaven—but can go in a direction opposite of the exhalation pushing it (no. 188). The starting point of the wind is above, as can be seen in a cloud in the sky, which is already moved by the wind before the wind is noticeable on earth. The material cause is the dry exhalation detached from the earth and the wind begins in the place to which the exhalation has moved (no. 189). Just as the water of the rivers comes together little by little, the wind that gathers from exhalations is feeble in the places where it begins, but acquires strength as it moves on (no. 190).

Lesson 9 (I.5) further explains how winds increase in strength or become weaker. Just as the sun moves the winds, it also makes them die down by dissolving the exhalation, or by preventing their formation by drying out the earth. During the summer heat, there may be a great calm (no. 191). The dying down of winds is also caused by a great cold that quenches the warmth—the origin of the exhalation. But even in the intermediate season, there may be calm periods when exhalations have not yet been formed (no. 192). Winds may get stronger at the rise of the constellation Orion and its setting may also be accompanied by severe and stormy winds. The reason is that, at that time, summer is ending and fall is coming. Likewise, at the setting of Orion, stormy winds are generated during several days because the rising and setting of Orion extends through a longer period due to its size (no. 193).

The Etesian (οἱ δ ἐτησίαι) winds[27] blow during and after the rising of the Dog Star, in July, that is, after the summer solstice; they do not blow when the sun is closest to us, nor when it is far away. These winds die down at night (no. 194), but blow particularly in the morning and in the evening as the accumulated moisture of the earth begins to exhale (no. 195). At night the cold freezes the humors, so that the exhalation stops; that is to say, what is frozen or what is dry does not exhale, but the earth that is moist exhales when warmed. One could also say that at night the sun is distant and cannot draw exhalations (no. 196). But there is a difficulty: why do the north winds blow after the summer solstice, but the south winds not after the winter solstice? Aristotle solves the difficulty by writing that these south winds do not blow uninterruptedly and are therefore less noticed. The Etesian winds blow over areas abounding with water warmed by the sun and so are continuous. The greater exhalation occurs after the rising of the constellation of the Dog, as there is more heat than before the solstice or during it (nos. 197–98).

In lesson 10 (I.5), we learn that the south wind does not come from the

---

27. Winds blowing from the north of the Aegean Sea during the summer.

Antarctic, but from the summer tropic. Aristotle had already explained that the southern winds do not blow from regions with much water and snow, such as the south. The south wind blows toward us from the region under the summer tropic, that is, under the constellation Cancer and not from the region under the (for us) invisible constellation at the South Pole (no. 199). Then he shows that the shape of the habitable earth resembles a drum, both with regard to our region in the north and with regard to that in the Southern Hemisphere. Thomas notes that Aristotle does not say whether the Southern Hemisphere is inhabited. Midway between the two poles is the equator, intersected by the Zodiac, which alternately moves north (the summer tropic) and south (the beginning of the winter tropic). Part of the celestial sphere lies between the two tropics. The part between the summer tropic and the adjacent zone is always manifest to us, while that between the winter tropic and the adjacent region is always hidden from us. As the earth is a sphere located in the center of the world, the parts of its globe must be considered from the viewpoint of the different parts of the celestial sphere. At this point, Thomas reproduces a schematic division of zones and circles of the earth, adding to the schematic divisions mentioned by Aristotle. He mentions, following Aristotle, that the lines drawn on the surface of the earth to indicate the habitable zones have the shape of a drum. The zone between the tropics is uninhabitable because of the excessive heat of the sun overhead. The zone under the constellation of the Bear (in the north) is uninhabitable on account of the cold there (no. 200).

The part of the world where we are living lies between two circles (the summer tropic and the circle that is the limit of that part of the heaven that is visible to us). The opinion that describes the inhabited earth as having a circular surface cannot be accurate, for this region is limited by habitable and inhabitable zones and extends east and west. However, the extent of this region is limited by the sea and concerns only half the circle involved. The length of this region exceeds its distance from north to south in a ratio of more than five to three. When going east or west, we will not experience differences of heat and cold. If the sea were not between the eastern and western limits of this zone, we would be able to traverse the whole distance from east to west. This also shows that the habitable part of the earth is not spherical. The other zones are not inhabited on account of the heat or cold there (no. 201).[28]

Next, Aristotle examines the origin and the path of the south wind. Just as the north wind blows from the arctic pole, so a wind must also blow from the

---

28. Thomas, following Aristotle, writes that the zone where we live extends from the Pillars of Hercules to India in the east. Access to what lies beyond is impeded so that we do not whether people live there or not (no. 201).

opposite pole. But just as the north wind cannot reach our part of the earth and not even all of the inhabited area, so the south wind does not come from the South Pole, but blows from the summer tropic (nos. 202–3). Aristotle had mentioned in lesson 7 that some explained the vehemence of winds by assuming that they blow from the poles. And he had adopted it, as Thomas signaled. But Aristotle now rejects it and provides another explanation of their strength, namely: it is on account of the size of the area and the mass of matter collected that the south wind is stronger and steadier than the north wind (no. 204).

At this point toward the end of II.5 (363a20), Thomas's commentary ends. As was said in the introduction, three additional chapters or lessons (nos. 13–15), covering Aristotle's chapters 7–8 on earthquakes (364a14–369a7), were later discovered and edited.[29] In the next paragraphs, these additional lessons are briefly discussed.

Aristotle regards earthquakes as affections of the winds, which move inside the earth and shake it. Thomas notes that before determining more precisely the nature of earthquakes (*secundum veritatem*), Aristotle examines the opinions of others (*secundum opinionem aliarum*) (W 70, 12), that is to say, Anaxagoras, Anaximenes, and Democritus. Thomas expands Aristotle's description of Anaxagoras's position, introduced by *circa quam sciendum*, and recounts how for Anaxagoras, ether's natural motion is up and as such it penetrates the hollows of the earth from below. The earth's pores are clogged by the rain falling from above and the rising ether becomes trapped and shakes the earth. Aristotle gives four reasons for why this explanation is "silly," such as the inability to explain particular times and places where earthquakes occur, for in Anaxagoras's view earthquakes can only occur during rainy seasons. The opinion of Democritus that earthquakes are the result of either excess water moving around in the cavities of the earth or by dry cavities attracting water from wet areas is not explicitly rejected by Aristotle, Thomas writes, because it runs contrary to Aristotle's view of the generation of rivers and wells exposed earlier in the treatise. But Democritus's opinion is also related to that of Anaximenes, who held that earthquakes are the result of frequent moistening and drying of subterranean cavities, so that they collapse and shake the ground. Thomas again enumerates Aristotle's three arguments against these views such as the inability to explain why earthquakes occur in places that not conspicuous to excessive drought or rain (W 73, 90–104).

Thomas's commentary on I.8 consists of two chapters or lessons. Contrary to the positions put forward by his predecessors, Aristotle argues that only

---

29. In what follows, I refer to White's edition as "W," followed by page and line numbers. In White's edition chapters 7 and 8 of Aristotle's text comprises chapters (*capitula*) 13–15 in Thomas's text.

dry exhalation in the form of wind can cause an earthquake. The reason is that only dry exhalation in the form of wind has the necessary power to cause an earthquake because it is the most violent, fastest, penetrating, and fine of the elements. Thomas notes that this causal explanation (*per rationem*) is followed by arguments based on observation (*per signa*) (W 77, 11). There is for instance the observation that most earthquakes occur when the weather is calm or at night when the sun is absent. Similarly, the most severe earthquakes occur where the sea is full of currents (*magnum fluxum*) or the earth is most porous. The most severe earthquakes also occur in spring and autumn when most winds are produced. In the remainder of I.8 (from 367b22 onward) Aristotle deals with a number of additional events such as the duration of an earthquake, its sound, locality, etc. Regarding the sounds accompanying an earthquake, Aristotle remarks that "the earth seems to bellow as they say it does in fairy stories" (368a25). And Thomas comments that it was customary with the ancients that when something unusual (*inconsueta*) happened one sought after an explanation involving a divine entity (W 90, 50).

Concluding Remarks

At the beginning of his commentary Thomas describes the treatise as a further elaboration of the basic description of the material world in the *De caelo* and the *De generatione et corruptione*. Despite what the title of the treatise suggests, the subject matter entails more than an investigation into the higher regions of the world (hence the name *meteoro-logica*) but also discusses earthquakes, storms, lightning, etc. Thomas's interest in these matters indicates that he has a keen sense of the value, the importance, and the all-embracing character of the science of nature. However, while the higher part of the world acts in a mostly regular fashion, the activities of the bodies in the inferior zone are less ordinated. Thomas admits that as a result not everything can be explained with certitude, that is to say, in some things one can reach the truth only to some degree (no. 7: *veritatem attingimus aliquo modo*). While fully supporting the goal pursued by Aristotle in the *Meteorologica* as being in line with and part of the entire investigation of the physical world, Thomas explicitly leaves open the question of the accuracy of Aristotle's descriptions and explanations.

Upon reading Thomas's commentary, we discover a number of statements where he expresses corrections or even doubts and criticisms. This is particularly the case regarding the eternity of the world and of time (nos. 19, 138,

160). In no. 54, Thomas adds a note that the planets are five: Saturn, Jupiter, Mars, Venus, and Mercury. When Aristotle writes that the flow of the Nile River is subject to changes, Thomas adds that the passage of the Bosporus is also becoming narrower (no. 137). In Book II, lesson 10 (no. 199), he notes that Aristotle does not say whether the Southern Hemisphere is inhabited, a remark that seems to indicate that Thomas himself is inclined to think it is. In Book II, lesson 7 (no. 187), Thomas adds a *considerandum est autem* saying that while in this lesson Aristotle writes that the southerly wind flows from the South Pole, he expresses a contrary opinion in lesson 10. In Book II, lesson 10 (nos. 200–201), Thomas gives some further details as to the schematic division of the earth into zones by adding that access to what lies beyond the inhabited zone, that is, beyond the Pillars of Hercules and India, is impossible. Apparently, Thomas had no inkling of the existence of China.

The commentary of Thomas makes us admire his grasp of the subject matter up to its smallest details and the faithfulness of his presentation to the thought of Aristotle. His interest in Aristotle's text as such and not merely as a preparation for his systematical works or scriptural commentaries is underscored by the fact that, as Kevin White has pointed out, other passages on earthquakes in Thomas's writings seem to rely on Albert's *Meteora* rather than on the text of Aristotle itself.[30]

---

30. White, "Three Previously Unpublished Chapters," 66–67.

7 ❧ THE COMMENTARY
ON THE *DE ANIMA*

The *De anima* is one of the major works of Aristotle and has been the object of intense study and research in classical antiquity, and again in the period extending from about the year 1000 to the end of the medieval period. Even in our time it still attracts the interest of scholars. The psychology of Aristotle is a new science, one concerned with the study of the soul, its faculties, and operations; it is of a higher rank than physics, as it teaches us what organic life is.

The text has come to us in three books. In the introduction to Book I, Aristotle tells us how valuable and how difficult the knowledge of the soul and of its actions is. Next, he mentions the opinions of early Greek philosophers about the soul and successively refutes their theories of the soul as a harmony, as a self-moving number, or as composed of the four elements and as present in all things. A note on the divisibility of the soul closes the first book. In Book II, he sets forth his own theory of the soul and its faculties or powers. After presenting two definitions of the soul—(1) the soul as the ἐντελέχεια (the actualization and form) of the living organic body and (2) the soul as that by which we live, have sense perception, and can move and think—he studies its faculties, in particular the external senses. In Book III, he deals with the *sensus communis* (αἴσθησις κοινή), imagination and thinking, and the passive and the active intellect. After comparing the intellect with the imagination, Aristotle turns his attention to the motive faculty and the question of the relations between the different faculties. The order between the books of the *De anima* is clear and logical. There is no need to recur to the hypothesis of an earlier and a later redaction of its different parts.[1]

The *De anima* is a most impressive treatise for its admirable analyses and its completeness. Aristotle was indeed the first to conceive a science of living

---

1. François Nuyens, *L'évolution de la psychologie d'Aristote* (Leuven: Institut supérieur de philosophie, 1948).

beings. His predecessors had only scraps of information to offer. In his lost early dialogue *Eudemus,* he presents the human soul and its destiny quite differently from his description in the *De anima*: the soul belongs to the higher world to which it migrates at the death of the body, a view in line with Plato's thought.[2] But the *De anima* studies the science of the soul by explaining what organic life is. Natural science must consider those activities in which the body is involved. Aristotle probably wrote the text after his return to Athens in 335, in about the same years as he composed his other major works, the *Physics* and the *Metaphysics.*

In his *De sophisticis elenchis*—the last of his books on logic—Aristotle writes that he has completed his program by constructing logic, where before there was nothing. He begs for the understanding of his readers when they discover defects, and he also asks them to show their appreciation for the task he has accomplished.[3] We may apply this observation also to the *De anima*. Compared to what his predecessors had said about life and the operations of the soul, this treatise marks an enormous amount of progress.[4] By one stroke, philosophical psychology becomes a scientific discipline, free from mythological or folkloric considerations. Observation and rational analysis constitute the basis of this treatise, which is an incredible accomplishment.

In the following centuries, the *De anima* put its stamp on philosophical studies of the soul. It was studied, commented upon, and referred to in antiquity by the Greek commentators and the Arab philosophers and it continued to be a source of inspiration for Renaissance thinkers.[5] No other work, apart from the *Categories,* has received so many commentaries in late antiquity. Theophrastus examines a number of problems treated by Aristotle but after Theophrastus, the *De anima* seems to have been forgotten for some two hundred years.[6]

One can notice again references to doctrines of the *De Anima* in Posidonius, Xenarchus, and Boethus of Sidon. The Platonist Atticus (fl. 175 A.D.) blames Aristotle for having deprived the human soul of its immortality and attributed thought to the body and the soul of man, instead of reserving it to the soul alone. While Aristotle accepts the immortality of the intel-

---

2. Anton-Hermann Chroust, "Eudemus or On the Soul: a Lost Dialogue of Aristotle On the Immortality of the Soul," in *Mnemosyne* 19 (1966): 17–30.

3. *De soph. elench.* 183b36.

4. See Düring, *Aristoteles,* 571.

5. See *Mind, Cognition and Representation: The Tradition of Commentaries on Aristotle's "De Anima,"* ed. Paul Bakker and Johannes Thijssen (Aldershot: Ashgate, 2005).

6. See Paul Moraux, "Le *De anima* dans la tradition grecque. Quelques aspects de l'interprétation du traité, de Théophrase à Thémistius," in *Aristotle on Mind and the Senses: Proceedings of the Seventh Symposium Aristotelicum,* ed. G. E. R. Lloyd and G. E. L. Owen (Cambridge: Cambridge University Press, 1978), 281–324.

lect, Atticus blames him for not being very clear with regard to the origin of the soul and reproaches him for having deprived the soul of its immortality. Moraux quotes the following text: Aristotle is like a squid that distracts its enemies by ejecting a dark liquid; the obscurity of Aristotle's text helps him to mask the difficulties of the subject itself.[7]

Galenus knows the *De anima* and often uses its doctrinal insights, but contrary to what Aristotle did, he places the seat of the intellect in the brain. Alexander of Aphrodisias (200 A.D.) wrote a commentary on the *De anima* but only fragments have survived in the writings of later authors such as Themistius, Philoponus, Simplicius, and others. Alexander, writing before the rise of Neo-Platonism, also published a treatise of his own on the subject, posterior to the commentary, of which the second book has received the title *Mantissa* or *Supplement*.[8] There Alexander develops, in a section known to Latin medieval authors as *De Intellectu* and translated from the Arabic by Gerard of Cremona toward the end of the twelfth century, his most influential theory, identifying Aristotle's active intellect with God.

In psychology, Plotinus takes up positions that differ from those of Aristotle. Porphyry often refers to the *De anima,* but remains a convinced Platonist in his paraphrase of the text. Later detailed commentaries on the *De anima* by Philoponus and Simplicius show some influence of Plotinus.[9] One should mention as well Themistius's paraphrase of the *De anima,* of which the Latin translation by William of Moerbeke was finished on November 22, 1267; Thomas was the first in the Latin West to be able to consult Themistius's paraphrase.[10]

Avicenna wrote his own treatise on the soul, while leaving aside Aristotle's historical considerations in Book I and concentrating on the soul itself and its faculties. In man, he argues, the intellect is turned to material things—the

7. Moraux, "Le *De anima* dans la tradition grecque," 287.

8. CAG Suppl. 2.1: *Alexandri Aphrodisiensis: De anima Liber cum Mantissa,* ed. Ivo Bruns (Berlin: Reimer, 1887). Both Part I as well as the Supplement have been translated as part of the Ancient Commentators on Aristotle series. The translator of the Supplement has also prepared a new edition: *De anima libri mantissa: A New Edition of the Greek Text with Introduction and Commentary* by Robert W. Sharples (Berlin: De Gruyter, 2008).

9. See Henry J. Blumenthal, "Neoplatonic Elements in the *de Anima* Commentaries," in *Aristotle Transformed: The Ancient Commentators and Their Influence,* ed. Richard Sorabji (London: Duckworth, 1990), 305–24. The commentary by Simplicius, whose authorship is disputed, can be found in CAG 11, Philoponus in CAG 15, and are both available in the Ancient Commentators on Aristotle series.

10. Gerard Verbeke published the Latin translations of the commentaries of Themistius and Philoponus. Themistius, *Commentaire sur le traité De l'ame d'Aristote. Traduction de Guillaume de Moerbeke. Édition critique et étude sur l'utilisation du commentaire dans l'oeuvre de Saint Thomas,* ed. Gerard Verbeke (Louvain: Publications universitaires de Louvain, 1957); Philoponus, *Commentaire sur le « De anima » d'Aristote. Traduction de Guillaume de Moerbeke. Éd. critique avec une introd. sur la psychologie de Philipon,* ed. Gerard Verbeke (Louvain: Publications universitaires de Louvain, 1966).

intellectus materialis—and only in part to what is higher than man.[11] Averroes, on the other hand, wrote three commentaries on the *De anima*: a compendium, the *medium*, and the *magnum*, the latter being available in the Latin translation by Michael Scotus.[12] In my review of the commentary of Aquinas, I shall mention some of the main theories of this Arab philosopher.[13]

The first Latin translation of the *De anima* was made by James of Venice—the *Vetus*—round about the middle of the twelfth century. Toward 1230, Latin versions of Arab translations of the *De anima*, as well as of the commentaries of Averroes, were available in the West. Around 1266, William of Moerbeke finished his revision of the *Vetus*—the *Nova*—which became the main translation used by Thomas when he wrote his commentary at Santa Sabina in Rome before his return to Paris in 1268 (see also below). The contents of the *De anima* in its novelty and depth will unfold for us when we follow the commentary by Aquinas, which is "one of the very greatest commentaries on the work."[14]

In the first thirty years of the thirteenth century, teaching Aristotle's books on nature was forbidden at the University of Paris because of deviations from, or negations of, some dogmas of the Christian faith, but after a bull of Pope Gregory IX (1231) the books were used again and numerous commentaries were published in the period from 1231 to the time Thomas composed his work on the *De anima*. The highly acclaimed and voluminous introduction by R. A. Gauthier to the critical edition of Thomas's text informs us about a number of these commentaries.[15] According to Gauthier, Aquinas is indebted to them for the technique and formulas used in his own commentaries. These earlier commentaries also gave Thomas an insight into the various lines of interpretation available for a particular passage. Gauthier contends that Thomas's knowledge of the interpretive history of the *De anima* comes largely from these arts faculty commentaries.

The time of composition of Thomas's commentary can be determined quite precisely. On the one hand, he used the new translation by William of Moerbeke, which the latter finished in 1267. On the other hand, it was written

11. See the critical edition *Liber de anima seu Sextus de naturalibus*, edited by Simone Van Riet in two volumes (Louvain: Peeters, 1968–72) and the valuable and extensive doctrinal introductions (1*–74*; 1*–90*) by Gerard Verbeke.

12. *Averrois Cordubensis Commentarium magnum in Aristotelis De anima libros*, ed. F. Stuart Crawford (Cambridge, Mass.: Mediaeval Academy of America, 1953). An English translation with an extensive introduction can be found in Averroes (Ibn Rushd) of Cordoba, *Long Commentary on the "De Anima" of Aristotle*, ed. Richard C. Taylor (New Haven, Conn.: Yale University Press, 2009).

13. See also my earlier study, "Le Commentaire de saint Thomas d'Aquin sur le *De anima* d'Aristote," in *L'anima nell' antropologia di S. Tommaso d'Aquino. Atti del Congresso della Società Internazionale S. Tommaso d'Aquino* (Sita), Rome, January 2–5, 1986, ed. Abelardo Lobato, O.P. (Milan: Massimo, 1987), 33–51.

14. *Essays on Aristotle's "De Anima,"* ed. Martha Nussbaum and Amélie Oksenberg Rorty (Oxford: Clarendon, 1992), 2.

15. *Sentencia libri De anima* (Rome / Paris: Commissio Leonina / Vrin, 1984), 251*–71* (Leonine ed., 45/1).

before 1271, as Book Λ of the *Metaphysics* was still called Book XI until the year when William of Moerbeke finished his translation of that text, namely toward the middle or end of 1271, when it came to be referred to as Book XII. It is also prior to the *De unitate intellectus contra Averroistas* (1270), as it does not show traces of the battle against the Averroists that then raged in Paris, nor of the theory that the human intellect is not part of the soul, refuted in the *De unitate intellectus*. The Italian family of manuscripts of Thomas's *Commentary* also points to its composition in Italy, so that we may safely assume with Gauthier that it was written in Rome at the Dominican convent of Santa Sabina before the departure of Thomas for Paris in the summer of 1268. As such, it constitutes the first of the twelve commentaries on Aristotle's works. In writing the commentary, it was Thomas's intention to bring together from the text of Aristotle the essential, eternally valid elements of a philosophy of the human soul with its different faculties and operations.

Whereas it seems that Thomas did not have a direct knowledge of Avicenna and Averroes,[16] he did rely heavily on Albert's *De Anima* paraphrase, composed in 1254–57, in lessons 12–13, which deals with I.5.409b18–411a25. Remarkably, after lesson 13, Albert seems to play no significant role.[17] Something similar occurred with the Themistius paraphrase, translated by William of Moerbeke. In regard to the first eleven lessons of Book I, Verbeke and Gauthier have noted a massive and literal correspondence between Themistius and Thomas whereas in the later books Themistius is almost absent. Gauthier gives the following plausible explanation: Thomas handled Book I so differently from the rest because at the time the contents of *De anima* I were considered either obscure or not doctrinal. Hence Book I was considered as less important and not commented upon by most masters (*non legitur*). Thomas was therefore forced to rely heavily on the work of others who had commented on it.[18]

In the years after Aquinas composed his commentary, the science of the soul was still hotly debated and considered an important subject in university teaching. Some doubted the possibility of a scientific study of the soul because of its imperceptibility, but Aristotle himself in the *De partibus animalium* (641a18ff.) considers the study of the soul to be part of the philoso-

---

16. *Sentencia libri De anima*, 224*: "L'Averroès que cite saint Thomas n'est donc pas l'Averroès directement lu dans son texte authentique: c'est l'Averroès scolaire."

17. For an excellent comparative analysis of Albert's and Thomas's commentary see Paul D. Hellmeier, *Anima et Intellectus. Albertus Magnus und Thomas von Aquin über Seele und Intellekt des Menschen* (Münster: Aschendorff Verlag, 2011), 145–89. He emphasizes the difference ("völlige Verschiedenheit," 188) between the two commentaries in "almost all important topics: the understanding of the soul as form, the teaching on the intellect and the epistemology."

18. *Sentencia libri De anima*, 281*–82*.

phy of nature.[19] Another disputed question was whether its proper subject is the soul or ensouled matter. Thomas leaves no doubt that the soul is the proper subject of this science because it fits entirely with Aristotle's position in the opening lines of *De anima* I.1 (401a1–7).[20] Regarding the proper order to be followed, Aristotle in II.4.415a14–22, and Thomas in his commentary, observe that one needs to begin with the acts, or more precisely, with the objects to which the acts are directed, and then discuss the powers and finally the essence of the soul. In the *Summa theologiae*, however, we are told to begin the soul's essence, then its powers, and finally its operations.[21] S. de Boer has observed that this difference in approach reflects the difference between the *ordo inveniendi* and the *ordo discendi*, that is to say, in the *De anima* one conducts a scientific investigation into the soul whereas in the *Summa* the material is ordered in such a way that the student can best follow and understand it.[22]

The Commentary of Thomas Aquinas

Book I

Thomas begins his commentary in lesson 1 (I.1.402a1–403a2) with Aristotle's observation in *De partibus animalibus* I.1.639a15–29 and I.5.645a36–b13 that, in order to avoid repetition, one should begin with what is common to a genus as a whole and only afterward what is proper to individual species.[23] Given that all living things form a certain genus in which the presence of a soul is something which the individual species share, Aristotle's treatment of living things begins with the soul (no. 1). Then Thomas turns to the text itself and distinguishes 402a1–403a2 from the rest of the treatise insofar as it constitutes a prologue (*prohemium*) to the entire text of the *De anima*. Following insights employed in Roman rhetoric, Thomas says that a prologue has three purposes: to make well-disposed (*beniuolus*), teachable (*docilis*), and attentive (*attentus*).[24] Aristotle achieves the first purpose, he

---

19. See Sander W. de Boer, *The Science of the Soul: The Commentary Tradition on Aristotle's De anima: c. 1260–c. 1360* (Leuven: Leuven University Press, 2013), 48–55.

20. Albert the Great and others considered the mobile body the subject of physics, but Thomas says that it is mobile being, leaving in this way room for the study of the soul as belonging to physics.

21. *ST* I, q. 75, *proemium*.

22. De Boer, *The Science of the Soul*, 75–76.

23. The excellent translation of Thomas's commentary by Kenelm Foster and Silvester Humphries has been very helpful: *Commentary on Aristotle's "De Anima"* (South Bend, Ind.: Dumb Ox Books, 1994).

24. See the learned footnote in *Sentencia libri De anima*, 4, note to lines 24–32, and White, "St. Thomas Aquinas on Prologues."

says, by showing the dignity (*dignitas*) and usefulness of the science (402a1–7), the second purpose by presenting the order and division of the treatise (402a7–10), and the third purpose by attesting to the difficulty of the science (402a10–403a2). Every science is good and venerable because it is man's perfection. There are theoretical and practical sciences. The science of the soul deserves our respect because of the greater perfection of its subject matter, the soul. The mode of this science also gives it its dignity or nobility insofar as everyone experiences that he has a soul, which gives him life and motion. We grasp the difference between a living being and inanimate things, and so we understand that the soul is the principle of life and of this we possess certainty (*certitudo*). The Latin translation used by Thomas had chosen *certitudo* for the Greek ἀκρίβεία (exactness or precision). The term *certitudo* is somewhat ambiguous because it seems to contrast with Aristotle's statement in 402a10–11 that to give a compelling account of the soul is a "most difficult" project.

Ross admits to having doubt as to why Aristotle assigns a high degree of ἀκρίβεία to the study of the soul and suggests that it is because soul is a pure form. Polansky suggests it has to do with the fact that exactness refers to principles which are more precise the more they include fewer assumptions, and the less variation there is in the subject matter of principles.[25] For Thomas, the term *certitudo* gives him the occasion to emphasize the experiential self-awareness of the soul (*experitur in seipso*) as the principle of life (no. 6). Regarding the usefulness of knowledge of the soul, Thomas writes that knowledge of our intellectual powers is a prerequisite for knowledge about immaterial substances studied in metaphysics. Given the connection between virtues and powers of the soul, knowledge of the soul is also necessary to gaining knowledge in the moral sciences. And finally, the natural sciences profit from such knowledge because much of what it studies are things which have their origin in the soul as moving principle (no. 7).

Thomas finds the second purpose of presenting the order and division of the treatise expressed in 402a7–10, where Aristotle writes that first the nature and essence of the soul and then its qualities are to be investigated. Thomas elaborates more on the structure of the treatise at the beginning of Book II. Whereas Book I deals with various opinions, Book II discusses what Aristotle holds to be the truth. The nature of the soul is treated in 412a6–414a28, which is the object of the first four lessons on Book II. The soul's powers are the object of the vast remainder of the treatise, first in general (414a29–415a22)

---

25. Aristotle, *De anima*, ed. David Ross (Oxford: Clarendon Press, 1961), 165; Ronald Polansky, *Aristotle's "De Anima"* (Cambridge: Cambridge University Press, 2007), 36.

and then in particular (415a22–434a21). The final chapters of Book III (12–13.434a22–435a25) discuss the connection between the various powers. The third purpose of attesting to the difficulty of the science takes up the remainder of the prologue, as it relates to the first chapter of Aristotle's text (402a10–403a2). In it, Thomas closely follows the text in enumerating the difficulties surrounding the definition of the soul, its essence, and its accidental qualities (nos. 9–15).

In lesson 2 (I.1.403a3–b24), the question is raised whether the passions and the acts of the virtues are common to the soul and the body. Thought is an activity of the intellect alone, although it requires objects presented to it by the sense faculties of the body. Thomas concludes that a faculty that has an operation by itself also exists by itself (no. 21).[26] On the other hand, in the passions we experience ourselves, the body is involved and therefore the science of the soul belongs to physics. Aristotle next examines what the ancients said about the soul: he will use what is right in those theories, but put aside what is wrong.

Lesson 2 (I.1–2.403a3–b24) points out that to determine the nature of the soul we must begin by gathering what seems to belong to the soul by nature. Previous philosophers started from what distinguishes ensouled beings from inanimate things, namely, sensation and movement. Aristotle first mentions those authors who approached the soul *from the point of view of movement*. Democritus advanced the theory that because the soul is in a high state of movement, it must be a kind of fire, that is to say, it must consist of atoms of a round shape, which are most mobile among all the particles in the world. Some Pythagoreans agreed with Democritus, while others said that the soul is the force which moves the particles. Anaxagoras also considered souls the source of motion—as is, according to him, the intellect, which itself, however, is motionless. It is not clear to what extent he distinguishes it from the soul. In conclusion, Aristotle writes that all these philosophers considered living beings from the standpoint of motion, that is, as self-movers (nos. 34–42).

In lesson 3 (I.2.403b24–404b8), Aristotle mentions those philosophers who investigated the soul *from the point of view of sense cognition*. According to them, the reason why the soul can know things is that it is itself made up of the principles of things, namely, the elements. Being earthly, the soul knows earth, Empedocles said, and through love we know love.[27] In his *Timaeus*, Plato makes the soul consist of two elements or principles, namely, Sameness and Difference, of which material things and also the soul are composed, while

---

26. No. 21: "Quod habet operationem propriam per se, habet etiam esse per se."
27. In addition to the four elements, Empedocles also mentions love and strife as cosmic principles.

purely immaterial beings consist of one principle. This theory, Aristotle says, rests on the same idea as that of Empedocles, namely that "like is known by like." When for instance our soul knows individual material things, it does so through identity and difference, and it brings them together in species and genera through sameness (no. 47). Plato was convinced that things we can think of as abstract, such as mathematical entities and universal Ideas, consist as subsistent realities. The ideas are of the nature of numbers, as they constitute the specific nature of things, which is characterized by numbers (nos. 49–50).

Lesson 4 (I.2.404b8) notes that the soul's knowledge of things is based on its own numerical composition. Aristotle observes that some philosophers combined movement and sensation in their description of the soul as a self-moving number, where "number" refers to the soul's cognition (no. 52). In lesson 5 (I.2.404b8–405b30), Thomas gives a summary: all philosophers regarded the soul as the cause of movement and cognition, yet their different views of its nature resulted from the difference of the elements they thought it to be composed of—some thought of material principles, others of immaterial principles—but all agreed that it is that which moves most. They also differed as to the number of principles the soul was thought to consist of; some admitted only one principle (e.g., air or fire, like Heraclitus), others several, like Empedocles. Plato understood the soul to be composed of immaterial principles (nos. 53–54). Democritus said that the soul is composed of round atoms, which cause movement and are the cause of cognition. Anaxagoras stressed the soul's role in cognition and movement, but distinguished between the intellect, which is simple and unmixed, and the senses. He attributed to the intellect both knowing and moving (no. 57). Aristotle next mentions Thales, Diogenes, and Heraclitus. According to Alcmaeon, the soul is related to the celestial bodies (nos. 58–61).[28] Some followers of Thales, who considered water to be the principle of living beings, made this element the principle of all things. Anaxagoras was the only one to deny the passivity of the intellect, but he did not say how it knows (no. 66).

In lesson 6 (I.3.405b31–406b15), the theory of the soul as a self-moving essence is studied.[29] Aristotle argues in general against the view that movement pertains essentially to the soul. He first objects to the theory that the soul moves *per se*; in this supposition, its movement must be one of the four species of motion: local motion, growth, decrease, and alteration. All four

28. Aristotle refers to the early Greek thinker Alcmaeon of Croton, who he also mentions in *Metaphysics* I.986a27–31. See Ross, *De Anima*, 182.

29. Chapter 3 extends over lessons 6, 7, and 8.

motions involve a position in space, so the soul would be in a place. Hence we must consider whether the soul while causing movement is moved itself. Aristotle advances six arguments against the view that the soul itself is moved. Thomas makes the following observation: although some of these arguments may not seem conclusive in relation to the particular theory discussed, they are effective because they destroy the position in question by pointing to its impossible consequences (no. 74).[30] For instance, if it moved itself, the soul would move in one of the four species of motion mentioned above and this would imply a position in space, so that the soul would be localized (no. 75). One might doubt that alteration involves a local movement. As to this point, Thomas explains that alteration is also happening with respect to place, as what causes alteration must draw near to what undergoes it, so that a change in place is the cause of an alteration (no. 76). It is not clear, however, according to which of these species the soul would move itself. If one does not see a difficulty in the theory that says that the soul is in a place, Thomas answers, then the soul would have to be assigned to a position in the body, and would no longer be the form of the whole body (no. 77).

A second argument against the view that the soul is in a place is that in such a case it could be moved violently and would stop moving when forced to do so. But this is impossible if its movement is spontaneous. Thomas points out an apparent weakness of this argument: the soul moves naturally and hence not under compulsion. He resolves it by saying that the philosophers who upheld this view said that the only bodies moving with a natural movement are the four elements. Now the four elements may undergo enforced movements (no. 79). A next argument suggests that the soul moving the body would be moved by the same movements as the body and might come back to the body that it left, returning life to it, something that is clearly impossible. Objections may be advanced against this argument, and Thomas says that it holds only for those who think that the soul is located in the body as in a vessel (nos. 81–83). Aristotle brings two more arguments and Thomas refutes some objections against them (nos. 84–86). The Platonists asserted that the soul is not moved by sensible objects, but moves itself toward them. But Aristotle proves that the possible intellect is reduced in act by the cognitive species of the objects.[31]

In lesson 7 (I.3.406b15–407a2), Aristotle brings forward some arguments against a theory of Democritus, who fails to explain that the soul is also the cause of rest and is at the origin of strivings and choice (no. 89). There is a

---

30. Polansky approvingly quotes this passage from Thomas in his *Aristotle's "De Anima,"* 83.

31. The theory that sense cognition is not passive but active became a central doctrine of the Stoa. See *Sentencia libri De anima*, 31, note to lines 248–50.

certain parallelism between the view of Democritus and that of Plato, because we read in the *Timaeus* that the soul moves the body insofar as it moves itself. Stating that the essence of all things consists of numbers, which are formed by one and two, Plato held that these numbers are the elements or causes of identity and difference, finitude and the infinite (nos. 92–93). Being placed, according to Plato, between the higher beings that never change and the material substances that change, the soul was said to consist of identity and difference (no. 94). Plato believed the soul to consist of the numbers 1, 2, 3, 4, 8, 9, and 27, in which harmonic proportions are found (no. 96), as it takes pleasure in whatever is harmonious. So it is attuned to the harmonious movements of the celestial spheres (nos. 97–98). The essence of the soul would be midway between abstract numbers and sensible substances, and so there is in the soul a direct grasping of the object and a return by which it reflects on itself. The intellect moves in a circle, as we find two circular movements in the heavens: the sphere of the first heaven, and the sphere of the planets, which execute circular motions in opposite directions (nos. 102–3).[32]

In the long lesson 8 (I.3.407a2–b26), in which Thomas comments on the last part of chapter 3, Plato's view of the soul, as Thomas had described it in the previous lesson, is refuted. Thomas observes that Aristotle does not reject Plato's view inasmuch as Plato's more profound intention is concerned, but just according to the impression his words make (*quantum ad sonum verborum eius*). Plato did not really think that the soul is a quantitative magnitude. Averroes and Albert the Great also say that Plato when speaking of the soul is using metaphorical language (no. 107).[33] Thomas recalls the basic principle that a faculty is known by its acts and the acts or operations by their objects (no. 110). In the case of the intellect and thought, these successive objects are like numbers in a series, where one number leads to another, as we understand one object after another and not like magnitudes (no. 111). A further important argument is the following: for Plato, understanding was not receiving intelligible forms, but making a sort of contact with these forms. Aristotle asks if it touches them partly or in their entirety. Thomas says that Aristotle presupposes here that the intellect is indivisible, as is each individual substance (nos. 112–16). Thomas also presents the other arguments that Aristotle advances against Plato (nos. 119–28). The main difficulty in Plato's theory is that he does not explain why the soul is joined to the body and neglects to elucidate the nature of the body that receives the soul (no. 130). Aristotle concludes his exposition by saying that one may see a connection between Plato's theory and

---

32. We may assume that Thomas found this information about Plato's theory of the soul in Themistius.
33. See *Sentencia libri De anima*, 38, notes to lines 3–13.

the Pythagorean fable that any soul can enter any body. But this is impossible because the body of each kind of living beings has its own form, its own way of moving. It is as if they say that the art of weaving can enter into a flute.

In lesson 9 (I.4.407b26–408a34), Aristotle deals with the view that considers the soul as a harmony. In Empedocles's theory, the four elements together with love and hatred form a certain harmonious whole. This view is rejected by Aristotle: being a substance, the soul is not a harmony, which is an accidental reality.[34] Moreover, the soul moves something, but harmony does not (nos. 134–35). Harmony belongs to the body rather than to the soul, for it is found in a mixture of continuous things. But this does not apply to the soul. We do not see nor know the parts of the soul that would form a harmony. Contrary to those philosophers who called the soul a harmony, Aristotle argues that harmony is just a disposition of the body in view of the soul (no. 144).[35]

In lesson 10 (I.4.408a34–b32), Aristotle examines the "movement" of the soul not from the point of view of its moving the body, but insofar as it is the source of activities. Already in lessons 6 and 8, Thomas gave a critical evaluation of some of Aristotle's arguments: sometimes when Aristotle has already formed his own opinion about a question, he nevertheless formulates objections and answers to this opinion; sometimes he does so before demonstrating the solution, basing objections and answers on the views of others, and not on his own opinion, as for instance in *Physics* III.4–8, where he deals with the theme of the infinite and presents some arguments that as such are false, but that are considered to be true by his opponents, for example, that bodies are both light and heavy. He does so also in *De caelo* I.3.269b15–270a10, where he examines theories about the infinite. In this lesson, he does the same, notably by presupposing that the Platonists are right in considering the passions to be movements in the soul by means of its own organs as the intellect. To them there is no difference between sense perception and the acts of the intellect; every kind of soul is considered to be immortal (nos. 147–48).

The only theory that Aristotle really attacks and rejects here is that the activity of the senses would belong to the soul alone, not to the body and the soul. He rejects the view that the passions are movements of the soul. Sensation takes place in certain parts of the body (no. 150) and is not a movement of the soul alone (no. 151): it proceeds from both the soul and the body (no. 152). Movements originate from the soul but are not in the soul itself

---

34. Thomas also ascribes the theory to Dynarchus and Simiates, a reference he found in Nemesius.

35. See Elisa Coda, "The Soul as 'Harmony' in Late Antiquity and in the Latin Middle Ages. A Note on Thomas Aquinas as a Reader of Themistius' In Libros De Anima Paraphrasis," *Studia Graeco-Arabica* 7 (2017): 307–30.

(no. 153), as such movements need not be in the soul itself (no. 156). Thomas warns the reader that this solution is only provisional, for movement is found in the activities of the soul in different ways (no. 157). Sometimes the soul is the terminus to which processes tend, for example when impressions are transmitted to it, but sometimes it seems to be the starting point, as in remembering (no. 158). Movements occur in the activities of the vegetative soul and, in a less strict sense, in the acts of the sensitive soul (no. 159); and they occur least strictly of all, in a metaphorical sense, in acts of the intellect, such as understanding. At this point, Thomas makes an important remark: love, hatred, delight, etc., are also found in the intellectual part of the soul, without being accompanied by feelings in the sensitive part (no. 162). The weakening of the activities in old age is not due to a decline of the soul, but to that of the organs of the body (no. 164); yet Aristotle does not want to say that the intellect has a special bodily organ, Thomas observes (no. 165). The intellect is more noble, godlike, and unalterable.

In lesson 11 (I.4–5.408b32–409b18), the theory of the soul as a self-moving number, taught by Xenocrates, is discussed. Xenocrates was the last head of the Academy (from 338 to 314) who had known Plato personally. He was generally respected, although his interpretation of Plato's philosophy was less impressive. Hundreds of years later he was still severally criticized by the Neo-Platonist Proclus for his belief in minimum indivisible lines. Aristotle, who does not mention him by name, refers to his definition of the soul as a self-moving number. By way of six arguments Aristotle shows that this is unreasonable (nos. 169–74). A first argument goes as follows: a number consists of units, and these units must consist of a moving part and a part that is moved, but a unit like a point cannot be divided. In another argument he says that a moving point makes a line, and a moving line a surface, but this does not cause life. In the last of his six arguments, Aristotle argues that a point cannot be separated from a line, but that the soul can be separated from the body (no. 174). It is impossible to define the substance of the soul as a self-moving number (nos. 176–77).

In lesson 12 (I.5.409b19–411a5), Aristotle says that we must still consider how the soul would be composed of the elements through which it would know, as some say it does. Knowledge would come to us by assimilation, and so these authors had a glimpse of the truth. But if so, he objects, we would only know the elements. He refutes this position by means of nine arguments, for instance: if the soul is composed of the principles of substance and accidents, it would be all these things at once, for example, substance, quantity, quality, etc. He also rejects the saying that "the same is known by the same":

some animals do have earth, bones, etc., in their body, but these parts of them have no sensation. He finally refutes the theory of Orpheus, who thought that the soul is the breath of animals: there are many animals that do not breathe at all (no. 190). As the imperfect is known by the perfect, the soul would not need to have all the elements within itself in order to know the physical world.

In lesson 13 (I.5.411a7–26), we read that some authors said that the soul is intermingled with everything in the universe, as Thales asserted that everything is full of gods. Thomas observes that he must have thought that the entire universe was alive and that life was divine, so that a god was everywhere in the universe. This idea was perhaps behind the rise of idolatry (no. 192). If there is a soul in the air and in fire, why does it not make animated beings of them? Why are the souls in the elements of higher rank than those in things composed of these elements? It is very improbable that air or fire are living bodies (nos. 193–95). As animals live by breathing air, the air came to be thought of as the cause of animal life and as being alive, and the soul was thought to be a part of the whole air (nos. 196–97).

In lesson 14 (I.5.411a6–27), Thomas addresses the last part of Book I, where Aristotle notes that we can distinguish three powers as underlying the different activities of the soul, namely vegetative, sensitive, and intellectual activities; but when one pays attention to these activities as such, one can distinguish five different faculties: nutritive, sensitive, locomotive, appetitive, and intellectual powers (no. 201). Do these different powers belong to the whole soul, so that with each part of the soul we can perform these different activities, or does each activity have its own special part of the soul? The answer is that the powers of the soul are distinct, but this should not be understood in the sense that the soul consists of several quantitative parts (nos. 204–5). There have been philosophers who went to the point of making these different powers into different souls, but it is difficult to see how one body could contain several souls. In that case, there would no longer be a unifying principle, for the body is unified by the soul (no. 206). If every operation of the faculties should have its own organ, what then about the intellect that has no special organ? The theory is also proved wrong insofar as in certain living beings one part of the organism may have several functions. And Aristotle adds that living beings of lower rank need fewer diversified organs, so that certain animals go on living after having been divided (nos. 207–8). In conclusion, it appears that life belongs properly to things that move and act of themselves. The word "life" also means the being of a living thing.[36]

36. See also Paul D. Hellmeier, "'Tote Wissenschaft'?—Thomas von Aquin als Kommentator von *De Anima* I," *Divus Thomas* 118 (2015): 114–47.

Book II

In Books II and III, Aristotle sets forth his doctrine about the soul and its faculties. In his commentary, Thomas explains the order in which Aristotle proceeds in his exposition about the soul (nos. 211–20). The subject matter is so difficult, says Aristotle, that we may assume that thus far the truth about the soul has not yet been discovered (no. 211). In the first four lessons of Book II, Thomas explains Aristotle's theory of the soul: we must determine what the soul is, before examining its parts. Aristotle presents two definitions, a definition being either the conclusion of a demonstration or else its starting point. The two definitions are explained and then followed by the study of the faculties of the soul, which occupies the rest of Book II and is continued in Book III. The division between Books II and III is not very obvious. As Thomas recalls, in the manuscripts of the Greek text, Book III begins at 424b22, that is, the section where Aristotle speaks of the "common sense"—one of the internal senses—in preparation for the study of the intellect and the locomotive power, which are treated in Book III. In his edition of the critical text of Thomas's commentary, Gauthier follows the division used in the Latin translations of the Arab version of the *De anima*, which has Book III begin at 429a10, where the study of the intellect starts.[37] We will follow the division of the Greek manuscripts. In the Latin versions Thomas uses, Book II consists of twenty-four lessons, which comment on twelve chapters.

Lesson 1 (II.1.412a3–b9) notes that the order in which Aristotle studies the soul and its operations is that from what is common to all living beings to what is less common. Obviously, Aristotle is most interested in the latter part. He first explains how to arrive at two definitions of the soul, which are respectively the conclusion of a demonstration and the principle or the starting point of the study of the soul. The soul is the formal principle of a compound, so that in its definition we must refer to the subject or matter that it determines (nos. 212–13). In fact, when attempting to define the soul, we must keep in mind three divisions: substance and accidents; the division in matter, form, and the compound out of them; and finally, the division into *habitus* and its operation (*actus secundus*).

In no. 219, when Aristotle distinguishes between inanimate physical bodies and living beings and qualifies the latter by the occurrence in them of nutrition, growth, and decay, Thomas observes that these activities alone do not

---

37. On the question as to which section of the text Book III should begin with, see Bazán, "Le commentaire."

define living beings, as some also have sensation and thought. A living body is a physical reality and a substance. Soul is that by which a body, its subject, has life (no. 220). Soul is neither the compound (of form and matter) nor matter; it cannot but be conceived as a form (no. 221)—the substantial form—which is the first actualization of matter (nos. 222–24). Thomas adds a note about the theory of Avicebron, who places several substantial forms in one and the same living body, namely that of a substance, of a body, and of a living being;[38] but he failed to see that the forms that come (to a subject) after the first substantial form only add accidental determinations. Thomas emphasizes that it is one single substantial form that gives all the perfections to a given substance; the soul animates a living being but also gives it corporeality and substantiality. As such the body is not the matter of the soul "but functions as if it were the matter of the soul."[39] Thomas writes: "But being a body, which is less perfect, is as it were matter [*quasi materiale*] with respect to life" (no. 225). Elsewhere Thomas explains that, in the proper sense of the term, the matter informed by the human soul is primary matter insofar as it is understood (*intelligitur*) as capable of receiving life.[40] Primary matter as such, being pure potency, cannot enter into the definition of the soul and neither does it exist as such before the body is actually ensouled.[41] The soul is compared to the *habitus* of a science, which is called a primary act; its use is a secondary act (no. 229). Aristotle's famous definition of the soul is: the primary actualization of a physical bodily organism (no. 233). This definition solves what for many had been (and still is) a difficulty, namely the way body and soul are joined. The form is the actuality of the matter, which is its subject (no. 234).

In lesson 2 (II.1.412b10–413a10), Aristotle further explains the definition of the soul as the substantial form of a physical organic body by means of a comparison with artificial forms. If we take away the form of a tool, for example an axe, we are still left with a piece of iron, which is the natural form of that thing. The soul is the natural form, and not an artificial form, of living beings (no. 238). It is the (primary) act of a body having life in potency, that is to say, it possesses this power but does not (yet) act by it. It may lack, however, some secondary acts (no. 241). But Aristotle says that it is not yet clear whether the

---

38. On the theory of Avicebron as Thomas mentions it, see Leo Elders, *Thomas Aquinas and His Predecessors* (Washington, D.C.: The Catholic University of America Press, 2018), 332–36.

39. De Boer, *Science of the Soul*, 137.

40. *De spiritualibus creaturis*, a. 3, ad 2. De Boer, *Science of the Soul*, 139, also discusses this text and notes that Thomas's position corresponds closely to Ackrill's interpretation in J. Ackrill, "Aristotle's Definitions of psuchê," in *Articles on Aristotle, vol. 4: Psychology and Aesthetics*, ed. J. Barnes, M. Schofield, and R. Sorabji (London: Duckworth, 1979), 65–75.

41. In the generation of a human being, a series of intermediate forms intervene, which are steps on the road to the complete human species. See *SCG* II.89.

soul is the form of a body in the way a sailor is of his ship, that is, as a mover only.[42] The description thus far given of the soul is incomplete (no. 243).

In lesson 3 (II.2.412a11–b13), Aristotle intends to demonstrate his definition of the soul. We must, he says, proceed from what is better known to what is less known. In certain things, that which as such is more knowable is not always so for us. In mathematics, we can start from what is more knowable by itself and also for us. But in natural things, the effects are usually more knowable than the things themselves (no. 245). Certain definitions can be demonstrated by indicating why things are such (no. 246). This way of demonstration must be used here. Many definitions can be demonstrated by indicating the cause of why a thing is such (no. 247). Aristotle gives an example taken from geometry: a square is a right-angled figure with equal sides: this definition has the nature of a presupposed demonstration (nos. 250–51).[43] Aristotle begins to demonstrate the definition of the soul he has given above by passing from the effects to their cause (no. 253) and showing that the soul is the source and principle of the activities of a living being, so that this source and principle is the form of living beings (no. 253). Things that have a soul are alive and differ from inanimate beings (no. 254). There are four modes of life: intellectual life, sensitive life, life that is the cause of motion in space, and life that consists in nutrition, growth, and decay (no. 255). A soul is involved in all these modes, namely as a principle of life (no. 256). That there is a soul in plants and not merely an inanimate nature is shown by the fact that a plant, for instance a tree, grows upward and downward, while nature by itself does not move in opposite directions (no. 257). Feeding and growing is caused by the vegetative soul. All animals have the sense of touch, and so the animal soul is the principle underlying the activity of this form of life. The vegetative soul can exist apart from the animal soul, but the latter is never without vegetative life (no. 258). The primary sense of the animal soul is touch. In some animals it is even the only sense, but higher animals also have the other senses and the power of local movement (no. 260). At the end of the treatise, Aristotle will indicate why vegetative life is found separated from sensitive life and why in the latter touch is sometimes the only sense.

In lesson 4 (II.2.413b13–414a28), the question is raised whether such powers as those of the vegetative soul and the senses are the soul itself or parts of it. In beings with vegetative life and sense activity, these powers are parts of the soul (no. 262). Some primitive animals when cut into parts retain in these

---

42. See *Sentencia libri De anima*, 76, notes to line 153, for the many references to texts wherein Thomas rejects the comparison of the soul to a sailor in a ship.

43. See *Sentencia libri De anima*, 78, notes to line 57, for an explanation of the terminology.

parts a sensitive soul, for besides vegetative life they have some sensation and local motion (no. 265). Aristotle concludes from this that these powers are not located in a special part of the soul, while other powers such as sight and taste are. Touch, however, is present in the entire body (no. 266).

With regard to imagination, one might wonder whether it has a special organ. In the lower animals it is indefinite, but in the higher animals it has well-defined activities, and so we assign a special organ to it (no. 267).[44] But the question regarding whether the intellect has any special organ has not yet received a clear answer. Is it separable from the body (no. 268)? Its function, such as forming opinions, differs from what the senses do, and so it must be a different faculty (no. 269). When there is only vegetative life, the soul itself is involved, but when there is sense activity, faculties intervene which are parts of the soul (no. 270). The soul being the form of a living body is the first principle of life; it is the primary principle, that is, the formal principle of a body capable of life, the principle of sense activity, movement, and understanding (nos. 272–73). The body that is determined by the soul is not just any body, but a physical, organic body (no. 277).

Aristotle speaks of the soul's powers in general in lesson 5 (II.3.414a29–b32), as they are found in plants, imperfect and perfect animals, and in man. In his elaborate commentary, Thomas notices that the soul has no other parts than these powers, and explains why in addition to the division of the soul into vegetative, sensitive, and intellectual souls, we speak of five classes of powers (no. 280). The reason is that we must differentiate between the various activities. The animate beings we are now studying consist of those that are material and from this point of view they are like inanimate things, that is, their matter is restricted to this particular thing. Those that have a certain immateriality, however, are not only these particular things but can also become, in a certain sense, other things through their power of cognition (nos. 282–83). In the intellect, things that are known exist without their individuality and material conditions, while in the senses things are known without their matter, but rather with their individual material determinations and by a bodily organ. Sense knowledge knows things in particular; the intellect knows its objects universally (no. 284). The vegetative soul has activities at a purely material level, the activities of the intellectual part of the soul are immaterial, and between these are those of the sensitive soul. Now every form has a certain tendency that makes it proceed to its operations. The tendency that results

---

44. See *Sentencia libri De anima*, 84, notes to lines 90–100, where a text from Averroes is quoted: in imperfect animals, imagination is always combined with the perception of the senses, but in perfect animals it can also be active when there is no activity of the exterior senses.

from a sensible form is called sensitive desire, and that from an intellectual form is an intellectual desire. The tendency that accompanies natural forms is called natural appetite, which is at the origin of local movement (no. 286). In some things we find all these powers, but in others only some, and in plants only one.

Thomas sees a beautiful order in nature. As Aristotle points out, the species of things succeed each other as numbers in a series, where each time the number one is added (no. 288). Next, Aristotle shows that appetition exists in all animals. Where there is any sensation, for example, of the sense of touch, there is pleasure, pain, joy, and sorrow, according to whether the thing touched is congenital or not. This also follows from the fact that the sense of touch is aware of whether the food is dry or moist, hot or cold, and provokes appetition. The acts of the sense of touch are always accompanied by desire (nos. 290–91). In addition to these powers, some animals also have the capacity to move from one place to another, and in human beings there is the power of understanding. The intellect has no special bodily organ. Now, Aristotle says that the definition of the soul is related to the powers mentioned above. But he does not give different definitions of the classes of souls, as we do not of successive figures. The idea of soul is one, in the same way as that of geometrical figures, where the triangle exists potentially in the other figures. A common definition can be applied to the different classes of souls (nos. 296–98).

In lesson 6 (II.3–4.414b32–415a22), Aristotle continues the study of the soul's powers and how they are related to the different genera of living beings. He intends to show what is particular to each class of these—plant, animal, man—and what is the principle of life of each of them. The vegetative soul can exist by itself, but the sensitive soul cannot exist without the vegetative principle, which assures its existence and is the basis of all other activities. Likewise, touch can be the only sense of some animals: by touch the animal senses the elements, and what things consist of and by what it is nourished (no. 300). There is a connection between the power of sensitive life and that of locomotion, although not all animals have the latter. The last class of souls is that which has understanding and reason, but which presupposes the other powers. Purely immaterial beings do not require the sensitive and vegetative souls (no. 301). The lower animals have a sort of imagination; but, in them, the imagination does not function independently from the apprehension of the senses (no. 302). The study of the powers of the soul must begin from that of their acts and pass from these to their objects (no. 304), which determine every type of operation. Some objects are active agents—for instance, the objects of the senses—but the objects of the active powers are final terms to be attained by the operations of these powers (no. 305). Different things can form the same object of a faculty, as a colored animal and a colored stone are of eyesight (no. 307). To know our intellect, the intellectual faculty must be actualized by an idea drawn from sense cognition; we do not know it by a direct intuition of its essence (no. 308).

The vegetative soul is studied in lessons 7, 8, and 9 (I.4). In lesson 7 (I.4.415a22–b28), because of its importance, nourishment must be examined before we are going to deal with generation. The vegetative power underlies the soul's other activities and is common to all living beings (no. 310). To generate beings of one's own kind is an act of the vegetative power. Aristotle now states, Thomas says, something that he had not mentioned before: all actions natural to all living beings proceed from the vegetative power. Reproduction is such an activity and is natural to all living beings (no. 312). Any living being can reproduce its like, provided it is mature and not defective. Thomas indicates the reason, namely, that it assimilates to the divine. Things of a lower level tend to the greatest possible assimilation with the divine and do all they can in view of this end (no. 315). Lower forms of life can only share in that of the perpetual divine being insofar as their nature allows (no. 317). The soul is the cause of the living being, as its essential form; it is the end for the sake of which we live (no. 318). It gives being to living things; it is the actuality of the body. Nature equips living beings in view of their form, the soul, so that the soul is also a final cause. Natural things without life are instruments of living beings, as plants are of animals (nos. 319–23).

Lesson 8 (II.4.415b28–416a18) recounts the theory that saw in fire the cause of growth and nutrition: fire feeds itself and "grows" (no. 330). Aristotle acknowledges the role of fire as a secondary agent in feeding. Each species of living beings has its own measure as regards its size, but this cannot depend on fire, which has no fixed limit (no. 332). In lesson 9 (II.4.416a19–b31), Aristotle further discusses nutrition. As food must become the nourished being, it must be its contrary, for becoming is from one contrary to another. Food must be such a contrary that it can change into the thing fed by it.[45] Among the four elements, only water seems to be food (no. 335). When food is processed and digested it is no longer contrary to the body that is fed (no. 339). No being is fed except that which has a soul (no. 342). Food is in potency to becoming the living body (no. 343). Finally, food is related to generation: seed, the cause of generation, is a residue of food (no. 344). Aristotle closes

---

45. Gauthier notes that Thomas borrowed some terms from Themistius and Averroes in this passage, but that his interpretation is quite different, see *Sentencia libri De anima*, 103.

the chapter with some definitions. The nutritive faculty is the power by which a living being keeps itself alive, and food is that by means of which it does so. He distinguishes between three functions of the vegetative soul: keeping alive, growing which makes the living being larger and augments its capacities, and reproducing (nos. 346–47). The separate instrument of nutrition is food; the united instrument is heat (no. 348).

In lesson 10 (II.5.416b32–417a20) and the following chapters, Aristotle deals with the senses. That is to say: in the remaining chapters of Book II, he focuses on the exterior senses, while Book III focuses on the interior senses and the intellect. Now, unsurprisingly, Aristotle first studies what is common to the senses, and next what is characteristic of each of them. Some of the earlier thinkers said that "like is known by like." But at the beginning of sensation, agent and patient are contraries. Aristotle then says that the senses are in potency and must be brought to act (no. 351). Empedocles thought that like is known by like and that the senses are the objects they perceive; they would somehow consist of them, that is, of the elements of which they are composed. But if that were true, we should also sense our senses and be able to sense things that are absent (no. 353). In fact, sensation is intermittent and can be in potency and in act (no. 355). By sensation in act is meant that a sense is acted upon by some agent that reduces it to act (no. 357).

This theme is further elaborated in lesson 11 (II.5.417a21–b16), where Aristotle, while dwelling on intellectual knowledge, explains the different ways in which a thing may pass from one state to another. He points to human beings who have a capacity to learn, but can also possess the habitual knowledge of the things they have learned before and that they may recall when actually thinking (nos. 361–62). Therefore, "potentiality" may be taken in two senses, namely a primary potentiality and a secondary one when one already possesses the habit. "Being acted upon" can also have different meanings, namely that of the destruction of a quality one possesses or that of a process according to the state of the potency that is actualized (no. 365). When the knowledge that one possesses is actualized, we have to do with an increase in perfection rather than with an alteration. Learning is a change to the possession of knowledge and maturity. Even when one goes from error to knowledge, there is no alteration in the true sense of the term (no. 370). When one acquires knowledge by oneself or by a teacher, one's potency is actualized by something already in act. This "something" is the light of the agent intellect and the first principles, or it is a teacher leading the one who learns from one principle to another (no. 372).

In lesson 12 (II.5.417b16–418a6), Aristotle applies the above to sensation.

He distinguishes between being in potency to have a sense faculty (as an unborn baby) and being in potency to actual sensation—the first comes to us by generation, the second by using the faculties (no. 374). The difference with actual thinking is that the objects of the senses are outside, whereas intellectual knowledge of the universals is somehow within the soul. Once we possess intellectual knowledge we can think, but in order to perceive by the senses, we must receive the objects from the outside (no. 375). Sensation apprehends individual things: the senses are individual realities, while the universal comes into being by abstraction from matter (no. 377). Thomas adds that the universal can be understood in two senses: (1) as something several things have in common; or (2) as something in itself, but then it has no real existence, contrary to what Plato thought (no. 378), who assigned real existence to it as an idea. Human nature as a universal exists only in our intellect. Abstracting the universal from individual beings is no falsehood, because its attachment to individuals is not denied (no. 379). In the last part of the lesson, Thomas recalls what he had said about proximate and remote potency.

Before dealing with the individual senses, we must first consider their objects, which Thomas does in lesson 13 (II.6.418a7–25). Aristotle distinguishes between the proper objects of the senses and the sense faculties. The proper objects (*sensibilia propria*) are either proper to one sense or common to more than one (no. 383). Each sense apprehends the object proper to it and is not mistaken about it (no. 384). The objects common to more senses are movement, rest, number, shape, and size. Touch and sight perceive all these five common objects. Common sense (*sensus communis*) perceives them through the proper objects of the senses. Thomas mentions an error we may come across, namely that some consider these common objects the proper object of the *sensus communis*, but he is quick to reject this view: the faculty called common sense has a different function.[46] The common objects are incidental to the individual senses, differentiating what the individual senses perceive by their proximity, shape, or movement. Thomas also introduces a distinction: what affects a faculty directly and modifies it may be called its absolute object of it, while the common sensibles may differentiate this object by their proximity, shape, etc. They do not immediately modify the faculty but cause a difference with regard to the mode of sensation, for example, being situated far or near, together or apart (no. 394).

When something is connected incidentally with the proper object of a sense, while in reality it is known by another sense (when, e.g., a white thing is seen as sweet), it is so because of previous experience (no. 395). We speak

---

46. Gauthier refers to Averroes as a possible source, see *Sentencia libri De anima*, 119, notes to lines 49–55.

of collaboration with the intellect and, in animals, with a natural instinct (no. 397). At this point, Thomas adds a note on the interior sense called *cogitativa*: it apprehends the individual thing as existing in a common nature because of its collaboration with the intellect. But the instinct of animals is not aware of the individual things as having a common nature, but experiences them only as the objects of passions or actions (no. 398). As appears from the notes in the text edition of the Leonine, Thomas compared the views of Avicenna and Averroes to establish the proper character of the *cogitativa*.

In the next two lessons, Aristotle deals with sight. In lesson 14 (II.7.418a26–b26), he deals with sight itself; and in lesson 15 (II.7.418b26–419b30), he investigates how color is seen. Now, the object of sight is the visible. What is visible is colored. Certain things like glowworms can be seen at night, although we do not see a color (no. 400). Color is a quality. It can directly affect air and water (the transparent), but is not visible without light. By itself, the transparent has no color but is receptive of it. The heavenly spheres of the planets are transparent. The fact of being transparent is consecutive on a general nature, as that of air and water (no. 404), which is in potency to light and darkness. By light this potency is actualized (no. 408). Light is not a body; as two bodies cannot simultaneously be in the same place, as, for instance, light is with the air.

On the following lines of the text (418a28ff.), Thomas gives a long commentary. Against Empedocles, he argues that light cannot be a body, as the illumination of a certain space is sudden and not due to a local motion (no. 409). If light were a body in a successive local motion from east to west, it would not escape our attention (no. 412). We must distinguish, Thomas writes, three questions: the nature of light; the nature of the transparent; and the need of light for seeing (no. 413). And he adds an argument of his own against the view that light is a body: if it were a body it would be suddenly multiplied over the whole hemisphere or disappear.[47] Other authors think that light is of a spiritual nature. Thomas objects that a spiritual nature cannot be the object of a sense—the light we see cannot be spiritual. It is true that we use the word light to signify spiritual realities; in fact, the sense of sight is more spiritual and noble than the other senses because its object comprises properties that the lower bodies have in common with the celestial bodies. Furthermore, the perception of their objects is accompanied by a material change, as the natural form of heat is received in the sense of touch, but with light this is different (no. 415). Some said that light is the manifestation of color, but that is impossible, because some beings shine at night without any col-

---

47. With regard to this argument, Gauthier (Leonine ed., 45/1:126, note to lines 205–6) refers to Albert the Great.

or being visible (no. 419). There were also some who thought that light is the substantial form of the sun or has an intentional being, but Thomas says that no substantial form can be the object of sense perception. He also observes that light rays cause material changes, and he thinks that light is an active quality of the celestial bodies (no. 420). It has no contrary and so there is no contrary disposition in the bodies that are illuminated. Illumination is instantaneous. This explains why the most perfect bodies are always lucent and the most material bodies opaque (no. 422). Light is necessary for seeing because the transparent medium must be actualized. Color, being a certain form, has the power to impress its likeness on the medium, but it has no activity that disposes the medium to receive its likeness; light, however, disposes the medium to receive it (no. 425).

In lesson 15 (II.7.418b26–419b3), we read how we see color and how the medium is related to it. As the same sense apprehends contrary qualities, sight also apprehends darkness (nos. 428–30). Certain things have some light in their constitution, and when they are close to a source of strong light they appear as colored. Light is necessary for colors to be seen. The medium for transmitting light is the transparent. A vacuum, however, is not a medium and cannot receive or transmit. In nos. 434–36, Aristotle gives a remarkable explanation of why distance diminishes visibility: everything is seen through light beams in the form of a triangle, the apex of which is in the eye; the further the object is removed, the longer the sides of this triangle (or pyramid) become, and the smaller is the angle at the apex. Also, for the other senses, there is each time a medium, as for instance the air for sound and odor, but for touch and taste the medium is less evident (no. 437).

Sound is studied in lesson 16 (II.8.419b4–33). Aristotle deals first with sound in general. The objects of sight, taste, and touch have a permanent existence in their subjects, but the case of sound is different. He explains the origin of sound and of its reverberation, the echo. Sound is more spiritual than the objects of smell, taste, and touch. Soft objects do not have the power to produce sound. Contrary to color, odor, etc., sound only exists when the medium is affected by a sound-producing body. Sound exists in the medium and in the faculty that hears it (nos. 440–41), but not in the sound-producing body; its cause is percussion and it is propagated by local motion in a medium. To produce sound, the object struck must be hard, and the medium in which sound is produced is air or water. Air can also serve as the object struck (no. 446). The echo is sound produced by reverberation. Thomas compares it with a stone thrown in water, which produces circular waves: when these waves meet an obstacle, they return (no. 447).

In lesson 17 (II.8.419b33–420b5), the difference between high and low sounds is explained. The air conveys the sound and, so that it may reach the ear, it must be in an uninterrupted movement (no. 452); but also the air inside the organ of hearing, which itself lacks motion, passes on the different sounds (no. 454). Thomas writes that "different books" say that we cannot hear in water. He means the text of some translations from the Greek and the Arab.[48] But this is not correct: we can hear as long as water does not flood into the inner ear (no. 457). Those who hear a continuous ringing in the ear suffer from a defect, as the air inside the ear is continuously moving (no. 458).

In lesson 18 (II.8.420b5–421a6), voice is studied as a kind of sound. Aristotle determines what kinds of animals have a voice and what its organ is. Bloodless animals and fish have no voice. Voice is a kind of sound produced by certain animals, and differs from sound produced by percussion. It differs because it can be prolonged (although the sound of certain instruments also can). Voice may be in the form of a melody (though high and low pitches are also sometimes produced by certain instruments). Voice consists of elements such as syllables with interruptions (yet the sound of certain instruments can also be interrupted) (nos. 467–69). The organ of voice is the same as that by which we breathe, namely, the windpipe. Nature uses the inhalation of air for the regulation of natural heat (the parts of the body around the heart must be cooled) and for making speech possible. The tongue is also involved (no. 473). Voice is the sound produced by striking on the air one breathes, proceeding from the windpipe and the mouth. Not every sound of animals is a voice (e.g., coughing). Voice must be a sound that has a signification by nature or by convention (nos. 475–76).

Lesson 19 (II.9.421b9–422a7) deals with smell and its object. Aristotle says that it is difficult to determine smell and its object, but a comparison with savors helps. In man, the sense of smell is weak and we cannot always distinctly observe the object that smells. The reason is that our brain—to which the organ of smell is close—is cold and moist, so that our sense of smell is less developed (no. 480). Taste, on the other hand, is a mode of touch. Man has a much superior sense of touch than the other animals. People with a more developed sense of touch are mentally more acute (no. 483). The excellence of man's mind corresponds to that of his sense of touch. The better the sense of touch, the greater man's intellectual capacity (no. 484). A good sense of touch results from a good and healthy body (no. 485). The different kinds of odor correspond to the kinds of flavor. But sometimes a pleasant odor does not go together with

---

48. See *Sentencia libri De anima*, 141, notes to 101.

a good taste, when the balance between the watery liquid in taste and the dry gaseous matter in smell is not well proportioned. A thing may smell good, but taste bad (no. 488). Odors are often more indistinct than flavors.

In lesson 20 (II.9.421b9–422a7), Aristotle considers the medium through which smells come to us, and next the organ of smell. Obviously, air is the medium, but water can be as well, as can be seen in aquatic animals traveling long distances for food they have apparently smelled (no. 481). Some authors thought that all sensation is consummated in touch,[49] namely, by our some-how "touching" the objects. In sight, this would happen by visual lines projected by the eye toward the object. When this object is "touched," it is seen by the eye. But in the case of the other senses the objects come to us (no. 492). The reason why these authors made a distinction between two forms of sensation was that they had not developed the theory of a spiritual modification of the medium, Thomas writes in an additional note. In the *De anima*, Aristotle does not mention it,[50] but we must assume such a modification because vultures, for instance, smell carrion at a distance of fifty miles, and this cannot be because something from the carrion has spread over such a distance. Hence the medium is affected spiritually, especially by the objects of sight (no. 495). The sense of smell in man and in animals is the same: animals suffer in the same way as man from strong vicious odors (no. 498). In man, respiration is required for smelling; in breathing animals, the organ of smell is covered, and by respiration the pores open (no. 499).

Taste is studied in lesson 21 (II.10.422a8–b16). After dealing with the objects of vision, hearing, and smell, Aristotle now considers those of taste. The tasteable is something tangible and is not perceived through a medium extraneous to the body, as is the case for vision, hearing, and smell (no. 502). Taste is a kind of touch, for it perceives its object by contact, but the flavor of the object of taste is not that of the qualities of the elements, which constitute the objects of touch. As the object of taste consists in moisture, it is related to touch. Thus one may distinguish between taste insofar as it concerns the basic qualities of nourishment and taste insofar as it concerns sensing flavors. Flavors are not the basic qualities of which natural bodies are composed. As to the first object, there is no such thing as temperance (no. 504). Nothing tasty is tasted without moisture, as appears from the role of saliva (no. 508). It would seem that the drinkable and the undrinkable are fundamental to taste, insofar as they are perceived as a species of touch (no. 510). The pleasure given

---

49. Gauthier writes that the issue was raised by Albert the Great; see *Sentencia libri De anima*, 132, notes to line 23.

50. But he does so in his *De sensu et sensato* IV.

by food and drink accompany taste inasmuch as it is a kind of touch (no. 511). As the tasteable is liquid, the organ of taste must be neither moist nor flavored, but able to become so (no. 512). The tongue is not able to taste when it is dry or excessively liquid (no. 513). At the end of the chapter, Aristotle mentions some of the species of flavor, such as sweet and bitter.

In lesson 22 (II.11.422b17–423b21), touch is examined as the last of the external senses. It is the least spiritual of them, but the foundation of all sense activity. Its study comprises that of tangible objects (no. 517). A first question is whether there are several senses of touch (because of the difference of its objects, such as cold and warm, soft and hard). Each of the senses studied in the previous chapters bears on *one* pair of contraries, while touch senses both hot and cold, heavy and light, moist and dry, etc. (nos. 519–21). Thomas resolves the difficulty by recalling that a genus may include several contraries besides the primary ones (no. 523), as there are, for instance, several contrary qualities in regard to a substance. A second question is whether flesh is the immediate organ of touch or only a medium. At first sight it is not clear whether touch has a distinct organ, as do sight, hearing, smell, and taste. But then Aristotle notes that flesh is the medium of the sense of touch, composed as it is of different elements, which transmit the objects of the manifold sensations of touch (nos. 526–28).

In lesson 23 (II.11.423a22–424a16), Aristotle explains how flesh is the medium of touch and what the organ of touch is. Can air or water be the medium of touch? This seems difficult, for these elements have tangible qualities, while the medium of a sense must be lacking the qualities that the sense perceives. Averroes resolves the difficulty by saying that in air and water there are extraneous bodies with tangible qualities, but that as such air and water do not affect us (no. 534).[51] Thomas calls this answer erroneous in several ways: our bodies are naturally subject to the influence of these elements, being somewhere in the middle between the extreme qualities of the elements; and they are related to these qualities as potency to act (nos. 535–36). Our body is so disposed that it is open to be influenced by elemental qualities. Averroes fails to distinguish between the elements as contrary to each other and as containing each other (no. 537). Thomas explains this as follows: from one point of

---

51. Here at no. 534 we find the only direct mention of Averroes in the entire commentary. Gauthier gives a chronological explanation for the "serenity" in regard to Averroes which he regards as a characteristic feature of Thomas's commentary. Written between two periods of virulent anti-Averroism (the *Summa contra gentiles* and the *De unitate intellectus*), Thomas enjoyed the tranquility of Rome during the time of its composition (*Sentencia libri de anima*, 234*). There might have been other factors as well: the literary genre of a commentary which requires to avoid discussions not directly linked to the text; and the use of *quidam* which implicitly refers to masters of the Faculty of Arts following Averroes.

view the elements are contrary to each other, but from another point of view they are related, as they are all related to and contained by the surrounding element and the body of the first heaven (no. 538). Another error of Averroes is that water and air as such would not undergo any change, but Thomas says that they are changeable, as at least water is to some extent capable of being destroyed. Air and water change more easily when they occur in small quantities. The objects of taste and touch are so close to us that the medium and the sense are affected together (no. 542). The notions of flesh and tongue appear to be related to touch and taste, just as air and water are related to the organs of sight, hearing, and smell (no. 543). If the object of vision is placed on the eye, we do not see it. This means that the organ of touch is within us and that there is a medium (no. 545). When tangible qualities, such as warmth, are the same as the sense of touch (e.g., temperature), we do not feel them. The organ of touch is in potency to a mean between these qualities (nos. 546–49).

Lesson 24 (II.12.424a17–b18), the last lesson in Book II, is a summary in which Aristotle determines some aspects of sense knowledge, in particular the relation of the object to the senses. As all recipients do, the senses receive the various forms (which are their objects) from agents. If the recipient is at the same level as the (material) agent, it receives the form together with its matter. But when the material disposition of the recipient differs from that of the agent, it receives the form without its matter. In such cases, the form received is adapted to the mode of being of the sense, which has a certain immateriality although it resides in an organ (nos. 553–55). If the impact of the object on the sense organ is too strong, the organ may be destroyed or neutralized (no. 556). Plants do not have sense perception (although they are affected by heat and cold, etc.). The reason is that they lack the balance between the extremes of the tangible objects, which is required for sensation. They do not have the mediate state between these qualities (no. 557). Animals that lack a particular sense cannot be affected by the object of this sense (no. 559). The objects of a sense may have a (physical) effect on the subject of the sense insofar as they are tangible things (no. 561). Tangible qualities have a greater active power than other sense objects and operate on bodies in general. At the end of the chapter, Aristotle observes that air is affected by odor, but that it does not smell it, because it lacks the corresponding sense potency.

Book III

In Book III, we pass to the study of the intellect and intellectual knowledge.[52] That is to say: the external senses are clearly different from the intellect, but

___

52. See the remarks above on the division of the treatise in Books II and III.

is the intellect perhaps an internal sense? In lesson 1 (III.1.424b22–425b11), Aristotle shows that there is an interior sense called common sense, because by it we perceive the activity of the other, external senses. Nevertheless, the five external senses with their organs allow us to perceive the whole range of sensible objects (no. 566). If one of the senses is lacking, it is because the particular organ is missing (no. 569). The organs of the senses are composed of air and water, which conduct themselves passively with regard to the objects of the senses. Fire, however, is not active in the sense organs (no. 571). Earth, as it is by itself, is not the organ of any sense, but is mixed with the organ of touch, which, in a sense, must be composed of all the elements in a certain proportion (no. 572). There cannot be a special organ for the so-called common sensibles—movement, rest, number, size, and shape—as they are perceived by several senses (nos. 572–79). The senses perceive the objects of other senses indirectly (no. 581). Because we have several senses, we acquire a more complete knowledge of an object that strikes a sense (no. 582). They help us distinguish between different accidental properties. As the objects of the senses are different, there must be different senses. Touch and taste are impressed by physical contacts, but the other senses receive their impressions through a medium.

Lesson 2 (III.2.425b12–426b7) opens with the question of whether we are aware that we are seeing by the sense of sight or by some other sense. Is there a general sense faculty that makes us perceive the acts of the different senses? A further question, to be treated in chapter 3, is that of how we distinguish between the proper objects of the five senses (no. 584). Both questions are difficult. Aristotle advances two arguments in favor of the opinion that it is by the sense of sight that we perceive that we are seeing (nos. 585–86). The act of seeing can have a dual meaning: seeing an object and being aware of seeing it. But then there are two different acts. An objection is raised (no. 587): if it is by sight that we are seeing, sight must be colored, as we only see what is colored. Now, this objection contradicts the supposition that in order to see colors, sight itself must not be colored (no. 587). The answer, as Thomas presents it, is that this "seeing that we are seeing" is a judgment on the reception of the object and so it is not colored itself. But according to the second argument, as Thomas explains, the same faculty is seeing color on the sense organ and our sight of it.[53] The sensible object and the receiving sense are identified in one subject, although they differ in thought. Thomas refers to the concepts of action and passion, which differ in thought, while the subject of action and

---

53. This answer is a clarification by Thomas: *Et dico* (no. 591).

passion is in the thing that receives the action (nos. 592–93). This would mean that seeing, hearing, etc., also imply awareness of these acts. Actual seeing, hearing, etc., cease when the object is no longer there (no. 594). An excessive object, as too much light or sound, can destroy the respective faculty.

Passing to lesson 3 (III.2.426b8–427a16), we are reminded that in the previous lessons this common sense was in the background of the theme treated. The conclusion reached was that seeing is perceived by the sense of sight, although not in the same way it perceives colors. To distinguish between the acts of the different exterior senses and their objects, for example, between white and sweet, a special sense is needed, which perceives the difference between the objects of the various senses impressed on the individual faculties (nos. 600–602). Touch, being a particular sense, cannot perceive both these different acts and their different objects (no. 603). To do so, a special faculty is needed that "understands" and "senses" these objects and their differences. Thomas writes that Aristotle uses the two verbs, understand and sense, because he has not yet demonstrated the difference between this sense and the intellect (no. 604) or because both faculties know the objects and their differences. There is a simultaneous apprehension of the different activities of the senses and of their objects (no. 605). Aristotle advances an impressive objection: different acts cannot be known simultaneously, for one and the same faculty cannot receive at the same time contrary determinations (no. 608). But he indicates the solution: our perceiving flows from a common root to the individual senses and their organs, and all sensations terminate in this root, just as a point is not only the beginning of a line, but also the end of another part of it (no. 609). He stresses that there is a common sensitive principle (no. 610). This faculty, which is called common sense, must have an organ, and Aristotle suggests that it is like the organ of touch spread through the entire body. It lies at the very root of our sense faculties (no. 612). The other senses share in the power of this common sense faculty.

In lesson 4 (III.3.427a17–b26), Aristotle examines whether rational judgment and understanding[54] are beyond the range of the sense faculties, and shows that the imagination (the sense faculty that forms images) is different from judgment and understanding (no. 615). The early philosophers identified sense knowledge and thought. A vague suggestion in the text, namely that the god(s) influence(s) our mind, is briefly elaborated by Thomas. He mentions the theory of the influence of the heavenly bodies on the sense faculties of

---

54. Foster and Humphries translate the *sapere et intelligere* of the Latin text quite correctly by "rational judgment and understanding." The Greek text has νοεῖν καὶ φρονεῖν. Thomas explains the verb *sapere* as *iudicare*.

animals and also on the intellect. But this would imply that the intellect is a material faculty. Why does Thomas introduce the heavenly bodies here, which are not mentioned by Aristotle? He probably wants to show that a material influence on the human mind is impossible, while keeping the door open for God's influence. Empedocles and Homer considered the sun the cause of understanding (nos. 618–19). But whoever ascribes to the stars a direct influence on the intellect obliterates the difference between the intellect and the senses. However, an indirect influence of the celestial bodies might be possible (no. 621). The ancients who affirmed that the intellect is corporeal did so because our thought also uses images, that is, the presence of a likeness. But if knowledge is acquired by likenesses, how do we explain error (no. 624)? Thomas answers that the ancients were not bothered by this problem insofar as, for them, that which seemed true, was true. In their view, knowledge is the contact of the soul with what is like itself, while error is contact with what is unlike (nos. 625–26). The response to this view is that like and unlike are contraries; if one knows one of them, one also knows the other as its contrary (no. 628). Rational judgment and understanding are not the same as perceiving. Wise judgment is also found in some animals, which share in a certain prudence, while ordinary perceiving is found in all animals (no. 629).

The perceiving of the senses is always according to the truth, but thought can be right or erroneous, both in scientific knowledge and in prudential judgments as well as in opinions (no. 630). To stress the difference between sense perception and rational reasoning, he says that all the animals have sense perception, but that rational judgment is found only in man, who investigates. The separate substances, however, Thomas adds, understand immediately without investigation (no. 631). In no. 632, he shows that having images in the imagination is not the same as having an opinion. A first difference between them is that images are called up at will, while opinions are not (no. 633). Opinions affect our feelings, but this does not need to be the case with imagination (no. 634). Opinion and thought have an effect on our feelings—they can make us feel sad, frightened, hopeful, happy, etc.—but as long as something is merely imagined, it does not affect us (no. 635). The reason is that things regarded as good or bad make an impression on us. Thomas must have felt that the argument is not very convincing for he adds that in brute animals natural instinct causes them to be affected by what they perceive.

In the previous lesson, imagination was already mentioned. Now, in lesson 5 (III.3.427b27–428b9), this interior sense is discussed from the point of view of what it is not. It is not a cognitive power by which we distinguish between truth and falsehood. Aristotle explains successively what imagination is not. First he notes that through imagination we perceive images together with their difference from other things. But discerning that the object perceived is not something else is also done by sense perception, opinion, scientific knowledge, and understanding (*intellectus*). The last three activities are different from sense knowledge. By understanding is meant the apprehension of things immediately known to us, such as the first principles (no. 639). These four activities were distinguished by Plato, who assigned the numbers one, two, three, and four to them, beginning with the understanding as "one." Imagination is not one of these four. It differs from the senses as it is working during our sleep, and some animals who have sense cognition do not have imagination; the senses are truthful but the imagination may present images to which nothing in nature corresponds; the imagination gives no certitude about the presence of the objects seen; it is like sense perception in the dark; phantasms appear during our sleep, when the senses are not active (nos. 641–57). "Understanding the principles" and "science," based on demonstration, are always true, but imagination is often false as opinion sometimes is. Animals have no opinions (nos. 648–49). Opinion leads to belief and sometimes to persuasion and rational inference, which animals do not have (no. 650). Imagination is not a combination of sensation and opinion (nos. 651–52). Thomas follows the exposition of Aristotle, carefully explaining the argument.

In lesson 6 (III.3.428b10–429a9), Aristotle explains that imagination is a movement. By this he means the actualization of a faculty by phantasms. It presupposes sensation, which causes these phantasms. Although the senses are true with regard to their proper object, errors may arise in the interpretation of the latter. Thomas gives the example of the interpretation of the identity of a white object that one has perceived from a distance (nos. 660–62). The common sensibles, such as size and movement, may also give rise to error in the imagination, which is mostly truthful as long as the proper object of a sense is present (nos. 663–64). In the absence of the proper sensible, the imagination is more exposed to errors, such as false combinations. Imagination is defined as the movement resulting from what the senses in act perceive. At this point, Thomas notes that Aristotle leaves unanswered the question whether it is a power (or faculty), and answers himself that because diverse movements imply diverse potencies, it is necessary to posit a potency distinct from the exterior senses (no. 667). In the absence of a sensible object, images can also stimulate the appetite, and determine to a considerable extent the behavior of animals (no. 669). When in human beings the intellect does not control their feelings, the imagination occupies the scene and passions may arise, as also happens during sleep or in the case of insanity (no. 670).

Lesson 7 (III.4.429a10–b4) is a long and detailed commentary by Thomas on a relatively short doctrinal text of Aristotle concerning the intellect. Thomas includes the following survey of the contents of chapters 4 to 8 (lessons 7–13): first, the (potential) intellect as such is studied in lesson 7; then its object, in lesson 8, while some difficulties are resolved in lesson 9; the agent intellect is the subject of lesson 10, while lesson 11 deals with intellectual operations; in lesson 12, the intellect is compared to the senses; and in lesson 13, some consequences are drawn.

Entering into the subject, Aristotle mentions the question—without answering it—as to whether the intellectual part of the soul is a separate entity, as Plato appears to have thought (nos. 671–74). The acts of the senses and of the intellect are similar, being both a kind of knowing, either potential knowledge or knowledge in act. But then this question arises, whether the intellect is merely passive with regard to its object by which it is determined, or is what happens something resembling a passion (no. 675)? The latter means that the intellect is actualized, that it is able to be determined by its object, as the senses are, and is closer to the truth; as such, it is impassible, but it receives the intelligible species (no. 676).

Aristotle proceeds to determine the nature of the intellect. He rejects the view of Empedocles, namely that the intellect knows all things because it is all things, but he follows Anaxagoras: the intellect is open to the knowledge of all things because it is not identical with any of them. If it had a determinate nature, it could not be open to the knowledge of all things (nos. 678–81). The intellect is in potency. Thomas observes that Aristotle is speaking of the intellect by which the human soul understands, and so excludes the intellect of God, who knows all things in act (no. 683).

The intellect has no bodily organ and no particular bodily nature (no. 685). It differs from the senses by being impassible, whereas the sense organs can be affected by excessive impressions of objects (nos. 687–88). Thomas stresses that it is not a faculty separated from the body and existing on its own, for *it is this individual man who understands*. The individual man as the agent and the immediate principle of his intellectual activity cannot be formally separated from it in being (no. 690). Some authors, Thomas says, tried to connect the intellect (conceived by them as separate) with our human being through the images or phantasms of our imagination.[55] But Thom-

---

55. This is the theory of Averroes. For an overview of the relation of Thomas to Averroes, see Elders, *Thomas Aquinas and His Predecessors*, 306–31.

as explains and strengthens the reasoning of Aristotle. The theory of Averroes, namely that our different ideas have as their subject phantasms in our imagination and that through them we are connected with them as present in an outside intellect, does not prove any continuity between that intellect and ourselves. Our intellect can only think when the intellectual cognitive species are in it and detached from or abstracted from the phantasms of our imagination. If, according to the theory of Averroes, there were a connection between that outside intellect and ourselves, we ourselves would not understand, but we would rather be what is known (*sed magis intellectus*), Thomas says (no. 694). Moreover, Averroes's theory is also contrary to Aristotle's doctrine insofar as Aristotle explicitly says that the subject of his present inquiry is a part of the soul and not a separate substance (no. 696). For further details, Thomas refers to what he has said elsewhere in greater detail.[56]

In lesson 8 (III.4.429b5–22), Thomas gives another detailed commentary on a relatively short text of Aristotle because of the importance of the theme or question at hand, namely: how does the intellect form universal concepts? In the previous lesson, Aristotle argued that the intellect must be actualized by intelligible objects. Here, he first recalls that a man of science already has a store of intelligibles that may be fully actualized by himself when he starts thinking about them. But in order to acquire these intelligibles in their first state of actuality in the mind, the intellect must be helped and brought to act by another (*ab altero*), Thomas says (no. 701). At this point Thomas leaves open what this other is, but it will become clear that the agent intellect using the images of the interior senses is meant. It is somewhat surprising that Aristotle first mentions the state of the habitual possession of ideas, which is perhaps a concession to the Platonists, who taught that our intellect is from the very beginning equipped with the ideas of the essences of things. Thomas also mentions the theory of Avicenna according to whom the ideas would disappear from the intellect when they are no longer actually used, although one who possesses the *habitus* of a science, has the power to actualize them (nos. 702–3). When in act, the mind can also think *of itself*, as the Latin translation used by Thomas suggests, while the Greek text rather says that it can think *by itself*.

In the remaining part of the lesson (regarding lines 429b10–b22), Aristotle points to the difference between the abstract form (the essence) and the concrete things of which it is the form. Thomas presents a long commentary extending over several passages (nos. 705–19); he rejects wrong theories and

---

56. "... que alibi diligencius perscrutauimus." One may think of *SCG* II.59–61 and *De unitate intellectus*. See *Sentencia libri De anima*, 227*.

helps the reader understand what Aristotle writes in this concise text. The essence of a material being differs from the individual concrete thing, but does so only at the accidental level. This is precisely what the intellect aims at: it draws the essences (ideas) from what the senses perceive, so that there is a difference *per accidens* between the essence and the concrete thing from which the essence is drawn (no. 705).

This is the case with all beings of which the forms exist in matter. What belongs to the individuality is not included in the essence. Socrates is not his human nature. However, this distinction does not apply to forms that exist without matter (no. 706). But mathematical entities whose forms are in matter are distinguished from the individual characteristics of their matter: there is a difference between the form, such as a triangle, and the concrete triangle (no. 708). Thomas adds that this distinction does not apply to the immaterial substances (no. 710). Sensitive things are known by the senses (no. 711), but their forms are known by the intellect. But we can, so to speak, bend back (*circumflexa*) and connect the universal form with the individual (no. 712). We do so when we return to the phantasm, so that we know the subject in which the form exists (no. 713). This also applies to mathematical objects. The intellect, which knows the essences, is distinct from the faculty that knows the objects as such, in their concrete form, namely the imagination (no. 715). Thomas explains the sentence, "As things are distinct from matter, so it is with what concerns the intellect" (429b21–22), with several arguments: first, what is separate from matter in being can be known only by the intellect; second, what is not separate in being, but only in thought, can be perceived in abstraction, although physical beings abstracted from individual matter cannot be completely abstracted from sensible matter (e.g., man consists of flesh and bones) (no. 716). It follows that essences are the proper object of the intellect, and not sensible things (no. 717). And Thomas adds an important note: the intelligible objects are not that which we know, but that by which we know things (no. 718).

In the last section of lesson 8 on III.4, Thomas mentions Averroes's theory of the uniqueness of the possible intellect of all men, which he had discussed and refuted at length in *Summa contra gentiles* II.73. Averroes believed that his interpretation was confirmed by Aristotle, where the latter writes (429b19–22) that "the possible intellect is not mixed (with the body), is impassible and separate," but these words of Aristotle do not oblige us, Thomas says, to say that our intellectual substance is not united to the body, as its form that gives it its being.[57] To explain this, Averroes repeatedly speaks of a *continuation*

---

57. *SCG* II.69.

of this unique intellect with us, without explaining how this continuation would come about from an ontological point of view. Regardless of whether the Parisian masters of the thirteenth century have correctly understood the doctrine of a single intellect of all men, here we only consider how Thomas formulated it. According to Averroes, an immaterial intellect cannot be individualized, as it is without matter. Therefore, it cannot be proper to each individual man, even less so because then the forms in our mind would all be individualized, whereas in reality they are universal concepts. Moreover, Averroes argued that the intellect must be one because different individual men have the same concept but, says Thomas, there is no reason why there could not be more concepts of one thing, if there are more intellects (no. 719).

In lesson 9 (III.4.429b22–430a9), two difficulties are discussed. (1) If the intellect is simple and separate, how can it receive the objects or impressions needed for understanding? (2) If the intellect knows itself, does it do so by itself? But then everything intelligible is also an intellect and intelligent (nos. 720–21). Aristotle answers that the mind is passive insofar as it is receptive of forms, but by itself it is empty like a sheet of white paper (no. 722). Answering the second difficulty, he says that in fact the intellect itself is intelligible, but through a concept, meaning that the concept of the thing understood is also that by which the intellect understands itself (no. 724). The (potential) intellect is known by a concept and not immediately by itself (no. 725). Thomas adds the observation that God is perfect actuality and knows himself through himself. The immaterial beings also do not need concepts to know themselves: they do so by their essence. But in material things the form as such is not intelligible, but only potentially so (no. 726).

In lesson 10 (III.5.430a10–25), Aristotle passes to one of the most debated and original chapters of his treatise, namely the theory of the agent intellect. He argues that, besides the (potential or passive) intellect, there must be an active power in us that renders the potential intelligibles in act (in the intellect). His main argument is that all through nature, in each class of things, there is potency and, different from it, a productive cause that reduces what is potential to act. So, in the human soul, there is the potential intellect in which intelligible concepts may become present, and an agent intellect that can make these intelligibles actual concepts. On the basis of 430a10–16, Thomas remarks that Aristotle "expressly says" (*expresse dixit*) that the agent and possible intellects are in the soul and thus "making it expressly clear" (*expresse dat intelligere*) that Aristotle takes them to be parts of the soul and not distinct substances (no. 736). Aristotle calls the agent intellect a ἕξις τις, a certain *habitus* or state. Thomas gives a detailed and excellent explanation. First, he says that the term *habitus* or state might give rise to misunderstanding as the term *habitus* indicates a reality that is not yet fully active, while here an active factor is meant, an actual presence, as light that makes colors visible in the medium (no. 730).[58] Thomas adds a further explanation: Plato did not need such an active power to actualize the intelligibles in our intellect, as the intelligible essences are already present in us, but according to Aristotle the essences are not actually intelligible in their existence in material things (no. 731). And he describes what is proper to this agent intellect: it is separated from matter, impassible, not composed of corporeal things, and not joined to a bodily agent. As for these properties, it agrees with the passive intellect, but differs from it in that it is in act (no. 732). It is essentially in act, but free from matter (no. 733). Certain philosophers conceived the agent intellect as a substance separate from man; by this Thomas means Avicenna and those who follow him. Avicenna considered the agent intellect a separate reality that contains all the intelligible essences in itself and gives them to us corresponding to the images that the senses present us. It is called the *Dator formarum*.[59] According to Avicenna, the agent intellect is an independent reality that has its seat in the last cosmic sphere surrounding the earth.

Thomas's main argument against this theory is that natural beings must dispose of the powers needed to perform their natural activities. For this reason, the agent intellect must be a natural function of man and one in being with the individual man (no. 734). The objects represented by the senses and by imagination become intelligible when they are abstracted from the images in our imagination (no. 735). Thomas formulates a difficulty: how can these images be in potency with regard to the intelligible species and already be present in act in the agent intellect (no. 737)? But this difficulty disappears if one considers that there are different ways of being in potency. The agent intellect does not contain all intelligible objects actually in itself, but is an immaterial power that can assimilate the images of the imagination to itself and render them immaterial. That is why Aristotle compares it to a light, and this also indicates that it is not a separate substance (nos. 738–39). He then describes the three properties of the intellect in act: (1) actual knowledge is identical with the thing known; (2) absolutely speaking (but not with regard to our intellect), considering the whole of reality, actual knowledge is prior in nature and in time—no potency would ever be actualized if there were not something in act (no. 740); and (3) the agent intellect is always in act (no. 741).

However, the part of the soul that has activities reserved to itself is indeed

<hr>

58. See Polansky, Aristotle's "De Anima," 463.
59. See Q. *de anima*, a. 15; Q. *de veritate*, q. 18, a. 8, ad 4.

separate (Aristotle says this in II.2.413b26: χωρίζεσθαι) and survives. In fact, according to Thomas, Aristotle "concludes [*concludit*] that the soul's intellective part alone is immortal and perpetual." Immortality does not imply eternity, Thomas adds, because in *Metaphysics* XI (read XII.3.1070a21–26), Aristotle says that forms cannot exist before their matter (no. 743). But the so-called passive intellect, that is, the part of the soul which has the passions, is corruptible, says Aristotle. Thomas explains this exceptional use of the term "intellect." In this context, it indicates a faculty that clearly belongs to the sensitive part of the soul, namely the sense faculties of the imagination or the *cogitativa*; it is in a sense intellectual and rational insofar as it partakes in reason.[60] Thomas says that in the current inquiry, Aristotle does not examine how after death the intellect knows and what it knows and does not know. This is not the intention of Aristotle or Thomas (nos. 744–45).[61] Thomas himself deals with this question in detail in *Summa theologiae* I, q. 89.

In lesson 11 (III.6–7.430a26–431b4), Aristotle deals with the two operations of the intellect: (1) the apprehension of essences and (2) the combining or separating of two things, subject and predicate, in judgment. The first operation is a direct apprehension of things (e.g., of man), and it is without falsehood (no. 746). But when there is a certain composition there can be falsehood. Speaking of composition, Aristotle refers to Empedocles, who attempted to explain how composite organisms come into being. At first there were only different parts that were later brought together by love. Similarly, the intellect combines separate objects. When it does so conform to reality, it is in truth (nos. 747–48). When, in this operation, it includes a reference to the past or to the future, falsehood may also occur in respect to time (nos. 749–51). The composition of the subject and the predicate may be false, and so truth or falsehood comes into the mind. Aristotle's concern is to show that when undivided (but potentially divisible) things are understood as simple objects, the intellect is true, and this understanding occurs in an undivided time (no. 752). Even if their consideration is protracted, they will be known as wholes at every instant (no. 754). If a whole is considered as a unity, it is understood in an undivided time, but this is no longer the case if one understands the parts separately.

---

60. *In VII Metaphys.*, lesson 10, no. 1495, Thomas says that the expression *intellectus passivus* sometimes signifies the imagination; in *ST* I, q. 79, a. 2, ad 2, we read that according to some, the terms mean the sensitive appetite and the passions, which Aristotle also calls "rational by participation." But others say that they mean the *cogitativa* or *ratio particularis*. In both ways of understanding the term, it indicates the acts of a bodily organ; whereas the potential intellect, which thinks the intelligible essences, is not passive except in the third way of the passions, insofar as it receives a determination.

61. No. 745: "Set quomodo tunc intelligat, non est presentis intentionis discutere."

Things that are specifically one but consist of discontinuous parts (e.g., man) are indivisible in their specific nature (no. 755), although this unity is not the same as that of the continuum (no. 756). What is totally one, as a point, is understood as the privation of the continuum (no. 757). The explanation is that our mind starts from sense data, all of which have some magnitude, so that what has no magnitude can only be defined negatively. And this explanation also applies to separated, immaterial, substances (no. 758). When the intellect considers contraries, it moves from the positive contrary to the opposite contrary. In the next sentence, Aristotle writes (430b24–26): "if there is anything—one of the causes—which has no contrary, it will know itself and its activity," an obvious reference to what he says in *Metaphysics* XII.1075b30ff. Thomas avails himself of this sentence to refer to the divine mind, which has itself as its primary and immediate object and is always in act (no. 759). In no. 760, Aristotle mentions again the second operation of the intellect, the combining or separating of the subject and the predicate. Whenever the intellect affirms or denies things, it is either true or false; true when it does so in conformity with the reality it understands. In the simple apprehension, however, it is always true (no. 761). The immaterial substances understand in a way that agrees with the first operation of the intellect, so that in their thinking they are always true. Yet deception in our (human) first operation can occur when a wrong definition is applied, or when its parts do not agree with each other.

Lesson 12 (III.7.431a4–b19) contains several remarkable observations on sense cognition and its comparison with the intellect. Objects actualize the senses, yet the senses are not passive as if something in them would be destroyed or as if they would lose something when they are determined by an object (no. 765). This actualization of the senses is different from a physical movement; it is the fulfilment, the completion of the senses (ἡ τοῦ τετελὲσμένου) (no. 766). What holds for the senses also applies to the intellect and the will, in which there are no passions but a pure apprehension of the object. The appetite, however, may show a desire for or an aversion to the object. Affirming or rejecting the object is an act of the intellect (no. 767). Aristotle distinguishes three stages: being actualized by the object; awareness of its being good or bad, which may be followed by pleasure or distaste (no. 770). These stages are found both in the senses and in the intellect. Thomas stresses the difference between what happens at both levels: the senses are impressed immediately by what is pleasant or disagreeable, whereas what the intellect perceives at once is the goodness or badness of the object (no. 771) and it affirms or denies these qualities, while the senses perceive them only "in a certain way" (*quasi affirmat vel negat*). Just as the senses need their objects to be active in order to sense, the intellect needs phantasms (no. 772). Pursuing the comparison between the senses and the intellect, Aristotle reminds us that the proper objects of the external senses come together in the common sense, as the lines from the circumference of a circle come together at the center (no. 773). In a similar way, all phantasms come together in the intellect, which perceives the differences between them (no. 774). The common sense distinguishes between the objects of the senses; the intellect does so between the different ideas (nos. 775–76). Thomas clarifies the meaning of the sentence at 431b2, namely that "the intellectual faculty understands form in the phantasms" (τὸ νοητικόν ἐν τοῖς φαντάσμασι νοεῖ), as follows: the intellectual part of the soul understands the intelligible forms abstracted from phantasms (*a phantasmatibus abstractas*), even if these are absent, that is, not present in the senses, but only present in the phantasms. The intellect can desire or reject them (no. 777). Sometimes phantasms or concepts make us deliberate on things of the future, as if they were actually present (no. 778).

In the next section (no. 779), Aristotle compares speculative knowledge with practical knowledge. Truth and falsehood in both of them belong to the same genus, namely, the class of good things or that of bad things. Thomas writes that we can understand this passage in two ways: (1) what is good or bad remains so both at the level of the speculative and that of the practical intellect; and (2) knowledge, if true, is a good for the intellect. Truth and falsehood are not reduced to the class of good and evil things, but form a genus in both the speculative and the practical intellect (no. 780). How do we understand what is outside the range of sensation, such as mathematical objects and immaterial things? When dealing with composed things, we can consider one part without the other, provided its concept is not included in that of the other part (nos. 781–82). We understand mathematical realities as if they were separate while physically they are not (no. 783). Likewise, in understanding physical beings, we abstract what is universal in them from individuating factors. In his *De anima*, Aristotle does not examine if our intellect can know substances separated from matter. Thomas says that when Aristotle speaks, at 431b18, of the intellect as not separate from size (μὴ κεχωρισμένον μεγέθους, *non separatum a magnitudine*), he wants to stress that it is one of the powers of the soul (nos. 785–86).

In lesson 13 (III.8.431b20–432a14), Aristotle recapitulates the main points of what he had said about the senses and the intellect. In a first important statement, he says that the soul is all things, as the ancient philosophers asserted, but not in the way they thought. The senses and the intellect, when in act, are the objects they actually know, but they are not their objects when in a state of potentiality (no. 788). Empedocles thought that the soul was simply identical with things, but this is not the case. The soul is able to assimilate intelligible and sensitive forms of being. In a certain sense, it even is identical with its intelligible objects (no. 790). This dependence of the intellect on the senses is determined more precisely: all the objects of our understanding are of the realm of sensible, space-bound things, and have their being in the objects of the senses. This means that in order to know them we must use the senses. When the intellect considers something, this must at the same time be present in us as a phantasm (no. 791). Phantasms are characterized by the fact that they are loosened from the concrete objects present in the senses. At this point, Thomas observes that Avicenna was in error when he declared that once we had the phantasms we no longer needed the senses.[62] To reflect on the knowledge we acquired, we need the phantasms (no. 792). By contrast, Aristotle shows that the imagination differs from the intellect in that the intellect composes and divides, and so is in truth or in falsehood, while the imagination just represents the sensible aspects of things (no. 793). The concepts of the intellect differ from phantasms by their universality, Thomas adds, as they are abstracted from individual characteristics.

In lesson 14 (III.9.432a15–433a8), Aristotle considers the power of local movement. What is the principle that makes us move locally? Is it a particular part of the soul, located in a special section of the body (no. 795)? Thomas qualifies this passage (432a17ff.) as written by way of a controversy or dispute, but one which leads Aristotle to certain conclusions. How do we divide the powers of the soul? Some said that the soul has infinite powers. The powers of the soul may also be divided into those of the rational part of the soul and those which do not fall under it (nos. 796–97). He mentions the vegetative and the sensitive, the latter with its concupiscible and irascible parts (nos. 798–99). The appetitive faculty seems to be distinct from the other parts of the soul. This faculty is in part rational and in part irrational. Aristotle seems to consider it one faculty. Having probably in mind Plato's division of the soul and its faculties (see the *Phaedrus*), he writes at 432b4–5 that it would be absurd to split the soul (καὶ ἄτοπον δὴ τὸ τοῦτο διασπᾶν). But Thomas, very politely taking up what Aristotle had admitted, namely that there are two appetitive faculties in the sensitive part of the soul and one in the rational part, says that these faculties differ according to what their objects essentially are (no. 803). The intellect apprehends the good

---

62. He compared the situation to a person who has finished his voyage and need no longer be on the road.

differently from the senses, namely in terms of the universal essence of the good, while the senses know it according to the kinds of good apprehended: some things appear as good because they give pleasure—the concupiscible appetite is ordained to them—but when obstacles make it difficult to enjoy what is pleasant, the irascible appetite intervenes (no. 804). All its movements—hating, fearing evil, and hoping to acquire the good—are directed to reaching the good (no. 806). It is remarkable how Thomas, while following the text almost to the letter, clarifies the argument and lays down the basic distinction of the (rational) will from the two appetitive powers.

In the remainder of this chapter, Aristotle turns to local movement, that is, insofar as it differs from generation, vegetative life, breathing, etc. (no. 807). The principle of local movement cannot be that of vegetative life, for it is caused by what animals imagine or desire, while the vegetative principle functions without imagination (no. 808). This follows from the fact that plants do not move about this way (no. 809). Some animals have sensation but are incapable of moving from place to place (no. 810). This is not because they lack the necessary organs, for nature never fails to provide what is necessary for each species of animals. Thomas adds a conclusion (*ex hoc autem accipere possumus*): when there is a vital principle, there will also be the corresponding organs (no. 811). A speculative consideration of practical affairs is not a principle of local movement (nos. 812–15). Not even the practical intellect is a principle of local movement: when people have reached a decision, they do not always follow up what they have decided; passing to action requires something else in addition to practical knowledge (no. 816). Even the appetitive part in us does not simply command our movements, for some people who need to do something and desire so, do not always move accordingly (no. 817).

In lesson 15 (III.10.433a9–b27), Aristotle discusses the principles of the movement of animals. In the previous lesson, he has shown that their vegetative and sensitive parts are not the principles of local movement. Apparently, the intellect and the imagination must be what move men and animals (no. 818). Animals, but also many people, follow their imagination rather than rational discourse (no. 819). The moving principle of the mind is practical reason, which connects knowledge with the action that must be performed. The last thing that the practical reason considers is the first thing that has to be done—that is, the starting point of the whole action (no. 821). The same applies to the imagination, which moves in virtue of the desire for its object (no. 822). Therefore, the object desired is the mover (no. 823). The intellect moves by virtue of the appetite for an object, that is, by the will (no.

824) which concentrates the appetite on one object. The appetite can independently move to action (no. 825). If we make a mistake in drawing conclusions from the first principles, our choice may not be directed to a real good.

The argument of no. 827 is important: in the final analysis, the power that makes us move is the soul acting through the appetitive faculty. Aristotle rejects the division of the motive power of the soul into rational, irascible, and concupiscible potencies. The motive force proceeds from the soul as such. But he distinguishes the reasoning part of the soul, which has to do with contingent matters, from the part devoted to scientific thought, which is concerned with necessary objects (no. 828). Desire as such is not a motive force. People often have contrary desires, resulting from the opposition between reason and concupiscence (no. 829). These happen to occur in beings who have a sense of time and are aware of the now and of the future. Movement depends on three factors: the mover, the organ by which it moves (which is a part of the body), and the thing moved (nos. 830–31). The primary organ and moving principle must be such that it is both the starting point and the end term of movement (nos. 832–33). This results from the fact that all movements of animals consist in pushing and pulling (ὥσει καὶ ἕλκξει). The agent that impels pushes the thing forward, while the one that pulls draws the thing to where it is itself.

In lesson 16 (III.10–11.433b27–434a21), Aristotle considers local movement insofar as it is present in the different animals. First he mentions what is common to all animals, namely appetition as the cause of movement. Appetition presupposes imagination (no. 836). Thomas reminds the reader that the term "intellect," as Aristotle uses it in the *De anima*, can mean imagination, but that here imagination also signifies intellectual knowledge (no. 837). In a passage admirable for its sharp observation, Aristotle writes that the imperfect animals form images of objects that give them pleasure or cause pain and make them move accordingly. They do not form images of distinct things in different places, but of what is present and pleases or hurts (no. 839).

The principle of movement in man is deliberative reason, which is sometimes rendered inactive by desire. Reason as moving is deliberative imagination, which is proper to rational beings (no. 840). Reason is able to make one phantasma out of many, meaning the selection of one among several. Thomas explains that in order to select and to decide or choose, reason must follow a rule or have an end in view of which it can determine which object to choose or what to do. One may see here a covered reference to natural law (no. 841). The lower appetite does not know deliberation, and deliberation may be hampered in man by passions (nos. 842–43). It is according to nature, Thomas writes, that the higher appetite dominates the lower. A comparison with the celestial bodies (in accord with the ancient image of the world) illustrates this: the sphere of the first heaven gives the first impetus; and planets like Saturn add their own motion (no. 844).[63] In the last two sections of the lesson, Thomas stresses again that it is not speculative reason that initiates movement, but practical reason, when applied to a particular subject (nos. 845–46).

Lesson 17 (III.12.434a22–435a10) notes that the vegetative power is found in all living beings, though not all of them have sensation. Those with a simple body cannot have the sense of touch, but all have a vegetative soul from the moment of generation until their corruption (no. 847). Animals that move locally must have sense perception, however, or else they cannot reach what they need (no. 848). The sense of touch requires a balance of contrary qualities and cannot exist in simple bodies (no. 849).

Generally, Thomas affirms, nature does nothing in vain but acts for an end (no. 851). It has adapted the bodies of mobile animals to allow them to move, so that they can get the food they need; to this effect they need sense cognition (no. 852). Immobile animals do not have to seek their food, as it comes to them (no. 853). Some have suggested that some living beings could reach their food by intellectual knowledge only. But at this point Thomas recalls that the human mind presupposes sense knowledge (no. 854). The view that the intellect cannot exist without sense knowledge seems to be in conflict with Aristotle's theory of the moving souls of the heavenly bodies, which are alive and intelligent but lack sense knowledge because their bodies are not adapted for it (no. 855). Hence, Thomas says, one should not understand the term "non-generated" (ἀγένητον, 434b5) as referring to heavenly bodies but to certain animals, airy beings, called demons by the later Platonists (no. 857). According to Thomas, Aristotle wanted to suggest that Plato was wrong in accepting these beings.[64]

In no. 858, passing to the main theme of the lesson, Aristotle proceeds to show that the sense of touch necessarily presupposes a mixed, composed body. Touch is found in the entire animal world, as every animal is a living body and all bodies are tangible, except the celestial bodies, which are outside the sphere of the elements (no. 859). Touch is necessary for animals to distinguish what is harmful and what congenial. Taste is a kind of touch, as

---

63. The comparison was made by Themistius and taken over by Averroes. See *Sentencia libri De anima*, 250.

64. On the theories of the Platonists, see Elders, *Thomas Aquinas and His Predecessors*, 84–100. See also Thomas's *Expositio in Boetii De Trinitate*, q. 3, a. 4.

it perceives food as convenient or not to our constitution (nos. 860–61). The other senses are not found in all animals (no. 862) but for those animals that move from place to place, they are absolutely necessary to perceive things at a distance (no. 863). The intermediate air between the distant object and the sense is affected by the shape, the color, etc., of the object (no. 864).

In lesson 18 (III.13.435a11–b25), Aristotle stresses again the central place of the sense of touch. While the other senses each use a medium, touch is in direct contact with the object (no. 865). The animal body must by itself be capable of touching and therefore in a state that holds the middle between various qualities (such as hard and soft, cold and warm). We do not feel with bones or hair because in them one element dominates (no. 867). All animals have touch. They die when they are bereft of it (no. 869). Excessive light or noise can damage hearing or vision, but do not threaten animal life (no. 870). But tangible qualities can directly endanger the life of animals. The destruction of touch leads to the death of an animal (no. 871). Thomas notes that, earlier on, Aristotle had considered taste to be essential to the animal, associated as it is with touch. Here, he considers taste from the point of view of savor. It can tell an animal that a type of food is agreeable and in this way is helpful to the animal. The same applies to smell, which from a distance draws the animal to food (no. 873). The lesson includes a note on hearing, which renders communication possible between animals and is helpful in the education of the young; while the tongue allows us to communicate feelings to others. Thomas also makes reference to the last observations of Aristotle about the senses of touch, taste, smell, and hearing, and concludes that as for now what has been said about the soul is sufficient (no. 874).

Concluding Remarks

With the *Sentencia libri De Anima*, Thomas produced the first of twelve commentaries on Aristotle's works in a period of just a few years. Although he had ample knowledge of the main elements of the treatise, both from his own formation as well as from previous works he had written, in particular Book II of the *Summa contra gentiles* and the *Quaestiones disputatae De Anima*, Thomas's commentary on this great and innovating treatise of Aristotle is a masterful accomplishment. It possesses an irresistible clarity because of the light it sheds on the nature of the soul and its different powers (such as the imagination, the common sense and, above all, the intellect), on the formation of concepts by the agent intellect, and on the intellectual appetite. He always stays close to the text that is available to him and the few digressions are clearly indicated as such. He does not only actively pursue to understand the content of the work but also intends to explain how Aristotle proceeds in his argumentation as well as how the text is structured. The commentary remains at the level of philosophical psychology and is faithful to the exposition of Aristotle. Even his affirmation of the immortality of the soul, which has to be distinguished from the Christian view of the personal continuity of the human soul after death, is entirely based on philosophical principles and constitutes a valid development of Aristotelian principles. Precisely because of his close reading of Aristotle, his commentary remains until today a trustworthy guide to reading Aristotle's often difficult text, something which cannot be said of many other medieval commentaries.

His first commentary on Aristotle forms part of larger project to recuperate the substance of Aristotle's doctrine. We are witnessing the construction of a genuine philosophy along the lines of Aristotle's principles. The use of certain conclusions of this philosophical undertaking within theology was certainly Thomas's intention but one would go too far by saying that this was the primary aim of Thomas's commentary on *De anima*. In fact, his careful and patient reading of Aristotle's text surpasses its use merely in theology.

8 ❦ THE COMMENTARY ON THE
DE SENSU ET SENSATO

In the *De sensu et sensato*, Aristotle describes the soul as the principle of the structure and functioning of the whole body, and so it probably dates to the second period of his teaching in Athens.[1] W. D. Ross thinks that the *De sensu et sensato* is earlier than *De anima* II, as Aristotle would not yet have considered the soul as the ἐντελέχεια, the act of the body. This conclusion, however, is by no means certain.[2] The treatise stresses the joined activity of the body and the soul, and considers the sense faculties insofar as the body is implicated in their functioning. In the first chapters of the text, Aristotle stresses that the activity of the senses he is discussing is common to all animals; these are activities of the soul and body combined. In the treatise, he does not deal with the sense of hearing, but with vision, smell, touch, and taste, and argues that their objects are mixtures of qualities, such as black and white, sweet and bitter. Odor is ingeniously connected with flavor, and the classification of its objects is quite interesting. The common sensibles (κοινὰ αἰσθητά) are size, shape, roughness, smoothness, sharpness, and bluntness. In the opening lines of the treatise (436a8–17), Aristotle also mentions that what is common to both body and soul, such as sense, memory, appetite, etc., is sometimes common to everything that participates in life but sometimes it is only common to animal life. He lists four pairs: wakefulness and sleep, youth and old age, inhalation and exhalation, and life and death. By and large, these remarks give us the nine small treatises known as: on sense perception and sense objects (*De sensu et sensato,* 436a1–449b3), on memory and recollection (*De memoria et reminiscentia,* 439b3–453b11), on sleep and waking (*De somno et vigilia,* 453b11–458a32), on dreams (*De insomniis,* 458a33–462b11), on prophecy in sleep (*De divinatione per somnum,* 462b12–464b18), on longevity and shortness of life (*De*

1. Nuyens, *L'évolution*; W. D. Ross, *Aristotle's "Parva Naturalia"* (Oxford: Clarendon, 1955), 14.

2. For a qualified treatment of this question see Stephen Menn, "Aristotle's Definition of Soul and the Programme of the De Anima," *Oxford Studies in Ancient Philosophy* 22 (2002): 83–139.

longitudine et brevitate vitae, 464b19–467b), on youth and old age, on life
and death, and on respiration (*De iuventute et senectute, De vita et morte, De
respiratione,* 467b10–480b30).

By the thirteenth century these treatises, with some small variations,
were grouped together and designated as *parvi libri* (or *parvi libri naturales*)
and later on became known as the *Parva naturalia.* Apart from Alexander of
Aphrodisias's commentary on the *De sensu et sensato,* these treatises received
little attention within the Hellenistic era. An important change was brought
about from the twelfth century onward due to the Greek-Latin translations
(*translatio vetus*) and the Arabic-Latin input of Averroes's *Epitome* of a number of the *Parva naturalia,* including the *De sensu et sensato.* A new translation (*translatio nova*) of the entire *Parva naturalia* by William of Moerbeke
in the 1260s as well as his translation of the commentary by Alexander of
Aphrodisias sparked a renewed interest.

Thomas's commentary on the *De sensu et sensato,* as Gauthier explains in
his introduction to the critical edition, is posterior to his *De anima* commentary and completed after 1268 in Paris.[3] Among the *Parva naturalia,* the *De
sensu et sensato* and the *De memoria et reminiscentia* are the only treatises that
have been commented upon by Thomas. With regard to the sources Thomas
used when composing his commentary, Alexander of Aphrodisias must be
mentioned in the first place. Gauthier, as did Mansion before him, examined
Thomas's use of Alexander's commentary and points to Alexander's presence
throughout the text; he is even mentioned by name on a number of occasions.[4] Alexander provides information not given by Aristotle himself, such
as the names of Democritus and Anaxagoras, which Aristotle had not mentioned in the passages where their theories are discussed. Alexander is also a
valuable source of information on the Stoics. Gauthier mentions 164 places
where Thomas appears to follow Alexander and eight where he distances himself from him.

Further sources are the *Epitome* of *Parva naturalia* by Averroes, which
was well known in the time of Thomas,[5] and the expositions of Albert the
Great and Adam of Bockfeld on these treatises.[6] Gauthier regards the most

---

3. Leonine edition, vol. 45/2. Gauthier calls Thomas's commentaries on the works of Aristotle "Sententia," but not all specialists consider this title appropriate, pointing to the frequent use of "expositio." See also
Robert Wielockx, "Thomas d'Aquin, commentateur du *De sensu,*" *Scriptorium* 41 (1987): 150–57.

4. Auguste Mansion, "Le commentaire de saint Thomas sur le *De sensu et sensato* d'Aristote," in *Mélanges
Mandonnet* (Paris: Vrin, 1930), 1:83–102; Gauthier (Leonine ed., 45/2), 103*ff. The text of Moerbeke's translation used by Thomas was a copy of the autograph of Moerbeke.

5. Gauthier (Leonine ed., 45/2), 113*.

6. For the critical edition see Albertus Magnus, *De nutrimento et nutrito. De sensu et sensato cuius secundus
liber est de memoria et reminiscentia,* ed. S. Donati (Münster: Aschendorff, 2017), and S. Donati, "The Critical

important contribution of Averroes that he brought the *De sensu* and *De memoria* together in one book.[7] Some commentaries on the treatises in the *Vetus* translation may also have inspired Thomas. The commentary is a prolongation of that on the *De anima,* shedding light on particular points. Thomas himself refers several times to his commentary on the *De anima.*[8] On the basis of his prologue and the beginning of lesson 2, one can reconstruct the following *divisio textus.* After stating his intention in the prologue (lesson 1, 436a–b8), Aristotle divides the treatise into three parts: a summary of what he has said in the *De anima* (lesson 2, 436b8–437a19), the application of the soul's sense-powers to the body (lessons 3–14, 437a19–445b2), and finally a discussion of remaining questions (lessons 15–19, 445b3–449b4). The second and largest part deals with the application of the sense-powers to the organs of the senses (lessons 3–5) and then to the objects of the senses (lessons 6–14).

The Commentary of Thomas Aquinas

The commentary, which consists of seven chapters and nineteen lessons, opens with a prologue in lesson 1 in which Thomas explains the place of the *Parva naturalia* among the works of Aristotle.[9] To this effect, he proposes a theory of the order of the different sciences, using as his starting point *De anima* III.4.429b21–22, according to which the sciences are distinguished from one another according to the way in which their objects are separated from matter, recalling the tripartition of the speculative sciences in *Metaphysics* E (physics, mathematics, theology). This applies also to the science of the soul, which by its very essence is ordered to the body: the parts of this science follow the order of the modes according to which their objects are separable from matter. What is more universal (and more separate) is studied first. For this reason, Aristotle first studies what the soul is, and then its qualities and the mode of composition (or its relation) with

Edition of Albert the Great's Commentaries on *De sensu et sensato* and *De memoria et reminiscentia*: Its Significance for the Study of the 13th-century Reception of Aristotle's *Parva Naturalia* and its Problems," in *The Letter before the Spirit: The Importance of Text Editions for the Study of the Reception of Aristotle,* ed. A. van Oppenraay and R. Fontaine (Leiden: Brill, 2012), 345–99.

7. Gauthier (Leonine ed., 45/2), 114*.

8. For an excellent annotated English translation see *St. Thomas Aquinas: Commentaries on Aristotle's "On Sense and What is Sensed" and "On Memory and Recollection,"* trans. Kevin White and Edward Macierowski (Washington, D.C.: The Catholic University of America Press, 2005).

9. See also André-Jean Festugière, "La place du *De anima* dans le système aristotélicien d'après S. Thomas," in *Archives de l'histoire doctrinale et littéraire du moyen âge* (Paris: Vrin, 1931), 25–47; and Kevin White, "St. Thomas Aquinas and the Prologue to Peter of Auvergne's Quaestiones super De sensu et sensato," *Documenti e studi sulla tradizione filosofica medievale* 1 (1990): 427–56.

the body. Finally, he determines what belongs to each class of animals and plants and deals with the different qualities and operations that the animals have in common, as well as those that are proper to some species, such as those proper to the different senses. Accordingly, there are three groups of treatises: The four treatises of the first group concern living beings in general, two other treatises deal with the movements of animals, and next come the texts on the senses and their activities: the *De sensu et sensato, De memoria et reminiscentia,* and *De somno et vigilia.*[10]

Aristotle distinguishes, Thomas continues, between the different degrees of living beings: plants, or vegetative life, without sensation and local movement; beings with sensation but without local movement; and those with both sensation and local movement (no. 3).[11] The study of the substances separated from matter belongs to metaphysics, but the different activities of a living body and its parts are studied in the treatise we are now dealing with (no. 4). On the ensouled body there are the *De morte et vita, De respiratione et expiratione,* and *De iuventute et senectute.* Next come the treatises on *The Length and Shortness of Life, Health and Disease,* and *Nutrition and Nourishing.* Other treatises deal with the movement of animals and what causes it, and the members of the body that allow them to move. Next follows the study of the internal and external sensitive faculties, considerations that are dealt with in the present treatise. Sleep and activity cause the difference between sense activity and its absence (no. 5).

After the discussion of the soul, there follows logically the study of the senses, which pertain in the first place to the soul (no. 6). This takes us to the treatise we are now dealing with. In the *De anima,* the faculties of the soul were considered from the point of view of the soul, while in the present treatise they are studied from the point of view of the body (436a1; no. 7), that is to say, we must examine which dispositions render the operations of the senses possible (436a6; no. 8). Thomas explains why Aristotle does not consider at this point the interior senses, such as the imagination and the estimative sense, except memory. The reason is that for the former the object they deal with is present or quasi-present in them, while this is not the case for memory (436a8; no. 9). With regard to local movement, its principle in animals is the irascible appetite (no. 10). Imperfect animals have only the sense of touch, and memory is found only in perfect animals (no. 11), as is anger which results from the irascible appetite. All these acts are the common operations

---

10. Thomas mentions six treatises, two of which he thinks are lost.

11. For the convenience of the reader, the numbers of the relative sections in the Marietti edition are given in brackets.

of the soul and the body. The concupiscible appetitive faculty seeks what is agreeable to the senses, while the irascible makes the animal act for what is laborious (no. 12).

In *On Being Awake and Being Asleep*, Aristotle mentions what pertains in any way to the nature of being alive, that is, being awake and being asleep, which are found in all animals but not in plants, while life and death are found in all living beings. The cause of all these states must be investigated (436a11; no. 13). Aristotle places the question of health and disease under the subject of natural philosophy and stresses the connection between the latter and medicine (436a17; nos. 14–16). All the above mentioned operations are common to the soul and the body, a fact that can be shown by induction and by argument: the sense powers are affected by the sensible object, which is material; when a sense organ is damaged, the operation of the sense faculty is obstructed (436b1; no. 17).

Passing to lesson 2 (1.436b8–437a19), Thomas notes that whereas the external sense-powers are the subject of the *De sensu*, the inner senses of memory and recollection are treated in the *De memoria et reminiscentia*, "which is part of the present book." As we will see in the next chapter, when Thomas comments on the *De memoria et reminiscentia*, he adds a separate prologue, indicating that he regards it as a distinct work. Thomas notes as well that Aristotle takes up certain things he said about the senses in the *De anima*, namely that animals have sensation: touch and taste are common to all animals (no. 20); they sense the things necessary to their life and useful both for adaptation to their environment (warm, cold; dry, humid) and for what they need to feed themselves (nos. 21–22). In the following section, the senses that are found only in perfect animals are considered. These animals have forward movement, and so they can perceive what is at a distance: sight and hearing sense from a distance what is good and what is harmful (436b18; nos. 23–24). Both are found in animals that have prudence and pursue what is good for them and shun what is bad or destructive. For those who have "intelligence," these senses help them to attain well-being (which is the reason why they have them; τὸ οὗ ἕνεκα, Aristotle writes in the original text).

The Greek φρόνησις was translated by "prudence," although in the context it is likely to have a wider meaning than that of the first of the four cardinal virtues. Thomas adds a note on the virtue of prudence, which directs us about what we must do to reach what we want or ought to do. It helps us to discern among the great number of objects presented to us by the senses. The other animals have no share in this consideration by the intellect, but distinguish a great number of different forms by their vision, smell, etc. (437a1–3). Another notion is that sight surpasses hearing: sight is altered by things themselves, hearing by sounds that are produced by the movements of certain things. Sight as such is better for animals for seeking what is necessary and avoiding what is harmful. It is also more helpful for giving knowledge, while hearing is useful for promoting understanding in rational instruction (437a3–15; no. 27). Vision is likewise superior in showing many differences in the objects, which become visible when the translucent is illuminated. All bodies have some color either by themselves or insofar as the basis of color, the translucent and light, is found in them (no. 28). Thomas adds an excellent observation: vision also lets us know better the common sensibles, for the more universal a cognitive power is, the more its power extends to many things, in particular to the subject of inherence, common to the different qualities, the continuum (no. 29). Hearing informs us only about the different sounds, which show what affects the interior of animals. Its function is to let us know the different affections (no. 30). Yet indirectly, hearing contributes most to intelligence thanks to instruction by rational discourse. This is confirmed by the fact that blind persons are wiser than deaf and mute people (437a15; nos. 31–32).

In lesson 3 (1.437a19–438a5), Aristotle examines the relation of the sense faculties to their bodily organs and to sensible objects. The Pre-Socratics connected these organs with the four elements because of their conviction that "like is known by like"; the soul has the same nature as all things and so it can know them. A difficulty was that there are five senses and only four elements. Some authors placed an intermediate between air and water, namely, vapor, which was related to smell. Touch was related to earth, taste to water, hearing to air, and sight to fire. Aristotle considers this last point here. In favor of the relation between vision and fire is the fact that we see a flash when the eye suffers a shock (437a22; no. 35). Aristotle objects that the eye at rest does not see fire and gives another explanation of our seeing a flash: the eye being smooth and polished has a shine, which explains the brightness; a rapid movement makes that this flash is noticed as being separate from the shine of the eye itself (437a35–b11; nos. 37–38). Next, Thomas gives the answer of Alexander to an objection that says that no movement would be fast enough to make this happen, namely that the pupil of the eye is divisible in parts and when part of it reaches the place of the shine, this is still coming from the rest of the pupil, so that the flash is seen as coming from elsewhere (no. 39). This happens in darkness because the flash is so small that it is obscured by light from outside. When one moves slowly this shine is not seen (437b5; no. 40).

Arguing against this theory that connects vision with fire, Aristotle mentions Plato's view in the *Timaeus* and the theory of Empedocles, who thought, first, that the organ of sight is related to fire and, second, that when something is seen light issues from the eye. But Aristotle criticizes this theory: even in dark surroundings, a burning lamp keeps shining (no. 41). Some details of Plato's theory are mentioned next. According to Plato, when light issuing from the eye encounters some light outside, vision results; if it encounters darkness, it is extinguished (470b13; no. 42). But this is unreasonable, according to Aristotle; not darkness but cold and moisture extinguish fire, according to a somewhat different reading of 437b15 by Alexander (no. 43). One might, however, say that the light emitted by the eye just dies out when not comforted by some light outside the eye (no. 44). But the light of fire is either darkened by a greater light or, like fire itself, extinguished in water. So the weak light issuing from the eye would be extinguished by daylight, and by water or ice, as happens to the flame of burning objects (437b19; no. 45).

As stated, Aristotle mentions the theory of Empedocles, who said that vision happens through light issuing from the eye, as from a lamp meaning that when this is prohibited by covering the lamp, it becomes dark outside. But inside the eye the light is preserved, shielded by the cornea, which, however, when letting through the light weakens it. Aristotle adds that Empedocles also suggested a different view, namely that visible things sometimes emit certain bodies, causing vision (437b23–438a3; nos. 46–47). Empedocles expressed the latter view in a poem, reproduced in the Greek text edited by Ross.[12]

In the next section, pertaining to lesson 4 (2.438a5–b2), Democritus's theory of vision is discussed. Aristotle approves Democritus for ascribing sight to water, but then says that he was mistaken in that he thought that vision is only the appearance in the pupil of the eye of the object seen. However, according to Aristotle, vision is not just the presence of an object in the eye, but an activity of an agent who has the power of sight. The appearance of an object is only a reflection. He shows this by pointing to the reflection of the human visage in a mirror, which receives an image but only reflects it. Why does a mirror (and similar bodies that receive images) not see the image (nos. 48–52)? Thomas adds an observation: according to Democritus, the soul is something corporeal so that we should not be surprised that he called an operation of the soul an affection of the body (no. 50). Thomas further explains it in a *sciendum est*: the first reception of the object is corporeal. This is not surprising, as vision is an act of the soul by means of a bodily organ. Yet bodily passion is not the same as vision (no. 51).

Democritus fails to explain why other bodies, in which a reflection of

---

12. Ross, *Aristotelis Fragmenta Selecta* (Oxford: Clarendon, 1955), fr. 84.

forms occurs as in a mirror, do not see (438a10; no. 52). Aristotle mentions that Democritus correctly assigned vision to water in the organ of sight because of its transparency, rather than to air (although it is also transparent). As water is denser and is preserved better (air disperses), so the pupil and the eye as the medium of sight are assigned to water (no. 53). We see this when the eye is destroyed and water flows out from it and also in the fact that the eyes of embryos (which retain much of the power of their origin) are quite cold and bright, properties that are characteristic of water. The pupil is surrounded by the white of the eye, which, fatty as it is, keeps the water of the pupil from freezing (438a17; no. 54). Aristotle also criticizes the theory according to which seeing happens by emitting rays: we see the faraway stars, but it is absurd to say that something goes out from the eye that far. It would mean as well that different bodies are in the same place (the emitted corporeal substance and the body seen). Moreover, according to the mathematicians who hold this view, the apex of the emission would be in the eye, the basis in the object seen. The size of the eye is insufficient for allowing emissions to faraway objects. Finally, it is not clear what is the nature of the body emitted. Is it air? But there is air everywhere around. Fire? If so, we would also see at night. Light? But light is not a body (no. 55). Plato has a different opinion: what is emitted by the eye goes only a certain distance until it merges with the light outside, and this merging would then cause vision. Aristotle rejects this view: if there is no outside light, the light coming from the eye will be extinguished. But if the outside light reaches the eye, there is no need for this emission; it is better that vision happens without a medium, so Aristotle, if the medium is not necessary (438a27; no. 57). Moreover, this theory of the union of the light from the eye with light outside is irrational: qualities do not melt together. Bodies of a different nature also do not coalesce. Finally, the cornea of the eye would impede the merging of two kinds of light (438a29; no. 58).

Lesson 5 (2.438b2–439a5) treats the elements of which the sense organs consist and the relation of the latter to parts of the body. Aristotle first repeats what he has shown in *De anima*, namely that vision is impossible without light, as vision needs a transparent medium and light makes the body between the eye and the object transparent. Whatever this medium is—illuminated air or something else like water—the movement that takes place through it causes vision (438b2; no. 59). Thomas notes that we should not consider this movement as a local movement in the way Democritus and Empedocles conceived it, namely, as an emission from the bodies seen, for then these would grow smaller. It is an alteration to the form of the object seen (nos. 60–61). But in the medium this form remains imperfect as a certain "intentional" being (no. 62). Next, Aristotle shows that we must assume that the pupil of the eye, which is the organ of sight, consists of watery matter, for water is translucent. As there must be light outside, so in the eye there must also be something transparent (438b5; no. 63). With regard to actual seeing, Aristotle writes that the faculty of vision is not on the outward surface of the eye, but that the sensitive part of the soul (which exercises vision) must be close to the brain. Further on he calls the eye with its vision an offshoot from the brain. When the passage from the pupil to this inner principle is cut, there is no vision (438b8–15; nos. 64–65).

In the following section, Aristotle treats of the organs of the so-called not-necessary senses and those of the necessary ones, connecting them with the four elements as his predecessors had done, although with some reservation.[13] This theory had been discussed in *De anima* III.1. In the present text, vision of the eye is attributed to water, hearing is connected with air, and smell with fire (no. 66), but Thomas notes that in *De anima* III.1, only air and water are said to constitute the sense organs, namely of vision and hearing, while the organ of smell might be formed of these two, and warmth is said to be an essential prerequisite of all sensitive activity. With regard to smell, Thomas also recalls another explanation of Aristotle: actual smelling is connected with "fire" (or heat), while potentially the sense may be said to be made of either air or water (no. 67). Aristotle shows that in fact the act of smelling is fire (i.e., connected with a vaporous exhalation), while the organ, which is potentially smelling, is contrary to the act of smelling and therefore cold and close to the brain as is the faculty of vision (438b21–30; nos. 68–69). The brain is humid and cold and hence is susceptible to heat in actually smelling something and also to water or air in the act of the organ of vision (no. 70). If this is the case, was Plato then not right in ascribing vision to fire, as Aristotle assigns smell to it? Thomas sees a difference: the organ of smell contains water insofar as water is potentially warm, while the organ of vision contains water insofar as it is translucent and shining in potency (no. 71).

With regard to the *organs* of the necessary senses (such as, notably, that of touch), Aristotle says that the organs of taste and touch are related to earth, which means that the element earth is present in the organ to a high degree

---

13. Thomas refers to *De anima* III.1.425a5–7, noting that assigning sense-organs to the elements was not "secundum sententiam Aristotelis" but that, because others did assign the sense-organs to the elements, Aristotle "condescended, as it were" to these philosophers and thus discussed this relation of the sense-organs with the elements. See no. 66: "considerandum est quod non fuit secundum sententiam Aristotelis quod organa sensuum elementis attribuerentur, ut patet in libro de anima, sed quia alii philosophi organa sensuum quatuor elementis attribuebant; ideo quasi in hoc condescendens, dicit quod suppositis his quae dicta sunt de visu, oportet, secundum quod aliqui dicunt, unumquodque sensitivorum, idest organorum sensus, attribuere alicui uni elementorum, sicut alii faciunt."

and in a greater amount than in the organs of the other senses. The organ of smell contains water but also earth, so that it is potentially the moist substance that conveys the different smells to the sense. The organ of touch is close to the heart, which is the warmest part of the body, so that the coolness of the earth is brought to a moderate temperature (438b30; nos. 73–74). Touch is present throughout the body; its medium is the flesh, but it senses best in the region of the heart: wounds inflicted there are most painful. People with small heads are impulsive, as the heat of the heart is not cooled off sufficiently, while in the case of large heads, there is too much evaporation upward.[14] Thomas adds a note: we should not say that there are two centers or principles of sensation, respectively near the heart and near the brain, as there is no sensation without heat, so that in the last analysis sensation proceeds from the heart to the brain (439a1–4; nos. 75–76).

We now pass to lesson 6 (3.439a6-b14). The subject of the lesson is the sensible objects of the five senses. They must be distinguished from the so-called common sensibles. How do they act upon each sense and how are the organs of the senses affected? This last question regarding the affection of the sense organs has been dealt with in *De anima* II.6ff. Aristotle now investigates what the objects of the senses are by themselves. And because hot and cold, moist and dry, and hard and soft, have already been examined in the *De generatione et corruptione* and *Meteorologica*, he now considers color, odor, and flavor (439a6–16; nos. 77–78). In *De anima* II.7–12, he explained what the sensibles are as the respective senses perceive them, but here he considers them for what they are by themselves. The visible in act is the same as the sense power, but the visible in potentiality is not (no. 80). The sensibles are capable of actualizing the sense faculties. Aristotle first considers color, and next odor and flavor. The principle of color is twofold: there is the formal principle, light, and there is the material principle, the *perspicuum*, that is, the transparent. The transparent must be determined by color: light is the color of the transparent (439a21; no. 80).

As we shall see, the concept of the perspicuous will be somewhat further developed by Thomas. Color in the "perspicuous" disappears when the light fails, whereas it remains in a colored body (no. 81). The perspicuous, Thomas says, is a kind of common reality, found in air and water and in many bodies in varying degrees; it is receptive (*susceptivum*) of light (nos. 82–83). It is present in the celestial bodies and goes through them, for they are transparent. The sun is filled with it, from where it goes to the other bodies, which let it pass through,

---

14. Aristotle is referring to persons who have less facility to cool off the warmth of the heart.

while the earth receives the light only at its surface (nos. 84–85).[15] Examining color first, Aristotle defines it as being a limit of the indeterminate perspicuous in the bodies; in these bodies, the perspicuous is something ultimate, that is, at the outside of them. Certain bodies are limited by themselves, others have no limits by themselves, but by other bodies. This is the case with the perspicuous, which itself has no limits and has nothing determinate by which it can be seen: the light it receives goes all through it (nos. 87–88). But the perspicuous or transparent existing in bodies has a limit, and that is their color. Color is a quality of the surface or limit of a body (439a25; no. 89). It is the same perspicuous that is receptive of color in such bodies as air and water, which are colored from the outside, and in bodies that have their own color, so that color is a limit of the perspicuous (nos. 90–92). Aristotle concludes this section by presenting the definition of a color as the outer limit (or extremity) of the perspicuous in those bodies that have color by themselves. Color is not something quantitative, but a quality. Inside bodies, color is potentially present; it is reduced to act by their division. In transparent things such as water, which by themselves are unlimited, color is only present at their limits (*secundum extremitatem*) when they are touching something (439a32–b11; nos. 93–94).

In lesson 7 (3.439b14–440a15), Aristotle determines the species of colors, first of the extreme, then of the intermediate colors. The presence of light in the air may be caused by the transparent, as this is present at the limits of bodies, while its absence causes darkness. As the color black is contrary to white, there must be some light in it, for contraries are in the same class (no. 95; 439b16). With regard to the intermediate colors, Aristotle sees similar proportions as there are in numbers. Because of the number one, numbers are commeasurable, while continuous quantities are not always so, but stand in a relation of more and less to each other. If they are commeasurable, they have a common measure, for example, a certain length (nos. 98–100). This is also found in qualities. The proportion between colors is the same as that between low and high tones in music. Harmonious colors based on numerical proportions are well adjusted and agreeable to watch (439b30; no. 101). Pure or primary colors have a numerical proportion to each other. When they are disordered, this proportion is lacking. This also happens when the colors are not pure and are unpleasant to look at. There is another way to obtain intermediate colors: when painters place a color over another, stronger and more telling color (440a7; no. 103).[16]

---

15. Gauthier (Leonine ed., 45/2), 38 and 246ff., notes that this theory was used by Maimonides to explain the darkness at the beginning of the creation of the world according to the Book of Genesis.

16. On Aristotle's theory of colors see Richard Sorabji, "Mathematics and Colors," *Classical Quarterly* 22 (1972): 293–308.

The theme of the generation of intermediate colors is further treated in lesson 8, where the two modes of the generation of colors are compared. The Pre-Socratics thought that colors are an emission from bodies, in the way Democritus and Empedocles taught that vision is caused by an emission of particles from bodies (440a7; nos. 103–4). Aristotle objects: if this emission entered the eye, the eye would be damaged and the bodies would lose their substance because of these continuous emissions (nos. 105–6). Some said that the intermediate colors are produced when the colors of the extremities of bodies are placed next to each other, but this would require time. As the distances of these bodies to the eye are not the same, colors would be seen at different times. If vision resulted from contact with a beam of particles, vision would be touch. But this is impossible, for our vision does not sense contraries as contraries (as touch does). Moreover, outside wind would affect the stream of particles and distort vision; light would no longer be necessary for vision (no. 107). Moreover, if the vision of various colors resulted from different emissions of particles, time would be needed for them to reach the eye in relation to the distance; the distance of the various kinds of particles to the eye would be different (no. 108), but the different arrival times would not be noticed, so that one could speak of an imperceptible time. But this conclusion would not apply when one holds the theory of the superimposition of one color upon another (no. 109).

According to the theory of those who say that vision results from contact with the particles of the different parts, there would not be simultaneous vision, but a body would be seen successively, as the particles would not reach the eye at the same time, although these time differences would be imperceptible (no. 110). But if a body is perceived as a whole, vision sees it simultaneously. But we can also consider one part of it as distinct from the rest and subsequently consider the other parts; if we do so, we notice the succession and therefore time (no. 111).[17] To explain the generation of intermediate colors we must expound the mixture of bodies, which happens not only when very small particles of them mix (no. 113), but also by the mixture of an entire body with another body (no. 114). Bodies share in the perspicuous according to more and less; the colors depend on the perspicuous. When the bodies are different and mixed, colors will also be mixed and different shades and varieties will result, depending on numerical proportions or on the respective mass of the bodies (nos. 115–16).

17. These two sections of the text are additional explanations by Thomas, perhaps inspired by Alexander. See Katerina Ierodiakonou, "Aristotle and Alexander of Aphrodisias on Colour," in *The "Parva naturalia" in Greek, Arabic and Latin Aristotelianism*, ed. B. Bydén and F. Radovic (Cham: Springer, 2018), 77–90.

In lesson 9 (4.440b28–441a29), odor and flavor are studied together because, as Aristotle says, they are almost the same affection: both result from a mixture of humid and dry, following on a change caused by heat. Flavor is more the result of moisture, odor that of dry air and vapor (no. 118). Because the sciences proceed from what is more evident to what is less so, Aristotle deals first with flavor, as the different flavors are more familiar to us than odors. The sense of smell is weaker in us than in other animals and is activated by a hot damp (*calidum igneum*), and its organ is near the brain, which is cooler and more moist than other parts of the body (no. 119).

The sense of touch in man is very precise (*certissimum*) because of the well-ordered and varied composition of the human organism. This holds also for taste, which is a kind of touch (no. 120). To determine the nature of flavors, Aristotle begins by observing that water as such is insipid, although it is the root and principle of all flavors. If it has a flavor, the reason of it is that some substance has been mixed to it (no. 122). To explain why it is the root of all flavors, Empedocles says that these flavors are actually present in water, but are not perceived because of their small quantities. A second view is that of Democritus and Anaxagoras as mentioned by Alexander, namely that water does not actually have those flavors, but consists of such a material that the flavors easily appear: they are already present as seeds (no. 123). Aristotle rejects these opinions: if Empedocles were right, a certain flavor would have to be collected and concentrated in a body, before its flavor would be tasted. But experience shows that the sun causes the flavor of fruits to change (441a10; no. 124). It is impossible that water should be the matter out of which flavors come to be: observation shows that the different parts of a plant have different flavors, so that these flavors are not caused by the water around it, which only has one flavor (441a18; no. 125). According to some authors, flavors would be produced by changes in the water caused by heat, but water is very subtle. Rather than being found in water, different flavors are present in different parts of plants and animals, that is, in bodies with a certain density (441a21).

The true cause of flavors is explained in lesson 10 (4.441a30–442a11). All flavors of the fruits of plants are derived from earth, which acquires them thanks to a small admixture of water and an alteration caused by heat. Aristotle advances two arguments: (1) the ancients said that water tastes like the earth it passes through; the water of sources differs according to the soil where these spring up (441a30; no. 130). Thomas notes that Aristotle does not say what the universal cause of flavors is, but speaks of the birth of flavors in water. (2) Flavors come from the earth as one can notice in plants which grow out of the earth. Water changes according to the savors of the earth mixed with it. At this point, Thomas recalls that the four elements are each characterized by a pair of contrary qualities: the earth is cold and dry; fire is hot and dry; air is warm and moist; and water cold and moist (no. 133; 441b8). Fire is the most noble of the elements and closest to the heavenly bodies; it is the most active (no. 134). Fire as such and earth do not act but, insofar as it is hot, fire does.[18] Some authors, including Alexander, said that heat is the substantial form of fire. A substantial form, however, is not perceptible by the senses. Heat is the proper accident of fire, which acts through it (no. 137). Thomas adds a note: according to Alexander, the Stoics teach that bodies act by themselves (i.e., by their substantial form) while, according to the Platonists, there are only accidental changes; substantial forms do not result from natural changes (no. 138). But the answer is that all things act according the way they are in act: the form of the main agent is reproduced by the agent that acts (no. 139). When a moist and watery substance filters through dry earth and when this process is directed by something warm, the moisture acquires the quality of a flavor (no. 140).

Aristotle defines flavor as a passion in a humid, watery subject caused by what is dry, that is, earth, to which heat is added, which actualizes the sense of taste from potency to actuality (441b19; no. 141). Flavors are not only present in moist or dry things, but also in combinations of both. They are an affection of the food, which is a mixture of dryness and moistness (441b23; no. 143). The food of animals serves a dual purpose, namely, to make them grow and to nourish them. The heat causes growth, while the cold causes contraction (no. 144). It is proper to heat to expand. A text in *De anima* II.3.414b7–8 that says that *touch* is the sense related to food does not contradict this, because there Aristotle places moisture, that is, flavor, under the tangible objects (no. 145). In the last section of the chapter, he confirms the foregoing exposition when he says that all animals are nourished by what is sweet and by admixing other ingredients. Their natural heat causes their growth by digesting the food, drawing from it what is light and sweet, and leaving behind what is salty and bitter. This is why the feces of animals are quite bitter and salty. Something similar happens in the universe: the heat of the sun in the bodies of the more exterior regions draws out moisture, leaving behind what is earthen and dense. Thus rainwater is sweet, although the sea from which most of it is drawn is salty. Other flavors are added to food for seasoning (442a3; nos. 146–47).

Lesson 11 (4.442a12-b26) treats of the species of flavors. Intermediate flavors are formed from a mixture of sweet and bitter, as colors are from black

---

18. Being hot is considered a quality of the substantial element fire.

and white. Heat causes sweetness by dissolving the moisture of food. In the absence of it, bitterness results. Intermediate flavors result when this moisture is not wholly digested. The relation to moisture determines the variety of flavors. A sour flavor is caused when the moisture is not fully digested (442a12; no. 148). Aristotle then says that those flavors please us best that are mixed according to a numerical proportion (442a13; no. 149). Bitter and salty flavors are caused by an excessive heat (no. 150). He enumerates seven flavors, as he counts also seven colors, but by a mixture of these flavors and colors new varieties are obtained (442b25; no. 152). Bitter and salty are the privation of sweet in moist food (no. 153). Aristotle mentions the theory of Democritus, who reduced all sensible objects to tangible things, to size and shape. This is clearly wrong, because touch perceives its objects directly, while the other senses do so through an external medium that need not be tangible (no. 154). Democritus called black rough and white smooth (442b4; no. 156). Aristotle rejects this view for three reasons: (1) no sense knows figures as its proper object; (2) all sensible objects are distinguished by contrarieties, but figures are not contrary to figures; and (3) figures are infinite in number, but the sense of taste does not distinguish an infinite number of flavors (no. 160; 442b13–24).

In lesson 12 (5.442b27–443b16), Thomas explains succinctly but masterfully the order of the themes that will be treated (no. 162). First, Aristotle shows what is passive in the generation of odors and then, what is active in it, namely, moisture that penetrates into what is dry. Water and air are receptive of odor, which is transparent in them insofar as it is saturated by something dry, receives moisture which cleans it (no. 163). So, not only the air but also water is receptive of odors. This is apparent in the case of fish that perceive their food from a distance although they cannot see it and there is no air in the water around them. Fish do not breathe. Air does not remain in the water but goes up (no. 164). The air and water that receive odors are moist. Odor is the form impressed by the "sapid dry"[19] diffused in a moist environment, that is, water and air (no. 165; 443a6). That the "sapid dry" (*enchymum*) is the cause of odor is shown by the following arguments. (1) The elements have no odor because they do not have this sapid dry. The sea does have an odor because the sapid dry mixes in it with the humidity of water, that is, substances coming from the earth are mixed in it. This is evident by its salty taste (no. 166). (2) Stones do not smell as they do not have this humidity, but wood smells because it has some of this greasy humidity, as is evident because it burns (no. 167). And (3) this is also seen in metals. Gold is lowest in odor, as it is clos-

---

19. The English translation by K. White and E. Macierowski transliterates this as "enchymous dryness."

est to earth, but certain metals such as tin have some odor (no. 168). Some consider odor a smoky evaporation. Smoke is an intermediary between air and earth. Heraclitus thought that vapor is the origin of things (no. 169) and some of the ancients believed that smoke is something like vapor, for example, an exhalation and/or an evaporation, but in reality evaporations are different as they consist of something common to air and earth. Aristotle rejects these views: vapor belongs to water, while smoke does not (443a29; no. 170). Some also thought that, insofar as odors are like emanations, an odor must be considered an evaporation. But it is wrong to speak of emanation in the case of colors, so that according to these authors evaporation (emanation) should not be said of odors; in both these views perception is thought to come about through touch (by an emanation). But in that case the bodies smelled or seen would get smaller and be finally dissolved (443b1; no. 172). Moreover, things can be seen and smelled at a distance. The conclusion is that moisture in the air and in water undergoes the influence of the "sapid dry" and so odors arise (443b3; no. 173). The "sapid dry" produces odors both in water and on the continent, just like dry land when washed by watery moisture produces savors (no. 174). Because of the proximity of odors and savors, odors, like savors, are produced in water and arise in air and water. The development of both odors and savors is hindered by frost (no. 176).

In lesson 13 (5.443b17–444b7), after explaining the generation and the nature of odors, Aristotle examines the species of odors and distinguishes between the odor of food as pleasant to those who have appetite and as losing its attractiveness when the appetite has been satisfied. This type of odor is related to savor and corresponds to its species (443b17; no. 177). It stimulates the appetite, but when we have eaten, it no longer impresses us. With regard to these odors, animals have a more acute sense than man. Odors of this kind are distinguished according to the species of savors (444a3; no. 178). But the second type of odors are those that are pleasant to smell and are only sensed by man, so that the sense of smell in man is richer than that of the other animals. Aristotle explains this by the fact that the human brain compared to that of other animals is larger in relation to the size of man's body. These kinds of odors are a remedy against excessive coolness of the brain; when used in the right way, they promote health, but they serve no further purpose, and Thomas observes with some regret that they are useless to help us in the investigation of nature, for which sight and hearing are very helpful (*cum tamen nulla alia utilitas appareat*) (444a8; no. 185). Yet for the purpose of health, the odors combined with the flavors of food are always pleasant and promote health (444a16; no. 186).

Because of its usefulness to temper the cold of the brain, smelling is done through respiration but only in man and in certain animals (no. 187). Odors have a sanitary power, namely that of warming the processes in the area around the brain, whereas breathing is used by nature, first to cool the brain area and, in second place, to sense odors (nos. 188–89). Those animals that have lungs and breathe can perceive odors of the second class that are related to flavors (444b2; no. 190).

Lesson 14 (5.444b7–445b2) notes that animals that do not breathe can nevertheless smell, and animals can also smell odors of the second group, not connected to food. Fish and insects sense their nourishment (which they cannot see) from a distance. Do they have another sense power beside the five senses? The answer is negative, as sense powers are distinguished by their objects, which would be the same for such an additional sense (444b15; no. 194). Aristotle has an ingenious explanation of how these animals perceive odors: when breathing and sensing something, a sort of cover is removed from the sense organ, while in animals that do not breathe there is no such cover. He compares it to the absence of eyelids in certain animals (444b21–28; no. 195). To further clarify this, he reconsiders the sense of smell. Some animals are not hampered in their search for food by a foul odor except insofar as it is harmful to their health when they perceive the changed condition of the food by touch (no. 197). Of the five senses, touch and taste perceive their objects directly, while sight and hearing do so through external media. Smell is in the middle and has something in common with both groups insofar as odor is an affection of nourishment and so goes together with touch and taste, but it also agrees with sight and hearing insofar as odor is an affection perceived through an external medium (445a4; nos. 198–201).

The Pythagoreans connected odors with food and went so far as to say that certain animals feed themselves with odors (445a16; no. 202) but against their theory pleads the fact that food must consist of several elements in order to be able to nourish. Animals, being composed of the elements, must feed themselves with food composed of the different elements (445a17; no. 204). Water alone cannot feed the animals. Furthermore, the odors when smelled manifest themselves to the sense of smell near the brain, while the air that carries the odors goes to the lungs. But neither the brain nor the lungs can digest food (nos. 205–6).

Starting with lesson 15 (6.445b3–446a20), Aristotle deals with some questions about sensible objects and the sense powers. A first question is whether sensible qualities are infinitely divisible as bodies are. If they were, the sense powers would also be divisible to infinity and would sense every magnitude, however small. Points, however, will not be visible, nor can one see a white color that has no extension, and this is also true of the other sensibles, because the senses are "powers in a magnitude."[20] The senses are the actuality of a bodily organ and cannot receive further determinations when these have no magnitude: the agent must be proportionate to the passive receiver. But there remains a difficulty, Thomas says, namely: how are we to understand that every magnitude is perceptible? Sensible qualities are not infinitely divisible (445b6–10; no. 210). This difficulty is discussed in two steps: (1) if sensible bodies are not infinitely divisible, there is a body that lies beyond the division of sensible qualities and has no such divisible qualities; it would not be perceptible (445b11–15; no. 211); and (2) if these minuscule bodies were not perceptible, our soul would no longer be able to know everything, as the intellect can only know what the senses present to it. In a note, Thomas writes that this is directed against Plato's theory of the existence of intellectual forms outside our soul; according to Aristotle, the forms of singular things are known by the intellect through abstraction (no. 213). He reaffirms that there are no indivisible magnitudes (no. 214).

The species of colors and savors are finite in number: in all the genera of sensible things, there are contraries that are furthest removed from each other, so that the intermediate species are finite in number (no. 215). If a finite continuum is divided in equal parts, the division can be continued to infinity, but this is not the case in a division into unequal parts. A continuum *per accidens*, as for instance a colored surface, is divided into a limited number of parts (no. 216). Sensible qualities exist in a continuum, as in their subject, but when parts of the continuum are separated, they exist actually by themselves. Before their separation they were parts in potency (no. 217) and were not perceived. Small parts of what is visible and small sounds can escape our vision or hearing. This also happens in the field of the other senses: minimal quantities are potentially perceptible (no. 218). The parts of a continuum are perceptible in potency, not in act (no. 219). While a mathematical body is infinitely divisible, a natural body is not. When the power that keeps the parts together becomes very weak, the body turns into something else, and there are no parts left of the previous substance (no. 220). When an object as such is less perceptible, the power of the sense faculty must be greater, so that perception is possible. But this power, no more than other powers, cannot increase indefinitely and so its objects in minimal quantities remain hidden (nos. 222–24).

Lesson 16 (6.446a20–447a11) addresses the following question: are the

---

20. Aristotle is referring to the bodily organ of the senses, which has a certain magnitude.

sense powers changed by the sensible objects they perceive? Those ancient philosophers who spoke of an emanation thought so, but Aristotle holds that the object causes an alteration in the medium, which then arrives at the sense. There is no problem with regard to touch and taste (where the senses are in direct contact with their objects), but with regard to light one can raise the question whether it first affects the medium before it does the sense. It seems reasonable to say that light first affects the medium (nos. 226–27). When a sense perceives something it has already perceived it, as the impression on the sense is instantaneous: a sense begins to perceive without any previous motion in it. When one perceives something, one has already perceived it. Thomas provides a fine explanation of Aristotle's argument in nos. 229–34, namely that there is no generation in things in which there is no becoming (*fieri*). Thomas explains that there is generation when a terminus is reached by a successive movement (no. 229), but when a previous disposition for a change is absent, the change is instantaneous: air is illuminated instantly and whoever perceives something has already perceived it (no. 230). Nevertheless, with regard to our hearing, there is a successive motion of the sound, which covers a certain distance before reaching the sense of hearing (no. 231). During this traversing, the sound of the voice can be disturbed in various ways (nos. 232–33). This may happen also in the transmission of light (nos. 234–35).

In the next section, Aristotle shows the difference between vision, on the one hand, and hearing and smelling, on the other. Air and water, as being the media in hearing and smelling, are subject to many different movements (nos. 236–37). Without naming him, Aristotle mentions the view of Gorgias that different persons with different organs cannot perceive the same sound (446b17).[21] However, that which moves the sense powers immediately is different in different persons, but what moves the medium is the same (no. 238). What reaches the individual senses is not an effluence of objects, but a movement and passion of the medium. The alteration caused by sounds is through local motion; that caused by light, however, is not through a successive motion, but rather the entire medium is moved as one mobile thing by the source of light (no. 240). The reason for this difference is that when what is received in a medium is received as in its proper subject, it can remain in it and be a principle of action; but when it is received as something added, it does not remain and is not a principle of action. Odors are received in the air and in water according to their own being, insofar as air and water are transformed

---

21. The editors of the Leonine edition refer to *De Melisso, Xenophane, Gorgia* 980b9–14, a first-century A.D. treatise falsely attributed to Aristotle. See J. Mansfeld, "De Melisso Xenophane Gorgia: Pyrrhonizing Aristotelianism," *Rheinisches Museum für Philologie Neue Folge* 131, nos. 3–4 (1988): 239–76.

by the "sapid dry" (no. 242); but the transparent does not receive its substantial form from the body that illuminates it, so that light is received in it as an adventitious form, which does not stay when the source of light is no longer present (no. 243). While sound arrives first in the medium before reaching the ear, light illustrates the whole medium (air) simultaneously, whereas sound first reaches halfway through the medium.

In no. 245, Thomas explains the effect of alteration. Alterations are not precisely measured by magnitude, as they are not motions in quantity. Sometimes a whole body is altered simultaneously. Mutations from being to nonbeing and vice versa are instantaneous (no. 246). In successive alterations, the distance between the point of departure and that of arrival is sometimes covered part after part. The first part is changed by the cause of the alteration (no. 247). One could object that, at first, some parts are not yet touched by the alteration, so that the whole does not change simultaneously (no. 249). Some say that, when changing from black to white, a body keeps some parts that are black, but this is not the view of Aristotle, Thomas says (no. 251). The former statement applies to local movement, but alteration is not simply a continuous motion. We may assume that the whole medium between the perceptible object and the sense power is not affected simultaneously in its totality, except in the transmission of visible objects, where there is no local movement (no. 252).

Lesson 17 (7.447a2–448a1) addresses the following question: does it happen that one sees something and hears a sound at the same time? In other words, can two sense powers sense their objects at the same time? Some things plead against it. (1) Certain objects cannot become one, for example, those which belong to different genera; therefore, we cannot sense objects of different sense faculties at the same time (no. 257). And (2) one sense power cannot sense two different objects at the same time, as it will perceive them as one (nos. 259–60). Thomas observes that one sense power has only one operation in the same indivisible time (no. 261). There is no other way in which the soul can judge whether something is numerically one, unless by perceiving as one what is present in it (no. 262). The same sense can judge about the objects it perceives, for example, sweet and bitter by the sense of taste, but not the objects of the other senses.

In lesson 18 (7.448a1–b16), Aristotle, after having shown that a sense power cannot sense two different objects simultaneously, considers the case of contraries. Contraries cannot be present in the same indivisible subject, but in a divisible subject they can. Contraries are the object of one sense, as sweet and bitter of taste, but they cannot be perceived simultaneously (no. 265). This applies also to what lies in the middle but is closer to one extreme than to the other (no. 266) and to things that are opposed to each other in different proportions, such as much and little, half and double, even and uneven (no. 267). If different qualities in the same genus cannot be perceived simultaneously, much less can objects in different genera (no. 268). According to some, the different harmonized sounds of a symphony would not really reach the ear simultaneously for the time difference in time is not perceived, although they seem to do so (no. 269). But Aristotle denies this suggestion that there is an imperceptible time: all time can be sensed (no. 270). He rejects it because time is perceived in something existing in time, so that if this thing were imperceptible, there would be no time we could speak about (no. 271). Yet it is possible that some part of time is imperceptible.

In nos. 272–75, Aristotle advances some arguments to show that even short lengths of time can be observed. The question is whether there could be some short length of time or tiny part of a body that because of their smallness are imperceptible? Aristotle says that time will always be perceived by some part of it, which will be sensed even if because of its smallness this part itself would not be sensed. If a part, taken separately, would not be perceived, insofar as it is considered as present in the whole, it falls under the sense power (nos. 274–75). But does such a part have the power to influence the sense (no. 276)? Thomas notes that if it is a part not separated from the whole, it will be sensed insofar as the sense is ordained to the whole, with no part of it left out (no. 277). All things, whether large or small, are sensible, but are not seen in the way they exist: what is far away is seen as being smaller (no. 278). What is indivisible can be understood in two ways: (1) as a body of minimal size which cannot be divided further; it is imperceptible; and (2) as part of a continuum that is not divided. Such an indivisible is not perceived by the senses.

In lesson 19 (7.448b17–449b4), the final lesson of the treatise, Aristotle comes back to the question of how the soul can simultaneously sense several different sensible objects. It is a fact that animals do sense several sensible objects at the same time. But can the soul simultaneously sense different objects? If so, the soul must comprise several parts or faculties (no. 282). Aristotle rejects this solution for it would lead us to say that a sense like vision sees different colors by its different parts (no. 283). If one says that there are two powers of vision, the answer is that it would not become apparent how they could be different in the same soul (no. 284). Furthermore, the objects of the different senses are each time the same, for example, visible objects correspond to the sense of vision as the objects of other senses correspond to their respective senses. There is only one faculty for each class of sensible objects (no. 285).

The sensible objects of the different senses are perceived by one soul, the different sensibles of one genus are sensed by one sense power, while the one and undivided soul senses the sensible objects belonging to the different genera. The different sense faculties together are the sensitive soul (no. 286). Thomas adds an observation: when there are several well-ordered sense powers, those of lower rank serve as instruments, so that Aristotle can say that the common sense senses through vision, hearing, taste, etc. (no. 287).

Aristotle indicates two ways in which one can conceive how the same part of the soul can sense different things: (1) the common sense is related to the different sense objects as a point is to the lines that come together in it; and (2) our body, which is numerically one, can receive and integrate different qualities or determinations. In this way, the soul perceives all sensibles (no. 289). But this does not explain how the same sense can sense contraries. The answer is that a physical body cannot receive at the same time contrary forms in their physical being, but the sense powers and the intellect receive forms spiritually and immaterially in their intentional being, when there are contraries (no. 291). Thomas adds an observation: the senses and the intellect must also judge contraries (in a single judgment) (no. 292). The words of Aristotle may give rise to a doubt, namely that color, odor, savor, etc., are not the objects of different senses but of one and the same faculty, as the Stoics teach.[22] If so, they would be different only in thought (no. 293). In a further remark, Thomas writes that whatever is sensed must have some magnitude. If the distance of the object to the sense is too great, the object cannot be seen or smelled. But a difficulty arises: at the limit of where it can just still be seen, the object will be both visible and invisible, but this is impossible (no. 295). Thomas also presents an objection that he found in Alexander's commentary: it would seem that larger bodies are seen from farther away, but what really happens is that each sensible thing is seen from a certain distance. What is indivisible has no proportional relation to any visible magnitude, and this means that the indivisible cannot be sensed, except insofar as it is the limit of a continuum (no. 296). In the final lines of the treatise, Aristotle recalls what he said about the objects of the senses and the sense faculties and says that we must now turn to the study of memory and recollection. The reason is the following, Thomas explains. In discussing the organs of sensing and the sensible objects, their relation to the senses and to each organ in the *De anima* and *De*

---

22. The Stoics accepted the different external senses, but taught that what we observe comes to our awareness in the so-called *phantasia katalēptikē* (imagination that receives and holds). Cognition is assent to cognitive representations. See F. H. Sandback, "Phantasia Kataleptike," in *Problems in Stoicism*, ed. A. A. Long (London: Athlone, 1971), 9–21.

sensu, what was dealt with belonged to the present. What remains is the past, which is known by memory and the object of the *De memoria et reminiscentia*, and the future, of which there is a certain foreknowledge in sleep and which is treated in the *De somno et vigilia*.

Concluding Remarks

William of Moerbeke's new translations of Aristotle's *De sensu et sensato* and of Alexander of Aphrodisias's commentary on the first treatise of Aristotle's *Parva naturalia* sparked a new interest into these parts of Aristotle's writings. On the basis of these new translations, Thomas offers a detailed and lucid discussion of the text. As such, the commentary offers important information on the sense organs and the sense objects, in particular the sense objects of colors, flavors, and odors. Partly on the basis of Alexander's commentary, Thomas is able to add historical information regarding Democritus and Empedocles. On several occasions Thomas provides an additional explanatory observation, often introduced by expressions such as *sciendum est* or *considerandum est*. This is the case for instance with regard to Thomas's criticism of the materialism of Democritus regarding vision (no. 51), the presence of prudence in animals (nos. 25–26), the distinction between generation and instantaneous production (nos. 229–30), and the presence of a sense-judgment (no. 292).

9 ❧ THE COMMENTARY ON THE *DE MEMORIA ET REMINISCENTIA*

In Plato's philosophy recollection plays a central role insofar as intellectual knowledge is a recollection of the respective Ideas or Forms. As such, Aristotle took a considerable interest in this phenomenon analyzed by his teacher. In Aristotle's early dialogue *Eudemus*, handed over in fragments, we find traces of Plato's theory, but when Aristotle abandoned Plato's theory of Forms, he also dropped the theory of recollection as found in Plato.[1] Aristotle's treatise *De Memoria et Reminiscentia* is part of the *Parva naturalia*, the collection of treatises concerned with capacities common to the body and soul of living things.[2] For Aristotle, memory lets us know what we have seen, heard, smelled, or learned before. It is always accompanied by a phantasm of the imagination. We speak of memory when a phantasm comes back into our awareness after an interval of time, and we become aware of having noted it before. Recollection is a conscious remembering of something. The crucial difference, therefore, is that, whereas memory is a passive state, recollection is a kind of active search and even a kind of deduction (451b2–5). For in trying to recollect, one has to find the correct starting point and pay attention to that starting point (451b18–20). Consequently, Aristotle argues that memory and recollection belong to different parts of the soul, respectively the sensing and the thinking soul (453a4–14). Both memory and recollection are nevertheless of past events. Moreover, they both require a physical substrate (453a14–31).[3]

When Thomas composed his commentary on the *De memoria*, during his second regency in Paris, he not only used the new translation prepared by William of Moerbeke (*translatio nova*) but also knew or at least had at his

1. See Helen S. Lang, "On Memory: Aristotle's Corrections of Plato," *Journal of the History of Philosophy* 18, no. 4 (1980): 379–93.

2. For the Greek text, see *Aristotle's "Parva naturalia,"* ed. W. D. Ross (Oxford: Oxford University Press, 1955).

3. For a thorough study of the treatise, see D. Bloch, *Aristotle on Memory and Recollection: Text, Translation, Interpretation, and Reception in Western Scholasticism* (Leiden: Brill, 2007).

disposal a number of texts dealing with Aristotle's text or at least with similar topics. Influential in this regard were Avicenna's *Liber de anima* and the Latin translation of Averroes's *Epitome* (or compendium) on the *Parva naturalia*.[4] Albert the Great's earlier commentary (*Liber de memoria*), which largely consists of Aristotelian paraphrases, although known by Thomas, does not seem to have had a decisive influence on Thomas's own commentary.[5] According to the *divisio textus* constructed by Thomas, one can divide the treatise into a prologue (449b4–8) and the text itself (449b9–453b11). The latter part treats first of memory (449b9–451a17) followed by recollection (451a18–453b11). Regarding memory, Aristotle first discusses its essence, followed by its seat and cause. With regard to recollection, Aristotle starts with distinguishing recollection from memory, then investigates the cause of recollecting, and finally asks about the sort of affection recollection is.

The Commentary of Thomas Aquinas

The fact that Thomas provides a prologue to the commentary in the opening lines of lesson 1 (1.449b4–30), as well as the fact that he describes the treatise as a "book," indicates that he regarded it as a distinct work. Although this seems to contradict a comment at the beginning of the *De sensu et sensato*, where Thomas writes about the *De memoria* as the "second treatise" of the "book" *De sensu et sensato*, traditional scholarship on the *De memoria* has regarded Thomas's commentary as a distinct work.[6] Thomas, moreover, regards the opening lines (449b4–8) as Aristotle's prologue to the text and this might have motivated Thomas to write his own prologue.[7]

He begins his prologue by recalling that in nature we observe a gradual progression from simple forms of life to more perfect living beings: from plants to animals and from more perfect animals to man. In this gradual pro-

---

4. *Averrois Cordubensis Compendia librorum Aristotelis qui Parva naturalia vocantur*, ed. A. L. Shields (Cambridge, Mass.: Cambridge University Press, 1949). The short commentary on the *De memoria* can be found on pages 47–72.

5. Leonine ed., 45/2, 124*. Apart from this introduction, see also chapter 4 of D. Bloch, *Aristotle on Memory and Recollection* for an extensive survey of the *De memoria*'s reception in the Latin West.

6. The Leonine edition has followed the remark at the beginning of the *De sensu et sensato*. This explains the full title of the edition: *Sentencia libri de Sensu et sensato cuius secundus tractatus est De memoria et reminiscentia*.

7. For the short commentary below in which I have tried to bring out the position of Aquinas with regard to the contents of the treatise, see the excellent pages of the already quoted book *Commentaries on Aristotle's "On Sense and What is Sensed" and "On Memory and Recollection,"* trans. Kevin White and Edward M. Macierowski (Washington, D.C.: The Catholic University of America Press, 2005), 167–266. For a more thorough study of the text, these pages should be consulted.

gression, the binding factor between some animals and man is some sort of prudence. These opening remarks are founded upon *Historia animalium* VIII.1.588b4–17 and *Nicomachean Ethics* VI.1.1144b26–28. The fact that Cicero in his *De inventione* II regarded memory (by which one apprehends past things) as a part of prudence, as well as the fact that Aristotle in the opening lines of his *Metaphysics* I.1.980a27–981a1 acknowledges the presence of prudence (arising from memory based on sensation) in some animals, allow Thomas to construct his prologue around prudence as its guiding theme. Just as animals have imperfect prudence, as they lack true foresight (*providentia*) and intelligence (*intelligentia*), so they also have imperfect memory (*memoria imperfecta*) because they only remember, whereas human beings both remember (*memorantur*) and recollect (*reminiscuntur*) (nos. 298–99). Thomas continues by remarking that those who are slow in learning may have a good memory, but recollection is found among intelligent people (nos. 300–301). Recollection is an action of finding again the knowledge one received but did not retain (no. 302).

Aristotle first examines memory and its object (no. 303): memory is not concerned with the future (nos. 304–5) nor with the present (no. 306), but with the past. When one has knowledge of what one did or of what happened in the past, we say that he remembers. It is not Aristotle's intention, Thomas notes, to say that memory cannot be of things which are themselves in the present. The act by which we remember points to what we have seen or done before, but also makes us aware when we see something, that we have seen it before, so that the act points to a time before the now. When we see something present, we do not say that we remember it. Thomas gives as an example a quotation from Virgil, *Aeneid* 3.628–29: "Ulysses had not forgotten Ithaca." The same verse was also mentioned by Augustine, *De Trinitate* 14.11.[8]

In lesson 2 (2.449b30–450a25), Aristotle examines if and how memory belongs to the intellectual part of the soul. He recalls that we cannot understand without an image marked by the continuum and time (no. 312). If we want to understand something of a certain magnitude, the intellect first needs a representation, that is, a phantasm of a particular size, although the intellect can understand it without any definite size, just as a magnitude (no. 313). We form our concepts by abstracting them from phantasms. Experience shows that we cannot consider scientific facts without the concurrence of some phantasms (no. 314). In this connection, Thomas recalls Avicenna's theory of intelligible species (or concepts): when one is no longer actually thinking of a particular concept it disappears (no. 315). He does not mention Avicenna by name, but

---

8. The verse reads: "Nec talia passus Ulysses / Oblitusve sui est Ithacus discrimine tanto."

says that this theory is patently contrary to what Aristotle holds. In our sense faculties, connected as they are with the body, images may be faint, but in the "possible intellect" the concepts have an unchangeable mode of being. But the intellect needs the phantasms because in a way it sees these intelligible contents present in these images (no. 316). Thomas adds a further explanation: an act or operation is proportional to the faculty, namely, the thinking power and the essence of the one who is thinking. Our human intellect operates in the domain of the sensitive, so that it knows the intelligible essences in the phantasms (no. 317).

Next, Aristotle shows to which part of the soul memory belongs. Magnitude, movement, and time are so much connected that they are known by the same part of the soul (no. 318). Movements are known when one knows the distance covered by a magnitude, and time is known when one knows the before and after in a movement. The senses perceive and know these objects in two ways: (1) by changes caused in them by the sensible object (this regards the proper as well as the common sensibles of the external senses and of the common sense); and (2) the first perception leaves a mutation in the sense, which remains when the sensible object itself is absent. The magnitude, movement, and time of the sensible object accompany this entire mutation process of the sense, which ends in reception by the common sense (no. 319). Memory is not only of what the senses have experienced, but also of what one has come to know and understand about something (no. 320). Imagination and memory are distinct faculties, as Avicenna has shown, as receiving and conserving impressions are different acts (no. 321).

At this point, Thomas makes an important addition: it happens that of the different powers or faculties, one of them is the origin and root of others, as for instance the nutritive power is the root of those of growth and of generation. In this way, the common sense is the root of imagination and of memory (no. 322). Memory is also found in certain other animals devoid of intellect, not just in man, and in whatever other "animals" that form opinions (the speculative intellect) and possess prudence (the practical intellect). If memory were an intellectual power, no other animals would have it, while in fact they do. Thomas adds the following note: the words "in whatever other animals" were added by Aristotle to remind the reader that some authors had doubts about certain animals that seem to show some form of intellectual activity (no. 324). Memory is only found in those animals which are aware of time and of a before and after (no. 325). Memory and imagination belong to the interior senses. And we remember material things more easily, while subtle and spiritual things are more difficult to remember.

In lesson 3 (1[3].450a25–451a17), the cause of remembering is analyzed. What we recall is absent, and one might wonder why we recall what is absent and do not rather remember the affection that is present in the internal senses (no. 327). The sensible object impresses its likeness on the senses and this impression remains in the imagination as a stamp, even when the sensible object itself is no longer present (no. 328). This image remains in us and is necessary for remembering the original. Certain persons do not receive this impression. Children and elderly people do not remember well (no. 331). But sometimes what one has learned in one's youth is established firmly in his memory. Also, what is new and unusual is impressed strongly. Those who are very quick in learning receive these images more easily (no. 332).

At this point a new question is raised: do we observe this past representation that is present in us? It would be strange if one would observe something both as absent and as present (nos. 335–39). Why would our memory not recall the thing itself, instead of recalling the representation of it? But how can one recall, with an interior sense, what is not present? Aristotle solves the difficulty by noting that the phantasm may be considered both as something by itself and as an image of something else to which it leads us (nos. 340–41). If we consider it in this second way we have to do with the principle of memory (nos. 342–43). We "remember" when we consider the phantasm as the image of what we have sensed before. There can be some movement of these phantasms without our knowing whether it is because of what we have sensed earlier. Thomas thinks this may be an allusion to the apparition of images in a dream. But sometimes we remember when we know that what we see now is what we have seen or heard before. This is remembering in the strict sense of the word (no. 346). In a third way, we remember when we think we remember something but when in fact we do not, as happened to Antipheron, who thought that he had seen before the phantasm (image) he was seeing now (no. 347).[9] Aristotle closes the chapter by noting that by frequently reconsidering the images (or concepts) acquired, we conserve them better (no. 348). Memory is the habitual conservation of these phantasms (no. 349).

In lesson 3 (2[4].451a18–b10), after having shown what memory is, Aristotle now considers recollection (*reminiscentia*). To explain what it is, he compares it with other forms of apprehension (nos. 350–51). First, he insists on the difference between receiving an image (*receptio*) and recovering it (*resumptio*). Reminiscence is not the recovering of an image or concept. When we first learn something, we do not speak of recovering it (no. 352).

9. Antipheron is mentioned in *Meteorologica* 373b4–10 as a person with impaired eyesight who always saw an image before him as he walked. W. D. Ross, *Aristotle's "Parva naturalia,"* 239.

Remembering something is not just receiving some knowledge, nor is it its presence in us. Memory consists in the factual presence of the knowledge of something, which becomes actualized and that one has seen or heard before (451a23; no. 353). But there is no memory in the first instant in which a certain knowledge is apprehended and has not yet become a habit. One does not remember something in the very instant one acquires its knowledge, but only after a certain interval of time (451a25; no. 354). Recollection is not a simple remembering, but is about what one has learned before. It is the action one undertakes in order to remember, so that memory follows upon recollection (451b2; no. 356). Yet in its search and attempt to retrieve what one has forgotten, it proceeds from memory (no. 357). But recollection is not learning for the second time; it is something more, as will be shown in the next lesson (451b6; no. 358).

Lesson 5 (2[5].451b10–452a4) treats of the cause of recollection and the way in which one recollects. The cause of recollection is the order of acts left in the soul when one first perceived the object. One movement follows a prior one either necessarily, so that when the first is present, the second follows— or else by custom and in most cases, for example, something a person usually does after a first movement (no. 360). Thomas adds some detailed comments on this whole section: the second way of recollection does not work in the same manner in different people; some are fast in making this connection either because of a natural disposition or because of intense interest (no. 361). In such cases, people search until they find the movement that followed immediately upon the first apprehension they do remember. The first movement from which they begin to search can be a time that they know, sometimes something else. One can, for instance, start from what is now to arrive at what one did some days ago, but one can also start from a point in the past that one remembers well and proceed from there (no. 363). But one can also recollect something because of a certain likeness, proximity, or a contrariety (no. 365). When one reaches the forgotten part unintentionally, we speak of simple remembering, but when it is by intention, we have to do with recollection (no. 366). We recall things or events of the past more easily when we often reconsider them (451b25–31; no. 368). Well-ordered things are recollected more easily. Thomas adds a conclusion in which he somewhat reduces the contrast Aristotle sees between remembering and recollecting. In order to remember or to recollect well, four points must be observed: (1) one must try to reduce what he wants to retrieve into a certain order; (2) one must concentrate one's attention on it; (3) one must frequently think of it in the right order; and (4) one must start the process of remembering from the beginning.

In lesson 6 (2[6].452a4–b6), Aristotle explains the difference between recollection and learning something again. Thomas notes that we must keep in mind that both the one who recollects and the one who learns something anew recuperate this knowledge just as it was (*absolute*) and not as if he draws it from something known before. But we do not arrive at the knowledge of something unknown unless we derive it from some principle known before. The principle from which we get to know something unknown must be of the same genus, so that we proceed from principles that we remembered from the beginning. This is not the case in learning something anew (no. 372). As a matter of fact, when recollecting, we move forward from something we kept in our memory, but when we do not succeed in recuperating the lost knowledge by something we had stored in our memory, the recollection becomes a case of learning again (no. 373).

It also happens that while searching in our memory we arrive at the series of acts on which depended what we have forgotten (nos. 374–75). The one who recollects must do so while thinking, speaking, or doing something else, by starting from a point, which for some is the place where something happened (452a12; no. 377).[10] People move easily from one contrary to another or, because of proximity, from one object to what is next to it (no. 378). Aristotle gives an example: from milk we move to white, from white to the clarity of the transparent. In a further example, he mentions the letters of the alphabet. We can sometimes recover the memory of a letter by passing to another (452a17; nos. 380–81). Custom is a real help: what we often see or hear is impressed on us and becomes like a second nature (no. 383). In natural processes, something may happen outside the order of nature. It also occurs in the field of what is customary that something happens outside the ordinary order we are used to, and our imagination is distracted so that we do not remember having known something before (452a30; no. 384).

Lesson 7 (2[7].452b7–453a4) points out that when one wants to recollect something, it is important to know the past, that is, the time the recollection is concerned with. It may happen occasionally that one remembers to have known, or dealt with, the item one is looking for just a few days ago. There is something in the soul that allows it to be aware of, and to judge, a greater or shorter length of time since something happened. This length is evaluated in relation with the present "now" (no. 387). But this does not mean that the soul knows a length of time or a magnitude by extending itself to it or touching it, as Plato seems to have suggested.[11] The soul does not know mag-

---

10. Macierowski has a valuable note on Thomas's reference to pseudo-Cicero, *Ad Herennium* III, 19:29–30.
11. In *De anima* I.3.407a3ff., Aristotle mentions an opinion expressed in Plato's *Timaeus* 36e, which holds

nitudes by a contact of the mind with them. The mind thinks abstract magnitude, and can conceive a much larger magnitude than the size of the world. Thomas adds the following comments. The soul knows magnitudes through a certain process; its concept is received in the soul and "resolved" so that it becomes proportional, and tuned in, to the outside magnitude (452b8; no. 388). But does it know greater and smaller magnitudes? The soul does know greater and smaller magnitudes by means of the forms (or species) it receives, which indicate larger or smaller bodies (nos. 389–90). This is visualized with the figure of an equilateral triangle: lines drawn at a certain distance from the base, but parallel to it, have angles equal to the original angles of the base with the sides. Such proportionality allows us to know different magnitudes. When the movement of the thing to be remembered and of past time are both present, we remember. But if there is no recording of the past, there is no remembering. Sometimes one thinks to remember something, but the memory of what we have forgotten does not come back. Remembering is to consider the phantasm of something insofar as it is an image of the thing apprehended before (452b23; no. 396). It also happens that one recalls something, but not as marked by a certain time, as the original impression was weak (452b29; no. 397).

Lesson 8 (2[8].453a4–b11) explains again the difference between recollection and remembering. A first cause of difference is different aptitude: there are people who remember easily but recollect with difficulty. A second difference is that recollection is a way to remember and is prior in time to it. A third difference is that remembering is found in many animals, but recollection only in man (no. 398). The reason is that recollection is like a sort of syllogism, as one notices that one has seen something before, from where one starts inquiring to arrive at the forgotten thing. But only man can deliberate (453a4; no. 390).

Some deny that recollection is a passion of the body. But that it is, says Aristotle, is shown by the fact that some people are disturbed when they cannot remember and feel uneasy (no. 401). Thomas adds a further explanation: activities in the intellectual part of the soul may be interrupted at will, but this is different when bodily organs are involved. We cannot stop these at will (no. 402). This happens most in people who have moisture in the region of the brain where the sense powers are located (no. 403). It also happens when bodily organs are involved in movements of anger, fear, and desire (no. 404). Something similar happens to people singing or reciting who continue when

---

that the soul of the world envelops the body of the world from the center to the circumference and communicates reason to all things.

they want to stop, as the movement of the imagination is still present (no. 405). Recollection is hindered by an indisposition of the body, as those whose upper part of the body is proportionally larger (like dwarfs who remember with more difficulty) than those who have a contrary disposition. This also happens to babies and very young children and to the very old, because of the movements caused by growth or, in old people, by decay. So it is evident that recollection is a bodily passion and an act of the sensitive part of man.

Concluding Remarks

In this short treatise, Aristotle mentions that memory has imperfect forms in certain animals. In its perfect form, it lets us know what we have seen or done before, so that it takes us back to a time before the present moment. Memory is not only concerned with what the senses have perceived earlier but also with what we had in mind and understood before. Memory is a distinct faculty, different from imagination. Reminiscence is not just simple memory but is an activity one carries out to recuperate what one has learned before. One examines the order of facts left in the mind when one observed something for the first time. The order of the observed facts left behind in memory is the cause of reminiscence. Certain people have a good memory, while their reminiscence functions with difficulty. Reminiscence is not found in animals, Aristotle says, because it is a kind of syllogism: one is conscious of having seen or heard something before and begins to seek in order to arrive at what he has known before.

Thomas provides the reader with a clear-cut exposition of the text that, by way of his prologue, locates the text within Aristotle's overall thought. In his exposition, he adds several explanatory lines and examples to guide the reader through Aristotle's text.

10 ❧ THE COMMENTARY ON
THE *METAPHYSICS*

The Greek geographer and historian Strabo (ca. 64 B.C.–ca. 24 A.D.) recounts how, after the death of Theophrastus, Aristotle's successor as the head of the Lyceum, a certain Neleus inherited the library of Aristotle and took it to Scepsis in Asia Minor where the books were locked away and eventually hidden in a crypt when the Attalid kings were looking for acquisitions for their library at Pergamon. Around 90 B.C. a wealthy Athenian, Apellicon, bought them and took them back to Athens. Strabo notes that as a result the early members of the Peripatos had hardly any works of Aristotle available to them. Some years later, the Roman general Sulla occupied Athens and, among numerous works of art, brought Apellicon's library to Rome.[1] Whatever is true in this story, it at least underscores the difficulties of the early Peripatetics to collect and study Aristotle's writings, so that knowledge about Aristotelian thought progressively weakened.[2] The Greek librarian Andronicus of Rhodes (first half of the first century B.C.) is credited with placing the works and papers of Aristotle in a certain order. After the works on logic and those on the philosophy of nature and natural science, he arranged the treatises he was unable to identify after the *Physics*. Hence the designation "the treatises after those on natural science" (τὰ μετὰ τὰ φύσικα).[3] The name indicates that these treatises should be studied

---

1. Strabo, *Geographyka* XIII.1.54.

2. The story of Aristotle's library includes many controversial details and many historians nowadays dismiss Strabo's account of a nearly total loss of the *Corpus Aristotelicum*. See John Patrick Lynch, *Aristotle's School: A Study of a Greek Educational Institution* (Berkeley: University of California Press, 1972), who discusses Ingemar Düring, *Aristotle in the Ancient Biographical Tradition* (Stockholm: Almqvist and Wiksell, 1957) and Paul Moraux, *Les listes anciennes des ouvrages d'Aristote* (Louvain: Éditions universitaires de Louvain, 1951). See also see Hans B. Gottschalk, "The Earliest Aristotelian Commentators," in *Aristotle Transformed* (ed. Sorabji), 55–81, and Paul Moraux, *Der Aristotelismus bei den Griechen*, vol. 1: *Die Renaissance des Aristotelismus im I. Jh. v. Chr.* (Berlin: De Gruyter, 1973): 1–31.

3. The name τὰ μετὰ τὰ φύσικα was formerly believed to date from the time of Andronicus, but Chroust gives good reasons to suppose that the term is earlier. Anton-Herman Chroust, "The Origin of '"Metaphysics,"' *The Review of Metaphysics* 14 (1961): 601–16.

after the books on nature. The exact nature of Adronicus's editorial role remains a vexed question.[4]

The same has to be said about the structure of what we now regard as the *Metaphysics*, consisting of fourteen books and traditionally designated by the first thirteen capital letters of the Greek alphabet plus the first small one.[5] In one of the ancient catalogues of Aristotle's writings the *Metaphysics* counts ten books with Books II (α), V (Δ), XI (K), and XII (Λ) absent. In another catalogue Book V (Δ) is regarded as an independent treatise. Books I (A) and II (α) appear to be introductions to two different editions of the *Metaphysics*.[6] One has to wait until Alexander of Aphrodisias around 200 A.D., and then only through Averroes's report of Alexander's view of the overall shape of the *Metaphysics*, to find a first description of the *Metaphysics* which fits the work as we know it.[7]

When discussing the *Physics* and the *De caelo* in previous chapters, I noted that the different books of which these works are composed do not necessarily form a harmoniously coherent whole. With *Metaphysics* the problem is even more serious. Books I (A) and II (α) seem to have been conceived as two separate introductions. Book III (B) is devoted to the presentation and discussion of a series of *aporiae* or philosophical puzzles which concern the status of metaphysics itself, its object, limits, and scope (*aporiae* 1–3, 5), the status and the nature of the principles, etc. While these *aporiae* address some of the most important topics of Aristotle's inquiry, it is not at all certain if and how Book III (B) determines the structure of the following books of the *Metaphysics*. Books IV (Γ) and VI (E) discuss the nature and object of metaphysics. Book V (Δ) seems to stand on its own as a collection of definitions. Books VII–IX (Z-H-Θ) constitute a fairly coherent group, often regarded as the so-called central books because they deal with central topics of Aristotle's metaphysics, such as substance, hylomorphism, essence and definition, universals and finally, in Book IX (Θ), act and potency. Book X (I) deals with the one as the most

4. See Moraux, *Die Renaissance des Aristotelismus*, 46–94; Jonathan Barnes, "Roman Aristotle," in *Philosophia Togata II: Plato and Aristotle at Rome*, ed. J. Barnes and M. Griffin (Oxford: Oxford University Press, 1997), 1–69.

5. Alpha Meizon (A = I), Alpha Elatton (α = II), Beta (B = III), Gamma (Γ = IV), Delta (Δ = V), Epsilon (E = VI), Zeta (Z = VII), Eta (H = VIII), Theta (Θ = IX), Iota (I = X), Kappa (K = XI), Lambda (Λ = XII), Mu (M = XIII), and Nu (N = XIV).

6. See Moraux, *Les listes anciennes*. Contemporary scholars such as Pierre Aubenque also have doubts about the authenticity of Book XI (K). See Aubenque's contribution as well as Vincent Décarie's for an opposite position in *Zweifelhaftes im Corpus Aristotelicum. Studien zu einigen Dubia*, ed. Paul Moraux and Jürgen Wiesner (Berlin: De Gruyter, 1983).

7. The only exception is that Book I (A) is placed after Book II (α), something which was not uncommon in antiquity. See Silvia Fazzo, "The *Metaphysics* from Aristotle to Alexander of Aphrodisias," *Bulletin of the Institute of Classical Studies* 55 (2012): 51–68.

important *per se* attribute of being as well as with dialectical notions, such as the same and the other, similar and dissimilar, contrariety, etc., which are closely related to the one. Book XI (K) seems to be a recapitulation of some elements of previous books. Book XII (Λ) is a treatise of its own, in which Aristotle presents his account of the divine. Finally, in Books XIII and XIV (M–N), Aristotle discusses in a rather heterogeneous manner the nature of mathematical objects (numbers and geometrical objects), primarily through a critique of a number of Platonic theories about these objects.[8]

The apparent differences between these books made Werner Jaeger conceive a theory of the development of Aristotle's philosophy: some of the latter's writings would date to a first period when he still adhered to Plato's fundamental doctrines, such as the theory of the Ideas, the preexistence of the human soul, and the increasing perfection of being in the universe which one observes when ascending from this material world toward the Ideas.[9] Jaeger spoke of stages in the development of Aristotle's philosophy and for a number of years his theory found supporters, such as François Nuyens, who traced the stages through which Aristotle's philosophy of the human soul would have passed.[10] Many specialists in ancient philosophy followed this path, trying to discover in Aristotle's works the passages in which he would adhere to doctrines close to Platonism and the theories of the early Academy. But in recent years, tracing the signs of such a doctrinal development in the extant works of Aristotle has no longer been the first concern of scholars.[11]

We know of a number of commentaries by the ancient Greek commentators.[12] While the commentaries by Aspasius (second century) and Simplicius

8. The literature on Aristotle's *Metaphysics* is immense. Influential resources are the following commentaries: William D. Ross, *Aristotle's "Metaphysics": A Revised Text with Introduction and Commentary* (Oxford: Clarendon Press, 1924); Giovanni Reale, *Aristotele. La Metafisica. Traduzione, Introduzione, Commento* (Naples: Loffredo, 1968); Horst Seidl, *Aristoteles Metaphysik. Mit Einleitung und Kommentar* (Hamburg: Felix Meiner Verlag, 1990). Both Reale and Seidl present a strongly anti-developmental account of the *Metaphysics* and make much use of ancient and medieval commentators. Detailed information can also be found in the following volumes of the *Symposium Aristotelicum*: *Aristotle's "Metaphysics" Lambda*, ed. Michael Frede and David Charles (Oxford: Clarendon Press, 2000); *Aristotle: "Metaphysics" Beta*, ed. Michel Crubellier and André Laks (Oxford: Oxford University Press, 2002), and *Aristotle's "Metaphysics" Alpha*, ed. Carlos Steel and Oliver Primavesi (Oxford: Oxford University Press, 2012). A helpful introduction into the recent debates on the *Metaphysics* can be found in Mary L. Gill, "Aristotle's Metaphysics Reconsidered," *Journal of the History of Philosophy* 43 (2005): 223–51.

9. Werner Jaeger, *Aristoteles: Grundlegung einer Geschichte seiner Entwicklung* (Berlin: Weidmann, 1923), appearing in English as *Aristotle: Fundamentals of the History of His Development* (Oxford: Clarendon Press, 1948).

10. Nuyens, *L'évolution*.

11. For a cursory overview see Georgios Anagnostopoulos, "Aristotle's Works and the Development of His Thought," in *A Companion to Aristotle* (ed. Anagnostopoulos).

12. See Gerard Verbeke, "Aristotle's *Metaphysics* viewed by the Ancient Greek Commentators," in *Studies in Aristotle*, ed. Dominic J. O'Meara (Washington, D.C.: The Catholic University of America Press, 1981), 107–28.

(sixth century) are lost, we possess a paraphrase of Book XII (Λ) by Themistius (fourth century) in a Hebrew-Latin translation as well as Syrianus's commentary on Aristotle's *Metaphysics* covering only books III, IV, XIII, and XIV. Asclepius (mid-sixth century), in his commentary on the *Metaphysics*, preserves two fragments of Syrianus's exegesis of Book VII (Z). But the author of the oldest and still extant commentary of Aristotle's *Metaphysics* is Alexander of Aphrodisias (ca. 200), known as the Commentator before Averroes took over that title. The received text of the commentary is in fourteen books, of which only the first five are by Alexander. The identity of the author of the remaining nine books—Pseudo-Alexander—is unknown, although most scholars ascribe the work to the late Byzantine commentator Michael of Ephesus (ca. 1070–1140).[13] Although Alexander's commentary was not translated into Latin until the sixteenth century, it became influential through its extensive use by Averroes (1126–98) in his *Long Commentary on the Metaphysics* in which he quotes extensively from Alexander's commentary on Book XII (Λ).[14] The Latin translation of Averroes's *Long Commentary* is attributed to Michael Scotus and dated ca. 1220–24.[15] This translation initiated a gradual replacement of Avicenna's (981–1037) *Liber de philosophia prima sive Scientia divina*, as it was known in its Latin translation from the second half of the twelfth century.[16] In fact, according Galluzzo, "in the first part of the XIII century and before Aquinas's masterly commentary, Averroes was the only instrument of which Latin commentators could avail themselves in order to become acquainted with Aristotle's *Metaphysics*."[17] By the time Thomas Aquinas writes his commentary, important commentaries on the *Metaphysics* were written by Richard Rufus of Cornwall, Adam of Bockfeld, Geoffrey of Aspall in Oxford, Roger Bacon in Paris (all written around the middle of the thirteenth century), and Albertus Magnus (ca. 1264), the latter of which relied heavily on Avicenna and Averroes.[18] Whether these and other sources had a significant influence on the

---

13. Many of these Greek commentaries are now available in an English translation in the Ancient Commentators on Aristotle series.

14. These fragments have been collected in Jacob Freudenthal, *Die durch Averroes erhaltenen Fragmente Alexanders zur Metaphysik des Aristoteles* (Berlin: Verlag der Königlichen Akademie der Wissenschaften, 1885).

15. The standard edition is *Commentarium Magnum in Aristotelis Metaphysicorum libros XIIII*, in *Aristotelis Opera cum Averrois Commentariis, vol. 8: Averroes Latinus* (Venice, 1562; reprinted in Frankfurt am Main: Minerva, 1962).

16. See Avicenna Latinus, *Liber de philosophia prima sive Scientia divina*, ed. S. Van Riet (Louvain / Leiden: Peeters / Brill, 1977–83).

17. Gabriele Galluzzo, *The Medieval Reception of Book Zeta of Aristotle's "Metaphysics"* (Leiden: Brill, 2013), 9.

18. See Amos Bertolacci, "Avicenna's and Averroes' Interpretations and Their Influence in Albert the Great," in *A Companion to the Latin Medieval Commentaries on Aristotle's "Metaphysics,"* ed. Fabrizio Amerini and Gabriele Galluzzo (Leiden: Brill, 2014), 95–135.

composition of Thomas's commentary will to a large extent have to await a critical edition by the Leonine Commission.[19]

The Date of His Commentary on Metaphysics
and the Use of *alia littera*

The *Metaphysics* is one of the main works of Aristotle, and Thomas's commentary is the most extensive of all the commentaries he wrote on Aristotle's books. Later on in this chapter we will have an opportunity to discuss the contents of the individual books that compose the *Metaphysics* more closely. At the time when Thomas composed his commentary, there were at least five Latin translations of the *Metaphysics*, four from the Greek and one from the Arabic. The partial twelfth-century translation (I–IV.4.1007a31), attributed to James of Venice, is known as the *Translatio Iacobi sive "Vetustissima."* Another anonymous translation, which also extends into IV.4, is referred as the *Translatio Composita sive "Vetus."* The *Translatio Anonyma sive "Media,"* attributed to Gerard of Cremona, has thirteen books, omitting Book Kappa (XI). Averroes's *Long Commentary on Aristotle's Metaphysics* also contains a translation of Aristotle's text. The Latin translation from the Arabic, known as the *Translatio nova,* attributed to Michael Scotus and dated from 1220s, is incomplete as well. More importantly, because of the absence of Book Kappa, the Latin version of Book Lambda becomes the eleventh book. Finally, between 1260 and 1261, William of Moerbeke revised the *Media* and added his own translation of Books Kappa (XI) and Mu (XIII). We also have a second revision of his own translation, dated 1266–68, so that there are in fact two versions of what is called the *Recensio et translatio Guillemi.* As a result of his translation of Book Kappa and its inclusion in the *Metaphysics,* Book Lambda became known as "Book XII."[20]

---

19. See, e.g., although not focusing on the *Metaphysics* as such, John F. Wippel, "The Latin Avicenna as a Source for Thomas Aquinas's Metaphysics," *Freiburger Zeitschrift für Philosophie und Theologie* 37 (1990): 51–90; reprinted in his *Metaphysical Themes in Thomas Aquinas II* (Washington, D.C.: The Catholic University of America Press, 2007), 31–64.

20. For more details see Marta Borgo, "Latin Medieval Translations of Aristotle's Metaphysics," in *The Latin Medieval Commentaries on Aristotle's "Metaphysics,"* ed. Fabrizio Amerini and Gabriele Galluzzo (Leiden: Brill, 2014): 19–57. The translations from the Greek are all critically edited by Gudrun Vuillemin-Diem in the *Arisoteles Latinus* series. For the Arabic-Latin translation see *Aristotelis Opera cum Averrois Commentariis,* vol. 8. Note however that this edition not only provides the thirteenth-century Arabic-Latin translation but also Bessarion's fifteenth-century translation. According to William of Tocco, Thomas actively asked for new translations to be made (by William of Moerbeke?). See *Ystoria sancti Thome de Aquino de Guillaume de Tocco (1323),* ed. Claire le Brun-Gouanvic (Toronto: Pontifical Institute of Mediaeval Studies, 1996), 133: "Scripsit etiam super philosophia naturalem et moralem, super methaphisicam, quorum librorum procurauit quod fieret noua translatio que sentente Aristotilis continent clarius ueritatem." On this passage, see Torrell, *Initiation,* 229.

These different translations are important for a number of reasons. First, they enable a fairly accurate dating of Thomas's commentary. Thomas refers to Lambda as Book XII from the beginning of Book VII to the end of Book XII as well as in Books II and III. According to R. A. Gauthier, Aquinas first came into contact with William's translation in 1271. However, if Thomas did follow the order of the books in composing his commentary, it is possible that he was only able to read William's translation from Book VII onward and subsequently revised his commentary on Books II and III. Second, it gives us an insight into the use of Averroes's commentary. And third, it allows us to catch a glimpse of his philological inquiry when commenting on Aristotle's text.[21] Thomas was in fact very attentive to the text itself and registers a large number of variants among the translations. These are the famous *alia littera* which have been extensively studied by James P. Reilly, Jr.[22] His analysis of the eighty-six explicit citations of variants and numerous implicit citations of the Latin translations has shown that Thomas made use of all of the five translations mentioned above, with a preference for the Moerbeke translation, as well as other translations available to him, probably as marginal or interlinear glosses. Reilly has also discerned four types of uses: "(1) some are simply synonymous or alternate readings; (2) others are explanatory in character; (3) fifteen of the *alia littera* are said to express better or more clearly (*melius uel planius*) the text of Aristotle as Thomas understands it; and (4) five *alia littera* are explicit corrections."[23] Particularly the third and fourth type emphasize that Thomas's choice of alternative readings "was not the result of random selection. Rather, as a commentator on Aristotle, Thomas's major concern was to clarify what he understood the intention of Aristotle to be. To do this, he paid particular attention to difficult passages in the text, citing different translations, both explicitly and implicitly, so as to avoid real or apparent contradictions."[24] One can add that Thomas also employs his philological talent, which also led him to rightfully reject the authorship of the *Liber de causis*, to argue that Averroes's interpretation of Aristotle's text is often not compatible with Aristotle's text.[25]

---

21. Sections preserved in Ms. Neopolitanus, Bibl. Nat. VIII f. 16 also contain traces of Thomas's dictating activities to his secretaries. See J. Cos, "Evidences of St. Thomas's Dictating Activity in the Naples Manuscript of His 'Scriptum in Metaphysicam,'" *Scriptorium* 38 (1984): 231–53.

22. James P. Reilly Jr., "The 'alia littera' in Thomas Aquinas's 'Sententia libri metaphysiciae,'" *Medieval Studies* 50 (1998): 559–83.

23. Ibid., 569.

24. Ibid., 576.

25. Two instances are *In II Metaph.*, lesson 1, no. 286, and *In XII Metaph.*, lesson 1, no. 2418.

The Structure of the *Metaphysics*
according to Thomas

Thomas was obviously not aware of the modern-philological approach to the *Metaphysics*, which I briefly mentioned above, and its doubts regarding the unity of the text of the *Metaphysics* as we have received it. On the contrary, for Thomas the text displays a remarkable unity.[26] On the basis of the *divisio textus*, given at the beginning of each book, one can deduce the structure of the *Metaphysics* as follows:

1. Introduction (A 1–2)
2. Investigation (A 3–Λ)
   2.1. The opinions of the philosophers (A 3–10)
   2.2. The truth of the matter (B–Λ)
      2.2.1. On things related to the knowledge of truth (α)
      2.2.2. On truth as such (B–Λ)
         2.2.1.1. Dialectically (*modo disputativo*) (B)
         2.2.1.2. Demonstratively (*determinare veritatem*) (Γ–Λ)
        (A) The nature of the science (Γ)
        (B) The contents of the science (Δ–Λ)
          (i) The terms of the science (Δ)
          (ii) The contents: being (E–Λ)
          (ii A) The different modes of being (E)
          (ii B) On being (Z–Λ)
          (ii B 1) Being *per se* (Z–I)
            —Being divided according to the ten categories (Z–E)
            —Being divided according to potency and act (Θ)
            —One
          (ii B 2) The principles of being *per se* (K–Λ)
            —Summary and preparation (K)
            —Separate substances (Λ)

---

26. While Thomas did not comment on Books M and N, although translated into Latin, he frequently refers to these books in the course of his commentary and in particular in his commentary on Book III (B) which indicates he has a good knowledge of their content.

A few comments on this somewhat complicated division are in order.[27]

- *Book I* (A): In an introduction to the whole of the text (I.1–2), Aristotle discusses the subject and defining features of this science. This is followed by a critical discussion of his predecessors' opinions on the four causes (I.3–10)
- *Book II* (α): Aristotle brings in the notion of truth as well as epistemological questions related to the acquisition of truth. Insofar as this book deals with methodological issues, it is still part of the introduction.
- *Book III* (B): Aristotle starts his exposition dialectically by raising questions which the ancient philosophers either had a different opinion about or neglected. These questions offer an outlook into the rest of the *Metaphysics*.
- *Book IV* (Γ): The determination of the truth starts with Book IV, first with regard to subject of this science (IV.1–2) and second with regard to first principles, in particular the principle of noncontradiction.
- *Book V* (Δ): Given the fact that Book VI notes that metaphysical terms are not used in a univocal sense, a preliminary investigation in the meaning of these terms is needed.
- *Book VI* (E): Aristotle takes up again the question of the subject of this science, this time differentiating it from the other sciences. He also determines which sense of being are dealt with in this science.
- *Book VII* (Z): Aristotle "begins to establish the truth about essential being [*ens per se*], which exists outside the mind and constitutes the principal object of study in this science" (no. 1245). It has two parts: Books VII–XI on being as being and Book XII on the first principles of being. Book VII deals with substance in general.
- *Book VIII* (H): Aristotle discusses matter and form as the concrete principles of substance.
- *Book IX* (Θ): After discussing essential being as divided into the ten categories, Aristotle discusses potency and act and establishes the priority of actuality.
- *Book X* (I): Given the fact that being and unity accompany each other, a discussion of unity and its attributes follows.
- *Book XI* (K): A concise treatment of some sections of Books B, Γ, and E and of the chapters of the *Physics* on potency, act, and movement in view of the separate substances, "the knowledge of which constitutes

---

27. See the introduction to the Marietti edition for more details, in particular at XVII–XXII, as well as Gabriele Galluzzo, "Aquinas on the Structure of Aristotle's Metaphysics," *Documenti e Studi sulla Tradizione Filosofica Medievale* 15 (2004): 353–86.

the goal to which the things studied both in this science and in the other sciences are ultimately directed" (no. 2146).

- *Book XII* (Λ): Aristotle first gives a summary of what has been said in the preceding books on being in its unqualified sense, that is, substance (XII.1–5), and adds a section on separate substances (XII.6–10) in order to "complete" his study.

Aristotle's *Metaphysics* contains the basic doctrines that are the core of the philosophical thought of Thomas, including the four causes and the first principles, being, actuality and potency, matter and form, and the first unmoved mover. They are so foundational and true that when resorting to them Thomas did not need to refer often to Aristotle's text as can be seen from the relatively few explicit references to the *Metaphysics* in his *Summa theologiae*.

Aquinas's commentary on the *Metaphysics* has been studied quite thoroughly by such Thomists as Étienne Gilson, Joseph Owens, James Weisheipl, James Doig, John Wippel, Gabriele Galluzzo, and others. In this introduction, a complete and detailed discussion of Thomas's appreciation of the contents of the entire *Metaphysics* is impossible. In what follows I shall attempt to examine the most difficult and controversial points.[28] By giving a summary of Thomas's commentary on the contents of the first twelve books, I intend to present an abridged but continuous survey of the text as Thomas read it, with his summaries, comments, corrections, and additions. In this way, my exposition is an invitation to read Aristotle's text guided by Thomas, while special attention is drawn to his interpretation of difficult passages and Thomas's additions.[29]

The Commentary of Thomas Aquinas

The Proemium

Right at the beginning of the treatise and in Books I (A), IV (Γ), and VI (E), seemingly divergent views are presented about the nature and unity of first philosophy, that is, metaphysics. In Book A, metaphysics is described as wisdom and the science of the principles of things. On the other hand, in Book Γ we encounter a description of it as a study of being *qua* being. In Book E, theology is said to be the highest theoretical science, which has

28. On the following pages I am quoting some passages of my essay "St. Thomas Aquinas's Commentary on the *Metaphysics* of Aristotle," *Divus Thomas* (Piac.) 86 (1983): 307–26.

29. We have made use of *Thomas Aquinas: Commentary on the Metaphysics of Aristotle*, trans. John P. Rowan (Chicago: Henry Regnery, 1961).

immobile, separate being as its object. Thomas brings these conceptions into unity by using Aristotle's own principles. He does so in a proemium in which he shows that there is but one metaphysics. Referencing *Politics* I.6.1254a35–b10, where Aristotle writes about the soul-body-relationship in terms of the natural relation between ruler (intellect) and subject (appetites), Thomas first argues for the necessity of a science which rules of the other sciences and is ordered to man's perfection, happiness. This science is called wisdom insofar as it pertains to wisdom to direct others (*Metaphysics* I.2.982a18).

Next, the natural, hierarchical role of the intellect gives an insight into which science this is, as well as its subject, for the "science which is intellectual in the highest degree," that is, "which treats of the most intelligible objects" (*maxime intelligibilia*) "should be naturally the ruler of the others." "Most intelligible objects," Thomas continues, may be understood in a threefold way: (1) as that which gives the greatest certitude; this can only be the science of the first causes;[30] (2) as the knowledge that is furthest removed from the level on which the senses function and from what they communicate to us; that is, the science that considers the most universal principles like being and what is subsequent to being; and (3) as that which is best adapted to the intellect in the sense of being most intelligible; God and the intelligences are entirely immaterial and therefore most adapted to the intellect. The next step in Thomas's argument is to show that these three kinds of knowledge belong to one and the same science. The reason is that it is up to the same science to study the proper causes of a genus and the genus itself. The causes of being are the separate substances.[31] In this way, Thomas succeeded in combining the three views of first philosophy as we find them in Books I (A), IV (Γ), and VI (E) of the text.

But there remains a difficulty. Book VI.1 (E) states that being which is separate from matter is the subject of metaphysics, so that a large sector of existing things would not come in under it. Thomas first identifies this (i.e., being separate from matter) with the causes of being, but in an attempt to come closer to Aristotle's intention, he writes that what he calls the subject, the *ens commune*, is that which is in reality separate from matter under the aspect of being and of formal content (*secundum esse et rationem*). Thomas goes on to explain that not only beings that can never exist in matter, such as God, are said to be separate, but also those which can be without matter, such as being in general (*ens commune*).

---

30. In his proem, Thomas uses the plural *causes* out of respect for Aristotle's text and in order not to anticipate the conclusion of Book Λ, chap. 10, on the unity of the first cause.

31. Thomas uses the plural "substances" in deference to the text, but in Book XII, the singular appears.

This remark is of great importance. Thomas concludes that the description of the subject of metaphysics in Book VI (E) coincides with that of Book IV (Γ), namely, that this subject is common being. He is able to do so because he transposes both conceptions to a higher level. Being, unity, etc., do not depend in their *esse* on matter. In light of statements elsewhere in the commentary, such as that metaphysics also studies sensible things inasmuch as they are beings,[32] this can only mean that prior to our entering metaphysics we must determine its proper subject by showing that being as such is not necessarily material. We can do so by demonstrating that the being that we call the human soul is immaterial or that the first cause is immaterial. This allows us to consider material things from a metaphysical point of view and to see being as such in them. The proemium is in perfect agreement with what Thomas wrote in his *Expositio in Boetii De Trinitate,* q. 5, aa. 2–3.

In this connection we must consider the commentary of Thomas on Book IV.1–2 (Γ) and on Book VI.1 (E). The text of Book IV (Γ) begins in an abrupt way and does not refer to Book I (A), but Thomas sees a positive connection between the themes treated in both books: the first science (or first philosophy) considers the first principles; but principles are always principles of something and the first principles are principles of being. Thomas also places Book IV (Γ) in the context of the entire metaphysics, connecting it with the preceding part and with what follows. While Book III (B) presents a dialectical treatment of some questions, in Book IV (Γ) Aristotle proceeds by way of demonstration and gives a survey of what metaphysics should consider. It deals with the principles of being and those of demonstration (no. 534). Book IV (Γ) takes us to some of these themes (no. 529) and in this way Book IV (Γ) is the real starting point of the science of metaphysics.

We should also notice that Thomas defines metaphysics by the expression *cuius subiectum est ens,* instead of the Aristotelian *cuius subiectum est ens in quantum ens* (nos. 529 and 533). Although Thomas uses the expression "being *qua* being," he repeatedly calls metaphysics the science whose subject is being. Apparently, he wants to stress that metaphysics deals with reality as such, with common being, that is, with that which properly belongs to being, whether it is being in actuality or in potency, being as substance or that of the accidents. This common being is not a manmade construction, but is being outside the human mind.[33] Thomas understands the expression "being *qua* being" as the

---

32. *In VI Metaph.,* lesson 1, no. 1165.

33. *In VII Metaph.,* lesson 1, no. 1245: "the Philosopher, having dismissed accidental being and being in its sense of the truth of statements, now begins to establish the truth about being as such (*per se*) *quod est extra animam.*"

negation of a particular aspect or of a class of being (no. 530). What is surprising is that in his commentary, Thomas writes that Aristotle makes being in its universality the subject of metaphysics, while in the *Summa theologiae* I, q. 44, a. 2, he says that Plato and Aristotle considered being under a particular aspect: *sub particulari quadam consideratione vel in quantum est hoc ens vel in quantum est tale ens.* They did not consider the cause of being because they did not study being as such. But this criticism is not brought forward in the commentary except in guarded terms, namely in the closing section regarding the first part of Book IV (Γ), lesson 2 (no. 563), where a distinction is made between "this science" (the study of being) and philosophy (the study of substance). The text might mean that in the following books Aristotle develops a philosophy of substance.

In Book VI.1.1026a10–15 (E), Aristotle presents the well-known tripartition of the theoretical sciences. After this passage the Greek text goes on with the words "it is necessary that all causes are eternal and especially those" (1026a16). Apparently, all the causes implied in the process of generation are meant insofar as they lie outside the sublunar world.[34] The Latin translation that Thomas used reads "common causes" instead of "all causes" and in this way Thomas avails himself of the text to show that the science of these common causes studies all beings as beings; in other words, he combines the three views of metaphysics (mentioned above). He even goes so far as to declare that this text shows that Aristotle considers the highest immobile and separate principles the causes of being and not only of motion, and so he writes: "From this it is quite evident that the opinion of those who claimed that Aristotle thought that God is not the cause of the substance of the heavens but only of their motion, is false" (no. 1164). To confirm his conclusion, Thomas refers to a text in Book I (A) that says that wisdom is concerned with the most universal causes (no. 36), a text that he understands as stating that God is the cause of things, but this probably goes beyond what Aristotle intended to say.

In his commentary, Thomas also writes that first philosophy not only studies things separate from matter and motion (as Aristotle suggests), but also sensible things inasmuch they are beings. This remark implies that the exclusion of the study of sensible things in first philosophy is invalid, but Thomas does not explicitly say so. If there are no other substances but material substances, the philosophy of nature will be the first science, but if there is an immobile being, its study will be prior, and the science investigating it will be the first philosophy. Thomas subscribes to this conclusion, which he also

---

34. See Ross, *Metaphysics,* 1:356.

expressed in his theory of *separatio* in his *Expositio in Boetii De Trinitate,* q. 5, a. 3. When we learn—for example by the discovery of the immateriality of thought and hence of our own mind—that there is immaterial being, we can develop the science of metaphysics. It is Thomas's contribution to the study of metaphysics to have established that it is not the assimilation of the mind to the different levels of reality that constitutes the theoretical sciences, but that these sciences originate through the progressive penetration by the intellect into the being presented to us by the senses. This also results from the first lesson regarding Book E, where Thomas says that Aristotle, in his tripartition of the sciences, deals with the *methods* of defining things that are used in physics, mathematics, and theology, rather than with different levels of reality.

Book I (A)

Returning now to the commentary on Book I (A) of the *Metaphysics,* we read in the first lesson (I.1.980a21–983a3) that all men by nature desire to know and that man, in contrast to other animals, lives by art and reasoning. Aristotle explains the role of experience and the difference between art and science. Wisdom, the highest form of intellectual knowledge, deals with the first causes and the principles of things. In the second lesson (I.2.982a4–b11), he argues that the most universal beings are furthest removed from sensible things, while in the *Physics* we are told that we come to know first what is more universal. Thomas connects these seemingly contradictory statements by pointing to the fact that Aristotle not only speaks here of universals in terms of causes, but also reaffirms that sense knowledge, which is of singular things, is prior (no. 46), meaning that the science and wisdom of which he is speaking here is naturally later than what we learn by the senses. Aristotle recalls the importance of the final cause, that is, that for the sake of which people do certain things. Thomas says that Aristotle mentions the final cause in passing (*tangebat*), to add that it is the first of the causes. The science that considers the prior and universal causes, must also consider the universal end of all things, which is the greatest good in the whole of nature (no. 51).

In lesson 3 (I.2.982b11–983a23), Aristotle mentions that people are curious about the causes of the events which they observe (no. 55). This points to the quest for a supreme and definite science, which is *free* in the sense that it is not pursued for any other ends but the acquisition of knowledge (no. 58). It is the most honorable science (no. 64); its starting point is wonder (no. 66); it is speculative and not a human but a divine science (*non humana sed divina*) (no. 68).

In lesson 4 (I.3.983a24–984a16), Thomas writes that Aristotle considered the first two chapters as an introduction to metaphysics. Aristotle is now going to say what metaphysics has to tell us about the causes of things; first by way of an exploration of the opinions of earlier philosophers and then, in Book II, by pursuing the truth of the matter. There are four causes (namely material, formal, efficient, and final causes) (no. 70) and Aristotle successively reviews what the Pre-Socratic philosophers and Plato taught about them. He begins by stressing the central role of the material cause (no. 74): nothing is either generated or corrupted in an absolute sense, for there is always the material cause (no. 75). When Aristotle mentions the chronology of the different philosophers, also in relation to historical events in Greece, Thomas adds the personalities or events in biblical history which chronologically correspond to these, such as Ahaz, Zedekiah (598–587 B.C.), the Babylonian captivity, etc. (no. 77).

In lesson 5 (I.3–4.984a16–b3), some intimations are mentioned of a full acknowledgment of the efficient cause: some philosophers spoke of an intellect as a cause, others of love as a first principle. Lesson 6 (I.4.984b32–985b4) mentions love and hate as the moving causes in the philosophy of Empedocles, while lesson 7 (I.4–5.985b4–986a13) analyzes the atomists and the Pythagoreans, who held that numbers are the substance of things. Lesson 8 (I.5.986a13–b10) recalls the views of the Pythagoreans on the contraries. Their principles must be classified under the material cause (no. 183). Lesson 9 (I.5.986b10–987a28) sets forth the thought of Parmenides and the Pythagoreans on the causes of things, while in lesson 10 (I.6.987a29–988a17) we turn to Plato's theory of Ideas: in addition to the Ideas as formal causes, he regarded the Great and the Small as a material cause (no. 169).

We find a summary of what the early philosophers taught about the material cause in lesson 11 (I.7.988a18–b21). Lesson 12 (I.8.988b22–989b24) examines the theories of those philosophers who studied the causes while using the methods applied in the philosophy of nature. In no. 188, we encounter a statement added by Thomas: the first cause in the whole universe must be the most perfect being. In lesson 13 (I.8–9.989b24–990a34), Aristotle advances several arguments against the theory of Pythagoras that numbers are the principles of things. In lesson 14 (I.9.990a34–991a8), Plato's theory of Ideas is discussed again. Seven arguments are brought forward against it, while other arguments advanced in defense of this theory are refuted in lesson 15 (I.9.991a8–b9): basically, the Ideas do not contribute to the coming-to-be nor to the movements of sensible things. Likewise, they do not help us to come to know the sensible things. In lesson 16 (I.9.991b9–992a24), Aristotle proposes some arguments against the views that the Ideas are numbers. He also argues against Plato's theory of mathematical magnitudes, such as lines, surfaces, and solids. In lesson 17 (I.9–10.992a24–993a27), arguments are advanced against the view that the Ideas are principles of being and of knowledge, for example by showing that Plato's theory on the principles of things does not consider efficient and final causality.

Thomas presents the foregoing arguments of Aristotle with great precision and objectivity, without advancing criticisms. In no. 51, he mentions the final cause of all beings, the greatest good in the whole of nature, a covert reference to God.

Book II (*a*)

The fact that the second book of the *Metaphysics* was given the small *alpha* as its number suggests that the editors considered the book a sort of supplement. A student or colleague of Aristotle may have put together the texts which make up the book, but the contents and style are those of Aristotle himself, as Alexander says in his commentary, so that the topics discussed in the book can be regarded as certain prolegomena (προλεγόμενα) to theoretical philosophy as a whole.[35] Thomas seems to be unaware of this discussion and rather views Book II as a continuation of Book I insofar as Aristotle, after criticizing the opinions of the ancient philosophers on the first principles of things, now turns to establishing what is true.

In the first lesson (II.1.993a30–b19), Thomas quotes the words of Aristotle that what an individual person can contribute to the quest for wisdom is little compared to all the knowledge to be acquired (no. 276). The quest for truth is difficult and errors may occur. Certain things are less knowable, such as matter, motion, and time, because intelligibility depends on actuality, as will become clear in IX.9.1051a4–33, Thomas writes. Yet the difficulty depends more on the weakness of our intellect (nos. 280–82). He quotes Aristotle's comparison with the eyes of owls, unable to see in full daylight (τά τῶν νυκτερίδων ὄμματα, 993b9).[36] Against this comparison one might argue that, in contrast to our eyes, the intellect cannot be damaged by too much intelligibility of the object. Thomas replies that the intellect is not well adapted to a too-intelligible object, as it operates through abstraction from the images of our imagination (nos. 283–85).

---

35. *Alexandri Aphrodisiensis in Aristotelis Metaphysica Commentaria*, ed. Michael Hayduck (Berlin: Reimer, 1891), 138, lines 10–11 (CAG 1). For a discussion on Book II (α) see Reale, *Aristotele. La Metafisica*, 1:73–75. He argues that the book can be considered as an appendix, complementing Book I (A).

36. The *translatio Media* Thomas is using has "nicticoracum oculi."

Thomas adds a comment of Averroes, who argued that Aristotle used the comparison of the owl unable to see the clarity of the sun incorrectly. According to Averroes, Aristotle did not demonstrate that for us it is impossible to understand abstract substances. Averroes argued that, if this were the case, nature would have acted in vain and made something contradictory, meaning that that what is most intelligible could not be known by us.[37] This argument is ridiculous and deficient, says Thomas. Given that the human soul can only come to know the truth about things insofar as it understands them through abstraction from phantasms, the end of separate substances cannot consist in being understood by our intellect. Rather, the opposite is the case: the separated substances are the end of our intellect. Moreover, that which is in vain (*frustra*) is that which fails to reach its end. Separate substances do not, therefore, exist in vain. Averroes's argument is also deficient because he does not take into account other intellects that are able to understand the essence of separate substances. Extending Aristotle's comparison about the sun, Thomas writes: "for even though it [the sun] is not seen by the eye of the owl, it is seen by the eye of the eagle" (no. 286).[38] In the final section of the lesson, we read that people help one another, also in the quest for truth, so that we should be grateful to those who have shown us the truth. Such gratitude extends as well to those who have made only "superficial" statements because they honestly attempted to discover the truth.

In lesson 2 (II.1–2.993b19–994b11), we read that knowledge of the truth—and here the so-called ontological truth is meant—is proper to first philosophy, because it is not a practical science, directed to the production of something, but a speculative one. Knowledge of the truth results from knowing the causes of things, and first philosophy, that is, metaphysics, seeks to know the first cause (nos. 290–92). That which is the cause of a univocal effect possesses this attribute (the effect) in the fullest sense. Thomas observes that sometimes the effect does not reach a full resemblance with its cause, as the cause is of a higher order (no. 293). The principles of eternal things are most true, and the causes are more true than their effects. Commenting on 993b28: "Hence the principles of things [ὄντων ἀρχὰς] that exist forever must be most true," Thomas identifies the principles of things with the celestial bodies.[39] More importantly, Aristotle's affirmation that these principles do not have a cause of

---

37. Averroes, *Commentarium Magnum in Aristotelis Metaphysicorum XIII* 281–29C.

38. Thomas finds Averroes's argument wholly ridiculous (*valde derisibilis*) probably because it is entirely apparent that it runs counter to the *intentio Aristotelis* which he, Thomas, seeks to understand. In his systematical writings Thomas insists on the same criticism against Averroes: *SCG* III.41–43; *ST* I, q. 88, aa. 1–2; *Q. de Anima*, a. 16.

39. See also *Alexandri Aphrodisiensis in Aristotelis Metaphysica Commentaria* 148.24–34.

their being but are the cause of the being of other things, brings Thomas to his conclusion that "even though the latter [the celestial bodies] are incorruptible, they have a cause not only of their motion, as some men thought [*ut quidam opinati sunt*], but also of their being [*esse*], as the Philosopher clearly states in this place."[40] In fact, going beyond the wording of Aristotle's text, Thomas assigns a reason for Aristotle's argumentation and formulates a version of the principle of causality when he writes: "Now this is necessary, because everything that is composite in nature and participates in being must ultimately have as its causes those things which have existence by their very essence. But all corporeal things are actual beings insofar as they participate in certain forms. Therefore a separate substance which is a form by its very essence must be the principle of corporeal substance" (no. 296). The remaining part of this lesson (nos. 297–300) deals with Aristotle's rejection of the possibility of an infinite number of causes, both in terms of material and efficient causes and in terms of final and formal causes.

In lesson 3 (II.2.994a11–b9), Aristotle shows that it is impossible to proceed to infinity in material causality. Thomas explains it with the help of some examples (nos. 306–10). In some cases of growth or of the transformation of the elements, there is a natural sequence, which is not reversible (a boy grows and becomes a man), but the process of air turning into water is reversible (no. 311). Aristotle assumes that there is a first material principle, which is eternal, so that there is no infinite regress.

In lesson 4 (II.2.994b9–31), Aristotle tells us that in final and formal causality there is also no infinite regress. If there were no first for the sake of which things exist or are done, the genus of final causality would disappear; as a result the nature and notion of the good would disappear as well (nos. 316–17). There also is no infinite regress in formal causality, for this would imply infinite regress in definitions (nos. 319–22) and understanding things would become impossible (nos. 324–26).

In lesson 5 (II.3.994b32–995a20), the method to be used in the study of truth is explained. Things we are accustomed to are better known, as we acquired a habit and so they become natural to us. When Aristotle writes that the positive laws of a city are intended to make people do what is good,

---

40. No. 295: "Et per hoc transcendunt in veritate et entitate corpora caelestia: quae etsi sint incorruptibilia, tamen habent causam non solum quantum ad suum moveri, ut quidam opinati sunt, sed etiam quantum ad suum esse, ut hic philosophus expresse dicit." For similar texts see *In I De Caelo*, lesson 6, no. 64; lesson 8, no. 91; *In VIII Phys.*, lesson 3, no. 996; *In VI Metaph.*, lesson 1, no. 1164. James C. Doig argues in *Aquinas on Metaphysics: A Historico-Doctrinal Study of the "Commentary on the 'Metaphysics'"* (The Hague: Martinus Nijhoff, 1972), 200–209, that Thomas refers here to Albert and Averroes. In an early text (*In II Sent.* d. 1, q. 1, a. 5, ad 1), however, Thomas relies on Averroes's *De substantia orbis* in favor of the view that Aristotle regards God as the cause of being.

Thomas adds that the divine law, given by God, directs us to true happiness because the divine law contains no falsehood (no. 333). The disposition of people in their study of truth has a considerable influence. The various dispositions, which may facilitate or may render difficult the search of truth, are described (no. 334). We must be trained in logic, for example, which is a general disposition for the study of truth (no. 335). We should, however, not expect to find everywhere the same clarity as mathematics gives us (no. 336).

Book III (B)

Book III is also likely to form part of the introductory treatises to the science of metaphysics. Some of the expressions used in the book show its connection with Book A, as does the expression "we Platonists" which recur a few times in both books. According to the generally accepted division by Ross, Book III contains fourteen *aporiae*. Thomas distinguishes seventeen but this is merely due to the fact that Thomas counts as *aporiae* some questions which Ross tends to view as subquestions.[41] He divides these questions into two sorts: *aporiae* concerning the nature of the science of metaphysics (lesson 2) and *aporiae* concerning the contents of this science (lessons 3–15). Thomas gives a very precise analysis of the arguments of each chapter and frequently points to solutions in subsequent books of the *Metaphysics* (no. 355). As such, Book III forms a program for the rest of the *Metaphysics*.[42]

In lesson 1 (III.1.995a24–b4) of his commentary, he says that Aristotle proceeds by way of questions and considers first the disputed issues, the more so because the ancient philosophers held a great number of different opinions (no. 338). In order to make some progress we must first investigate the main problems we are facing; otherwise we cannot reach a solution (nos. 339–40). In order to form a judgment we must know the different aspects of the question under discussion (nos. 342–44). According to Averroes, this way of proceeding results from the fact that metaphysics is akin to logic.

In lesson 2 (III.1.995b4–27), the first set of problems concerning the nature of the science of metaphysics is discussed. Does one science investigate all four causes (no. 346)? Does it study all the first principles and which are the first principles of substances (no. 347)? Are sensible substances the only ones (no. 351)? Does one science study all substances (no. 348)? Does it study

---

41. Ross, *Metaphysics*, 1:221–25.

42. This view is shared by Reale and Seidl and to a lesser extent by Ross but criticized by Owens (*The Doctrine of Being*, 211ff.) as well as by Crubellier and Laks in their introduction to *Aristotle, "Metaphysics" Beta* (Oxford: Oxford University Press, 2009), 22–24.

both substance and accidents (nos. 352–53)? In lesson 3 (III.1.995b27–996a17), the question is considered whether universals are the principles of things (nos. 355–56) and what the relation is between the specific form and the individuality of things (no. 361). Are the principles universals or singular things (no. 364)? Are they in potency or in act (no. 365)? Are mathematical objects—such as numbers, lengths, and solids—substances (no. 366)?

Thomas treats of each of the book's *aporiae* in a separate lesson. In lesson 4 (III.2.996a18–b26) the question is raised whether the causes are studied in one science. The answer is negative (no. 370). Which causes does first philosophy study? Thomas notes that when discussing this issue Aristotle uses some sophistical arguments (no. 371). The study of all the causes does not belong to one science (no. 372). Do immobile things have a final cause (no. 374)? In the mathematical sciences there is no final cause (no. 375). One thing can be the effect of all the causes (no. 377). The science which deals with the end is called wisdom (no. 378). Insofar as metaphysics studies being, it considers the formal cause, the final cause, and in a certain sense (*aliqualiter*) the cause of motion (no. 384), but not the material cause. The study of the three causes mentioned belongs to it (no. 385).

With lesson 5 (III.2.996b26–997a15) the second part of the book begins, namely the study of the principles of demonstration proper to this science. All demonstrations proceed from some common principles, but not every science must study these principles. This would be a waste. And the science which deals with the principles, metaphysics, must have one subject matter. But is not substance its subject? The answer to this, says Thomas, can be found in Book Γ (IV), namely that first philosophy is the science of being.

The question discussed in lesson 6 (III.2.997a15–34) is that of whether both substance and accidents are studied in this science. A demonstrative science considers accidents as they belong to the *per se* accidents of the genus which is the subject of such a science (no. 395). When their principles are different, sciences differ, but one science can demonstrate the principles of another science by resorting to higher principles, as metaphysics does. When the principles are the same, the sciences do not differ from one another, as long as the accidents (i.e., the specific differences) and the genus are the same (no. 397). In Book Γ (IV) it will be determined that the science which studies being as being considers all substances (as substances) and the accidents common to them. The study of substances follows a certain order. Particular accidents are studied in particular sciences, for example, natural science studies the accidents of mobile substances. The study of the higher, more noble substances belongs to first philosophy (no. 398).

In lesson 7 (III.2–3.997a34–998a21), Aristotle argues about questions concerning substances. Are sensible things the only substances and if there are other substances besides the latter, are they of one genus (no. 404)? Some authors accept mathematical entities as a third group of substances between the pure Forms (or Ideas) and the sensible things. Thomas explains the theory of the intermediate beings as resulting from the second type of abstraction (no. 405). Recalling the arguments put forward in Book A, Aristotle says that some philosophers placed the (abstract) essences of things at the level of the heavenly bodies, claiming that they are the specific forms of the sensible things and calling these forms "forms *per se*," for example, man *per se* or horse *per se* (nos. 407–8). But it is absurd to believe that a corruptible being is specifically the same as an incorruptible one (no. 409).

Aristotle argues next against those who hold the theory that mathematical entities are intermediate between the Ideas and sensible things (no. 410). According to them there are lines, surfaces, etc., in addition to the sensible ones we observe, but this creates difficulties in astronomy: there would be another heaven and moon besides the present ones. Would they have motions? What is separate from matter is not mobile (no. 411). Thus, according to this theory, there would be intermediate entities between the Ideas and the sensible things, as well as an intermediate science dealing with these entities (nos. 413–14). After summarizing two more arguments against the same theory, Thomas says that in Books XIII and XIV (which he does not comment upon) Aristotle shows that there are no self-subsisting forms of mathematical figures (no. 422).

The question whether universals are principles is discussed in lesson 8 (III.3.998a20–999a23), as well as the problem regarding whether there are principles separate from matter. Are the genera we predicate of things elements and principles of them (no. 423)? Empedocles thought that the elements are intrinsic constituents of things, but he did not say that the genera of things are elements and principles (no. 425). This is also obvious when one considers products of art: a bed has "parts" but is not composed of the genus. But a contrary argument says that things are known by their definition, which mentions the genus (no. 427). Two more arguments follow (nos. 428–29). Yet, against this contrary argument Aristotle pleads that "being" and "one" are the most common genera. But if being and one were principles, genera would not be principles (no. 432). Moreover, being and one cannot be genera because no specific differences can be added to them, as being and one are said of all things (no. 433). The ultimate species, rather than the genus, are principles (no. 436). This is confirmed by two more arguments (nos. 437–39).

The conclusion is that the principle of things is their ultimate species rather than their genus (no. 440). However, another contrary argument says that the more universal something is, the more it qualifies as a principle (no. 441). The principles of sensible things are form and matter, the form constituting their species (no. 442). However, lesson 9 (III.4.999a24–b20) asks, are the universals separate from the individual and material things? If not, they are not the principles of these things; yet some of the most eminent philosophers said that they do exist and are principles (no. 443).

Thomas notes that in Book VII (Z) Aristotle shows that the universals are not substances existing *per se*. The universals are innumerable and are not principles (no. 446). The question is whether these exist as something apart from the beings composed of form and matter, as Plato affirmed by saying that concrete things participate in the universal essences (no. 447). If there is nothing separate from matter, there will be no science because the individual is sensible, not intelligible, whereas science is of the intelligible (no. 448). If nothing is eternal, generation becomes impossible because things are generated from other things and one cannot go back forever in a series of generations, that is, an infinite regress is not possible. So there is a material principle that is not generated (no. 450). After stating this argument centered on the material principle, Aristotle proves the same for the formal cause: the form is generated but, because an infinite regress is not possible in a series of generation, there must be some form that is not generated (no. 452). He also writes that if there is some matter that is ingenerate, it is reasonable to assume that there is also a form that is not generated (no. 453). Aristotle demonstrates this, Thomas says, in Book XII (Λ), no. 2488, where he shows that there are substances separate from sensible things.

The problem discussed in lesson 10 (III.4.999b20–1000a3) is whether the principles are one or many. In lesson 15, the question is examined whether they exist potentially or in act. Is there one formal principle of all the beings of a species (no. 456)? Two reasons are advanced against a positive answer: the things belonging to one species are many and different; if the substantial form were one, how could the different individuals of this species have this form, as each of them is a substance by itself (no. 458)? In this lesson, Aristotle does not advance an argument to defend the opposite, for he has shown already that there are no separately existing universals (no. 459). In Book VII (Z), lesson 5, he will show that the essence of something is nothing else but this thing itself. Are the principles of things numerically the same? Three arguments defend this position (nos. 461–63): (1) if the principles were not numerically the same, the thing composed of them would not be numerically one, but only specifically; but (2) if they are numerically one, so that each principle considered by itself is one, the principles of immaterial substances will differ from the principles of sensible things that are numerically different but specifically one; and (3) they will be by themselves, and be nothing else, but this is unsustainable, because a principle must be a principle of something (no. 464). In Book XII (Λ), Aristotle will show, Thomas says, that the principles of all things (matter, form, or privation) are numerically different, but specifically the same. But the principles that are the separate intellectual substances are each numerically one in themselves. God is one in himself and in being; from him is derived the numerical unity found in all substances (no. 465).

In lesson 11 (III.4.1000a5–1001a3), the question is raised whether the principles of corruptible and incorruptible things are numerically the same. First, it is argued that they are not the same. If they were, all things would be perishable or imperishable (no. 467). Why are certain things corruptible but others not? Aristotle brings in Hesiod who said that those gods who did not drink nectar and eat manna became mortal.[43] Aristotle's point seems to be that either the gods are in need of food to survive, in which case they are not immortal, or they have no need for nourishment. In no. 469, Thomas writes that some truth may be hidden in this fable, if by nectar and manna we understand the supreme goodness of the first principle. Some things could be or become incorruptible by participating in the first principle, whereas things far remote from it cannot remain in existence as individuals. This could be a valid reading of what is intended by the gods not eating or drinking. Thomas opines that this nourishment of the gods could be an intimate participation in the first principle, but Aristotle rejects that they can render the gods immortal (no. 470) and argues against Plato's method of using fables to convey a certain truth.

If we ask the philosophers of nature why certain things are perishable and others not, they have no answer (no. 472). Empedocles says that what causes corruption is hate (no. 473), but his arguments do not hold, because God and the heavenly bodies, involved in these processes, would be without hate (no. 474). Opposing Empedocles's theory, Aristotle says that according to this view God would not know the elements and certain things we know because he does not have hate. The question is elaborately discussed in *Metaphysics* XII.10 (Λ) (no. 476). Here, Aristotle shows that love is not the cause of generation (no. 477), as Empedocles held; neither did the latter say why friendship and hate alternate in the cosmic process (no. 478). Thomas quotes Boethius's

---

43. The word *manna* is found in the Latin translation used by Thomas. The Greek original has ἀμβροσία, meaning a special elixir.

translation of some verses of Empedocles: at first there was concord, then hate (no. 479). But what could be the cause of such an alternation in the whole world (no. 480)? According to this Empedoclean theory, there are two kinds of corruption: that of the whole universe, including the gods, and that of singular things (no. 482). Toward the end of the lesson we are told that the principles of perishable and imperishable things are not the same (no. 486), a fact confirmed by the common belief of all men.

Passing to lesson 12 (III.4.1001a4–b25), we are confronted with what, in the words of Aristotle, is the hardest question of all: are being and unity (i.e., Being and the One, for previous philosophers) the substance of all things? Is unity really a constituent of things as Plato and the Pythagoreans hold? Empedocles reduced the One to love, while other philosophers introduced one element as a first principle, for example, fire or air (no. 489). In support of Plato's theory, one may put forward that if the One, which is most universal, is not a substance, no other universal will be, so that there are only singular things in the world (no. 490). Moreover, if the One is not a separately existing substance numbers also will not be separate (no. 491). If the One itself exists and is predicated of things, it must be the substance of all the things of which being and unity are said (no. 492). But the argument of the opposite view runs as follows: if something is one and being, existing by itself, the One and Being are *the* reality—the theory of Parmenides—and besides the One there is only nonbeing (no. 493). Again, if the One is not a substance, number also is not (no. 494). But if the One is a substance and exists separately, there will not be a multitude of different beings, as Parmenides in fact denied.

If there is another one (that is, another ultimate being or separate substance) besides the One itself, it must consist of something that lies outside the One and the thing out of which it becomes, is not a being (*non sit ens*) (no. 495). But if this other and separate one is indivisible, it follows that nothing really exists, according to Zeno, for it has no magnitude. That which does not make a thing greater does not exist because Zeno thinks that continuous quantity is the same as being (no. 496). Points and "one" do not become larger, and in Zeno's theory they are nonbeings. Whatever is being has a bodily magnitude. Lines and surfaces, which allow a limited addition, are beings in a limited sense (no. 497). Aristotle criticizes Zeno's argument: we must make a distinction between making something larger and making something more in terms of being (no. 498). According to Aristotle, the difficulty Zeno as well as the Platonists are facing is how a magnitude can be caused by indivisibles (no. 499). In fact, Aristotle states, how can a magnitude be caused by an indivisible one, or by more ones (no. 499)? How can numbers and magnitudes be formed from what is formally one and from a second material principle (which is not one), above all when this material principle is inequality (no. 500)?

Thomas notes that the answer is found in the following books, especially in Book XII (Λ), and goes beyond the discussion of the principles regarding the Pre-Socratic philosophers by concluding that there is a separate being that is one and being by itself, being a substance, although it is not the substance of all things but rather their cause. If we speak of "One" besides God, it is interchangeable with being. In another sense the word is used insofar as it has the character of a basic, first measure, either in an absolute sense or with respect to some genus (no. 501).

In lesson 13 (III.5.1001b26–1002b11), Aristotle further discusses if numbers and continuous magnitudes are the substances of things. "One" is the principle of numbers, whereas the point and the line (determined by the number two) are principles of continuous quantity, and surfaces are determined by the number three (nos. 502–3). According to this theory, a body is less a substance than a surface and a surface less than a line, a line less than a point (no. 504). When this theory is thought through, it suggests that lines and surfaces are not the substances of things and that there will not be being (no. 506). Now, Aristotle first argues in favor of the opposite position: if points, lines, and surfaces are not substances, bodies also are not substances; consequently there will not be substances. But Aristotle then says that points, lines, and surfaces are indeed not substances, but rather the limits of bodies, the dimensions of bodies (no. 508). This is shown by two more arguments (no. 509). Substances that at first did not exist but later came into being did so by way of generation. But points, lines, and surfaces are not generated or corrupted (no. 510). Points, lines, and surfaces begin to exist or cease to exist when, for instance, a body is split or two bodies are united (no. 511). But one cannot say that points, lines, and surfaces are generated, for there is no matter from which they would be generated (no. 512). The argument is illustrated by the example of the "now" in time, which also is not generated (no. 513). Thomas adds a comment, namely that mathematical entities are accidents, and he refers us to Books XIII and XIV.

In lesson 14 (III.6.1002b12–32), the question is raised whether there are separate forms comparable to the objects of mathematics in Plato's philosophy. In regard to the existence of forms above sensible substances, the following argumentation is advanced. There are many different individuals in a species of sensible things. If there were nothing besides these sensible things and the mathematical entities, the substance of a form (species) would be numerically one and the principles of things would not be determined with regard to the individuals but only according to their species. However, that would yield an infinite number of principles (no. 517). Thomas again refers the reader to Books XII and XIV for a solution.

Lesson 15 (III.6.1002b32–1003b17) addresses the questions: are the principles of substances in act or in potency, and are they singular or universal? For Aristotle, the principles are in potency, not in act. If they were in act, there would be something prior to them, namely potency. But if the principles of substances are in potency, there will not be any being in act. What is possible is not yet a being, and so the principles will not be actual beings (no. 521). This question will be determined, Thomas writes, in Book IX, where it is shown that act is prior to potency, and in Book XII where it is shown that the first principle actually exists (no. 522). Regarding the singular or universal nature of the principles of substance, Thomas explains that the universality of the principles leads to untenable consequences such as Socrates being three particular subsisting things (Socrates, man, animal). A contrary argument says that a science has universals as its subject. If principles are not universal, there will not be a science of them. This theme is treated further, Thomas remarks, in Book VII.

Book IV (Γ)

How did Thomas see the relation of Book Γ to the other books of the *Metaphysics*?[44] As is intimated by him in his commentary on the previous books, Book Γ gives an answer to certain questions raised in Book B concerning the principles of being and the object of the first science. Book Γ determines this object in general, while the following books do so in a more particular way.[45] The book is divided by Thomas as follows: Aristotle first shows what the subject matter of this science is, and next gives an answer to the questions raised in Book B.[46] This second part is subdivided by Thomas in several sections. The idea of these numerous subdivisions is to study the theme of a selected passage carefully, often separately from the rest of the chapter. These subdivisions presuppose that one is very familiar with the whole book.

---

44. For a useful commentary on Book Γ see Barbara Cassin and Michel Narcy, *La décision du sens: Le Livre Gamma de la « Métaphysique » d'Aristote. Introduction, texte, traduction et commentaire* (Paris: Vrin, 1989).

45. See the commentary in no. 529, where this is expressed as follows: Γ determines the subject and themes *de quibus est consideratio huius scientiae*, while the following books investigate *de rebus quae sub consideratione huius scientiae cadunt*. See also Leo Elders, "Le commentaire sur le quatrième livre de la *Métaphysique*," in *Atti del Congresso Internazionale Tommaso d'Aquino nel suo settimo centenario* (Naples: Dominican Editions, 1976), 1:203–14.

46. See no. 534: "Secundo procedit ad solvendas quaestiones motas in libro praecedenti."

A first question we must consider concerns the conception of metaphysics that Thomas reads in the text of the first two chapters. According to Thomas, Aristotle has not demonstrated the existence of first philosophy. In the first lesson (IV.1–2.1003a21–b22), he writes that Aristotle assumes (*supponit*) that there is a science of which the subject matter is being (no. 529).[47] Thomas is probably thinking of the demonstration of the existence of metaphysics by means of what he calls the *separatio*, that is, the judgment that not all beings are material.[48] We do in fact find, in lesson 5, the same expressions he used in his *Expositio in Boetii De Trinitate,* q. 5, a. 3.[49] At the beginning of his commentary of Book Γ, Thomas makes another important observation. With regard to this first philosophy he writes: *cuius subiectum est ens.* The same expression is repeated somewhat further on, in no. 531: *sic igitur huiusmodi scientia cuius est ens subiectum.* We also read the same affirmation in no. 533: *habet ens pro subiecto.* Thus, he affirms that metaphysics has real being as its subject.

We also find here a doctrinal development about the need of this science that deserves to be stressed (no. 531). The use of the particle γάρ in the Greek text (1003a24, in the Latin translation *palam*) provides an opportunity to speak of the necessity of this science: our knowledge of other things depends on our knowledge of being and of what essentially belongs to it, just as the knowledge of what is proper depends on what is common (no. 531). This science considers universal being insofar as it is found in all beings (no. 532). Aristotle proceeds by pointing out that what is *analogically* predicated, that is, what is conceptually partly different from, but refers to the same thing according to a certain relation, also belongs to the subject of the same science (no. 535). This subject is one and has a certain nature (no. 536). With some examples, Thomas explains the different types of analogous predication (nos. 537–38). The word being (*ens*) is also used in different ways, but it is always said with respect to one first being, that is, the subject that has being by itself; other things, such as generation and corruption, are ways to being and nonbeing; accidents have their being in another; and finally substance has firm and solid being, as existing by itself (nos. 539–43).[50] Metaphysics is mainly concerned with substance, although it extends its consideration to all beings insofar as they are in the genus "being" (nos. 545–47).

---

47. Joseph Owens, in *The Doctrine of Being in the Metaphysics of Aristotle: A Study in the Greek Background of Mediaeval Thought,* 3rd ed. (Toronto: Pontifical Institute of Mediaeval Studies, 1978), 150, thinks that Aristotle makes no attempt to show that there is a science of being *qua* being, but this is not quite exact.

48. This is demonstrated by the immateriality of thought, and consequently of the human soul, as well as by the existence of a first unmoved mover.

49. "In his autem quae secundum esse possunt esse divisa, magis locum habet separatio quam abstractio."

50. Thomas writes "quasi per se existens," apparently to intimate that in the last analysis, substances depend on divine causality.

The remaining part of the second chapter is studied by Thomas in three successive lessons. In lesson 2 (IV.2.1003b22–1004a9), Aristotle explains what comes in under the study of being and how to consider these themes. First, he says that this science studies the one (τὸ ἕν [*unum*]). Now, unity (one) and being are one and the same (*natura*), but they signify this according to different conceptual contents (*rationes*). This is obvious as being and unity (one) are said of the same thing: a man is, and is one man. Unity adds to being that it is undivided (nos. 549–53). This is also obvious because both being and unity (one) are predicated essentially of things (no. 555). Thomas notes that according to Avicenna, being and one do not signify the substances, but signify that something is added: being (*ens*), for instance, signifies something added to the essence.[51] Of "one," which is interchangeable with being, Avicenna also said that it is the same "one" as the principle of numbers. But "one" as the principle of numbers signifies something that is added to a substance as an accident in the class of quantity. Thomas adds that as regards the first point, Avicenna is wrong because the act of being (*esse*) differs from the essence, but must not be understood as something added to it by way of an accident; it is as it were established by the principles of the essence. Both names, the act of being (*esse*) and the essence, are taken from the same verb "to be" (nos. 556–68). Regarding the second point, "one" as the principle of numbers belongs to the class of quantity and is not interchangeable with being and differs from unity as a property of being. In this last sense, it signifies being by adding the sense of indivisibility, while one as the principle of numbers, when said of a substance, adds the sense of measure, something which belongs to the science of mathematics (no. 560). As being and unity signify the same reality, the predicaments of being (substance, quantity, quality, relation, etc.) are also those of unity (no. 561). In a last passage of this lesson, expanding on Aristotle's claim for the need of a first philosophy, Thomas writes that this science is divided into the study of immaterial substances and sensible substances. Its study begins with sensible being, as this is better known (no. 563).

Lesson 3 (IV.2.1004a9–34) notes that, as it is the task of one science to investigate opposites, it pertains to metaphysics to study also negations and privations (no. 564). Negations are of two kinds: absolute negation and the negation of being within a genus, which says that something is not present within a genus. The negation that is included in the concept of unity is a ne-

---

51. According to Avicenna, who admits the real distinction between essence and existence, essences are already quasi-realities (in the order of the essences), not created by God. They are placed in the world of existing things by a sort of injection of being. This was widely taken to be Avicenna's position, at least by his Latin readers. See Wippel, "The Latin Avicenna as a Source for Thomas Aquinas's Metaphysics."

gation in a subject, and approaches a privation (no. 565). Thomas observes that we should not say that unity is the privation of plurality. The reason is that a privation is subsequent to that of which it is a privation, but plurality is not prior to unity. Unity (which is interchangeable with being) implies the privation of division. The absence of a quantitative division is not meant here, but the absence of a formal division, such as "this is not that." We first form the concept of being, next that of nonbeing, and finally of unity, which is the privation of division. Only then the concept of plurality results (no. 566). Unity and plurality are opposites and it is the task of one science to deal with opposites and contraries (no. 567). Terms that have different meanings but always in reference to one terminus, that is, analogous terms, belong to the same science. It is the task of a philosopher to verify the different ways in which something is said (no. 568).

Aristotle shows in lesson 4 (IV.2.1004a34–1005a18) that first philosophy considers all contraries, and examines such questions as that of the one and the different, of substance as such and of the substance as determined by its accidents (no. 570). It considers being and what affects being, that is, its passions. Being *qua* being has certain properties that are common to any being (no. 571).[52] Dialecticians and sophists deal with these questions, so that philosophy must do so too (nos. 572–73). But philosophy provides demonstrations, whereas logic remains at the level of *entia rationis*, and is extrinsic to what things are in their natural existence. The concepts we use in logic do not directly represent the things of the outside world, but are so-called secondary intentions, such as species and genus (nos. 573–74). Thomas explains the difference between sophistry and philosophy as follows: a sophist attempts to gain the reputation of a man of knowledge, although he really does not possess it, while the philosopher seeks to know the truth (no. 575). Nevertheless, in a

---

52. The expression "being *qua* being," which Thomas understands as that which is characteristic of being, has been interpreted differently. Some see it as referring to substance; e.g., Albert Schwegler, *Die Metaphysik des Aristoteles* III (Tubingen: L. Fr. Fues, 1847), 152. G. L. Muskens thinks that the terms denote, at least in Book K of *Metaphysics*, incorporeal being; "De ente qua ens Metaphysicae Aristoteleae obiecto," *Mnemosyne* 13 (1947): 130–40. Philip Merlan thinks that the expression signifies the most eminent being, namely, divine being; *From Platonism to Neoplatonism* (Leiden: Martinus Nijhoff, 1953), 179. Auguste Mansion thinks it means being in its whole extension, everything that is being, as stated in his "L'objet de la science philosophique supreme d'après Aristote, Métaphysique E.1," in *Mèlanges de philosophie grecque offerts à mgr. Auguste Diès* (Paris: Vrin, 1956), 151–68. Giovanni Reale proposes that the formula "being *qua* being" (ὄν ἦ ὄν) can be read in both an extensive as well as an intensive sense so that it integrates a study of being, a study of substance, a study of divine substance, and a study of principles and causes; see *Aristotele. La Metafisica*, 1:324. This approach somewhat resembles that of Patzig and Frede who argue for two levels of focal meaning: the horizontal level in which everything other than substance depends on substances and the vertical level in which changing substances are dependent on a changeless substance for their being. Günther Patzig, "Theologie und Ontologie in der 'Metaphysik' des Aristoteles," *Kant-Studien* 52 (1960): 185–205; and Michael Frede, "The Unity of General and Special Metaphysics: Aristotle's Conception of Metaphysics," in *Essays in Ancient Philosophy*, ed. Michael Frede (Oxford: Clarendon Press, 1987), 81–95.

certain sense dialectics and sophistry are also a science insofar as they show how to arrive at conclusions in probable subject matters (no. 576). Whatever comes in under unity and being must be considered by the philosopher who studies being. All contraries are reducible to unity and to being, because one of the two contraries is a privation and as such reducible to nonbeing (nos. 579–80). All beings are reduced to contraries: either they are contraries or they come from contraries (no. 584). Thomas adds a note: when Aristotle says that all beings are contraries or are from contraries, he does not state his own opinion nor that of the ancient philosophers for immobile beings, such as Plato accepted, are not contraries (no. 585). In the last section of the lesson, Thomas summarizes what belongs to the subject of first philosophy (no. 587).

In lesson 5 (IV.3.1005a19–b8), Aristotle solves another question raised in Book Γ: does the first science also deal with the first principles of demonstration? In this lesson, he treats of these principles in general; in the next lesson, lesson 6, he treats of the first of these principles (no. 588). Whatever is present in all beings, and whatever is used by all sciences, belongs to the subject of first philosophy (no. 590), but the sciences use the first principles of demonstration insofar as they concern their particular subject matter (no. 591). Yet thus far no one tried to say something about these first principles themselves (no. 592). Particular sciences, indeed, must not be concerned about them, for it is the task of first philosophy, which studies common being, to deal with these principles (no. 593). There have been philosophers who attempted to demonstrate them. At this point, Thomas quotes a variant reading of the text and notes that in one translation the text says that students must not consider these first principles as statements to be demonstrated. But another better version of the text says: those who acquire knowledge must come to know them, but not seek to demonstrate them (no. 594).

Lesson 6 (IV.3–4.1005b8–1006a18) argues that the knowledge of a person who devotes himself to the study of first philosophy will be most certain when he knows the principles (no. 596). The firmest and strongest principle is a principle about which one cannot lie; it is not a supposition and it is not acquired by demonstration (nos. 597–99). These properties belong to the first principle. It is most firm, for it is impossible that at the same time the same attribute is in a thing and is not (nos. 600–601). Contradictory statements cannot be true at the same time (nos. 602–3). In the first operation of the mind, by which we form concepts, we cannot think something if we do not have the concept of being; in the second operation, we cannot proceed if we have not first understood this noncontradiction principle (no. 605). Some natural philosophers denied the truth of the principle that contraries cannot belong to the same subject at the same time (no. 606). If there were infinite regress in a demonstration, there would be no demonstration. This implies that not all things can be demonstrated (no. 607). Yet, in a certain respect, one can demonstrate this first principle, namely by pointing out that if one denies it, his words lose their sense (no. 608). Thomas then quotes another and better translation of the last lines of this section: if one wants to convince someone who denies the principle, it will be possible to make a syllogism that refutes his argument, but not a demonstration of the principle (no. 610).

Lesson 7 (IV.4.1006a18–1007b18) discusses the first principle within a dialectical disputation. Thomas says that Aristotle first refutes the opinion of those who say that contradictory statements can be true at the same time (in lessons 7–15) to show next that there is no intermediate between contradictory statements (in lesson 16). He refutes those who say that these contradictory statements may both be false at the same time. In a discussion, the point of departure (the principle) must be a term of which both the one who speaks and the one who listens know the meaning. "Man" signifies a two-footed animal and does not signify the contrary (no. 620). It is apparent, then, that the term signifies something distinct from its contradictory (no. 621). Being a man and not being a man are totally opposed, more than "man" and "white" (no. 622). This point is also argued as follows: those who say that "man" and "non-man" are the same destroy all predications of the substance (nos. 625–26). A term that signifies something does not at the same time signify something else (no. 628). It is impossible that everything that is predicated of a subject is predicated accidentally. If this were the case, nothing would be predicated *per se* of it, in virtue of itself, and one could go on forever (no. 629). With regard to this argument of Aristotle, Thomas adds a note: although an accident is not the subject of another accident, it can nevertheless be a cause of it, as warm and moist are the cause of sweet (no. 635).

In lesson 8 (IV.4.1007b18–1008b2), Aristotle brings forward some more arguments against those who deny the principle of noncontradiction. A third argument against those who do not accept the principle is that if an affirmation and a negation are both true at the same time, all things will be one (no. 636). The theory of Protagoras, that whatever seems true to us is true, leads to contradictions. According to Anaxagoras, all things are one but in a certain confusion: everything is in everything; but in fact he was talking about things in a state of potency (nos. 637–38). A fourth argument against those who say that contradictory propositions are true of the same subject leads to the conclusion that all things must be one (nos. 647–48). Without the principle of noncontradiction, everyone would have the truth (no. 649) and a dispute would be impossible (no. 650). The definition of true and false would no longer apply (no. 651).

In lesson 9 (IV.4–5.1008b2–1009a16), Aristotle advances a fifth argument against the rejection of the principle of noncontradiction: one cannot enter into a discussion with those who hold that affirmations and negations about the same subject are true. These persons seem to be similar to plants (no. 653). A sixth argument is based on the simple conduct of people, who know that going to a place is different from staying home. Saying that the number four is five is not the same as saying that it is one thousand. In the first affirmation, one is closer to the truth, but when we say "closer" there must also be something that is simply true. The opinion of Protagoras is similar to those views that have already been refuted (no. 662).

In lesson 10 (IV.5.1009a16–38), Aristotle argues against those who for some sophistical reasons did not accept the first principle. Here we must appeal to their ordinary way of thinking to help them see the truth (no. 663). Others, however, must be brought to insight by arguments (no. 664). Next, he gives a first solution to the question why some think that contradictory statements are both true: they see that some contraries come from the same thing, as air and earth from water. This made Anaxagoras say that everything is mixed in everything (nos. 665–66). We can help them by saying that in one way they are right but in a limited sense, namely that contraries can be present in potency (no. 667). Thomas reads 1009a36–38 as a second solution but he does not see clearly what Aristotle intends to say. Rather, he connects it to the Platonists who posited unchangeable separate Ideas in order to achieve certain knowledge, claiming that sensible things contain a mixture of contraries and hence are unable to procure certain knowledge.[53] Hence, Thomas prefers the first solution (no. 668).

Next, in lesson 11 (IV.5.1009a38–b12), Aristotle explains why some thought that whatever appears to us is true. The reason is that people perceive sensible qualities as sweet and bitter in different ways (no. 669). In such cases, it is impossible to say which opinion is correct. One is tempted to assume that somehow each opinion is true (no. 670). Some say that what the majority of people deem to be the case is what is true (no. 671).

In lesson 12 (IV.5.1009b12–1010a15), two reasons are mentioned why some have thought that the truth of things is what appears to us: sense cognition corresponds to the nature of things and shows the truth, but error may occur

---

53. According to Reale, Aristotle is saying that the claim (i.e., contradictories can both be true at the same time) cannot be extended to the whole of being because the divine is entirely free of any becoming, so that in it contradictions and contraries do not even exist in potency. *Aristotele, La Metafisica*, 1:345–46.

with respect to the common sensibles, and our senses may not be in a good disposition (no. 673). Now Empedocles seems to believe that our judgments are in conformity with the dispositions of our body. Here, Thomas quotes two or three different translations, and we must admire the efforts he makes to discover what Aristotle wanted to say precisely (no. 675). Next, Aristotle refers to Parmenides, who speaks of the intellect, but, as he sees it, the intellect follows the condition of the body and so the outcome is not different from what the others like Empedocles say (no. 676). According to Anaxagoras, things are the way we perceive and evaluate them (no. 677). But if so, the quest for truth is impossible (no. 680). The reason why these philosophers developed their theories was that they attempted to derive true doctrine just from sensible things, but much in these things is indeterminate because of the nature of matter present in them (no. 681). They went wrong when they said that there is nothing determinate in sensible things (no. 682) and that everything is always in motion (no. 683), a theory of which Heraclitus proposed an extreme version.

In lesson 13 (IV.5.1010a15–b1), Aristotle continues his arguments against the above-mentioned theories. Something true can be said of a thing that is changing, namely that it is not that which it was before, and therefore we can make a true statement (no. 685). Another argument says that a thing that is changing has already reached something of that into which it is changing (no. 686). Opposing the theory that all things are always in motion, Aristotle writes that there is not necessarily continuous motion in qualities and in the forms of things (no. 688). Moreover, contrary to what the protagonists of these theories say, a good number of sensible things are immobile (no. 689). A fifth argument declares that certain things are immobile by their very nature, so that it is not true that all things are always in motion (no. 690). Moreover, the thesis that all things are in motion does not agree with the theory, held by the same philosophers, that contrary statements are true of the same thing, as their theory implies that things are at rest.

Turning now to lesson 14 (IV.5.1010b1–1011a2), Aristotle tells us that truth does not consist in appearances. It is not our senses, but our imagination that is the proper cause of falsity (no. 693). In the next section, Aristotle explains why when we see things from afar, they look smaller than when we see them from close quarters, or why sick people experience certain things differently from when they are healthy (nos. 694–99). That truth does not consist in appearances is also shown by the case of a physician who is familiar with a certain disease and knows what will happen to a sick person (no. 700). The judgment that a sense makes about its proper object is acceptable and more trustworthy than what the other senses may say about this object. This applies also to what is akin to this proper object, namely the common sensibles, although here a sense may more easily be deceived. Hence not all judgments, based on what the senses tell us, are equally true (no. 701). Another argument against the view that all statements are true points to the fact that no sense tells us about its object that it is simultaneously so and not so (no. 703). In the theory that contradictory statements are true, nothing necessary is left, except what appears at this moment to the senses (no. 704).

In lesson 15 (IV.6.1011a3–b22), Aristotle argues against those who out of obstinacy defend the theory that contradictory statements are true. Sophists think that demonstrations are possible of all things, but the judgment of a healthy and of a sick person need not have the same value (no. 709). It is a sign of a sick mind to seek a demonstration of things of which there is no demonstration (no. 710). Those who say that whatever appears to us is true, make all beings relative to opinion or to the senses (no. 712). When every appearance is true, it follows that contraries will both be true at the same time (no. 713). We must oppose these sophists from the standpoint of the truth of things and not just from what people think (no. 716). Aristotle concludes by saying that of all opinions and views the most certain is that contraries are not simultaneously true (no. 718).

In lesson 16 (IV.7.1011b23–1012a28), he argues against those who accept an intermediate between two contradictory statements. If a person says something, it must be either true of false; if false, it is not; if what he says is true, it is so in reality. One of the two statements must be necessarily true (no. 721). If there were an intermediate between contradictory statements, this would be an intermediate either by participating in both the extremes or by being of a different genus. In the latter case, there would be no changing of one of the extremes into the intermediate (no. 724). This follows also from the fact that the intellect either affirms or denies something; it must think the truth or think that something is not. Every opinion must be either true or false (no. 725); true and not true are contradictory and there is no intermediate (no. 726), otherwise there would be something between being and nonbeing. If there were an intermediate between contradictory propositions, there would be something between true and not true, but there is no such intermediate (no. 726). In numbers also there is no intermediate between being even or odd (no. 728). Another argument Aristotle mentions is that if there were an intermediate, we would have an affirmation, a negation, and an intermediate, but this intermediate could be denied, so that we would have four propositions, and this could go on indefinitely (no. 729). To the question of whether something is white, we must answer affirmatively or negatively (no. 730). There is no intermediate between the two. Why do some hold the opinion that there is an intermediate between contradictory statements? Aristotle indicates two reasons: (1) when people are not able to solve a dispute between two views, they accept an argument, a view, somewhere in the middle; also (2) some of them want to demonstrate everything. The first principle of noncontradiction, however, cannot be demonstrated, and so they deny it (no. 732). These views lead to the theory of Heraclitus that everything is in movement, that is, that things are and are not (no. 734).

In lesson 17 (IV.8.1012a29–b31), Aristotle argues against certain positions that follow from the above opinions. A philosopher must first refute those who deny the principles of logic and of the particular sciences; all principles are based on the first principle, namely that there is no intermediate between an affirmation and a negation. This principle is consequent on the concept of being, which is the primary subject of metaphysics. Errors against the principles lead to errors about being and nonbeing, rest and motion (no. 736). Some say that nothing is true and that everything is false; others say that things are equally true or equally false (no. 737). The one who says that these positions are correct is simply wrong because he is contradicting himself (no. 738). There are certain contradictions that cannot possibly be true and not true at the same time (no. 739). A second way of arguing against such adversaries is to ask whether words signify something. If so, we advance some definitions and argue on the basis of these and from the definition of truth, namely: what is, is, and what is not, is not. This shows that not all things are true (no. 740). The one who says that everything is true declares that the contrary statement is also true (no. 742). In this connection, Aristotle also mentions the opinion of those who say that everything is at rest and nothing will change from the state in which it is at a given moment, and that whatever is true will always be true. But this opinion is absurd (nos. 747–48).

Book V (Δ)

Book V determines the sense of the main terms used in metaphysics. Thirty terms are defined and described. The commentary of Thomas has twenty-three lessons for thirty chapters of Aristotle's text. Thomas describes the contents of the book as follows: first, Aristotle considers the meaning of the terms that signify causality; second, the meaning of those that signify the subject of the first science, metaphysics, or part of it; and finally, the meaning of the terms that signify the passions of being *qua* being (nos. 749–50).

In lesson 1 (V.1.1012b34–1013a23), the different meanings of the term *principle* are set forth: a principle is that from which movement starts and each thing begins to move; and next what is first in being. If we say that a foundation is the principle of a house, the principle exists *in* the house. In another sense, principle is that from which things begin, as is the case in generation, but remains outside that which is generated. The term is also used in the field of moral actions and of cognition, as in the expression "the first principles" (nos. 755–62).

In lesson 2 (V.2.1013a24–b16), Thomas mentions and comments on the different genera of causes as mentioned and described by Aristotle, who reduces them to four. The general meaning of cause is that from which a thing comes to be, something intrinsic (the material cause), as different from privation and the contraries; for instance, a statue is made out of bronze and bronze is the statue. In another sense, the species and the model are formal causes. The definition is related to the form (no. 764). A third kind of causality is the first principle of movement and change, that is, the moving cause (no. 765). At this point Thomas writes that according to Avicenna, there are four modes of exercising efficient causality: perfective, dispositive, assisting, and advisory (nos. 766–69). The causality of the efficient cause extends to what makes things be in whatever way (no. 770). The fourth kind of causality is that of the final cause, namely, that for the sake of which something is done (no. 771). The term *cause* is used in many ways and a thing can have several causes (no. 773). It can also happen that two things are mutual causes in different genera of causality (no. 774). The four causes form two pairs: the efficient and final cause; matter and form (no. 775).

In lesson 3 (V.2.1013b16–1014a25), Thomas comments on the last part of chapter 2: all forms of causality are reduced to these four genera. Some difficulties are explained: seed is an efficient cause, but the menstrual fluid is a material cause (in Aristotle's view) (nos. 777–80). Thomas notes that the end may be last to be attained but that from the point of view of causality it is always first (no. 782). Aristotle closes his explanation of the sense of the term cause with a section on the modes or varieties of causality. These modes are given in accordance with the different ways a cause is related to the effect, for instance, *per se* or *per accidens,* and as prior or later, as universal or particular, as proximate or remote (nos. 783–88). Thomas adds a note, saying that a thing can be an accidental cause in two ways: (1) of something that is accidental to the cause, for example, the old age of a sculptor; and (2) of something that happens to the effect, for instance by removing an obstacle or good luck as the cause of finding a treasure (no. 789). The effects can be divided into prior and later effects (nos. 790–91). Some causes are simple, others are composite (nos. 793–94).

In lesson 4 (V.3.1014a25–b15), the term *element* is defined (no. 795ff.). Four properties of elements are mentioned: (1) element signifies the material cause; (2) it is a principle from which something is formed first; (3) it is intrinsic, and so it is different from the contraries; and (4) the species to which it belongs is not further divided in subspecies. This definition is illustrated by examples: letters are the elements of words; the elements are that into which a compound is resolved; we also speak of the elements of a doctrine. Finally, Aristotle mentions the metaphorical use of the term (nos. 802–7) to signify something that is one, small, and useful for other things. The most universal things are called elements. Thus a point is called an element. A genus is not divided into different things and is also called an element (no. 805).

The term *nature* is treated in lesson 5 (V.4.1014b15–1015a20). Thomas says that nature may also mean substance (no. 808). The following senses of the term are mentioned: (1) nature signifies the generation of living beings; (2) it is the principle out of which something is generated; (3) it is the source from which motion begins; (4) it means matter in the sense of the principle of a thing with respect to its being and becoming; and (5) it is the form of things seen as the principle of what they are (nos. 808–20).

In lesson 6 (V.5.1015a20–b15), the senses of *necessary* are listed. As has been explained in lessons 2 and 3, a cause is a principle from which something follows by *necessity*. Four modes of being necessary are distinguished. Thomas explains how the absolutely necessary differs from the other types of necessity, namely that it belongs to what is intimate in things as form, matter, or essence. What is necessary in a relative sense depends on an external cause, such as the end and the efficient cause (nos. 833–35). At the end of the lesson, some remarks are made on "necessary" in matters of demonstration (no. 836).

In lesson 7 (V.6.1015b16–1016b3), after having explained the different senses of the terms *cause* and *necessary*, Aristotle turns to the study of terms that signify things that are the subjects considered in metaphysics. He first deals with what is considered as common to all things, the terms *oneness* and *being*, and next with what is the main subject of this discipline, *substance* (no. 842). The essentially one is distinguished from what is accidentally one, for example, the musical Coriscus (no. 844). Among things essentially one, Aristotle mentions the essentially continuous, which has only one motion essential to it (no. 852). Thomas explains why here, contrary to what he said in the *Categories*, Aristotle defines the continuum by its movement, and not by the unity of its different parts, namely that this definition allows him to consider different grades of unity (nos. 854–55). Next, Aristotle indicates five modes of essential oneness: (1) being one not by contact but as continuous; (2) being one in species; (3) being of the same genus; (4) having one definition; and (5) when their concept is indivisible (nos. 856–65). In no. 858, Thomas corrects the *translatio anonyma*: instead of *curvitas* we must read *reflexio*.[54]

The study of the one is continued in lesson 8 (V.6.1016b3–1017a6). The indivisible in every way is most one, as all other modes of being one are reducible to it. If something is indivisible in a particular sense (*secundum quid*), this can only be with regard to its quantity or to its nature, namely, with regard to its subject or to its form (nos. 866–67). From these modes other modes of being one are derived, for example: by joining forces, a group of men, pulling a ship ashore, are one; or by undergoing a certain situation imposed on them, people are said to be one; or when some people possess a property (a piece of land) together (no. 868). But the first of all these modes is to be one in substance. A circular line is most one, being complete (no. 871). The following property is mentioned as flowing from oneness: one is the principle of number, even numbers are measured by it. This measure has the nature of a principle, because through this measure we come to know the things that we measure, and oneness is for all things the principle by which we know them (no. 872). But being one is not the same for all classes of beings as, for instance, we use a minimum weight as measure, but also the daily movement of the sun as the measure of time (no. 873). The first measure is indivisible (in its quantity or in its kind). A point is entirely indivisible and has no position (no. 874). The one as the principle of numbers is their measure, but this sense of "one" is not the same as that which is interchangeable with "being." In an analogous way, "one" is also predicated of other genera of things (no. 875). And there are other modes of being one by analogy like the term *healthy* can be said of food, the climate, exercise, etc. (no. 879). The chapter closes with a note on the different ways in which things are said to be many.

In lesson 9 (V.7.1017a7–b9), the different senses of *being* (*ens*) are listed. First, there is the distinction between essential being (being *per se*) and accidental being (being *per accidens*). Here, accidental being has the sense of an accidental connection of the predicate with the substance. "A man is white" is a being *per accidens* (no. 885). The different ways of using this accidental predication are mentioned in nos. 886–88. Being *per se*, as independent from our thinking, is divided into the different predicaments. Thomas points out that being is not a genus and that the different ways of predication signify ways of being (nos. 889–90). He adds a *sciendum est* by pointing out that a predicate

---

54. This is an instance of Thomas, when revising his commentary, decided that the text, as found in the *translatio anonyma*, was false and replaced it with the text found in the Moerbeke translation. For more details see Reilly, "The 'alia littera' in Thomas Aquinas's 'Sententia libri metaphysiciae,'" 574–77.

can be referred to a subject in three ways: (1) it is the subject, that is, it signifies the first substance; (2) it signifies what is in the subject; and (3) it signifies what is taken (in different ways) from outside the subject (nos. 891–92). In some predications, the verb "to be" itself is not used (e.g., a man walks) but the above division applies also to them. Avicenna says that when accidents are predicated of a substance, they signify in the first place the substance. But this is wrong, Thomas notes, as they signify the substance only by implication (no. 894). Being is also used to signify that a statement is true; the truth of a thing determines the truth of a proposition (no. 895). This use of the verb "to be" is related to the first sense of the term, namely as an effect to its cause (no. 896). At the end of the chapter, Aristotle divides being into actual and potential being. All the predicaments are divided by actuality and potency (no. 897).

The four senses of the term *substance* are explained in lesson 10 (V.8.1017b10–26), namely the following: (1) simple bodies (earth, water, etc.) are called substances, but also compounds of them, such as animals and their parts, the statues of idols, and even demons;[55] (2) the cause of the being of the substances listed in (1); (3) all the parts present in such things as lines, surfaces, and numbers, according to the Platonists, but Thomas rejects that these parts are substances (no. 901); and (4) the quiddity as the complete essence (nos. 898–902). Reduced to two senses we remain with, first, the ultimate subject in propositions, namely this particular thing, and, second, the form and the species, but not matter (nos. 903–5).

In lesson 11 (V.9.1017b27–1018a9), we find the explanation of the way in which things are said to be essentially or accidentally *the same*. There are three ways in which things are the same in an accidental way: (1) when two different accidents belong to the same subject; (2) when a predicate is said to be the same as the subject of which it is predicated (e.g., a man is musical); and (3) when two predicates are in the same subject (nos. 908–9). In all modes where "the same" is predicated *per accidens*, none of these names is used universally (no. 910). Things are said to be the same *per se* (essentially) in the same way as they are said to be one *per se*, that is, things the matter of which is one or the substance of which is one (no. 911).

Lesson 12 (V.9–10.1018a9–b8) discusses the ways in which the term *other* or *different* (*differens*) is used. Things can be other in kind (dog, cat) or individually other (two individuals of the same species). "Other" is opposed to "the same." Whereas things that are "other" or "different" differ in some

---

55. Thomas mentions that Apuleius defines demons as animals composed of an ethereal body, a rational mind, with a passive soul, but which exist eternally. This definition is reported by Augustine, *De Civitate Dei* VIII, 16. For Thomas's theory of the demons, see Q. *de potentia*, q. 6, a. 6.

particular respect from each other, things that are *diverse* (*diversum*) do not (no. 916). Things of the same species differ only by accidental differences (no. 917). Aristotle also shows when things are said to be "like" (*simile*), and distinguishes between three modes of likeness: first, oneness in quality; second, when things undergo the same thing. This can be considered from the point of view of the subjects which undergo and from that of what affects them (no. 918); and third, things which are similar to others in several qualities (no. 920). Next he distinguishes the ways of being opposed, namely, the four classical ways: contradictory, contrary, by privation, and by relative opposition (no. 922); and he explains how we recognize that things are opposed, namely by comparing them from the point of view of motion and from that of their subjects (nos. 923–24). In addition, he mentions the different ways in which we call things contrary (nos. 925–28).

Lesson 13 (V.11.1018b9–1019a14) explains the ways in which things are said to be *prior* and *posterior*. Prior is what is nearest to some determinate principle (no. 936), either a natural principle or some extrinsic principle. A thing can be prior in motion and quantity (no. 937). There is priority with regard to place (nos. 938–39), time (no. 940), and motion (no. 943). Something can also be prior in knowledge, for instance with regard to the intellect, such that universals are prior to singular things and an attribute is prior to the composite ("musical" is prior to "musical person"). Some properties are prior to others too (nos. 947–49). Aristotle also discusses what is prior in the order of being: things that can be without other things are prior to the latter; and substance is prior to accidents. Finally, the relationship of act and potency is mentioned.

Lesson 14 (V.12.1019a15–1020a6) deals with the meanings of *act* and *potency*. Four ways of being possible are distinguished: (1) being the principle of motion and change, that is, active potency; (2) being able to undergo, that is, the principle of passive potency;[56] (3) potency as the (active) principle of being able to do something; and (4) all determinations or dispositions that render a thing incapable of being acted upon and make it immovable or at least not easily so (nos. 955–60). Aristotle next mentions the modes of "capable" or "potent," which correspond to the senses of potency. Finally, he explains the different senses of *incapacity* (nos. 967–69), which are reduced to a primary incapacity (nos. 975–76).

The meaning of *quantity* and of related concepts is explained in lesson 15 (V.13.1020a7–32), while the next two lessons treat of quality and relation. Quantity means the divisibility of a subject into its constituent parts—a divis-

---

56. In no. 958, Thomas mentions the Moerbeke translation of 1019a22–23.

ibility which is different from other divisions, such as that into the elements (no. 977). Quantity is either multitude or magnitude; multitude can be counted, while magnitude can be measured; and quantity is divisible into continuous parts according to the three dimensions (no. 978). Some properties of magnitude are mentioned, such as large and small, broad and narrow, low and deep (nos. 979–83). Thomas adds an important note here: quantity is closest to the substance, so that some philosophers thought that such forms of quantity as lines, surfaces, and numbers are substances (no. 983). Division into parts is only found in the category of quantity (whiteness cannot be divided). Certain things are called quantitative in an accidental way (motion, time) (no. 985). Thomas also observes that in the *Categories*, Aristotle writes that time is essentially quantitative, while here he says that it is accidentally so. This difference can be explained by the fact that in the *Categories* he distinguished the species of quantity from the point of view of measure, while here from that of what quantity is by itself (no. 986).

In lesson 16 (V.14.1020a33–b25), *quality* and related concepts are examined. Four modes are distinguished, which are later reduced to two. One meaning of quality is the qualification of a substance, as part of the definition—this sense is lacking in the enumeration in the *Categories* (no. 987). A second use of the term is the qualification of the objects of mathematics, such as a square being a qualification of figures and a compound of numbers (nos. 989–90). A third use is the determination of mobile substances insofar as they undergo alteration. This is the third species listed in the *Categories*. The fourth use is that of disposition, which is mentioned first in the *Categories*. Thomas notes that potency in the sense of a passive principle is omitted here (no. 995). These four modes are reduced to two: (1) quality is what differentiates a substance; quality in mathematics is reduced to this first sense; and (2) quality is also the passion of things that undergo motion. Virtue and vice are reduced to this last sense. They occur in living beings that have the faculty of choice (no. 999).

The term *relative* is dealt with in lesson 17 (V.15.1020b26–1021b11). The directly or essentially relative is found in three modes: (1) in the field of numbers, in quantity (e.g., double) and in what contains (no. 1006); (2) the relative in the field of action and passion; and (3) the measurable as relative to its measure, though this is not a mutual relation. Thomas adds two notes with regard to (1): quantity is derived from number (no. 1007); and the ratio or proportion in numbers is divided into equality and inequality, which can be larger and smaller, more and less (no. 1008). The following paragraphs mention different ways in which numbers relate to each other. Thomas adds that the first species of proportionality (*ratio*), namely multiplicity, consists in comparing a number with unity (one). But the term *multiple*, as used here, also implies a numerical relation to unity. When numbers of different size are compared, the smaller one will be seen as one (*accipit rationem unius*) (no. 1015). Some continuous quantities have a proportion to one another, which is not a numerical proportion, for example incommensurable continuous quantities (no. 1020). In no. 1023, Aristotle deals with relations in things that are active and passive. Such things are related either for what they are or by the actualization of their power. Thomas observes that although knowledge seems to be relative to both the knower and to its object, it is in fact only relative to its object (no. 1028).

After having discussed the meaning of terms like *cause, subject,* and *parts of the subject*, etc., Aristotle turns in lesson 18 (V.16.1021b12–1022a3) to the term *perfect* and analyzes its different meanings in ordinary language. "Perfect" can be transferred to bad things, such as a perfect lie or a perfect thief. Thomas gives a fine exposition of the text, but does not add special remarks or propose corrections.

Lesson 19 (V.17–18.1022a4–36) discusses the senses of the terms *limit* (*terminus*), *according to which, itself,* and *disposition*. Thomas calls these terms conditions that make a thing perfect. Something is perfect when it has everything that befits it. "Limit" implies that nothing lies outside what is limited. Aristotle distinguishes four senses of the term (nos. 1045–48). In no. 1050, the sense of "in itself" and "according to which" is mentioned. In lesson 20 (V.19–23.1022b1–1023a25), the different meanings of the terms *disposition, having* (*habitus*), *privation,* and *to have* are mentioned. When explaining "to have" or "to hold," Thomas comments on Aristotle's observation at 1023a20–21 that "the poets make Atlas holds the heavens" as follows: Atlas was a great astrologer, who made an accurate study of the motion of the celestial bodies, and from this arose the story (*fictio*) that he holds up the heavens (no. 1083). In lesson 21 (V.24–27.1023a26–1024a28), such terms as *to come from something, part, whole,* and *mutilated* are explained. Thomas presents a clear survey of Aristotle's text, but does not make additions or corrections. Lesson 22 (V.28–30.1024a29–1025a34) mentions the different uses of the terms *genus, false,* and *accident.*

Book VI (E)

According to Werner Jaeger the first chapter of Book E (VI), together with Books A, B, Γ, and Δ, would be part of an introduction to the science of being,[57] while chapters 2–4 would prepare the study of substance as it

---

57. Werner Jaeger, *Aristotle: Fundamentals of the History of His Development,* 2nd ed. (Oxford: Oxford University Press, 1948), 204–27.

is developed in the following books. W. D. Ross argues that Book E takes up what Aristotle had said in Book Γ and proceeds to define the subject of metaphysics as compared to that of the other speculative sciences.[58] As we shall see, there is a difficulty, as Book Γ seems to qualify the subject of first philosophy as being *qua* being, while in Book E this subject is more precisely defined as things that exist separately from matter and are immovable.

Thomas sees Book E as the continuation of Book Δ. After having explained the meaning of being and unity (the one) in Book Δ, in Book E and the following books, in particular in Book Z, Aristotle concentrates on being and what is subsequent to it. The first chapter of Book E presents the well-known tripartition of the theoretical sciences, which I mentioned at the beginning of my summary, namely physics as concerned with movable being, while in mathematics those things are studied which are immovable but embodied in matter, whereas the first science deals with things that exist separately and are immovable.[59]

In lesson 1 (VI.1.1025b3–1026a32), Thomas says that the study of being and the principles and causes of being are the contents of Book E (no. 1146). Sense knowledge does not deal with the causes of things, but is only concerned with what is communicated to the senses. While the other sciences deal each with a particular genus (no. 1147), they do not determine the quiddity of their subject, but explain it by means of what the senses present, or they borrow it from other sciences. Geometry, for instance, accepts what it knows about magnitude from first philosophy (no. 1149). Particular sciences do not determine the whatness of things, nor do they consider whether the genus of their subject exists or not (no. 1152).

Mobile being is the subject matter of the science of natural things (no. 1155), which have sensible matter in their definition (no. 1158). Mathematics considers sensible things devoid of motion (no. 1160). Aristotle then turns to the science of being: if there is something that is immobile in being and consequently separable (in being) from matter, it will be studied in a theoretical science, different from mathematics and physics (no. 1162). The first causes of beings that are generated are themselves not generated, for there is no infinite regress. These immaterial and immobile beings are the causes of the sensible things that are known to us. They are the causes of all beings and the subject of first philosophy, as was shown in I.982a4–10 and II.993b19–994b11. First philosophy studies being as such *(ens simpliciter)* and therefore all beings insofar

---

58. Ross, *Aristotle's "Metaphysics,"* xvii.

59. This tripartition recalls Plato's hierarchy of being: the world of Ideas, the sensible things, and the mathematical entities (τὰ μεταξύ). In Plato's thought, the intermediates do exist by themselves.

as they are beings, including their essences. And Thomas adds: "From this the falsity of the opinion is clearly evident who claimed that Aristotle thought that God is not the cause of the substance of the heavens, but only of their motion" (no. 1164).[60]

Another important point Thomas stresses is that first philosophy also studies sensible things insofar as they are beings. Unless one accepts Avicenna's explanation that the things with which this science is concerned are separate from matter, not in the sense that they always exist without matter, but in the sense that they do not necessarily exist in matter (no. 1165). But judging from the wording of the sentence, Thomas himself does not agree with Avicenna's explanation. Aristotle mentions the reasons why this science can be called theology: if the divine exists somewhere, it will exist in such a nature, that is, as immobile being separate from matter; the most noble science will be that of the most noble class of beings, among which the divine beings are counted (nos. 1167–68). If there is an immobile substance, it will be prior to natural things, and the science that studies it will be first philosophy. Because it is first, it will be universal and study being *qua* being and what comes with it, as well as the essence (no. 1170).

In lesson 2 (VI.2.1026a33–1027a28), the subject matter of this science is determined. First, the accidental is excluded (nos. 1172–76). Accidental being is only being by name. The sophists used arguments based on the accidental (no. 1178). But Aristotle explains what the accidental is. There is no generation nor corruption in the accidental (no. 1179). The accidental can only happen in things and processes that take place in most cases, because of matter that is not totally subject to the agent (no. 1186). What happens for the most part (*in pluribus*) is found in some beings (no. 1188). Because sciences treat of what happens always or for the most part, there is no science of the accidental.

In lesson 3 (VI.3.1027a29–b16), Aristotle notes that according to some authors, all causes are causes *per se*; given the cause, the effect follows necessarily. This is also the theory of Avicenna (no. 1191). Thomas writes that we should understand him as wanting to say that, if no obstacle interferes, the effect will follow (nos. 1192–93). But if the effect always follows upon the cause, all things

---

60. John Wippel reminds us that most modern interpreters of Aristotle do not think that Aristotle presents the unmoved mover as the cause of being, but Thomas says that here and in Book II, to which he refers, Aristotle considers the immobile immaterial beings as the causes of things. Did Thomas force upon Aristotle a position different from what he held? Wippel suggests that to Thomas this position was so evident that Aristotle must have accepted it; see his "Thomas Aquinas' Commentary on Aristotle's *Metaphysics*," in *Uses and Abuses of the Classics: Commentaries on Classical Philosophical Texts*, ed. J. Gracia and J. Yu (Aldershot: Ashgate, 2004), 137–63, esp. 149. I would like to call attention to the presence of Plato's metaphysical views in Book α (II), and to Thomas's particular use of some of Aristotle's texts, to show that basically his philosophy is not in disagreement with the Christian faith with respect to the dependence of all things on God.

will be necessary when their proximate or remote causes are present (no. 1198). A living being will necessarily die because all bodies composed of contraries will be corrupted (no. 1199). Thomas adds a long section (nos. 1203–22) on fate and Providence due to the impression that Aristotle does away with fate and Providence, something which is held by other philosophers. Central to Thomas's response is the principle "the higher a cause the more extensive is its causality," on the basis of which it can be said that what seems unrelated on the level of a lower cause is in fact related when referred to a higher common cause. Thomas distinguishes three grades of causes: (1) a corruptible and mutable cause determined to particular effects; (2) an incorruptible but mutable cause which is universal insofar as it extends to everything that is being generated; and (3) an incorruptible and immutable, that is, a divine cause, which is universal *simpliciter* "because its proper effect is existence [*esse*]."

On the basis of the first grade of causes only, it seems that many things will happen accidentally because of defects in the agent or because of two not necessarily connected causes being involved (no. 1210). On the basis of the second grade, however, when one takes into account the causality of the celestial bodies, the effect of their action is not accidental but may become so because of an indisposition of the matter in the sublunar world (no. 1212). Thomas underlines that in our part of the world there are agent causes that can act by themselves, without depending on the celestial bodies, for instance, rational souls. He mentions his view, which we find in all his works, that the celestial bodies can produce changes in human bodies by which the respective souls may become inclined to do certain acts, but in these cases there is no necessity to obey these inclinations (no. 1213). Hence fate—the determination of things by cosmic causes—does not do away with all those events that happen accidentally (no. 1214). Thomas adds that if we go back to the ultimate cause of contingent things, we must conclude that nothing can escape God's causality (no. 1215).

When we relate whatever happens in the world to the first cause, it is obvious that all things are ordained by it, even if some events take place accidentally compared to their proximate causes of a lower order (no. 1216). How, then, can we explain that fate and divine Providence do not take away contingency in what happens in our world? Of fate and divine Providence we had an explanation in the lines above. Divine Providence cannot fail to produce its effects: God is the cause of being as being and of whatever comes with being. He gives being to things but also necessity or contingence, and the means to act accordingly that come with it. Whatever is subject to divine Providence is necessary, but at our level it may be contingent. Seen from the side of God, things and events are necessary, but from the point of view of proximate causes, they can be or not be, and they can happen necessarily or contingently (nos. 1220–22).[61]

In lesson 4 (VI.4.1027b17–1028a6), the truth of our words and statements is studied. Propositions can be true or false, that is, express what is not (*non ens*). These propositions can be either affirmations or negations; "Man is an animal" is true, "A horse is rational" is false. This truth and this falsehood are found in the intellect (no. 1231), namely, in the second operation of the intellect (no. 1233). Our senses may correctly represent the terms (subject, predicate), but they do not expressively know this conformity (no. 1235). In its first operation, the intellect acquires the likeness of things, is aware of it; it expresses and pronounces it in the second operation, that is, in a judgment (no. 1336). Things may be called true or false with regard to this judgment (no. 1237). True and false as objects of our knowledge are in the mind (no. 1240). The judgment by which the intellect combines or separates things is only in the mind, not in the things (no. 1241). This (logical) truth is excluded from the subject matter of first philosophy because it is a being *per accidens*.

Book Z (VII)

Together with Books H and Θ, Book Z is considered to constitute the main and central part of the *Metaphysics*, that is, the study of being as such (*per se*), which is the subject matter of this science. Referencing Book VI.1025b3–5 (E) and Book IV.1003a1 (Γ), Thomas divides the *Metaphysics* into the study of being as being which starts with this book and the study of the first principles which starts with Book XII (Λ). In lesson 1 (VII.1–2.1028a10–b32), Thomas also explains the place and role of Book X (I), a book that is considered by some students of Aristotle as a different and independent treatise. Thomas sees it as connected with our main subject insofar as its subject—unity—is a property of being. He says that we must first deal with being as divided into the predicaments, and next with being as divided into actual and potential being, which is the subject of Book IX (Θ) (no. 1245). Among the predicaments, substance is first and it is this particular thing, while the accidents are determinations of the substance (nos. 1249–52). When they are considered in abstraction from their subject, they are no longer beings, although the intellect can consider them as beings by

---

61. The commentary of Thomas on this lesson is eight to ten times more detailed than the short text of Aristotle. Undoubtedly this is due to the fact that divine Providence is a central topic in the condemnations of 1270: of the thirteen propositions condemned by Bishop Tempier, nos. 10 (*Quo Deus non cognoscit singularia*), 11 (*Quod Deus non cognoscit alia a se*), and 12 (*Quod humani actus non reguntur providentia Dei*) deal with this topic. The condemnations of 1277 will also address this topic in propositions 3, 21, 53, 55, and 62.

themselves (nos. 1253–55). But they are only beings when considered as determinations of a substance (no. 1256).

Substance is the first of things in our cognition, by its definition and according to time, meaning that substance can be considered separately from the accidents. It is first in definition because when defining accidents, we must always mention the substance, their subject; it is first in our knowledge as we must always know the subject of the things we are dealing with (nos. 1257–59). The ancient philosophers, in their quest for what being is, were in fact seeking substance (no. 1260). Therefore, we must investigate being and try to clear up what substance is. Living beings as well as their parts and the elements, and bodies composed of them, and the celestial bodies are all called substances. It is another question whether besides them there are other substances, as the Platonists thought (nos. 1263–64). Thomas mentions the Pythagoreans, who held that the limits of bodies (e.g., surfaces) were substances, and Plato, who considered the Ideas and the mathematical entities as substances. Next, Thomas mentions Speusippus,[62] Plato's first successor at the Academy, as distinguishing between first and secondary substances. Aristotle will examine these theories in Book XII (nos. 1265–69).

In lesson 2 (VII.3–4.1028b33–1029b12), Aristotle considers substance itself, determining first the order to follow in the treatment before dealing with substance itself and dividing it into its parts. The first sense of substance is that of quiddity, that is, the essence or nature of things. A second sense is that of a universal (the theory of Ideas as separate Forms). A third meaning is what makes things exist by themselves: in this sense, being and one are the substance of all things. In a fourth sense is the subject, that is, the particular substance is called substance. This can be the genus, the species, the specific differences, or common accidents.

The subject, however, is not essentially predicated of other things. What is here called "subject" is said to be the first substance in the *Categories* (no. 1273). The genus and species are the so-called second substance. But here "that which something was to be" (*id quod quid erat esse*) is treated. It is the formal principle of the genus, the species, and the individual substance (nos. 1274–75). The subject as a particular substance is divided into three: matter, form, and the compound, and Aristotle compares these three with one another. The form is substance in a higher degree than matter, it is prior, and is being

---

62. The context of no. 1266 makes it clear that "Leucippus" is most likely a scribal error. The same error occurs in Book XII, no. 2545. See Georges Ducoin, "Saint Thomas commentateur d'Aristote. Étude sur le commentaire thomiste du livre Λ des Métaphysiques d'Aristote," *Archives de Philosophie* 20 (1957): 78–117, 241–71, 392–445, at 84 for a list of corrections to the Marietti text based on a selection of manuscripts.

to a greater degree. Matter becomes being through the form. Form is also prior to the compound (which has matter in it). What he says about substance thus far puts its universal meaning forward: substance is that which is not said of a subject; but this sense is general and does not manifest the proper principles on which our knowledge of things depends (nos. 1276–80).

Aristotle says that the ancients argued that matter is substance more than other things: when we remove from physical bodies the passions, motion, generation, and corruption, which belong to the genus of quality, and the dimensions, which come in under quantity, the subject in which these are found is the substance, that is, matter. It would seem that matter alone is the substance (nos. 1281–83). But the ancients were mistaken in their reasoning, as they did not know the substantial form and did not distinguish it from matter. They did not really know matter: matter is not something, it is neither quantity nor a quality. It is the first subject, which underlies motions and changes. It differs from quantity, quality, and the other accidents (nos. 1284–86). Aristotle does not prove that matter is different from all forms by the substantial changes it can undergo, but by an argument from logic, a science that Thomas says is close to metaphysics.[63] There must be something of which all predicates can be said but which differs in being from the subject of which they are said and from each of the things that are predicated of it, namely, that the quiddity and essence of the latter is different.

Thomas adds a note: there is no question here of a univocal predication (as a genus is predicated of its species), but of a denominative predication, as for instance we predicate "white" of man. As we cannot say that man is whiteness, we cannot say either that matter is a man. Matter differs essentially from the substantial forms (nos. 1287–89). Just as Forms are outside the essence of matter, but in a way relate to it accidentally, negations of Forms, which are privations, also relate to matter accidentally. Aristotle adds this remark to reject the opinion of Plato, who did not distinguish between privation and matter. Next, he shows that matter alone cannot be the substance. Two things seem most proper to substance: first, that it is separable, for an accident is not separable from its substance, but the substance can be separated from an accident and, second, that it signifies this thing (*hoc aliquid*). These two qualifications do not belong to matter. Matter by itself cannot exist without the form, as it is only potential; it becomes this thing by a form. It is evident therefore that the compound (the species) out of matter and form is the substance rather than matter (nos. 1290–93). But as for now, we should concentrate on matter and

---

63. In his commentary on Book Z, Thomas stresses several times the affinity of metaphysics with logic.

form, as the substance is subsequent to matter and form, being composed of them, so that knowing the latter precedes knowing the substance as composed of them. A second reason is that the composite substance is accessible to the senses, while matter is only known up to a certain extent, as by itself it cannot be known, the form being the principle of knowledge. Matter is known in an analogous way (nos. 1294–96).

Aristotle recalls the division of substances into sensible and immaterial substances, and turns to the study of the quiddity of sensible things, because the latter are for us more manifest than the immaterial substances, which, as such, are more knowable. For us, things that lay open to the senses are more accessible (nos. 1299–1302). And we must proceed from what is better known to us. Thomas illustrates the text by some examples. An army obtains the victory by different individual fights. Accidents, motion, privation, etc., possess little or nothing of being, yet are better known to us, as they are open to the senses. We must proceed from their knowledge to that of the things that in themselves are perfectly knowable.

In lesson 3 (VII.4.1029b12–1030a19), the essence of sensible substances is studied with regard to what it is, and in lesson 17 (VII.17.1041a6–b33), insofar as it is a cause and principle. Aristotle first removes from the study of the essence whatever is said of it accidentally, and next the terms that are predicated by way of properties. He examines the "what it was to be being" from the way we attribute predicates to it. Thomas adds a note here: in the following chapters, Aristotle means by "being this" or "belonging to this," the "what it was to be." "Being musical" lies outside what you are essentially, namely a man, that is, a living being, a rational substance, etc. (nos. 1308–10). The proper passions of things that do not contain the definition of the subject pertain to the quiddity (nos. 1311–14). Which things have a quiddity (essence)? This question concerns also the things that have accidents. Quiddity is only proper to things that are something (no. 1323) and that belong to a species, of which there is a definition; it is composed of a genus and the specific differences (nos. 1327–28).

In lesson 4 (VII.4–5.1030a17–1031a14), Aristotle explains in which way the accidents can be defined (which is different, to be sure, from the way we determine the subject). Because "the what a thing is" (the *quod quid est*) is not said of accidents but of substances, we must explain how to define accidents, each time we ask what a particular accident is. Accidents signify the sort of things we are dealing with; they are beings in a limited sense. As being is said of all predicaments, but in different ways, and in the first place of substance; "that what a thing is" is said of the subject *tout court* but it is said in a qualified way of the accidents (no. 1331). A quality, for instance, does not signify being in an absolute sense, but tells us how a substance is (no. 1334). The "what a thing is" (whatness) is found primarily in substances, and secondarily, in an analogous way, in the accidents (nos. 1335–37). The so-called compound accidents (like "snub" in snub nose) cannot be defined separately from the thing they are attached to (nos. 1339–46). Aristotle concludes that there are only definitions of substances (nos. 1347–50). Accidents have being insofar as they are in a subject, and their quiddity depends on this subject (nos. 1352–53).

In lesson 5 (VII.6.1031a15–1032a11), Aristotle investigates how an essence is related to the thing of which it is the essence. Is it the same? A particular thing does not differ from its own substance; it has the same essence. But in those things that are said of it accidentally, the essence is not the same as the thing of which the essence is said. In the case of essential predication, the essence, and that of which it is the essence, must necessarily always be the same. If the essence of a thing were to differ from the thing itself, this would also be the case in all the things that have an essence. It leads to unacceptable conclusions (nos. 1358–66). If one separates the essences from the things themselves, as the Platonists do, things will not be known. If we can explain our knowledge of things in another way than by recourse to the Ideas, there is no reason to resort to the theory of Ideas (nos. 1367–71). Aristotle presents some more arguments to show that the essence of a thing and the thing itself are the same (nos. 1374–77). At the end of the lesson, Thomas notes, by way of a *Sciendum est autem* and in support of Aristotle's argument, that the quiddity of a thing is expressed in its definition. When a definition of a thing is given, its quiddity is also expressed. The quiddity is what is essential of a being, such as man, but it excludes the accidents (nos. 1378–79).

Lesson 6 (VII.7.1032a12–1033a23) presents Aristotle's arguments supporting the thesis that the Forms of becoming things are not generated by Forms outside our world of becoming. The cause of generation is either a proper cause (the intrinsic principle of motion—nature—or art as an extrinsic principle), or an accidental cause like chance or fortune (nos. 1380–82). In natural generation, things are generated from matter by an agent, and the particular things generated are called substances. Matter and form in the agent are only the principles of a composite substance (nos. 1383–86). All things that come to be have matter from which they come to be, for matter is in potency to forms. The form coincides with what the generation is ordained to (nos. 1387–93). There are processes of generation that are the result of art, power, mind, or chance. Thomas mentions that Aristotle seems to hold that some things can be generated both from seed and without seed, by the action of the sun (nos.

1393–1400). The more perfect a thing is, the greater the number of factors required for its generation. For things produced by art, the productive form exists in the mind of the agent. Health may be caused by a form, namely the medical science in the mind of the physician (no. 1406), or by other intermediate things by which health is brought about (no. 1410). As everything is generated from matter and by what is alike to itself, something must preexist, which becomes part of the thing generated, that is, the matter. But we use the term matter to signify both the matter out of which and in which things come to be, and also the privation, for example, a sick person becoming healthy (no. 1415).

In lesson 7 (VII.8.1033a24–1034a8), Aristotle explains that what is generated is the composite thing. The form is generated only accidentally, for it does not have being itself but exists in matter. The essence of a thing, which refers to the form, also is not produced in the strict sense of the term. Thomas adds a correction (*non tamen proprie dicitur*) here: the text says that a form comes to be in matter, but what comes to be is the composite, which is generated from matter according to a certain form (no. 1423). Everything that comes into being is divisible, as it is the concrete whole that comes to be. Matter is present in everything that is generated. Aristotle argues that when forms are not directly generated, recourse to the Ideas is no longer necessary (no. 1427). Moreover, what is generated is this particular thing (no. 1428). Thomas notes that those who fail to see that Forms do not come to be, face the difficulty of having to explain where Forms do come from (no. 1430). Separate Forms cannot be the cause of things as exemplary causes: whatever is generated receives its likeness from the thing generating it. Moreover, every Form that is generated is some singular thing (no. 1435). This statement is important as it indicates the principle of individuation, that is to say, matter as determined and prepared to receive the form. Individuation must not be ascribed to the form.[64]

In lesson 8 (VII.9.1034a9–b19), we learn about generation, by art and by nature, of composite beings as well as of accidental forms. Why do certain things only come about by art, while others, such as health, can also result from natural factors? The answer lies in the matter that in these cases has an aptitude to the form and can be moved by an intrinsic or extrinsic principle (nos. 1436–39). At this point, Thomas adds an extensive note (*Sciendum est autem*) on the theory of *inchoatio formae* or incipient formality, that is to say, the theory that "matter contains some active principle, which is the form pre-

---

64. Thomas's doctrine of the principle of individuation is that matter, as marked by quantity and determined by it at the moment of generation, is the disposing cause to which the generating power adapts the new form.

existing potentially in the matter and a kind of beginning of form" (1142a).[65] He admits that Aristotle's words in 1034a11 about matter as the principle of generation (ἡ ὕλη ἡ ἄρχουσα τῆς γενέσεως) can be wrongly interpreted.[66] Proponents (*quidam*) of this theory argue that without an active principle, generation would be violent. Thomas likens this theory to the one that claims that the beginnings of forms lie hidden, that is, that there is a latency of forms in matter.[67] But matter cannot have an intrinsic active principle. Such a principle would mean that something has the ability to effect change in itself, which only occurs in living beings, not in inanimate things. Hence the matter about which Aristotle writes should be understood as referring to living beings only. Thomas finds confirmation in a text where Averroes writes about Aristotle's equivocal use of the term *principle* (no. 1442).[68]

In the next section, Aristotle explains how we must understand the principle that everything that is generated is generated by something having a similar form. The principle does not apply to accidental generation, but to generation in its proper sense, such that the likeness of the form generated must preexist in the cause, either in the same mode of being or as a part of it (as is the case in medicine) or in a different way (as a house preexists in the mind of the builder) (nos. 1443–47).

In the case of artificial things, what is produced may preexist in part in the cause that produces it. In healing a disease by medicine, we have a non-univocal generation. The form of the generating force can be referred to the form in the effect in four ways: (1) it is totally in the generating cause (e.g., the form of a house); (2) when a part of the form generated is in the generating cause (e.g., restoring health by heat, which is only a part of health); (3) when only a part of this form is found virtually in the generating cause (e.g., health is only virtually present in some medicines); and (4) when the whole form is virtually present (nos. 1448–49), as a builder possesses the form of a house only virtually, and as the seed in natural generation does not actually possess the soul of the animal to be born. The seed is not univocal with the

---

65. Thomas consistently rejects the theory of *inchoatio formae*; see *In II Sent.*, d. 18, q. 1, a. 2; *In II Phys.*, l. 13, no. 58; *ST* III, q. 32, a. 4. In the *Scriptum*, while arguing that matter assists in generation, not by actively contributing to the process, but by reason of its aptness to receive forms, he concedes that this aptness may be called *appetitus materiae* or *inchoatio formae*, but it nevertheless is a purely passive potency.

66. Ross (*Aristotle's "Metaphysics,"* 190) also admits that the "phrase might seem peculiar, in view of the passivity commonly ascribed to matter by Aristotle. The explanation is that it is only prime matter that is entirely passive; other matter has some quality of its own and can thus initiate movement."

67. Thomas refers to his contemporaries or early predecessors. For an identification of these, see the important contribution by Marta Borgo, "Les raisons séminales entre théologie et philosophie: d'Alexandre de Halès à Thomas d'Aquin," *Documenti e Studi sulla Tradizione Filosofica Medievale* 23 (2012): 143–72.

68. Averroes, *In libros Physicorum Aristoteles* II, 1, in *Aristotelis Opera cum Averrois Commentariis*, vol. IV, 48E–F.

living being to be born, but this is the being from which the seed comes. There is also generation by chance (e.g., animals born from decaying material) when their matter is moved by itself (nos. 1450–54). Some argue that in this case the form of these things comes from subsistent Forms, as what is accidental cannot give a form. But Aristotle argues that in the active power of the seed the animal is virtually present, although this is accidental. In things generated from decaying material, there is a principle at work similar to the active power of the seed (nos. 1455–57). Finally, we are reminded by Aristotle that the Form as such does not come to be, but the composite. A substance is always generated from a substance (nos. 1458–59).

In lesson 9 (VII.10.1034b20–1035b3), the parts of which the essence is composed are examined as well as the relation of these parts to the whole. A definition expresses each of the parts of the things it defines. But the parts of a circle are its segments, which are not mentioned in its definition; and in the definition of man no integral parts are signified. A second difficulty arises from the question of the priority of the parts. But in some ways the whole seems to be prior, as a man is to his finger. Averroes advanced the view that the form of the whole is the same as that of the formal parts of a thing, such that, for instance, humanity would be the same as the soul (nos. 1463–67).[69] But this is wrong, for sensible matter is part of the essence of natural substances. There cannot be a species of natural bodies without sensible matter. The form of the whole differs from that of a part, as the whole itself also differs from its parts. The quiddity of a species is composed of matter and form, but not of this individual matter and form, as Avicenna says.[70] This provides three arguments against the theory of Ideas: (1) the essence of a thing does not exist separately from the things of which it is the essence; (2) forms existing apart are not the causes of generation; and (3) the concept of a species includes sensible matter as common to material things. We should be aware that the word "part" is used in several senses. It can be a quantitative part, but the parts of substance are matter and form. This matter is individual matter, but matter as part of a species is common matter in a universal sense (nos. 1468–73). The parts into which a thing is dissolved are not always parts of its substance, but the whole is constituted of these parts as of their matter. All things that signify something composed of matter and form are dissolved into material parts, which are the principles of these things (nos. 1474–80).

Lesson 10 (VII.10.1035b3–1036a25) addresses the following question: are

---

69. Averroes, *Commentarium Magnum in Aristotelis Metaphysicorum XIII* 177C.

70. Avicenna, *Liber de Philosophia prima sive Scientia divina V–X*, ed. S. Van Riet (Louvain: Peeters, 1980), tr. V, c. 5, p. 275.

the parts prior to the whole? The parts that together make up our concept of a thing must be prior to the thing of which they are the parts. This is shown by an example: to define properly a part of any animal, one can only define it by its proper operation, that is, one must have recourse to the soul. The *formal* parts are prior to the composite, while the body and its parts are subsequent to the form, which is the soul (nos. 1482–87). But they are not prior in the sense that they can exist independently of the concrete whole. Matter is part of the essence of physical things, but it is unknowable in itself and is known only by means of the form. Sensible matter refers to such things as bronze and wood, and the elements, whereas intelligible matter refers to what exists in sensible things but not *as* sensible things like the objects of mathematics. Now, if things are the same as their form, the parts of these things will be subsequent to the parts of their form as conceived in thought and in the definition. But if one says that the soul differs from the animal of which it is the soul, we must at the same time say that parts are prior to the whole and are not prior, because we must distinguish between common matter (matter as conceived in the species) and individual matter (nos. 1488–1500).

The question relating the parts of a species, as distinguished from those of the individual thing, is examined in lesson 11 (VII.11.1036a26–1037b7). A circle can exist in different materials, so that it is obvious that the material is not part of its essence. But other things, for example, man, always come to be in the same material they exist of, so that we wonder whether these parts belong to the definition of man (nos. 1501–6). With regard to mathematical figures, some Platonists went so far as to say that the species are numbers. But this creates difficulties: specifically different things may share in the same number, such as "three." Aristotle also objects that if neither sensible things nor lines are parts of the species, no sensible matter is. But the Platonists consider matter as consisting of the number two. If the number one would be the only species, there would be only one species of all things (nos. 1507–15). He points out that although we can define a circle without bringing in the material out of which it is made, an animal cannot be defined without stating that it is a principle of motion and activities, for which bodily parts are necessary (nos. 1516–19). The soul is the form of the animal, the body its matter, both in a universal way but also in particular beings like Socrates.

A next question is whether besides the substance of material and sensible things there exist some substances outside these sensible things, namely their Forms or Ideas. The question typically belongs to first philosophy, which deals with the first and immaterial substances, and with sensible substances only insofar as they are substances and beings (nos. 1523–28). As the individual is individualized by its matter, each thing is placed in its species by its form. Thus the definition of the species is taken from the form and those parts are placed in the definition in which the form is first and mainly found. The substance is the form that is in matter, and form (species) and matter (individuality) together are called the whole substance. In the immaterial substances, the essence of each of them is the same as the thing of which it is the essence. Primary substance here means the thing that does not exist in something else. Thomas notes (no. 1535) that Aristotle now excludes two kinds of things from the previously stated identity of each thing and its essence: accidental things and material substances. If an individual thing has matter as part of its species, it also has individual matter, which, however, does not belong to its essence.

In lesson 12 (VII.12.1037b8–1038a35), Aristotle examines how a thing composed of parts can be one. It is obvious that one thing cannot come forth from many specific differences, although it consists of a genus and a specific difference (nos. 1537–38). A genus does not exist separately from the things which it contains, namely, the species. It can be predicated of its species, and so somehow it signifies the whole thing. The so-called differences (which determine the species of a genus) are added as already contained implicitly in the genus. Sometimes one of these differences is subdivided (e.g., dividing feet into winged and wingless) but in these divisions we must come to an ultimate one, and this will be the specific form and the substance (no. 1559). The genus is not something apart from its differences, and a thing is defined by an ultimate specific difference. But in the substance there is no order of differences or parts, because it is complete such as it is. If a definition has several parts, it does not mean a multiplicity of essential parts (no. 1564).

In lesson 13 (VII.13.1038b1–1039a23), we read that universals cannot be substances, as they are predicated of many things. Thomas adds a note on the different meanings of the term *universal*. The term can be taken to mean the nature of things (species, genus), and in this sense it can signify the substance of the things of which it is predicated quidditatively; and it can signify the nature of things in a universal way as a one-in-many (no. 1570). A substance is exclusively proper to a thing and does not belong to something else. It is not predicated of a subject, while a universal is always predicated of some subject. From the point of view of first philosophy, the substance is its subject (no. 1576). Singular things, which are particulars, cannot be composed of universals when these are conceived as existing apart from individual things. If universals were substances, there would be in Socrates both the substance "man" and the substance "animal." This theory is also refuted by the argument of "the third man," namely that which stands above the individual and the species "man." Thomas presents a detailed commentary on these arguments of Aristotle, which shows the admirable grasp he had of the problems involved.

Lesson 14 (VII.14.1039a24–b19) deals with the rejection of universals as separate substances, in the sense of existing apart from sensible things. "Animal" as present in man and as present in a horse are the same in intelligible contents, but for the Platonists "animal" as one individual and subsistent Idea is said of a man and of a horse (no. 1593) and is present in them as a distinct reality. But if so, it will be incapable of existing in many species. When a genus is held to be one substance, it will have contrary properties, such as two-footed and many-footed (no. 1597). "Animal" must be assumed to be one in all species of animals. Aristotle ends his long and detailed exposition by concluding that there are no Ideas of the species and genera of sensible things (no. 1605).

In lesson 15 (VII.15.1039b20–1040b4), three arguments are given for why Ideas cannot be defined. The essence or intelligible structure of things does not have individual matter in it and is not capable of being corrupted. Of singular substances there is no definition. An Idea, however, is also a singular thing, so that it is impossible to define (nos. 1607–12). To define a singular thing we need several words that are also applicable to other things, so that we come to know its class. If only one word is used, the thing still remains unknown. For this reason, Ideas will lack definitions (nos. 1613–18). It is impossible to define singular, eternal things. The descriptions that some authors gave, for example, of celestial bodies such as the sun, are defective and do not express the essentials of them (nos. 1627–30).

In lesson 16 (VII.16.1040b5–1041a5), we return to the study of sensible things. It is shown that unity and being are not substances. The parts of which a substance is composed are not actually existing things, but potential beings, as none of them are separate, although they may be close to being actual (nos. 1632–34). As certain parts of some souls may be close to actuality, these souls can be divided while the animal is alive and the parts can go on living. Unity and being are interchangeable; they are not the substance of a thing but are predicated of it. They are closest to the substance, signifying it as it is, but because they are common attributes, they themselves are not substances (nos. 1635–41). If unity (the One) would exist by itself, it would no longer be said of other things. It also seems impossible that a form exists by itself and at the same time in many other things, in particular as an incorruptible form by itself in corruptible things. In Book Z, Aristotle has not yet shown that there are separate substances apart from our sensible world, but, Thomas says (no. 1646), he will do so in Book XII. It has become evident that no universal predicates are substances (nos. 1642–57).

Lesson 17 addresses the role of nature and substance as principles, which is explained in the last chapter of Book Z (VII.17.1041a6–b33). After having rejected the Platonist view that the universals (separate forms) are substances, Aristotle now shows that substance in the sense of the essence really exists in concrete things. From the study of these sensible things it will be possible to understand also the substances separate from this sensible world. Substance in the sense of essence is a principle, for things exist because of it (no. 1649). This brings us to the question of the "why" (*propter quid*) of things. This question, that is, the question "Is it a fact that a thing is such?" presupposes the thing's existence as evident. The question does not, therefore, ask about why a thing is itself but about why a thing is something else (no. 1654). When asking for the why of something, like thunder, we may ask for the cause taken as form in the matter (*causa, quae est forma in materia*); whereas, in other cases, our question can concern the (efficient or final) cause of the form in the matter (*causa ipsius formae in materia*). The former question asks about the quiddity of a thing and is the concern of the logician. The latter is the concern of the philosopher as it regards the truth of the matter (*secundum rei veritatem*) (nos. 1659–60). Now the "why" sometimes concerns the form, but sometimes the agent or the goals of a thing (no. 1667). Substances composed of form and matter can be known, but simple substances without matter will be examined in Book XII. Thomas explains that we come to an understanding of these separate substances from the sensible substances (no. 1671). With regard to the sensible substances, Aristotle argues that in every composite, which is one, there is something in addition to its parts. This "something" appears as the cause of the being of the elements of the composite. It is the substance, or in case the composites are not substances (e.g., syllables and artificial things) it is a formal principle (nos. 1675–80).[71]

Book VIII (H)

As the continuation of Book Z, Book H deals with the principles of sensible substances, that is, form and matter as individually determined. In lesson 1 (VIII.1.1042a3–b8), Aristotle explains what the matter of sensible substances is. Thomas recalls that while, in the previous book, Aristotle spoke about matter, form, and essence from the viewpoint of dialectics (*modo logico*), he now discusses the sensible substances in their own principles and as substances (no. 1681). As has been shown before, first philosophy is mainly

---

71. For a more extensive analysis, see Gabriele Galluzzo, "Aquinas's Interpretation of Aristotle's Metaphysics, Book Z," *Recherches de théologie et philosophie médiévale* 74 (2007): 427–81, as well as his *The Medieval Reception of Book Zeta of Aristotle's "Metaphysics,"* 1:235–324.

concerned with substance (no. 1682). The existence of sensible substances is admitted by all philosophers. But some of them make the forms and the objects of mathematics substances, which exist on their own (no. 1683). In line with this, the universals and the genus are seen as substances. But the other view holds that substance is the quiddity of any natural substance (no. 1684). As the essence is substance and is expressed in the definition, it was determined in Book Z which parts of the definition are parts of the thing, and that neither the universal nor the genus is substance (no. 1685).

Here, Aristotle first shows that matter is a principle of sensible things. It is called substance, not that it has actual existence, but because it is something capable of being actualized and becoming this particular thing. Form is called substance because it actualizes matter, and the thing composed of both is capable of existing by itself and is the subject of generation and corruption. Form and matter are generated and exist because of something else. A form is separable in thought (no. 1687). In all changes taking place in sensible substances, matter is the subject common to the changing substance and the new generated being. In every change there is a subject common to the termini of the change. In generation and corruption this common subject is primary matter, which has no form of its own. If it were a bodily thing by itself, there would not be real generation and corruption, but alteration. Generation helps us to determine the nature of primary matter (no. 1689). This primary matter, undetermined in itself, is lacking in the celestial bodies, in which there is change of place and alteration, but no generation and corruption (no. 1690).

In lesson 2 (VIII.2.1042b9–1043a28), Aristotle determines the formal principle of sensible things. Democritus thought that the material principle of all material things is of the same nature, and the only differences between these beings are position, shape, and arrangement (no. 1692). But there are many other differences, such as the way the parts and the qualities of the parts are combined (no. 1693). These differences constitute the being of things. This becomes evident when we reduce them to some classes (no. 1694). These differences signify the form (the quiddity) of their subject. So, for instance, "rational" signifies something having an intellectual nature (no. 1697).

The nature of forms is further determined in lesson 3 (VIII.3.1043a29–1044a14). Aristotle does so by paying special attention to Plato's theory of separate Forms, which are realities besides matter and sensible things and are neither generated nor corrupted (no. 1704). Does a term like *house* signify only its form as a shelter or also the material out of which it has been made? According to the Platonists, the first and real meaning of these universal terms is that of the form alone. When applied to the concrete whole, they become analogous terms (nos. 1706–7). The form alone of sensible substances and the essence of the latter are not the same, as the essence also comprises intelligible matter.[72] But of things that are only form, the forms are identical with their essences, for they have no individuating matter. The specific names of things pertaining to our sensible world signify their form and intelligible matter, but these things are not the same as their essence (nos. 1708–11).

Aristotle shows that forms themselves are not produced, but come to be in particular things (no. 1716). The forms of corruptible things, when incapable of existing apart from their matter, are not separate (no. 1718).[73] In definitions of sensible or intellectual things, a part that is as a form is joined to a part that is as matter. This means that, if the species of things were forms only, they could not be defined. After having defined what is true of forms in relation to the Ideas, Aristotle considers their relation to numbers. Concrete numbers, applied to things, cannot be divided to infinity, although continuous quantity can. A definition cannot be divided, similar to when something is added to a number, the number is no longer the same. If, however, a small part is added to (or subtracted from) the essence, there results another definition (nos. 1721–25). As a number consists of units, a definition signifies a thing as a number, but the substance signified by it is essentially one thing (nos. 1726–28).

In lesson 4 (VIII.4–5.1044a15–1045a7), Aristotle determines how matter is present in sensible things and what it is. As things come to be from matter, a first question is whether there is one kind of matter for all things or several kinds. Things seem to have some proper matter, but this impression "perhaps" comes from some prior material. Thomas explains the *perhaps* (ἴσως or *forsan*) in Aristotle's text at 1044a20 in terms of leaving the question open for incorruptible things, which may have a different matter (no. 1729).[74] We nevertheless speak of matter in a secondary sense, as the proper matter of the different things that is different each time. As ultimately all bodies are subject to generation and corruption, they come from one first matter. We must assign all the causes, including the proximate causes, of material things. The knowledge of the first causes is general and incomplete. The material cause of man is not the elements (which are general to all corruptible things), but flesh (nos. 1736–38).

If the celestial bodies have matter, it is not the matter of corruptible things, but the potentiality to motion and to different places (nos. 1739–42).

---

72. To be sure, the individualized matter is not the essence of material things.

73. Thomas probably has in mind the human soul, which is capable of existing when separated from the body.

74. For a similar use of ἴσως or *forsan* see Book VII, lesson 16, no. 1646.

Accidents do not have matter out of which they come to be, but the substance, which they determine, functions as their matter because it receives the accidents, although it exists independently from them. Everything which comes to be, comes from matter and is composed of form and matter. Aristotle also discusses the way we must understand the matter from which something comes into being. For instance, a corpse comes from a living body but the living body is not its matter; rather, it is the components out of which the living body consisted.

Lesson 5 (VIII.6.1045a7–b23) discusses the question of what makes a definition and a thing one and of the union of matter and form. A pile of loose parts is not one thing. One may ask: what makes a thing that has several parts one? Why does man not consist of two connected forms, namely "animal" and "two-footed"? When we hold that in definitions one part is as matter and the other as form, the problem is easily solved (nos. 1756–59). Matter is of two kinds, sensible and intelligible. Mathematics abstracts from sensible matter. The objects of mathematics consist of the continuum but abstract from sensible qualities, yet they have intelligible matter. Substances that do not have this intelligible matter are only forms, and these forms give them their unity (nos. 1760–62). The predicaments are each their own being (no. 1763). What is entirely separated from matter is but its own essence and is one thing. It has no matter that awaits a determination by a form. The Platonists thought that individual things, such as "this man," participate in the form "man" and "man" in its turn in "animal," etc. But the cause of man's unity was not clear to them. Some suggested that there is a certain togetherness or cohesion of "substances." But the theory that there is a mean uniting the forms is false. What is potential becomes actualized and there is no need of a bond (nos. 1764–67).

Book IX (Θ)

The relation of act and potency is further examined in Book Θ. While in the previous books Aristotle mainly dealt with substance, the categories, sensible and intelligible matter, he now turns to the study of act and potency.

Lesson 1 (IX.1.1045b27–1046a35) recalls that all forms of being refer to substance. In the definition their proper subject, substance, is enclosed. But besides the division into the categories, being is also divided into actual and potential being (nos. 1768–69). Aristotle does not speak here of potency insofar as it is found in mobile beings, but as found in being in general, first in sensible things, next in intelligible things (nos. 1770–72). In the first four lessons, potency and incapacity are examined; in lessons 5 and 6, actuality is treated; and in lesson 7, the relation of potency and actuality is considered. He leaves aside potency as the active agent by which things are moved and potency in the sense of a disposition by which a thing cannot undergo a change for the worse, that is, corruption. These two potencies relate to potency in the sense of active power (nos. 1773–79). Aristotle observes that in our language the expression "capable of" often includes the sense of being able to do something well. Having an active power means that there is also something else that can be acted upon (nos. 1780–81). If active and passive potencies are understood in reference to the subject, in which they are present, they are different. A patient that receives the influence of an active agent has some principle in itself by which it is capable of undergoing this action, which is called passive potency. And this is not present in the principle of action, except in an accidental way. By incapacity we mean the privation of the potency to undergo a particular action by an agent. There are as many senses of incapacity as there are of potency (nos. 1782–85).

In lesson 2 (IX.2.1046a36–b28), we learn about the difference in potencies according to the difference of their subjects. Those found in rational souls differ specifically from those found in nonrational souls. Irrational potencies cannot lead to contrary determinations, but the conception of a thing in the mind can lead to the contrary of what has been conceived, such as health and sickness, eyesight and blindness. First we know the existing thing, next its privation. But the same science deals with both (nos. 1787–91). Natural things do not produce contrary effects, but the person who acts by science may conceive opposites. A rational power can produce contrary effects (no. 1792).

In lesson 3 (IX.3–4.1046b29–1047b30), both the view that a thing only has potency when it is acting and the opinion that everything is possible are rejected. According to the former view, no one has a capacity or an art except when actually exercising it. But Aristotle objects to this. If one did not have it before, one would not have it later. Moreover, if he had at one moment an art, he must still have it later unless he would lose it, for example, by forgetfulness (nos. 1796–97). Another argument against this view refers to such qualities as hot and cold, bitter and sweet. It would be nonsense to say that these would only be what they are when being sensed, which was the view of Protagoras, who said that all such properties exist only when being apprehended by the senses. And we would have the sense faculties only when we are actually sensing (nos. 1798–1801). If one understands potency and faculty in this way, one does away with generation and change: in this view a man who stands will always stand. The conclusion is that potency and actuality are distinct. Those who remove potency do away with generation (nos. 1802–3). Aristotle says that the possible is that from which nothing impossible follows when it is assumed to be actualized (no. 1804). Actuality signifies what is fulfilled (ἐντελέχεια) and perfect. The word "actuality" was first applied to motion, as this is best known to us, and from motion to other things. Being moved means to be in act and actualized (no. 1805).

Aristotle next refutes the opinion of those who say that everything is possible. In fact, however, only those things are possible (even if they will never exist) from which nothing impossible follows when they would come into existence (nos. 1807–8). Thomas notes that "possible" is also used for things that exist necessarily, which are evidently possible, while the common meaning of the word is to be capable of being and of not being (no. 1812). When something is possible, nothing impossible follows when it exists (no. 1813). And Thomas adds a further note: if the consequent is impossible, the antecedent also is, but the opposite is not true because we can draw a conclusion from an impossible antecedent. An example makes clear what is meant: if a man is a donkey, he is an animal.

Lesson 4 (IX.5.1047b31–1048a24) deals with the question of the priority of act and potency. Some potencies are in us by nature, while others are acquired, as for instance becoming a harpist. We must determine the different ways of being capable of something, as some of them are irrational, such as the power of growth, and others rational. The irrational potencies are acted upon when an active power comes into contact with them; for instance, wood burns when in contact with fire. The rational powers that are capable of producing different effects do not necessarily actualize passive potencies (nos. 1815–19). They must be determined to bring about a particular effect; this is done by appetite or choice. A rational power acts when it desires an object it is capable of (no. 1820).

Lesson 5 (IX.6.1048a25–b36) deals with the notion of *act* (actuality) by explaining and explains the different senses of the term and what it means when something is in potency to an act. Act means that a thing is, but act is not not-being in potency. "Apollo" is potentially in a piece of wood, but this wood actually becomes Apollo when it has been carved. Thomas notes that Aristotle shows by examples what act is, and that we should not look for a definition (nos. 1824–26). The term *act* is used in different senses: it means the determination of a potency, for example, an operation. Things are in act in different ways. As sight is in the eye, the substance (that is the form) is said to be in matter (nos. 1828–29). Certain things are only actual when they are actually seen, but potential when they are capable of being seen. The infinite, such as the infinite divisibility of a line, is at the same time in act and in potency (no. 1831).

In lesson 6 (IX.7.1048b37–1049b3), Aristotle explains what it means that a thing is in potency. To be healed, one must have a definite disposition to be so and there must be nothing that obstructs it: nature or art reduce this disposition to actual health (nos. 1833–34). What applies to healing also applies to other activities, produced by other arts. Certain things require to be brought into a good disposition before they can be reduced to act (nos. 1836–38). Composite things receive their names from matter. What is produced is not called a "that" but an ἐκείνινος, a "that there," to indicate the material from which it comes to be. Wood, earth, etc., are "those things there" from which objects come to be; but if there is a matter that does not refer to particular objects made out of it, it is first matter. This is not a universal but something subsistent (nos. 1839–42). Accidents have the substance as their subject, but in all material things that have a substantial form, matter is the ultimate subject. And this material thing may conveniently be called "that there" (no. 1843).

The question of priority with regard to act and potency is debated in lesson 7 (IX.8.1049b4–1050a3). As has been established in Book Δ (V), the term *prior* is used in different senses. *Potency* has been defined as a principle of motion in a universal way. Act is prior to all these forms of potency. It is prior in intelligibility, in substance, and—in a sense—in time. This is shown by the fact that potency can only be defined by an act: for instance, a builder is one who can build. The knowledge of the act is prior to that of potency (nos. 1844–46). But in individual things the potential is prior in time to act, as seed is prior to grain. But prior to things that were potential beings, there were agents that brought them to actuality. What is potential must always be brought to act by agents in act. There is always some first agent that moves the potential. Aristotle recalls that it has been shown in Book Z (VII) that everything that comes to be comes from something (matter) and some agent (nos. 1847–49). With regard to our operative potencies, it is also clear that, in a way, act is prior; for instance, to become a builder one must begin to build something. A sophistical contrary objection is that one who practices an art already has it. The answer is that whatever is being moved has already partly been moved. Who learns a science, must already have it, although imperfectly (no. 1855).

In lesson 8 (IX.8.1050a4–b6), the priority of act to potency with regard to substances is further explained. To be prior with regard to substance is to be more perfect; "perfect" is related to the form and to the end that has been reached. Act is not only prior to potency in intelligibility and in time, but also with respect to form and substance: the end of the process of generation is the perfection of the form. A second proof of the priority of the act is that in the process of becoming and in activity, the end is the act. Act is the goal of potency: we have the power of sight in order to see, and not the reverse. Matter is in potency until it receives its form. If the perfection of things does not consist in being actualized, there would be no difference between dumb and learned. Actualization and activity are the goal of potencies but, in the case of operative potencies, this goal lies in the thing produced. In cases where nothing is produced, the operation itself is an act, such as seeing. Thomas comments on an aside in the text on happiness (1050b1): happiness consists in the activity of the person who is happy, and is not something external; it consists in understanding and willing (nos. 1856–66).

In lesson 9 (IX.8.1050b6–1051a3), Aristotle shows that also in incorruptible beings act is prior. As such, these beings are not in potency, whereas corruptible beings are. What is capable of being, may be or may not be. This potency is a potency to opposites. Therefore, what has this potency is corruptible (nos. 1867–70). Hence incorruptible things do not have this potency; but they may have a limited potency for change of place or qualities. Now, nothing necessary is potential: necessary things exist always. If there is eternal motion, that motion is only potential with regard to place (nos. 1871–74). The things that move eternally are always active. There is no danger that someday the motion of the heaven will cease: incorruptible things do not tire in their activity. For corruptible things it is not natural always to undergo motion. Thomas adds the following remark: what Aristotle says here about the eternity of the heavenly bodies does not encroach on God's power, as the being and movement of the heavenly bodies depend on his will (nos. 1875–79). Bodies such as fire and earth resemble the heavenly bodies as they are always acting, but their potencies are to opposite terms. In the last part of the lesson, Aristotle rejects Plato's view of science and motion as separate Forms because these would be merely potential whereas acting and thinking, being acts, are of higher rank (*potior*) (nos. 1880–82).

In lesson 10 (IX.9.1051a4–33), act and potency are compared from the point of view of good and evil. A thing can be in potency to contrary determinations, but being good in act is just good. What is absolutely evil is worse than what is evil in a qualified sense. A potency for evil is not yet evil and actual evil is worse than this potency. Evil accompanies potency, but it is further removed from perfection. There is no evil in eternal things, but Thomas adds that they can be deprived with regard to place or similar accidents (nos. 1883–87). In the following section, we read that in geometry the truth is discovered by drawing figures and by their division. Those divisions exist potentially, and the truth is not immediately evident. By means of the example of the angles of a triangle and the angles in a semi-circle, Aristotle shows that certain truths about lines and angles become evident when brought from potency to act. A potency is known when it is actualized (nos. 1888–94).

In lesson 11 (IX.10.1051a34–1052a11), truth and falsity are examined in relation to act and potency. True and false are properly said of what actually is or is not. He who thinks that two things are separated when they actually are, has the truth; he who thinks that things are combined that are actually separated is in error. When you are white and we think so, our judgment is true. Thomas adds an explanation: when the intellect combines two things, such as a subject and a predicate, it has the truth when these are really combined (e.g., Socrates is a man). For things that cannot be otherwise, statements can always remain true, while other sentences (e.g., Socrates is sitting) can be true and become false when he (Socrates) gets up (nos. 1895–1900). The truth of simple things is reached when the intellect apprehends and signifies it in words. Not apprehending it is not an error. As a sense power is always true with regard to its proper object, the intellect is true with regard to the quiddity of things, its proper object (nos. 1901–7). One is deceived about a quiddity when one commits an error in combining or separating the components of a composite substance, for example, saying that a donkey is a rational being, and also when the definition we give consists of incompatible parts. Error about the being of simple substances can only result from a mistaken combination or separation. Truth always concerns actuality, namely, how things are. Simple substances are beings in act, that is, forms existing by themselves that are neither generated nor corrupted. There is no error or falsity in them, although we may be deceived about them accidentally (nos. 1908–10). The truth about them is to consider them as they are. Ignorance about them is not like blindness, as we do have the power to come to know them. Thomas notes that, according to Aristotle, the human intellect can acquire understanding of simple substances. About immobile things there is no error in regard to generation and corruption, as there may be about contingent beings, for they exist always (nos. 1911–19).

Book X (I)

Book X is dedicated to the study of the one (τὸ ἕν, *unum*) and of its opposites. A close analysis of it presents many intricate problems, in particular with regard to Aristotle's theory of the principles, of the opposites and contraries and evokes the issue of his adherence to some of Plato's later theories. The commentary of Aquinas is not a historical study, but an attempt to explain the doctrinal contents of what Aristotle wrote in this book, especially about oneness and what accompanies it. [75]

75. The important place that Aristotle assigned to the One and its opposites must be explained by its

Lesson 1 (X.1.1052a15–b19) opens with a remark aimed to show the coherence of the different books of the *Metaphysics*. Aristotle makes an inquiry into the one because he has already established in Book IV that metaphysics has as its subject being and the one that is convertible with being (no. 1920). Aristotle points out that the term *one* is used in different senses, but its primary meaning is "essentially one," the continuum, and second, "continuous by nature," that is, what has a form that makes it continuous by nature. This form can be a uniform whole or something which is not uniform.

In lesson 2 (X.1.1052b19–1053b8), which discusses the second part of X.1, Aristotle mentions a central property of the one, namely that it is a measure. The one as a measure is found foremost in quantity, from where it is transferred to other predicaments. Its essential characteristic is being indivisible (to which nothing can be added or from which nothing is subtracted), which makes it a measure that allows us to know a quantity. Qualities like heavy and light are in a way subject to measure when compared to something else, for example, earth is heavier than water (nos. 1937–42). From its meaning as a number, the one as a measure is transferred to length and size, where for instance the foot is used. A smallest thing is taken as the measure, and allows us to know the different quantities. With regard to the rapidity of motions, a simple (but the fastest) motion is taken as their measure (e.g., the daily motion of the first heaven). In sounds, the measure is the difference between two half tones. All measures are something that is one (nos. 1943–50). It is not strictly necessary that a measure is numerically one.

To measure lengths we use several measures, which in themselves need not be indivisible (such as the foot), except in relation to the thing measured. Aristotle adds a second property: a measure must be of the same kind as the thing measured, a length of length, etc. (nos. 1951–54). "One" as the measure of numbers is not itself a number; but, numbers being a plurality of units, it is better to say that the one is the measure of units. Next, Aristotle explains that "measure" is also used in the case of intellectual knowledge insofar as it measures what is intellectually cognoscible, as sense perception measures what is perceptible by the senses. But this is a rather figurative use of the term *measure*. What we know is in a sense the measure by which we can see whether we really know things. Thomas adds an important note: if there is a science that is the cause of things, it is the measure of the beings produced by it. In this

---

prominence in the speculations of his predecessors, who spoke of the One as a principle, an ἀρχή, as well as by his own initial reception of several of Plato's main theories. On this subject, see Elders, *Aristotle's Theory of the One: A Commentary on Book X of the "Metaphysics"* (Assen: Van Gorcum, 1961) as well as *"Metaphysics" Book Iota*, trans. Laura M. Castelli (Oxford: Clarendon Press, 2018).

way, divine science is the measure of all things. Protagoras, on the other hand, said that man is the measure of things, which are what they are because we perceive them in this way (nos. 1955–60).

In lesson 3 (X.2.1053b9–1054a19), Aristotle enquires whether the one constitutes the very substance of things. After having determined how the one relates to quantity and to other categories, he now examines its relationship with substance. Is the one a substance; does it exist by itself, as the Pythagoreans and the Platonists taught? According to Empedocles, one of the two agent principles besides the four elements is love, which he identified with the one. Diogenes said that air is the one and the principle of things (nos. 1961–62). But the one cannot be a substance because no universal, being common to many, is. As a universal it is not a cause, as a cause is not predicated of its effects. No genera are substances and the one is not the very nature of what is said to be one. Aristotle shows that in the predicament of quality, there is each time an underlying quality (e.g., white in the class of colors), which is the subject of the one. Likewise in the class of tunes, number is not their substance, but tone. The same applies to all things (nos. 1963–73).

Next he shows that the one and being signify the same thing, which follows from the fact that the one is predicated of all the categories, and also of substance. "One" just adds to being that it is not divided. When we call a thing one we do not express a different nature, but just state its unity. Beings are called one: when they are dissolved, they lose this unity. Thomas raises a difficulty (*videtur autem*): just before Aristotle said that oneness is not the substance of things, but here he seems to say the contrary (no. 1978). The answer is given by the fact that substance has a dual sense, namely, of first and of second substance (the universal essence). The one does not signify the individual subsistent thing, but the unity of the species (nos. 1974–80). Thomas also mentions the view of Avicenna, who said that oneness is simply a nature added to things, as a number is added to things. In reality, however, oneness is interchangeable with the being of each of the categories, as the term being also signifies each of the ten categories (nos. 1981–82).

In lesson 4 (X.3.1054a20–1055a2), Aristotle examines the different ways in which "one" and "many" are opposed. First, the concomitant attributes of both terms are mentioned. The one is opposed to the many as the indivisible is to the divisible. They are not opposed as contradictory terms but as contraries (and also not as relative terms, for both are absolutes). One of the contraries is a privation. Thomas adds (no. 1990) that if "one" is a privation of plurality, it is no longer first, as composites are known first. Even if the one is first in nature, we come to know it by the privation of division (no. 1991). If the one is considered as a certain thing by itself, it is opposed to plurality; as such it is prior, but from the viewpoint of division, multitude comes first (nos. 1992–97). We first form the concept of being, then of division, and next of oneness and after that of multitude, Thomas says (no. 1998). Some attributes, such as sameness, likeness, and equality, follow from unity. "The same" can be used in different ways, such as numerically the same and the same in the intelligible structure (e.g., the genus or the species).

The different ways of "being like" are mentioned. Thomas observes that the sentence where it says that when there is oneness of substance we also have oneness in quantity and quality, must be understood in such a way that in order to have likeness we must have diversity of substances. Things are also said to be like when they both have a certain quality, although in different degrees (nos. 1999–2012). The notion that something is either the same or other in relation to everything else is true for beings but not for nonbeings. Diversity is not said of the latter. Thomas notes that to the objection that "sameness" should only be used for substances, we can answer that substance is the root of the other genera and that what we say of the substance also applies to the other predicaments (no. 2016). Finally, Aristotle shows the difference between "diverse" and "different." Things that are diverse are so in themselves, while they are different in particular respects. Those things are diverse that are not generated from each other (nos. 2017–22).

In lessons 5–10, Aristotle examines contrariety. In lesson 5 (X.4.1055a3–33), he shows that contrariety is the greatest difference between things. Between beings that differ in genus there is no greatest difference, as there is in specifically different things where contraries constitute the greatest difference, as they go to the extreme end and there is nothing beyond them. One thing cannot have many contraries, because contrariety is the greatest difference and there cannot be more than two extremes, and there is nothing beyond the extremes. Aristotle mentions four definitions of contrariety by other philosophers: (1) contraries are things that differ most; (2) contraries are things that differ most in the same genus; (3) contraries are attributes that have the greatest difference in the same subject; and (4) contraries are attributes that have the greatest difference in the same art or faculty (nos. 2023–35).

In lesson 6 (X.4.1055a33–b29), contrariety is compared to possession and privation. A perfect privation requires some positive reality (*natura*) which is furthest removed from possessing its opposite. The other contraries refer in different ways to possession and privation (nos. 2037–39) because they are all derived from this "first contrariety." Aristotle shows by induction that contrariety is a privation of one of the contraries. As there are different kinds of privations, some contraries have an intermediate. Another difference of privations is that one kind has a subject, but others do not (nos. 2040–58).

In lesson 7 (X.5.1055b30–1056b2), the opposition of the equal to the large and the small is explained. We ask if a thing is equal to, or more or less than, another; but we do not say that the equal is contrary to it (no. 2061). The equal is opposed to the unequal, and the unequal means something characteristic of the great and the small. Hence, the equal is opposed to both the large and the small as a negation or a privation (nos. 2066–68). It is capable of being either large or small but it is neither of them; rather, it is intermediate between them (nos. 2069–71). To be one of the two extremes, an intermediate subject is required to be capable of being either one of the extremes (no. 2073).

The opposition between the one and the many is discussed in lesson 8 (X.6.1056b3–1057a17). There is a special difficulty here insofar as "the many" can have many senses. "The many" are opposed to "the few." Does this mean that "the one" signifies "a few"? But "a few" is a plurality, so that one would be a plurality (nos. 2075–79). "Many" is used in the sense of a plurality that is "much," but also as the plural of "one." "Two" is the first instance of a few. "One" is opposed to the many as a measure. In its meaning of indivisible, "one" is interchangeable with being (nos. 2080–90). When the term *plurality* signifies a measurable number of things, it refers to the predicament of quantity, but in its sense of multitude it is not limited to a particular genus. Just as being is not a genus, "one" also is not. In its sense of the principle of number, "one" is not contrary to the many as a species of quantity. When there is a number, there is "one," but the opposite need not be the case (nos. 2091–94). Aristotle explains that the relation of "one" to "the many" is similar to that of the knowable object to knowledge. The cognoscible object is the measure of knowledge, as a number is measured by "one" (nos. 2095).

In lesson 9 (X.7.1057a18–b34), the nature of contrariety is determined more precisely. Intermediates are defined as that through which a thing passes when changing from a contrary to its opposite, as we see happen in colors and sounds. They stand between opposites and belong to the same genus. It follows that they must be composed of the contraries, as they are of the same genus. Aristotle illustrates this by way of the example of colors and shows that there are differences in degree with regard to the extremes (nos. 2097–2111).

In lesson 10 (X.8.1057b35–1058a28), Aristotle explains that things that differ specifically belong to the same genus. The difference is added to the genus, not as a part of it but as embracing and determining it to this or to that species. The genus is related to the specific difference as matter is to the form. While matter is present in both parts of something we divide, it is not both of them, but the genus "animal" is both man and horse (nos. 2112–17). Against the Platonists, Aristotle asserts that the common genus is differentiated specifically. He also rejects the theory of those who say that what belongs to the nature of the genus does not differ in its different species. This difference is contrariety, for only contrary things can be present within the same subject or genus. Things opposed contradictorily or by privation are not in the same genus. Contraries, however, belong to the same genus. They differ from each other in species. But no species is specifically different from its genus, nor is it the same (nos. 2118–26).

Lesson 11 (X.9.1058a29–b26) deals with the specific differences. Some contraries do not cause different species but are within the same species, as female and male. The reason is that the latter differences are not related to the specific form of things, as white and black are not. Male and female pertain to the animal by reason of its matter (nos. 2127–35).

In lesson 12 (X.10.1058b26–1059a14), Aristotle shows that some contraries make things differ in genus. The corruptible and the incorruptible are opposed, as matter and the capacity to change are opposed to the absence of them. "Corruptible" does not belong accidentally to some species, but necessarily to the things in which it is present. If not, the same thing would be at one time corruptible and later incorruptible (nos. 2136–39). At this point, Thomas is thinking of the Christian doctrine of the resurrection of the human body and adds a remark: this notion of corruptibility does not prevent divine power from being able to keep some things corruptible by their nature from being corrupted (no. 2140). Corruptible and incorruptible pertain to the very nature of a genus, and cannot have their genus in common from the point of view of the philosophy of nature, although from that of logic they can, as they can have a common definition (e.g., both corruptible and incorruptible things are substances). This entails a refutation of Plato's theory of the specific identity between the Idea of man and an individual man. And Thomas adds a further note: Aristotle said that some contraries (such as black and white) do not cause things to differ specifically in general, although they do cause a specific difference within the genus of color. But corruptible and incorruptible do cause such a generic difference, namely, the difference between "capable of not being" and "incapable of not being" (nos. 2141–45).

Book XI (K)

From the opening lines of his commentary in lesson 1 (XI.1.1059a18–1060a2), it becomes clear that Thomas regards the *Metaphysics* so far as a study of the common attributes of being in general (*ens commune*).[76] As a universal and first science, however, it must also study the separate substances. At this point in the *Metaphysics*, Aristotle looks back at what has been achieved and summarizes the results of the preceding books and of the *Physics*, in particular those that are useful for knowing the separate substances. This summary runs until Book XII.5 (Λ) after which, at 1017b3, the separate substances themselves are studied (no. 1246).[77]

In Book A, he showed that wisdom is the science of principles. Are the principles one or many? The answer is that the principles are reduced to one genus. A next question is whether wisdom considers all substances. If it does, it seems to become doubtful how the same science can embrace several subject matters. At this point, Thomas notes that it treats all substances, as all belong to the common class of beings (nos. 2146–53). Wisdom considers both substances and accidents. When Aristotle wonders which kind of wisdom is concerned with all four causes, Thomas clarifies this point and says that this science studies the kinds of causes mentioned, especially the formal and final cause, and also the end, which is the first cause of motion (no. 2557). This science does deal with sensible substances inasmuch as they are substances, but not insofar as they are sensible. If the objects of mathematics are not separate beings, it is difficult to explain what its subject matter is. It does not seem to deal with sensible things as such. Here, Thomas adds the following observation (no. 2162): the objects of mathematics are not separate from sensible things in being, but only in thought. Wisdom deals neither with separate forms nor with the objects of mathematics as separate things, but studies them insofar as they are beings (nos. 2163–68). Being and "one" are not genera because whatever differences there are, they are qualified as beings and as one. The genus contains the specific differences potentially (nos. 2169–71). And Thomas adds a closing remark: universals are principles of knowledge, and so genera also are. These are divided into species (no. 2172).

---

76. Because of the absence of certain essential themes of Aristotle's metaphysics, such as primary matter, and the apparent equation of pure being with that which is unmoved and transcendent, Jaeger concluded that Book K, chaps. 1–8 is strictly Platonic, in *Aristotle: Fundamentals of the History of His Development*, 214. Ross writes that the book consists of two parts: chapters 1–8 (1059a18–1065a26), "a shorter version" of the contents of Books III–V and chapters 9–12 (1065a26–1069a4), containing extracts from *Physics* II–IV (*Aristotle's "Metaphysics,"* 305). Reale, while agreeing with Ross, argues that Book K serves as a summary and preparation for Book XII (*Aristotele. La Metafisica*, 1:92). See also Giovanni Reale, *The Concept of First Philosophy and the Unity of the Metaphysics of Aristotle*, ed. and trans. John R. Catan (Albany: State University of New York Press, 1980), 247–94. Originally published as *Il Concetto di Filosofia Prima e l'Unità della Metafisica di Aristotele* (Milan: Vita e Pensiero, 1967).

77. Thomas must have been troubled by the first chapters of this book because on several occasions (nos. 2153, 2167, 2181, 2189, 2191, 2193) he adds a final note, which seems to slightly correct the preceding passage and which begins with *Veritas est.*

In lesson 2 (XI.2.1060a3–b3), the question is examined whether there are nonsensible substances. These seem to be apart from individual things, so that the question comes up whether wisdom deals with genera and species. But this is impossible because they are not principles. Thomas (using, again, the somewhat critical expression "the truth of the matter is") says that there exist only individual things; the rest exist only in the consideration of the intellect. Is there something separate from sensible things? The true answer is that there are certain substances that are separate from sensible things, not as forms or ideas, but as movers (nos. 2174–79).

If there is a first separate principle, why are some things that proceed from it eternal, but other things not? The answer is that certain things are corruptible because of their great distance from the first principle. Not all things are substances. Some authors claimed that the principles of things are the one and being, but the one and being do not exist separately, as being, for instance, is predicated of all existing things. Both do not signify substances. The Platonists accepted the One as the principle of things, but how can, for instance, a number, composed as it is of "units," be one? Lines and surfaces are limits of bodies and cannot exist apart. Neither the one nor lines and surfaces are principles (nos. 2180–87). Aristotle continues by considering whether substances are principles. As a particular thing, a substance is not a universal, so it is not a principle. Again, Thomas intervenes with a note: "the truth is" that we must consider the natures of subsisting things in general; genera and species are placed in the class of substances, and so scientific knowledge of them is possible. The form is the specifying principle of the concrete whole. Is the form sometimes separate? Thomas answers as follows: "the truth is" that there is some principle apart from matter, but this is not the form of sensible things. Aristotle asks if the principles of all things are related and are one numerically or specifically. Thomas intervenes again: "the truth is" that the extrinsic principles of things are the same numerically, but the intrinsic principles (matter and form) are not (nos. 2188–93).

In lesson 3 (XI.3.1060b31–1061b17), we are informed more precisely about the subject matter of this science. The term *being* is used in many senses. If these have a common meaning, there can be one science of all beings. He then explains the analogous use of such terms as "healthy," which is midway between the unequivocal and equivocal use of words. Being signifies what exists by itself, but it can also mean what belongs to a thing and determines it as, for instance, qualities do (nos. 2194–97). Also all contraries, which accompany beings, are reduced to a primary contrariety, such as "one" and "plurality." "One" and being are interchangeable. There are contraries of which one opposite is not seen as a full privation of a form, but rather as that of its perfection, so that intermediates become possible. Mathematics investigates things by leaving out sensible qualities while retaining quantity. In a similar way, in this science of being are left out all particular beings, and it considers only what belongs to being in general (nos. 2198–2205).

Lesson 4 (XI.4.1061b17–33) notes that this science studies the first principles of demonstration. Mathematics and other sciences use the first principles of demonstration in a particular way, but this science uses them in a general way as they are common to all, and, for instance, not insofar as they are related to quantity or to motion. In common principles, the predicate is included in the definition of the subject and is known to all (nos. 2206–10). In lesson 5 (XI.5–6.1061b34–1062b19), the principle of contradiction, the first of all these principles, is studied; it is immediately evident and cannot be demonstrated by some other principle better known, because it is the first. The truth and the necessity of this first principle are obvious: our words must signify some one thing and not other things. Opposite affirmations with regard to the same subject cannot be true at the same time. Aristotle argues against Heraclitus that if, as Heraclitus says, one and the same thing can both be and not be, this statement will also not be true; and when Heraclitus says that no affirmation is true, this statement will also be false. Protagoras held that an affirmation and a negation can be true at the same time, as man is the measure of all things and the being of things depends on our apprehension; but if so, the same thing is and is not (nos. 2211–24).

In lesson 6 (XI.6.1062b20–1063b35), Aristotle shows against opponents that contradictories cannot be true at the same time. According to Anaxagoras, things that come to be preexisted in minuscule size within the subject, in which the coming to be takes place. In reality they come to be from matter, in which the new thing is present in potency. If the senses or the intellect of some persons judge differently about things, we should accept what the person whose faculties are not impaired says. But Aristotle rejects the theory that every appearance is true (nos. 2225–32). Truth must not be based on sensible things that are changing all the time, but on the heavenly bodies, which contain the world. Heraclitus thought that increase or growth takes place all the time, but often in minuscule quantities, so that there is always change. By contrast, Thomas refers to *Physics* VIII, where Aristotle says that a body grows during a certain time (no. 2235). Even if a body were continuously changing in quantity, it could remain the same in its qualities. If our judgments about things become different when we are changing ourselves, this must not be attributed to the things outside. If we remain the same there will be something permanent in the world and some truth we can express in sentences (nos. 2236–40). Contrary statements cannot be verified of the same subject at the same time. The reason is that one of the contraries is a privation. This applies also to intermediates, because they imply the privation of both extremes; the definition of intermediates says that they are neither the one nor the other of the contraries. Aristotle concludes that the opinions of Heraclitus and Anaxagoras are not true. And this also goes for the view of those who say that all statements are true (nos. 2241–46).

In lesson 7 (XI.7.1063b36–1064b14), Aristotle explains to what extent metaphysics differs from all other sciences. Every science, both doctrinal and practical, seeks certain causes and principles of its proper object, that is, of a particular class of beings. It tries to demonstrate certain properties of the quiddity of its subject, but there is no demonstration of the quiddity itself (nos. 2247–52). Thomas adds an explanation of the difference between speculative sciences and productive sciences: in the former, the act remains in the agent, but in the productive sciences it passes over to some external matter (no. 2253). The things that are considered in the philosophy of nature have their principle of motion in themselves. Next, Aristotle shows how the mathematical sciences differ from the philosophy of nature: sensible matter is excluded from their consideration, whereas the subject of the philosophy of nature is precisely what includes sensible matter (nos. 2254–58). First philosophy studies being as being. Does it also consider things that are separate from matter? Its difference from the philosophy of nature is obvious, for natural things have matter as a principle of motion. Mathematical sciences study immovable things, but their objects are not separate from matter. First philosophy deals with a substance that is apart from sensible things and in every respect immovable, "if there is such a substance," Aristotle writes, for its existence has not yet been proved, Thomas notes. The science that considers separate beings must be called the divine science and the science of the first principles. Aristotle concludes by saying that there are three classes of speculative sciences. These sciences are most noble, because they seek knowledge for its own sake. Moreover, "theology" deals with the most noble object. Is first philosophy also the most universal of sciences? It deals with all things and with immovable primary being, which is the principle of the other things, and so it is universal (nos. 2259–66).

In lesson 8 (XI.8.1064b15–1065b4), Aristotle shows that no science considers the accidental, that is, what happens accidentally, for what happens accidentally has no determinate cause. Sciences consider their subject and what is proper to it. The accidental is not a being in the proper sense. What happens always or for the most part can be the object of scientific study, but what happens by chance is accidental and is not the object of scientific study. The accidental has no necessary cause and no principles. It has been objected that once a cause exists, the effect follows necessarily and so there will not be a possibility of accidental effects. But things that are accidental have no determinate cause from which they necessarily follow. Next, Aristotle summarizes what has been said about accidental events and luck in *Physics* II. We speak of luck when something happens for the good of the agent, without being intended. Luck is an accidental cause and therefore it is not the primary cause of things (nos. 2268–88).

The definition of motion is presented in lesson 9 (XI.9.1065b5–1066a34) whereas in the next chapter a property of motion is discussed, namely, infinity. Being is divided by act and potency. Thomas gives two possible readings of τὸ μὲν ἐνεργείᾳ μόνον τὸ δὲ δυνάμει in 1065b5 (no. 2289):

> He [Aristotle] says that one kind of being is actual only, such as the prime mover, which is God; another is potential only, such as prime matter; and others are both potential and actual, as all intermediate things. Or: by the phrase "actual only" he means what already has a form completely, as what is now completely white; and by "potential only," what does not have a form, as what is not white in any way.

Furthermore, Aristotle reminds us that being is divided by the ten categories and that motion is an imperfect act. Some things in the different genera are found to be perfect and others imperfect, such as a form and its privation, respectively. There are as many species of motion as there are kinds of being. The definition of motion is as follows: motion is the act of what is in potency insofar as it is in potency. This definition is explained as applying to things as they are moveable and whose motion has not yet been completed. Other definitions of motion, such as otherness, are not adequate. The act of the mover and that of the thing set in movement are the same motion. Yet as the act of the mover it is called action, while as it is received in the thing moved it is called passion, which is one of the categories (nos. 2289–2313).

After having explained the meaning of motion, Aristotle deals with the infinite, which is an attribute of motion, in lesson 10 (XI.10.1066a35–1067a37). First, he distinguishes the various senses of the term *infinite*. What is infinite cannot be measured, it is not traversable. This may mean a thing that has not yet been traversed, or that is traversed with difficulty. The proper sense of the term is that which has no limit, as a limitless line. Some things are potentially infinite by addition, subtraction, or division. The actually infinite exists neither as separate from sensible things nor as an accident of them. If the infinite existed by itself, it would not have continuous quantity (which is the subject of what is infinite), and so it would be indivisible, for whatever is divisible has magnitude (nos. 2314–22). Another argument insists on the fact that infinity is said of numbers and continuous quantities, that is, accidents that do not exist by themselves. The infinite in act does not exist in sensible things: there is no body without a definite surface. There are also no infinite numbers (the infinite cannot be counted, while numbers are measured by "one"). If one of the elementary bodies like air would be infinite, the other elements would be pushed aside. And there is no other simple body apart from the four elements (nos. 2323–36).

At this point, Thomas observes that here Aristotle does not speak of the heavenly bodies, which exist apart from the four elements. The natural philosophers had no knowledge of the fifth element, the ether. But even this fifth body is not infinite (no. 2338). A sensible body is in a place, while the infinite is not. If a body has heaviness or lightness, it has a place in the universe and cannot be infinite (no. 2343). Thomas intervenes again, noting that in the *De caelo* we learn that there is a body that is neither heavy nor light. This observation suggests that Thomas considered the text of Book K as written before the theory of the fifth element had been fully developed (no. 2350). Yet another argument says that the infinite should be somewhere, but that it cannot be in a place, as it is not contained by any limits. In the final section of the chapter (no. 2354), Aristotle deals with the potentially infinite, which is found in what is continuous, in motion, and in time. This must be understood as infinite divisibility. Time is a numbered motion; its continuity exists in a subject.

Motion and change are dealt with in lesson 11 (XI.11.1067b1–1068a7). A thing may change: (1) when that to which it belongs changes; (2) when some part of it changes; or (3) when it is changed in its totality—and this division also applies to the mover (nos. 2355–58). Aristotle also presents another division of change, namely into generation, destruction, and contrariety. But none of these changes is motion. Next he speaks of being and nonbeing: a first sense is the combination and separation in propositions; then comes the sense of act and potency (the potential is a nonbeing). Now, while the subject can be moved, nonbeing cannot. This also appears from the fact that everything that is moved is in a place, and nonbeing is not. Changes that involve contradictories are not motions (nos. 2359–75).

In lesson 12 (XI.12.1068a8–b25), Aristotle shows that motion occurs in only three predicaments: quantity, quality, and place. There is no motion in substance and relation, nor in action and passion. Is there motion in the predicaments of time (the moment when something happens [*quando*]), of the position in a place, and of being dressed or equipped? In these predicaments there is no motion either (nos. 2376–92). There is no change of change. If there were, change would happen because of a preceding change, and this would have to go on forever. Aristotle gives two more arguments against the possibility of change coming about from change. Motion occurs only in the predicaments of quantity, quality, and place. In a final note, the different senses of *immovable* are explained (nos. 2401–3).

Lesson 13 (XI.12.1068b26–1069a14) discusses the end of Book K, where some terms related to motion are further explained, such as being together in a proper place, being separate, and being in contact (i.e., when the extremities are touching). The term *subsequent* is used for what comes after some starting point. *Contiguous* is what is subsequent to something it is in contact with. In the continuum, on the other hand, the points of contact are one and the same extremity. The contiguous is prior to the continuous (nos. 2404–15).

Book XII (Λ)

Book Lambda is a notoriously difficult text which has sparked new interest in recent times.[78] Numerous questions have been raised regarding the systematical and chronological relation of Book XII to the other books of the *Metaphysics*, and the internal structure of Book XII as well as its goal. A discussion of these various, more recent interpretations falls outside the purpose of this book.[79] It is however important to realize that these newer interpretations differ to a large extent from the "traditional interpretation," which conceives Lambda as containing Aristotle's theology and as the culmination of the *Metaphysics*.[80] As we will see, Thomas places himself firmly within this tradition as it was commonly held from Alexander of Aphrodisias onward until twentieth-century commentators such as Jaeger, Ross, and Reale.[81]

78. There have been two new critical editions: Silvia Fazzo, *Il Libro Lambda della Metafisica di Aristotele* (Naples: Bibliopolis, 2012) and Alexandru Stefan, *Aristotle's "Metaphysics" Lambda: Annotated Critical Edition Based upon a Systematic Investigation of Greek, Latin, Arabic and Hebrew Sources* (Leiden: Brill, 2014), as well as two important collections: *Aristotle's "Metaphysics" Lambda* (ed. Frede and Charles) and *Aristotle's "Metaphysics" Lambda—New Essays*, ed. Christoph Horn (Berlin: De Gruyter, 2016). In addition, see *"Metaphysics" Book Λ*, trans. Lindsay Judson (Oxford: Clarendon Press, 2019).

79. The introduction by Michael Frede in *Aristotle's "Metaphysics" Lambda*, 1–52, presents a good overview.

80. The term "traditional interpretation" stems from Silvia Fazzo who strongly endorses a *tabula rasa* when it comes to reading Lambda. She also claims the abandonment of Lambda as containing a theology has been "quasi a condition of possibility for the renewal of Aristotelian studies." Silvia Fazzo, *Commento al Libro Lambda della Metafisica di Aristotele* (Naples: Bibliopolis, 2014), 38–42.

81. See also Leo Elders, *Aristotle's Theology: A Commentary on Book Lambda of the "Metaphysics"* (Assen:

Book Λ agrees with Book K insofar as the knowledge of separate substances "constitutes the goal to which the things studied both in this science and in the other sciences are ultimately directed," as Thomas writes at the beginning of his commentary on Book XI (K) (no. 2146).[82] But it goes much beyond Book K insofar as it is the only treatise that presents Aristotle's theology and describes the activity of God.[83] In lesson 1 (XII.1.1069a18–30), Thomas sees Book Λ (XII) as a summary of what Aristotle said about substance in Books VII and VIII as well as in *Physics* I. It reaffirms that the main inquiry of first philosophy has to do with substance, as substance is prior to the other kinds of beings, so that this science of first philosophy investigates the first principles of being, that is, of substances. Thomas distinguishes four arguments. First, if the universe of things is a kind of "whole" (*totum*), substance is the first of all beings both in the ontological and the chronological order. Thomas writes that Averroes does not notice that Aristotle used "whole" in an analogous way. Averroes thinks that the meaning of the text is that things are either related by a genus, or have nothing in common because things merely succeed one another (nos. 2416–18).[84] Second, the other predicaments are not beings in an unqualified sense. Only substance subsists, and the accidents refer to what the substance has or what is in it. Therefore, metaphysics as the study of being is mainly concerned with substances. Thirdly, because the accidents cannot exist apart from the substance, their study is included in that of substance. Finally, the ancient philosophers also testified to this because they were looking for the causes of substance (nos. 2419–23).

In lesson 2 (XII.1–2.1069a30–b32), we read that there are three classes of

---

Van Gorcum, 1972), and Ralph McInerny, *Praemabula Fidei: Thomism and the God of the Philosophers* (Washington, D.C.: The Catholic University of America Press, 2006), 219–83, esp. 283n1.

82. See also *In XI Meta.*, lesson 7, no. 2262, where Thomas notes, commenting on 1063a35–36 ("if indeed there is such a substance, that is, one which is separate and immovable, as we shall try to show"): "He says here, 'if there is some such substance' apart from sensible substances which is immovable in every respect. He says this because the existence of some such substance has not yet been proved, although he intends to prove this." According to Reale (*Aristotele. La Metafisica*, 2:221), Aristotle's remark "as we shall try to show" can only refer to XII.6–7.

83. For studies of Thomas's commentary on Book Lambda, see André-Jean Festugière, "Notes sur les sources du commentaire de S. Thomas au Livre XII des Métaphysiques," *Revue des sciences philosophiques et théologiques* 18 (1929): 282–90, 657–63; Georges Ducoin, "Saint Thomas commentateur d'Aristote. Études sur le commentaire thomiste du livre Lambda des Métaphysiques d'Aristote," *Archives de philosophie* 20 (1957): 78–117, 240–71, 392–45; Gabriele Galluzzo, "Aquinas's Commentary on the *Metaphysics*," in *A Companion to the Latin Medieval Commentaries on Aristotle's "Metaphysics,"* ed. Fabrizio Amerini and Gabriele Galluzzo (Leiden: Brill, 2014), 209–54, esp. 242–54; Ruedi Imbach, "Quelques observations sur la réception du livre XII de la 'Métaphysique' chez Thomas d'Aquin," *Revue des sciences philosophiques et théologiques* 99 (2015): 377–407.

84. Averroes, *Commentarium Magnum in Aristotelis Metaphysicorum XIII* 290–92. For a detailed analysis, showing that Thomas is indebted to Themistius, via Averroes, see A. Festugière, "Notes sur les sources du commentaire de S. Thomas au Livre XII des Métaphysiques," 282–90.

substance: sensible eternal substances, sensible perishable substances, and immovable substances. The Platonists posited the universal Forms as separate substances; the Pythagoreans did so with the objects of mathematics. Sensible substances, both the perishable and the eternal ones, are the objects of the philosophy of nature, but separable immovable substances are studied in first philosophy. As to sensible substances, Aristotle shows that there is matter in them, that is, a substrate of the things that change into one another. The things undergoing this change must be in potency to the forms they have at the beginning of the change and to those of the end term. In substantial changes, the substrate (matter) has no determinate form. Aristotle solves the difficulty of the ancient philosophers who denied generation, as nothing can come from nothing. In reality, what is changed, changes from the potential to act. A philosopher like Anaxagoras, who did not know the potential, thought that all things were mixed. Aristotle affirms that matter in the celestial bodies is different, as they are not subject to generation, but they know a change of place (nos. 2424–36). Then he explains that things that are capable of being generated each have a definite matter from which they come to be. Primary matter is first in potency to the forms of the elements, and through these to other specific forms (nos. 2437–39).

In lesson 3 (XII.2–3.1069b32–1070a30), the subject treated by Aristotle is the form. Form is a principle of changeable substances, its contrary is the principle of privation, and the third principle is matter. In every change there is a subject and contraries. The last (most basic) matter, that is, primary matter, is not generated. Also, the form as such is not generated, but becomes present by the action of an agent that is similar to the form to be produced. Luck and chance are privations of nature (nos. 2441–45). Speaking about forms from the viewpoint of the composite substance, we must distinguish matter, the natural form, and the substance composed of matter and form. Certain forms do not exist outside the composite things (e.g., a house) except insofar as they are present in the mind of the builder. Natural forms are in natural things (nos. 2447–48). Plato said that the specific form of things, of which he affirmed the existence, are natural forms. Thomas, following Aristotle, writes that Plato was not wrong that the separate Forms exist by nature but only if one has established their existence, that is, the existence of other Forms besides those of the composite substance (no. 2449).[85] The form results when the process of change is terminated; it disappears when the composite is disintegrated, but Aristotle wonders whether the rational soul, which has an operation without

---

85. Here the expression *dico autem* refers to Aristotle himself and not to Thomas's opinion.

the body, remains after the disintegration of the composite. Here, he does not further discuss this question because it belongs to the science of the soul, Thomas writes. Thomas also adds two important observations. First, Aristotle rejects Plato's view on separately preexisting Forms only insofar as it involves the preexistence of the human soul. Second, Aristotle's words cannot be read as saying that only the possible intellect or only the agent intellect survives as a separate substance because such a separate soul would preexist the composite and could not be its form.[86] In a final section, Aristotle reaffirms that there is no need for the existence of the Ideas: in our part of the world, the causes known are sufficient to explain the formation of things (nos. 2450–54).

The principles of movable substances are examined in lesson 4 (XII.4–5.1070a31–1071b2). Are they the same as those of the other categories, such as relations, which seem furthest removed from substances? Relations have being only in reference to something else. With two arguments, Aristotle shows that they are not the same. First, principles are of the same kind as what they cause; as substance and accidents are very different, they cannot have the same principles (no. 2455–60). A second proof runs as follows: that elements are not the same as the things composed of them is obvious; if they were the cause of both the substance and the accidents, they would be different from them, but this is impossible because whatever exists must belong to one of the predicaments (no. 2461). The principles of things are proportionally the same. Aristotle mentions the elements hot and cold as the principles of things, but the bodies formed out of them are something different (no. 2466). The simple bodies, in turn, and what is composed of them, have the same principles and elements, while other things have other proximate principles. Not all things have the same principles, but they have principles proportionate to them. Elements and principles differ as intrinsic and extrinsic causes, but the term "principle" can mean both an intrinsic and extrinsic cause. Privations are a cause *per accidens*. Thomas notes that Aristotle omits the final cause here, as it is only a principle insofar as it is present in the intention of the mover. The cause of motion and the form are of the same species. There must be a first among the moving causes (no. 2475), but also in the genus of substance we must arrive at some first. According to Aristotle, Thomas says, the celestial bodies are ensouled; but if they are, they have no other faculties but intellect and appetite. Act and potency amount to the same thing as matter, form, and privation (no. 2480). Potency and act are proportionally the principles of all

---

86. No. 2543: "Ex quo etiam patet quod non potest hoc depravari, sicut quidam depravare conantur dicentes intellectum possibilem tantum, vel agentem tantummodo esse incorruptibilem." This is the topic of his *De unitate intellectus contra Averroistas*.

things, so that they are universal (although not in the sense of Plato's universals). Things that are not in the same genus, as substance and the accidents have different causes (nos. 2480–86).

With lesson 5 (XII.6.1071b3–22) we have arrived at Aristotle's theology because he now begins to determine the truth about "immovable substances, which are separate from matter" (no. 2488). Thomas divides the remainder of Book Lambda as follows. First, Aristotle shows that there is an immovable and eternal substance, separate from matter (1071b3–1072a26). Next, starting at 1072a26, he asks about the attributes (*conditio*) of this substance and more in particular its perfection (1072a26–b14), whether it is one or many (1072b14–1073b17), and its operation (1074b15–1076a4). These last questions deal with the immaterial substance as an intelligence and an intelligible object (1074b15ff.; lesson 11) as well as a desirable good (1075a11ff.; lesson 12).

In lesson 5 (XII.6.1071b3–22), it is argued that an eternal, immovable substance must exist. If all substances are perishable and are destroyed, all other beings (such as the accidents) will perish. But it has been shown in *Physics* VIII that motion is eternal: it neither began to exist nor can it perish. Time must also be eternal. In order to account for the eternity of motion, there must exist an eternal, moving substance, which is always acting. Plato's theory of eternal Forms does not explain the presence of motion because as universals they are not able to move (nos. 2488–93).[87] Now, Aristotle shows that this eternal substance, causing motion, exists and that its essence is act. If this mover had potentiality in its essence, it could not exist, for whatever is in potentiality may possibly not be. And this substance must be immaterial, for matter is in potency. In the last section of the lesson (nos. 2497–99), Thomas adds the observation that the arguments put forward in *Physics* VIII are not demonstrative but at most probable (*probabiles rationes*) although Aristotle firmly thought (*firmiter opinatus*) that motion and time must be eternal. For if we suppose that at some moment time began to be, there would only be an imaginary "before" preceding time. Likewise, if we suppose that there is no body outside the world, "outside" only refers to something in our imagination. It is therefore not necessary that there be a time before time began to be or a time after time will cease to be, even though "before" and "after" signify time. In a somewhat surprising way, Thomas continues by claiming that, even if Aristotle's arguments are only probable, what Aristotle says about the eternity and immateriality of the first substance necessarily follows:

---

87. In light of other passages (see note 60) and in particular no. 1164 one might conclude that Thomas's use in this passage of expressions such as *substantia motiva et effectiva sempiterna* and *substantiam sempiternam moventem et agentem in actu* points to efficient causality.

Even if the world were not eternal, it would still have to be brought into being by something that has prior existence. And if this cause were not eternal, it too would have to be produced by something else. But because there cannot be an infinite series, as has been proved in Book II [2.994a1–b8], it is necessary to posit an eternal substance whose essence contains no potentiality and is therefore immaterial.

In lesson 6 (XII.6–7.1071b22–1072a26), Aristotle investigates whether act is absolutely prior to potency. As not everything that is able to act is actually acting, it would seem that potency is prior. But if potency were absolutely prior, at some time nothing would exist. What is potential does not exist actually and does not come into being by itself. There must always be something existing. Absolutely speaking, act is prior to potency, although in one and the same subject that is brought to act, potency is prior (nos. 2500–2509). If there is a never-ending series of generations, the motions of the celestial bodies must be eternal. There must be an eternal agent that always acts in the same way so as to cause the eternal motion of things (no. 2510). While the cause of the eternity of things is the first heaven, the sun that is at one time nearer to the earth and somewhat later farther removed from it, causes generation and corruption of the lower bodies as a secondary agent. If these motions explain what happens in the sublunar region, it is not necessary to look for other causes such as the Ideas to intervene. In the final section of the lesson, Thomas comments on the first part of XII.7, where Aristotle very briefly says that there must be an unmoved mover, which is not a being in potency, but whose essence is act (no. 2517–18).

Lesson 7 (XII.7.1072a26–b14) deals with the question of how the first mover causes motion, that is to say, in which way a desired object causes movement. In the case of voluntary motions, the will and the sensible appetite have the character of moved movers. In human beings we distinguish between what causes motion as a desirable good (e.g., which causes pleasure to the senses) and that which causes motion as an intelligible good. This distinction does not apply to the first unmoved mover who is desired as good by himself. And the object of the concupiscible appetite is only good when it is desired in conformity with reason (nos. 2518–22). Now, that which is good and that which is desirable belong to the same class. The first intelligible being in act is prior to the potentially intelligible and is a simple, not composite, substance. The good and the desirable belong to the same class of things. The greatest good will be a simple substance in act. This leads to the conclusion that the first mover is identical with the first intelligible, desirable being and good. The first mover is an end, as things by their motion tend to participate to some degree in it (nos. 2523–28). The first heaven is the first being moved and which in turn moves the other things in the world. The primary motion of the first heaven is a local motion, so that the heaven remains the same substance. The first heaven can in no way become different, and it moves necessarily in the sense that the order of the whole demands that its motion goes on forever. The whole of nature depends on it. The necessity of the first motion is a necessity in view of the end to be reached. Thomas observes by way of conclusion (no. 2535):

> It should also be noted that Aristotle says here that the necessity of the first motion is not absolute necessity but the necessity that is from the end, and the end is the principle which he later calls God inasmuch as things are assimilated to God through motion. Now assimilation to a being that wills and understands (as he shows God to be) is realized according to will and understanding, just as things made by art are assimilated to the artist inasmuch as his will is fulfilled in them. This being so, it follows that the necessity of the first motion is totally subject to the will of God.[88]

In lesson 8 (XII.7.1072b14–1073a13), we read about the perfection of the first substance, which causes motion as intelligible and as desirable. According to Aristotle, the first heaven has a soul and understands and desires the perfection of the first mover.[89] It is concerned with what is best, and the pleasure experienced in intellectual activity is of a higher kind than that of the senses, something which is also expressed in *Nicomachean Ethics* X. The act of understanding found in the first mover consists in the identity of its intellect and its intelligible object (nos. 2536–39). Material substances become actually intelligible by their likenesses abstracted by the agent intellect. In us, however, this intelligible form is not a substance, but in the first mover it is his substance. The intellect of the first heavenly sphere is brought to actuality by its contact

---

88. We notice that Thomas does not speak of a soul of the first heaven to explain this appetite for the good of God. As we have seen before, he is reluctant to accept Aristotle's theory of the animation of the first heaven. Wippel remarks that Thomas's attribution of will to Aristotle's God has no textual support, in his "Thomas Aquinas' Commentary on Aristotle's *Metaphysics*," 264. Moerbeke's translation of 1072a28–30, however, reads: "Concupiscibile QUIDEM ENIM *IPSUM* apparens bonum, UOLUNTABILE autem primum IPSUM EXISTENS bonum." Moreover, as Brock has pointed out, this attribution might be due to Alexander, as reported by Averroes (*Commentarium Magnum in Aristotelis Metaphysicorum libros XIIII* 320F–G), who presents the first mover as a lord and king to whose will the others conform. Themistius also compares the first mover to a living law or a king that the first heaven wants to obey and imitate. See Stephen L. Brock, "The Causality of the Unmoved Mover in Thomas Aquinas's *Commentary on Metaphysics XII*," in *Nova & Vetera* (English edition) 10 z(2012): 805–32, esp. note 66. Brock relies on Enrico Berti, "Il movimento del cielo in Alessandro di Afrodisia," in *La filosofia in età impériale*, ed. A. Brancacci (Naples: Bibliopolis, 2000), 227–43. See also Themistius, *Paraphrase de la Métaphysique d'Aristote (Livre Lambda)*, trans. Rémi Brague (Paris: Vrin, 1999), 94, no. 29.

89. Thomas reiterates his hesitance when he observes that the animation of the heaven is "secundum opinionem Aristotelis" (no. 2536).

with the first mover (nos. 2540–42). The following sentence of Aristotle's text (at 1072b25–26) says that God is in a pleasurable state in a much a higher degree than we sometimes are. Thomas adds that what causes the perfection of a thing has that perfection in a higher degree, an important principle that he uses in the fourth of the five ways of the *Summa theologiae*, concluding to the existence of God, namely that the more and less of a perfection requires a greatest (no. 2543).[90] God is life itself in the form of thought: his substance is act and most intelligible, and his intellect is its activity. His intellect is identical with his own understanding (*Intellectus enim eius est ipsum suum intelligere*). In passing, Aristotle rejects the view that goodness is only found at the end of a series (nos. 2545–46).[91] The first mover has neither magnitude nor parts, and moves in infinite time. Its power is infinite in the sense of being not limited to some definite effect (nos. 2544–52).

In lesson 9 (XII.8.1073a14–b17), the question of the moving powers of the numerous revolving heavenly spheres is discussed. Introducing the chapter, Thomas suggests that this question is about the immaterial substance, whether it is one or many (no. 2553). Those who posited the Ideas said that there are Ideas of all specific essences. When the Ideas were considered to be numbers, there also was no clear answer as to their number.

Now, as follows from *Physics* VIII, Thomas comments, the first unmoved mover is eternal and it is an eternal mover which causes an eternal motion just as a single mover causes a single motion. Besides sharing in the revolution of the first heaven, the planets perform circular local movements, each of which is caused by an eternal unmoved substance (nos. 2553–56). Thomas explains this as follows: the stars (read: the planets) are eternal substances; their movers must also be eternal and be substances. They are as numerous as the stars. Thomas observes that here Aristotle computes only the planets and their motions, because the motions of the fixed stars, contrary to the primary motion, had not yet been detected: above the sphere of the fixed stars another sphere was posited that turns the whole in its daily motion. Thomas also introduces an argument which he ascribes to Avicenna and which is based on the axiom *ex uno non nisi unum*.[92] Hence this first sphere is moved directly,

---

90. In all perfections a certain inclination or motion is found toward their source in which they participate.

91. This view is found in later Pythagoreanism and Speusippus. See Hans J. Krämer, *Der Ursprung der Geistmetaphysik* (Amsterdam: Schippers, 1964), 213. Thomas probably found this information in Averroes, who disposed of the commentary of Simplicius, *In II De caelo*, chap. 6 (CAG VII, 422ff.). But in his description of the movements of the celestial bodies Averroes does not sufficiently distinguish between the fixed stars and the planets, nor does he inform us about the chronology of the various astronomers.

92. See Avicenna, *Metaph.* IX, 4 (ed. Van Riet, 451.50–51): "Nosti etiam quod ex uno, secundum quod est unum, non nisi unum." This axiom is also related to several of the 219 articles condemned in 1277 by the

not by the first principle, but by an intelligence, which is caused by the first principle. This intelligence also produces the substance of the body of a star and its soul. This process is repeated in the following lower orbits. But Thomas rejects Avicenna's argument as unnecessary because, if it is characteristic for a superior substance to possess the cause and the thing caused in their intelligible existence, then from such a superior substance, understanding many things, also many effects can be produced.[93]

However, Thomas signals a difficulty in Aristotle's text: the sun revolves in a much lower orbit, but has an enormous influence, something which seems to stand in opposition to Aristotle's claim in 1073b1–3 that the order of separate substances corresponds to the order of motions and bodies moved. Referring to Ptolemy's *Quadripartitum*, he lists successively the effects caused by Saturn, Jupiter, Mars, Venus, Mercury, and the sun. The motions of the planets seem sometimes irregular, but by introducing different spheres moving into different directions, this seeming irregularity can be reduced to an order.[94] Regarding the exact number of planetary motions, Aristotle advises to investigate oneself but also to listen to experts and, while respecting different opinions, accept those that are more certain. Thomas emphasizes the need to search for the truth and not an opinion that one likes and adds that the same applies to views that might appear later on (nos. 2557–66).[95]

Lesson 10 (XII.8.1073b17–1074b14) deals with the number of unmoved movers. Plato and Eudoxus introduced the so-called revolving spheres of the heavenly bodies, so that the apparent irregularities could be explained. Ptolemy explained apparent irregularities in the motions of the fixed stars by introducing eccentric spheres and epicycles.[96] But this hypothesis implies that not every movement will be around the center of the world. Moreover, a sphere with epicycles is not of equal density as a sphere without them. It will be expanded and compressed when a body on these epicycles is moved. Eudoxus suggested a solution regarding the motion of the planets: each planet would have several concentric spheres, each with its own motion; and all mo-

---

bishop of Paris. See R. Hissette, *Enquête sur les 219 articles condamnés à Paris le 7 Mars 1277* (Louvain: Peeters, 1977), 70–72.

93. On the refutation of Avicenna's position see Wippel, "The Latin Avicenna as a Source for Thomas Aquinas's Metaphysics," esp. 50–64.

94. As Ducoin has pointed out ("Saint Thomas commentateur d'Aristote," 85n21), no. 2565 is almost identical to Averroes's text in *Commentarium Magnum in Aristotelis Metaphysicorum XIII*, 328I.

95. In his commentary on the *De Caelo*, Thomas says that certain hypothetical explanations about cosmic events were abandoned because of later discoveries and replaced by better ones (*In II De caelo*, lesson 17, no. 235). This text shows that for Thomas the scientific explanations about the cosmos had a provisional value.

96. Ptolomeus did his astronomical work in the second century A.D.; Eudoxus was a contemporary of Plato and Aristotle.

tions together account for the seemingly irregular movements of the planet. He posited four spheres for each of the five planets. Calippus, a contemporary of Aristotle, added two spheres to those of the sun and the moon to account better for the increase in speed and slowing down, which are visible in their motions. He also added one sphere to each of the remaining planets. Next he introduced the so-called revolving spheres, the function of which was to allow the planet next in order to have the right position with regard to the revolution of the first heaven (nos. 2567–86).

Some authors assumed that there are certain celestial bodies without a corresponding motion. But Aristotle maintains that every immutable substance must be considered the end of some motion, and that the number of celestial motions corresponds to that of the separate substances, so that there are no immutable substances besides the number of celestial motions. Thomas notes that the assumption that every immaterial substance has a corresponding motion is not necessary, as there are immaterial substances too perfect to be tuned to some celestial motion. Immaterial substances do not exist for the sake of corporeal things (no. 2589). Another objection against the above explanation is that there are more motions in the world than those that have thus far been noticed. Aristotle answers that there cannot be any other motions besides those observed. Thomas explains this "probable conclusion" as follows: every mover exists for the sake of something moved. There is no motion that exists just for itself. All motions must exist for the sake of the stars. A third objection suggests that there are many worlds, each of which would have a great number of spheres and motions, and hence also of unmoved movers.

Thomas explains the argument of Aristotle as follows: things that are specifically one (as the numerous immaterial movers would be) and numerically many contain matter. But these first principles do not contain matter. The first unmoved mover is one in number, and there is only one heaven, that is, one first eternal motion. Aristotle sees a confirmation of this in the religious tradition of mankind (1074b1–15). The immaterial substances are called divine beings, but only the first principle is God. In a final note, Aristotle says that the traditions about the gods have been introduced in the form of a myth. If among these traditions the thought emerges that the first principle is God and that God is only one, this will be considered a divine statement (θείως ἂν εἰρῆσθαι νομίσειεν, 1074b9–10). But tradition was obscured, got lost, and was rediscovered again. Thomas makes an observation on this periodical reemergence of arts and philosophical-religious insights. Aristotle, he says, had to uphold this theory because of his conviction about the eternity of the world: mankind could not have been without these arts and religious beliefs for an infinite period of time.[97]

In lesson 11 (XII.9.1074b15–1075a10), there is a further examination of the understanding and knowledge of the first mover, who is said to cause motion as an intelligible object. The first mover as a desirable good will be the topic of the next lesson, lesson 12 (XII.10). The intellect of the first sphere, which knows the first mover, has a nobler intelligible object than itself, so that one might think that this applies also to the first mover, but this mover is the noblest being, without any potentiality. This means that its essence cannot be related to its intellect as its object, for in that case the essence would be something potential. The essence can only be the best if it is identical with the act of understanding. This takes us to the question of what the first mover contemplates.

Given the dependence of the intellect on its object, it is unfitting and even absurd to think that the nature of the object does not matter. On the contrary, we must remove low-graded, contingent beings from its consideration and retain noble objects. Hence, the first intellect knows what is most divine and most honorable. For the same reason, God does not shift from considering his divine essence to other objects. If the first intellect's activity, that is, his act of understanding, were not identical with his substance, his intellectual activity would be tiresome, that is, involve potency, and would not be continuous. This would mean, so it seems, that a continuous intellectual activity must be received from something else and therefore does not belong to the nature of the first intellect. But, Thomas remarks, this conclusion is merely probable because it assumes that what is received is contrary to one's nature. This is true of humans but not of the continuity of the motion of the heavens, which depends on an external principle but is not tiresome (nos. 2600–2610). Given that there is no potency in the first intellect, it follows that, if the first intellect does not understand himself, something other would be first, that is, more worthy. Hence, in understanding himself, the intellect of the first intellect is the same as its object. As if to express the importance of this reasoning Thomas adds the following remark (no. 2614):

<hr>

97. For similar claims regarding the infinite revival of opinions see *Meteorologica* I.3.339b27–30 and *De caelo* I.3.270b19–20. As Fabienne Baghdassarian explains in *La question du divin chez Aristote. Discours sur les Dieux et science du principe* (Louvain: Peeters, 2016), 291–96, this is due to Aristotle's cyclical conception of history. Similar to the "divine statement" passage here, Thomas responds in *In I De Caelo*, lesson 7, no. 77, that "the minds of men are naturally inclined to the truth" so that true opinions can indeed be reached. And in *In I Meteorologica*, lesson 3, no. 19, Thomas again comments about the infinite revival of opinions as follows: "[Aristotle] says this in keeping with his opinion that the world and human generation have been going on from eternity, as indicated in previous books."

It should be noticed that the Philosopher's aim is to show that God does not understand something else but himself, inasmuch as the thing understood is the perfection of the one understanding and of his activity, which is understanding. But it is manifest that nothing else can be understood by God in such a way that it would be the perfection of his intellect. Nor does it follow that all things different from himself are not known by him; for by understanding himself he knows all other things.

Thomas continues along these lines with the idea that what is derived from principles is virtually contained in the principles, so that the perfect understanding of a principle entails the perfect understanding of its effects.[98] "Therefore, as the heavens and the whole of nature depend on the first principle which is God, as has been said, it is obvious that God knows all things by understanding himself" (no. 2615). If he knows things at a lower level, his nobility is not lessened, as these objects are understood in his understanding of the most noble things (no. 2616).

Aristotle raises two questions. First, understanding one's own act of thinking seems accessory to the principal act of understanding; second, how could it be God's very life? However, in the speculative sciences, the concept by which we know a thing is the thing understood. It is just one act of understanding. This also resolves the second question about what it is that confers goodness to the first intellect, his act of understanding, or the thing understood (nos. 2617–20). A further question is whether God understands by way of a simple apprehension (as we ourselves know concepts) or by composition (as we do in the so-called second operation). In God, it cannot be this second way, as the intellect then shifts its attention from one part of the judgment to the other (e.g., Peter runs). Having no matter, the first intellect is simple. Finally, the intellect that is concerned with composites attains its knowledge over a period of time, while God has and is his knowledge always (nos. 2621–26).

Lesson 12 (XII.10.1075a11–1076a4), the final lesson of Book Lambda, consists in a further investigation into the first mover as a good and as an object of desire. The chapter is divided into Aristotle's position (1075a11–25) and a discussion of his predecessors' positions (1075a26–1076a4). According to Thomas, Aristotle asks whether the whole universe has the good as something separate or as the order of the whole. Given that the good functions as an end, the question becomes whether the end is extrinsic (or transcendent) to the whole or intrinsic (or immanent). Aristotle argues for both. The universe has the first mover as its separate end and good. But this ordination requires an internal order of the parts of the universe as well. Aristotle's example of

---

98. At this point Thomas implicitly introduces the notion of participation.

the relation between an army and its commander shows that the good of the whole is to be found both in the whole itself (the army) and the one who presides over the whole (commander). The former, however, is subordinated to and depends on the latter because the order of an army exists in order to attain victory, which is the good of the commander. The separate good of the universe is a greater good because "the whole order of the universe exists for the sake of the first mover inasmuch as the things contained in the mind and will of the first mover are realized in the ordered universe. Hence the whole order of the universe must depend on the First Mover" (no. 2631). The things in the universe are ordered to this good as to one end, but in different ways, so that they are also related to each other. Things have an inclination, implanted in them by the first mover, to act in view of their proper end and of their common end, even if they do not know it. Things that never fail in acting in view of their own proper end contribute in all their actions to the whole. But lower bodies may sometimes be subject to chance and to what is contrary to their nature (no. 2631–37).

There are however different views concerning the order of the universe, for example, according to one opinion all things come from contraries, while no explanation is given of how they come from contraries. Contraries, however, cannot be acted upon by one another. For Aristotle, the difficulty is resolved by the introduction of (the principle of) primary matter. Others considered matter as one of the contraries (e.g., the equal and the unequal, or plurality), as Plato did (nos. 2627–42). But Aristotle rejects this theory because, if true, all things would participate in evil as well as in the good. Yet no evil and destruction are found in the celestial bodies. Others held that the good is the principle of things. Empedocles, for instance, made love a moving material principle but failed to show how it works. Furthermore, how can strife be an incorruptible principle? In IX.9.1051a19, Aristotle had already rejected the possibility of evil itself existing as something apart from a thing. Anaxagoras made the good and the intellect the moving principles but never answers why and how the intellect causes motion. The answer is that the intellect and its intelligible object must be the same, as we (Aristotle) explained in regard to the first mover (no. 2648). Those who made contraries first principles did not explain how things come from contraries. What about indestructible things? To avoid the problem, Parmenides and Melissus asserted that all things are one. But they were unable to explain why generation is eternal. Those who said that contraries are the first principles had to make of one of these a higher principle, the other one being a privation. But because the first principle is immaterial, there is nothing contrary to it.

Finally (1075b24–26), Aristotle deals with another group of different opinions, that is, the opinions of those who held that the principles of things are separate natures (no. 2656). By referring back to XII.6.1071b3–22, he repeats his main conclusion: without a first mover there will be no ultimate principle of change and hence no nature, no orderly change in the sublunary world, and no regular celestial movements. Those who posit Forms and numbers as separate substances face a number of difficulties. First, these Forms and numbers do not seem to be the causes of anything. Second, how can continuous quantity come from numbers? Third, if separate Forms and numbers are first principles, how can contrariety come from them? And if not, there is no generation or motion because these Forms and numbers cannot be moving causes because these forms are not efficient causes. Generation and motion would no longer be eternal. First principles must therefore be movers. Thomas refers us back to the beginning of XII.6 as well, but also to I.2.982b4–11, for understanding the way in which first principles are movers. There Aristotle had argued that metaphysics as *scientia architectonica* must be concerned with the final cause of all things as "the greatest good in the whole of nature" (nos. 50–51). Fourth and finally: given that Forms and numbers are not able to move, an explanation of why something comes to be unified becomes unintelligible unless one accounts for a mover, as was stated in VIII.6.1045a29–33.

These opinions have in common that there exists a certain connection between these separate substances. In the last lines of Book Lambda, Thomas discovers the opinion of those who, while positing separate substances, even rejected such a connection.[99] This would reduce the substances of the universe and their principles to unrelated beings. Aristotle rejects this and writes: "Beings do not want to be governed badly: 'To have many rulers is not good: let there be one ruler'" (1076a1–4). Thomas comments on the first part of the final sentence of Book Lambda by arguing that if each thing in nature is seen to be disposed in the best way suited to it, all the more have we to suppose that the whole universe is ordered in the best way possible (no. 2262). The second part of the final sentence leads Thomas to conclude: "Aristotle's conclusion is that there is one ruler of the whole universe, the first mover, and one first intelligible object, and one first good, whom above he called God, who is blessed for ever and ever. Amen" (no. 2263).[100]

---

99. Aristotle is thinking of Speusippus; see Book VII.2 (1028b21–24).

100. Thomas nor the Moerbeke translation, which has "Entia uero NON UOLUNT DISPONI male, nec bonum PLURALITAS PRINCIPATUUM. Vnus ergo PRINCEPS," recognize the last line as a quotation from the *Iliad* II.ii.204. Note also the similarity between these lines and the final lines of his commentary on the *Physics* ("Et sic terminat philosophus considerationem communem de rebus naturalibus, in primo principio totius naturae, qui est super omnia Deus benedictus in saecula. Amen").

Concluding Remarks

Despite the somewhat less well-ordered composition of the *Metaphysics*, Thomas attempts to show that Aristotle's treatise is nevertheless coherent. He brings the somewhat divergent views on the nature of metaphysics, as present in Books Α, Γ, and Ε, to harmony and unity: metaphysics is the science of being *qua* being or, rather, the science of being. He concludes with Aristotle that there is a first cause of the eternal movement of the first heaven, but he goes beyond the wording of the text—albeit not beyond the gist of Aristotle's entire philosophical thought and principles—by arguing in the last chapters of Book XII that this first mover is the cause of the being of all things. When contemplating himself, God knows the world, which depends on his causal influence.

The text of the commentary is subtle and nuanced because Thomas is in search of the *intentio auctoris*. In most lessons, it also reflects Thomas's own metaphysical doctrine, which almost everywhere agrees with what Aristotle writes. Besides some obvious corrections and additions, introduced by *sciendum est autem* and similar expressions, Thomas has some inconspicuous ways of marking a certain distance between what Aristotle writes and his own doctrine, notably by phrases such as *hic dicit* or *hic supponit*.

Thomas does not favor the view that the celestial bodies are ensouled, and he notes that certain texts are in conflict with the Christian faith regarding the creation of the world, while adding the explanation that Aristotle had to uphold his theory of the eternity of the world in order to explain the recurrent reappearance of philosophical and religious doctrines. For the patient and careful reader, the commentary is a mine of priceless information about Thomas's own thought, besides being an admirable presentation of Aristotle's greatest work.

11 ∾ THE COMMENTARY ON THE NICOMACHEAN ETHICS

Aristotle's *Nicomachean Ethics* (hereafter *NE*) is surely the most famous and influential text in the formation of Western moral thought. In more recent times, ever since Anscombe's rejection of modernity's utilitarianism and Kantian ethics in favor of an account of the good based on moral psychology and moral virtue as well as MacIntyre's emphasis on human beings as social animals, Aristotle's text and its account of virtue, practical wisdom, and happiness has become the central text for developing a contemporary virtue ethics.[1] Many contemporary scholars of Thomas Aquinas have come to rediscover his emphasis on virtues and happiness as an alternative to modern ethical theories.[2] This renewal has led to a great number of studies devoted to this text and a resulting variety of interpretations of difficult passages. Obviously, we cannot discuss in detail all these suggestions and must restrict ourselves to the most important ones.

NE constitutes the first of a two-part "philosophy of human affairs" (ἡ περὶ τὰ ἀνθρώπεια φιλοσοφία, X.9.1181b15), which Aristotle completes in his *Politics*. Leaving aside the *Magna Moralia*, whose authenticity is doubtful, the other extant writing on ethics, the *Eudemian Ethics*, is an exposition on man's moral life in many parts parallel to *NE* (the so-called common books, *Eudemian Ethics* 4–6 and *NE* 5–7). Werner Jaeger wrote extensively on what he calls the original ethics of Aristotle and the relation of *Eudemian*

---

1. See G. E. M. Anscombe, "Modern Moral Philosophy," *Philosophy* 33 (1958): 1–19, and Alasdair MacIntyre, *After Virtue* (Notre Dame, Ind.: University of Notre Dame Press, 1981). For a good overview of the recent fate of Aristotle's ethics, see Jennifer Welchman, "The Fall and Rise of Aristotelian Ethics in Anglo-American Moral Philosophy," in *The Reception of Aristotle's Ethics*, ed. Jörn Müller (Cambridge: Cambridge University Press, 2012), 262–88.

2. In the area of moral theology Servais Pinckaers's *Les sources de la morale chrétienne. Sa méthode, son contenu, son histoire* (Fribourg: Editions Universitaires, 1985), translated as *The Sources of Christian Ethics* by M. T. Noble (Washington, D.C.: The Catholic University of America Press, 1995), has been instrumental. For a review of his work see *Renouveler toutes choses en Christ: vers un renouveau thomiste de la théologie morale: hommage à Servais Pinckaers*, ed. Michael S. Sherwin and Craig Steven Titus (Fribourg: Academic Press Fribourg, 2009).

Ethics to the partly lost Aristotelian dialogue *Protrepticus.* In what Aristotle writes in these two earlier works, he shows a proximity to Plato's thought. *NE,* on the other hand, present Aristotle's definite moral doctrine.[3] While the Pre-Socratics and the Sophists proposed only vague sketches of a moral science as such,[4] Plato devoted a considerable part of his dialogues to the study of such central questions as man's happiness, the virtues, and the difficulties people run into in their search of happiness; he taught the doctrine of the virtues as holding the middle between excess and deficiency.[5] Human conduct depends also on the education a person received, especially in early youth.[6] Aristotle, however, was the first to give a systematic form to his reflections on moral questions, especially in *NE.*

The text as it has come down to us comprises ten books. The first book serves as an introduction insofar as it analyzes man's longing for happiness and fleshes out various convictions about happiness. Toward the end of the first book (I.12), Aristotle makes the transition from the analysis of happiness to that of virtue in general and, in Book II, moral virtue in particular. Given that his concern is of a practical nature, that is to say, directed toward becoming virtuous (1103b26–29), an investigation into actions and their circumstances is needed. And so the first five chapters of Book III are devoted to the relation between virtue and voluntary action, choice and deliberation. At III.6.1116a6, Aristotle begins his extensive analysis of eleven moral virtues: fortitude (III.6–9), temperance (III.10–12), liberality (IV.1), magnificence (IV.2), magnanimity (IV.3), ambition (IV.4), meekness (IV.5), friendliness (IV.6), truthfulness (IV.7), and wittiness (IV.8). The eleventh virtue, justice, comprises the entire fifth book. In Book VI, Aristotle returns to what he had already announced in Book II (1103b31–34), that is, a study of what it means to choose a mean according to right reason. Hence it contains a study of the intellectual virtues and their relation to prudence. In Book VII, Aristotle discusses continence and its opposite, or self-restraint and the lack thereof; but in the final chapters (VII.11–14), he also deals with pleasure. Books VIII and IX contain a lengthy discussion of friendship. In Book X, he first turns to

3. Jaeger, *Aristotle,* 228–58. For a discussion of Jaeger, see Chris Bobonich, "Aristotle's Ethical Treatises," in *The Blackwell Guide to Aristotle's "Nicomachean Ethics,"* ed. R. Kraut (Oxford: Oxford University Press, 2006), 12–36.

4. The sophist Protagoras raised the question whether virtues can be taught. His motto that man is the measure of all things seems to exclude universally valid rules of conduct. Socrates insisted on the avoidance of all excess (μηδὲν ἄγαν) and dealt with many themes, but did not reach a systematic presentation of his teaching on the virtues.

5. Plato proposed the doctrine of the four cardinal virtues and described, especially in his dialogue *Phaedrus,* the difficulties we encounter from the side of our sensual appetite (τὸ ἐπιθυμητικόν) when we strive to act well.

6. See Plato's *Laws* VIII.

pleasure as a preface to his concluding discussion on happiness in chapters 6–8; in the final chapter (X.9), he prepares the transition to the *Politics*.

The earliest extant commentary on an Aristotelian text is the commentary by Aspasius (fl. ca. 143 A.D.) on—precisely—*NE* I–IV and VII–VIII, which, according to Gauthier, gives us "the most precious" text from antiquity for understanding Aristotle's ethics.[7] The manuscript tradition has supplemented this incomplete commentary with (anonymous) commentaries and scholia by Byzantine scholars such as Eustratius (twelfth century) for Books I and VII, an anonymous Byzantine scholar for Book VII, and Michael of Ephesus (twelfth century) for Books IX–X.[8] The fact that the compiler had to take recourse to much later commentaries already indicates that *NE* was not much commented upon.

The Church Fathers took over a considerable number of the ethical teachings of the Greek and Roman classical authors. Despite their fundamental dismissal of the pagan way of life and immorality, many were convinced that there is a fundamental correspondence between much of what these non-Christian authors wrote and Christian moral doctrine. Especially definitions and divisions of the virtues as well as detailed considerations about the virtues were borrowed from this classical literature.[9] A decisive factor in the reception history occurred, according to Gauthier, when Nemesius (fl. ca. 390 A.D.) extensively, although without mentioning Aristotle, used *NE*'s Book III to discuss human freedom in his *De natura hominis*. Its reception in Maximus the Confessor and John Damascene, and through them later on in Thomas Aquinas, who, as many other medieval authors, attributed the *De natura hominis* to Gregory of Nyssa, indirectly gave the Christian world many important elements of Aristotle's psychology of the will.[10]

According to Anna Akasoy the impact of *NE* in the medieval Arab world was "fairly small." This is suggested by Averroes's remark that he had at first

7. *L'Éthique à Nicomaque, introduction, traduction et commentaire* by René Antoine Gauthier and Jean-Yves Jolif, 2nd ed. (Louvain: Nauwelaerts, 1970), I:1.100. The entire third chapter (91–240) of ibid., devoted to the literary history of *NE*, remains a rich source of information. For an analysis of Aspasius's commentary, see P. Moraux, *Der Aristotelismus bei den Griechen. Band 2: Der Aristotelismus im I. und II. Jh. n. Chr.* (Berlin: De Gruyter, 1984), 249–93.

8. Aspasius's text can be found in CAG 19.1. Much of the anonymous commentaries can be found in CAG 19.2, 20, and 22.3. These texts have been translated into English in the Ancient Commentators on Aristotle series.

9. See Charles Norris Cochrane, *Christianity and Classical Culture* (Oxford: Oxford University Press, 1939); Gerard L. Ellspermann, *The Attitude of the Early Christian Latin Writers toward Pagan Literature and Learning* (Washington, D.C.: The Catholic University of America Press, 1949); J. Liebard, *Les enseignements moraux des Pères apostoliques* (Gembloux: J. Ducalot, 1970).

10. *L'Éthique à Nicomaque* (trans. Gauthier and Jolif), I:1.102. See also Beatrice Motta, "Nemesius of Emesa," in *Cambridge History of Philosophy in Later Antiquity*, ed. Lloyd P. Gerson (Cambridge: Cambridge University Press, 2010), 1:509–19, esp. 516–17.

only the first four books at his disposal and only later with much difficulty was able to acquire the remaining books. His so-called *Middle Commentary* on *NE*, translated into Latin around 1240, "remained almost unknown in the rest of the Islamic world."[11] Neither Avicenna nor Averroes will have a major influence on the development of Aquinas's ethical thought.[12]

Toward the end of the twelfth century the Latin West will gradually become acquainted with the text of *NE*, first by way of the appearance of the so-called *Ethica Vetus*, consisting of only Books II and III, and then by the *Ethica Nova*, of which Book I as well as some excerpts from the other books have survived. Both these two early versions are the work of Burgundio of Pisa.[13] These partial translations serve as the basis for the earliest reception among canonists, theologians, and philosophers. In fact, numerous (mostly anonymous) commentaries from the Faculty of Arts, dating from the first half of the thirteenth century, when a course on *NE* at the university of Paris first became optional and later mandatory, have survived. The most important impetus, however, in the study of *NE* occurred in 1246–47 when Robert Grosseteste published not only a complete translation of Aristotle's text but also of a number of Greek commentaries such as those of Aspasius, Eustratius (eleventh century), and Michael of Ephesus (twelfth century) together with his own explanatory notes. The value of this compilation became immediately apparent. Albert the Great was the first to adopt Grosseteste's translation in his Cologne lectures between 1248 and 1252 (published as *Super Ethica*); therein he refers to the compilation as "the Commentator" almost three hundred times.[14]

Turning to the commentary of Aquinas on this treatise, the *Sentencia libri Ethicorum* (hereafter *SLE*), we have at our disposal an excellent critical edition of the text in the Leonine Edition, prepared by R. A. Gauthier.[15] Based on the influence of the early Parisian commentaries and his use throughout

11. Anna Akasoy, "The Arabic and Islamic Reception of the Nicomachean Ethics," in *The Reception of Aristotle's Ethics*, ed. Jörn Müller (Cambridge: Cambridge University Press, 2012), 85–106.

12. See Elders, *Thomas Aquinas and His Predecessors*, 298–99 and 327.

13. For more details on all *NE* translations see *L'Éthique à Nicomaque* (trans. Gauthier and Jolif), I:1.111–32, as well as the first part of the critical edition of the Latin translations in vol. 26 of the Aristoteles Latinus series: *Ethica Nicomachea. Translatio Antiquissima libr. II–III sive 'Ethica Vetus', Translationis Antiquioris quae supersunt sive 'Ethica Nova', 'Hoferiana', 'Borghesiana', Translatio Roberti Grosseteste Lincolniensis sive 'Liber Ethicorum' (Recensio Pura et Recensio Recognita)*, 5 vols., ed. R. A. Gauthier (Leiden / Brussels: Brill / Desclée De Brouwer, 1972–74).

14. *Super Ethica*, ed. Wilhelm Kübel (Münster: Aschendorff, 1968–87), edit. colon. T. 14; see the indices on 817–18. For detailed studies of this commentary, see Georg Wieland, *Ethica—Scientia practica. Die Anfänge der philosophischen Ethik im 13. Jahrhunderts* (Münster: Aschendorff, 1981), and Jörn Müller, *Natürliche Moral und philosophische Ethik bei Albertus Magnus* (Münster: Aschendorff, 2001).

15. *Sententia libri Ethicorum* (Rome: Ad Sanctae Sabinae, 1969), which constitutes vol. 47 in the Leonine edition and in particular Gauthier's "Praefatio" at 1*–275*. See also his "Appendix: Saint Thomas et l'Éthique à Nicomaque," in *Sententia libri Politicorum / Tabula libri Ethicorum* (Rome: Ad Sanctae Sabinae, 1971), v–xxv.

his writings of the *Ethica vetus* used in Paris before 1250, Gauthier argues that Thomas studied *NE* in Paris in 1246–47. It is also generally agreed that in 1248–52 Thomas drew up a *reportatio* of Albert's lectures, which Albert used for the composition of his *Super Ethica*. Gauthier has established the massive influence of Albert's *Super Ethica* on the composition of *SLE*.[16] Thomas used a version of Aristotle's text, the *Recensio recognita*, a revision of a version of Grosseteste's translation.[17] According to Gauthier, *SLE* was written during his second regency at Paris in 1271–72, that is to say, posterior to the composition of *Prima Secundae*.[18] Its close temporal proximity to the moral part of the *Summa theologiae* has led many to believe that Aquinas wrote *SLE* as a kind of preparation and help for the construction of his moral theology. Some sections of the commentary, however, seem to have been written later than the parallel passages of the *Secunda Secundae*.[19] Apparently, Thomas wanted to present the text as a study in philosophical ethics and as a faithful summary of what Aristotle exposits in his book. For him, Aristotle is a witness to human nature. On the other hand, all through his works, Thomas is intent on coordinating the philosophical analysis of human moral actions and the Gospel message. This raises, however, the question of the precise relationship between Aristotle's philosophical treatise and Thomas's moral theology. Are there intrusions of theological views in the explanation of Aristotle's moral doctrine? While studying and analyzing the text of *SLE*, I shall examine the relevant passages where such theological themes appear.

The influence of *SLE* on the later Middle Ages and the Renaissance is considerable.[20] Jörn Müller, for instance, writes: "Its popularity outranked by far the later commentaries on *NE*, even the ones which were fashioned in the form of questions on Aristotle's text (e.g., the quite influential *Quaestiones su-*

---

16. Gauthier has counted 350 passages in *SLE* where Thomas depends on Albert, not only for Albert's explanations but also for his knowledge of the Greek commentaries translated by Grosseteste (praefatio, 235*–56*).

17. Gauthier offers arguments against attributing this *recensio* to William of Moerbeke ("Saint Thomas et l'Éthique à Nicomaque," xviii–xx), arguments which are contested by Jozef Brams, "The Revised Version of Grosseteste's Translation of the Nicomachean Ethics," *Bulletin de Philosophie Médiévale* 36 (1994): 45–55.

18. See also René-Antoine Gauthier, "La date du commentaire de saint Thomas sur l'Éthique á Nicomaque," *Recherches de théologie ancienne et médiévale* 18 (1951): 66–105, and Auguste Mansion, "Autour de la date du commentaire de saint Thomas sur L'Éthique à Nicomaque," *Revue philosophique de Louvain* 50 (1952): 460–71.

19. This position is argued for in James C. Doig, *Aquinas's Philosophical Commentary on the "Ethics": A Historical Perspective* (Dordrecht: Kluwer, 2001), esp. 197–229. Vernon J. Bourke has argued for a composition in Orvieto in 1261–64 and subsequent revision in Paris: "The Nicomachean Ethics and Thomas Aquinas," in *St. Thomas Aquinas 1274–1974: Commemorative Studies* (Toronto: Pontifical Institute of Mediaeval Studies, 1974), 1:239–55.

20. For Thomas's influence following the condemnations of 1277, see R.-A. Gauthier, "Trois commentaires 'Averroistes' sur l'Éthique à Nicomacque," *Archives d'histoire doctrinale et littéraire du Moyen Âge* 16 (1947–48): 187–336, and Iacopo Costa, "L'Éthique à Nicomaque à la Faculté des arts de Paris avant et après 1277," *Archives d'histoire doctrinale et littéraire du Moyen Âge* 79 (2012): 71–114.

per decem libros Ethicorum by John Buridan)."[21] Although Thomas's *SLE* has been studied more extensively than most of his other Aristotelian commentaries, its doctrinal wealth has not always been recognized.[22] While most scholars praise the light it sheds on Aristotle's often difficult text, there are those who feel that it is not a reliable presentation of Aristotle's ethical thought.[23] Others, like Gauthier, consider it "une oeuvre manquée" (a failure); it is surpassed by far by the second part of the *Summa theologiae,* Gauthier writes, and is of no help for the understanding of Aristotle's text.[24] This statement seems to be close to the view of those Christian authors who think that a perfectly developed natural ethical science without Christian revelation is not possible.[25]

In the following exposition and summary of the commentary, special attention will be given to passages where Thomas seems to depart from what Aristotle says or where he completes the text. Above all, I shall try to determine if and where the commentary may have been influenced by Christian moral doctrine.[26]

The Commentary of Thomas Aquinas

The Nature of Ethics

Unlike some of his other Aristotelian commentaries, *SLE* is not preceded by a proemium. The reason for this absence could be that Thomas felt that the first chapter of Book I (1094a1–18) provides a good opportunity to ex-

21. Jörn Müller, "Aquinas's Commenting Strategy in his *Sententia libri Ethicorum.* A Case Study," *Divus Thomas* 118 (2015): 148–84, at 148. Müller refers to David Lines, *Aristotle's Ethics in the Italian Renaissance (ca. 1300–1650): The Universities and the Problem of Moral Education* (Leiden: Brill, 2002), 158–66, and Lines, "Sources and Authorities for Moral Philosophy in the Italian Renaissance: Thomas Aquinas and Jean Buridan on Aristotle's Ethics," in *Moral Philosophy on the Threshold of Modernity,* ed. Jill Kraye and Risto Saarinen (Dordrecht: Springer, 2005), 7–29.

22. Apart from the study by Doig mentioned earlier, there is *Aquinas and the "Nicomachean Ethics,"* ed. Tobias Hoffmann, Jörn Müller, and Matthias Perkams (Cambridge: Cambridge University Press, 2013).

23. Jaffa, *Thomism and Aristotelianism,* 7.

24. *L'Éthique à Nicomaque* (trans. Gauthier and Jolif), I:1.193. In his "Saint Thomas et l'Éthique à Nicomaque"—printed as an appendix to vol. 48 of the Leonine edition (Rome: Editori di san Tommaso, 1971), xxiv—Fr. Gauthier is better advised and calls the commentary *une œuvre de sagesse.* The disappointment regarding the doctrinal content of *SLE* compared to that of *ST*'s *Secunda Pars* is explained by the fact that Thomas wants to present the philosophical ethics of Aristotle which, on certain points, was not as developed as his own exposition in the *Secunda Pars.*

25. On the role of reason in moral science one may compare Leo Elders, "The Primacy of Reason according to Aquinas," in *Logica et Musica: In honorem Summi Pontificis Benedicti XVI,* ed. Elzbieta Szczurko, Tadeusz Guz, and Horst Seidl (Frankfurt am Main: Peter Lang, 2012), 87–115.

26. In our exposition of Aquinas's commentary on the *Nicomachean Ethics,* the translation by C. I. Litzinger, O.P., has been a great help, in particular for the translation of certain terms: *St. Thomas Aquinas: Commentary on Aristotle's "Nicomachean Ethics"* (Notre Dame, Ind.: Dumb Ox Books, 1993). Note, however, that this translation is not based on the critical edition.

pound the nature of ethics as a science. Indeed, from the very beginning of his commentary, Thomas recalls the division of the sciences in order to determine the nature of ethics and to assign to it its place among the sciences. The wise man studies the realm of beings, brings about order in what he does, and attempts to explain the order he discovers in the world. The order in the physical world is the subject matter of natural philosophy, while ordering the acts of the intellect is the task of logic, and ordering the acts of the will that of ethics; the arts and crafts help us to bring about order in the work we carry out.[27] Liberal arts belong to the productive sciences but may prepare one for the study of ethics and help man to organize his moral life.[28] Because ethics considers man's actions, it presupposes knowledge of philosophical anthropology. But ethics differs from the latter because it is based on the first principles of the practical intellect, just as the theoretical sciences are based on the first principles of the speculative intellect. For this reason there is no real continuity between the theoretical sciences and ethics, but there is a certain dependence. It is impossible to study the ethics of Aquinas without drawing on the insights reached in the philosophy of nature. The importance of this connection will appear in every chapter of the commentary.[29]

Subscribing to a fundamental doctrine of Aristotle, Thomas points out from the very beginning of his commentary that man is a social being and belongs to such communities as the family and the state, societies he needs to develop himself and to live a well-ordered life.[30] Consequently, the study of man's actions is divided into three branches: (1) ethics, which deals with man's life as an individual; (2) the discipline that considers what man has to do in the context of a family; and (3) the science of man's life in a political community. The commentary is mainly restricted to the first and second themes, although in dealing with the virtues, in particular with justice, man's special duties toward the political society are also examined.

In the introduction to his commentary, Aquinas makes it clear that ethics is not merely about insight in what one ought to do. Does not Aristotle write that ethics, rather than explaining what virtue is, aims at making us virtuous?[31] Large sections of the text consist indeed of prudential reflections on the vir-

---

27. This division of the sciences and arts had been developed in the Academy and after Aristotle it was vigorously propagated by authors of the Stoic school.

28. See Gérard Verbeke, "Arts libéraux et morale d'après Saint Thomas," in *Arts libéraux et philosophie au Moyen Âge* (Paris: Vrin, 1969), 653–61.

29. Leo Elders, "El método en la ética según santo Tomás de Aquino," *Medioevo* 18 (1992): 71–84.

30. *SLE* I, lesson 1, no. 4: "ut homo non solum vivat, sed et bene vivat."

31. *NE* II.2.1103b27.

tues. But it is noteworthy that Thomas slightly modifies Aristotle's statement. He writes that the purpose of ethics is indeed *not only* knowledge, but also human action, as is the case with all practical disciplines.[32] Ethics is a philosophical discipline and the knowledge it gives us is of a general nature insofar as it considers the principles of our actions; but, in contrast with the theoretical sciences, these general considerations are ordered to the performance of good actions. Nevertheless, how one should act in concrete circumstances is not determined by the science of ethics, but by the virtue of prudence.[33]

Book I

Aristotle's opening words are that every art and inquiry aims at some good. Thomas begins his commentary by introducing the idea of order, referring to *Metaphysics* I.2.982a18: it is the task of the wise man to order his own life and his natural environment. But to introduce order is the task of the intellect. We have already noted that ethics is a practical science. Hence it does not tell us so much what virtue is as aim at rendering us good persons, as Aristotle says.[34] Yet certain chapters of the treatise seem to depend on speculative rather than on practical reason, such as the section of the text dealing with man's happiness. Other chapters, however, treat of our individual actions. Aristotle also repeatedly reminds his readers that certitude cannot be reached in the field of ethics. For this reason it is not surprising that the Oxford scholar H. H. Joachim considered *NE* an "utterly pragmatic treatise," although other students of Aristotle are inclined to make ethics dependent on the speculative intellect.[35]

What is the position of Thomas in this respect? In his commentary, he stresses the cognitive nature of ethics more than Aristotle does. For Aristotle, ethics is helpful to man so that he may act in view of his true happiness, but the determination of the end is probable rather than certain, for knowledge about what one should do also depends on one's character.[36] Thomas, on the other hand, calls the knowledge of the end necessary: to lead a life as one ought to

32. *SLE* I, lesson 3, no. 40: "Finis enim huius scientiae non est sola cognitio ad quam forte pervenire possunt passionum sectatores, sed finis huius scientiae est actus humanus, sicut et omnium scientiarum practicarum."

33. See Leo Elders, "The Ethics of St. Thomas Aquinas and Its Importance for Our Age," in *Faithfulness to Reality: Essays in Honour of M. A. Krapiec*, ed. Wiernosc Rzeczywistosci (Lublin: Catholic University of Lublin Press, 2002), 396–418.

34. *NE* 1103b27.

35. See *Aristotle: The "Nicomachean Ethics": A Commentary by the late H. H. Joachim*, ed. D. A. Rees (Oxford: Clarendon Press, 1951); Takatura Ando, *Aristotle's Theory of Practical Cognition* (Amsterdam: The Hague, 1958), 210ff.

36. *NE* 1094a22.

lead, one must have a true knowledge of one's last end.[37] Furthermore, when Aristotle writes that the purpose of the study of ethics is not knowledge but action, Thomas restricts this by adding that ethics does *not only* aim at knowledge.[38] As mentioned above, the change in wording is significant because it witnesses to a clear distinction between the science of ethics, on the one hand, and prudence, on the other. Ethics acquires an epistemological status somewhat different from the one Aristotle assigned to it.

And when Aristotle writes that ethics regulates the arts and sciences, Thomas observes that this applies to the question of whether the use we make of them is morally sound but not to these pursuits as such.[39] Ethics has a well-defined task of its own. There is among Thomists some diversity of judgment with regard to the question of whether an independent moral science is possible.[40] As appears in the commentary, the intuition of moral duties is unique: there is no simple identity between the *is* and the *ought,* yet moral law and our duties are the expression of our (personal) nature. But because ethics must lead us to an end we do not really know, it is necessarily an imperfect science. In his commentary, Thomas hints several times at the imperfect nature of the happiness that Aristotle declares to be the end of the virtuous life.

In lesson 1 (I.1.1094a1–18), after explaining the role of reason in the differentiation of the sciences as set forth in the introduction, Thomas excludes those actions from the subject matter of ethics that are not subject to our will and reason (no. 3). When Aristotle writes that all men desire the good, Thomas explains that beings that have no knowledge are moved by the divine intellect. The supreme good, God, is in some way desired in all movements (no. 11).[41] We must distinguish between immanent and transient operations. But some operations are concerned with external things only insofar as they are of use, but not in order to change them. As immanent actions, these operations do not produce something (no. 13). There are many different operations and so there are different ends (no. 15), some of which are subordinated to others (no. 16). It makes no difference to the order of ends whether the end is an activity or a product.

In lesson 2 (I.1.1094a18–b11), Aristotle shows that human life has an end that is not desired on account of other ends: if there were infinite re-

---

37. *SLE* I, 2, no. 22.

38. *SLE* I, 3, no. 40: "Finis enim huius scientiae non est *sola* cognitio"; and II, 2, no. 256: "non enim in hac scientia scrutamur quid est virtus ad hoc *solum* ut sciamus huius rei veritatem."

39. *SLE* I, 2, no. 25.

40. See Vernon J. Bourke, "Moral Philosophy Without Revelation?," *The Thomist* 40 (1976): 555–70. I will return to this question in *SLE* I, lesson 2 (below).

41. The good accomplishes us as our end. Our striving reaches its end in the desired thing which is its good (*ST* I-II, q. 26, a. 2).

gress in ends, all desires would be useless because one would never get what one wants. Now the good is what all things desire and this desire is natural. Thomas adds a note: a natural desire is an inclination that the first mover has given us and that cannot be frustrated (no. 21). There must be some last end, and we ought to know about it in order to direct ourselves to it (nos. 22–23). But as Thomas says, Aristotle points to the limits of our knowledge of it. Its consideration belongs to the most important science in this field, which is political science. He mentions next its role in ordering the different pursuits in the city, and its use of the other practical sciences, calling it an architectural science (nos. 24–29).

Some years ago there was a diversity of opinion among Thomists regarding whether an independent philosophical ethics is possible.[42] The commentary shows beyond doubt that Thomas does admit natural ethics, despite the fact that man's sole final end is supernatural contemplation, and reason alone cannot answer questions about the precise nature of this contemplation of God and the way to attain it. Reason, however, does discover that we are ordained to the contemplation of God. This finds its expression in a *natural desire* for this end. This insight entails the possibility of natural ethics: reason discerns the major obligations of natural law—as will appear in the following books of *NE* that deal with the moral virtues—and tells us how to live in conformity with the exigencies of our human nature. Thomas explains that it is desirable that political science aims at the good of a whole people and also at that of the different countries. This good shows a greater likeness to God, who is the ultimate cause of all goods. Political science is the most momentous of the practical sciences, while theology is the most important science *simpliciter*. By "theology," Thomas may mean here in the first place philosophical theology but implicitly also Christian theology (nos. 30–31).

In lesson 3 (I.3.1094b11–1095a13), which discusses teaching and learning ethics, Aristotle draws attention to the fact that opinions about what is good and what should be done often vary in different people and in different countries, where material goods are not always used in the same way. Because of these differences, we must proceed from simple principles and go from there to what is more complex (nos. 32–35). We should not expect total certainty in contingent matters. A special difficulty is that young people are not good students of political science because they are inexperienced (nos. 36–38). People

42. Jacques Maritain and Étienne Gilson tend to give a negative answer, but J. Ramírez, O. Lottin, and others argue that even without recourse to revelation reason can prove man's moral obligations. See Bourke, "Moral Philosophy Without Revelation," 355–70, as well as Ralph McInerny, *The Question of Christian Ethics* (Washington, D.C.: The Catholic University of America Press, 1993), and Leo Elders, *The Ethics of St. Thomas Aquinas* (Frankfurt am Main: Peter Lang, 2005); reprinted edition 2019.

at large may not follow the instructions of ethics either because they choose to satisfy their concupiscence or when, contrary to their resolve, they are overcome by a passion. Thomas repeats that the end of moral science is not knowledge alone (*non est sola cognitio*) but good human actions.

In lesson 4 (I.4.1095a14–b13), Aristotle, according to Thomas's *divisio textus*, begins his treatise on moral science. He first determines what happiness is, after which in I.13 (lesson 19, see below), Aristotle turns to the study of the virtues, which occupies the following books. There is a general agreement that happiness comes with living well and acting well (no. 45). But then opinions differ on what this entails: some see it in some sensible good, while for the Platonists it is the good itself. Aristotle stresses how important it is for a good moral life to have been brought up well, but he nevertheless leaves open the possibility of learning by oneself what one ought to do (nos. 53–54), and stresses the principle that certain things must be accepted just the way they are (*quia ita est,* says Thomas).

Aristotle warns us not to overlook the difference between arguments from principles and arguments toward principles.[43] Thomas explains that the arguments from principles are restricted to *propter quid* demonstrations, like those that are used, for example, in mathematics. Then he adds that we always go from what is better known to us to what is less known. We must, however, distinguish between what is by itself better known (the principles and the causes) and that which is so for us. In ethics, the effects are better known and so we argue from the effects to their principles, as we also do in the philosophy of nature (no. 51).

In lesson 5 (I.5.1095b14–1096a10), some opinions about happiness are reviewed. The majority of people place what they assume to be happiness in things that bring them a life of pleasure. Such sensual goods, however, like eating well and sexual intercourse, are also pursued by animals (nos. 56–61). Others place happiness in an active or public life (no. 62). They seek honor, but the things that cause one to be honored (such as virtue) are better. Aristotle discards also this opinion: virtuous people may not have an opportunity to practice the virtues and be ill-favored by fortune (nos. 63–73).

The theory of those who place happiness in a separated good is discussed in lesson 6 (I.6.1096a11–35). Aristotle shows a certain reluctance to discuss and to reject the doctrine of the venerable Plato but, he says, it is more in agreement with good morals to oppose a friend for the sake of truth, for truth is

---

43. Aristotle's text is difficult. Some scholars hold that it is deductive, others feel that we must proceed in both ways. See W. F. R. Hardie, *Aristotle's Ethical Theory* (Oxford: Clarendon, 1968), 34.

something divine (nos. 74–77).[44] Thomas mentions a view of Andronicus[45] and adds a note: while rejecting a subsistent Idea of the good in which good things would participate, Aristotle does not deny that God is the good itself, on which all good things depend, for he teaches this in *Metaphysics* XII.10. What he does reject is the view of a subsistent Idea of goodness in which good things would participate. Three arguments are advanced against Plato's theory. First, substance is being by itself from which are derived all other beings and so substance replaces the subsistent Idea of the good. The second argument insists on the fact that "good" is not predicated univocally of different things. The different categories each have their own essence and goodness. Finally, if Plato's theory were right, there would be one single science of all good things, but this is clearly wrong (nos. 80–82).

In lesson 7 (I.6.1096a34–b29), the discussion about Plato's Idea of the Good is continued. An error of this theory is that the participated form is the same as its Idea. Thomas adds a clause beginning with *considerandum est* to stress that the separate good which is the cause of all good things has to be placed in a higher degree of goodness than the goods we find in this life (*quam ea quae apud nos sunt*), precisely because it is the last end of all of them (no. 84). He even suggests that Aristotle is closer to a correct notion of this good than Plato was. If one says that the good things here are perishable and thus of lower rank, Aristotle replies that when the good is eternal, it does not mean that it is better, for then the difference is in duration. In our world, we can add "goodness" to things, so that what lasts longer will be better, but to the pure idea of the good nothing can be added (nos. 83–86). Contrary to Plato, the Pythagoreans did not hold that the good has only one nature. An absolute good cannot be an Idea common to all good things. Some goods are good by themselves, but other things are called good in reference to what is good in itself: they are useful (nos. 87–91). But what is good by itself? Is it sought for itself? If nothing else were a good by itself except the Idea of the good, this Idea would impress its likeness on other things that are not good by themselves. But if so, the same nature of goodness would appear in very different things (honor, prudence, etc.). But these things differ, so that there is no common form of goodness. Aristotle explains that in reality "good" is predicated of things analogically, according to the different ways in which analogy is used. Thomas explains that this is the case when different things are ordered to the

44. Aristotle does not mention Plato by name. Nuyens, *L'évolution*, 181, reads in the text that when writing these lines Aristotle was still close to the Academy, but his interpretation is not very convincing.

45. Thomas refers to a pseudo-Aristotelian text *De laudabilis bonis*, sometimes attributed to Andronicus of Rhodes.

same end or depend on the first principle of goodness they are ordered to. He adds that the separate good is the ground plan, the core (*idea et ratio*) of all good things, their principle and end (nos. 92–96).

In lesson 8 (I.6.1096b30–1097a15), Aristotle tells us that even if the Idea of the good existed, it could not be the object and cause of our happiness, as it would not be the result of human acts, nor is it produced by man. One could reply that it is the model of all the goods we seek to attain and that it helps us to understand them. Aristotle refutes this argument: all the sciences and arts tend to some good, but never resort to the knowledge of this separated good; in their practice of the arts, craftsmen never turn to this separate good; a physician, for instance, does not seek health as such, but the health of this person (nos. 97–102).

The nature of happiness is discussed in lesson 9 (I.7.1097a15–b21), at first in general. The discussion extends over several lessons. The good we seek to reach in our different activities is that for the sake of which we act. It is called the end. Beyond these different ends we pursue, there is the human good, that is, happiness. Commenting on 1097a28–29, Thomas insists that that there must be *one* last end for all men because of the unity of human nature (no. 106). For Thomas this is man's sole end, namely, the vision of God, but he is very much aware of the fact that what Aristotle is describing as the happiness of man is different: it is the imperfect happiness of this life, as he repeatedly points out. Thomas notes the complex nature of what Aristotle presents as man's last end and he adds a long explanation: there is a parallelism between the manner in which an agent moves to an end and the way in which the end moves the desire of the agent. Now, certain agents move only owing to a movement they received; others move partly by their own form, and partly need to be moved by the main agent. Finally, there is the most perfect agent which moves without being moved by others. Similarly, there is a good which is desired in view of something else (the useful); then there is a good which is desired partly because of its own perfection and partly in view of a further end; finally, there is a most perfect good which is never desired for the sake of something else. Thomas adds that in the text Aristotle distinguishes between these three types of ends (nos. 108–9). This remark helps to solve some of the difficulties raised against Aristotle's account of the last end. Happiness satisfies our desire, but because we are social beings, it also extends to the good of others, though this does not go on indefinitely. Aristotle, however, Thomas says, is discussing happiness as attainable in this life, "for happiness in a future life is entirely beyond the investigation of reason" (no. 113). Happiness implies self-sufficiency because it brings with it what is necessary and what we absolutely need (nos. 107–17). Bernard William and Anthony Kenny argued that Aristotle apparently admits other ends besides happiness, but these can only be subordinated goods, not our real end.[46]

In lesson 10 (I.7.1097b22–1098a20), happiness is defined. Aristotle shows that happiness consists in an activity proper to man. His well-being and good are found in the operations proper to him. The reason is that things are perfected by their activity. When something extrinsic to man is called his happiness, this is only so because he attains it through his operations, either by making it, by using it, or by enjoying it. If man has an operation proper to him *qua* man, *human* happiness must consist in this operation (nos. 118–19). At this point, Thomas observes that if happiness is thought to consist in something else, it will be something that makes a person capable of this operation, or it is what he attains by it, namely "as God is said to be the beatitude of man," Thomas adds quite naturally in line with the argument, but creating an opening to the Christian doctrine of beatitude (no. 120). Man must have a proper operation resulting from his being and form, as already each organ of the body has its typical operation. This is his operation as a rational being: it comprehends the appetite as controlled by reason. It is an activity according to virtue, that is, pertaining to the best of the virtues. Aristotle adds that for happiness, continuity is required. But real continuity and perpetuity, and so perfect happiness, cannot be had in the present life, Thomas says. Happiness in the present life results not just from one good action but from the continued performance of good deeds (nos. 121–30).

In lesson 11 (I.7.1098a20–b8), Aristotle explains the conditions to which we must pay attention by further determining happiness, namely by proceeding from what is common to what is proper. Our reason has the characteristic that it grasps the truth little by little. The passage of time will also help, provided we remain concentrated on the subject. We must also be aware that there are differences in the principles we use: some are manifest by themselves, others by induction, and still others are derived from custom. Induction helps our reason to find the right thing to do. Following Aristotle's indications, Thomas distinguishes between several types of induction. The first is called *ex particularibus imaginatis*. An example is the induction made in arithmetic that num-

---

46. Anthony Kenny, "Aristotle on Happiness," *Proceedings of the Aristotelean Society* 66 (1965): 93–102; Bernard Williams, "Aristotle on the Good: A Formal Sketch," *The Philosophical Quarterly* 12 (1962): 289–96. According to Hardie, Aristotle does not clearly distinguish between a "comprehensive plan" and "paramount objects" (Hardie, *Aristotle's Ethical Theory*, 23). Ever since Hardie's distinction between Aristotle's conception of happiness as "dominant" and "inclusive," that is, happiness is either a single activity (*theoria*) or the exercise of several ethical virtues, both these positions have been defended. For an overview see Terence Irwin, "Conceptions of Happiness in the Nicomachean Ethics," in *The Oxford Handbook of Aristotle*, ed. Christopher Shields (Oxford: Oxford University Press, 2012), 495–528.

bers are either even or odd. A second type is the induction in natural sciences: through sense experience we learn certain things, for example, that all living beings need food. Finally, there is also induction in ethics: certain principles may be drawn from experience, such as "concupiscence decreases when one does not give in to one's desires" (no. 137). But this should not be understood in a restrictive sense, as if there would not be any other inductions in ethics. Aristotle acknowledges considerations based on man's nature, and Thomas mentions moral principles known to us by an analysis of nature, so that he can write that in ethics we proceed *modo compositivo*, as we do in all productive arts (nos. 131–38).

In lesson 12 (I.8.1098b9–1099a7), we see that what is commonly said about happiness agrees with what Aristotle has laid down thus far. The philosophers he discusses assert that the goods of the soul are the most important goods. The view that happiness is an operation of the rational soul is in agreement with this old conviction. But it is an operation that remains in the agent; it is an immanent action. Yet some philosophers taught that happiness consists in the moral virtues, such as prudence, provided pleasure is added. Some added external goods as an element of happiness. But the more distinguished authors placed happiness in the goods of the soul, in virtuous actions more than in virtue itself (nos. 139–53).

The discussion is continued in lesson 13 (I.8.1099a7–1099b8), that is to say, the view of some is set forth that happiness is virtue together with pleasure. Aristotle agrees: ordinarily virtuous actions are pleasurable, and this pleasure is preferable to others, although for some people pleasure accompanies vicious acts, not in agreement with nature but due to corrupt habits. Virtuous men find pleasure in good acts. Their life has nobility and goodness in itself, and pleasure necessarily belongs to virtue, for virtuous acts are in conformity with the habit of the virtues and are ordered to the right end and are noble. The good man judges that actions in accordance with the virtues are pleasurable. Are external goods necessary to happiness? Happiness needs external goods as instruments, Aristotle explains with the help of some examples (nos. 154–64).

In lesson 14 (I.9.1099b9–1100a5), Aristotle investigates the cause of happiness. If happiness proceeds from a human cause, that cause could be learning or practice, in the case of moral virtues, or by further exercise of them. But it may have a divine cause, Aristotle says, for the gods bestow gifts on men: now happiness is a supreme gift. Thomas adds that it is reasonable that happiness as man's ultimate end should come to him from the supreme God (nos. 165–68). His arguments runs as follows: to arrive at a higher end a higher power is needed; now happiness is man's last end. This is illustrated by the fact that our bodies and intellects receive their perfections from the beings above them, namely, from heavenly bodies and separated substances. Hence happiness comes to man from the highest power, that is, God. But the details of this argument belong to metaphysics.[47] Thomas uses the opportunity provided by Aristotle's text (namely his allusion to happiness as a gift of the gods, 1099b12) to bring in God as a cause of man's (imperfect) happiness.

How do we have to understand in this passage Thomas's reference to God's help? In this context, it cannot but mean God's general motive force, which is the source of all created activity and which leads things to their respective ends. The need to admit this divine motion is given with Aristotle's theory of actuality and potency, so that Thomas's explanation is in line with Aristotle's own principles.[48] Nevertheless, it is acceptable (*tolerabiliter*) to say that happiness has a human cause insofar as it comes to man by study, exercise, and training. Thomas admits Aristotle's affirmation "even if it is not sent us by God, but comes to us because of virtue" (1099b14–15) but he adds the following reading: "if it is not sent to us *immediately* by God" (no. 169).[49] However, insofar as "divine" not only indicates what comes from God but also what makes us like God in goodness, happiness is divine, Thomas adds. It is not a product of chance, for it would be strange if our best good depended on chance. Happiness is an activity of rational man in accord with virtue. It cannot be attributed to irrational animals. Aristotle excludes children from experiencing real happiness because they do not have the full use of reason. Happiness belongs to what constitutes the end of human nature. Nature does not fall short in providing the means to reach its end. If therefore happiness is the end of human nature, it must be attainable by those who possess human nature, or at least by most of them. This is the case if it proceeds from a human cause. Likewise, it is not the result of good luck: what results from good luck lies outside the activity of reason, for happiness is an act of virtue and what is according to virtue is according to reason. Thomas adds that happiness results from some proximate human cause but principally and in the first place from a divine cause. On several occasions Thomas reminds the reader that Aristotle's view is an *opinio* or *sententia* (nos. 170–76).[50]

Lesson 15 (I.9–10.1100a5–b7) asks: can anyone be called happy in this life? Solon thought that we should call happy only the one who is close to death

<hr>

47. At the background is the condemned proposition 173, which says that happiness cannot be given by God. See Hissette, *Enquête*, 268–69.

48. See *SCG* II.17.

49. This affirms that Thomas has God's general motive force in mind and not any special intervention.

50. In his commentary, Thomas does not further determine how God is the cause of man's happiness.

but Thomas says that death is the worse of evils and happiness the greatest of perfections.[51] Moreover, the former is unreasonable, as happiness is a kind of activity. Thomas recalls that here Aristotle is not speaking of the happiness of life to come, but of that in this life. Solon's argument was that a definite statement can be made about a person's happiness during his life. But evil in the sense of dishonor—or the shameful conduct of his family—can happen even to a dead person. Fortune very often turns, so it is difficult to declare one happy or unhappy (nos. 177–86).

The discussion on happiness and changes of fortune is continued in lesson 16 (I.10.1100b7–1101a21). Virtuous actions, and not external goods, are predominant in declaring someone happy. They are among the most lasting goods. The habit of a virtue is more firmly fixed in man than science, because it is used more often. Vicious actions, on the other hand, are a main factor in causing the opposite state. Even frequent evils happening to the virtuous man will not eliminate virtuous actions entirely. Virtue makes good use even of misfortune. According to the Stoics, sorrow does not affect the virtuous man at all, but this is not right, even if the wise man will not be moved easily from happiness to unhappiness. Aristotle calls the man happy who acts in accord with perfect virtue and has sufficient goods for virtuous activity. In such a case, Aristotle says, man has to be called happy "but as a human being." Some commentators consider the last words, if not the whole clause, a later interpolation, but it would seem that in the context they make sense: man's happiness is never fully secure and is always exposed to the danger of unexpected changes.[52] Thomas takes the words to convey a limitation: men are happy insofar as those who live in this world subject to mutability can possess perfect happiness. Moreover, the Latin translation used by Thomas clearly suggests this limitation (*beatos autem ut homines*). Thomas adds that because "a natural desire is not in vain, we can correctly judge that perfect beatitude is reserved for man after this life," but refrains from developing this idea (nos. 187–92). Doig comments correctly that Thomas "never introduces into the *SLE* more than is needed for the understanding of the *Ethics* and for the realization that Aristotle's moral thought does not contradict Aquinas's vision of Christian theology."[53]

In lesson 17 (I.11.1101a22–b9), Aristotle explains the role of friends as affecting the happiness of the dead. Do things happening to friends affect the

---

51. See *Compendium theologiae*, chap. 227: "Omnium autem malorum humanorum gravius est mors."

52. *L'Éthique à Nicomaque* (trans. Gauthier and Jolif), II:1.84–85.

53. Doig, *Aquinas's Philosophical Commentary*, 133. For an analysis of Thomas's use of "beatos ut homines" in other works, see ibid., 122–33.

dead in some way? The dead are outside the present life and only have contact with us insofar as they live in the memory of the living. Changes of fortune do not affect the dead. The influence of the changing fortune of friends on the dead will be insignificant and will not make them happy or unhappy. Occasioned by Aristotle's remark that the happiness of the dead is fragile and insignificant, Thomas adds an important note: Aristotle intends to speak of the dead as they live in the memory of men; the question of whether their souls survive in some way after death does not belong to the present inquiry. He adds that he had discussed this topic elsewhere in greater detail. The fact that Thomas uses the first person (*disseruimus*) indicates that on the question of the afterlife he is speaking in his own name and not in that of Aristotle (nos. 203–12).[54]

In lesson 18 (I.12.1101b10–1102a4), the question is raised if happiness is a good to be honored or to be praised. Praise consists only in words, while honor is a testimony signifying a person's excellence by word or deed. We praise a man because of his vigorous mind or the strength of his body. But in the latter case, it is a question of the powers of the body and is not related to virtue. The separated substances—Thomas replaces "the gods" of Aristotle's text with "separated substances"—are not praised for things men are praised for: they have no concupiscence nor fear (no. 218). Praise is given to things whose goodness is considered in relation to something else. But the gods deserve something better than praise. Happiness is to be honored because it is a perfect good. People look upon the principle and cause of the good as something to be honored. Thomas adds that God is the first principle of all that is good, while happiness is the principle of all human good, because people do all they do for the sake of happiness. Therefore happiness is to be honored (no. 223).

In lesson 19 (I.13.1102a5–31), the discussion of the treatise on virtue begins. Happiness was described as an action in the line of perfect virtue, so that at the end of the treatise on virtues he will return to study pleasure and happiness. As of now, virtue will be studied insofar as the citizens of a political society need to be virtuous. This implies also the study of the soul as the basis of the virtues. As was explained, one part of the soul is rational, another part irrational. Aristotle raises the question of whether these parts are distinct from each other but does not answer it here (nos. 224–30).

---

54. The historical context in which he wrote *SLE* apparently demanded such a personal remark for the question of man's afterlife was very much debated. Certain medieval commentators thought that Aristotle denied the happiness of life hereafter and the text of *NE* seems to go into this direction. See Gauthier, "Trois commentaires," 258–64, and Hissette, *Enquête*, 310, proposition 218 ("Quod nihil potest sciri de intellectu post eius separationem").

In lesson 20 (I.13.1102a32–1103a12), the irrational part of the soul is subdivided and its functions are explained. One part of it, the vegetative soul, is common to all living beings "here below." Its function is assimilation and growth, and its effects are more evident in the lowest living beings. In human beings it is particularly active during sleep (nos. 231–34), although our imagination is also at work during sleep and may reflect what we have experienced while awake. Besides this vegetative part, there is another part of the soul that participates to some extent in reason but has nothing to do with virtuous behavior (nos. 235–36). The sensitive appetite is meant, which in a continent person obeys reason, that is to say, practical, not theoretical reason. Reason can restrain the movements of the sensitive appetite. Thomas adds that our reason is not governed by the motions of the heavenly bodies, which can affect the sensitive appetite (nos. 237–41). Virtues are divided according to the parts of the soul: some virtues are in that part that is rational by nature, while other virtues are placed in that part that is rational by participation (nos. 242–44).

Summarizing his observations on the Aristotelian treatise of happiness (lessons 8–15), it is clear that Thomas accepts the definition of happiness as the good in light of which we pursue whatever we seek to achieve. It consists in the first place in the activity of the intellect in accordance with virtue, because happiness must result from a natural activity of man. A second observation is that in the present life perfect happiness is not possible. Thomas finds support in what Aristotle says: external causes can deprive us of the leisure and goods necessary to exercise this contemplative activity; and, second, in his conclusion, where he writes that we are only happy as men (lesson 15, no. 180), Thomas distinguishes between imperfect happiness accessible in this life and the perfect happiness consisting in the contemplation of God. Aristotle does not mention the latter, but Thomas says that it is in agreement with what Aristotle writes in *Metaphysics* XII.10. This perfect happiness has a human cause, but primarily a divine cause (lesson 14). What is remarkable is the integration of all the elements of Aristotle's doctrine of happiness, namely as consisting in an intellectual activity and as the true end of man. According to Thomas, all elements of Aristotle's doctrine can be taken up as a vague prefiguration of the Christian doctrine of the true happiness of man in the vision of God. Thomas uses Aristotle's correct analysis in presenting happiness as the last end of man.[55]

55. See Jörn Müller, "Duplex beatitudo. Aristotle's Legacy and Aquinas's Conception of Human Happiness," in *Aquinas and the "Nicomachean Ethics"* (ed. Hoffmann et al.), 52–71.

Book II

In lesson 1 (II.1.1103a14–b25), Aristotle explains that intellectual virtues are in general developed by teaching and experience—they are ordered to knowledge—but that moral virtues are the product of actions and custom. In the following books up to Book VII, the moral virtues are analyzed, but in Book VII some special questions are discussed. Moral virtues are in the appetitive part of the soul and consist in a certain inclination to something desirable. They are not in us by nature, but acquired by habituation: if we act repeatedly according to reason, an impression is made in the appetite, and so the habit of the corresponding virtue is formed (nos. 245–54).

In the opening lines of lesson 2 (II.2.1103b26–1104b3), Aristotle notes that it is not the purpose of the practical science of ethics to know what virtue is, but that it aims at making man good. As mentioned earlier, Thomas restricts this affirmation considerably: in *this* science we must *not only* investigate what virtue is in order to know the truth about it, but we must also become good by acquiring virtue (no. 256). In this chapter, Aristotle explains how virtues are caused by actions. Now actions causing virtues are actions in accord with right reason (nos. 255–59). Immoderate actions in certain fields lead to excesses, and the lack of exercise leads to weakening of strength. This happens also in the case of the virtues (nos. 260–62). At this point of his exposition, Thomas observes that virginity, which abstains from particular pleasures, is not a defect. It does not make one abstain from all pleasures (no. 263).[56] A virtue produces the same sort of actions as those that have led to its formation (no. 264).

Lesson 3 (II.3.1104b3–1105a16) explains the role of pleasure and sorrow in the formation and practice of the virtues. At the beginning, when practicing a virtue, one experiences difficulties and even reluctance, but having acquired it, acting according to it is pleasurable (nos. 265–66). Thomas adds that we must not conclude that every moral virtue is concerned with pleasures and sorrows as its proper matter; justice and fortitude are not, although the purpose of all moral virtues is to make man well-ordered in regard to his pleasures and sorrows (no. 267). This is reached by training and instruction. Aristotle presents several reasons to show that some virtues are concerned with particular pleasures and sorrows. Men become evil by the

---

56. The topic of virginity, generated by what was thought to be Aristotle's position on temperance and insensibility, was heavily discussed in thirteenth-century commentaries on Aristotle's *Ethics*. The 1277 condemnation precisely contains the thesis (no. 169) that "perfect abstinence from the act of flesh corrupts virtue and the species." See Gauthier, "Trois commentaires," 298; Hissette, *Enquête*, 299–300. This context explains the impressive number of quotations from Aristotle in *ST* II-II, q. 152, a. 2. See Elders, "St. Thomas Aquinas's Treatise on Temperance," *Nova & Vetera (English edition)* 16 (2018): 465–87, esp. 478–79.

excessive pursuit of pleasures when they ought not to do this (nos. 268–71). Thomas notes that the Stoics thought that virtue consists in the cessation of all passions, but we say that only inordinate passions should be excluded (no. 272). The virtuous man takes the right attitude with regard to what is pleasurable and what causes sorrow (nos. 273–79).

Lesson 4 (II.4.1105a17–b18) compares virtue and art. There is no likeness between art and virtue. The perfection of art consists in the good produced, while virtuous actions remain in the agent but are subject to conditions, such as that the acts should not be carried out in ignorance nor out of passion. They should be done for the sake of the virtuous work itself, and should have a background of stability. Acts are called just when they are similar to those that a just and temperate man performs. If one wonders how a man who does not yet have a certain virtue can acquire it by acting according to this virtue, Thomas gives the following answer: the first principles of reason allow the formation of correct thought, and nature has also given man the first principles of the moral order, so that by acting according to these principles a man makes himself virtuous (no. 286).

In lesson 5 (II.5.1105b19–1106a13) virtue is defined. There are three principles in the soul involved in its operations: passions, powers, and habits. By passions here are meant states related to the appetite, not those related to the perceptive faculties, nor to the intellectual appetite. In this lesson, Thomas presents a clear and complete survey of the faculties of the human soul which reveals the didactic purpose of his commentary. The sensitive appetite is divided into the concupiscible and the irascible appetite (nos. 289–93). He enumerates the different passions and the powers or faculties from which they proceed. Habits are dispositions of the powers resulting from repeated actions so that the powers become suited to only one of the opposites (good or bad). Virtues are not passions but habits. The difference with the passions is seen in the fact that we are praised for the virtues we have, but not for our passions. A further difference is the fact that the acts of virtues are not without choice, while passions arise prior to deliberation and choice. Moreover, we are moved according to the passions, but by virtues we are disposed to certain actions. Finally, he explains that virtues are not faculties: we are not called good for having certain faculties (powers), but for being virtuous (nos. 294–305).

In lesson 6 (II.6.1106a14–b28), we read that virtues are habits that make the person who has them, and the work that he does, good. Aristotle adds that this is done by actions and works according to the mean, that is, the middle between excess and deficiency. But the mean stands in proportion to the agent and is not the same for all. He illustrates this by the differences of the diet of athletes and sportsmen. In the case of fear, there is also a mean (nos. 306–18).

In lesson 7 (II.6.1106b28–1107a27), Aristotle adds a third reason why virtue lies in the middle between extremes: there is only one way of acting right, but many ways of going wrong. Thomas adds Dionysius's principle: evil results from any defect, while the good requires a complete cause. We see this in health and sickness, physical beauty and ugliness. Aristotle then presents the definition of a virtue: a virtue is a habit by which we act according to choice, the object of which is the mean in regard to us, as determined by reason. Thomas understands λόγῳ in 1107a1 as meaning "by reason" but, as several scholars have pointed out,[57] the sense of the term more likely is "by a norm." Aristotle probably has in mind the exigencies of human life and the example of a prudent man. This norm is far from being absolute. While Thomas fully recognizes the role of objective elements with regard to the morality of our acts, he nevertheless holds that reason must formulate the laws of conduct (nos. 319–26). The extremes belong to vices. Certain actions imply vices, such as adultery and theft. They are evil in themselves (nos. 327–32).

The definition of virtues is explained in detail in lesson 8 (II.7.1107a28–b21), where it is applied to individual cases. The passions are marked by an inclination that can be contrary to reason, either by drawing reason into the wrong direction, or by making one shrink from what is good. The root of the virtues is the rectitude of reason by which we must direct our actions (nos. 333–36). Thomas notes that some authors, like Cicero and Seneca, conceived some virtues as comprehensive categories, distinguishing prudence, justice, fortitude, and moderation, while they made all other virtues species of them. But this is not appropriate. The four main virtues are of such a nature that no specific differences can be added to them. The Stoics distinguished them by the different ways in which our reason is involved, but Thomas agrees with Aristotle that virtues are distinguished by their objects (nos. 337–38). Prudence, for instance, is not concerned with all acts of knowledge but with reason commanding how to conduct ourselves, and justice bears on the equality of acts in our dealings with others. Prudence and justice are studied in Books V and VI. For now, the virtues concerned with the passions are examined, and we are reminded how in the opposite vices excess

---

57. See *L'Éthique à Nicomaque* (trans. Gauthier and Jolif), II:1.147–49; and Aristotle, *"Nicomachean Ethics" Books II–IV*, trans. C. C. W. Taylor (Oxford: Clarendon Press, 2006), 66.

and deficiency occur. In particular, the virtues concerning the use of money are briefly discussed (nos. 337–44).

In lesson 9 (II.7.1107b21–1108b10), the virtues concerning honors are mentioned, such as magnanimity and liberality, ambition and mildness. With regard to truth there is truthfulness, and with regard to amusement there are also virtues and vices. In our relations with other people, there is the virtue of friendliness and righteous indignation as a mean between envy and enjoyment in wickedness (nos. 345–57).

Lesson 10 (II.8.1108b11–1109a19) deals with the opposition between virtues and vices. Aristotle distinguishes the opposition between the vices (which have a virtue as a mean between them) and that between each of these vices and the respective virtue. Insofar as the virtue in the middle partakes in the two extremes, it has a certain opposition to them, although the opposition between the two extremes is greater (nos. 358–64). There are cases in which one extreme is more opposed to the virtue than the other extreme, because it has a greater dissimilarity with it (nos. 365–66). Thomas gives a further explanation. What Aristotle says happens in the virtues concerned with the passions: a vice concerned with restraining them is more like the virtue than the opposite vice, while in the case of fear the extreme which discards fear is closer to the virtue which strengthens us in dangers. One may add that vices that move us in the direction of what we are naturally inclined to, such as pleasure, are more contrary to the respective virtue than the contrary vices (nos. 367–68).

Lesson 11 (II.9.1109a20–b26) describes the ways of becoming virtuous, which, according to Aristotle, is the central theme in the study of moral behavior. It is difficult to discover the mean, but easy to deviate from it. To attain the mean one must try to avoid the extremes, that is, the vices most opposed to the virtue, and take into account what one is personally most attracted to and move in the opposite direction (nos. 369–75). Thomas adds an observation: while Aristotle advocates striving vigorously for the opposite of what one likes most, the Stoics propose an easier way, namely to withdraw little by little from the things one desires most, a method most adapted to the halfhearted (no. 376).[58] But the following advice is valid for all: everyone is naturally inclined to bodily pleasure so that whoever aims at acquiring the virtues ought to be on his guard—the desire for bodily pleasure leads to many sins. Finally, Aristotle explains how difficult it is to determine the mean. For this reason, minor deviations from it are not censured (nos. 377–81).

---

58. He refers to Cicero's *Tusculaneae Disputationes* IV, chaps. 31–35.

Book III

In the first seven chapters of Book III, Aristotle interrupts the study of the virtues to present some general remarks on virtuous and sinful actions. Lesson 1 (III.1.1109b30–1110a19) deals with the subject of voluntary and involuntary actions. An involuntary act contrary to virtue deserves pardon, and an involuntary act in accordance with virtue does not merit praise. The involuntary proceeds from simple causes, such as ignorance or violence, while many factors are involved in a voluntary action. Not every action instigated from the outside is a forced action, but only that action with which our will does not concur. Actions like throwing merchandise overboard during a storm are mixed, although closer to the voluntary than to the involuntary, for we judge it as a particular action. The example shows that we must also take into consideration the time when the action was performed (nos. 382–91). In this sort of action, people are sometimes praised when they are made to do something disgraceful in order to obtain great goods, for example, to prevent their relatives being executed by a tyrant.

In lesson 2 (III.1.1110a19–b17), Thomas does not commit himself to the legitimate or sinful character of such acts, while Grosseteste writes that our Christian religion teaches and holds that we must not sin for the sake of some usefulness.[59] If we consider the text itself, it is not clear how far Aristotle is willing to go on this road. Thomas knows that some understood the passage as allowing us to do what is wrong for the sake of a good purpose.[60] But in his commentary he presents a text similar to that of Albert the Great, to which the Latin translation more or less entitles him. The verb *sustinere* does not have the sense of "undertaking," which the Greek ὑπομεῖναι may sometimes have (1110a30).[61] Thomas writes that out of fear or threats one may be led do something shameful or sad, but not to commit a sin (*sed non quidem peccatum*; no. 393).[62] Thomas understands Aristotle as saying that it is sometimes better to endure something ignoble to obtain a greater good, but he takes the precaution to add that this does not mean that one may commit a sin for the sake of such a good.

---

59. Quoted after Gauthier (Leonine ed., vol. 47), 122.6–7.

60. *Q. de malo*, q. 15, a. 1, obj. 5 and ad 5 (Leonine ed., 23 and 269, note to line 43).

61. That is, "to stand one's ground" (*sustinere*). Thomas writes: "quandoque difficile est iudicare quid sit eligendum, propter hoc quod aliquis evitet malum, et quid mali sit sustinendum propter hoc quod non deficiat ab aliquo bono" (no. 396).

62. Thomas is firmly holding the doctrine of intrinsically evil acts, especially in a context where, following the lead of Aristotle, it would have been understandable to attribute a decisive role to the intention. For deviating interpretations, see John F. Dedek, "Intrinsically Evil Acts: A Historical Study of the Mind of St. Thomas," *The Thomist* 45 (1979): 385–413.

This explanation agrees quite well with the general trend of Aristotle's text, except insofar as Aristotle admits that one may do something unlawful (ἃ μὴ δεῖ) to escape from great suffering. But in this context Aristotle also writes that one should rather die than commit horrible crimes. Some actions done out of fear do not deserve praise. But there are actions that are so bad that no amount of force should compel one to perform them. Thomas gives the example of St. Lawrence, who endured roasting on the gridiron to avoid sacrificing to idols (nos. 392–95). Those who cannot be forced to perform disgraceful things are worthy of praise. Aristotle mentions a view according to which pleasurable goods cause forced actions because they force a person to act without the intervention of his reason, so that all actions done for something that is good or pleasurable would be enforced, but this is unreasonable. Actions performed when one is necessitated are unpleasant. But there are actions done on account of external goods that are not enforced, but voluntary (nos. 396–405).

Lesson 3 (III.1.1110b18–1111a21) examines involuntary actions resulting from ignorance. A distinction is made between acting in ignorance and acting on account of ignorance. A person can be ignorant of what he ought to do or avoid. But this ignorance cannot happen to someone who has the use of reason, so that what he does in this state is not involuntary and does not excuse from guilt. But there is another ignorance concerning particular aspects of an act, such as the circumstances, which may exculpate a person by rendering an act involuntary (nos. 406–14). Aristotle distinguishes six circumstances. Thomas refers to Cicero, who also mentioned time and place as circumstances (no. 415).[63] Thomas says that some explain Aristotle's expression "by what an action is carried out" as "by what means" (no. 415).[64] Surprisingly, Aristotle adds to the list of circumstances "that which the act is about," which is the object of an act, rather than one of the circumstances.[65] Thomas silently corrects the sentences, saying that what one does *pertinet ad genus actus* (no. 415), to avoid criticizing Aristotle.[66] Only insane people are ignorant of all these circumstances. Aristotle gives some examples of ignorance concerning what one is doing or the instruments one is using. In some cases there can be ignorance of the end, when the acting person does not know to what end his action is leading. The most important circumstances are "what one is doing" and "for the sake of what one acts" (nos. 416–24).

63. Cicero, *De inventione* I.44.

64. Cicero speaks of "quibus auxiliis."

65. See *L'Éthique à Nicomaque* (trans. Gauthier and Jolif), II:1.188.

66. In *ST,* Thomas mentions that in *NE,* Aristotle seems to make the *quid* and the *finis* of the act circumstances. He resolves the difficulty by suggesting that what is meant by Aristotle is not the essential specification of the act nor its end but secondary and additional aspects as, for instance, the quantity of the act or a secondary purpose one also has in mind when performing a particular action (*ST* I-II, q. 7, a. 3, ad 3).

In this lesson, the problem of morally wrong actions is also discussed from the point of view of ignorance. Aristotle writes that a drunk person, or a man in anger, do not act out of ignorance, but rather they do not realize what they are doing. He seems to extend this explanation to all those who commit morally wrong actions, adding that just not realizing what one is doing is wrong. But the examples quoted do not seem to apply to all sinful acts in general. In a number of cases, a different type of ignorance is involved, namely, *not wanting to know or consider what one is really doing*. Thomas indicates that in sinful acts there is a sort of ignorance with regard to the particular choice: a person who sins does not "know" what he must do in this particular case and what evil he should avoid, insofar as he decides that he has to do this morally wrong deed and abstains from a particular good action. Thus, Thomas intimates that this "knowledge" is dependent on the will. However, with an admirable restraint, he does not elaborate on his own theory of the *absentia considerationis* as the formal cause of the morally wrong act, apparently because at this juncture such a detailed account was not necessary and would tend to show the shortcomings of Aristotle's text.

In lesson 4 (III.1.1111a22–b3), Aristotle defines the voluntary by removing what causes the involuntary, such as violence and ignorance. When the agent himself knows the circumstances, and the action originates from him, his action is voluntary. Some authors, however, objected and argued that in some cases one knows the circumstances but that when an action results from a passion, it is not voluntary. Aristotle answers that the passions are intrinsic, and that animals and children act voluntarily, that is, by an intrinsic movement. So things done in anger or by sensual desire are voluntary. And he adds five more arguments to show that actions resulting from passions are voluntary, as proceeding from the human agent himself (nos. 425–31).

In lesson 5 (III.2.1111b4–30), Aristotle deals with choice, which is closely connected with the virtues. Whether acts are virtuous or not is judged by the choice the agent makes. Choices are voluntary. Voluntary is the genus, of which choice represents a species. Choices are made after deliberation, but things done on the spur of the moment are not the effect of choice. Aristotle refutes the opinion that choice is sensual desire or that it results from anger. In the continent person, sensual desire is opposed to choice. Things done out of anger are not done by choice, for they are done without much deliberation and often suddenly. Choice and desire or wishing are acts of the same appetite, but nevertheless differ. Wishing indicates an act of the appetite in general, which desires what is good, while choice is an act of the appetite concerning a particular act ordering us to a good. Wishing may concern things not done by ourselves, while choice is directed to our own activity. The difference between wishing and choosing is also visible in that choice concerns the means, but wishing regards the means as conducing to the end. Finally, choice is directed to things within our power (nos. 432–47).

The topics discussed in the first lessons of Book III have raised a number of issues. A central question is whether Aristotle recognizes the will as a faculty, something which is denied by Gauthier. Nevertheless, according to Thomas, the act of willing succeeds the judgment of the intellect. On this issue, the exposition of Thomas is in agreement with Aristotle. Thomas regards *voluntas* (βούλησις) as the first act of a faculty rather than the faculty of the will as such. But there is a difference with Aristotle insofar as for Thomas choice (*electio*, προαίρεσις) is an act of the rational appetite, whereas for Aristotle it is part of the acts of the intellect. Thomas remains close to Aristotle's text insofar as he affirms that the voluntary acts proceed both from the intellect and from the will, something which is contrary the position of Duns Scotus.[67]

The relation between choice and opinion is the subject of lesson 6 (III.2.1111b30–1112a17). Having shown that choice is not the same as desire, anger, and wishing, Aristotle now explains how it differs from opinion. Opinion can concern anything, but choice only those things that are within our capacity. Opinion is about what is true and false, choice about what is good and bad. If we choose what is good we are said to be good, but having an opinion about what is good does not yet make us good. A man is good on account of his actions, not because of his opinions. Furthermore, opinion relates mostly to things, choice to our actions. The good of a choice consists in the rectitude of our appetitive faculty, but the perfection of an opinion is truth. Choice is accompanied by certitude, while opinion is not. Opinion pertains to the cognitive faculty, choice to the appetitive faculty. Finally, he says that choice is voluntary, resulting from deliberation, so it is an act of reason and the intellect (nos. 448–57).

In lesson 7 (III.3.1111a18–1112b11), after having explained what choice is, Aristotle turns to counsel. People take counsel about things that deserve careful consideration. No one asks advice about things that exist always, as the separate substances, or about things that are in a perpetual uniform motion, or about things that usually follow the same pattern. We do not seek counsel about what happens by chance, because it is unforeseen. Likewise, we do not consult others about necessary and natural things. Counsel being ordered to action, we take counsel about what is in our power and on how to proceed in matters that are not certain. Now counsel is more necessary in the arts and in

---

67. On this matter see Matthias Perkams, "Aquinas on Choice, Will and Voluntary Action," in *Aquinas and the "Nicomachean Ethics*," 72–90.

situations where the outcome has not yet been determined than in the sciences (nos. 458–72).

In lesson 8 (III.3.1112b11–1113a2), we are informed about the method and order of taking counsel. We take counsel about the means to reach the end, but not on the end; likewise, we do not seek advice on the principles, but about the conclusions. If the end has been taken for granted, we seek advice about the means needed to reach the end. If the means are not at hand, we take counsel on how to acquire them. Aristotle also explains the limits of seeking advice: when we arrive at the point where we can do the rest by ourselves, we no longer need advice. There are also limits in seeking advice on our side. If a man were always taking counsel, he could go on to infinity (nos. 473–82).

Aristotle compares counsel and choice in lesson 9 (III.3.1113a2–14). The object of choice is the same as that of counsel. Counsel precedes choice, because after deliberation and advice a judgment is due (nos. 483–87). In lesson 10 (III.4.1113a15–b2), Aristotle begins his study of willing. Willing concerns primarily the ends that the will has chosen and wants. The will does not always have what is really good as its object. A vicious person may choose an object that is not a real good, while the virtuous person passes a correct judgment on the objects and ends of man's activity, which are in accord with right reason. Aristotle's text (1113a29–34) seems to assign a decisive role to the morally excellent or wise man (σπουδαῖος, *studiosus*). However, the wise man does not proceed in an arbitrary way. He is excellent precisely because he knows reality and understands what one must do or not do in certain circumstances. Thomas interprets this (no. 494) in the sense of conveying an objective rule of morality by adding that what is good without any restriction and what is according to right reason appears as such to the wise man, who sees what the true good is. The morally excellent or wise man, therefore, is as it were the rule and the criterion of what one should do (nos. 488–95).

Lesson 11 (III.5.1113b3–1114a3) explains that virtue and vice are within our power. Choice is voluntary and consequently virtuous actions are within our power. When affirmation is within our power, then negation also is: virtuous and vicious actions differ as affirmation and negation do, and so they lie within our power. Aristotle refutes the error that no one is voluntarily evil: vice is something voluntary, our good and bad actions are in our power. We see this in education and in public life, where evildoers are punished and good actions promoted by honors. This also shows in cases where we ourselves are the cause of our ignorance and held responsible. Ignorance of things a man should know is considered to be blameworthy. He should have learned them and have been diligent instead of negligent (nos. 496–506).

In lesson 12 (III.5.1114a3–11), the maxim that "no one is voluntarily evil" is refuted. In the previous lessons, Aristotle says that it is in the power of man to be diligent, but some deny this, saying that there are people with a lazy temperament. Thomas explains this in greater detail: there is no direct influence of physical agents on the intellect and will, as Aristotle shows in *De anima* III.4, but an influence on the sensible faculties of man, such as by his passions, is possible. Influences from the outside do not affect reason and will more than the passions, which are open to persuasion (no. 508). Habits of the soul are voluntary at the beginning, but after their formation they are no longer so. There are different evil habits: some remove men from doing good, other habits give an inclination to perform bad acts. Now, habits are produced by operations. Some are willed for themselves, others in their cause (no. 507–14).

The opinion that we have no faculty that discerns what is good is discussed in lesson 13 (III.5.1114a31–b22). A thing must be perceived as good in order to be desired. According to some, it is not in our power to perceive certain things as good. Now a thing can be judged good, first, by a theoretical consideration and, in a second way, by practical knowledge as an action performed in special circumstances (throwing merchandise overboard during a storm). An adversary argues that what a person desires depends on how he was at his birth. But Aristotle says that those who argue this way do not distinguish between the senses and the intellect. Once again we read that the heavenly bodies can cause a disposition in the human body, but not in the mind. One's temperament also cannot decisively determine the will, which is able to reject what comes from the sensitive appetite. An interlocutor agrees that virtue is voluntary, but denies that vice is. The virtuous and the vicious man are alike in regard to the end. If virtues are voluntary because we cause the habit ourselves, the same applies to the vices. The lesson ends with a summary of what has been explained in the previous lessons: habits produce the same actions as those by which they were produced themselves, and they are in our power (nos. 515–27).

In lecture 14 (III.6.1115a6–32), having treated the virtues in general, Aristotle begins to study individual virtues. He begins with fortitude, a virtue mainly concerned with fear about what threatens our life and other terrifying evils, the most frightening of which is death. Fortitude is concerned especially with the danger of death in battle, in storms at sea, and sickness. A person is brave when he is not afraid of death for a good cause. But Aristotle mentions especially fortitude shown in war, exposing oneself to death for a noble cause. When Aristotle writes (1115a26–27) that death seems to be greatest of evils and that there is nothing left to the dead, Thomas adds (no. 536) "that is, of those things which belong to our present life and which we know. For the things that belong to the state of the souls after death are not visible to us" (nos. 528–42).

In lesson 15 (III.7.1115b7–1116a16), Aristotle studies the acts of fortitude by comparing them with the acts of the opposite vices, such as fear. Some evils exceed man's power, such as earthquakes, tidal waves, etc., but the brave man will not lose his judgment when facing them, but will endure terrifying things. What a brave person accomplishes by his courageous conduct is fortitude in action. There are people who lack fear and others who are excessive in daring. Aristotle distinguishes between the defect of fear and the excess of recklessness. Who is reckless exceeds in daring. Fortitude makes one sustain sufferings in order to bring about some good. Who lays hands on himself to escape poverty and other things that cause sorrow is not brave but rather a coward: he seems unable to bear sorrows and when he suffers death, it is not for something honorable but to escape painful evils (nos. 543–58).[68]

Lesson 16 (III.8.1116a16–b23) discusses acts that seem courageous but are not acts of real fortitude because of a lack of knowledge (as when one is brave by ignorance). Furthermore, there is a type of fortitude that operates by anger, hope, and ignorance. Civic fortitude can be that of the citizens who conduct themselves with bravery in view of being honored. Another type of fortitude is that of soldiers who are brave for being honored or to avoid blame. The fortitude of the citizen is practiced between fear and shame. Soldiers are brave in war because of previous experience they have acquired. "No one fears to do what he has learned to do well," Thomas adds, quoting from the fourth-century Roman writer Vegetius's *Epitome rei militaris*. When soldiers see that the enemy is stronger, they may flee, while the citizens remain after the soldiers have left. The brave man fears disgrace more than death (nos. 559–70).

In lesson 17 (III.8.1116b23–1117a28), counterfeit forms of fortitude are described, for instance, when one acts in rage. Rage does in fact incline to acts of fortitude, while the brave perform the acts with the intention of the good. There is a likeness between virtues and certain acts done in rage or anger. Another type of fortitude is that of those who are brave because of their hope and confidence. Those who are confident in this way do not persist in their efforts when they fail to get what they expected. The brave man, however, endures dangers and terror by the interior inclination of the virtue of fortitude. When Aristotle asserts that the courageous person defends his position even

---

68. On this topic see the excellent analysis in Jennifer Herdt, "Aquinas's Aristotelian Defence of Martyr Courage," in *Aquinas and the "Nicomachean Ethics"* (ed. Hoffmann et al.), 110–28, esp. 117–20.

if there is no hope, just because it is beautiful to do so (1117a17–19), Thomas adds that the courageous holds his position in order that some good may come from it (no. 578).[69] But with praiseworthy restraint he refrains from introducing here the theme of Christian hope. Another counterfeit of fortitude is the conduct of those who are ignorant of the fact that the evils they fight are dangers (nos. 571–82).

Lesson 18 (III.9.1117a29–b22), which closes the discussion of fortitude, explains the properties of fortitude as related to pleasure and pain, to fear and daring. Fear appears in man when he faces a threat from something stronger than himself. He acts daringly when he thinks that the person he is going to attack is not too powerful. Pain is an evil that afflicts us but fortitude makes us not withdraw from a good to escape pain. The relation of fortitude with pleasure is more difficult to describe. Fortitude consists in enduring distressing things, but when reaching the end of his courageous behavior man may experience some pleasure. Rejecting the error (of the Stoics) that the wise man suffers no grief, Aristotle says that the more perfect a person is in virtue, the more he is saddened by the imminence of death. Thomas notes (no. 590) that to some virtuous men death is desirable because of the hope of a better life and adds that it did not pertain to Aristotle to treat of things that belong to the condition of another life. Although in the previous books it was argued that virtuous acts are pleasurable, we now see that the acts of every virtue are not always pleasurable (nos. 583–94).

The last lessons of Book III deal with temperance.[70] In lesson 19 (III.10.1117b23–1118a26), Aristotle points out that this virtue is concerned with pleasurable actions and things. Whereas fortitude is concerned with feelings of the irrational part of man, namely his irascible appetite, temperance has its seat in the concupiscible part of the soul where are found the pleasures of food and sex, which we have in common with animals. Temperance is not concerned with pleasures of the soul, such as learning, honor, and having friends, but with bodily pleasures, though not with all such pleasures; for example, it does not concern the delight taken in seeing, hearing, and smelling. Thomas provides an explanation: the appetite of other animals is moved only by natural instinct, but in man these experiences also serve his intellectual knowledge (no. 611; see also nos. 595–610, 612).[71]

The relation of temperance to touch and taste is examined in lesson 20

69. On the difference between hope in Aristotle and Christian hope, see *L'Éthique à Nicomaque* (trans. Gauthier and Jolif), II:1.233–34.

70. See Elders, "St. Thomas Aquinas's Treatise on Temperance and Aristotle."

71. Insofar as *NE*, in separating the lower pleasures entirely from those of the intellectual soul, presents a dualistic view of man, Thomas discreetly points to the unity of man.

(III.10.1118a26–b28), which deals with the pleasures of taste insofar as taste is ordered to touch in eating and drinking, which concern certain parts of the body. Touch is the most common of the senses and all men desire nourishment, food, and drink, although not all want expensive types of food. In those natural desires that are common to all men, not many deviate. Transgressions occur when people take more than nature requires. People sin against temperance in many ways by excesses (nos. 613–25).

In lesson 21 (III.11.1118b28–1119a20), we find an explanation of how sorrows, pleasures, and desires may affect a temperate person. Sorrows result because of the absence of those pleasures one expected. The intemperate man desires all possible pleasures but his desire is not directed by reason. There is also the vice of not desiring pleasures at all, which is a defect not in keeping with human nature. The temperate man follows the golden mean with regard to pleasure, sorrow, and desire, avoiding all excessive desires. He desires those pleasures that are good for the health of the body, but he does so in right measure (nos. 626–34).

In lesson 22 (III.12.1119a21–b18), intemperance is compared with cowardice and childish behavior. It is more voluntary than cowardice, as the intemperate man rejoices in what he does, while cowardice is caused by something involuntary. This also follows from the fact that the intemperate man seeks pleasure. For this reason, intemperance is more disgraceful than cowardice. Visited by great pain, a soldier may throw away his arms, an act that at that moment is not disgraceful, while in general it would be cowardly. In the case of intemperance, the fact of desiring singular things is highly voluntary, but considered on the whole and in general, things are less voluntary (e.g., adultery in general). Intemperance is compared with the sins of children: the intemperate must be chastised and restrained. Children strive most of all after pleasure. If they are not restrained, sensual desire will dominate their lives. The desire of pleasure is insatiable. The more one gives in to it, the more it comes to dominate. It must be corrected by reason, so that people become so disposed that they desire the right things in the right way (nos. 635–48).

Book IV

In this book, Aristotle considers those virtues that concern external things. In the first five lessons, liberality and the opposite vices are examined. In lesson 1 (IV.1.1119b22–1120a14), we read that liberality has a certain likeness with temperance, insofar as temperance moderates the desire of acquiring and possessing external goods. The proximate matter of temperance is desire and pleasure. In liberality, extravagance and stinginess in the use of wealth are the excesses and deficiencies with regard to the use of money. One who squanders his wealth is extravagant. The virtue of liberality leads to the correct use of wealth. It is more proper to liberality to distribute wealth to the right persons than to look after a lawful increase of one's possessions. It is more characteristic of this virtue to bestow than to receive benefits. The virtue of liberality is especially ordained to making donations. In the course of this lesson Thomas notes that there is a wider use for this virtue than indicated by Aristotle. What Aristotle mentions is the *materia remota*, the different ways in which wealth can be used. But there is also the *materia propria*, which is the desire to possess wealth (nos. 649–65).[72]

In lesson 2 (IV.1.1120a23–b24), Aristotle explains the act of donating. The liberal man gives cheerfully or at least without sadness. For him wealth is the means of giving to others. Giving for a wrong purpose is not an act of liberality. The liberal man does not take income from wrong sources, and is more eager to give than to accept benefits from others. He keeps less for himself. One who gives from moderate means is also acting according to the virtue of liberality. Those who inherited money from their parents make donations more easily than persons who acquire their wealth by their own efforts. The liberal man is not very much disposed to accept and to keep riches for himself (nos. 666–77).

In lesson 3 (IV.1.1120b24–1121a15), Aristotle deals with extravagant spending, when one is spending beyond his means, whereas the liberal man disposes of his funds with right measure, gives away both in large and in small amounts and does so with pleasure; the liberal man prefers what is reasonable to the desire for greater wealth. He is disposed to share his wealth and, being intent on giving, he is saddened by inappropriate hoarding of money. The spendthrift, on the other hand, commits excesses in spending, while the miser falls into the opposite vice (nos. 678–85).

In lesson 4 (IV.1.1121a16–b12), we read that the desire of lavish giving is cured by dwindling means and by old age, when one is more prone to keep one's wealth. Contrary to the liberal man, the spendthrift does not spend properly, but rather than being evil, this proneness to spend is caused by stupidity. Yet being a spendthrift is much better than being a miser. His defect is that he is inclined to take and even to acquire dishonestly, and to waste his belongings in food and sex. If, however, such a person is attracted to virtue, he will easily find the mean (nos. 686–96).

The meaning of illiberality is explained in lesson 5 (IV.1.1121b12–1122a14).

---

72. As a Christian and a mendicant friar, the regulation of this desire itself belongs to the moral life.

Our human life tends to become weaker, and earthly goods tend to decrease, so that people become easily parsimonious. Illiberality can lead to excess in acquiring goods and stinginess in giving. But not all illiberal people sin in both ways. Some illiberal people keep what is theirs but do not take the goods of others, because that would be shameful or it would oblige them to give things to others in their turn. But other illiberal persons are immoderate in taking or in making profit from sordid or unlawful dealings, such as gambling, robbing, etc. Illiberality as a vice opposed to liberality is worse than extravagance (nos. 697–706).

In lessons 6 (IV.2.1122a18–b18) and 7 (1122b19–1123a34), magnificence is discussed; this is a virtue concerned with wealth, not with income and donations, but only with considerable expenditures. The opposed vice is meanness. The magnificent knows what it is proper to spend and that the project on which he spends his wealth must be worthy. It is also characteristic of the magnificent to spend cheerfully. But a person may fall into excessive spending beyond good reason (nos. 707–18). The objects of magnificence are more precisely determined in lesson 7, namely, in the first place, votive offerings in temples and gifts spent for the worship of the demons. At 1122b21 Aristotle uses τὸ δαιμόνιον which in the Latin text version Thomas is using is translated as *daemonium* although Grosseteste's *recensio pura* more correctly has *divinum*.[73] Hence Thomas comments that the gentiles venerated not only their gods, but also demons, whom they considered to be intermediaries between the gods and men. Aristotle expresses himself according to the cult of the gentiles, which manifestly has been abrogated (no. 719). In the second place there are contributions to public welfare, and next the construction of one's own home.

Finally, expenditures must be proportionate to the wealth and position of the giver. Great gifts should be made by those who possess considerable riches, indifferently whether they inherited their fortune or acquired it. Highborn and renowned persons should disburse important donations, and perhaps more on account of honor than of need. But in each donation they should spend what is fitting. One can sin against the right proportion by excess. The stingy person falls short in every respect and always tries to spend the least possible (nos. 719–34). The chapter contains a difficulty when Aristotle states that, because the exercise of magnificence requires large resources, the poor cannot be magnificent (1122b26–27). This idea met with sharp criticism from Bonaventure and was included in the 1277 condemnations.[74] Thomas takes up

73. *SLE* 222, note to lines 26–28. Albert for instance correctly uses *divinum* (*Super Ethica*, IV, l. 6, p. 248) and hence makes no mention of demons.

74. *L'Éthique à Nicomaque* (trans. Gauthier and Jolif), II:1.270.

Aristotle's suggestion that in the virtues one must consider both *who* is acting and *what* is being done and adds that one must consider whether we have to do with a prince or with a private citizen, a nobleman or a person devoid of nobility, but also whether he has large or limited resources, for his contribution must be proportionate to his situation and means (no. 721). This addition is unobtrusive and remains strictly limited to what is required for the correct understanding of this particular question. Any assertion which might give the impression that Aristotle's account is incomplete or inaccurate is avoided.[75]

The following four lessons are concerned with the virtue of magnanimity. In lesson 8 (IV.3.1123a34–1124a4), Aristotle explains that this virtue concerns great things. The magnanimous thinks himself worthy of great things and must be so himself.[76] The pusillanimous thinks himself worthy of less than he really is, while a conceited person is excessive in thinking what his merits are. But what is the mean of this virtue? There is a mean insofar as the magnanimous considers himself deserving praise according to his worth. At this point, Thomas adds a few lines: if those in eminent positions deserve honor, much more so does God (no. 742). Honor is the best of all external goods. Magnanimity is related to the other virtues: the one who performs a great act of any virtue is worthy of great honor. Some think that the magnanimous must rely on his own opinion and not hesitate to do injustice to others, but this is wrong, says Aristotle. One who is not virtuous cannot be magnanimous. Magnanimity is the ornament of all the virtues (nos. 735–49). Insofar as the magnanimous man seeks honor and knows his own value, it would seem that this attitude conflicts with the humility required from Christians. The three anonymous commentaries studied by Gauthier express such an opposition.[77] Thomas rejects the suggestion that humility is a form of modesty, a virtue that is discussed by Aristotle.[78] For, according to the text of Aristotle, his "humility" is the attitude of mediocre people, who acknowledge that they do not deserve great honors. For Thomas humility is the virtue which makes us acknowledge our condition as creatures and act in accordance with it. Thus, one can be at the same time magnanimous and humble. But in *SLE* he does

75. In *ST* II-II, q. 134, a. 3, ad 4. Thomas furthermore observes that the main act of a virtue is one's inner choice, which one can make without disposing of any substantial means, so that even a poor man can be magnificent.

76. Magnanimity was for Thomas a delicate subject because of the apparent contrast of certain statements of Aristotle with the Christian virtue of humility. Thomas explains Aristotle's description in such a way that magnanimity becomes acceptable as a virtue. In the *ST* II-II, q. 129, he gives a transposition of magnanimity that allows him to consider this virtue as an important element of the moral life. See R.-A. Gauthier, *Magnanimité. L'idéal de la grandeur dans la philosophie païenne et dans la théologie chrétienne* (Paris: Vrin, 1951), esp. 298–374 and 443–65 for the position of Thomas.

77. Gauthier, "Trois commentaires," esp. 294–328.

78. *ST* II-II, q. 164, a. 4.

not dwell on this point. However, that this solution was present to him appears from the commentary on 1123b31, where Aristotle writes that the magnanimous is not a man who first claims honors, but who withdraws himself as soon as he meets with criticism.[79] Thomas adds this remark: some think that the magnanimous man always clings to his own view and that he never follows the advice of others nor feels any qualms about inflicting injustice on others. However, this view is wrong. The magnanimous does not care so much for money, etc., that he would do anything to obtain more of it (no. 747).

In lesson 9 (IV.3.1124a4–b6), acts of magnanimity are described. The main act of this virtue is to conduct oneself well with regard to honors, in which the magnanimous takes a moderate delight, but he is not cast down by insults. He is honored for riches and power as belonging to good fortune, but is moderate in case of misfortune. Material goods are the only ones recognized by some people; they seem indeed to add something to magnanimity. But in reality only the virtuous man should be honored. Possessions without the presence of the virtues cannot make a man magnanimous. Those who lack this virtue cannot bear good fortune gracefully (nos. 750–58). Aristotle seems to suggest in this passage that the magnanimous, inasmuch as he knows that he is worthy of honor, disregards insignificant signs of consideration bestowed upon him and he is not afflicted when he does not receive the honor due to him. Thomas points to 1124a5–6 (*in magnis honoribus moderate delectabitur*) and notes when the magnanimous attaches little value to honor (which is nevertheless one of the greatest external goods of man) he will also consider insignificant many other things. This could create the impression, Aquinas adds, that the magnanimous are haughty, but what really is the case is that they disregard external goods and only value virtue which is inside man (no. 755). Thomas suggests the way in which Aristotle's magnanimity becomes acceptable to Christians, or rather the way it is a true natural virtue.[80]

The properties of magnanimity are discussed in lesson 10 (IV.3.1124b6–1125a16). Because the magnanimous values few things as important, he will not easily expose himself to dangers, but when in danger he will not spare his own life. He does good to others, gives important rewards; although he does not like to receive benefits, does not remember well those who did him favors, and does not even want to hear about such favors, he nonetheless likes to hear

---

79. The Greek text has "runs away shaking his arms," which was translated as *fugere commoventem*. Thomas has this wording in *ST* II-II, q. 129, a. 4, ad 2. But because its meaning is hard to discern, he follows another translation in *SLE*, namely *fugere commonentem*, so that the meaning is: "does not run away from criticism." See *SLE*, 222, note to lines 184–87.

80. See also no. 756: "Sed secundum rei veritatem solus bonus, id est virtuosus, est honorandus, quia scilicet honor est proprium praemium virtutis."

the favors he himself bestowed commemorated. According to Gauthier, this "chocking" passage merely gives a portrait of the magnanimous according to popular ideas rather than expressing Aristotle's own opinion.[81] Thomas, however, takes the text as it stands and tries to interpret it. To this effect, he uses the (at first sight) surprising distinction between *ex dispositione* and *ex electione*: the disposition of the magnanimous is such that he enjoys bestowing benefits but is reluctant to receive something from others. Now, it is a fact that we often think of things we like but that we seldom remember what we do not enjoy. But it is the firm decision of the magnanimous to return greater benefits in exchange for what he received, insofar as he remembers his benefactors (no. 764).

A further property is that the magnanimous man does not engage in a great number of activities. He is more solicitous about the truth than about what people say. He divulges what he has done, but cares little for others and hardly associates with them. Thomas notes that the magnanimous man does not show contempt for others, that is, a disregard which would deprive them of due reverence; he just does not pay them a greater tribute than they are entitled to receive (no. 774). The magnanimous is slow in showing admiration but easily forgets injuries. Thomas adds an example: Cicero said of Julius Caesar that he had the habit of forgetting nothing but injuries (no. 778). Being largely self-sufficient, the magnanimous man does not need revenue from other sources. The magnanimous man does not talk much about trivial things. Aquinas comments that this is because he does not attach great weight to particular events in human life, but his whole attention is turned toward the common good and to divine things (*circa bona communia et divina*). These comments are all in line with Aristotle's principles and even with the wording of the text. Aristotle himself intimates that the magnanimous man is seeking a contemplative life. A further property is that he does not care whether people praise him or not (no. 779). In order to live magnanimously, certain natural dispositions seem to be required (nos. 759–83).

The vices opposed to magnanimity are mentioned in lesson 11 (IV.3.1125a17–35). A first vice is small-mindedness, as when a person does not think himself worthy of many good things, ignores his own ability, and fails to strive for greater things. If he does not engage in great and good works, he becomes worse. There is also the vice of excess: the presumptuous are ignorant because they do not know their own limits. They greatly exalt themselves. Small-mindedness is more opposed to magnanimity than conceit. It leads to avoiding those virtuous deeds that are within reach (nos. 784–91).

---

81. See *L'Éthique à Nicomaque* (trans. Gauthier and Jolif), II:1.287.

In lesson 12 (IV.4.1125b1–25), we read about an unnamed virtue that has to do with ordinary honors. It is related to magnanimity, which concerns great honors, but this virtue, together with liberality, gives us the right disposition with regard to mediocre things. The mean in these matters is valuable, but the extremes are blameworthy, as when one desires more than one is capable of, or less than one should (nos. 792–99).

A different virtue is analyzed in lesson 13 (IV.5.1125b26–1126b10), namely, meekness and the opposed vices. Thomas notes that the term *meekness* is used here to signify a virtue that seeks a mean between extremes. The word *meek* indicates a lack of anger (no. 803). The disordered lack of anger has no name, but the other extreme is called violent anger. It is praiseworthy to be angry about the right things and the right people. Contrary to the Stoics, Thomas says, Aristotle shows (no. 804) that a lack of anger can be wrong, for it means that one does not grieve at evil and does not punish what should be punished. But there occur excesses in anger, especially by hot-tempered people, who, however, often quiet down soon. Punishment calms down the angry, although there are people who remain angry. Finally he says that it is not easy to determine for how long one should stay angry (nos. 800–815). In this chapter, Aristotle remarks that to support injuries is characteristic of the servile mind (1127a7), a remark for which he is sharply criticized by Bonaventure.[82] Thomas suggests by way of explanation that the servile mind does not react to injuries the way he should (*debito modo*, no. 806) and observes that such a man is by nature inclined to take revenge when one has inflicted injury on him (no. 812). In this way, he reduces the entire text to a description of the spontaneous inclinations of natural, pre-virtuous man. It is not an expression of how one should behave.[83]

In lesson 14 (IV.6.1126b11–1127a12), amiability is considered as a virtue related to our actions. It makes us conduct ourselves agreeably toward others. An extreme is to be obsequious, trying to please everyone. The other extreme is to be contrary and make life unpleasant for others. But Aristotle sees a difference in pleasing or displeasing those who are close to us and outsiders. The one who has this virtue will also behave differently according to whether the persons he is dealing with are high-class people, friends, or casual acquaintances (nos. 816–30).

The virtue of veracity, which is dealt with in lesson 15 (IV.7.1127a13–b32), makes us truthful in our words and actions. Truthfulness makes us present

82. See ibid., 302–3.

83. Thomas interprets the ἀνθρωπικώτερον (literally "more human," in Latin, *humanius*) in 1126a30 as "homo magis inclinatur naturaliter ad puniendum."

things as they are. One extreme is impostery, which makes one say false things for the sake of glory or gain. A rare but real case is someone who chooses impostery, seeks it for its own sake, and delights in deceit.[84] The other extreme is the vice of minimizing the truth about oneself, as Socrates did in denying that he was wise. Impostery is more opposed to the virtue than belittling oneself because lying is *per se* evil. Thomas explains Aristotle's claim by an implicit reference to Augustine (no. 837): "Signs were instituted to represent things as they are. Therefore, if someone represents a thing otherwise than it is by lying, he acts in an inordinate and vicious manner" (nos. 831–49).[85]

Aristotle deals with amusement in lesson 16 (IV.8.1127b33–1128b9): a man should find some relaxation from work, stress, and worries. He describes several ways in which people amuse themselves and others. Like the jesting of a well-educated person, it can even be a virtuous act. Excesses are buffoonery and mockery. Aristotle's statement (1128a33) that the cultivated and civilized person is a sort of law unto himself is explained and qualified by referring to free choice by which the wise man avoids what the law prohibits and does what the law allows him to do. In this way, he seems to be his own law. By "law" Thomas here (no. 862) means in the first place the positive law, but secondarily also natural law and the principles of moral life (nos. 850–66).

In lesson 17 (IV.9.1128b10–35), Aristotle considers shame, which is not a virtue. People abstain from doing certain things because of shame. Shame regards voluntary misconduct, for which blame is due, so it is not becoming to the virtuous person. The morally good man must not do shameful things (neither according to truth nor to opinion). The absence of shame after a disreputable action seems evil, so that shame would be good. Nevertheless, shame is not a virtue, for it does not exist in a virtuous person (nos. 867–84). The goods that one desires are not always beneficial. Thomas notes that quite opportunely Aristotle adds a few words on continence. Although this habit is not a virtue, it follows right reason, although the continent person is still plagued by concupiscence (no. 883).

---

84. As Kevin Flannery notes in his detailed analysis of this passage, "the word 'impostery' is archaic. There is no other word, however, that so well represents the quality of being an imposter (ἀλαζών). The word ἀλαζονεία is sometimes translated as 'boastfulness,' but that does not capture Aristotle's sense. As we shall see, Aristotle says that the man who boasts 'for no reason' (1127b10) does not qualify as an imposter (an ἀλαζών); obviously, however, he would be a boaster." See Flannery, "Being Truthful With (or Lying to) Others," in *Aquinas and the "Nicomachean Ethics"* (ed. Hoffmann et al.), 129–45, at 131n3.

85. *SLE*, 252, notes to lines 85–88.

Book V

In lesson 1 (V.1.1129a3–b10), having dealt with the virtues concerning the passions, Aristotle addresses the virtue of justice, which deals with human actions in the context of the human community. At the beginning of the lesson, Thomas notes explicitly that the virtue of justice of which Aristotle speaks does not concern the passions but is the principle of external actions (no. 889). From a habit like justice proceed only just actions. With regard to injustice, he says that what is contrary to the law is unjust. The covetous man, who wants to have too much, is unjust. Goods coveted are not always beneficial for the individual. Men seek these goods (from God, Thomas adds) and pray for them, they desire them as if such things were always beneficial. Because of this, they become covetous and unjust, but it should not be this way. A man ought to pray that those things that are good in themselves be also good for him. May each person choose what is good for him (no. 897).[86] Referring to cases of unjust behavior, Aristotle mentions the man who desires too little of what is arduous. The one who acts against the law is also unjust (nos. 885–99).

Lesson 2 (V.1.1129b11–1130a14) deals with legal justice. In a democratic state, the people govern and, instead of observing what is simply just, they act according to their laws, which are in some measure just according to the different cities. Legal justice makes us act perfectly in relation to others, while other virtues aim at the good of the individual. Aristotle says that legal justice embraces every virtue (nos. 900–912).

In lesson 3 (V.2.1130a14–b29), particular justice is dealt with as part of general justice. Aristotle argues that particular justice is a particular form of equality in our dealings with other people in regard to our duties toward them, while every unjust action or situation consists in a certain inequality (nos. 913–26).

Distributive and commutative justice are mentioned in lesson 4 (V.2–3.1130b30–1131a29). One form of justice is the distribution of common goods. Another species is justice in transactions (commutative justice), as for instance in selling and buying. He mentions several forms of injustice (theft,

---

86. Aristotle's references to traditional religion and its practices are often understood as not presenting Aristotle's own convictions. *L'Éthique à Nicomaque* (trans. Gauthier and Jolif), II:1.337, even considers the passage on prayer (1129b4–6) as a possible gloss incorporated into the text. Jean Pépin distinguishes between the internal efficacy of prayer (the act of prayer could be beneficial to the one who prayers, regardless of whether the gods hear prayers) and the external efficacy (the act of prayer could be beneficial because they are heard and answered by the gods). Only the former might be attributed to Aristotle. "Aristote, 'De la Prière,'" *Revue Philosophique de la France et de l'Étranger* 157 (1967): 59–70. For an analysis of Aristotle's texts on prayer see Robert Mayhew, "Aristotle on Prayer," *Rhizai* 4 (2007): 295–309.

adultery, assassination, etc.). The just is a mean and is proportionate between the more and the less (nos. 927–37).

Lesson 5 (V.3.1131a29–b24) points out that the just is what is characterized by the right proportion, because what is just should be regulated according to a certain proportionality with regard to the persons to whom the distribution is made and the things that are distributed. What is unjust lies outside this proportion, for example, by reason of more and less. A man acts unjustly if he takes too many goods for himself (nos. 938–46).

In lesson 6 (V.4.1131b25–1132a25), the mean in commutative justice is determined. Here what is equal is observed according to an arithmetical proportion. A judge attempts to reduce an injustice to equality and to require compensation for the loss one party has suffered. The just is a mean between gain and loss. When mediating between the quarreling parties, a judge tries to determine what is just (nos. 947–55). The study of this theme is continued in lesson 7 (V.4.1132a25–b20). To establish equality, the amount exceeding the mean must be taken from one of the parties and given to the one who has less. In transactions, one should receive what is just for the work one has done or for the object of art produced. So it appears that justice means that before and after a transaction, one possesses what is an equal amount (nos. 956–64).

In lesson 8 (V.5.1132b21–1133a18), the Pythagorean theory of the mean in justice is mentioned, namely that it consists in reciprocation. This is patently wrong in distributive justice, by which the citizens get a proportional share of the common good. But in transactions of commutative justice, the mean does indeed consist in reciprocation. However, in questions of damage and injury, when the injury is personal, the compensation changes according the rank of the injured person. It also makes a difference whether the injury was inflicted voluntarily or not. With the help of a drawing, reproduced by Thomas, Aristotle shows that in commutative justice reciprocation must take place according to what is called a diagonal proportionality (nos. 965–77).

The subject of lesson 9 (V.5.1133a19–b28) is money. To obtain proportionality in exchanges, what is commensurate should be established and the things exchanged should be equaled. To this effect, money was introduced by mutual agreement. It replaced a thing-for-thing exchange, and was a guarantee that with money one could provide for future needs. But in buying and selling, before a compensation in money is given, an equality in what is exchanged has to be established (nos. 978–91).

Lesson 10 (V.5.1133b30–1134a16) shows that justice intervenes to establish the mean between, on the one hand, what has been done or inflicted as unjust and, on the other, what one has suffered as being unjust to him. Justice is a habit of the just man that makes him do what is just by deliberate choice. By contrast, being unjust is a habit by which one chooses to do what is unjust. Injustice is to take benefits in excess and to avoid onerous things one should support (nos. 992–99).

Lesson 11 (V.6.1134a17–b18) deals with the person who is unjust. Committing unjust acts occurs in many ways. If these acts are not committed by deliberate choice they proceed from passion, not from the vice of injustice. If in distributive justice one who governs does not attribute to himself more than to others (according to a correct ratio of distributive justice), he will be honored. Thomas adds that above this reward proffered by man, the just may expect a reward from God (no. 1011). The justice of a master or of a father is not the same as political justice but shows a certain similarity (nos. 1000–1015).

A division of political justice is presented in lesson 12 (V.7.1134b18–1135a15). A first division is that into natural and legal justice. At this point Thomas takes issue with a discrepancy between Aristotle's view and that of Roman lawyers (*iuristae*) for, unlike Aristotle, they understood natural justice in contrast with civil justice, which seems to be identical to political justice. Thomas notes, however, that the terms *civil justice* or *political justice* are used in two different senses: for Aristotle it refers to the perspective of the agent as a citizen of a given state, whereas for the Roman lawyers it refers to the cause of justice. So, while some laws have their origin in human conventions, others originate from natural relations, that is, from that to which nature inclines men (no. 1017). Natural justice has everywhere the same force and power to promote the good and to prevent evil. It arises from nature, like the indemonstrable principles, for instance, that theft must not be committed.[87] Nature inclines us to them.[88] Thomas recalls the difference between Aristotle and the Roman lawyers when he emphasizes that this "nature" can be taken in two ways: that which is common to all animals and that which is proper to man as a rational animal. The Roman lawyers referred to the former in using "natural right" whereas they called the latter the "right of the peoples" (*ius gentium*), to

87. Thomas's comparison of indemonstrable speculative principles to indemonstrable practical principles, on the basis of 1034b19, is central to his doctrine of natural law in *ST* I-II, q. 94.

88. Jaffa (*Thomism and Aristotelianism*, 180) claims that Thomas incorrectly attributes the immutability of the natural law to Aristotle but Jaffa failed to see to what extent nature and the nature of man is foundational to his ethics. See Max Salomon Shellens, "Aristotle on Natural Law," *Natural Law Forum* 40 (1959): 72–100; Fred D. Miller, Jr., "Aristotle on Natural Law and Justice," in *A Companion to Aristotle's "Politics,"* ed. David Keyt and Fred D. Miller Jr. (Oxford: Blackwell, 1991), 280–304; Jean-François Balaudé, "Nature et norme dans les traités éthiques d'Aristote," in *Aristote et la notion de nature: Enjeux épistémologiques et pratiques*, ed. Pierre-Marie Morel (Bordeaux: Presses Universitaires, 1997), 95–129; Tony Burns, "Aristotle and Natural Law," *History of Political Thought* 19 (1998): 142–66; George Duke, *Aristotle and Law: The Politics of Nomos* (Cambridge: Cambridge University Press, 2019), 129–48.

refer to specifically rational and social outcomes of man as a rational animal such as that agreements are to be kept (*pacta sunt servanda*), etc. Aristotle's natural justice, therefore, includes both the natural right and the right of the peoples as used by the Roman lawyers.

Next Aristotle gives the different meanings of *legal justice*, namely, what is universally imposed by law; what has been determined by law in particular cases; and the sentences passed by judges. Legal justice has its origin in natural justice—in his commentary, Thomas refers to Cicero (no. 1023)—but it is not derived from it by way of a conclusion but by a determination in its application. It may coexist with an admixture of human errors. But there are so many particular applications that some have wondered if there is anything determined by nature. Aristotle answers affirmatively, but allows that in the application of what is naturally right there occur exceptions, yet what belongs to the very nature of man is invariable. Finally, Aristotle defines what a just action is, namely, when a person does what is just either by nature or by law (nos. 1016–34).

In lesson 13 (V.8.1135a18–1136a9), we learn what sorts of actions make people just or unjust. Aristotle distinguishes between voluntary and involuntary acts. Furthermore, there are the circumstances of our actions. What is done in ignorance is not in the power of the agent. We do some acts with previous deliberation, others without. One who inflicts injury by deliberate choice is obviously acting against justice. Some involuntary acts are deserving of pardon (nos. 1035–49).

In lesson 14 (V.9.1136a10–b13), suffering injustice is analyzed. Can a man voluntarily wish that something unjust be done to him, or is every suffering of injustice involuntary? The incontinent person voluntarily harms himself and suffers injustice from himself, so that suffering injustice is not always involuntary. Another example: when while visiting a prostitute a man is robbed, he somehow willingly suffers injustice. But Aristotle says that no one wishes with full consent (*completa voluntate*) to suffer injustice, although he does what is harmful to himself. Actually, suffering injustice is involuntary, while committing an injustice is voluntary (nos. 1050–64).

In lesson 15 (V.9.1136b15–1137a30), an interesting question is raised in regard to distributive justice: who commits an injustice, the one who distributes too much to a particular person without regard to his merits and of what is fair, or the one who accepts it? Aristotle shows that it is the one who distributes who commits an injustice, and not the one who accepts. Next he argues that one does not commit unjust actions readily and with pleasure. It is also not true that one does always with great facility what is just. In the final section of the lesson, he describes different attitudes with regard to riches: for some (presumably the gods) there is no excess in their use of it, while for the very wicked whatever they do with it is bad, and for others again riches becomes harmful at a certain point (nos. 1065–77).

The subject treated in lesson 16 (V.10.1137a31–1138a3) is equity. Aristotle describes the equitable as better than the legally just, but as comprised of what is naturally just. The law is formulated in a universal way, but it is difficult to comprehend all particular situations. Exceptions made by equity do not destroy the universal validity of the law. In a given case the equitable is the just thing to do and is better than what is legally declared as just. It completes the law, where this is defective. Equity, then, is a particular species of justice (nos. 1078–90).

Lesson 17 (V.11.1138a4–b14) discusses injustice done to oneself. In the strict sense of the words, one cannot do injustice to oneself. Nevertheless, whoever takes his own life because of anger does what the law forbids and is unjust, for he deprives the state of a citizen, but he does not commit an injustice to himself. It is impossible for the same person to do injustice and to be the one against whom an injustice is committed. No one unwillingly does injustice. It is worse to do injustice than to suffer injustice (nos. 1091–1108).[89]

Book VI

In lesson 1 (VI.1.1138b18–1139a15), having shown that the mean of the virtues must be determined by right reason and lies between excess and deficiency, Aristotle distinguishes between that part of the rational soul that considers necessary things, and another part that is deliberating and reasoning. At this point (no. 1119) Thomas raises a difficulty: in *De anima* III.4, Aristotle distinguishes between the active and the potential intellect, which is in touch with all things. It would be contrary to the nature of both, Thomas writes, if one of them would understand necessary things, another part contingent ones. One can also say that the same faculty that knows the object in its perfect form also knows it in its imperfect state. Moreover, a sense like sight sees perfect things, such as the heavenly bodies and imperfect things on earth. So it is obvious that not every differentiation of the object requires a different power; for instance, the intellect knows substances and accidents. Thomas explains that the natural sciences examine both necessary and corruptible contingent things, but that one can also take corruptible things as they exist in their individuality as variable. In this way, they are known by

---

89. On Book V, see Jeffrey Hause, "Aquinas on Aristotelian Justice," in *Aquinas and the "Nicomachean Ethics"* (ed. Hoffmann et al.), 146–64.

the senses, in particular by the sense power called "particular reason," which gives a sensory judgment and compares particular impressions that become the object of deliberation and action (nos. 1109–23).

In lesson 2 (VI.1–2.1139a15–b13), after recalling that he has distinguished two parts of the rational soul, Aristotle examines which is the most excellent habit of each of these parts. But he first indicates that the act of the appetitive faculty corresponds to the affirmation or negation of the intellect, that is, it is a tending and adhering, on the one hand, and a withdrawing, on the other. When choosing, reason must deliberate and indicate a good option; the appetitive faculty concurs and must be right in order for the choice to be virtuous. Thomas again points out a difficulty in Aristotle's text (at 1139a27–31): the truth of the practical intellect depends on its conformity with the right appetite, while the appetite is right when it agrees with right reason. This seems to be a circular argument. Therefore, Thomas distinguishes between the end and the means: the truth of the practical reason is the rule for the rectitude of the appetitive faculty with regard to the determination of the means, but practical reason corresponds to the appetite, which acquires its rectitude from its inherence to the end, that is, it depends on the finality of man's natural inclination (no. 1131).

Thomas also resolves another difficulty: Aristotle's text seems to suggest that the speculative and the practical intellect are different parts, something which is denied in *De anima* II.10. The solution is that the practical intellect has its beginning in the consideration of the universal, but terminates its consideration in a particular action (no. 1132). The choice results when the appetitive faculty tends to and approves a particular object. The effect of choice is action. Reason, when it ordains itself to an individual thing or act to be done, is practical reason. A good action is the end. Reason can take counsel about contingent things. But what was done is not contingent anymore and cannot become undone, not even by God, as the poet Agathon says.[90] Thomas approves and adds that God is the universal cause of being whose power extends to all being; only what is inconsistent with being is subtracted from it (no. 1139).

In lesson 3 (VI.3–4.1139b14–1140a23), the intellectual virtues are mentioned: art, science, prudence, wisdom, and understanding. Science is to know with certitude what cannot be in any other way, that is, what is necessary and eternal. Of perishable things, the science of what is universal in them is possible. Every science can be taught, and what is knowable can be learned. It can be taught by reasoning (syllogism) and by induction. As there

---

90. An Athenian tragic poet who lived in the second half of the fifth century B.C. and is mentioned in Plato's *Symposium*.

is no reasoning to infinity, there are certain syllogistic principles, which one must know in order to have science. In the domain of the contingent, there is prudence concerning what has to be done and art concerning what can be made under the guidance of reason. In art, there are two things that must be noted: the action of the craftsman and the work he makes. Art is not about necessary things, nor about natural things, which have the principle of motion in themselves (nos. 1142–60).

Lesson 4 (VI.5.1140a24–b30) deals with prudence. Prudence is a virtue concerned with our actions, giving good counsel about what to choose and what to do with regard to our whole life. It does not concern things that are absolutely impossible or fully beyond our power. Thus, prudence deals with the good of man. It is called φρόνησις, while temperance (σωφροσύνη), which moderates pleasures and pains, as its Greek name indicates, evaluates its objects. By seeking intense pleasure, one's judgment can be distorted. Prudence is a habit ordained to action, guided by correct reason, and ordained to the good of man. Its seat is in the estimative part of our reason and it requires the rectitude of the appetite (nos. 1161–74).

Lesson 5 (VI.6–7.1140b31–1141a19) is an exposition of the habit of the first principles. Above the other intellectual virtues there must be the understanding of the principles of moral life, as the principles of demonstration must be known in the sciences where we proceed from indemonstrable principles to conclusions. Wisdom shows us what to do but bases its demonstrations on principles. It is the understanding that is concerned with them. The term "wisdom" has several meanings, such as the ultimate perfection in an art. But we also use the term to indicate the overall wisdom and the knowledge of the most general principles. Wisdom consists in knowing and confirming these principles and knowing the things that are inferred from them (nos. 1175–83).

Lesson 6 (VI.7.1141a19–b22) describes wisdom as the main intellectual virtue. Political science or prudence is not the most noble of the sciences, for the most noble is the knowledge of the most honorable and divine things. Usefulness is not the highest criterion. A second argument says that wisdom is the same everywhere, while prudence, which is said of people proportionally, may differ in different persons. What is healthy differs for different animals and people, but wisdom is one, for it considers what is common to all beings. The heavenly bodies, for instance, are more being than man. Thomas adds: we do not treat here of God and the separate substances, as they do not come in under the object of the senses. In no. 1189, he distinguishes between the separate substances and the heavenly bodies. Wisdom is the science of what is most honorable, prudence of what is useful to us, a distinction that several great philosophers neglected. The prudent man must have knowledge of the universal but he must also know the individual, because action has to do with individual things (nos. 1184–94).

In lesson 7 (VI.8.1141b22–1142a32), prudence is shown to be very important in daily affairs. Civic prudence is distinguished from prudence as such, although they are substantially the same habit: prudence as such is about what is good or bad for oneself, while civic prudence is about things that are good for all, and so it is more important than individual prudence. It is directed to the application of the laws. The city is more important than the household, the household more than the individual. The good of the individual cannot be attained without civic and domestic justice. Civic and domestic prudence are not sufficient without personal prudence. Youth do not yet have a sufficient experience of practical things, although they can become proficient in a science like mathematics. Just as in the sciences there are indemonstrable principles, in prudence there is a singular thing, which is taken as an ultimate, that is, a singular practicable thing, which functions as a principle of action (nos. 1195–1216).

In lesson 8 (VI.9.1142a32–b33), we hear of the virtue of εὐβουλία, which concerns deliberation. It is not a science, nor is it opinion, but a deliberation combined with inquiry. It supposes a certain acuteness of the senses and imagination, but, as the name says, it is an inquiry of reason. It deliberates correctly and it aims at attaining a good end. *Euboulia* as such directs deliberation in view of the end of human life. Particular *euboulia* directs deliberation in view of some special end (nos. 1217–33).

Lesson 9 (VI.10–11.1142b34–1143b17) deals with σύνεσις, the habit of judging correctly in individual cases. The person who has this habit is called sensible, because of his sensible deliberation in matters of prudence, but *synesis* differs from prudence insofar as it gives a right judgment when one deliberates about what has to be done. But the impulse to pass to action does not come from *synesis* but from prudence, which prepares us for the final choice. At this point Aristotle mentions yet another virtue, γνώμη, which is considerateness. Thomas explains it by comparing it to the relation of equity to legal justice (it intervenes in cases in which the law is deficient), so *gnome* provides a correct judgment in cases where the overview of *synesis* is insufficient or defective. These different habits belong to the same person and aim at the same thing, so that *gnome, synesis,* and prudence all deal with what is doable. Aristotle next mentions νοῦς (*intellectus*), that is, understanding which is a habit of both the speculative and the practical intellect and concerns the first principles; at the practical level, it concerns the singular and contingent, which are principles as final causes (the ends of our actions). All these habits concern singulars and are in contact with the senses. Some people are inclined to them by a natural disposition. They develop them while growing older, so we must be attentive to what elderly, experienced people say. Commenting on this text, Thomas refers again to a more objective norm by adding that experienced people see the principles of what they have to do.[91] By "principles" he means the synderesis (or synteresis) and rules of conduct derived from it. Thomas adds that in the understanding of particular things, the sensory power of judgment, called particular reason (no. 1255), intervenes (nos. 1234–56).

In lesson 10 (VI.12.1143b18–1144b1), the usefulness of these virtues is discussed. Wisdom does not consider operations but first principles, so it hardly contributes to man's happiness. Likewise, prudence does not contribute to happiness, as we perform the necessary actions because we already possess the respective habits. It is not necessary to have prudence in order to become virtuous, provided one is instructed by wise men. However, wisdom and prudence do something for happiness in the following way: because happiness results from virtue, the man who acts with wisdom and prudence does have the necessary virtues, so that happiness can result. Prudence cannot exist without the moral virtues. Aristotle then argues that a certain skillfulness or cleverness is required that enables us to do the things ordered to an end. This habit is used by prudence to reach our good (nos. 1257–74).[92]

Lesson 11 (VI.13.1144b1–1145a11) deals with the relation between the moral virtues and prudence. Moral virtues cannot exist without prudence. Aristotle argues that there exist some natural virtues, in the sense that people have a natural disposition to virtuous actions. There is a basic orientation to these in the intellect as well as in the will but, when acting according to this disposition, one needs the guidance of reason. This applies to the practice of all the virtues. Just as in the discursive part of the soul there are shrewdness and prudence, so in the appetitive faculty there are natural dispositions to virtue and the moral virtues. All virtuous actions are done with right reason, which means with prudence. When there is prudence, the other virtues are also present, connected as they are with one another (nos. 1275–91).

Book VII

Lesson 1 (VII.1.1145a15–b20) deals with continence, which is imperfect in the genus of virtues. When a man's practical reason is right, so that he knows

91. For other instances see his commentary above on 1113a29–34 (no. 494) and 1128a33 (no. 862).

92. On the question whether the goal of moral actions is determined by reason or by desire see Tobias Hoffmann, "Prudence and practical principles," in *Aquinas and the "Nicomachean Ethics"* (ed. Hoffmann et al.), 165–83.

what to do but inclines to the contrary because of a passion, he is incontinent.[93] But if the perversity of the appetitive faculty is considerable, man's reason will follow this inclination and become perverted in its judgments. Perversion can become so great that it is called brutishness. Opposed to it is heroic virtue, which Aristotle calls divine, in the sense that it exceeds the ordinary human mode. Heroic virtue and brutishness are seldom found. Aristotle's remark on the existence of a heroic, divine virtue provides Thomas with an opportunity of enlarging the perspective and making an opening to supernatural grace. To understand Aristotle's reference, he says, we must recall that the human soul holds the middle between higher and divine substances, with which it communicates through the intellect, and the brute animals, which have the sensitive faculties in common with man. In the same way that the sensitive faculties are sometimes corrupted to a subhuman level (such as in the case of bestiality), the rational part is sometimes perfected above the common mode of human perfection, as it were, into a similitude with separate substances (no. 1294).[94] At the end of the lesson, Thomas gives an overview of what Aristotle is going to do in the next chapters.

For Aristotle continence is a preparation rather than a virtue itself. The reason is that a good number of people show some self-control, but nevertheless occasionally sin by following their passions. Hence they cannot yet be called virtuous in Aristotle's eyes, because he who is virtuous acts rightly. This view is not taken over by the Stoa: the virtuous man struggles to gain self-control. In the Christian tradition continence was also considered a virtue, so that is not surprising that among the 270 theses condemned in 1277 there is the proposition that continence is not a virtue.[95] However, in this debate, much depends on what is called continence. Here, Thomas adopts Aristotle's view of continence as a not yet perfect state of virtue, although in the *Summa theologiae* he also mentions the Christian use of the term in the sense of virginity.[96]

Lesson 2 (VII.2.1145b21–1146b7) presents several doubts about continence and incontinence. How can one who judges correctly be incontinent? Socrates

93. When discussing one's inability to act on one's knowledge contemporary authors often speak about "weakness of the will" whereas Thomas speaks about *incontinentia* or incontinence, the common Latin translation of Aristotle's ἀκρασία.

94. One can contrast this addition (*considerandum est*) with the way in which John Cooper writes about this passage ("little needs to be said") in "Nicomachean Ethics VII. 1–2: Introduction, Method, Puzzels," in *Aristotle: "Nicomachean Ethics," Book VII. Symposium Aristotelicum*, ed. Carlo Natali (Oxford: Oxford University Press, 2009), 9–40. On heroic virtues in Aquinas see Daniel Ols, *Ex amore Veritatis* (Florence: Edizioni Nerbini, 2015), 83–110.

95. See Hissette, *Enquête*, 297–99.

96. *ST* II-II, q. 155. Regarding the question whether there is development in Thomas regarding the issue of continence as a virtue see Doig, *Aquinas's Philosophical Commentary*, 225–65.

thought that a man who judges correctly does only what is best. Against this position speaks the fact that some people do what they know is wrong. Others weaken this position by saying that those overcome by their passions did not have knowledge but only opinion. Yet if they have a strong opinion, it comes down to their having prudence, which opposes the desire. But this is impossible, for performing base actions cannot go together with prudence, which is conjoined with the virtues. On the other hand, when one is incontinent it does not mean that he has given up all right insight (nos. 1310–27).

Lesson 3 (VII.3.1146b8–1147b19) gives the solution to several difficulties raised in the previous lesson. Thomas first gives an excellent analysis of the problems involved with continence and incontinence that became apparent in the previous lesson (nos. 1328–34). Aristotle reminds us that continence and incontinence bear on concupiscence and the pleasures of touch. The incontinent judges that pleasure should always be pursued. He may not consider or may suppress the general proposition that getting drunk, for instance, is wrong and choose to enjoy excessive drinking now. Passion is not present when one is concerned with general statements, which relate to the universal, but it may influence particular judgments (nos. 1335–53).[97]

In lesson 4 (VII.4.1147b20–1148b14), the discussion about continence and incontinence is pursued. One can be incontinent in various ways according to the kind of pleasure one is seeking. We must distinguish between pleasures that accompany certain necessary bodily acts (food, drink, sex, some material goods), while other pleasures are unnecessary, such as those given by riches, etc. Those who, contrary to right reason, pursue one of the latter are called incontinent with a restriction, for example, incontinent in matters of money. But incontinence is considered a vice when both reason and the appetitive faculty tend to evil or when the appetitive faculty alone does so and not reason. People may also be called incontinent with regard to necessary things if they strive for them contrary to right reason, but, unlike the intemperate, they do this not with deliberate choice (nos. 1354–67).

Lesson 5 (VII.5.1148b15–1149b24) deals with different kinds of pleasure. A first distinction is that between human and bestial pleasures. He calls *bestial* those pleasures that are unnatural and horrible, like eating human flesh and engaging in homosexual activities. Some people do these things because of a tendency or due to having become accustomed to it. People who use their reason scarcely, or women who do not control their emotions, cannot be called continent or incontinent without qualification. There are excesses of vice with

97. For a further analysis of what is known as the "syllogism of the incontinent" see Martin Pickavé, "Aquinas on Incontinence and Psychological Weakness," in *Aquinas and the "Nicomachean Ethics,"* 184–202.

regard to all virtues, which may be caused by different factors. He quotes timidity as an example: some people are timid by temperament, others by a pathological condition. One may occasionally experience something of these unnatural passions but not be overcome by them. In such cases we speak of continence. He concludes that unqualified continence and incontinence concern those passions and vices that temperance and intemperance are about (nos. 1368–84).

Lesson 6 (VII.6.1149a24–1150a8) describes different kinds of incontinence, first with regard to anger. This is less disgraceful than incontinence in the pleasures of touch. In anger one still listens somehow to reason, but in sensual pleasures the incontinent man enjoys them without any reasoning. Moreover, anger does not act deceitfully, while the desire of pleasure springs up in secret and paralyzes reason. The irate acts with some sadness because of the injury he suffered. His act is a mixture of the voluntary and involuntary. Some bodily pleasures are natural, others not. Temperance and intemperance have to do with pleasures that are human and natural; they proceed from deliberate choice. Badness in man is imputable because he remains master of his actions (nos. 1385–1403).

In lesson 7 (VII.7.1150a9–b28), continence and perseverance are considered. Both continence and incontinence share the same matter with temperance, namely the pleasures pertaining to touch and taste. He who overcomes them is continent, but the one who gives in is considered incontinent. Whoever intentionally pursues these pleasures beyond measure is intemperate. The intemperate man who sins by deliberate choice is worse than the one who sins when overcome by passion. Aristotle also mentions the vice of effeminacy, the vice of shunning fatigue, and that of seeking amusement to an excessive degree. Incontinence is divided into impetuosity and weakness. Sometimes the incontinent man deliberates but is overcome by passion, while others follow a passion as soon as it arises. In this latter case we speak of impetuosity. Still others pull themselves together when they feel a passion arise of which they have previous knowledge, and resist desire (nos. 1404–21).

In lesson 8 (VII.8.1150b28–1151a28), we read that intemperance is worse than incontinence. The intemperate man sins by deliberate choice, whereas the incontinent man gives in to a passion by weakness. The intemperate man is incurable because of a lasting habit, while the incontinent man is curable when the passion passes. Some incontinent men are weak and easily dragged along by a passion, while others are impulsive and are overcome by a violent passion. The incontinent man sins without deliberate choice, while the intemperate man acts with deliberate choice and is unrepentant. Aristotle explains that in the field of action, virtues are what principles are in reason. They represent the end for the sake of which we act. This end is not taught by reasoning, but we acquire the correct view of it by considering the things to be done. The incontinent person keeps the right evaluation of the end but abandons right reason in his actions (nos. 1422–34).

Lesson 9 (VII.9.1151a29–1152a6) compares continence and obstinacy. May a man who abides by a principle and a choice be called continent even if incidentally he adheres to a false principle? Such a man is essentially continent. Aristotle compares the one who is stubbornly attached to his own view to the continent man, but says that he is different in many ways. The continent man does not change his opinion by passion or desire of the senses, but can be convinced by arguments to change. The obstinate does not change his view, and the incontinent who seeks pleasure pertinaciously is on this point like the obstinate person. Aristotle shows next that continence is related to virtue; it also seeks the mean, insofar as the continent wants neither too much pleasure nor too little. The difference between the continent and the temperate man is that the latter does not have evil desires, because his sexual desire is fully controlled by his virtue. The intemperate man has a perverse judgment about pursuing pleasure, while the incontinent man has a correct judgment (nos. 1435–54).

In lesson 10 (VII.10.1152a6–36), prudence and incontinence are compared. Can prudence coexist with incontinence in the same person? Prudence is accompanied by the moral virtues, while in the incontinent person passions are strong. Moreover, the incontinent man fails to follow the commands of reason and his choice is wrong, although there is a limited similarity in conduct. The incontinent man is like a city with good laws that are not observed. Those who are incontinent by habit are more easily cured than those who are so by temperament (nos. 1455–68).

In lesson 11 (VII.11.1152b1–24), the relevance of pleasure and pain for the moral life is considered.[98] Virtues and vices are concerned with pleasure and pain. Aristotle himself holds that happiness, our common end, is related to pleasure, which is to be reached by virtuous actions. Some philosophers, however, thought that no pleasure is good. This view was defended by them with several arguments: pleasure is a means to an end, not the end itself; a temperate man is praised for avoiding pleasures, but one does not avoid what is good; the prudent man seeks to be free from pain and pleasure; prudence is obstructed by great pleasures; the products of the arts are good, but pleasure

---

98. See the detailed and excellent analysis by Kevin White, "Pleasure, a Supervenient End," in *Aquinas and the "Nicomachean Ethics"* (ed. Hoffmann et al.), 210–38.

is not such a product; and pursuing pleasures is childish. One can also say that some pleasures are harmful; they are not the highest good.

Lesson 12 (VII.12.1152b25–1153a35) provides answers to these arguments. Some pleasures are absolutely good, others bad, and others are sometimes good relative to a certain individual. Perfect pleasure is found in the good that consists in an activity. The pleasure of contemplative activity is not accompanied by further needs or desires. The pleasures that accompany the acts of our good habits are true pleasures. Now, answering the arguments against pleasure put forward in the previous lesson, Aristotle says that when we associate happiness with pleasure, we mean pleasure as the connatural unimpeded actualization of an existing habit. No habit is hindered by the pleasure resulting in its actualization, but perhaps sometimes by pleasures alien to it. By the arts we can make things that cause pleasure, but pleasure itself is not a product of the arts. That the wise man avoids pleasures applies only to certain pleasures. Physical pleasure as such is not good in an unqualified sense (nos. 1483–97).

In lesson 13 (VII.13.1153b1–1154a7), Aristotle explains that there is one pleasure that is the highest good. Speusippus and some Platonists argued that the opposition of pleasure and pain is that between the more and the less. But this would make pleasure an evil, as pain is. Other Platonists did not hold that pleasure is an evil but considered it as something imperfect. Aristotle answers that even if some pleasures are evil, this does not imply that pleasure cannot be the highest good. Happiness is an unimpeded activity of good habits. Unimpeded actions are pleasurable. Now, one pleasure must be the best, which comes with the highest activity, namely, that in which happiness consists. But to be happy one also needs health and external goods so that one is not hindered in undertaking activities. The view that a man can be happy even when suffering from great misfortune—the Stoic theory, says Thomas in no. 1507—is nonsense. On the other hand, too much of good fortune becomes an obstacle, hindering man's central activity. Also, tendencies differ according to different people, so that the highest good for all does not seem to consist in the same pleasure. But Aristotle maintains that the contemplation of truth is the highest good for all, as all naturally desire to know. Thomas comments on Aristotle's claim that "all things by nature have something divine in them" (1153b31) by saying that this desire is grounded in an inclination of nature, which depends on the substantial form of a thing as derived from the first principle (no. 1511).[99] Some authors denied that pleasure is the highest good, resulting from the fact that they identified pleasure with bodily pleasure (nos. 1498–1515).

99. See *L'Éthique à Nicomacque* (trans. Gauthier and Jolif), II:2.810.

The last chapter of the book is addressed in lesson 14 (VII.14.1154a8–b34) and discusses physical pleasure. The difficulty is whether bodily pleasures are good. The majority of men are only concerned with physical pleasures. Aristotle argues that they are good up to a certain point, insofar as they remove pain. In fact, bodily pain brings people to seek a remedy in excessive pleasure, that is, in general bodily pleasure. People also seek these pleasures because of their intensity as a remedy for pain and their lack of experience of other pleasures. Yet they are not universally good, as some result from evil activities; other bodily pleasures are remedies for some defect and satisfy natural desires, such as that of food, so that they cease when the need is satisfied. Excessive physical pleasures lead to pain in those who pursue them, as they suffer at the least lack of them. People who pursue them have no knowledge of the delight of intellectual activities. Melancholic persons have a continual need of some pleasure as a remedy for their disposition. Intellectual pleasures are better because there is no opposite pain: the activity of reason is proper to our nature and so it is delightful, although not always, because of our composite nature and the intervention of other factors. But God, who is simple and unchangeable, rejoices always in the contemplation of himself, whereas for men change is delightful, because human nature is not capable of remaining in the same condition (nos. 1516–37).

Book VIII

In Book VIII, after having discussed the moral virtues, Aristotle now considers friendship, as it is based on virtue and is an effect of virtues, as he indicates in lesson 1 (VIII.1.1155a3–b16). Friendship is based on free choice and so accompanies the virtues. Ethics studies the things required for human living. Friendship occupies an important place in our lives: without friendship external goods lose much of their meaning, namely when there is no one to share in what we have, no one to receive help from to conserve our possessions. Friends are needed for the young and are useful for the old. Work is more effective when friends collaborate with us. Moreover, there is a natural friendship for our fellow men that share human nature with us. Lawmakers try to promote friendship between citizens. Perfect justice promotes and protects friendship. Nevertheless, there are conflicting opinions on friendship. Some say that it is based on likeness, whereas others say that people who do the same work become enemies. In fact, while Empedocles says that likeness is loveable (like desires like), Euripides and Heraclitus say that contraries seek one another. Aristotle concludes that, incidentally, the contrary is sought as it is believed to be helpful, but there are more kinds of friendship (nos. 1538–50).

In lesson 2 (VIII.2.1155b17–1156a5), he explains what friendship is, considering it from the point of view of goodness. There are pleasurable and useful goods, but their goodness depends on our condition and position. Everyone loves what is good for him, in the sense of what seems to be good to him, regardless of whether it is really good or only apparently so. Next he points out that mutual return is necessary in a friendship: the one loving is loved in return. Finally, mutual benevolence is required, which is recognized by both friends. Aristotle defines friendship as a bond of men who wish well to one another, who both recognize some good and have mutual appreciation or love of the good, of the pleasurable, or of the useful.

The different forms of friendship are discussed in lesson 3 (VIII.3.1156a6–b35). As there are three types of love, there are also three kinds of friendship, based on the good as such, on the pleasant, and on the useful. These three answer to the definition of friendship, namely mutual support and help, and wishing the good of one another according to the kind of friendship. Friendships of the last two types are more easily dissolved because the friend is not loved for himself but for his usefulness or the pleasure he provides. Next Aristotle shows among which age groups we find these types of friendships most frequently. Useful friendship is often found among the elderly, who need the help of the young, and also among adolescents. Friendship based on pleasure is found among young men, who live more according to the impulses of passion. But as people grow older, other things are considered pleasant, and the young themselves are in a state of change. They fall in love as easily as they change. But in the so-called virtuous friendship, friends wish to another what is good and love each other because of their goodness. This friendship is durable. It provides pleasure and is also useful, but it is not often found, as virtuous people are rare and friendship needs time to develop.

Useful and pleasant friendships are compared in lesson 4 (VIII.4.1156b35–1157b5). In these friendships, durability requires exchange and return, but it does not necessarily happen between people who love each other sexually, because one party takes pleasure in seeing the beauty of the beloved, while the beloved does so in receiving attention. When these begin to fail, this friendship also languishes. If friends have like habits, their friendship is more durable. But if the advantages disappear, the friendship also does. A friendship is destroyed when one discovers in a friend something contrary to their friendship, but this does not happen in virtuous people. Only good people can be real friends.

The act and habit of friendship is examined in lesson 5 (VIII.5.1157b5–1158a1). Some people are friends by habit, even if they are not actually practicing their friendship, while others live together pleasantly doing good to each other. Friendship may cease because of the absence of friendly acts (as other habits are weakened by lack of practice) or forgetfulness. Neither the old nor the surly are disposed for friendship. There are also people who are not inclined to associate with others. Being together and rejoicing in the same things is proper to friendship. Mutual love, characteristic of friendship, presupposes rational choice. But what is done by choice implies habit. Friends who are loved for their own sake are loved from habit and not from passion. The one who loves a friend loves what is good in himself, but wishes good to his friend for the friend's sake. In friendship mutual love is required.

In lesson 6 (VIII.6.1158a1–b11), Aristotle examines the different friendships in relation to the persons involved. The young, who take pleasure in company, easily make friends, but elderly and sullen people find little pleasure in the company of others. With regard to those who enjoy the perfect friendship, they cannot be a friend to many people. This also results from the fact that a friend is pleasing, but that one does not easily find many people who are pleasing. It is also difficult to become very well acquainted with many people. In the other types of friendship, it is easier to have many friends. Sometimes these friendships are both useful and pleasant.

The subject of lesson 7 (VIII.7.1158b11–1159a12) is about the question of whether friendship between unequals is possible, for instance, between a father and a son, a husband and his wife, a superior and a subordinate. These relationships are different as are those between the partners involved in them: the attitude of a son to his father is not the same as that of the father to his son. Many qualities can be present in one within a pair of friends and not in the other. Aristotle argues (1158b25–29) that the better person should be loved more by an inferior man than he himself loves one who is mediocre. This assertion seems to contradict the Christian faith with regard to God's love for the world. Thomas presents Aristotle's view and then says that it applies to the friendship about which we are speaking now, *de qua loquimur* (no. 1635). The friendship between God and man apparently is entirely beyond the horizon of Aristotle's outline of ethics, just as man's supernatural happiness was not intimated either. I would like to stress the importance of this short clause, *de qua loquimur*, because it qualifies the doctrinal value of a whole book of *NE*. In the absence of a certain proportion, Aristotle also argues, friendship between men and the gods (τῶν θεῶν), which Thomas replaces with the singular "God," is not possible. Aristotle has no idea of a totally gratuitous love of God for man.[100] Thomas admits the view of Aristotle but restricts its validity to a friendship characterized by social intercourse and sharing in each other's life.[101] Furthermore, he notes that according to the custom of the gentiles Aristotle calls the separate substances gods. Now, it is obvious that there is no friendship between these beings and man in the sense that they lead a common life.[102] But if this is so, wishing a friend to become virtuous runs the risk of losing that friend because he becomes more godlike. Aristotle says that in such cases we must assume that the friend remains the same person (nos. 1624–38).

Lesson 8 (VIII.8.1159a12–b24) inquires about love and being loved in friendship. Loving is more characteristic of friendship than being loved, although many want to be loved rather than to love, as they expect to obtain benefits and honor. But because friendship is a habit and a habit should be actualized in its act, loving is more proper to friendship than being loved. When one of the friends lacks in goodness, great love can make up for this deficiency. Often parents are more loving of, rather than being loved by, their children. Which friendship lasts longer? The one based on virtue will last, for virtuous people do not easily change. Wicked people, however, have nothing in which they repose and do not long stay like-minded. Friendship between persons of unequal conditions are directed to utility. Sometimes people say that contrary seeks contrary, but what people really seek in such cases is the mean (nos. 1639–56).

Lesson 9 (VIII.9.1159b25–1160a30) deals with friendship in civil society. Aristotle argues that there friendships must be understood as civic associations. People united in associations share with one another, yet the same rights are not found in all associations. Friendships are greater when people have more things in common. Aristotle stresses that friendship and justice are found in the same person. Justice is differentiated according to the type of friendship. All associations are contained in civic associations, for in all these

100. In *ST* II-II, q. 23, Thomas explains that man's friendship with God is based on grace and the infused virtues. For the extensive use of Aristotle in this respect see Guy Mansini, "Aristotle and Aquinas's Theology of Charity in the Summa Theologiae," in *Aristotle in Aquinas's Theology*, ed. Gilles Emery and Matthew Levering (Oxford: Oxford University Press, 2015), 121–38.

101. Elsewhere, at 1162a4–5, Aristotle says that "the friendship of children to parents, and of men to gods, is a relation to them as to something good and superior," something which Thomas (no. 1715) describes as "paternal friendship."

102. In an excellent study Avital Wohlman observes that St. Thomas scrupulously remains at the level of ethics. God's love for man, in the form of divine friendship, is a free gift which Aristotle could not know about. In places where the text allows a reference to God's love, Thomas avails of such an opening to point out that we may safely assume that God is the source of all good things and that the wise man will be agreeable to God (*NE* VIII.13). See Avital Wohlman, "L'élaboration des éléments aristotéliciens dans la doctrine thomiste de l'amour," in *Revue thomiste* 82 (1982): 247–69, at 249.

unions people come together for their common interest. Even those that are formed for pleasure are for some utility, for example, for religious acts such as sacrifices to render honor to the gods. Aristotle has the plural "gods," but Thomas changes it to the singular "God" (no. 1670). Friendships are formed in analogy to these associations and are hidden in or contained by them (nos. 1657–71).

In lesson 10 (VIII.10.1160a31–1161a9), different kinds of states are distinguished. Having connected friendships with civic associations, Aristotle now distinguishes them according to the divisions of political regimes. There are three forms of polity: kingdom, aristocracy, and timocracy—and three corrupted forms: tyranny, oligarchy, and democracy. By timocracy he understands the rule of the masses, by which the common good of the rich and the poor is promoted, and all citizens are equal, while in a democracy only the good of the poor is intended; the latter is not very different from a timocracy, which is a kind of good government. Aristotle shows next what in a household corresponds to these regimes. The position of a father resembles that of a king. But in Persia the fathers are like tyrants in treating their sons as slaves. The way a husband and his wife govern the family corresponds to aristocracy. When the husband does not leave the wife in charge of anything, their household resembles an oligarchy. This happens also when the wife has complete authority. Brothers are equal, so they form a timocracy. Groups living together without a leading authority resemble a democracy in which each individual has equal power (nos. 1672–87).

Lesson 11 (VIII.11.1161a10–b10) compares the different forms of friendship with the kinds of political regimes. Aristotle compares the friendship of a father to that of a king: as a father is a ruler of his son, so a king is ruler of his subjects, and both are distinguished by their excellence; parents and ancestors are honored. The friendship between husband and wife corresponds to the regime of aristocracy, where a few are entrusted with authority and do not take away the belongings of others: a husband is placed over the wife, but, Thomas adds, he does not command (*praeripit*, no. 1694) in things proper to his wife. The friendship between brothers is similar to that of comradeship or of a political club, where people have the same training, and one does not have all the power. But there are also forms of friendship corresponding to corrupt forms of government, where real friendship is minimal, especially in a tyranny, where nothing is shared between the ruler and his subjects. A tyrant does not work for the common good but for himself. When Aristotle writes that there cannot be any friendship between a master and his slave, except as men, Thomas comments that a master can have friendship with a slave as a human being (no. 1700). The chapter closes with the remark that in the corrupt political system of a democracy, friendship is fully realized (nos. 1688–1701).

In lesson 12 (VIII.12.1161b11–1162a33), a subdivision of friendship is presented. The point of departure is that friendship brings with it common participation. Consanguinity and comradeship imply a common origin or upbringing, but in civic friendships (between soldiers, students) people are more involved in associations. Aristotle next mentions friendships between relatives, between man and wife, a father and his son; parents love their children as part of themselves, while children love their parents as the source of their being. Parents love their children more than the children love them, because they engendered them. They love them as themselves. As long as children have not attained the use of reason or, Thomas adds, at least the capacity to distinguish their parents from others, they—very young children—do not yet love their parents (no. 1709). Fraternal friendship is similar to that of comrades, but it is strengthened by common upbringing and likeness in their way of living. Nephews are also more or less related. Aristotle then turns to the friendship between man and wife, which is almost natural. The domestic society of man and wife is antecedent to civil society and more necessary. Thomas adds a conclusion: man is by nature more a conjugal than a political animal (no. 1720). The union of man and wife is not only for the generation of offspring, but also for the things that are necessary for human life. These functions are divided between man and wife. When both are virtuous, their friendship will be based on virtue. Each must do what is just to the other. Children strengthen their union (nos. 1702–25).

Lesson 13 (VIII.13.1162a34–1163a23) discusses quarrels and complaints, which we find especially in utilitarian friendships. When in a noble friendship the friends are intent on serving each other, quarrels do not easily occur. Quarrels in friendships based on pleasure occur seldom. In friendships directed to the utility, there may arise conflicts when legal utility differs from moral utility. To avoid conflicts, those who receive benefits should make an adequate return (nos. 1726–43).

Lesson 14 (VIII.14.1163a24–b28) deals with complaints in friendships between unequals. In friendships based on virtue, the better person thinks that it is reasonable to receive a greater benefit, as does the more useful person in friendships based on utility. The other party, the needy, etc., think that they should receive the same. Aristotle solves the difficulty in this way that the more noble party should receive greater honor—in compensation for acts of virtue—while the less noble or poorer party should receive greater "gain" and assistance. It is sufficient to return what is feasible, as not all benefits can be re-paid. No one can ever to adequately repay his parents or God (nos. 1744–56).

Book IX

In lesson 1 (IX.1.1163b32–1164b21), Aristotle discusses matters of preserving and destroying friendships. How is it possible to preserve a friendship be-tween persons unlike each other? The answer is: by exchanges analogical-ly proportional to both friends. The difficulty is that affection and services cannot be computed in money. They are to be judged according to, first, the interior act of love and, second, to external gifts and services. When the be-loved does not provide utility or pleasure to the lover, friendship may be broken. But friendships based on virtue are more durable. In friendships based on utility, the one who receives a benefit should make a fair estimate of what is due. He who helped a friend or bestowed a gift leaves the esti-mate of the repayment to the receiving party. But when those who receive are negligent, problems arise. Aristotle mentions teaching philosophy, the value of which is not measurable in terms of money, and says that the re-turn should be similar to what we give to our parents and God (Thomas again changes the plural "gods" to the singular; no. 1768). The amount of help or pleasure is best known by the one who receives help or pleasure. Re-payment should be made according to his judgment (nos. 1757–72).

In lesson 2 (IX.2.1164b22–1165a35), Aristotle raises some doubt about the duties of assistance and repayment in a friendship. Must one assist one's father in all matters or help a friend rather than a virtuous person? A general rule is that we must pay a debt or make a return to a benefactor before giving a present. But settling difficulties with certitude is not easy. It is also not easy to determine which honors are to be paid to different persons, such as one's parents, brothers, friends, or benefactors. Children should provide for their parents and help them. One should always try to give everyone what is appro-priate (nos. 1773–84).

Lesson 3 (IX.3.1165a36–b31) deals with the dissolution of friendships. It is not surprising that friendships based on pleasure or utility are broken when the advantages no longer exist. When in a friendship based on virtue the persons in question are no longer virtuous, the friendship ceases. An evil-doer, who is clearly wicked, cannot be loved by a virtuous man. We should not immediately break off with all who have done some evil, but only with those of excessive wickedness. One who is advancing in virtue cannot remain friends with one who has ceased to progress. This happens in friendships with persons of our past, who no longer have the same tastes and enjoy the same pleasures. Friends have to be delighted and saddened by the same things. But when a friendship is dissolved, a man should act kindly toward those who were his friends (nos. 1785–96).

In lesson 4 (IX.4.1166a1–b29), we read about the practice of friendship. A first act is to willingly offer help and gifts for the sake of a friend. A second act is to want his well-being, as a mother loves her children. Aristotle mentions as a third act sharing joys and sorrows, having the same tastes. Next he lists the main qualities of the good man as a basis for his attitude toward his friends: he works for the intellectual element that is foremost in his life; he wishes himself life and virtue and continued existence. Adding to a dubious mention of God in the Greek and in the Latin translation at 1166a20–22, Thomas writes: "the being that remains identical in his existence is God; he does not wish himself some good he does not now possess, but possesses perfect good in himself. He is always what he is at any time, as he is unchangeable. Now, we are like God most of all by our intellect, which is incorruptible and unchangeable. Therefore every man's existence is thought of in terms of his intellect" (no. 1807).[103] This addition remains within the limits of the theory of the first unmoved mover as explicated in *Metaphysics* X. When Aristotle suggests that the virtuous man is at peace with himself because he practically never regrets (*impaenitibilis enim ut dicere*), Thomas qualifies it as follows: "as he always acts in accord with reason, he will not easily feel regret" (no. 1809). His feelings toward his friend are like those to himself, for a friend is so to speak another self. In virtuous people these feelings, which I have described as ordered to friends, are also those directed toward themselves. But wicked people cannot converse with themselves, as they remember many distressing evils they committed that they forget when in company of others or engaged in external activities. But they cannot find internal peace. Finally, he observes that after the gratification of his passions, a bad person is often saddened (nos. 1797–1819).

Lesson 5 (IX.5.1166b30–1167a21) explains that the works of friendship are beneficence, good will, and concord. First, goodwill is explained (the Latin word *benevolentia* translates the Greek word εὔνοια). It is the beginning of friendship, but it is not yet friendship: the person to whom our goodwill is directed may not know it or may be a stranger. It is not love, because love is accompanied by familiarity. There is no goodwill in a friendship based on pleasure, but it can have a place in a friendship based on utility. In general we have goodwill for a person because of his virtue (nos. 1820–29). Lesson 6

103. On the difficulties involved in this passage, see Don Adams, "Aquinas on Aristotle on Happiness," *Medieval Philosophy and Theology* 1 (1991): 98–118.

(IX.6.1167a22–b16) examines how concord is related to friendship. Concord consists in making the same choices rather than in having the same views; it concerns what has to be done. Concord is found among virtuous men. Bad people want more than their share of the advantages and less of the labor and burden (nos. 1830–39).

Beneficence is studied in lesson 7 (IX.7.1167b17–1168a27). Aristotle notes that benefactors seem to love the people on whom they bestow their benefits more than these do their benefactors. The reason might be that the beneficiaries feel themselves in debt, whereas the benefactors do something good, and feel some love for the good they do, as craftsmen and poets love their products, because they love their activity and their being. On the other hand, it is not a virtuous act to receive benefits, so the benefactor is less worthy of love. Finally, giving and loving is like an activity, as is love. Being loved is more like being passive. Conferring gifts may entail some work, while people who receive them can remain passive, so that benefactors love their beneficiaries more than vice versa (nos. 1840–54).

In lesson 8 (IX.8.1168a28–b28), a doubt is raised on love of oneself. Bad people do everything for gain and nothing for the good of others, while the virtuous do not act for themselves alone. But, Aristotle says, all the good things one does for others are found in one's basic attitude to oneself, as is confirmed by many proverbs. However, love of self can also be blameworthy, when one assigns to oneself more than one's share. Most people try to acquire an excessive amount of goods and use them to satisfy their desires. They follow the irrational part of their soul (nos. 1855–65).

Lesson 9 (IX.8.1168b28–1169b2) is about the love of self of the virtuous person. A person loves himself more when he seeks to excel in virtue and collect the noblest goods. He gives precedence to the noblest part of his being, the intellect. One who seeks to be eminent in good works loves himself best. Whoever follows reason is continent, and his actions are voluntary, not dictated by impulses. So he who loves himself best is intent on virtuous actions and will perform many actions for his friends and his country. He is willing to die for his friends, preferring a splendid act of virtue to a long, quiet existence. He also gives up honors for a friend and chooses virtue above other things (nos. 1866–84).

Lesson 10 (IX.9.1169b3–1170a13) addresses two questions. (1) Does a happy man need friends, or is he self-sufficient? (2) When one enjoys divine favor does one still need friends? A proverb says that when the spirit is benign there is no need of friends. Thomas notes that the Platonists believed that human affairs were governed by divine dispensation through intermediary spirits, some good, some malevolent. One who enjoys the favor of divine Providence does not seem to need friends (no. 1887), but Aristotle says that he does need friends both when prosperous and in misfortune. Man is a social animal and should not live alone all the time. He will come to know the virtues better by seeing virtuous behavior in others. In a sense, the actions of his friend will be his own and his own activity will be more consistent. As he lives on good terms with his friends, a companionship in virtue will be formed (nos. 1885–99).

In lesson 11 (IX.9.1170a13–b19), some fundamental reasons are set forth as to why a happy man needs friends. First of all, existence and life are desirable. But life means that man's capacity for perception and thought is operating. Thomas adds a remark: potentiality as such is indeterminate; it is determined by an act. A man becomes good when his potentiality is actualized. Life is naturally good, therefore also for the virtuous person (no. 1904). This is apparent because all desire it. It is also true for the virtuous man. The perception of being alive is pleasant to the virtuous person. We are conscious that we are alive by reflective acts, by which we experience that we are alive. This delightful perception is good. But one also perceives existence and action in a friend, through a close togetherness and association. Without such friends there would be a deficiency (nos. 1900–1912).

Lesson 12 (IX.10.1170b20–1171a20) considers the number of friends one should have. In the case of useful friendships, a great number of friends would mean that a person must show many favors, which would be burdensome. As far as pleasure goes, a few friends would be sufficient to provide the needed relaxation. With regard to friendships based on virtue, Aristotle makes a comparison with the number of citizens: an enormous number would make a country, but very few would not be sufficient for civic life. As one cannot associate with a multitude of people, one cannot have a great number of virtuous friends nor entertain close contacts with them. It is also difficult to share in the joys and sorrows of a great number of friends. So one should not seek too many friends. It is not possible to practice real friendship with a great number of them (nos. 1913–24).

Lesson 13 (IX.11.1171a21–b28) notes that friends are needed both in prosperity and adversity. Do we need friends more in prosperity than in adversity? When suffering reverses our fortune, we need friends to help us, but in times of prosperity we should have virtuous friends. In days of sorrow the presence of a good friend is delightful, for when we perceive that a friend sympathizes with us, his sympathy gives us comfort. The virtuous man also sees to it that on his account a friend is not saddened too much. But when he finds himself in pleasant circumstances, he will see to it that his friends share in his well-being. On the one hand, he should ask his friends only with some reluctance to share his misfortunes; but, on the other, he should readily go to his friends who are suffering from misfortune to comfort them. The conclusion is that in all circumstances the presence of friends is desirable (nos. 1924–43).

Lesson 14 (IX.12.1171b29–1172a15) tells us about the pleasure of living together with friends as the most proper and pleasant way of practicing friendship. As consciousness of ourselves is delightful, so is that of a friend's existence. We also see that sharing one's favorite pursuits and interests with a friend is delightful. Friends become better by being together, working together, and loving each other. A friend provides a model of a virtue (nos. 1944–52).

Book X

In lesson 1 (X.1.1172a19–b8), after having treated the different virtues and their effects, Aristotle considers the end of the virtues, namely, pleasure and happiness. In Book VII, he already dealt with sensible and bodily pleasures; but he now discusses pleasure as accompanying happiness. The role of pleasure, rewards, and presents in the education of children and in social life is obvious. Pleasure is important and present in all phases of human life. People should enjoy the things they ought to enjoy and grieve over what they ought to be saddened by. Pleasure and pain are found in the different phases of human life. One must not choose to do evil or avoid what is good to obtain pleasure or to avoid pain. But there are different opinions on pleasure: for some it is a kind of good, for others it is very bad, and there are also those who say that it is better to withdraw from pleasure as it can make us slaves. Yet this view does not agree with what people commonly seek and do (nos. 1953–78).

Passing to lesson 2 (X.2.1172b9–1173a13), we read about the opinion of those for whom pleasure is a good. Aristotle cites the theory of Eudoxus who considered it as the greatest good. His first reason was that all creatures seek pleasure so that it must be proper and good to them, and his arguments were accepted because of the moral excellence of Eudoxus himself. Moreover, pain ought to be avoided, so that pleasure should be sought. Pleasure added to the good makes it more desirable. But Plato tried to show that pleasure is not a good in itself, but only so when combined with a virtue, like prudence. Thomas observes that according to Plato, the essentially good is the very essence of goodness to which nothing can be added. Whatever is good in things is derived from the very essence of goodness (no. 1972). But Aristotle rejects this line of reasoning, according to which nothing is good in itself because it would render human life undesirable at all and void of any good. Consequently, Aristotle also rejects Eudoxus's idea that what all desire is not necessarily good. On the contrary, "that which all men believe to be true, we say is really so" (1172b36). Thomas justifies this idea by adding that "it is impossible that all men are mistaken in their natural judgment" (no. 1975).[104] Even in wicked people there are desires of natural goods, on which all agree. As all seek to avoid pain and attain pleasure, pleasure and pain are opposed to each other as good and evil (nos. 1964–79).

Lesson 3 (X.3.1173a13–b20) is a detailed discussion of Plato's theory of pleasure, namely, that pleasure does not belong to the category of the good. Good comes in under the genus of qualities, but pleasure is not a quality, so it is not a good. The reply is that good is said of all categories, not only of quality. The Platonists also argue that the good is determinate, but pleasure indeterminate, so that it does not come in under the genus of the good. In addition, they say that pleasure, which admits degrees of more and less, is not marked by oneness and so it does not belong to the genus of good. Aristotle rejects this argument by saying that the same can be said of justice and the other virtues, which all admit more and less; health does too. The Platonists also say that pleasure is a movement, that is, something imperfect. Now every motion is fast or slow but swiftness and slowness are not attributable to pleasure. We do not say that someone is pleased quickly. They also hold that pleasure is a process of generation. If so, it would be dissolved into that from which it is generated, that is, pain. But this argument is at the level of bodily passions, while pleasure is a passion of the soul. For instance, pleasure in mathematical studies has no opposite pain. Finally, Aristotle observes that many pleasant memories and hopes exist without there being preceding defects that are being replenished. There are pleasures without the defect of pain, so that pain is not a correlative of every pleasure (nos. 1980–96).

In lesson 4 (X.3.1173b20–1174a12), another argument that pleasure is not a good is discussed. The Platonists pointed to such pleasures as adultery and drunkenness, but Aristotle says that disgraceful pleasures were not pleasant in an absolute way; real pleasure is what is pleasant according to reason. He also points out that pleasures from virtuous actions and from shameful actions differ in kind, and that pleasure is not a good in itself; if it were, it would have to be chosen under any circumstances. Aristotle argues that there are many

104. On this so-called *consensus omnium* idea, see Klaus Oehler, "Der Consensus omnium als Kriterium der Wahrheit in der antiken Philosophie und der Patristik," *Antike und Abendland* 10 (1961): 103–29.

things we want to do: to see, to hear, to remember, to know, etc., without paying attention to eventual pleasures as good in themselves, which pleasures apparently are not (nos. 1997–2004).

In lesson 5 (X.4.1174a13–b14), Aristotle is clearing the way for the definition of pleasure. Just like seeing is perfect in its very act, pleasure is too, whereas motion involves duration, as in the construction of a temple. But pleasure is complete in every part, without an interval of time, so that it is not a motion, nor a process of generation (nos. 2005–21).

In lesson 6 (X.4.1174b14–1175a21), the nature of pleasure is defined: pleasure accompanies a perfect activity as its achievement. People are especially active in the things they love most. As we grow weary of activities, pleasure is not durable. The most perfect action is also the most pleasant. Pleasure perfects the action as a form that co-determines it, and not as an agent. It does so because of favorable conditions that accompany the action. Also, life is a certain activity, and so all people desire life and seek pleasure. Aristotle does not answer at this point the question regarding whether pleasure is more important and more desirable than life and contemplation, for in his view they go together. Thomas clarifies it by an ingenious argument: we must live according to reason; hence we should want only so much pleasure as is convenient, that is to say, insofar as we have the operation which is consequent upon the pleasure (nos. 2022–38).

Lesson 7 (X.5.1175a21–b24) describes different kinds of pleasure; first as being consequent on the different kinds of activities, and next with regard to their goodness or badness. Activities differ in kind: those of the senses differ from each other and from the activity of the intellect. Therefore, pleasures that perfect these activities will also differ specifically, as they have an affinity with their actions. Pleasures intensify these activities and may prolong them. But some activities may be hindered by pleasures arising from another activity. That which is more pleasant (e.g., eating and drinking) may hamper another activity (e.g., thought) (nos. 2039–49).

In lesson 8 (X.5.1175b24–1176a29), we are instructed about the morality of pleasure. Aristotle reminds the reader how closely linked activity and pleasure are, though they are not the same, for pleasure pertains to our appetitive part. As activities differ according to virtue and vice, so do pleasures. Things of the same species have similar pleasures, for they follow the nature of the species. In contrast to animals of the same species that have the same pleasures, men have quite different pleasures because reason is not determined to one kind of behavior. The pleasure that virtuous men experience is the main form of human pleasure. Virtue is the measure by which we should judge all human actions and undertakings. There is one principal pleasure among those of the virtuous man and which accompanies the activity proper to man (nos. 2050–64).

After considering the nature of pleasure, Aristotle takes up a new subject in lesson 9 (X.6.1176a30–1177a11), namely that happiness is not a habit, because habits remain even during our sleep. But because sensation ceases and intellectual activity is imperfect, happiness does not remain, "if there was any," Thomas notes (no. 2066). Habits remain in periods of misfortune, but happiness does not. Aristotle next determines that happiness accompanies those activities that are desirable in themselves, and where nothing further is sought. Some think that amusement is such an activity; tyrants especially stress this kind of amusement, but princes may not be well behaved. Thomas observes that Aristotle calls people in power tyrants (no. 2072). As tyrants whose lives are not always virtuous devote much of their time to amusement, our happiness does not consist in amusement. But as a virtuous activity arises from good habits, it is most desirable to a good person, and happiness must be placed in this activity, and not in amusement. In a next argument, he shows that happiness is the purpose of our whole life, something we do not say of amusement. Anacharsis[105] says that one can amuse oneself for a certain time, so that one can work harder, but one cannot work all the time. Finally, Aristotle says that some pleasure is found in amusement, but that the joy that accompanies virtuous activities is different. As happiness is the highest good of man, it must consist in his best activity (nos. 2065–79).

This conclusion is further elaborated in lesson 10 (X.7.1177a12–b4). The best activity is the one that is in accordance with the highest virtue, and flows from what is best in us, that is, the intellect. Aristotle's suggestion that the intellect is either divine or the most divine element in us offers Thomas the opportunity to develop somewhat further the nature of the intellect. Compared to divine things, only the intellect understands things that are essentially (Thomas adds *essentialiter* to the text) divine and it possesses a certain connaturality to divine things (no. 2083). He also uses this opportunity to point out, against the Averroists, that according to Aristotle the intellect is part of the soul and that it is not simply something divine and separate, but the most divine of whatever there is in man insofar as, like separate substances, its operation is without a corporeal organ. As Doig has noted, Thomas is influenced by Albert, who uses information gathered in the Commentator, that is, the Greek commentaries, to distinguish between two positions: on the one hand,

---

105. A Hellenized Scythian sage (600 B.C.), later considered one of the Seven Sages.

there is Plato, for whom the soul understands through the light received from the divine separated intellect and, on the other, Aristotle and the Peripatetics, for whom the intellect is part of the human soul.[106] Thomas also has in mind Avicenna and his followers, who placed separate intellects in the different revolving heavenly spheres, as well as Averroes who taught that there is only one intellect common to all men. Thomas shows that an Averroistic version of man's happiness did not impose itself as authentically Aristotelian; and this was not only a threat to Christian views but also at variance with Aristotle's principles (no. 2084).

We can persevere in contemplation longer than in other activities, as the body is used very little in it. Yet there is some fatigue, as the intellect needs the phantasms existing in the sense faculties. The resulting pleasure is pure because the mind deals with immaterial objects, which cannot be destroyed. The contemplation of truth comprehends investigation and reflection. The man who practices justice needs other persons in order to do so, while the contemplation of truth is an internal activity, and requires little assistance of others, although companionship in a life of contemplation promotes intellectual activity. Happiness in contemplation is never sought for the sake of other things (nos. 2080–97).

In lesson 11 (X.7.1177b4–1178a8), happiness and leisure are examined. There is a form of rest we take when we have to interrupt an activity because of fatigue, but another form of rest and leisure results when we have reached a particular goal. Among the activities in the field of the moral virtues, there are none which in themselves bring leisure. They are directed to a further end, while the contemplative activity of the intellect places man at leisure and, if he is able to conduct this activity over many years, his happiness is assured. To engage in intellectual activity over many years makes him practice an activity proper to the superior substances. So the contemplative life compared to that of the moral virtues is like the divine life compared to ordinary human life. The poet Simonides[107] advised us to stay at a purely human level, but Aristotle says that we must strive to attain immortality and direct all our efforts at living a life according to reason. What is best in us is most proper to us and therefore most delightful. This contemplative life is not human considering our composite nature, but it is most properly human considering what is best in us (nos. 2098–2110).

The theme of happiness in its connection with the moral virtues is further examined in lesson 12 (X.8.1178a9–b32), where Aristotle introduces a

106. Doig, *Aquinas's Philosophical Commentary*, 268–69.
107. Born at Ceos, Simonides was an author of epitaphs in honor of those fallen during the Persian wars.

secondary type of happiness resulting from the practice of the moral virtues, which have to do with external goods, bodily goods, and the passions. Moral virtues, including prudence, regulate the passions and are concerned with man as composed of body and soul. They may give us a certain happiness. Happiness based on contemplation has not much need of external goods, just what is necessary for life, but in the practice of the moral virtues more goods are required. This leads to the question of what is more important in moral virtue, choice or external acts. And the answer is: choice is more important, but external acts are necessary. For contemplation none of these things are required, and external goods may even distract us; nevertheless, a man needs the necessities of life. The example of the gods shows that perfect happiness consists in contemplation: we cannot ascribe to them the acts of the moral virtues, which would be unworthy of them. Indeed, no other activity can be attributed to them except contemplation. When Aristotle concludes by saying that the life of the gods is completely happy, Thomas adds: "the gods, that is, the intellectual substances" (nos. 2111–25).

Lesson 13 (X.8.1178b33–1179a32) has as its subject the relation of happiness to external goods. Human nature is not self-sufficient for a life of contemplation, because the body needs external goods for its sustenance, rest, and health. But we do not need many of these goods. Modest wealth allows us to do good to those who need help. Aristotle quotes the wise Solon in confirmation. Anaxagoras concurs too. And the life of those who seek happiness must harmonize with their doctrine. Thomas adds that this is not the case with the Stoics, who teach that external goods are not human goods but nevertheless seek to acquire them. Aristotle writes that the man who lives in such a consistent and harmonized way will please the gods and will be beloved by them, if the gods have any care of us, as is generally believed they have. Thomas changes the plural to the singular God and confirms divine Providence—*sicut rerum veritas habet*: God exercises solicitude over human affairs (no. 2133). It is reasonable that God should confer his greatest favors on those who honor their intellect. Aristotle places ultimate happiness in man's activity of wisdom. Again Thomas adds in a final note that Aristotle does not explain perfect happiness, but happiness such as there may be in man's mortal life (nos. 2126–36).

In lesson 14 (X.9.1179a33–1180a24), Aristotle argues that in order to accustom ourselves to a life according to the virtues, legislation is required so that we acquire the habit of practicing the virtues. For most people, persuasive words alone are not enough and they have to be coerced by the fear of punishment. Habituation is required for a man to become virtuous. Aristotle mentions that there are three opinions on this issue: some say that men are virtuous by nature (by temperament and the influence of the heavenly bodies); others say that they become so by practice; and others again say that they do by instruction. As to the first view, being inclined to virtue by nature is not in our power. Where Aristotle speaks of an influence of the heavenly bodies in regard to the movement of man's mind to what is good, Thomas adds the words "and from God who alone governs the intellect" (no. 2145). With regard to instruction, in order for it to be effective, we must become receptive by good customs. Whoever lives by his passions will not eagerly welcome advice. By legislation people should get accustomed to the practice of the virtues. To live a temperate and hard life is unattractive to many. The young must be reared under good laws but adults also must discover the goodness of a life according to the virtues. While the virtuous comply with the requirements of a good and noble life insofar as they are convinced of its goodness, the insubordinate need punishments. Some say that those punishments or pains should be inflicted that are directly contrary to the inordinate pleasures some people seek. To become virtuous, men should receive a good education and observe the right moral code. The law should have coercive power (nos. 2137–54).

In lesson 15 (X.9.1180a24–b28), Aristotle insists that there should be some supervision of the education of children and the activities of the citizens. One can contribute to it by becoming able to make good laws and being a legislator. Public regulations and laws hold a similar place as what a father tells his sons and household, although what a father imposes does not have the same coercive power as the regulations of public government. Aristotle insists on the necessity of a general knowledge: legislators should try to acquire a universal knowledge of the way of life and the activities that make people virtuous. A comparison with what is needed to heal people by the art of medicine confirms what he says in this lesson (nos. 2155–63).

In lesson 16 (X.9.1180b28–1181b23), some instructions are given on how to learn to make laws by experience or education. There is a noticeable difference with the other arts, where those who teach them are also practicing them themselves. But in political science, the Sophists pretend to teach the laws but do not observe them. Politicians do not publish on political science nor make their sons good statesmen. Experience in politics is a help but it is not enough. Political science must be studied. But the Sophists are a long way from teaching political science, as they identify it with rhetoric and think that it is easy to make laws, namely that one collects different laws and chooses the best. But legislators must also make new laws. Choosing the best does not depend on the intellect alone; to know which kind of laws are the best, one should have much experience and know what is suitable. Collections of written laws and the constitutions of the different states are helpful. So at the end of his treatise on ethics, Aristotle prepares the way for his books on the state and the different regimes.

Concluding Remarks

This summary of Thomas's commentary shows that his explanation of the text develops on the level of philosophy. As an attentive reading of what he says on human happiness in his comments on Books I and X show, there is no confusion of this philosophical exposition with the Christian doctrine of the vision of God, for we read that the happiness that can be reached in this life remains imperfect. However, as it consists mainly, as Aristotle shows, in the contemplation of the intellect, it really and ultimately consists in the vision of God, which according to the Christian faith is man's final destination.

Thomas also does not discuss the question of whether the souls of the deceased survive after death, as that does not form part of the present inquiry (Book I, lesson 17). As Wohlman says, Thomas stays scrupulously at the philosophical level, while he writes in other works, such as the *Summa contra gentiles*, that Aristotle holds the view of the soul's immortality because he teaches that the intellect is incorruptible. When Aristotle speaks of sacrifices to the gods, Thomas changes the plural to the singular (God) and notes that the cult of the pagans has been abolished (Book IV, lesson 7), a statement that remains within the limits of philosophy and of what Aristotle writes in *Metaphysics* XII.

On several occasions, Thomas makes important additions to what Aristotle writes, as in the question of how to acquire a virtue, namely by acting in conformity with the first principles of the practical intellect and by following the example of wise and virtuous persons (Book II, lesson 4). Induction based on experience helps us to distinguish between different virtues (Book II, lesson 8). All through his commentary, Thomas informs his readers about certain Stoic doctrines concerning the moral life. In Book III, lesson 1, there is an interesting example of how Thomas respects Aristotle's text: the question is raised whether a good intention can render an imperfect or even bad act acceptable. Without criticizing Aristotle, he writes at the end of the passage that we cannot commit a sin to obtain a greater good.

In general, Thomas's method in commenting on Aristotle's text is to remain faithful to the explication of its literal sense. He nevertheless occasionally broadens the perspective by means of occasional observations on what Aristotle writes elsewhere, for example, in the *Metaphysics,* and the general principles of his philosophy. He does not introduce theological considerations in a commentary on a philosophical text and does not try to "improve" Aristotle.

12 ❧ THE COMMENTARY
ON THE *POLITICS*

The *Politics*, as Aristotle's treatise on man's life as a member of local communities and as a citizen of the state is commonly called, is comprised of eight books. As is the case with the *Metaphysics*, it is not a uniform work, but consists of a series of treatises. The book was probably put together by Aristotle himself or by his school. Aristotle bases his exposition of man's life in communities on ethical and metaphysical views. A central idea is that man is a ζῷον πολιτικόν (social animal); he finds his fulfillment only in the civil community of the state, which is conceived by Aristotle not as an empire but as a city of modest size consisting of the union of different villages and comprised of several classes of citizens. The end of the individual as well as that of the state is the perfect life of the citizens, and Aristotle sees a parallel between the (ideal) political community and a well-functioning organism.

Sir David Ross suggested that the treatise may date to the time Aristotle was in Lesbos, Troad, or Macedonia, but many think that it might have been composed in Athens during the years at the Lyceum.[1] Throughout the book education to adult citizenship is stressed. The treatise is a realistic description of the need for man to live in a community, of the different forms of government, and also of the ideal civic society. The state is not just the result of a convention, but based on human nature and ordained to the well-being of the citizens.

In Book I, Aristotle examines how community life developed in the family, in the village, and in the state, which is not an outgrowth of the family. In Book I, we find Aristotle's theory of slavery. He stresses the necessity of producing what is necessary for man's life (ἀναγκαῖα), and slavery is one of the necessary means for this. Book II describes different constitutions, for example, Plato's Utopia, and the constitutions of Sparta and Carthage. Book III

1. W. D. Ross, *Aristotle* (London: Methuen, 1923), 235–69.

presents a classification of constitutions and of different forms of government. Books IV, V, and VI give an account of the existing constitutions and regimes, such as oligarchy and democracy and their varieties. Finally, Books VII and VIII describe the ideal state and the best constitution. According to Werner Jaeger, this last "utopian" part of the *Politics* is earlier that the empirical part, but Christopher Rowe rejects this suggestion whereas Charles Kahn finds it convincing.[2]

As is the case with *NE*, the arguments in *Politics* are based on teleology.[3] In the last chapter of *NE*, Aristotle says that the study of man's life in a city will complete his exposition of man's moral life. Laws and government are needed to make the life of adults and the young better disciplined. When necessary, the government must impose punishment and penalties on the ill-conditioned citizens. Those who want to make the lives of other people better must acquire the science of legislation; thus *NE* leads us to expect a study on the ideal form of civic life. As W. L. Newman writes in his magisterial study of the *Politics*, Aristotle's political science is concerned with the constitution of an ideal state, but also with the improvement of the actual forms of government and the ways and means to educate people to become wise and useful citizens.[4]

In subsequent centuries Aristotle's *Politics* received little attention either in terms of translations from the Greek or in terms of commentaries. By the twelfth century both the Arabs and the Latin West were merely aware of its existence. This changed when William of Moerbeke around 1265 composed the first complete translation from Greek into Latin and in doing so offered "this hidden treasure to the European world and from there on to the whole world."[5] Moerbeke's translation, known as the *translatio completa*, builds on his earlier and incomplete translation, composed around 1260, which ends at II.11.1273a30. It would remain the only complete Latin translation until Leonardo Bruno composed his own translation in roughly 1438. Apart from its reception by way of commentaries on Aristotle's text and its use in commentaries on Peter Lombard's *Sentences*, there are the influential

---

2. Jaeger, *Aristotle*, 263; Christopher J. Rowe, "Aims and Methods in Aristotle's *Politics*," *Classical Quarterly* 27 (1977): 159–72; Charles H. Kahn, "The Normative Structure of Aristotle's 'Politics,'" in *Aristoteles' "Politik." Akten der XI. Symposium Aristotelicum*, ed. Günther Patzig (Göttingen: Vandenhoeck and Ruprecht, 1990), 369–84. See also Peter L. Simpson, *A Philosophical Commentary on the Politics of Aristotle* (Chapel Hill: The University of North Carolina Press, 1998), xvi–xx.

3. See Rudolf Stark, "Der Gesamtaufbau der aristotelischen Politik," in *La Politique d'Aristote* (Genève: Fondation Hardt, 1961), 3–35, esp. 11.

4. W. L. Newman, *The Politics of Aristotle*, vol. 1 (Oxford: Clarendon, 1887).

5. L. Minio-Paluello, "Die Aristotelische Tradition in der Geistesgeschichte," in *Aristoteles in der neueren Forschung*, ed. P. Moreau (Darmstadt: Wissenschaftliche Buchgesellschaf, 1968), 314–38, at 327.

fourteenth-century treatises by Dante (*De Monarchia*) and Marsilius of Padua (*Defensor Pacis*).[6] Moerbeke's translation provided scholars in the West with the terminology to give a scientific expression to human life in political societies as well as an independent textual basis for developing politics as a scientific discipline.[7]

Thomas's early biographers, William of Tocco and Ptolemaeus of Lucca, both confirm the existence of an unfinished commentary on the *Politics* which is now dated as composed between 1268 and 1272. In subsequent printed editions his unfinished commentary was often supplemented by Peter of Auvergne's commentary but there were also alterations to Thomas's text or interjections of Peter's commentary into Thomas's text. The critical edition has established that Thomas's commentary breaks off at III.6.1280a7, as well as the fact of his exclusive use of Moerbeke's *translatio completa*.[8] Most likely, it is Albert the Great who has to be credited with the first Latin commentary on the *Politics*.[9] These first two Latin commentaries will prove to be highly influential in subsequent centuries.[10]

The Commentary of Thomas Aquinas

The text of the commentary begins with a prologue in which Thomas, referencing *Physics* II.2.194a21–23 and II.8.199a15, points out that in the operations of his mind, man must imitate what nature does and let himself be guided by what he sees in nature, the cause of which, Thomas writes, is the divine intellect. With this addition regarding the divine intellect Thomas possibly had in mind a remark in *NE* I.1.1094b9–12, where Aristotle compares the good of one person with the good of the *polis* (πόλις) and describes the latter achievement as more divine (θειότερον, *divinius*). Man can know the different processes in nature with a theoretical knowledge, but

6. See C. Flüeler, *Rezeption und Interpretation des Aristotelischen Politica im späten Mittelalter* (Amsterdam: Grüner, 1992).

7. Rolf Schönberger, "Die aristotelische *Politik* in der Philosophie des Thomas van Aquin," in *Die Politik des Aristoteles*, ed. Barbara Zehnpfennig (Baden-Baden: Nomos, 2012), 195–212, at 209.

8. Leonine edition, vol. 48. I have also consulted the English translation based on this critical edition: Thomas Aquinas, *Commentary on Aristotle's "Politics,"* trans. Richard J. Regan (Indianapolis, Ind.: Hackett, 2007).

9. See pages 8–10 of the introduction in the Leonine edition as well as Francis Cheneval, "Considérations presque philosophiques sur les commentaires de la *Politique* d'Albert le Grand et de Thomas d'Aquin," *Freiburger Zeitschrift für Philosophie und Theologie* 45 (1998): 56–84.

10. Some even go so far as to characterize a large number of subsequent commentaries on the *Politics* as plagiaries of Thomas's and Peter of Auvergne's text. See J. Dunbabin, "The Reception and Interpretation of Aristotle's Politics," in *The Cambridge History of Later Medieval Philosophy*, ed. N. Kretzmann, A. Kenny, and J. Pinborg (Cambridge: Cambridge University Press, 1982), 723–37.

making things comes in under the practical intellect (nos. 1–2). The intellect proceeds from what is simple to what is complex. This order is also visible in human communities, where some are simple, others more complex: the city (*civitas*) is the most perfect community or society (nos. 3–4).

In the second part of the prologue, following the rules with regard to the aim of a prologue, Thomas deals with the necessity of a political science, its nature, dignity, and relation to other sciences, as well as its proper order. Given that philosophy deals with everything that can be known by reason and the order of the city falls under the work of (practical) reason, philosophy would not be complete without a science that deals with the city (*scientia civilis*). As the city must be organized and governed and its subjects are deliberating agents, this science is a practical science and forms part of the moral sciences (nos. 4–6). Its dignity derives from the teleological nature of all the other human societies, that is, all other human societies are ordered toward the city. As such, its corresponding political science is both the most important science and the one directing the other practical sciences (*principaliorem et architectonicam*). This time Thomas explicitly refers to *NE* X.10.1181b15–23 but other passages, such as *NE* I.1.1094a9–16 and *NE* VI.8.1141b22–25, also come to mind. Commenting on one of these passages, Thomas describes *architectonica* as "directing the others in what they should do."[11] The order in which we proceed in this science is that we go from its parts to the study of the whole. This procedure is, however, common to both the speculative and the practical sciences. Its distinguishing feature consists in manifesting "how each thing [within the city] may be perfected." One notes that Thomas does not refer to a set of specifics proper to the practical sciences, such as the appropriate amount of exactness and life experience which Aristotle develops in *NE* I.2–3 (nos. 7–8).

In the final lines of *NE* (1181b13–23) Aristotle himself already provides a brief outline of the *Politics*. If one combines Thomas's remarks on these lines with some remarks made at the beginning of his commentary on Books II and III, one can arrive at the following *divisio textus* of the eight books of the *Politics*. Book I deals with aspects belonging to the household and, as such, serves as a link connecting *NE* with the *Politics*. Books II–VIII deal with the *civitas*. First, in Book II, the views of Aristotle's predecessors are discussed. Books III–VIII contain Aristotle's own opinions. He starts with distinguishing between various forms of government in Book III and determines their differences in Books IV–VI. In Books VII–VIII, he writes about the best regime's features and how it is to be established.

11. *In Eth.* I, 2, no. 25.

Book I

In the first lesson (I.1.1252a1–1253a38), Thomas considers Aristotle's introduction to the detailed discussions that will take place in the following
chapters.[12] As all communities seek some good, the city as being the highest form of community life will seek to attain the highest good (nos. 9–11).
It includes the other communities, and its end is most comprehensive. The
city has more members than a village or a family, but numbers alone do
not make the nature of communities specifically different, as some have
argued, who saw only a little difference in the tasks of those in charge of
each of these communities (nos. 14–15). That this position is wrong becomes clear when we analyze the different groups in their elements (nos.
16–17). The domestic community of male and female is ordered to the generation of offspring; husband and wife cannot be without one another. Yet
it is proper to the male to lead by reason; he also has the power to generate offspring (no. 18).[13] Aristotle passes to a discussion of the association
of ruler and subjects. Those who excel in bodily strength are able to do the
work that the ruler has assigned to them. Without the wisdom of the ruler,
the bodily strength of the slave would be of no use (no. 19). But women and
slaves cannot be placed on the same level. A woman is not robust insofar
as her body is concerned, but has an aptitude for having children. Aristotle says that nature does not make one single thing perform different functions. Those of slaves and women differ: a woman has no natural aptitude
for hard work as slaves have. Things are made for one main purpose. According to some authors, women and slaves belong to the same order, but
Aristotle says that they are different by their nature.

Then Thomas comes to speak of the term *barbarus* and mentions its different senses, such as people who do not know the language of the society in
which they are living or people who are not ruled by any civil laws (no. 22).[14]
Thomas sees a common factor insofar as by the word *barbarus* something foreign is meant. The term also signifies people lacking in reason as, for instance,
happens to those who live in intemperate regions of the earth where extreme
climatic conditions predominate, or by other factors prevailing in a land that

---

12. See *In Pol* I, 2, no. 42: "Posito prohemio in quo ostendit conditionem ciuitatis et partium eius, hic
accedit ad tradendum scientiam politicam."

13. In this section of the text, Aristotle does not dwell on the role of women, but passes to the leading
function of the ruler.

14. At this point one encounters the first of nine quotations from or references to Scripture. The text of
1 Cor 14:11, "but if I do not know the meaning of the language, I shall be a foreigner to the speaker and the
speaker a foreigner to me," serves as an illustration of the term *barbarus*.

make people irrational and, as it were, brutal. The word may also mean people who do not live under laws or who live under irrational laws. Finally, it can signify people who do not understand one another's language or who do not know the art of writing (no. 23). As Aristotle says, among barbarians there is no government based on nature. Most barbarians have a strong physique but are deficient with regard to their mind. Among them there are no governors and subjects, but they do use female and male slaves. So the poets say that it is appropriate that the Greek rule over the barbarians. And Thomas adds that, when the opposite takes place, there is a perversion of order, as indicated in the Bible, Ecclesiastes 10:7: "I have seen servants on horses and princes walking as servants" (no. 24).

Returning to the domestic community, Aristotle distinguishes two types of association: of man and woman, and of master and slave. One may add to these that of father and son (no. 25). The household management of the family came into being to facilitate the work that has to be accomplished every day (no. 26). He speaks next of the village made up of several households: it is not instituted for everyday life, but in view of external acts that are not performed daily (no. 27). The village community is a natural development as families are growing and spreading out over their environment. In this way, a village is a natural community (no. 28). As households are ruled by an aged member, so the village is ruled by one who is first in the order of kinship. The rule of a king derives from this original order (no. 29). And because human beings think that the gods are similar to them in their outward appearance, the gods would also be ruled by a king. Thomas interprets Aristotle's words on ancient polytheism as concerning the separate substances, who—according to the philosophy of the Platonists—were created, he says, by the only one and supreme God. By this remark he tries to place what Aristotle writes on the level of natural theology (no. 30).

The communities of the families and the villages are ordained to the city, that is, to a civil society made up of several villages. It is the task of the city to provide sufficient means and assistance to the citizens to lead a human life and to promote the good life for all, so it will become a perfect society. Thomas adds the words "the good life ordered to the virtues," which is not in Aristotle's text but is in line with what he writes in several other texts (no. 31). The civil society is a natural community, just as the family and the village are, for man is a political animal. The city is the end of the family and of the village and provides what is needed for a true human life. It is a natural community for it originates from natural principles, namely, the family and the village (nos. 32–33). As a member of the city, man is naturally a political animal (no.

34). Not all men are city dwellers but this does not affect the argument, as natural things are sometimes defective—or, Thomas adds, some men may have found in themselves a more perfect life in the solitude of the desert. Aristotle's use of the expressions *melior quam homo* (1253a4) and *deus* (1253a29) leads Thomas to name John the Baptist and Anthony as examples. Vicious people are unfit to live in a political community (no. 35).

Next Aristotle proves man's social nature by the faculty of speech. Animals utter sounds as an expression of pleasure and pain (no. 36), but do not have speech. By speech, man signifies what is useful or harmful and what is just or unjust; man is by his nature an animal living in the communities of a family and of the state (no. 37). The city is by nature prior to the household and to the human individuals (no. 38). The individual is related to the city as a part to the whole (no. 39). All men are naturally inclined to live in a civil society (no. 40). In the last section of the lesson, Thomas goes into details, showing that without laws and justice, man would be the worst of all animals by the corruption of both his concupiscible and of his irascible appetites (no. 41).

In lesson 2 (I.2.1253b1–1254a17), Aristotle treats of the domestic society with regard to the place and function of slaves.[15] For Thomas, chapter 1 of the treatise is an introduction. Aristotle now begins to discuss the two communities of which the state is composed. The state itself is the subject matter of Book II (no. 42). The domestic community (the household), if it is complete, consists of free persons and slaves, husband and wife, father and son (in poor families animals are the servants). This last relationship depends on the second (no. 44). The main task of this domestic society lies in the field of economy and has to do with financial matters (nos. 45–46). Aristotle first discusses the relationship of master and slave, so as to explain, first, what is useful for a person to know in order to exercise his authority in these matters and, second, to show that this relationship is better than what many think it is. Thomas introduces a slight change to obtain a more positive evaluation of the relationship of master and slave, and ascribes to Aristotle a better insight into the moral aspects of slavery (no. 47). Aristotle mentions two opinions about the relationship of master and slave: first, (1) the idea that governing a domestic society is similar to directing the city; and (2) a second view involving a somewhat better understanding of these matters (1253b17, τὶ πρὸς τὸ εἴδεναι

---

15. Aristotle is very detailed in his treatment of the question of slaves, while Plato says almost nothing about it. In his view, serfdom is a sort of *Notbehelf* ("temporary solution for lack of better"), to procure what is necessary for the community; see Olof Gigon, "Die Sklaverei bei Aristoteles," in *Entretiens XI: La politique d'Aristote* (Genève: Fondation Hardt, 1965), 247–67. A slave is open for *logos*, and one can discuss with him, something an animal does not have, but a slave may suffer from such vices as gluttony, cowardice, etc., and seems unable to reach the εὖ ζῷον (the good life), but he helps to make the life of the nobler class possible.

περὶ αὐτῶν). Thomas understands these words as saying that we shall get a deeper comprehension of what master and slave are than the ancients had, so that he sees an opening in the text to a better moral evaluation of slavery.

Aristotle quotes two views of this master-slave relation: (1) one view holds that a master has the knowledge to direct and to govern the household and the slaves; he exercises a sort of despotic authority; and (2) another view holds that it is against nature that one has slaves, both the master and the slave being of the same human nature (no. 49). Aristotle, however, argues that it is impossible to live in a domestic community without having at one's disposal what is needed for life; one must have the means to obtain what is necessary as an artist needs his tools (no. 51). Certain tools are inanimate, while other tools, as slaves, are ensouled beings. From certain tools some effects proceed, while the tools remain what they are. Slaves, however, share in the actions of the master and are not simply tools to produce an effect (*factio*) wholly different from themselves (no. 53). A slave is not just a thing owned by his master, but is as a part of his master (*non solum est servus domini sed est simpliciter illius*) (no. 54). A man who does not by nature belong to himself but to another is by nature a slave and a thing possessed (*res possessa*). The definition of a slave is: a slave is a living, separate instrument of another, but he is a human being, associated to the activity of the master. He is different from the servant or the artisan who participates in the work (*factio*) of his master. A slave belongs to someone else, but he exists as a human being, not as a brute animal (no. 55).

Lesson 3 (I.3.1255a3–b15) takes on the following question: is it natural for some men to serve as slaves or is all slavery contrary to human nature? To rule and to be ruled is not only something depending on what is necessary, or what results from violence, but it is also one of the things useful for man's well-being. What is useful for a person is also in conformity with his dignity and with justice. We also notice that some people are from their birth in a condition to be subject to others, while other people are apt to direct. Furthermore, there are many ways in which one can be subject to others, just as there are several ways of directing: a husband and his wife, a master and his slaves, a king and his subjects. Moreover, it is always better to rule over worthier subjects—over human beings—than over animals (no. 59).

In things consisting of several parts, we find a leading, important part, and other parts that are naturally subordinated. This is apparent in inanimate things, in the human body, in animals, and in man (nos. 60–61). In things that are devoid of life, there is a ruling principle, such as harmony in melodies, which we may understand, Thomas says, as signifying a key tone; or also among the elements of the human body, where one element always dominates. Aristotle does not dwell on these points because they do not belong to the present subject (no. 62). But this state of things is visible in the components of man, body and soul, namely that the body is subject to the soul, which rules. It is obvious when we consider a healthy, well-disposed person whose bodily members execute their functions at the command of the soul (no. 63). And it is advantageous for the body to be governed by the soul and for the appetite to be directed by the intellect and reason as by a political way of governing, for instance as a king rules over free citizens.

Aristotle sees this principle at work in domesticated animals, which are better off than wild animals, as they share more in reason (no. 65). It is also applicable to the different sexes: the male rules and the female is by nature subject (no. 66). Aristotle applies the principle to social and political life at large. Given the ruling role of reason in human life, those who suffer from a deficiency of their reason should be subject to others. Thomas sees a confirmation in Proverbs 11:29: "The stupid will serve the wise." Those who are best for manual work will become slaves: for them it is better to be ruled by the wise, as they cannot be governed by their own reason (no. 68). These men have no desire to use their reason (*sensum rationis*), but insofar as they experience good and bad they are incited to serve. In bodily work, a slave can in many ways serve better than animals because he has the use of reason (no. 69).

Nature, Aristotle says, shows a certain inclination to bring about a difference between the bodies of free persons and of slaves. The latter are strong so as to carry out such tasks of working in the fields, while the bodies of the free citizens have a delicate complexion and are not suitable for these servile tasks, although sometimes they are well-disposed for fighting a war and carrying out civic tasks in times of peace. Expanding on a sentence of Aristotle, Thomas notes that in a minority of cases this reasoning does not hold: sometimes those who have the souls of free men have the bodies of slaves (no. 70). Thomas adds that a better soul also leads to a better inner disposition of the senses and the physical forces, although deviations occur in the bodily appearance and disposition of the members (no. 71). Aristotle insists that we notice a considerable difference in the respective bodies of free persons and slaves. It is the intention of nature to bring about such a difference (no. 72). As the souls of some excel, it is fitting that others serve them, but it is not so easy to notice the beauty of the soul as that of the body. The conclusion of the chapter is that some people are free by nature, while others are slaves (no. 74).

In the previous lesson, Aristotle argued that some people are by nature destined to be slaves. In lesson 4 (I.4.1255a3–b15), however, he writes that the opposite view is also true to a certain extent. That is to say: slavery has a twofold meaning, namely according to a natural disposition of some people and according to a manmade law (e.g., when prisoners of war become the slaves of the victorious party). This law is generally observed and is called the law of the nations (no. 75), but it is doubtful if the one beaten by the stronger party should be made a slave (no. 76). The one who inflicts violence always excels in some way (no. 77). But it is doubtful whether the one who gains the upper hand must rule. Some say that the law concerning prisoners of war has been introduced as a concession to those who win a battle to incite them to fight bravely. Others are of the opinion that it seems to be just that those who appear to be better are ruling. Thomas quotes Proverbs 12:24: "For the strong authority, for the slack forced labor." They say that we must accept the common opinion (no. 78). Aristotle, however, observes that the law concerning slavery resulting from war is not a natural right but that it is only just in a certain respect and relative to what is advantageous for man, for all laws have been made for the benefit of people. It is not by natural justice that all those who are prisoners of war are made slaves; it often happens that the wise are overcome by the uneducated. Those who have been beaten in war are kept by the winning party and are forced to live in subjection to it. This has its advantages for the winner as it stimulates him to fight better. Related to this, there is the policy that to prevent crime in a city there must be strong guardians (no. 79).

A victory resulting from superior strength has been considered a sign of excellence. What we have here is "being just" in only one respect. Yet even the virtuous must observe this order, for the common good is superior to private interest (no. 80). Aristotle notes that when the cause of going to war is unjust, the slavery that eventually results from it is no longer simply just. A second reason advanced against making the captives of a war slaves is that it may not be fitting that certain captives become slaves, for instance those belonging to the aristocracy (no. 81). People also commonly do not say that when aristocrats have been made prisoners, they should become slaves. Only the uneducated should become so (no. 82). Those who say so have natural slavery in mind. Persons of high birth are not slaves by their nature nor have been so (no. 83). They are free in their own land and everywhere on earth. But barbarians (that is, the non-Greeks) are only free men in their own country. This view is confirmed by the famous poet Theodoctes,[16] who wrote that those whose parents are both noble should not be called slaves. The poet used the term *divine*, and Thomas, overlooking the figurative meaning of the word, notes that the parents were erroneously called divine according to the error

---

16. The poet Theodoctes was a disciple of the Academy and also of Aristotle.

of the gentiles (no. 84), summarizes the argument as follows: what they want to say is that being free citizens or slaves is determined by the virtue of the mind, so that those who have a powerful mind are free and noble, according to what the God says in 1 Samuel 2:30: "Those who honor me, I honor in my turn." The reason is that a man is born from men, that good people beget a good man. But there are exceptions (no. 86). It happens that by a different education and a different way of life people become dissimilar to their parents (no. 87). Finally, Aristotle says that certain differences between freedom and slavery do not result from nature. A slave is related to his master as the body is to the soul, but he is also a part of his master as an ensouled instrument, so that friendship between both is possible (no. 88).

In lesson 5 (I.5.1255b16–40), Aristotle examines the opinion according to which despotic rule is the same as political rule and implies knowledge. Political rule, however, is that of free citizens, whereas despotic rule is that of a master over his slaves. Better subjects demand a better government (no. 89). Political rule also differs from household rule, which is monarchical, insofar as the household is governed by one person. Thomas advances a difficulty here: not every household is under despotic rule; when both husband and wife rule, it becomes aristocratic; or when brothers share in ruling, it becomes a timocratic regime, as is explained in *NE* VIII.12. And he notes that Aristotle is speaking of the ideal form of household rule. That brothers direct the household, for instance, is only temporary until the inheritance has been divided and each has his own house. The rule of the housewife is relative, as she is subject to her husband. When the situation is different, we have to do with a corrupt form of ruling (no. 90). Thomas also rejects that despotic rule is called a science: those who rule despotically do so by a natural disposition (no. 91). However, this regime may be accompanied by an exchange of knowledge insofar as the family father may instruct the young and the slaves to carry out different household tasks. One has the science proper to a despotic ruler when one knows how to employ the slaves well (no. 93). But this is not a highly qualified knowledge. Masters who do not need to instruct them are free for nobler pursuits and for political life (no. 94). Finally, Aristotle mentions the "knowledge" of how to acquire slaves, for example waging a just war. An unjust war does not lead to a "true knowledge" of how to acquire slaves (no. 95).

Lesson 6 (I.6.1256a1–b39) outlines the ways of acquiring property. As slaves are part of one's property, Aristotle now turns to a study of the ways of acquiring property in general. First, he asks whether the art of making money is entirely the same as that of the economics of the household or, if it is a part of it, whether it is subservient to governing one's household (no. 98). Second, he asks whether this art is only subservient to governing the household or whether it has a wider function by providing the things needed in addition to being a tool of the economics of the household (no. 99). The art of moneymaking differs from the art of economics insofar as the former concerns acquiring money, while the latter instructs us how to use it (no. 100). But is moneymaking a part of its use or does it just provide the material? The question concerns agriculture in particular (no. 102) and the ways to acquire the necessary alimentation.

In order to deal with this in more detail, he first discusses what is necessary for the feeding of animals. There are, for instance, carnivorous and vegetarian animals (no. 103), and their way of life differs according to the food they eat and the way in which they acquire it, for example, by taking their food from spoils. As to the diversity of food that human beings need, Aristotle distinguishes three basic forms of acquiring food: (1) sheep herding; (2) raiding or stealing from people; and (3) fishing and hunting. As man needs a great variety of products, the above-mentioned ways of acquiring food are often mixed (no. 104). To stress that acquiring food is quite natural, he refers to animals who do not immediately produce a perfect progeniture, but intermediate forms of life (e.g., chickens who produce eggs), as these animals always provide sufficient food for further development. Plants are food for animals, which in turn are food for man, who also uses other parts of them, such as their skin for vestments, etc. (no. 105). Thomas adds an observation here: nature does not leave things in an imperfect state (no. 106), so that for man acquiring what he needs for his life is natural, even if it means taking spoils. Acquiring what is needed for one's life is part of being a member of a household and also of the state (no. 107). Next, Aristotle points out that there are acquisitions and riches that go beyond what a man needs, the pursuit of which does not satiate his desire. The things necessary for human life are finite in number, as tools used by man are neither infinite in number nor in size. Therefore, there is a natural acquisition of property (nos. 108–10).

Lesson 7 (I.7.1256b40–1257b23) focuses on acquiring what one needs by exchanging things that have become useless for the seller, and by buying with money what has become necessary. While procuring what is necessary for life is natural, using money to do so is not, but was invented to facilitate exchanges (no. 111). Aristotle examines exchanges in detail. Things like footwear have their first use, but may also serve in exchanges (no. 112). All sorts of things can be used in exchanges; for example, one can barter wine for bread (no. 113). When community life developed beyond the households and the villages, and cities made their appearance, people had to obtain what they needed for their lives from others locally distant from them. One still finds this form of exchange among barbarian nations, who do not yet know the use of money (no. 114). This form of exchange is natural because it aims at procuring the things one needs (no. 115). When this form of exchange expanded to people far away and merchandise had to be transported over longer distances, the use of money was invented, being easy to transport and having some value from the metals of which it consisted, namely bronze, iron, silver, gold, and other things of this kind. At first, the metal had a certain size and weight, but later certain marks were stamped on it, which made it easily recognizable (no. 116).

Later on, a kind of monetary exchange was introduced by which money was exchanged for money. As a result, people began to seek how to make the greatest profit (no. 117). From the time when the exchange of money was introduced in view of making profit in an artificial way, the art of "making money" developed, which looked for ways to gain the most and so to amass a great amount of money (no. 119). Aristotle says that it is childish to say that none of the natural things—such as wheat, wine, etc.—constitute wealth, but only money as introduced by law. If these manmade regulations about money changed, money would lose its value and no longer contribute to what man needs for his life, for instance when the king of a community were to decide that money was without value. On the other hand, it is foolish to say that money is worthless, if one does not have much of it. And he adds that it can happen that one who is wealthy needs food and is starving, which is exemplified by the story of Midas who died for hunger as whatever he touched was changed into gold (no. 120). Money and riches are different; some form of wealth is in accord with nature. Those who have plenty of natural things are wealthier than those who are rolling in money (no. 121).

Lesson 8 (I.8.1257b23–1258b8) notes that the desire to make money in commerce has no limits, contrary to the desire in all the other arts. As such, however, the desire of things that are ordered to an end is limited and has a terminus according to the rule and the measure of the end, as medical treatment is limited to what is useful for healing. But the end as such is desirable for itself. The unbridled desire for more money should be limited, as our need of it also is. In fact, however, all households try to increase their financial means without any limit (no. 125). A first reason is that they are not satisfied with a good, virtuous life, or else they would be content with those natural means that would allow them to live well. Yet man's concupiscence knows no limits. Some think that bodily pleasures necessarily belong to the virtuous life and that money can help to acquire them. They also seek wealth for the members of their household. The reason for this abuse is that they do not have a correct concept of man's life and tend to strive for money without limit (no. 126). A second abuse is that they seek an excess of bodily pleasures, which is rendered possible by "productive money" (*nummularia*). Then money is no longer subservient to its natural end (no. 127). When it becomes impossible to obtain all the money needed to satisfy their desires, people resort to other means, such as using their ascendency or military means, though this is contrary to the nature of these means (no. 128). Yet managing a household in the strict sense of the term is procuring those things that are necessary according to our nature (no. 129). Moneymaking is not the same as the economy of the household and the state but is and should be subservient to it. One form of moneymaking is praiseworthy, while another form must be rejected (no. 130). People are prior to the economy of the family or the state, and nature provides different types of nourishment, such as fruits or fish, so that it is not the task of the economic administration to make this food, but to distribute it and see to it that the households obtain what they need, just as a weaver does not make the wool himself. Moneymaking (*pecuniativa*) should be at the service of man (no. 131). As the members of a household need to be healthy and must do what is necessary for life, one could ask: is the art of medicine not part of the domestic economy? Aristotle answers that they must use the advice of doctors, for to determine by which means health is restored is the task of the specialists of medicine. In a similar way, to consider how money can be acquired is part of the art of moneymaking (no. 132).

Nature must provide the things that the household or the state economy needs. And the trades and arts that support it also get their material from nature. Nature provides alimentation to what is generated; for instance, an animal is born from menstrual blood, and it makes milk from the remains of food. Because man is composed of things that are according to nature, the other existing natural things serve as food for him, such as fruits and animals. But making money, not by trading in natural things, but from money by lending it out against interest, is not according to nature (no. 133). Aristotle shows which form of moneymaking is praiseworthy and which form is reprehensible. Obtaining money for natural products, such as fruits or animals, which are necessary for man's life, is praiseworthy. But moneymaking may go from what is necessary to what greed wants, when it does not come about from natural things, nor is ordained to provide what is necessary for human life, but lets man make money out of money. And then there is a form of moneymaking by way of interest only, by which money grows (increases) by itself. This way of making money is totally against nature (no. 134).

Lesson 9 (I.9.1258b9–1259a36) identifies the things that those who are intent on making money must know: markets, interest, and the comparative value of merchandises. Here the prudence of the philosopher Thales may serve as an example.[17] For the use and management of money it is important to know the value of the things one owns, which of them are most valuable, and where their value is greatest, for instance where cattle, horses, and sheep are highest priced (no. 137). In the second place, one should acquire a great quantity of this merchandise by cultivating the land, exploiting vineyards and orchards. One should also be an expert in apiculture, fishing, rearing birds, and in whatever is helpful for our life. By means of these things, it becomes possible to acquire the money to support oneself (no. 138). These are the first and most proper ways of making money. Next, there is a form of making money by selling things that are not necessary for human life, so that the things exchanged are non-necessary objects. This is done in commerce and by transportation of goods, either by ship or overland or by assisting services (no. 139). Another way of making money consists in charging interest on the money one lends to someone else. One can also make money by earning a salary, and finally by mining stones and metals under the earth (nos. 140–42). In addition, one should distinguish between different kinds of work: for some tasks, little skill is required, for others much more. Furthermore, a great deal of luck sometimes helps (no. 144). Some wise men have written about these ways of gaining money, such as Chares of Paros[18] and Apollodorus of Lemnos.[19] Thomas adds the Roman author Palladius (no. 145).[20] Aristotle quotes the anecdote of Thales who made a profit thanks to his meteorological knowledge (no. 147). Finally, he mentions a way of making money by buying up the entire supply of a certain product to sell it later at a higher price (no. 149). Some authors who studied political regimes seemed to be intent on ways to increase the money in the public treasury (no. 150).

In lesson 10 (I.10.1259a37–1260a36), after having discussed in the previous lessons the relation of master to slave, Aristotle turns to the study of the relation between man and wife, father and son. A father rules over his wife not as over a slave but with what he calls political authority, while he rules over his sons with regal power. His power over his wife does not extend to all things, but extends so far as matrimonial law stipulates. This authority of the father of a family is according to the nature of things (no. 152). In political rule, those who rule exchange roles with their subjects, as they hold office for one year

---

17. Thales, foreseeing that the next harvest of olives would be bad, bought up a great quantity to sell it later at a higher price.

18. A contemporary of Aristotle.

19. Lived in the fourth century B.C., quoted by Varro and Plinius.

20. A Roman landowner from the fourth century A.D. who wrote on agriculture.

and are the equals of their subordinates. But as officials they are honored and are addressed with respect (no. 153). In the next section, the authority of a father is compared to regal power: a father's power is indeed regal, but it is distinguished from that of a king because a father loves his sons and is older, which gives him a certain priority. A king has a natural superiority, but must be of the same race as his subjects. Thomas adds a few lines: love is what distinguishes regal authority from civil authority, which is authority over one's equals, but the presence of love makes the difference with a tyrannical regime. In the latter, one does not rule out of love but in view of one's own advantage (no. 154). Obviously, one who manages a household is more engaged in looking after the human persons than in acquiring possessions. He is more intent on the virtues by which people live well than on the means to enlarge his property. He is also more interested in the virtues of the free citizens than in those of the slaves. Thomas explains that Aristotle has his reasons for saying so: material things and slaves are for the sake of man, and the end of them all is what our activity is aiming at (no. 155).

Slaves must possess a minimal aptitude to carry out the tasks their masters assign to them. Do they also have moral virtues? If they have them, by what would they then be distinguished from free persons? On the other hand, why should they not have them as human beings (no. 156)? The same question concerns wives, children, and, in general, all the subjects of rulers. If they have these virtues, why are they subjects? If one says that the difference is one of having more or less of these virtues, this does not lead to a specific difference (no. 157). The answer is that both those who rule and their subjects must have the virtues, but that there are differences, as is the case in the human body, some parts of which are directing, while other parts are executing these directives (no. 158). Slaves do not deliberate; women do, but their power is weaker and they are easily influenced by emotions. Likewise, children cannot deliberate on all the particular things that must be considered when decisions are to be taken (no. 159). These different groups of people partake in the virtues in different ways. Courage is different in men from what it is in women. The same must be said of the other virtues, so that the difference is not just according to more or less but according to their conceptual content (*ratio*). When speaking about the virtues one must go into details, as the sophist Gorgias did.[21] Aristotle refers to a text from Sophocles's *Ajax* (293), namely that for women silence is an embellishment (γυναιξὶ κόσμον ἡ σιγὴ φέρει). And Thomas quotes two biblical texts in confirmation: women should not speak in

---

21. Gorgias is mentioned by Plato in his dialogue *Meno*.

the assembly (1 Cor 14:24) and one should not allow independence to one's child (Eccl 30:11) (no. 160).

In lesson 11 (I.11.1260a21–b24), Aristotle considers the virtues that craftsmen, women, and children should have. If slaves must have the virtues so as not to fail in their tasks because of a lack of self-control, the same applies to craftsmen, who must have good dispositions (virtues), for it often happens that because of a lack of restraint and temperance, defects show up in the work they do, when their attention is elsewhere while they are working (no. 162). The situation of a craftsman is very different from that of a slave. A slave is associated with his master and family, so he must have some moral virtues, whereas a craftsman is removed from these contacts with people. Some of them, however, have a stable service, like cooks, and so they must have the moral virtues (no. 163). Furthermore, a slave is a slave by nature and virtues are ordained to what we have by nature. There is in us a natural inclination to them (no. 164).

People acquire virtues when these are explained to them by instruction as the lawmakers present them to the citizens (no. 165). When dealing with matters concerning the city, one must treat of the virtues that women and children should have, and of the contacts fathers and their children should have with one another to show what is good for them, but one cannot do so before dealing with the political life of the city as a whole (no. 166). The reason is that when one deals with a part, one must consider its relation with the whole, meaning that men, women, and children are indeed part of the city. In our exposition of the state, Aristotle argues, we must show how women and children should be instructed. Thomas quotes these arguments of Aristotle without further comment.

Book II

In the previous book, Aristotle dealt with the communities of which the state consists. Now, in lesson 1 (II.1.1260b27–1261b15), he examines the state itself and the forms of government as proposed by some philosophers. By comparing the different regimes we see better which one is the best (no. 169). Thomas adds that it is characteristic of the best political regime that people live in the way they want. Different views about the end of human life lead to different conceptions of civil life. Those who place the end of life in pleasure, power, or honors, consider that regime the best where they can live in a pleasurable way, acquire riches, and be honored. Those, however, who consider the moral good as the reward of a virtuous life and the true end of the state, will think that the state is best in which people live in peace and practice the virtues. Hence we can say that the best political order is the one that corresponds to the different expectations of the people. Aristotle discusses those political regimes that were established by wise people (no. 170). Thomas concludes this section by saying that for people the best political regime is that in which they can live as they wish.

Before presenting his own views, Aristotle discusses what some other philosophers have said, but what in many ways is not right (no. 171). He deals first with the form of government and of civil life that Plato called the best. And because the state is a certain community, the question is to what extent the citizens should have everything in common, or share in some things and not in others (no. 173). Obviously, they should at least live in the same territory (no. 174). According to Plato's *Republic*, wives and children should be shared (no. 175). Aristotle points out the inconvenience of this idea and shows that the arguments brought forward in support of it, namely to obtain total unity, are unreasonable. Plato also failed to explain how to apply his project (nos. 176–77).[22] A total unity is impossible, as it would do away with the state itself, which consists of a certain multitude; also, when a family would become totally one, it would become a single person (no. 179). If one says that Socrates[23] only wanted to exclude inequality, Aristotle answers that a state should consist of citizens of different conditions. He shows this in three ways: (1) a state is not the same as an army where the soldiers are equal; (2) the citizens of a state do not live spread out over villages, as the Arcadians, among whom the families[24] were on their own, although at least associated;[25] and (3) to obtain a perfect whole the things of which it consists must be specifically different, like the parts of the human body (no. 180). There should be exchanges between citizens in proportionally equal returns, as was explained in *NE* V.8. Here, "proportionally" does not mean exactly equal, and there is no question of quantitative equality. A state should not be unified in the highest degree, as Socrates proposed (no. 181).

In a state, it is not possible that all rule except in the sense that those who govern alternate after a limited period of time. But even so there will be difficulties, for when people who were shoemakers or carpenters are holding positions of government (no. 182), the question of competence arises. It is better that the state be so organized that certain citizens more capable than others

22. In the following lessons, Thomas mentions Socrates as the philosopher who proposed this regime, obviously because in his *Republic* Plato lets Socrates propose and explain this theory (no. 172). He may have wanted to dissociate Plato himself somewhat out of respect for his philosophy and so he did not use his name.

23. The main speaker in Plato's *Republic*.

24. We must probably read *unusquisque* as signifying the different families.

25. In Aristotle's time, the Arcadians in Megalopolis formed a league and had their general assembly.

should always govern. Not all are equal in virtue and naturally industrious. Those among the best should alternate in office. In a state, a diversity of those who hold positions of authority and their subjects is necessary. Total unity (or total uniformity) would destroy the state (no. 183). In no. 180 the argument was founded on the necessity of differences between the members of a community. Aristotle now bases his argument on the end of the state, namely a fair measure of well-being for all the citizens. A family is in a better position to secure this aim than a single citizen, and a state as such can provide for this better than a family or an individual. He concludes that what has less uniformity will provide this general well-being better than what is entirely one (no. 184). Socrates was wrong when he said that the greatest unity and uniformity is best for the state.

Lesson 2 (II.1.1261b16–1262a24) explains Socrates's belief that the cause of strife within a state was private property, because it caused everyone to look only after his own belongings. If property were held in common, all could then say "this is mine," meaning that what belongs to all is also his; this might be acceptable in a sense, but those who own something collectively will not say "this woman is mine," for no one would be the real partner or owner. The argument of those who say that some collective property is theirs, is a sophism if understood in a collective sense (no. 185). What Socrates wanted would even cause great harm, because people do not care much about what is common property; all people care most about what is their own. People ordinarily think that someone else should look after what belongs to the community, and they would also care less about "their" children (no. 186). People would not even know which child is theirs when a woman is shared by several men. Aristotle argues that in the state special relations can be established with the young, with sons, cousins, disciples, etc., which are pleasant and useful, but in Socrates's theory there would not be room for such relations (no. 187). People love and promote more what is their own. A final reason is that the law of Socrates will not and cannot prohibit that there is a special similarity between children and those who begot them. The law of Socrates cannot avoid this (no. 188).

In lesson 3 (II.1.1262a25–b36), Aristotle advances six arguments to explain the evils that would accompany Socrates's theory of sharing wives and sons. (1) If there is no relationship between people, it is not easy to avoid brawls; crimes against people are committed more easily when there is no kinship than when they are related to us (no. 189). (2) Improper behavior would result, such as fathers having intercourse with their daughters; Socrates was aware of this and tried to avoid such unworthy things by special laws, but these would be insufficient (no. 190–91). (3) When all children are raised up in the same way there will be less friendship between important persons; friendship develops better when there is proportional equality between them. Thomas adds a reference to the *NE* IX.1.1263b33 (no. 192). (4) When wives and children are shared, friendship will become weaker. People take better care of what they consider their own than of what is common property. Love is often love of one or of a few persons and becomes weaker when it extends to many (no. 193). (5) In a state governed according to the program of Socrates, children would be transferred from their mothers to other women to be brought up. This would create great confusion and would totally efface awareness of whose child a baby was and to whom it was given (no. 194). And (6) children who have grown up while in custody of people who are not their relatives more easily commit offenses than when they have grown up with relatives (no. 195).

In lesson 4 (II.2.1262b37–1263b30), Aristotle discusses a topic closely related to a previous topic, namely, common property. There are three ways in which citizens can share the possession of property: (1) when the yield of the harvest is common and divided over the citizens, although the land is privately owned; (2) when the land is also common property and the crops are divided for proper use by the individual citizens; and (3) when both the land and the crops are common, as Socrates wanted it (no. 196). The law of common property leads to bad effects. Aristotle names three. (1) Who will cultivate the fields? If foreigners have to do so, the problem is where they would come from and whether they would be available in sufficient numbers. If the citizens have to do it themselves, the question arises as to which of them should cultivate the land. Others would attend to important business affairs and receive much money, a situation which would lead to conflicts. (2) It would be very difficult to share income and possessions, as what we see is that people who do something together, such as traveling, often disagree about sharing expenses. And (3) people who do not work together have few disagreements, but there is frequent discord when they share in business undertakings (no. 199).

Aristotle shows next the harm the proposed legislation would cause. The current legislation, distinguishing between property belonging to individual citizens and to the community, is far better than what Socrates proposes, because each will take care of his private property, but also enjoys the advantages of common citizenship and the generosity of others because of the virtues practiced by the citizens (no. 200). This last point is further explained: in some states, like Lacedaemonia, people gladly lend their slaves, horses, and dogs to their friends, as if these were common property.[26] This common use

---

26. Laconia, as Lacedaemonia is usually called, was a state in the southeastern part of the Peloponnesus. Xenophon wrote a book about this republic (*De republica Lacedemoniae*), which may have been consulted by Aristotle.

must be regulated by good laws (no. 201). A second reason is that it is very enjoyable to dispose of one's own things. Those who want to introduce common property do not understand how pleasurable the possession of one's own things is (no. 202). Helping others with one's own belongings also gives much satisfaction, something that the legislation proposed by Socrates renders impossible (no. 203). Those who introduce the common possession of women and children make the practice of two virtues impossible, namely, temperance and liberality or generosity (no. 204). But the law proposed by Socrates is attractive insofar as it seems to promote friendship, to do away with the causes of strife and conflict, and to bring about the equality of the rich and the poor. Nevertheless, if all shared common property, there would be far more conflicts (no. 205). Finally, Aristotle says that one should not only speak of the evils that the people who have property and wives in common avoid, but also the many good things they are deprived of (no. 206).

Lesson 5 (II.2.1263b30–1264b25) presents arguments as to why what Socrates proposed is unsuitable and inadequate. His point of departure is false, namely the belief that total unity is best. It is obvious that for a city no such total unity is possible, for instance in the sense that there would be only one type of work or one craft and no different offices. When people sing all on the same note, there is no harmony (nos. 208–9). To make good laws, much experience over many years is required in order to find out if laws work or cannot be applied. In a totally unified state, as Socrates wants to establish, how would one proceed to divide the goods and the different tasks? It would take so much time that the citizens would have no time left to devote themselves to the important task of, say, farming (no. 210). Coming back to the incongruousness of the proposals of Socrates, Aristotle argues that to have a state where things function, there must be a certain division of the community goods among different clans or associations. Socrates does not tell us whether, in his conception of the state, the farmers would still have their own lands, wives, and children separated from those of the other citizens, or whether they would really have everything in common (no. 211). A political community consists of a multitude of different people, but Socrates says nothing about this diversity, nor does he make clear how the farmers would be distinguished from, say, the guardians. And there is no reason either why some citizens would take upon themselves the burden of governing. Such excellence in virtues is not always evident (no. 212).

One might suggest that agriculture should be left to slaves, as they do in Crete, but in a state as Socrates sees it, certain citizens would be farmers and others craftsmen, and besides them there would be guardians, who would not work but still receive rewards. This would lead to friction, which would not occur if possessions were not held in common (no. 213). If in a state everything were held in common, citizens would complain that not all do the same work but receive the same rewards (no. 214). Socrates wanted to give farmers the right to dispose of the land, so that they would be helpful to the other citizens, but the opposite is likely to happen (no. 215). Another insufficiency of the way in which Socrates would organize political life is the question of what kind of laws would be introduced and what the education would be (no. 216). Furthermore, if wives were common to farmers and guardians, they could not be "used" by both parties at the same time (no. 217). A further difficulty is that women cannot do the same work as men, such as till the land and fight in wars (no. 218). It would also be dangerous to have always the same persons as leaders of the state, for this would provoke uprisings, as happened in the past (no. 219). Socrates explained why he wanted the same class of people to occupy always leading positions in the government, namely by pointing to the fact that a precious metal like gold is always found in the same mines, as are silver, bronze, and iron (no. 220).[27] Finally, according to Aristotle, Socrates takes away happiness from individual citizens as he does not allow them to have individual possessions, nor wives or children, in which people find happiness, as we read in *NE* I.13.1099a31–b7.

In lesson 6 (II.3.1264b26–1265b26), Aristotle examines Plato's theory of the state and governmental system as put forward in the latter's last major dialogue, the *Laws*. While Aristotle observes that Plato's theory of the state in the *Republic* is full of difficulties, many objections can also be raised against what the latter proposes in the *Laws* (no. 223). Socrates failed to say, in the *Republic*, if farmers and artisans should also exercise governing functions and take part in national defense, while he does assert that women should be enrolled in the army (no. 224). Leaving aside that women would be possessed in common like material property as proposed in the *Republic*, some regulations he proposed in the *Laws* require a different education than the one proposed in the *Republic* (no. 226). Moreover, according to what Socrates proposes in the *Laws*, women would also have their clubs and social gatherings, and there would be at least one thousand soldiers in the army, with up to a maximum of five thousand (no. 227). But much of what Socrates proposes is superficial (*leve*) and has not been tested in practice (no. 228). To be able to maintain an army of five thousand soldiers with their wives and children, the city would have to be very large. The size of a city must be adapted to the region and to

---

27. Aristotle seems to think that the citizens of the state have a general aptitude to different functions.

the people who live in it. Relations with other states should also be taken into account, and armaments should be appropriate for military campaigns in other regions and sufficient to deter enemies (no. 229). A city should be adapted to the region in which it was established.

Aristotle criticizes Socrates's words that a city should have enough means to allow its citizens to live soberly, for this could mean that they would be living in poverty. In reality, the citizens should be able to live moderately and agreeably (*liberaliter*). Temperance and liberality give people the right attitude with regard to the use of their financial means (no. 231). Next, he denies that Socrates can limit the territory of a city to a certain size, but allow at the same time for an indefinite increase of the population in numbers (no. 232).[28] The reasoning would be that some women do not have children, while others have several, so that the total population remains the same (no. 233). But this argument does not hold. If people have private property, they seek to promote what their children need, while in the state according to Socrates this would be different: the mighty would dispose of ample financial means, while the poor would have none or only a few (no. 234).

Lesson 7 (II.3.1265b26–1266a30) contains Aristotle's criticism of Socrates's theory of the different groups of citizens in the state. At the beginning of the lesson, Aristotle lists the six types of government mentioned in the *Laws*, which he will discuss in detail in Book III of the *Politics*. The first three of them he considers as correct constitutions, the other three as deviations. Thomas discusses the first three, namely: (1) a government by one person, either a king or a tyrant; (2) a government by a small number, either of persons elected because of their virtue or chosen because of their wealth and power; and (3) a government by many capable, virtuous men, which is called a *politia* or, when the entire population wishes to govern, it becomes a people's government (*democratia, id est potestas populi*) (no. 242). Socrates divides the citizens into two groups, one of them consisting of warriors (who are more numerous), the other one of artisans and farmers, who dwell outside the city (no. 243). The government is an oligarchy that ranks second after the regime of a king, but Aristotle says that a government by virtuous persons is better (no. 244). According to some, the best regime would be that of a mixture of the above-mentioned types of government, so that the administration would stay within reasonable limits insofar as numbers are concerned. Aristotle then mentions two concrete (kinds of) government, those of Lacedaemon (another name for Sparta) and Ephesus (no. 245). Now, in the *Laws*, Socrates

---

28. Aristotle seems to favor a certain form of birth control, but Thomas does not comment on the relevant passage although in his own works he will disapprove such a practice.

proposes (as the best regime) a mixture of monarchy and democracy, so that a certain equilibrium is reached (no. 246). The tyrannical and the democratic regimes are the worst of the different forms of government (no. 247). Aristotle observes that, in fact, Plato establishes a regime similar to an oligarchy where the power is in the hands of a few elected persons from whom the actual rulers would be chosen by lot (no. 248). One of their tasks was to call the assembly together. Plato, through Socrates, wanted most rulers to come from the wealthy class (no. 249). The citizens were to be divided into four groups from each of which an equal number of councilors would be elected. There would be fewer councilors from the lower classes, as the citizens of these classes are not obliged to vote (no. 250). This way of choosing from among those who have been previously elected is dangerous, as these are few and could easily become corrupt. Yet, despite his present criticism, Aristotle's own description of the best political regime in Books VII and VIII shows many similarities with that of Plato in the *Laws.* Some authors suggested that the present chapter was not written by Aristotle himself but by one of his disciples.[29]

In lesson 8 (II.3.1266a3–1267a21), Aristotle reviews the regime conceived by Phaleas,[30] who proposed certain regulations to avoid conflicts in a city. To him as well as to other legislators, the regulation of property seemed to be most important to this effect. Such regulations could be done easily at the foundation of a city, but would be much more difficult in an already established state (no. 256). With respect to possessing temporary goods, Plato ordered that those of the wealthy citizens should not exceed five times those of the citizens with the smallest fortunes (no. 257). But Aristotle notes that besides issuing regulations about the size of one's possessions, there should also be regulations about the number of children. After having reached a certain number of children, no one should engender any more or, in case of an excessive number, people should found other cities. When the number of children in families is different, the parents with one child will become wealthier, those with many children will become poor and may even become thieves. Thomas adds that this does not happen if the size of the property each citizen is allowed to possess is not limited (no. 258).

Aristotle agrees with the above-mentioned regulation with regard to the size of one's property. The ancient legislators, such as Solon of Athens and those of the city of Locri in Calabria, were aware of the good effects of limiting the property of the citizens. Individual citizens were not allowed to sell their possessions (no. 259). In places where no limits have been imposed, the

---

29. See Willy Theiler, "Bau und Zeit der aristotelischen *Politik*," *Museum Helveticum* 9 (1952): 65–73.
30. A contemporary of Plato.

poorer citizens will increase their property, while the rich will be losing (no. 260). According to Aristotle, prescribing equal possessions is not enough, but an average size should be set to avoid that some would pursue a luxurious life while others are forced to live in hardship (nos. 261–62). But better than merely regulate the size of people's property, concupiscence should be brought under control. This will happen by sufficient instruction, something Phaleas did not organize (no. 263), to teach people not to try to outdo others in wealth and honors (no. 264). Disparity in honors is also a reason for dissent. The law should regulate that honors are awarded according to what people do, and honors bestowed on people deficient in virtue should be different (no. 265). Citizens should not insult others, neither should they desire what they cannot have immediately, nor should they take away by force or deception what belongs to others to satisfy their concupiscence. A legislator must think of ways to prevent these evils. For those who are wronged, philosophy offers a remedy, something Phaleas overlooked (no. 266). People commit unjust acts to acquire wealth and honors. Phaleas did not propose any remedy against the injustices committed by tyrants (no. 267) or anything to improve the daily life of the citizens (no. 270). It is in this context that Aristotle seems to approve the killing of a tyrant. Again, one finds Thomas staying close to the text without interjecting his own opinion.

In lesson 9 (II.4.1267a21–b21), Aristotle advances some further criticisms of the constitution proposed by Phaleas, who insufficiently regulated the property the citizens were allowed to have. The possessions of a city should be sufficient to provide for the needs of the people and to defend itself against its equal city-states but not so large that more powerful states would desire to conquer it (no. 269). An example of a sufficiently armed city is Arcadia.[31] Upon the advice of Euboulos, probably a disciple of Plato, the tyrant Autophradates renounced an attack on Arcadia because a siege would cost more than the conquest of the city would yield. A next observation is that the property of simple and ordinary citizens may be equal, but that higher-class people, who deserve more, are likely to make difficulties if what they receive is equal to that of lower class citizens (no. 271). A third criticism of Phaleas's legislation is that many persons have unlimited greed, so that greed should be regulated more than actual possessions; the citizens should be educated so as to love justice while bad, greedy people should be degraded to the lowest rank, so that they cannot do harm (nos. 272–73). Aristotle also criticizes Phaleas for taking into account only immobile property, as there are other

---

31. A city and mountainous area in central Peloponnesus.

possessions where equality should be established in order to avoid agitation. In addition, Aristotle considers the legislation of Phaleas insufficient with regard to artisans, who would be obliged to put their products in common to distribute them among the citizens according to the latter's needs, a ruling that would make them slaves of the citizens instead of an important part of the population. Furthermore, there should also be artisans at the service of the city, as there are in Epidaurus and in Athens (nos. 274–75).

In lesson 10 (II.5.1267b22–1268a15), the constitution made by Hippodamus for the city of Milete is reviewed. Hippodamus proposed the introduction of different classes of citizens and the establishment of suburbs. Although he was ambitious and went into some excesses in lifestyle, including singularities in his way of dressing, Hippodamus was the first who developed a theory of the organization and administration of the city. He considered ten thousand citizens a good number for the people of a city, divided into artisans, farmers, and warriors. With regard to the financial means of the city, one part was destined for the religious cult, another public part for the soldiers, and a third part would be for distribution among farmers (no. 278). Concerning legal proceedings, Hippodamus said that people filed lawsuits on three matters, namely personal offenses, damage to property, and death (understood as anything that is harmful to his or her person). He also proposed to establish a court of appeal, where those causes that had not been judged correctly would be reviewed. Its judges would be senior citizens, distinguished by their virtuous life. They should not confer with one another, but express their decision in writing. If a judge wanted the accused to be absolved, he had to turn in his writing tablet blank. When they found the accused guilty or partly guilty they wrote their decision on a tablet. He did not approve of the actual praxis of judges conferring with each other on the case to be judged (no. 279). Hippodamus also introduced some ordinances about the way of life of the citizens; those who made proposals for improvements would receive a reward. Expenses for the education of the children of those who had died fighting for the city would be defrayed by the public treasury. Rulers would be elected by the entire people. A last measure was that magistrates charged with the administration of the affairs of the city must also look after foreigners, orphans, and others needing help (no. 280). Aristotle praises several of the measures proposed by Hippodamus.

In lesson 11 (II.5.1268a16–b22), some critical remarks are brought forward regarding the proposals of Hippodamus. A first criticism of Aristotle relates to the proposal concerning farmers, artisans, and soldiers, who must all take part in the government of the city, namely by pointing out that the farmers have land but no arms, while the artisans have neither arms nor land and would be like slaves, performing tasks for the others. In fact, leaders would only be selected from the warriors, so that discontent among the artisans could easily become a cause of sedition (no. 282). Aristotle is also critical with respect to what Hippodamus ordered about the warriors: in order to carry out their task of defending the city against enemies and to repress uprisings, they were to be strong in numbers and virtue, so much so that they could govern without the farmers and artisans sharing in the government (no. 283). If the farmers provided the food for the warriors, they would be part of the city, but from what Hippodamus writes they would actually be on their own as a separate group (no. 284). According to the latter's proposals, the city was to have common property from which the warriors would live, but who would till the fields for them? If the farmers had to provide the food for the warriors, Hippodamus should have given all the land to the farmers (no. 285). In addition, Aristotle is critical of the proposed regime concerning judicial verdicts: the judges should give their opinion separately, but they could easily previously discuss the issues with one another at their homes. There should not be any private discussions of a case. The best way to reach a verdict about the penalties to be imposed is when the judges confer about it (nos. 286–87). If the votes of the judges would be counted, no one would be forced to commit perjury (no. 288).

Lesson 12 (II.5.1268b26–1269a28) contains more critical observations on the constitutional laws proposed by Hippodamus. That those who (claim to) have done or invented something useful for the city should receive a reward could give rise to discussion and strife. Next, Aristotle discusses the possibility of changing laws if these have become inadequate or are unwise. In many sciences, Thomas adds, it has been advantageous to change the theories that had been advanced before, as in medicine.[32] The same is true for physical training and other skills, so that there is the saying that, in the question of political regimes, we should not hesitate to change the regime our ancestors observed if something better presents itself (no. 290). Ancient laws and customs are sometimes barbaric and irrational, as the custom of selling women (no. 291).

At this point, Aristotle mentions the possibility that ancient laws should not be followed when they stem from primitive ancestors or survivors of a catastrophe who were foolish people (*insensatos*). Thomas adds a lengthy di-

---

32. Here one should keep in mind that Aristotle presents a theory of periodical beginnings and rediscoveries, so that the history of man is not that of an endless rectilinear progression. See *Physics* 223b28, *Meteorologica* 339b28, *Metaphysics* 1074b10, and *Politics* 1329b25. Plato mentions the theory of a cyclical return in his *Republic* 272d and *Laws* 677b. But in the first book of the *Metaphysics*, we also find the theory of continuous progress realized through the never-ending efforts of many wise men down through the ages.

gression in which he places this claim within Aristotle's defense of the eternity of the world.[33] He does not fail to observe that according to Aristotle the world is eternal, but that it is also said the different regions began to be inhabited during certain periods, which does not seem to agree with the theory of an eternal world. Aristotle suggests a solution, namely the periodical flooding of the earth and new beginning of the human race generated from the earth—but this would be contrary to the way nature proceeds, where living beings are generated from seed. Only God can produce human beings, Thomas writes. Here one notes that it is Thomas who mentions the issue of the eternity of the world but also that he offers no judgment from the perspective of the Christian faith. Aristotle also mentions the solution that some people survived such a natural disaster and could make a new start, as in the ancient myth of Deucalion (no. 292).[34]

Even laws made by wise legislators can be changed because they could not foresee all circumstances and often wrote their laws in a general way (no. 293). Some object to changing the laws, noting that the advantage of new laws may be small while changing the rules one is used to observe causes disturbances, so that it seems better to tolerate small defects in the old laws (no. 294). Finally, Aristotle says that the argument of the continuous progress of knowledge in the arts and sciences does not apply here because, with regard to laws, custom is very important, so that occasionally only very small changes should be made (no. 295). Concluding the chapter, he notes that many questions remain to be discussed.

Lesson 13 (II.6.1269a29–1270b6) focuses on the regime of the republic of Lacedaemonia (Sparta). We must consider which of their laws and customs are in favor of a virtuous life and which are not (no. 297). All agree that a state must have at its disposal what is necessary for daily life, such as slaves or people needed for rendering services, who must observe the right discipline (no. 298). The slaves became a menace when the Spartans were in a difficult situation and could not very well keep them in check. This never happened to the Cretans, whose city-state was too far away from others to be attacked, whereas Sparta was beleaguered by all its neighbors: the Argives, Messenians, and Arcadians. From the very beginning, the Spartans also had conflicts with the Thessalians and waged wars with the Achaeans, Perrhebians,[35] and

---

33. No. 292 begins as follows: "Ad cuius intellectum considerandum est, quod Aristoteles opinatus fuit mundum ab aeterno fuisse, ut patet in octavo physicorum et in primo de caelo . . ."

34. In *The City of God* XVIII.8, Augustine mentions such a deluge that would have killed all except those who escaped in the ark. This flood was bigger than that in the time of Deucalion. Thomas mentions the biblical story of the survival of Noah and his family in Gn 6:14–8:14.

35. A tribe occupying a mountainous district on the northern border of Thessaly.

Magnesians, so that they often ran into difficulties when their slaves rebelled against them (no. 299). It is, indeed, difficult to deal with slaves: when a master is friendly, they get bold and consider themselves as equals, but if he gives them harsh treatment, they will hate and threaten him. One should treat them in a way that holds the middle (no. 300).

As regards the question of women in a state, Aristotle notes that a lack of discipline leads to abuse (no. 301). The Spartans had forgotten to make rules for women, so that these began to live voluptuously and even turned to crimes (no. 302). Aristotle mentions four unfortunate consequences of this situation: (1) the women claimed a good part of the fortune of their husbands, so that getting money became their main concern; (2) when men began to stay away from women, they fell into the vice of homosexuality (this was the more so in the case of soldiers who are inclined to immorality); (3) women in Sparta became presumptuous and meddled with everything, which was dangerous because they showed a lack of reason; and (4) because of their quarrelsome attitude, they were good for fighting in a war but their audacity was also even damaging, as became apparent in a war with Thebes, when the Spartan women refused to render the services that women perform elsewhere (no. 303). The singular position of women in Sparta is explained by the fact that their husbands were frequently fighting wars, so that their wives, who remained at home, lived by themselves. Here, Thomas comments that being a warrior can foster many virtues. Aristotle reiterates that, during their war with Thebes, the Spartan women were of no use and meddled with everything, causing considerable difficulties. This situation also led to a greater love of money (no. 304). Some of Spartans had very large possessions, while those of others were modest. Almost all of the territory was in the hands of a few citizens (no. 305). The citizens could not buy or sell land. Women owned two-fifths of the land, as they were made heirs by their dying husbands. They also received important dowries when marrying, although it would be better, Aristotle says, if such dowries remain small. In Sparta, one could leave one's property to whomever one wanted (no. 306). The territory of their state was so large that it could support fifteen hundred cavalry and thirty thousand infantry, but the Spartans became so few that there were only one thousand warriors left. It was also rumored that at one time they had ten thousand armed men. But equalized property must provide the city with sufficient men because if the poor possess too little they leave the city (no. 307). Spartan legislation promoted having several children. If a man had four sons, he was exempt from all taxes. But the above-mentioned regulations did not prevent there being many poor (no. 308).

In lesson 14 (II.6.1270b6–1271b19), Aristotle discusses the situation of the so-called *ephors*,[36] the senior citizens and the kings in Sparta. The *ephors* were very powerful; they decided about war and peace, selected the military officers, and did other similarly important things. They were elected from the people, but when some poor people were elected, they were open to bribery (no. 309). Aristotle thinks that the *ephors* had too much power: their authority was almost equal to that of a tyrant, and so they checked the power of the king, who was forced to allow the people to govern. The merit of this regime was that the people remained quiet (no. 310), but the way of electing the *ephors* was childlike (no. 311). The *ephors* could judge according to their own opinion because there were no written laws (no. 312). Sometimes their lifestyle was reprehensible (no. 313).

Aristotle criticizes the Spartan regulation that elderly citizens always retained their functions and could not be removed; they could even prohibit sentences from being executed (no. 314). The way they were elected was childish, Aristotle says. The candidates presented themselves, something which people greedy for honors often do. But the common good should prevail over individual wishes (no. 315). We might suppose that it is better to have kings, but kings in Sparta did not hold their office for a lifetime, as if the Spartans thought that the candidates were not good enough to stay in power. But it seems better, Aristotle writes, that they retain their royal jurisdiction for their whole lifetime (no. 316). With regard to common public meals (*convivia*), it would be better if these gatherings were paid by the state rather than by the contributions of all the people, even of the poor (no. 317). The fact that there was a supreme commander of the army and another of the navy could also give rise to conflicts (no. 318). In Sparta, all laws concerned warfare and so they were ordained to promote one kind of virtues and not those concerned with a peaceful life, yet prudence and justice are more important than courage in a war (no. 319). The Spartans had no public funds and contributions were requested from individuals. The above-mentioned defects made certain aspects of the Spartan regime objectionable (no. 320).

Lesson 15 (II.7.1271b20–1272b23), compares the regime of Sparta with that of Crete. On some points the regime of Crete is close to that of Sparta, but it differs in several ways. In certain things it is better, in other respects it is less perfect (no. 321). It is older than that of Sparta, which took over several institutions from the Cretans; Lycurgus, the founder of the state of Lacedaemonia (Sparta), lived for quite some time in Crete (no. 322). Crete

---

36. They were five, representing the five villages of the Spartan community, and combined the judiciary and executive powers. They were elected for one year.

is well-suited for a leading position: its cities are close to the sea and not far from the Peloponnesus and Asia Minor (no. 323). In three points, there are correspondences between both cities: agriculture is done by slaves; they both organize public meals; and their regimes show similarities (no. 324). In some respects, however, the regime of Crete is better according to Aristotle: taxes were set aside to pay for the public meals and for the religious cult. People were admonished to eat with measure at those common meals. Cretan law also attempted to prevent too much intermixing of men and women (no. 325). To the *ephors* in Sparta correspond the *cosmoi* in Crete, a counsel of aristocrats chosen from certain families and not, as in Sparta, from the entire population. This applies also to the *gerontes* (the elders), who were chosen from the *cosmoi* and kept their function during their lifetime. The people had no share in the government by the *cosmoi* (no. 326), who could not be deposed and remained in office for life; they ruled without written laws (no. 327). One cannot allege the absence of attacks and uprisings in Crete as a sign of good government, as this is explained by their geographical position, far away from enemies (no. 328). The *cosmoi* were frequently debarred, when they wanted some powerful people to be condemned or when their whole office was temporarily forbidden, but it would have been better if their term of office would have been regulated by law (nos. 329–30). Even if the suspension of the *cosmoi* looked like an intervention by the people, in most cases it led to a one-man government (no. 331). When there is no concord among the citizens, a state is not viable and is exposed to the danger of enemy attacks. Foreigners coming to Crete could not hold positions of power. Recently, Aristotle notes, foreign invaders attacked the island and the Cretans could not very well defend themselves (no. 331).

In lesson 16 (II.1272b24–1273b26), Aristotle discusses the regime of the city of Carthage by pointing out its similarities with the political organization of Sparta and Crete, as well as some of its defects. The regime was good, as appears from the absence of unrest of any importance and it did not degenerate into a tyranny (no. 332). One hundred and four officials, similar to the *ephors* in Sparta, governed the city; only virtuous people were elected to this office, while the Spartans chose just anyone. Carthage also had kings, as did Sparta (no. 333). But it would have been better if they had been chosen by election rather than because of their age (no. 334). Some defects were common to the three regimes of Crete, Sparta, and Carthage, namely: for some questions they resorted to an administration by the lower classes, while in others they gave the power to a small number of people (judges). In Carthage, when the one hundred and four officials had disagreements, the kings put the issue before the people. A committee of five men, chosen by the kings, could look into important questions. The leaders were not elected by bribery but because of their virtue (no. 335). The regime tended to be a government of a minority who were not paid, so that poor people could not exercise these functions (no. 336), as they would not have the leisure to engage themselves in the affairs of the state. Virtuous men with enough free time were charged with directing public affairs. This regime was aristocratic because virtue was highly regarded, but it was wrong to give the offices to wealthy people (no. 338). One man could be charged with several tasks, but then the execution of some of these would suffer. Except where the population of a city is not numerous, it is more democratic (*populare*) when different people are charged with different tasks, as we see it happen in an army and aboard ships (no. 339). Carthage found ways to avoid uprisings by sending some of their citizens to administer the cities controlled by them. They were fortunate that there were no rebellions in those cities (no. 340).

In lesson 17 (II.9.1273b27–1274b38), Aristotle discusses some political institutions and laws. Some of those who conceived laws were private citizens like Plato, Phaleas, and Hippodamus, while others were engaged in political life, but did not actually introduce their laws into their respective cities, something which, however, Lycurgus did in Sparta and Solon in Athens (no. 341). Solon is reputed to have been a good legislator because he put an end to the regime of a very exacting minority in Athens and freed the people from the domination of the wealthy, while allowing them to share in the government. He left the council of the Areopagus intact, a council which consisted of high-class citizens, but instituted a judiciary administration, whose power rested with the people (no. 342) and whose members were elected by lot and who had extensive powers, so that he was blamed for having given the power to the lower classes who tyrannized over the well-to-do citizens, and thus for reducing the power of the Areopagus (no. 343). But Solon had not intended this. Because of the Persian wars, Athens put stress on strengthening its naval power. He intended to free the people from oppression by the wealthy, giving them some political power. The government was committed, first, to noble and wealthy citizens, then to a group of five hundred citizens of modest property, and finally to the soldier-warriors. The lowest class consisted of people who worked as paid employees without political power (no. 344).

In the next section, Aristotle mentions several legislators, such as Zaleucus, Thales, etc. (no. 345). Philolaus[37] made laws for Thebes (no. 346) and Charondas introduced legislation that made giving false testimony a

---

37. A Pythagorean of Croton, contemporary with Socrates.

crime. Philolaus proposed a law to restrict the number of citizens, such that the total number of the population should remain the same. He also introduced legislation to reduce inequalities in property. Charondas made giving a false testimony a crime. Aristotle also mentions that Plato proposed four rules or regulations: (1) women, children, and property should be held in common; (2) there should be common dinners for women; (3) a law against drunkenness should be enacted; and (4) men in the army must train to become ambidextrous. Finally, Pittacus proposed a law imposing heavier fines for aggressions committed by drunkards, but did not consider the reduced accountability of the latter, while Androdamus of Reggio in Calabria introduced legislation on homicides (no. 347).

Book III

In lesson 1 (III.1.1274b32–1275b34), Thomas gives a summary of this third book. Aristotle presents a survey of the different political regimes followed by a detailed description of the different states (no. 348). Before examining the different political regimes, we must determine both what a state is and what a citizen is (no. 350). Just living in a city does not yet make one a citizen. There are visitors, foreigners, and slaves staying in a city without being citizens. Those who are subject to the laws are citizens, including the children born from them and not yet registered, as well as the aged who can no longer fulfill the tasks of the younger citizens. Fugitives and those condemned elsewhere are citizens in a certain way (no. 352). The best way to determine if someone is a citizen is to see if he takes part in political and judicial deliberations (no. 353). But there are differences between states; in some states ordinary citizens do not take part in judicial matters (no. 354). A citizen is a person, so Aristotle defines, who can take part in the sessions of the courts and in the public authoritative assemblies. And a state is the assembly of those who can live by themselves and are self-sufficient (no. 355). Some say that one is a citizen when born from parents who both are citizens, and some even want to extend this to the third or fourth previous generation. A certain Gorgias[38] said ironically that citizens are those who are begotten by other citizens of the state, but Aristotle prefers the definition he has given above (no. 356).

Lesson 2 (III.1.1275b34–1276b15) addresses the following question: does a state remain the same when the composition of the body of citizens changes by the introduction of foreigners and slaves? Aristotle thinks it does if the

---

38. Not the sophist Gorgias but a citizen of Leontini in Sicily, who seems to have been influenced by Empedocles and Zeno of Elea.

newcomers partake in some ruling power (no. 358). When there is a change of regime in a state, do the agreements made before still hold (no. 359)? Aristotle seems to think so. The main questions are whether the people and the location are still the same. The question of whether or not there are city walls is not decisive (no. 361). To guarantee the unity of a state, its size must be relative to what the surrounding territory produces. Important is also whether the citizens are of the same lineage (nos. 362–63). When the regime is transformed, a state does not remain the same, for the regime determines the nature of a political community. The question of whether what was previously agreed upon must be honored will be examined later (no. 364).

Lesson 3 (III.2.1276b12–1277b32) is an inquiry about the virtues of the citizens. Are the virtues of good citizens the same as those of good men in general (*alicuius civis*) (no. 365)? Sailors have different tasks aboard a ship, but common to all is that they help to make the ship sail safely. The same applies to the virtues of the citizens: they have different duties but each must diligently accomplish the task assigned to him. A good citizen works for the good of his city, but this differs according to the regime so that he must be prudent and ascertain how to accomplish best his task (no. 366). In a city, all should have the virtues of good citizens, but they may not always have the virtues of good men, as not all of them are morally virtuous. In fact, Aristotle argues that, just as the animal body and the human soul are composed of different parts, civil society consists of different members: men and women, masters and slaves, etc., and that therefore there is not one and the same virtue for all, while the virtue of the good man is everywhere the same. Apparently, the virtue of the good citizen is not simply the same as that of the good man (no. 368). It might be objected that to be good citizens people must have the virtues of good men (no. 371). Actually, the ruler must have prudence, so that he has the same virtue as the good man (no. 370). Yet a good citizen must be able to rule and to be ruled (no. 372).

It is true, however, that a ruler does not need to know what the tasks are of his subjects, such as artisans, cooks, and other workmen with jobs by which they dirty themselves. In the old days, these people had no share in the government. A ruler does not need to learn this kind of work (no. 373). But there are other regimes where a ruler governs not as a master over his slaves, but over free men who are his equals. In this type of government, those in power change office and learn to rule by having been subjects themselves (no. 374). A virtuous citizen knows how to do both, ruling and being ruled, and this applies not only to the virtue of justice but also to the other virtues, such as temperance and fortitude (no. 375). The virtue of a ruler is prudence in governing.

Other moral virtues are common to rulers and subjects, but subjects should also have a share in prudence, so that they know how to introduce order into their lives (no. 376). The forgoing text tells us in which respect the virtues of the good man and of the good citizen are the same and how they are different (no. 377).

In lesson 4 (III.2.1277b33–1278b5) some questions are raised about the precise definition of a citizen. Must every citizen be able to function in leading and administrative positions? What about artisans, who are neither foreigners nor traveling salesmen (no. 378)? Artisans are not citizens in the full sense of the term, but are imperfect citizens, as youngsters are (no. 379). To be a full citizen one must be free from those servile tasks that are necessary for sustaining the life of a city. Only those who have been freed from these tasks can be full citizens, and those who are not are citizens in a restricted sense (no. 380). States are different because of their regimes, and so there are different ways in which people are citizens. In some states, mercenaries are citizens and can even accede to positions of authority if they have been residents for a sufficiently long time, something which in other states is impossible, particularly under aristocratic regimes. Mercenaries have not been prepared for civil functions and do not have sufficient means at their disposal. For artisans this is easier, for they have more ways to collect a fortune (no. 381). Especially in democracies that are short of population (*defectum turbae*), foreigners and immigrants can more easily become citizens. When the number of citizens is on the increase, they exclude the children of slaves from becoming citizens, but those born from free women, even if the father is a foreigner, are considered citizens (no. 381). In any regime, a person who has held an office is a citizen, but it would be a mistake to consider all those who live in a state to be its citizens (no. 382). In some deficient states, one who holds a position of authority, without having the right virtues, is considered a real citizen (*bonus cives*); but in an aristocratic state a good man and a good citizen are identical, while they differ in a corrupt regime (no. 383).

In lesson 5 (III.4.1278b6–1279a21), Aristotle notes that a city is nothing else but the way in which the different offices are organized, especially the highest office, which rules over all others depending on it. The supreme office determines in fact the type of the regime pertaining to the different states (no. 385). Man is a social animal and seeks to live together with others in order to reach a better life, such that the different partners all contribute, and people make common life pleasant (no. 387). In domestic communities there is a dual form of ruling: that of the master and his slaves, which is useful to the master, but also advantageous to both; the second is that of the husband over his wife and children, which we call domestic rule. This kind of rule can also accidentally be advantageous to the master, as the different hands on deck are to the captain of a ship (no. 388). Political power is ordained to the good of the subjects, particularly when it was established on the basis of the equality and equal rights of the citizens. If this latter is so, it is only fair that for one stretch of time some are in power and others in a next period, except in cases where some citizens so much surpass the others that they are worthy to stay in power. But the evaluation of this being worthy (*dignum*) varies according to the period of time in which people live. At the beginning, those in power were serving the good of others, but because of the advantages they enjoyed and the share of the common good they appropriated while in power, they wanted to hold on to their office forever (no. 389). In whatever regime, the rulers are right from the point of view of justice when they are intent on the advantage and good of the people. But a regime in which the advantage of the rulers is the criterion is corrupt and against justice; then the citizens are being used as slaves (no. 390).

Lesson 6 (III.5.1279a22–1280a6) notes that a regime is nothing else but the way in which rulers govern. Regimes are distinguished according to the difference in the number of those who govern, namely one man, a small group, or many. If they govern for the common good the regime is just, but when they rule for the interests of those in power, either of one person or of many, this is a violation of the true nature of a regime (no. 392). With regard to the just government that seeks the good of the whole community, it is called a regime of the noble either because the best persons are in power or because it is ordained to what is best for the state and for all involved. But when the totality of the citizens is governing the state in view of the common good, we speak of a republic (no. 393). The perversion of the first is called a tyranny, while the perversion of an aristocratic regime is called an oligarchy; the latter has a small number of rulers and is intent on what is advantageous to the wealthy. The perversion of the republic is called a democracy. None of these perverse regimes is intent on promoting the common interest (no. 394). A tyranny is a certain monarchical regime that uses the citizens as slaves; when the poor are governing, we have a popular regime (no. 395). But are these descriptions correct? When in a state the wealthy citizens who govern are more numerous than the poor, it seems to be a government by the masses, that is to say, a democracy. And when the lower-class people are less numerous, but influential and governing the city, we have an oligarchy, so that the division of regimes given above does not seem right (no. 396). To solve the difficulty Aristotle says that when we speak of a government by a small number we must add that these persons are wealthy, and by a regime of the many, that they are poor. But these additions may not be sufficient, for there may be a government of quite a number of rulers who are rich, or a government of only a few who are poor (no. 397). For this reason, Aristotle concludes by saying that an oligarchy and a democratic regime are not so much characterized by the large or small number of rulers, but that poverty and wealth are what distinguishes them best (no. 398). Thomas's commentary on the *Politics* ends here.

Concluding Remarks

The commentary on the *Politics* remained unfinished. In his observations on the text, Thomas states that we must let ourselves be guided by what nature teaches us (no. 1). For both Aristotle and Thomas the basic principle of political science is that man is made for life in a community, much more so than other living beings. Hence the point of departure for the study of the state is that people form communities by living together. He mentions, however, that in some exceptional cases such as that of St. John the Baptist and St. Anthony, a solitary life may be better. Nevertheless, the state is the most perfect community. Thomas follows the text of the *Politics*, summarizing what Aristotle writes about the different communities up to the evaluation of the constitutions of Hippodamus, Phaleas, and those of Sparta, Crete, Carthage, and Milete. With regard to the evaluation of slavery, he not only writes—following a text of Aristotle—that according to some it is against human nature to keep slaves, but he also reproduces the answer of Aristotle, namely that the constitution of some people suggests that for them a life subordinated to, and under the direction of, a master is best. Thomas follows Aristotle in his criticism of Plato's theory of the common possession of wives and children. Throughout his commentary, Thomas stresses the importance of the practice of the virtues in community life. References to Christian doctrine are avoided. There are nine references to scripture but these either confirm or illustrate what Aristotle writes.[39]

---

39. For a book-length discussion, see Bernhard Stengel, *Der Kommentar des Thomas von Aquin zur "Politik" des Aristoteles* (Marburg: Tektum Verlag, 2011).

SELECT BIBLIOGRAPHY

Primary Sources

Albertus Magnus. *Super Ethica*. Edited by Wilhelm Kübel. Münster: Aschendorff, 1968–87.

———. *Meteora*. Edited by P. Hossfeld. Münster: Aschendorff, 2003.

———. *De nutrimento et nutrito. De sensu et sensato cuius secundus liber est de memoria et reminiscentia*. Edited by S. Donati. Münster: Aschendorff, 2017.

Alexander of Aphrodisias. *De anima Liber cum Mantissa*. Edited by Ivo Bruns. Berlin: Reimer, 1887.

———. *Commentaire sur les Météores d'Aristote*. Edited by A. J. Smet. Louvain: Publications Universitaires de Louvain, 1968.

———. *Supplement to "On the Soul."* Translated by R. W. Sharples. Ithaca, N.Y.: Cornell University Press, 2004.

Ammonius. *Commentaire sur le Peri Hermeneias d'Aristote: Traduction de Guillaume de Moerbeke; Édition critique et étude sur l'utilisation du commentaire dans l'œuvre de saint Thomas*. Edited by Gérard Verbeke. Leuven: University of Leuven Press, 1961.

Aquinas, Thomas. *Expositio libri Peryermeneias*. Volume 1*/1 of *Opera omnia iussu Leonis XIII P. M. edita*. Second edition. Introduction by René Antoine Gauthier. Rome: Leonine Comission, 1989. Translated by Jean Oesterle as *Aristotle on Interpretation: Commentary by St. Thomas and Cajetan*. Mediaeval Philosophical Texts in Translation 11. Milwaukee, Wis.: Marquette University Press, 1962. Reprinted, with a new introduction, as *Commentary on Aristotle's "On Interpretation."* Notre Dame, Ind.: Dumb Ox Books, 2004.

———. *Expositio libri Posteriorum*. Volume 1*/2 of *Opera omnia iussu Leonis XIII P. M. Edita*. Second edition. Rome: Leonine Commission, 1989. Translated by Richard Berquist as *Commentary on Aristotle's "Posterior Analytics."* South Bend, Ind.: St. Augustine's Press, 2007.

———. *Commentaria in octo libros Physicorum Aristotelis*. Volume 2 of *Opera omnia iussu Leonis XIII. P. M. Edita*. Rome: Leonine Commission, 1884. Translated by Richard J. Blackwell, Richard J. Spath, and W. Edmund Thirlkel as *Commentary on Aristotle's "Physics."* Rare Masterpieces of Philosophy and Science. New Haven, Conn.: Yale University Press, 1963. Reprinted in the Aristotelian Commentary Series. Notre Dame, Ind.: Dumb Ox Books, 1999.

———. *In libros Aristotelis De caelo et mundo expositio*. In volume 3 of *Opera omnia iussu impensaque Leonis XIII P. M. edita*. Rome: Leonine Commission, 1886. Translated by Fabian Larcher and Pierre Conway as *Exposition of Aristotle's Treatise "On the Heavens."* 2 vols. Columbus, Ohio: College of St. Mary of the Springs, 1964. Available at isidore.co/aquinas/english/DeCoelo.htm,

———. *In libros Aristotelis Meteorologicorum expositio*. In volume 3 of *Opera omnia iussu impensaque Leonis XIII P. M. edita*. Rome: Leonine Commission, 1886. Translated by Pierre Conway and F. R. Larcher as *On Meteorology*, 1964, pro manuscripto. Available at isidore.co/aquinas/english/Meteora.htm.

———. *Sentencia libri De anima*. Volume 45/1 of *Opera omnia iussu Leonis XIII P. M. edita*. Rome: Leonine Commission, 1984. Conway, Pierre, and F.R. Larcher, trans. On Meteorology. 1964, pro manuscripto. Available at isidore.co/aquinas/english/Meteora.htm.

———. *Sentencia libri De sensu et sensato cuius secundus tractatus est De memoria et reminiscencia*. Volume 45/2 of *Opera omnia iussu Leonis XIII P. M. edita*. Rome: Leonine Commission, 1984.

Translated by Kevin White as In *Commentaries on Aristotle's "On Sense and What Is Sensed" and "On Memory and Recollection."* Thomas Aquinas in Translation. Washington, D.C.: The Catholic University of America Press, 2005.

———. *Sententia libri Ethicorum.* Volumes 47/1 and 47/2 of *Opera omnia iussu Leonis XIII P. M. edita.* Rome: Leonine Commission, 1969. Translated by C. I. Litzinger as *Commentary on the "Nicomachean Ethics."* 2 vols. Library of Living Catholic Thought. Chicago: Regnery, 1964.

———. *Sententia libri Politicorum.* In volume 48 of *Opera omnia iussu Leonis XIII P. M. edita.* Rome: Leonine Commission, 1971. Translated by Richard J. Regan as *Commentary on the "Politics."* Indianapolis, Ind.: Hackett, 2007.

———. *In duodecim libros Metaphysicorum Aristotelis expositio.* Second edition. Edited by M. R. Cathala and R. M. Spiazzi. Turin: Marietti, 1971. Translated by John P. Rowan as *Commentary on the "Metaphysics" of Aristotle.* 2 vols. Chicago: Regnery, 1964.

Aristotle. *Aristotle's "Metaphysics": A Revised Text with Introduction and Commentary.* Edited by William D. Ross. Oxford: Clarendon Press, 1924.

———. *Aristotle's "Physics": A Revised Text with Introduction and Commentary.* Edited by William D. Ross. Oxford: Clarendon, 1936.

———. *Aristotelis Fragmenta Selecta.* Edited by William D. Ross. Oxford: Clarendon, 1955.

———. *Aristotle's "Categories" and "De Interpretatione."* Translated with notes and glossary by J. L. Ackrill. Oxford: Clarendon, 1963.

———. *De interpretatione vel Periermenias. Translatio Boethii. Translatio Guillelmi de Moerbeka.* Aristoteles Latinus II 1–2. Edited by Gerard Verbeke, revised by Lorenzo Minio-Paluello. Paris: Desclée De Brouwer, 1965.

———. *Aristotele. La Metafisica. Traduzione, Introduzione, Commento.* Edited by Giovanni Reale. Naples: Loffredo, 1968.

———. *Analytica posteriora. Translationes Iacobi, Anonymi sive 'Ioannis', Gerardi et Recensio Guillelmi de Moerbeka.* Edited by L. Minio-Paluello and B. G. Dod. Paris: Desclée De Brouwer, 1968.

———. *L'éthique à Nicomaque.* 4 vols. Second edition. Edited by R. A. Gauthier and J. Y. Jolif. Paris / Leuven: Publications Universitaires / Béatrice-Nauwelaerts, 1970.

———. *Ethica Nicomachea. Translatio Antiquissima libr. II-III sive 'Ethica Vetus', Translationis Antiquioris quae supersunt sive 'Ethica Nova', 'Hoferiana', 'Borghesiana', Translatio Roberti Grosseteste Lincolniensis sive 'Liber Ethicorum' (Recensio Pura et Recensio Recognita).* 5 vols. Edited by R. A. Gauthier. Leiden / Brussels: Brill / Desclée De Brouwer, 1972–74.

———. *De generatione et corruptione. Translatio Vetus.* Edited by J. Judycka. Aristotles Latinus IX.1. Leiden: Brill, 1986.

———. *Physica. Translatio Vetus.* Edited by F. Bossier and J. Brams; *Translatio Vaticana.* Edited by A. Mansion. 2 vols. Aristoteles Latinus VII.1–2. Leiden: Brill, 1990.

———. *Aristoteles. Metaphysik. Mit Einleitung und Kommentar.* Third edition. Edited by Horst Seidl. Hamburg: Felix Meiner Verlag, 1990.

———. *Posterior Analytics.* Second revised edition. Translated with a commentary by J. Barnes. Oxford: Clarendon Press, 1993.

———. *Peri Hermeneias.* Translated with commentary by Hermann Weidemann. Berlin: Akademie Verlag, 1994.

———. *Meteorologica.* Edited by G. Vuillemin-Diem. Turnhout: Brepols, 2008.

———. *Il Libro Lambda della "Metafisica" di Aristotele.* Edited by Silvia Fazzo. Naples: Bibliopolis, 2012.

———. *Aristotle's "Metaphysics" Lambda: Annotated Critical Edition Based upon a Systematic Investigation of Greek, Latin, Arabic and Hebrew Sources.* Edited by Stefan Alexandru. Leiden: Brill, 2014.

———. *"Metaphysics" Book Iota.* Translated with an introduction and commentary by Laura M. Castelli. Oxford: Clarendon Press, 2018.

———. *"Metaphysics" Book Λ.* Translated with an introduction and commentary by Lindsay Judson. Oxford: Clarendon Press, 2019.

Averroes (Ibn Rushd) of Cordoba. *Commentarium magnum in Aristotelis De anima libros.* Edited by F. Stuart Crawford. Cambridge, Mass.: Mediaeval Academy of America, 1953.

——. *Long Commentary on the "De Anima" of Aristotle.* Translated by Richard C. Taylor. New Haven, Conn.: Yale University Press, 2009.

——. *Commentarium Magnum in Aristotelis Metaphysicorum libros XIIII.* In Aristotelis Opera cum Averrois Commentariis, vol. 8 (Averroes Latinus), Venetiis apud Iunctas 1562. Frankfurt am Main: Minerva, 1962.

Avicenna Latinus. *Liber de philosophia prima sive Scientia divina.* Edited by S. Van Riet. Louvain / Leiden: Peeters / Brill, 1977–83.

——. *Liber de anima seu Sextus de naturalibus.* 2 vols. Edited by Simone Van Riet. Louvain: Peeters, 1968–72.

Grosseteste, Robert. *Commentarius in Posteriorum analyticorum libros.* Edited by P. Rossi. Florence: Olschki, 1981.

Johannes Philoponus. *Commentaire sur le « De anima » d'Aristote: Traduction de Guillaume de Moerbeke;* édition *critique avec une introduction sur la psychologie de Philopon.* Edited by G. Verbeke. Leuven: University of Leuven Press, 1966.

Martinus de Dacia. *Opera.* Edited by H. Roos. Corpus philosophorum danicorum medii aevi 2. Copenhagen: Gad, 1961.

Peter of Auvergne. *Peter of Auvergne Questions on Aristotle's "De caelo": A Critical Edition with an Interpretative Essay.* Edited by G. Galle. Leuven: Leuven University Press, 2003.

Simplicius. *Simplicii Aristotelis Physicorum in libros quattuor posteriores Commentaria.* Edited by Hermann Diels. Berlin: Reimer, 1895.

——. *Commentaire sur le traité du ciel d'Aristote: Traduction de Guillaume de Moerbeke.* Volume 1. Edited by F. Bossier, C. Vande Veire, and G. Guldentops. Corpus Latinum Commentariorum in Aristotelem Graecorum 8, 1. Leuven: University of Leuven Press, 2004.

Thémistius. *Commentaire sur Le traité de l'âme d'Aristote: Traduction de Guillaume de Moerbeke;* édition *critique et étude sur l'utilisation du commentaire dans l'oeuvre de Saint Thomas.* Edited by G. Verbeke. Leiden: Brill, 1973.

Secondary Sources

Adam, James, ed. *The Republic of Plato.* Vol. 2. Cambridge: Cambridge University Press, 1938.

Adams, Don. "Aquinas on Aristotle on Happiness." *Medieval Philosophy and Theology* 1 (1991): 98–118.

Adamson, Peter. "Al-Kindī and the Reception of Greek Philosophy." In *The Cambridge Companion to Arabic Philosophy,* edited by P. Adamson and R. C. Taylor, 2–51. Cambridge: Cambridge University Press, 2005.

——. "Aristotle in the Arabic Commentary Tradition." In *The Oxford Handbook of Aristotle,* edited by Christopher Shields, 645–64. Oxford: Oxford University Press, 2012.

Aertsen, J., K. Emery Jr., and A. Speer, eds. *Nach der Verurteilung von 1277: Philosophie und Theologie an der Universität von Paris im letzten Viertel des 13. Jahrhunderts.* Berlin: De Gruyter, 2001.

Akasoy, Anna. "The Arabic and Islamic Reception of the Nicomachean Ethics." In *The Reception of Aristotle's Ethics,* edited by Jon Miller, 85–106. Cambridge: Cambridge University Press, 2012.

Amerini, Francesco. "Aquinas's Philosophy of Language in his Commentary on De Interpretatione." *Divus Thomas* 118 (2015): 80–113.

Anagnostopoulos, Georgios. "Aristotle's Works and the Development of His Thought." In *A Companion to Aristotle,* edited by Georgios Anagnostopoulos, 14–28. Malden, Mass.: Wiley-Blackwell, 2009.

Ando, Takatsura. *Aristotle's Theory of Practical Cognition.* The Hague: Martinus Nijhoff, 1965.

Anscombe, G. E. M. "Modern Moral Philosophy." *Philosophy* 33, no. 124 (1958): 1–19.

——. *Three Philosophers.* Ithaca, N.Y.: Cornell University Press, 1961.

Ashley, Benedict. *The Way toward Wisdom.* Notre Dame, Ind.: University of Notre Dame Press, 2006.

Bäck, Allan. "Aquinas on Predication." In Braakhuis and Kneepkens, *Aristotle's "Peri Hermeneias" in the Latin Middle Ages*, 321–38.

———. "Sailing through the Sea Battle." *Ancient Philosophy* 12, no. 1 (1992): 133–51.

Badawi, Abdurrahman. *Histoire de la philosophie en Islam.* Vol. 2. Paris: Vrin, 1972.

Baghdassarian, Fabienne. "Aristote, De Caelo, I 9: L'identité des 'etres de là-bas.'" *Philosophie antique* 11 (2011): 175–203.

Balaudé, Jean-François. "Nature et norme dans les traités éthiques d'Aristote." In *Aristote et la notion de nature: Enjeux épistémologiques et pratiques,* edited by Pierre-Marie Morel, 95–129. Bordeaux: Presses Universitaires, 1997.

Barnes, Jonathan. "Theophrastus and Hypothetical Syllogisms." In *Theophrastus of Eresus: On His Life and Work,* edited by W. W. Fortenbaugh, 125–41. Oxford: Clarendon, 1985.

———. "An Aristotelian Way with Skepticism." In *Aristotle Today: Essays on Aristotle's Ideal of Science,* edited by M. Matthen, 51–76. Edmonton: Academic, 1987.

Bayer, Greg. "Coming to Know Principles in Posterior Analytics II 19." *Apeiron* 30, no. 2 (1997): 109–42.

Bazan, B. C. "Le commentaire de S. Thomas d'Aquin sur le Traité de l'âme." *Revue des sciences philosophiques et théologiques* 69, no. 4 (1985): 521–47.

Bertolacci, Amos. "Avicenna's and Averroes' Interprétations and Their Influence in Albert the Great." In *A Companion to the Latin Medieval Commentaries on Aristotle's "Metaphysics,"* edited by Fabrizio Amerini and Gabriele Galluzzo, 95–135. Leiden: Brill, 2014.

Biard, Joël. "Les commentaires sur le De generatione et corruptione comme lieu de réflexion épistémologique dans quelques textes du XIVe siècle." In *Lire Aristote au Moyen Âge et à la Renaissance: Réception du traité sur la génération et la corruption,* edited by Joëlle Ducos and Violaine Giacomotto-Charra, 119–34. Paris: Champion, 2011.

Bicknell, P. J. "The Fourth Paradox of Zeno: An Interpretation of Aristotle *Physics* 239 B33–240 A18." *Acta Classica* 4, no. 1 (1961): 39–45.

Black, Deborah. "Aristotle's *Peri Hermeneias* in Medieval Latin and Arabic Philosophy." *Canadian Journal of Philosophy* 21, supplement 1 (1991): 25–83.

Blumenthal, Henry J. "Neoplatonic Elements in the de Anima Commentaries." In *Aristotle Transformed: The Ancient Commentators and Their Influence,* edited by Richard Sorabji, 305–24. London: Duckworth, 1990.

Bloch, David. *Aristotle on Memory and Recollection: Text, Translation, Interpretation, and Reception in Western Scholasticism.* Leiden: Brill, 2007.

———. "Robert Grosseteste's *Conclusiones* and the Commentary on the Posterior Analytics." *Vivarium* 47, no. 1 (2009): 1–23.

Bobonich, Chris. "Aristotle's Ethical Treatises." In *The Blackwell Guide to Aristotle's "Nicomachean Ethics,"* edited by R. Kraut, 12–36. Oxford: Oxford University Press, 2006.

Bochenski, Joseph M. *Formale Logik.* Freiburg: Alber, 1978.

Borgo, Marta. "La *Métaphysique* d'Aristote dans le *Commentaire* de Thomas d'Aquin au I livre de *Sentences* de Pierre Lombard: Quelques exemples significatifs." *Revue des sciences philosophiques et théologiques* 91, no. 4 (2007): 651–92.

———. "Les raisons séminales entre théologie et philosophie: D'Alexandre de Halès à Thomas d'Aquin." *Documenti e Studi sulla Tradizione Filosofica Medievale* 23 (2012): 143–72.

———. "Latin Medieval Translations of Aristotle's Metaphysics." In *The Latin Medieval Commentaries on Aristotle's "Metaphysics,"* edited by Fabrizio Amerini and Gabriele Galluzzo, 19–57. Leiden: Brill, 2014.

Bossier, Fernand. "Traductions latines et influences du commentaire In de caelo en occident (XIIIe-XIVe s.)." In *Simplicius, sa vie, son oeuvre, sa survie: actes du Colloque International de Paris (26 Sept.–1er Oct. 1985),* edited by Ilsetraut Hadot, 288–325. Berlin: De Gruyter, 1987.

Bourke, Vernon J. "The Nicomachean Ethics and Thomas Aquinas." In *St. Thomas Aquinas 1274–1974: Commemorative Studies,* 1:239–55. Toronto: Pontifical Institute of Mediaeval Studies, 1974.

———. "Moral Philosophy without Revelation." *The Thomist* 40, no. 4 (1976): 555–70.

Bowen, Alan C., and Christian Wildberg, eds. *New Perspectives on Aristotle's "De caelo."* Leiden: Brill, 2009.

Braakhuis, H. A. G., and C. H. Kneepkens, eds. *Aristotle's "Peri hermeneias" in the Latin Middle Ages: Essays on the Commentary Tradition.* Groningen: Ingenium, 2003.

Brams, Jozef. "La Recensio Matritensis de la Physique." In *Guillaume de Moerbeke*, edited by Brams and Vanhamel, 193–220.

———. "The Revised Version of Grosseteste's Translation of the Nicomachean Ethics." *Bulletin de Philosophie Médiévale* 36 (1994): 45–55.

Brams, Jozef, and Willy Vanhamel. *Guillaume de Moerbeke: Recueil d'études à l'occasion du 700e anniversaire de sa mort.* Leuven: University of Leuven Press, 1989.

Bronstein, David. "The Origin and Aim of Posterior Analytics II.19." *Phronesis* 57 (2012): 29–62.

Burns, Tony. "Aristotle and Natural Law." *History of Political Thought* 19, no. 2 (1998): 142–66.

Burnyeat, Myles. "Aristotle on Understanding Knowledge." In *Aristotle on Science: The Posterior Analytics*, edited by E. Berti, 97–139. Padua: Editrice Antenore, 1981.

Burr, David. "Peter John Olivi and the Philosophers." *Franciscan Studies* 31 (1971): 41–71.

Carroy, Bertrand. "Héritage et différences: Thomas d'Aquin et Albert le Grand, commentateurs du *De generatione et corruption*." In *Lire Aristote au Moyen Âge et à la Renaissance: Réception du traité sur la génération et la corruption*, edited by Joëlle Ducos and Violaine Giacomotto-Charra, 102–17. Paris: Champion, 2011.

Casazza, Fabrizio. "Il Commento dei San Tommaso d'Aquino alla Politica di Aristotele." *Archivio teologico torinese* 11 (2005): 97–110; 12 (2006): 63–80.

Celluprica, Vincenza. *Il capitulo 9 del "De interpretatione" di Aristotele. Rassegna di studi 1930–1973.* Bologna: Il Mulino, 1977.

Cerami, Cristina. "The De Caelo et Mundo of Avicenna's 'Šifā': An Overview of Its Goal, Its Structure and Its Polemical Background." *Documenti e Studi sulla Tradizione Filosofica Medievale* 28 (2017): 273–29.

Cheneval, Francis. "Considérations presque philosophiques sur les commentaires de la Politique d'Albert le Grand et de Thomas d'Aquin." *Freiburger Zeitschrift für Philosophie und Theologie* 45, nos. 1–2 (1998): 56–83.

Cheneval, Francis, and Ruedi Imbach, eds. *Thomas von Aquin: Prologe zu den Aristoteleskommentare.* Frankfurt am Main: Klostermann, 1993.

Chenu, M.-D. *Introduction à l'étude de saint Thomas d'Aquin.* Paris: Vrin, 1950.

Chroust, Anton-Hermann. "*Eudemus* or *On the Soul*: A Lost Dialogue of Aristotle on the Immortality of the Soul." *Mnemosyne* 19 (1966): 17–30.

Cochrane, Charles Norris. *Christianity and Classical Culture.* Oxford: Oxford University Press, 1940.

Coda, Elisa. "The Soul as 'Harmony' in Late Antiquity and in the Latin Middle Ages: A Note on Thomas Aquinas as a Reader of Themistius' *In Libros De Anima Paraphrasis*." *Studia Graeco-Arabica* 7 (2017): 307–30.

Cohen, S. M., and P. Burke. "New Evidence for the Dating of Aristotle Meteorologica 1–3." *Classical Philology* 85, no. 2 (1990): 126–29.

Cooper, John. "Nicomachean Ethics VII. 1–2: Introduction, Method, Puzzles." In *Aristotle: "Nicomachean Ethics," Book VII. Symposium Aristotelicum*, edited by Carlo Natali, 9–40. Oxford: Oxford University Press, 2009.

Cornford, Francis. *Plato's Cosmology.* London: Routledge and Kegan Paul, 1952.

Cos, Joseph. "Evidences of St. Thomas's Dictating Activity in the Naples Manuscript of His 'Scriptum in Metaphysicam.'" *Scriptorium* 38, no. 2 (1984): 231–53.

Costa, Iacopo. "*L'Éthique à Nicomaque* à la Faculté des arts de Paris avant et après 1277." *Archives d'histoire doctrinale et littéraire du Moyen Âge* 79 (2012): 71–114.

Craig, William Lane. *The Problem of Divine Foreknowledge and Future Contingents from Aristotle to Suarez.* Leiden: Brill, 1988.

Crubellier, Michel, and André Laks, eds. *Aristotle's "Metaphysics" Beta: Symposium Aristotelicum.* Oxford: Oxford University Press, 2002.

Cullen, Christopher M. "Bonaventure's Philosophical Method." In *A Companion to Bonaventure,* edited by Jay M. Hammond, J. A. Wayne Hellmann, and Jared Goff, 121–66. Leiden: Brill, 2014.

De Boer, Sander. *The Science of the Soul: The Commentary Tradition on Aristotle's "De Anima," 1260–1360.* Leuven: University of Leuven Press, 2013.

de Couesnongle, Vincent. "La causalité du maximum: L'utilisation par Saint Thomas d'un passage d'Aristote." *Revue des Sciences philosophiques et théologiques* 38, no. 3 (1954): 433–44.

Dedek, John F. "Intrinsically Evil Acts: A Historical Study of the Mind of St Thomas." *The Thomist* 43, no. 3 (1979): 385–413.

De Haas, Frans. "Mixture in Philoponus: An Encounter with a Third Kind of Potentiality." In *The Commentary Tradition on "De Generatione et Corruptione": Ancient, Medieval and Early Modern,* edited by Johannes Thijssen and Henk Braakhuis, 21–46. Turnhout: Brepols, 1999.

De Haas, Frans, and Jaap Mansfeld, eds. *Aristotle, "On Generation and Corruption," Book I: Symposium Aristotelicum.* Oxford: Oxford University Press, 2004.

De Haas, Frans, Mariska Leunissen, and Marije Martijn, eds. *Interpreting Aristotle's "Posterior Analytics" in Late Antiquity and Beyond.* Leiden: Brill, 2009.

de Leemans, Pieter. "Alia translatio planior: Les traductions latines du De generatione et corruptione et les commentaires médiévaux." In *Lire Aristote au Moyen Âge et à la Renaissance, Réception du traité sur la génération et la corruption,* edited by Joëlle Ducos and Violaine Giacomotto-Charra, 27–53. Paris: Champion, 2011.

Del Punta, Francesco. "The Genre of Commentaries in the Middle Ages and its Relation to the Nature and the Originality of Medieval Thought." In *Was ist Philosophie im Mittelaalter?,* edited by Jan A. Aertsen and Andreas Speer, 138–51. Miscellanea Mediaevalia 26. New York: De Gruyter, 1998.

de Tocco, Guilelmus. "Vita S. Thomae." *Revue Thomiste* 21, supplement (1913).

———. *Ystoria sancti Thome de Aquino de Guillaume de Tocco (1323),* édition critique, introduction et notes Claire le Brun-Gouanvic. PIMS Studies and Texts 127. Toronto: Pontifical Institute of Mediaeval Studies, 1996.

Doig, James Conroy. *Aquinas on Metaphysics: A Historico-Doctrinal Study of the "Commentary on the 'Metaphysics.'"* The Hague: Martinus Nijhoff, 1972.

———. *Aquinas's Philosophical Commentary on the "Ethics": A Historical Perspective.* Dordrecht: Kluwer Academic, 2001.

Donati, S. "The Critical Edition of Albert the Great's Commentaries on *De sensu et sensato* and *De memoria et reminiscentia*: Its Significance for the Study of the 13th-century Reception of Aristotle's Parva Naturalia and its Problems." In *The Letter before the Spirit: The Importance of Text Editions for the Study of the Reception of Aristotle,* edited by A. van Oppenraay and R. Fontaine, 345–99. Leiden: Brill, 2012.

———. "Commenti parigini alla Fisica degli anni 1270–1300 ca." In *Die Bibliotheca Amploniana im Spannungsfeld von Aristotelismus, Nominalismus und Humanismus,* edited by Andreas Speer, 136–256. Berlin: De Gruyter, 1995.

Donati, S., F. Del Punta, and C. Trifogli. "Commentaries on Aristotle's Physics in Britain, ca. 1250–1270." In *Aristotle in Britain during the Middle Ages,* edited by John Marenbon, 265–83. Brepols: Turnhout, 1996.

Ducoin, Georges. "Saint Thomas commentateur d'Aristote. Étude sur le commentaire thomiste du livre Λ des Métaphysiques d'Aristote." *Archives de Philosophie* n.s. 20, no. 2 (1957): 78–117, 241–71, 392–445.

Ducos, Jöelle, and Violaine Giacomotto-Charra, eds. *Lire Aristote au Moyen Âge et à la Renaissance, Réception du traité sur la génération et la corruption.* Paris: Champion, 2011.

Duhem, Pierre. *Essai sur la notion de théorie physique de Platon à Galillée.* Paris: Hermann, 1908.

Duke, George. *Aristotle and Law: The Politics of Nomos.* Cambridge: Cambridge University Press, 2019.

Dunbabin, Jean. "The Reception and Interpretation of Aristotle's Politics." In *The Cambridge History of Later Medieval Philosophy,* edited by Norman Kretzmann, Anthony Kenny, and Jan Pinborg, 723–37. Cambridge: Cambridge University Press, 1982.

Düring, Ingemar. "Aristotle on Ultimate Principles from 'Nature and Reality': Protrepticus fr. 13." In *Aristotle and Plato in the Mid-Fourth Century,* edited by Ingemar Düring and G. E. L. Owen, 35–55. Gothenburg: Almquist and Wiksell, 1960.

———. *Aristoteles: Darstellung und Interpretation seines Denkens.* Heidelberg: Winter, 1966.

Elders, Leo. *Aristotle's Theory of the One: A Commentary on Book X of the "Metaphysics."* Assen: Van Gorcum, 1961.

———. *Aristotle's Cosmology: A Commentary on the "De Caelo."* Assen: Van Gorcum, 1966.

———. *Aristotle's Theology: A Commentary on Book Lambda of the "Metaphysics."* Assen: Van Gorcum, 1972.

———. *Faith and Science: An Introduction to St. Thomas' "Expositio in Boetii De Trinitate."* Rome: Herder, 1974.

———. "Les citations d'Aristote dans le Commentaire des Sentences de saint Bonaventure." In *San Bonaventura, maestro di vita francescana e di sapienza Cristiana,* 831–42. Rome: Pontificia Facolta Téologica San Bonaventure, 1974.

———. "Le commentaire sur le quatrième livre de la *Métaphysique.*" In *San Tommaso d'Aquino nel suo settimo centenario. Atti del Congresso Internazionale Roma-Napoli, 17–24 aprile 1974,* 1:207–18. Naples: Edizioni domenicane italiane, 1975–76.

———. "Le commentaire de saint Thomas d'Aquin sur le *De Caelo* d'Aristote." In *Proceedings of the World Congress on Aristotle,* edited by Ioannes N. Theodorakopoulos, 2:173–87. Athens: Ministry of Culture and Sciences, 1981.

———. "Saint Thomas Aquinas' Commentary on the *Physics* of Aristotle." In *La Philosophie de la nature de Saint Thomas d'Aquin,* edited by Leo Elders, 107–33. Rome: Libreria Editrice Vaticana, 1982.

———. "St. Thomas Aquinas's Commentary on the *Metaphysics* of Aristotle." *Divus Thomas* 86 (1983): 307–26.

———. "St. Thomas Aquinas's Commentary on the *Nicomachean Ethics.*" In *The Ethics of St. Thomas Aquinas,* edited by Leo Elders and Klaus Hedwig, 9–49. Vatican City: Libreria Editrice Vaticana, 1984.

———. "Le Commentaire de saint Thomas d'Aquin sur le *De anima* d'Aristote." In *L'anima nell'antropologia di S.Tommaso d'Aquino. Atti del Congresso della Società Internazionale S.Tommaso d'Aquino (Sita), Roma 2–5 gennaio 1986,* edited by A. Lobato, 33–51. Milan: Massimo, 1987.

———. "Averroes et saint Thomas d'Aquin." *Doctor communis* 44 (1992): 46–56.

———. "The Greek Christian Authors and Aristotle." In *Aristotle in Late Antiquity,* edited by Lawrence P. Schrenk, 111–42. Washington, D.C.: The Catholic University of America Press, 1994.

———. "El método en la ética según santo Tomás de Aquino." *Medioevo* 18 (1992): 71–84.

———. "The Ethics of St. Thomas Aquinas and Its Importance for Our Age." In *Wiernosc Rzeczywistosci (Faithfulness to Reality): Essays in Honour of Prof. M. A. Krapiec,* 399–418. Lublin: Catholic University of Lublin Press, 2001.

———. *The Ethics of St. Thomas Aquinas.* Frankfurt am Main: Peter Lang, 2005. Reprinted in Washington, D.C.: The Catholic University of America Press, 2019.

———. "The Aristotelian Commentaries of St. Thomas Aquinas." *The Review of Metaphysics* 63, no. 1 (2009): 29–53.

———. "La *Sententia in Librum Ethicorum* de Santo Tomás de Aquino." In *Tomás de Aquino, Comentador de Aristóteles,* edited by Héctor Velázquez, 43–73. México City: Universidad Panamericana, 2010.

———. "The Primacy of Reason According to Aquinas." In *Logos et Musica: In Honorem Summi*

Romani Pontificis Benedicti XVI, edited by Elzbieta Szczurko, Tadeusz Guz, and Horst Seidl, 87–115. Frankfurt am Main: Peter Lang, 2012.

———. "St. Thomas Aquinas's Commentary of Aristotle's *Physics*." *The Review of Metaphysics* 66, no. 4 (2013): 713–48.

———. *Thomas Aquinas and His Predecessors: The Philosophers and the Church Fathers in His Works*. Washington, D.C.: The Catholic University of America Press, 2018.

———. "St. Thomas Aquinas's Treatise on Temperance and Aristotle." *Nova & Vetera (English Edition)* 16, no. 2 (2018): 465–87.

Ellspermann, Gerald L. *The Attitude of the Early Christian Latin Writers toward Pagan Literature and Learning*. Washington, D.C.: The Catholic University of America Press, 1949.

Fazzo, Silvia. "The *Metaphysics* from Aristotle to Alexander of Aphrodisias." *Bulletin of the Institute of Classical Studies* 55, no. 1 (2012): 51–68.

———. *Commento al Libro Lambda della Metafisica di Aristotele*. Naples: Bibliopolis, 2014.

Ferejohn, Michael T. "Empiricism and the First Principles of Aristotelian Science." In *A Companion to Aristotle*, edited by Georgios Anagnostopoulos, 66–80. Malden, Mass.: Wiley-Blackwell, 2009.

Fernandez Garrido, María Regla. "Los comentarios griego y latinos al *De interpretatione* aristotelico hasta Tomas de Aquino." *Emerita: Revista de lingüística y filología clásica* 64, no. 2 (1996): 307–24.

Festugière, André-Jean. "Notes sur les sources du commentaire de S. Thomas au Livre XII des Métaphysiques." *Revue des sciences philosophiques et theologiques* 18, no. 2; no. 4 (1929): 282–90; 657–63.

———. "La place du '*De anima*' dans le système aristotélicien d'après S. Thomas." *Archives de l'histoire doctrinale et littéraire du moyen âge* 6 (1931): 25–47.

Flannery, K. "Being Truthful with (or Lying to) Others." In *Aquinas and the "Nicomachean Ethics,"* edited by Hoffmann, Müller, and Perkams, 129–45.

Flashar, Hellmut, ed. *Die Philosophie der Antike 3: Ältere Akademie Aristoteles – Peripatos*. Grundriss der Geschichte der Philosophie A3. Stuttgart: Schwabe, 1983.

Flüeler, Christoph. *Rezeption und Interpretation des Aristotelischen Politica im späten Mittelalter*. Amsterdam: Grüner, 1992.

Fontaine, Resianne. "The Reception of Aristotle's Meteorology in Hebrew Scientific Writings of the Thirteenth Century I." *Aleph: Historical Studies in Science and Judaism* 1 (2001): 101–39.

Frede, Dorothea. "The Sea-Battle Reconsidered: A Defence of the Traditional Interpretation." *Oxford Studies in Ancient Philosophy* 3 (1985): 31–87.

Frede, Michael, and David Charles, eds. *Aristotle's "Metaphysics" Book Lambda: Symposium Aristotelicum*. Oxford: Clarendon Press, 2000.

Freudenthal, Jacob. *Die durch Averroes erhaltenen Fragmente Alexanders zur Metaphysik des Aristoteles*. Berlin: Verlag der Königlichen Akademie der Wissenschaften, 1885.

Galle, Griet. "The Relation Between the Condemnations of 1277 and Peter of Auvergne's Questions on De caelo." *Ephemerides Theologicae Lovanienses* 91 (2015): 223–38.

Galluzzo, Gabriele. "Aquinas on the Structure of Aristotle's Metaphysics." *Documenti e Studi sulla Tradizione Filosofica Medievale* 15 (2004): 353–86.

———. "Aquinas's Interpretation of Aristotle's Metaphysics, Book Z." *Recherches de théologie et philosophie médiévale* 74, no. 2 (2007): 423–81.

———. "Aquinas's Commentary on the *Metaphysics*." In *A Companion to Latin Medieval Commentaries on Aristotle's "Metaphysics,"* edited by Fabrizio Amerini and Gabriele Galluzzo, 209–54. Leiden: Brill, 2013.

———. *The Medieval Reception of Book Zeta of Aristotle's "Metaphysics."* Leiden: Brill, 2013.

García Cuadrado, J. A. "La consignificatio verbal (Per hermeneias 16b 8–10): Ammonio, Boecio y Tomás de Aquino." *Revista Española de Filosofía Medieval* 19 (2012): 87–100.

Gauthier, René Antoine. "Trois commentaires 'Averroistes' sur l'Éthique à Nicomacque." *Archives d'histoire doctrinale et littéraire du Moyen Âge* 16 (1947–48): 187–336.

———. "La date du commentaire de saint Thomas sur l'Éthique á *Nicomaque*." *Recherches de théologie ancienne et médiévale* 18 (1951): 66–105.

————. *Magnanimité*. Paris: Vrin, 1951.

Gigon, Olof. "Die Sklaverei bei Aristoteles." In *La "Politique" d'Aristote; sept exposés et discussions*, 247–76. Geneva: Fondation Hardt, 1965.

Gomez Nogales, Salvador. "Saint Thomas, Averroes et l'averroisme." In *Aquinas and the Problems of His Time*, edited by Gerard Verbeke and Daniel Verhelst, 161–77. Leuven: University of Leuven Press, 1976.

Grabmann, Martin. *Mittelalterliches Geistesleben: Abhandlungen zur Geschichte der Scholastik und Mystik*. Vol. 2. Münich: Heuber, 1926.

Grant, Edward. *God and Reason in the Middle Ages*. Cambridge: Cambridge University Press, 2001.

Gutas, Dimitri. *Greek Thought, Arabic Culture: The Graeco-Arabic Translation Movement in Baghdad and Early 'Abbasid Society (2nd–4th / 8th–10th centuries)*. New York: Routledge, 1998.

Guthrie, W. K. C. "The Presocratic World Picture." *The Harvard Theological Review* 45, no. 2 (1952): 87–104.

Hardie, W. F. R. *Aristotle's Ethical Theory*. Oxford: Clarendon, 1968.

Hause, Jeffrey. "Aquinas on Aristotelian Justice." In *Aquinas and the "Nicomachean Ethics,"* edited by Hoffmann, Müller, and Perkams, 146–64.

Heath, Thomas. *Aristarchus of Samos: The Ancient Copernicus*. Oxford: Clarendon, 1913.

Hellmeier, Paul. "'Tote Wissenschaft'?– Thomas von Aquin als Kommentator von De Anima I." *Divus Thomas* 118 (2015): 114–47.

————. *Anima et Intellectus. Albertus Magnus und Thomas von Aquin über Seele und Intellekt des Menschen*. Münster: Aschendorff Verlag, 2011.

Herzberg, Stephan. *Wahrnemung und Wissen bei Aristoteles*. Berlin: De Gruyter, 2011.

Hissette, Roland. *Enquête sur les 219 articles condamnés à Paris le 7 mars 1277*. Leuven: Peeters, 1977.

Hoffmann, Tobias. "Prudence and Practical Principles." In *Aquinas and the "Nicomachean Ethics,"* edited by Hoffmann, Müller, and Perkams, 165–83.

Hoffmann, Tobias, Jörn Müller, and Matthias Perkams, ed. *Aquinas and the "Nicomachean Ethics."* Cambridge: Cambridge University Press, 2013.

Horn, Christoph, ed. *Aristotle's "Metaphysics" Lambda: New Essays*. Berlin: De Gruyter, 2016.

Hossfeld, Paul. "Der Gebrauch der aristotelischen Übersetzung in den *Meteora* des Albertus Magnus." *Mediaeval Studies* 42, no. 1 (1980): 395–406.

Humbrecht, Thierry-Dominique. "Thomas d'Aquin s'intéresse-t-il à la physique?" In *Lire Aristote au Moyen Âge et à la Renaissance*, edited by Joëlle Ducos and Violaine Giacomotto-Charra, 85–94. Paris: Honoré Champion, 2011.

Ierodiakonou, Katerina. "Aristotle and Alexander of Aphrodisias on Colour." In *The "Parva naturalia" in Greek, Arabic and Latin Aristotelianism*, edited by B. Bydén and F. Radovic, 77–90. Cham: Springer, 2018.

Imbach, Ruedi. "Quelques observation sur la réception du livre XII de la 'Métaphysique' chez Thomas d'Aquin." *Revue des sciences philosophiques et théologiques* 99, no. 3 (2015): 377–407.

Irwin, Terence. *Aristotle's First Principles*. Oxford: Clarendon Press, 1988.

————. "Conceptions of Happiness in the Nicomachean Ethics." In *The Oxford Handbook of Aristotle*, edited by Christopher Shields, 495–528. Oxford: Oxford University Press, 2012.

Isaac, Jean. "Saint Thomas, interprète des œuvres d'Aristote." In *Scholastica ratione historica-critica instauranda*, 360–61. Rome: Pontificum Athanseum Antonianum, 1951.

————. "Le Peri Hermeneias" en Occident de Boèce à saint Thomas: Histoire littéraire d'un traité d'Aristote. Paris: Vrin, 1953.

Jaeger, Werner. *Aristotle: Fundamentals of the History of His Development*. Second edition. Oxford: Clarendon, 1948.

Jaffa, Harry V. *Thomism and Aristotelianism: A Study of the Commentary by St. Thomas Aquinas on the "Nicomachean Ethics."* Chicago: University of Chicago Press, 1952.

Jenkins, John. "Expositions of the Text: Aquinas's Aristotelian Commentaries." *Medieval Philosophy and Theology* 5, no. 1 (1996): 39–62.

Joachim, H. H. *Aristotle: The "Nicomachean Ethics": A Commentary by the late H. H. Joachim.* Edited by D. A. Rees. Oxford: Clarendon Press, 1951.

Jordan, Mark D. "Thomas Aquinas's Disclaimers in the Aristotelian Commentaries." In *Philosophy and the God of Abraham: Essays in Memory of James A. Weisheipl, O.P.*, edited by R. James Long, 99–112. Toronto: Pontifical Institute of Mediaeval Studies, 1991.

———. *The Alleged Aristotelianism of Thomas Aquinas.* Etienne Gilson Series 15. Toronto: Pontifical Institute of Mediaeval Studies, 1992.

Judycka, Joanna. "L'attribution de la Translatio nova du De generations et corruptione à Guillaume de Moerbeke." In *Guillaume de Moerbeke. Recueil d'Études à l'occasion du 700e anniversaire de sa mort*, edited by J. Brams and W. Vanhamel, 247–52. Leuven: Leuven University Press, 1989.

Kaczor, Christopher. "Thomas Aquinas's Commentary on the Ethics: Merely an Interpretation of Aristotle?" *American Catholic Philosophical Quarterly* 78, no. 3 (2004): 353–78.

———. "Reading Aquinas's Commentary of Aristotle's Nicomachean Ethics: A Reply to Mark D. Jordan." In *Theology Needs Philosophy*, edited by Matthew Lamb, 279–92. Washington, D.C.: The Catholic University of America Press, 2016.

Kahn, Charles H. "The Role of Nous in the Cognition of First Principles in Posterior Analytics II 19." In *Aristotle on Science: The "Posterior Analytics,"* edited by Berti, 385–414. Padova: Editrice Anenore, 1981.

———. "The Normative Structure of Aristotle's 'Politics.'" In *Aristoteles' "Politik." Akten der XI: Symposium Aristotelicum*, edited by Günther Patzig, 369–84. Göttingen: Vandenhoeck and Ruprecht, 1990.

Kenny, Anthony. "Aristotle on Happiness." *Proceedings of the Aristotelean Society* 66 (1965–66): 93–102.

Kerferd, G. B. "Anaxagoras and the Concept of Matter before Aristotle." In *The Presocratics: A Collection of Critical Essays*, edited by A. P. D. Mourelatos, 489–503. Princeton, N.J.: Princeton University Press, 1974.

Kirk, G. S., and J. E. Raven. *The Presocratic Philosophers.* Cambridge: Cambridge University Press, 1957.

Knuuttila, Simo. "Medieval Commentators on Future Contingents in De Interpretatione 9." *Vivarium* 48, nos. 1–2 (2010): 75–95.

Krämer, H. J. *Der Ursprung der Geistmetaphysik.* Amsterdam: Schipper, 1964.

Lang, Helen S. "On Memory: Aristotle's Corrections of Plato." *Journal of the History of Philosophy* 18, no. 4 (1980): 379–93.

Lewry, P. Osmund. "Two Continuators of Aquinas: Robertus de Vulgarbia and Thomas Sutton on the *Peri hermeneias* of Aristotle." *Mediaeval Studies* 43 (1981): 58–130.

Liebard, Jacques. *Les enseignements moraux des Pères apostoliques.* Gembloux: Ducalot, 1970.

Lohr, Charles H. "The New Aristotle and 'Science' in the Paris Arts Faculty (1255)." In *L'enseignement des disciplines à la Faculté des arts (Paris et Oxford, XIIIe–XVe siècles)*, edited by Olga Wijers and Louis Holtz, 251–70. Turnhout: Brepols, 1997.

Long, A. A., ed. *Problems in Stoicism.* London: Athlone, 1971.

MacIntyre, Alasdair. *After Virtue.* Notre Dame, Ind.: University of Notre Dame Press, 1981.

Mahoney, Edward. "Aristotle and Some Late Medieval and Renaissance Philosophers." In *The Impact of Aristotelianism on Modern Philosophy*, edited by Riccardo Pozzo, 1–30. Washington, D.C.: The Catholic University of America Press, 2004.

Mansfeld, Jaap. "De Melisso Xenophane Gorgia: Pyrrhonizing Aristotelianism." *Rheinisches Museum für Philologie Neue Folge* 131, nos. 3–4 (1988): 239–76.

———, ed. *De generatione et corruption: Symposium Aristotelicum.* Geneva: Fondation Hardt, 1999.

———, ed. *Aristotelian Logic, Platonism, and the Context of Early Medieval Philosophy in the West.* Aldershot: Variorum, 2000.

Mansini, Guy. "Aristotle and Aquinas's Theology of Charity in the Summa Theologiae." In *Aristotle in Aquinas's Theology*, edited by Gilles Emery and Matthew Levering, 121–38. Oxford: Oxford University Press, 2015.

Mansion, Auguste. "Le commentaire de saint Thomas sur le *De sensu et sensato* d'Aristote." In
　Mélanges Mandonnet, 1:83–102. Paris: Vrin, 1930.
———. "La théorie aristotélicienne du temps chez les péripatéticiens médiévaux. Averroès - Albert le
　Grand - Thomas d'Aquin." *Revue néoscolastique de philosophie* 41 (1934): 275–308.
———. *De jongste geschiedenis van de middeleeuwse Aristoteles-vertalingen aan eigen bevindingen getoetst.*
　Letteren en Schone Kunsten van België 3.2. Brussels: KVAB, 1941.
———. "Autour de la date du commentaire de saint Thomas sur L'Éthique à Nicomaque." *Revue
　philosophique de Louvain* (3rd series) 50, no. 27 (1952): 460–71.
———. "Review of J. Isaac, 'Le Peri Hermeneias en Occident de Boèce à saint Thomas.' Paris: Vrin,
　1953." *Revue philosophique de Louvain* (3rd series) 51, no. 30 (1953): 315–19.
Marabelli, Constante. "Note preliminari allo studio del commentario di San Tommaso al 'Secondi
　Analitici' di Aristotele." *Divus Thomas* 88 (1985): 77–88.
Marenbon, John. *Le temps, l'éternité et la prescience de Boèce à Thomas d'Aquin.* Paris: Vrin, 2005.
Mayhew, Robert. "Aristotle on Prayer." *Rhizai* 4 (2007): 295–309.
McInerny, Ralph. *The Question of Christian Ethics.* Washington, D.C.: The Catholic University of
　America Press, 1993.
———. *Praemabula Fidei: Thomism and the God of the Philosophers.* Washington, D.C.: The Catholic
　University of America Press, 2006.
Menn, Stephen. "Aristotle's Definition of Soul and the Programme of the *De Anima*." *Oxford Studies
　in Ancient Philosophy* 22 (2002): 83–139.
Merlan, Philip. *From Platonism to Neoplatonism.* The Hague: Martinus Nijhoff, 1953.
Miller, Fred D., Jr. "Aristotle on Natural Law and Justice." In *A Companion to Aristotle's "Politics,"* edit-
　ed by David Keyt and Fred D. Miller Jr., 280–304. Oxford: Blackwell, 1991.
Minio-Paluello, Lorenzo. "Die aristotelische Tradition in der Geistesgeschichte." In *Aristoteles
　in der neueren Forschung,* edited by Paul Moraux, 314–38. Darmstadt: Wissenschaftliche
　Buchgesellschaf, 1968.
Mora-Márquez, Ana María. "*Peri hermeneias* 16a3–8: Histoire d'une rupture de la tradition interpréta-
　tive dans le bas Moyen-Âge," *Revue Philosophique de la France et de l'Étranger* 136 (2011): 67–84.
Moraux, Paul. *Les listes anciennes des ouvrages d'Aristote.* Louvain: Éditions universitaires de Louvain,
　1951.
———. "Recherches sur le *De caelo* d'Aristote." *Revue Thomiste* 51 (1951): 113–36.
———. *Der Aristotelismus bei den Griechen, Von Andronikos bis Alexander von Aphrodisias.* 3 vols.
　Berlin: De Gruyter, 1973–2001.
———. "Le *De anima* dans la tradition grecque de Théophraste à Plotin." In *Aristotle on Mind and the
　Senses,* edited by Lloyd and Owen, 281–324.
———. *Le commentaire d'Alexandre d'Aphrodise aux 'Seconds analytiques' d'Aristote.* Edited by P.
　Moraux. Berlin: De Gruyter, 1979.
Motta, Beatrice. "Nemesius of Emesa." In *Cambridge History of Philosophy in Later Antiquity,* edited
　by Lloyd P. Gerson, 1:509–19. Cambridge: Cambridge University Press, 2010.
Müller, Jörn. *Natürliche Moral und philosophische Ethik bei Albertus Magnus.* Münster: Aschendorff,
　2001.
———. "*Duplex beatitudo*: Aristotle's Legacy and Aquinas's Conception of Human Happiness." In
　Aquinas and the "Nicomachean Ethics," edited by Hoffmann, Müller, and Perkams, 52–71.
———. "Aquinas's Commenting Strategy in His *Sententia libri Ethicorum*. A Case Study." *Divus
　Thomas* 118 (2015): 148–84.
Newman, W. L. *The Politics of Aristotle,* vol. 1: *Introduction to the "Politics."* Oxford: Clarendon, 1887.
Nussbaum, Martha C., and Amélie Oksenberg Rorty, eds. *Essays on Aristotle's "De Anima."* Oxford:
　Clarendon, 1992.
Nuyens, François. *L'évolution de la psychologie d'Aristote.* Leuven: Institute of Philosophy, 1948.
O'Donnell, J. R. "Themistius' Paraphrasis of the *Posterior Analytics* in Gerard of Cremona's
　Translation." *Medieval Studies* 20 (1958): 239–315.

Oehler, Klaus. "Der Consensus omnium als Kriterium der Wahrheit in der antiken Philosophie und der Patristik." *Antike und Abendland* 10 (1961): 103–29. Reprinted in Oehler, *Antike Philosophie und byzantisches Mittelalter: Aufsätze zur Geschichte des griechischen Denkens*, 234–71. Münich: Beck, 1969.

O'Leary, De Lacy. *How Greek Science Passed to the Arabs.* London: Routledge, 1957.

Ols, Daniels. *Ex amore Veritatis.* Florence: Edizioni Nerbini, 2015.

Olshewsky, Thomas. "Self-Moved Movers and Unmoved Movers in Aristotle's Physics VII." *The Classical Quarterly* 45, no. 2 (1995): 398–406.

———. "The Bastard Book of The Physics." *The Classical Quarterly* 64, no. 1 (2014): 58–74.

Owen, G. E. L., and G. E. R. Lloyd, eds. *Aristotle on Mind and the Senses: Proceedings of the Seventh Symposium Aristotelicum.* Cambridge: Cambridge University Press, 1978.

Owens, Joseph. "Aquinas as an Aristotelian Commentator." In *St. Thomas Aquinas on the Existence of God: Collected Papers of Joseph Owens, C.Ss.R.*, edited by J. R. Catan, 1–19. Albany: State University of New York Press, 1980.

———. *The Doctrine of Being in the "Metaphysics" of Aristotle.* Toronto: Pontifical Institute of Mediaeval Studies, 1951.

Pellegrin, Pierre. "The Argument for the Sphericity of the Universe in Aristotle's *De Caelo*: Astronomy and Physics." In *New Perspectives on Aristotle's "De Caelo,"* edited by Alan C. Bowen and Christian Wildberg, 163–86. Leiden: Brill, 2009.

Pelzer, August. "Les versions latines des ouvrages de morale conservés sous le nom d'Aristote, en usage au XIIIe siècle." *Revue néoscolastique de philosophie* 23 (1921): 316–41; 378–412.

Pépin, Jean. "Aristote, 'De la prière.'" *Revue Philosophique de la France et de l'Étranger* 157 (1967): 59–70.

Perkams, Matthias. "Aquinas on Choice, Will and Voluntary Action." In *Aquinas and the "Nicomachean Ethics,"* edited by Hoffmann, Müller, and Perkams, 72–90.

Peters, Francis E. *Aristotle and the Arabs: The Aristotelian Tradition in Islam.* New York: New York University Press, 1968.

Pieper, Josef. *Hinführung zu Thomas von Aquin.* Münich: Kösel, 1953.

Pinckaers, Servais. *Les sources de la morale chrétienne. Sa méthode, son contenu, son histoire.* Fribourg: Editions Universitaires, 1985. Translated by M. T. Noble as *The Sources of Christian Ethics.* Washington, D.C.: The Catholic University of America Press, 1995.

Quin, John F. *The Historical Constitution of St. Bonaventure's Philosophy.* Toronto: Pontifical Institute of Mediaeval Studies, 1973.

Ravitzky, Aviezer. "Aristotle's *Meteorology* and the Maimonidean Modes of Interpreting the Account of Creation." *Aleph: Historical Studies in Science and Judaism* 8 (2008): 361–400. Originally published in Hebrew in *Jerusalem Studies in Jewish Thought* 9 (1990): 225–50.

Reale, Giovanni. *The Concept of First Philosophy and the Unity of the Metaphysics of Aristotle.* Edited and translated by John R. Catan. Albany: State University of New York Press, 1980. Originally published as *Il Concetto di Filosofia Prima e l'Unità della Metafisica di Aristotele.* Third edition. Milan: Vita e Pensiero, 1967.

Reilly, James P., Jr. "The 'alia littera' in Thomas Aquinas's *Sententia libri metaphysiciae*." *Medieval Studies* 50 (1998): 559–83.

Richardson, Hilda. "The Myth of Er (Plato, *Republic*, 616b)." *Classical Quarterly* 20, no. 3–4 (1926): 113–33.

Rosenthal, Franz. *Das Fortleben der Antike im Islam.* Zürich: Artemis, 1965.

Ross, William D. *Aristotle's "Parva Naturalia."* Oxford: Clarendon, 1955.

———. *Aristotle.* London: Methuen, 1923.

Rowe, C. J. "Aims and Methods in Aristotle's Politics." *Classical Quarterly* 27, no. 1 (1977): 159–72. Reprinted in *A Companion to Aristotle's "Politics,"* edited by David Keyt and Fred D. Miller Jr., 57–74. Oxford: Blackwell, 1991.

Sandback, F. H. "Phantasia Kataleptike." In *Problems in Stoicism*, edited by A. A. Long, 9–21. London: Athlone, 1971.

Schneider, Jakob Hans Josef. "Physik und Natur im Kommentar des Thomas von Aquin zur aristotelischen Ethik." In *Mensch und Natur im Mittelalter*, edited by Albert Zimmermann and Andreas Speer, 161–92. Berlin: De Gruyter, 1991.

Schönberger, Rolf. "Die aristotelische Politik in der Philosophie des Thomas van Aquin." In *Die Politik des Aristoteles*, edited by Barbara Zehnpfennig, 195–212. Baden-Baden: Nomos, 2012.

———. "Aristoteleskommentare." In *Thomas Handbuch*, edited by Volker Leppin, 216–38. Tübingen: Mohr Siebeck, 2016.

Schwegler, Albert. *Die Metaphysik des Aristoteles*. Vols. 1–3. Tübingen: Fues, 1847.

Seeck, G. A. Über *die Elemente in der Kosmologie des Aristoteles*. Münich: Beck, 1964.

Seidl, Horst. "Über die Erkenntnis erster, allgemeiner Prinzipien nach Thomas von Aquin." In *Thomas von Aquin. Werk und Wirkung im Licht neuerer Forschungen*, edited by A. Zimmermann, 103–16. Berlin: De Gruyter, 1988.

Shellens, Max Salomon. "Aristotle on Natural Law." *Natural Law Forum* 40 (1959): 72–100.

Sherwin, Michael S., and Craig Steven Titus, eds. *Renouveler toutes choses en Christ: vers un renouveau thomiste de la théologie morale: hommage à Servais Pinckaers*. Fribourg: Academic Press Fribourg, 2009.

Shiel, James. "Boethius' Commentaries on Aristotle." *Medieval and Renaissance Studies* 4 (1958): 217–44. Reprinted in *Aristotle Transformed: The Ancient Commentators and Their Influence*, edited by Richard Sorabji, 349–72. Ithaca, N.Y.: Cornell University Press, 1990.

Simpson, Peter L. *A Philosophical Commentary on the Politics of Aristotle*. Chapel Hill: The University of North Carolina Press, 1998.

Smet, A. J. "Alexander Van Aphrodisias en S. Thomas van Aquino: Bijdrage tot de bronnenstudie van de commentaar van S. Thomas op de meteorologica van Aristoteles." *Tijdschrift voor Filosofie* 21, no. 1 (1959): 108–41.

Smith, Robin. "The Relationship of Aristotle's Two Analytics." *Classical Quarterly* 32, no. 2 (1982): 327–35.

Solmsen, Friedrich. *Die Entwicklung der aristotelischen Logik und Rhetorik*. Berlin: Weidmann, 1929.

———. "Aristotle's Syllogism and Its Platonic Background." *Philosophical Review* 60, no. 4 (1951): 563–71.

———. *Aristotle's System of the Physical World: A Comparison with His Predecessors*. Ithaca, N.Y.: Cornell University Press, 1960.

Sorabji, Richard. *Matter, Space and Motion*. London: Duckworth, 1988.

———, ed. *Aristotle Transformed: The Ancient Commentaries and Their Influence*. London: Duckworth, 1990.

———. "Aristotle, Mathematics, and Colour." *Classical Quarterly* 22, no. 2 (1972): 293–308.

Souchard, Bertrand. "Le commentaire de Thomas d'Aquin du *De generatione et corruptione* d'Aristote: de la critique aristotélicienne des matérialistes à la critique thomasienne des spiritualists." In *Lire Aristote au Moyen Âge et à la Renaissance: Réception du traité sur la Génération et la Corruption*, edited by Joëlle Ducos and Violaine Giacomotto-Charra, 55–83. Paris: Champion, 2011.

Stark, Rudolf. "Der Gesamtaufbau der aristotelischen Politik." In *La Politique d'Aristote*, edited by Fondation Hardt pour l'Étude de l'Antiquité Classique, 3–35. Geneva: Fondation Hardt, 1961.

Stengel, Bernhard. *Der Kommentar des Thomas von Aquin zur "Politik" des Aristoteles*. Marburg: Tektum Verlag, 2011.

Taylor, A. E. *Plato: The Man and His Work*. London: Methuen, 1952.

Taylor, R. C. "Separate Material Intellect in Averroes' Mature Philosophy." In *Words, Texts and Concepts Cruising the Mediterranean Sea: Studies on the Sources, Contents and Influences of Islamic Civilization and Arabic Philosophy and Science*, edited by Ruediger Arnzen and Joern Thielmann, 289–309. Leuven: Peeters, 2004.

Theiler, Willy. "Bau und Zeit der aristotelischen Politik." *Museum Helveticum: Schweizerische Zeitschrift für klassische Altertumswissenschaft* 9, no. 2 (1952): 65–73.

Thijssen, Johannes. "An Introductory Survey." *The Commentary Tradition on Aristotle's "De*

Generatione et Corruptione": *Ancient, Medieval and Early Modern*, edited by Johannes Thijssen and Henk Braakhuis, 9–20. Turnhout: Brepols, 1999.

Torrell, Jean-Pierre. *Initiation à* Saint Thomas d'Aquin. Sa personne et son œuvre. Paris: Cerf, 2015. Translated by Matthew K. Minerd and Robert Royal as *Thomas Aquinas: His Person and Work*. Third edition. Washington, D.C.: The Catholic University of America Press, 2022.

Van Steenberghen, Fernand. *Aristotle in the West: The Origins of Latin Aristotelianism*. Leuven: Nauwelaerts, 1970.

———. *La philosophie au XIIIe siècle. Deuxième édition, mise à jour*. Louvain: Peeters, 1991.

Vansteenkiste, Clemente. "San Tommaso d'Aquino ed Averroe." *Rivista degli Studi Orientali* 32 (1957): 585–623.

Verbeke, Gerard. *Themistius: Commentaire sur le traité de l'âme d'Aristote. Traduction de Guillaume de Moerbeke*. Leuven: University of Leuven Press, 1957.

———. "Een onvoltooide commentaar van Thomas van Aquino (Peri hermeneias)." In *Mededelingen van de Koninklijke Vlaamse Academie van Wetenschappen van België, Klasse der Letteren* 22, no. 8. Brussels: Paleis der Academiën, 1960.

———. "Arts libéraux et morale d'après Saint Thomas." In *Arts libéraux et philosophie au Moyen Âge*, 653–61. Paris: Vrin, 1969.

———. "L'argument du livre VII de la Physique. Une impasse philosophique." In *Naturphilosophie bei Aristoteles und Theophrast. Verhandlungen des 4. Symposium Aristotelicum veranstaltet in Göteborg, August 1966*, edited by I. Düring, 250–67. Heidelberg: Stiehm, 1969. Reprinted in Verbeke, *D'Aristote à Thomas d'Aquin. Antécédents de la pensée moderne*, 148–65. Recueil d'articles. Leuven: Leuven University Press, 1990.

———. "Aristotle's *Metaphysics* viewed by the Ancient Greek Commentators." In *Studies in Aristotle*, edited by Dominic J. O'Meara, 107–28. Washington, D.C.: The Catholic University of America Press, 1981.

———. "Saint Thomas et les commentaires grecs sur la Physique d'Aristote." In *La philosophie de la nature de Saint Thomas d'Aquin*, edited by Leo Elders, 134–54. Vatican City: Libreria Editrice Vaticana, 1982.

Viano, Cristina. *La matière des choses: Le livre IV des* Météorologiques *d'Aristote et son interprétation par Olympiodore*. Paris: Vrin, 2006.

Wardy, Robert. *The Chain of Change: A Study of Aristotle's "Physics" VII*. Cambridge: Cambridge University Press, 1990.

Weisheipl, James A. "The Commentary of St. Thomas on the *De caelo* of Aristotle." *Sapientia* 29 (1974): 11–34.

———. "Albert's Disclaimers in the Aristotelian Paraphrases." *Proceedings of the PMR Conference* 5 (1980): 1–27.

Welchman, Jennifer. "The Fall and Rise of Aristotelian Ethics in Anglo-American Moral Philosophy." In *The Reception of Aristotle's Ethics*, edited by Jörn Müller, 262–88. Cambridge: Cambridge University Press, 2012.

Whitaker, C. *Aristotle's "De interpretation": Contradiction and Dialectic*. Oxford: Clarendon Press, 1996.

White, Kevin. "St. Thomas Aquinas and the Prologue to Peter of Auvergne's *Quaestiones super De sensu et sensato*." *Documenti e studi sulla tradizione filosofica medievale* 1 (1990): 427–56.

———. "Three Previously Unpublished Chapters from St. Thomas Aquinas's Commentary on Aristotle's *Meteora: Sentencia super Meteora* 2.13–15." *Mediaeval Studies* 54 (1992): 49–93.

———. "St. Thomas Aquinas on Prologues." *Archivum franciscanum historicum* 98 (2005): 803–13.

———. "Pleasure, a Supervenient End." In *Aquinas and the "Nicomachean Ethics,"* edited by T. Hoffman, J. Müller, and M. Perkams, 220–38. Cambridge: Cambridge University Press, 2013.

Wieland, Georg. *Ethica – Scientia practica. Die Anfänge der philosophischen Ethik im 13. Jahrhunderts*. Münster: Aschendorff, 1981.

Wielockx, Robert. "Thomas d'Aquin, commentateur du *De sensu*." *Scriptorium* 41, no. 1 (1987): 150–57.

Wilder, Alfred. "St. Albert and St. Thomas on Aristotle's *De interpretatione*: A Comparative Study." *Angelicum* 57, no. 4 (1980): 496–532.

Williams, Bernard. "Aristotle on the Good: A Formal Sketch." *The Philosophical Quarterly* 12 (October 1962): 289–96.

Wilson, Malcom. *Structure and Method in Aristotle's "Meteorologica": A More Disorderly Nature.* Cambridge: Cambridge University Press, 2013.

Wippel, John F. "Thomas Aquinas' Commentary on Aristotle's Metaphysics." In *Uses and Abuses of the Classics: Commentaries on Classical Philosophical Texts*, edited by Jorge Gracia and Jiyuan Yu, 138–64. Aldershot: Ashgate, 2004.

———. "The Latin Avicenna as a Source for Thomas Aquinas's Metaphysics." *Freiburger Zeitschrift für Philosophie und Theologie* 37 (1990): 51–90. Reprinted in *Metaphysical Themes in Thomas Aquinas II*. Washington, D.C.: The Catholic University of America Press, 2007.

Wohlman, Avital. "L'élaboration des éléments aristotéliciens dans la doctrine thomiste de l'amour." *Revue Thomiste* 82 (1982): 247–69.

Zimmermann, A. "'Ipsum enim ("est") nihil est' (Aristoteles, *Periherm.* I, c.3). Thomas von Aquin über die Bedeutung der Kopula." In *Der Begriff der Repraesentatio im Mittelalter*, ed. A. Zimmermann, 282–95. Berlin: De Gruyter, 1971.

INDEX NOMINUM

Ancient and Medieval Authors
(Aristotle and Aquinas are not listed)

Albertus the Great, 5, 9–10, 12, 16, 15, 52,
61–2, 88, 98n71, 158, 191, 203–4, 207–8, 232,
237n17, 238n20, 243, 255n47, 258n49, 280,
303, 314, 327n40, 404–05, 424, 434n73, 467,
475

Alexander of Aphrodisias, 14–15, 18, 30–31, 33, 35,
40n57, 46, 61, 87, 89, 117, 126, 147, 157, 159–60,
166, 169, 171, 173–77, 186–87, 190, 193, 201, 207,
235, 280, 284–85, 290–92, 300–301, 312, 314,
325, 386, 392n88

Al-Farabi, 15

Al-Kindi, 158

Ammonius, 14–57, 61

Anaxagoras, 93, 96, 100–101, 108, 111, 113, 119, 136,
138, 141, 153, 180, 183–84, 195, 203, 209–10, 212,
215–16, 222, 230, 240–41, 265, 280, 291, 340–42,
382–83, 388, 398, 469

Anaximander, 111, 153, 182

Anaximenes, 180, 182, 210, 230

Andronicus, 14, 18, 191, 311, 412

Apuleius, 39, 348

Aristarchus, 172

Aspasius, 15, 18, 31, 87, 313, 403–4

Atticus, 234–35

Augustine, 1, 5, 46n64, 49–50, 304, 348n55, 439,
500n34

Avempace, 117

Averroes, 1, 3–5, 12, 15, 18, 49, 62, 87–89, 94–95,
99–100, 115, 118, 120, 124–29, 131–38, 142,
145–49, 158, 161, 171, 173, 175–77, 184, 190, 201,
236–37, 243, 250n44, 252n45, 254–55, 259–60,
265–68, 276n63, 280–81, 303, 312, 314–16,
326–28, 361–62, 387, 392n88, 393n91, 394n94,
403–404, 468

Avicenna, 12, 71n17, 91, 103–04, 106, 117, 132, 145,
158, 173, 235, 237, 255, 266, 269, 273, 303–5, 314,
315n19, 337, 345, 348, 353, 362, 376, 393–94,
404, 468

Boethius, 15–19, 22–25, 27n40n, 28, 30–35, 40n57,
45n60, 46–47, 50, 53–54, 56–57, 332

Bonaventure, 4–5, 434, 438

Calippus, 155, 176, 187, 395

Cicero, 49, 156, 304, 422, 423n58, 425, 437, 443

Democritus, 101, 106, 119, 130, 136, 153, 164,
166, 167, 180, 183, 192, 195, 196, 209–10,
215–16, 230, 240–43, 280, 285–86, 290–93,
301, 367

Diodorus Cronos, 47

Diogenes, 222, 241, 376

Empedocles, 100–101, 108, 136, 138, 153, 156,
166–67, 179–80, 185, 191–93, 195, 222, 225,
241–41, 244, 253, 255, 263, 265, 270, 273,
284–86, 290–91, 301, 324, 330, 332–33, 342, 376
398, 454, 505n38

Epicurus, 46, 166n38

Étienne Tempier, 20, 51n82, 355n61

Gerard of Cremona, 61, 158, 193, 207, 235, 315

Gilles of Rome, 62, 88

Gorgias, 297, 488

Heraclides of Pontus, 154, 172, 179

Heraclitus, 99, 130, 139, 166, 182, 241, 294, 342,
344, 382–83, 454

Herminus, 15, 18

Hesiod, 115, 182, 222, 332

Hipparchus, 176

Hippocrates, 209, 215

Hippodamus, 498–99, 504, 509

Homer, 222, 263

Iamblichus, 15, 157

James of Venice, 3, 61, 79, 87, 89, 236, 315
John Damascene, 15, 403

Leucippus, 183, 192, 195–96, 356
Lycurgus, 502, 504

Maimonides, 289
Martin of Dacia, 17
Melissus, 90, 96, 99, 119, 181, 398
Michael Scotus, 87, 158, 236, 314–15

Nemesius, 244n34, 403

Olympiodorus, 15, 206

Parmenides, 13, 96, 99–102, 153, 181, 198, 324, 333, 342, 398
Peter Abelard, 16, 50
Peter of Auvergne, 159, 281, 475
Peter of Ireland, 16, 54n90
Peter of Saint-Amour, 16–17
Peter of Spain, 34, 50
Philoponus, 15, 31, 61, 85, 87, 89, 162–63, 170, 188, 190, 193, 206, 235
Plato, 2, 5, 8, 12, 14, 24, 27, 35–39, 42, 61, 64–67, 71, 77n21, 91, 94–95, 98, 100, 102–4, 111, 114, 116, 132, 134–5, 137–38, 141, 153–57, 160–61, 166, 168–69, 176, 182–83, 188–90, 196, 205, 223–24, 234, 240–41, 243–45, 254, 264–65, 269–273, 276, 284–87, 296, 301, 308, 313, 322, 324–25, 331–34, 339, 341, 352n59, 353n60, 356–57, 367, 373–74, 379, 388–90, 394, 398, 402, 411–12, 445n90, 464–65, 468, 479n15, 488n21, 490, 494, 496–97, 499n32, 504–505, 509
Porphyry, 15, 30, 34, 40, 56, 85, 235
Posidonius, 234
Protagoras, 340–41, 370, 376, 382, 402n4
Ptolemy, 394

Robert Grosseteste, 4–5, 61–62, 404–405, 424, 434

Robert Kilwardby, 16, 20
Roger Bacon, 3n8, 314
Robert of Vulgarbia, 17

Seneca, 422
Siger of Brabant, 88
Simonides, 468
Simplicius, 85, 87, 89, 126, 154n13, 155n18, 157n25, 158–62, 169, 171, 173–74, 177–78, 182, 186, 188–90, 193, 235, 313, 393n91
Socrates, 29, 34, 38–39, 42, 53, 55, 63, 267, 355, 363–64, 374, 402n4, 439, 449, 490–96
Solon, 416–17, 469, 496, 504
Sophocles, 488
Speusippus, 356, 393n91, 399n99, 453
Stephen of Alexandria, 15
Syrianus, 18, 314

Thales of Milete, 153, 179, 182, 241, 246, 487
Themistius, 61, 83, 87, 89, 118, 158, 173, 235, 237, 243n32, 244n35, 252n45, 276n63, 314, 387n84, 392n88
Theodoctes, 482
Theophrastus, 14, 23n34, 234, 311
Thomas de Vio Cajetan, 17
Thomas of Sutton, 17

Virgil, 304

William Arnaldo, 16
William of Auvergne, 4
William of Moerbeke, 15–20, 46, 56–57, 61, 79n23, 87, 89, 126n77, 158, 194, 207–8, 235–37, 280, 301–2, 315–16, 347, 349n56, 392n88, 399n100, 405n17, 474–75
William of Tocco, 475, 315n20

Xenarchus, 234
Xenocrates, 166, 245

Zeno, 47, 93, 116, 127–130, 135, 143, 333, 505n38

Modern Authors

Ackrill, J. L., 15n4, 248n40
Adam, J., 154n9
Adams, D., 461n103
Adamson, P., 158n19
Akasoy, A., 403–404n11
Amerini, F., 58
Anagnostopoulos, G., 86n4, 313n11
Ando, T., 408n35

Anscombe, G. E. M., 59n2, 401
Ashley, B., 88n13

Bäck, A., 52n34, 56n95
Badawi, A., 158n29
Baghdassarian, F., 157n22, 396n97
Balaudé, J.-F., 442n88
Barnes, J., 23n34, 59n2, 60n5, 80, 85n1, 312n4

Bataillon, L. J., 208
Bayer, G., 60n4
Bazan, B., 4n14, 247n37
Berquist, R., 66
Bertolacci, Amos, 314n18
Biard, Joël, 204n11
Bicknell, P. J., 130n79
Black, Deborah, 15n6,
Bloch, David, 61n11, 302n3, 303n5
Blumenthal, Henry J., 235n9
Bobonich, Chris, 402n3
Bochenski, J. M., 15
Borgo, Marta, 7n27, 315n20, 361n67
Bossier, Fernand, 159n34
Bourke Vernon, J., 405n19, 409n40, 410n42
Braakhuis, Henk, 16n9
Brams, J., 87, 405
Bronstein, David, 60n5
Burns, Tony, 442n88
Burnyeat, Myles, 60

Carroy, Bertrand, 203–4
Cassin, Barbara, 335n44
Celluprica, Vincenza, 52, 84
Cerami, Cristina, 158n30
Cheneval, Francis, 6, 85, 475n9
Chenu, Marie-Dominique, 10
Chroust, Anton-Hermann, 234n2, 311n3
Cochrane, Charles N., 403n9
Coda, Elisa, 244n35
Cohen, S. M., 206n4
Cooper, John, 449n94
Cornford, Francis, 153n8, 154n10
Cos, Joseph, 316n21
Costa, Iacopo, 405n20
Craig, William L., 52, 84

Darwin, Charles, 108n76
de Couesnongle, Vincent, 137n88
Dedek, John F., 424n62
De Haas, Frans, 192n3
Del Punta, Francesco, 6, 10, 11n31, 87n7
Doig, James C., 319, 327n40, 405n19, 406n22, 417, 449n96, 467, 468n106
Donati, Silvia, 87n7
Dondaine, Antoine, 208
Ducoin, Georges, 356n62, 387n83, 394n94
Duhem, Pierre, 187n53
Duke, George, 442n88
Dunbabin, Jean, 475n10
Düring, Ingemar, 157n23, 205n2, 234n4, 311n2

Elders, Leo J., vii, 2n1, 4n13, 12n12, 148n93, 157n22, 159n36, 185n44, 248n38, 335n45, 386n81, 406n23, 407n29, 408n23, 410n42
Ellspermann, Gerard, 403n9

Fazzo, Silvia, 312n7, 386n78
Ferejohn, Michael T., 60n6
Fernández Garrido, Maria R., 17n14
Festugière, André-Jean, 281n9, 387n83
Flannery, Kevin, 439n84
Flüeler, Christoph, 475n6
Fontaine, Resiane, 207n8
Frede, Dorothea, 52n84
Frede, Michael, 338n52, 386n79
Freudenthal, Jacob, 314n14

Galle, Griet, 159n35
Galluzzo, Gabriele, 314, 315n20, 318n27, 319, 366n71, 387n83
García Cuadrado, José A., 29n42
Gauthier, René A., 16–18, 24n35, 25, 33n52, 38n55, 43, 45n60, 46n64, 49n73, 50n80, 51n82, 53, 54n90, 55n93, 58, 62, 79n23, 83n26, 88n9, 89, 236–37, 247, 252n45, 254n46, 255n47, 258n49, 259n51, 280, 281n7, 289n15, 316, 403–406, 417n52, 418n54, 420n56, 422n57, 424n59, 425n65, 427, 431n69, 434n74, 435, 437, 440n86, 453n99
Gigon, Olof, 479n15
Gilson, E., 11, 88, 319, 410,
Gomez Nogales, Salvador, 4n14
Grabmann, Martin, 207
Grant, Edward, 3n6
Guthrie, William K. C., 153n3, 156n19

Hardie, William F. R., 411n43, 414n46
Hause, Jeffrey, 444n89
Heath, Thomas, 153n4
Hellmeier, Paul D., 237n17, 246n36
Herzberg, Stephan, 60n60
Hissette, Roland, 394, 416, 418, 420, 449
Hoffmann, Tobias, 406n22, 448n92
Horn, Christoph, 386n78
Hossfeld, Paul, 207n7
Humbrecht, Thierry-Dominique, 88n12

Ierodiakonou, Katerina, 290n17
Imbach, Ruedi, 6n22, 85n1, 387n83
Irwin, Terence, 60n4, 414n46
Isaac, Jean, 9n29, 15n7, 16, 19, 21n27

Jaeger, Werner, 86, 313, 351, 380n76, 386, 401, 402n3, 474
Jaffa, Harry V., 6, 406n23, 442n88
Jenkins, J., 7n26
Joachim, H. H., 408n35
Jolif, Jean-Yves, 403n7, 404n13, 406n24, 417n52, 422n57, 425n65, 434n74, 437n81, 440n86, 453n99
Jordan, Mark D., 6, 11
Judycka, Joanna, 194

Kaczor, Christopher, 6n21, 10–11
Kahn, Charles, 60, 474n2
Kenny, Anthony, 414
Kerferd, George B., 195n8
Kirk, Geoffrey S., 153n5, 193n5
Krämer, Hans J., 393n91
Knuuttila, Simo, 52n84

Lewry, Osmund, 17n15
Liebard, Jacques, 403n9
Lohr, Charles, 88n10
Lottin, Odo, 410n42

MacIntyre, Alasdair, 401
Mansfeld, Jaap, 297n21
Mansini, Guy, 457n100
Mansion, August, 89n14, 280, 338n52, 405n18
Marabelli, Constante, 62n13
Marenbon, John, 16n8, 52n84
Maritain, Jacques, 410n42
Mayhew, Robert, 440n86
McInerny, Ralph., 386n81, 410n42
Menn, Stephen, 279n2
Merlan, Philip, 338n52
Miller, Fred D., 442n88
Mora-Márquez, Ana M., 25n38
Moraux, Paul, 61n8, 157n24, 191n1, 234n6, 235, 311n2, 312n4, 403n7
Motta, Beatrice, 403n10
Müller, Jorn, 404n13, 405, 406n21, 419n55

Newman, John H., 3n7
Newman, William L., 474
Nuyens, François, 233n1, 279n1, 313, 412n44

O'Donnell, J. R., 6n9
Oehler, Klaus, 465n104
O'Leary, De Lacy, 2n5
Ols, Daniel, 449n94

Olshewsky, Thomas, 131
Owens, Josep, 6, 11, 319, 328n42, 336n47

Pépin, Jean, 440n86
Perkams, Mattias, 427n67
Peters, Francis E., 2n5
Pieper, Josef, 88
Pinckaers, Servais, 401n2

Quin, John F., 4n13

Ramirez, Santiago, 410n42
Raven, J. E., 153n5, 195n8
Ravitzky, Aviezir, 207n8
Reale, Giovanni, 313n8, 325n35, 328n42, 338n52, 341n53, 380n76, 386, 387n82
Reilly, James P., 316, 347n54
Richardson, Hilda., 153n7
Rosenthal, Franz, 2n5
Ross, William D., 59, 80, 86, 126, 130–31, 133, 156, 239, 241, 279, 285, 302, 306, 313, 322, 328, 352, 361, 380, 386, 473n1
Rowe, Christopher J., 474

Sandback, F. H., 300n22
Schneider, Jakob H. J., 105n75
Schönberger, Rolf, 6, 475n6
Seeck, G. A., 157n27
Schwegler, Albert, 338n52
Seidl, Horst, 82n25, 313n8, 328n42
Shellens, Max S., 442n88
Shiel, James, 18n19
Simpson, Peter, 474n2
Smet, A. J., 207
Smith, Robin, 59n1
Solmsen, Friedrich, 59n1, 157n27
Sorabji, Richard., 170n40, 289n16
Souchard, Bertrand, 203
Spiazzi, R., 21
Stark, Rudolf, 474n3
Stengel, Bernhard, 509n39

Taylor, A. E., 77
Taylor, Richard C., 2n5, 236n12
Theiler, Willy, 496n29
Thijssen, Johannes, 191n2, 193n3
Torrell, Jean-Pierre, 208, 315n20
Trifogli, C., 87n7

Van Steenberghen, F., 2n5, 4n12
Vansteenkiste, Clemens, 12n35

Verbeke, Gerard, 16, 18–19, 30, 48n72, 57, 87n6, 89n15, 131, 235–37, 313n12, 407n28
Viano, Cristina, 205n1

Wardy, Robert, 131
Weidemann, Hermann, 15n4, 53n89
Weisheipl, James A., 11, 88n13, 185n44, 319
Welchman, Jennifer, 401n1
Whitaker, C., 52n84
White, Kevin, 21n28, 207n11, 208, 230n29, 232, 238n24, 281n9, 293n19, 303n7, 452n98

Wieland, Georg, 404n14
Wielockx, Robert, 280n3
Wilder, Alfred, 16n12
Williams, Bernard, 414n46
Wilson, Malcolm, 206, 222n23
Wippel, John F., 315n19, 319, 337n51, 353n60, 392n88, 394n93
Wohlman, Avital, 457n102, 471

Zimmermann, Albert, 31n45

INDEX RERUM

abstraction, 73, 83, 93, 97, 104, 134, 254, 267, 296, 325–26, 330, 355

academy, 8, 77, 86, 154, 245, 313, 356, 407, 412, 482

accidental being, 347, 353, 384

accident(s), 67, 71, 76, 78, 99–102, 111–12, 174, 203, 321, 329, 336, 345, 348, 355–58, 369, 385, 387, 389–90

act and potency, 8, 312, 319, 321, 348–349, 369–74, 384–85, 389, 416

action(s), 27–9, 49, 51, 63, 72, 75, 101, 106–7, 110, 133, 138, 145, 174, 177, 186–187, 192–3, 233, 252, 255, 261–62, 274–75, 297, 370, 384; human actions, 405, 407–67–; involuntary action, 402, 424–32; voluntary action, 424–32

actuality, 30–31, 55, 248, 252, 266, 296, 318, 325, 365, 371, 374, 392

addition, 28–31

alteration, 92, 132–35, 143, 162–63, 191–204, 242, 253, 298, 367

amiability, 438

amusement, 439, 451, 467

analogy, 8, 347, 412

anger, 282, 309, 426–27, 430, 438, 444, 451

aporiae, 312, 328–29

appetite: concupiscible, 273–75, 283, 391, 421, 479; irascible, 273–85, 283, 421, 431, 479

aristocracy, 458, 482

Aristotelianism, 4, 5, 7, 188

authority, 138, 148, 458, 479–80, 482, 487–88, 502, 507

atomists, 110, 153, 183, 324

augmentation, 92, 132, 192, 200–202

being *qua* being, 8, 137, 319, 321, 336, 338, 344, 352–53, 400

being and unity, 333–34, 337–39, 376–77

beneficence, 461–62

brain, 235, 257, 287, 288, 291, 294–95, 309

brave man, 429–30

causality, principle of, 327

cause: divine, 354, 415–16, 419; efficient, 66–67, 105, 109–10, 132, 227, 324, 327, 345–6, 399; final, 67, 72, 79, 105–9, 115, 167, 157, 189, 206, 252, 323–25, 327, 345, 380, 389, 399, 447; formal, 79, 324, 327, 329, 331, 345, 426; material, 67, 78–79, 324, 345–46, 368

celestial bodies, 47, 49, 57, 92, 94, 104, 106, 110, 120, 122, 132, 139, 146, 153–57, 161, 168–78, 186–89, 213–14, 241, 256, 263, 276, 326–27, 351, 354, 356, 368, 388–89, 391, 395, 398, 400

certitude, 22, 45, 50, 63, 73, 83, 92, 231, 264, 320, 408, 427, 445

chance, 44, 48–49, 52, 58, 73, 86, 106–8, 148, 164, 172, 384, 398, 416, 427

change, 127–31, 137–38

children, 134, 306, 416, 432, 457–61, 464, 488–98, 504–5, 508

choice, 48–52, 426–28, 442–52

Christian faith, ix, 6, 10, 13, 137–38, 149–50, 170, 188–89, 236, 353, 400, 456, 471, 500

circumstances, 425–28

cogitativa, 255, 270

comets, 209, 215–17

concept, 24–25

concupiscence, 69, 275, 411, 414, 418, 439, 450, 485, 497

contemplation, 8, 410, 419, 453–54, 468–69, 471

continence, 448–52

contingency, 47–52, 57–8, 354

contradiction, principle of, 33, 41, 52, 68, 96, 341, 382

contrariety, modes of, 125–26, 377–78

copula, 55, 99

corruption, 111, 114, 123–28, 142–44, 168–77, 191–204, 217, 223, 332–33, 367–70

counsel, 427–28, 446

courage, 488, 502

cowardice, 432

533

creation, 1–2, 4, 7, 123, 136–38, 147, 149, 161, 167, 170, 188, 207, 289, 400

dator formarum, 71, 269
death, 234, 237–38, 416–18, 429–31, 471
definition, 26–34, 36, 59–60, 65–71, 76–81
demonstration, 62–75
division, method of, 77, 81

earth, 153–55, 178–81, 219–20; counter-earth, 179
earthquake, 210, 230–31
education, 277, 402, 428, 464, 470, 473, 483, 494, 498
elements, 80, 93, 97–98, 104, 112–13, 117–19, 132, 149, 153–54, 156–160, 164–65, 167–73, 179–80, 183–86, 189, 191–98, 206, 208, 210–14, 240–46, 259, 284–87, 292, 346, 376, 385, 389
ens commune, 320, 380
ephors, 502
eternity: of movement, 97, 142, 169, 197; of the world, 139, 159, 185–88, 197, 221, 224, 231, 396, 400, 500
equity, 404
evil, 373, 422, 425–26, 428–29, 439
exhalation, 209–18, 221, 225–31

fear, 430–1
fifth element, 117, 155–56, 208, 210, 212, 385
first mover, 8, 10, 87, 90, 92–95, 132, 139–42, 145–47, 156–57, 165, 168, 178, 181, 183, 186, 391–93, 396–400
first philosophy, 105–7, 319–22, 326, 329–30, 336–39, 352–55, 383, 387–88
first principles, 8, 51, 60, 65, 68, 72–75, 79, 82, 84, 90, 101, 194, 253, 264, 275, 318–19, 321, 325–26, 339, 345, 355, 382–83, 387, 395, 398–99, 407, 421, 446–48, 471
form, 91, 102–4, 107–9, 356–64, 367
fortitude, 429–31
fortune, 106–7, 359, 411, 417–18, 436
friendship, 454–464
future, 20, 24, 43–47, 50, 121–23

generation, 104–7, 114, 123–31, 142–43, 181–85, 191–204, 359–62
God, 2, 10, 26, 46, 49–51, 78–79, 84, 93, 124, 137–39, 148–49, 151, 158, 161–63, 165–68, 174, 177, 187–89, 193, 203, 235, 265, 268, 320–22, 325, 328, 332, 334, 353–54, 384, 387, 392–93, 395–97, 400, 409–10, 412–16, 419, 435, 440, 442, 445, 456, 460, 461, 469, 471, 478, 483, 500; as cause, 49, 79, 148–49, 161, 168, 203, 354, 445; eternity of, 138; friendship with, 456–58; intellect of, 25, 50, 265, 396–9; –goodness of God, 162, 177–78; will of, 50, 392
Good, Idea of, 412–13
growth, 199–202

habit, 75, 269, 421–22, 429
hail, 218–19
happiness, 8, 78, 107, 320, 328, 373, 401–3, 408–419, 448, 452–53, 467–69, 471, 494
heaven, first, 94–95, 113, 117–18, 123, 126, 136, 138, 142, 145, 147–49, 153–55, 158, 160, 163, 174–75, 187, 260, 276, 375, 391–93, 400
honor, 435–36
hope, 430–31
humility, 4, 435

ignorance, 70, 425–26
illiberality, 433–34
imagination, 250–51, 262–64, 266, 269, 273–75, 277, 305–6, 310
incontinence, 449–52
individuation, 360
induction, 12, 60, 95–96, 414–15, 471
infinite, the, 91, 93, 110–15, 126–27, 129–30, 163, 193, 244, 371, 384–85
instruction, 470
intellect: agent, 4, 84, 134, 253, 265–66, 268–69, 277, 389, 392; divine, 26, 49, 409, 475; passive, 242, 268–69, 305; possible, *see* passive; practical, 25, 272, 274, 305, 407, 445, 447, 471, 476; speculative, 25, 305, 407–8
intuition, 409

judgment, 63–4, 262–63, 355
justice, 440–44; domestic, 447; and friendship, 457; legal, 447; natural, 482

knowledge, 8, 24, 50, 59–61, 64–65, 71–75, 82–84, 239, 253–54, 263–65, 272, 276, 320, 336, 408

law, 439, 440, 442–44, 470, 482; divine law, 328; natural, 275, 410, 439, 442
leisure, 468
liberality, 432–33
light, 255–56
love: as friendship, 457, 459; as mutual love, 456; as principle, 69, 240, 244–45, 324, 332, 398; of self, 462

magnanimity, 4, 435–38

magnificence, 4, 434

man: as political animal, 459, 478; as rational animal, 442–43; as social animal, 463, 473, 507

mathematical entities, 155–56, 241, 330, 334, 356

mathematics, 70, 79, 97, 104, 156, 160, 350, 352, 369, 380, 382

matter, 91, 102–4, 356–64, 367

mean, 421–23, 441

medium, 120, 147, 256–60, 286, 297–98

meekness, 438

memory, 83, 282–83, 302–10

metaphysics: *cuius subiectum est ens*, 321, 336; subject of, 319–23; as theology, 353, 383, 386–87, 390, 410; as wisdom, 319–23, 380

money, 433, 441, 483–87

moon, 76, 153, 155, 172–78, 185

motion, *see* movement

movement, 8, 27–29, 86–87, 104, 109–10, 121–23, 128, 134–48, 153–80, 186–87, 242; circular, 91, 147, 153, 160–61, 164, 167–68; continuous, 94; division of, 123–24, 127–30, 163; local, 96, 115, 132, 143, 160, 164, 274–75, 393; natural, 85, 153, 158, 164, 180, 183–84, 186; *per accidens*, 124–28, 142; perpetuity of, 94, 142, 146, 148, 163, 203; of the soul, 242–45

natura difformationis, 175

nature, 1, 3, 5, 174–75, 189–90, 346–47, 442–43; acts for an end, 96, 106, 108, 276; art imitates nature, 104, 108; does nothing in vain, 175, 189, 276, 326, 417; necessity in, 63; order in, 95, 251; principles of, 101, 178

negation, 23, 33–36, 41–45, 54–57, 337–38

nonbeing, 99–100, 102–3, 110, 136, 197–99, 298, 336, 338–39, 343–44, 385

now, the, 80, 121–23, 127–29, 138, 275, 304

number(s), 101, 110–16, 119, 127, 143–44, 183, 241, 243–45, 324–25, 334, 350–51, 363, 368, 375–76, 385, 393, 399; principle of, 183, 334, 337, 347, 378

odor, 256–58, 288, 291, 293–95

oligarchy, 458, 495–96, 508–9

one, the, 374–79

opinion, 427, 447; and knowledge, 74–75

order: in nature, 251; as task of the intellect, 408

pain, 431–32, 452–54, 464–65

participation, 31, 78, 103, 134, 332, 397, 419, 459

passion(s), 134, 240, 244, 270–71, 411, 421–23, 426, 429, 440, 442, 449, 450–52, 465, 469–70; as accident, 29, 64, 67, 101, 110, 112, 124, 133–34, 182, 182, 192, 199–200; of being, 338, 343

past, the, 43–44, 50, 55, 121–22, 270, 301, 304, 307–8

phantasm(s), 264–67, 272–73, 302–306, 326, 468

philosophy of nature, 5, 10, 58, 75, 86, 88–90, 95–97, 107, 149–50, 152, 311, 322, 324, 379, 383, 388, 407, 411

place, 91–93, 115–21; natural, 115, 118–19, 140, 155, 164, 169, 180, 210, 212, 222–24; proper, 115, 117, 118, 130, 223, 386

planet(s), 69, 142, 147, 154–55, 163, 169–79, 185–87, 215, 217, 232, 243, 255, 276, 393–95

Platonist(s), 2, 5, 103–4, 111–12, 132, 135, 137, 161, 166, 186, 200, 242, 244, 266, 276, 292, 328, 333, 341, 348, 356, 359, 363, 365, 367, 369, 376, 379, 381, 388, 411, 453, 462, 465, 478

pleasure, 106, 134, 243, 251, 258, 271, 274, 391–92, 411, 415, 420, 423, 431–33, 446, 450–56, 460–61, 464–68

polity, forms of, 458–59

praise, 418, 424–25

privation, 29, 33, 55, 86, 91, 102–3, 115, 125, 127, 148, 167, 178, 198, 271, 293, 332, 337–39, 345, 349, 351, 357–58, 360, 370, 376–79, 382–84, 388–89, 398

private property, 491–92, 495

providence, 2, 4, 50, 58, 106–7, 149, 174, 190, 354–55, 463, 469

prudence, 75, 283, 301, 304, 408, 422, 445–48, 450, 452, 502, 506–7

punishment, 438, 469–70, 474

Pythagoreans, 110–12, 119, 153, 168, 173–74, 179, 183, 215–16, 240, 244, 295, 324, 333, 356, 376, 388, 393, 412, 441

quality, 124, 128, 133–34, 197, 289, 350, 357, 376–77, 385–86

quantity, 99, 104, 112, 114–15, 124, 133, 165, 197, 199, 201–3, 337, 347, 349–50, 357, 378, 382, 385, 399

regime(s), 458, 483, 487–90, 495–96, 499, 503–9

revelation, 11, 148, 406

secundum intentionem Aristotelis, 9–10, 94, 150

sense perception, 60, 83, 233, 244, 256, 260, 263–64, 276, 279, 375

shame, 439

slavery, 474, 479–83, 509

sorrow, 417, 420–21, 430, 432, 461, 463

soul, 83–84, 134, 154–55, 158, 168, 173, 177–78, 182, 188–89, 233–285, 296, 299–300, 363, 392, 415, 415–19, 421, 429, 431, 444, 462, 465, 467–68, 481; concupiscible, 273–75, 283, 391, 421, 479; definition of the, 240, 245, 248–51; human, 105, 313, 389, 449; immortality of the, 2, 4, 233–34; intellectual, 173, 181, 189, 250; irascible, 273–75, 282–83, 421, 431, 479; rational, 5, 168, 177, 354, 370, 388, 415, 444–45; sensitive, 173, 245, 250–51, 300; vegetative, 245–46, 249–53, 273–76, 419

sphere(s), 117–18, 153–54, 165–66, 168–69, 171–81, 207–10, 212, 229, 243, 269, 276, 392–96

stars, 153–57, 171–79, 181, 187–89, 208–09, 211–17, 263, 393–95

substance(s), 8, 27–28, 30, 64, 76, 91, 94, 102–4, 112, 114, 124, 147, 155, 181–83, 194–99, 243–45, 248, 317–19, 322, 328–38, 346–48, 355–59, 362–69, 372, 374, 376, 378, 381, 387–91, 412; eternal, 390–91; immaterial, 239, 267, 271–72, 358, 363, 395; immovable, 388, 390; natural, 181, 362, 367; separate, 71, 161, 163, 165–66, 168, 174–75, 178, 189, 263, 266, 269, 282, 317–20, 326, 365, 389–90, 394, 399, 416, 418, 427, 446, 449, 457, 467, 478; spiritual, 132, 147; vs. accidents, 99–100, 203, 349–50, 389

sun, 109, 155, 169, 171, 175–78, 185, 209–10, 213–18, 222–29, 263, 288, 291–92, 326–27, 347, 359, 365, 391, 394–95

supposition, 71, 77–78, 95–97

syllogism, 62–64, 70–71, 73–78, 82, 309–10, 340, 445

temperament, 429, 451–52, 470

temperance, 431–32, 451, 489, 493, 495, 506

time, 27–29, 50, 121–23, 126–31, 135, 137–40, 144–47; as measure, 86; vs. the infinite, 113

touch, 110, 173, 193, 249–62, 276–77, 287–95, 431–32, 450–51

transparent, the, 255–56, 288–89, 298; as *diaphanum*, 174, 255

truth, 4–5, 9–10, 12–13, 22, 23, 25–26, 32, 40, 45–46, 52–53, 63, 65, 75–76, 91, 101, 270, 325–28, 341–43, 348, 355, 373–74, 381–83, 411, 445; contemplation of, 453, 468; as *veritas rerum*, 166, 198, 366

truthfulness, 438–39

tyranny, 458, 488, 496, 503, 508

unity, 43, 49, 54, 73, 82, 333, 337–39, 369, 490–91, 493; of being, 365, 376; of an effect, 82; of the first mover, 94, 146; of human nature, 413; of a motion, 125; of a science, 7; of the world, 149, 164–65, 172

universals, 38–9, 44, 60, 65–66, 329–31, 364–67, 380, 390

vapor, 209–10, 213, 215, 218, 220, 223, 226–27, 294

virginity, 420, 449

virtue, 78, 133–34, 177, 350, 400–401, 407–08, 415–24, 428–72; definition of, 421–22; intellectual, 420, 445–48

vision, 173, 215, 217, 258, 260, 284–87, 290, 299–301; of God, 413, 419, 471

voice, 257

void, 116, 119–121, 156, 166, 184

weakness of the will, *see* incontinence

wealth, 433–34, 487, 496–97, 504, 507–8

will, 426–30; free, 16, 19, 51, 57; God's, 50–51, 169

wind, 210, 218, 226–32

wisdom, 75, 84, 446

world, oneness of the, 165

Reading Aristotle with Thomas Aquinas: His Commentaries on Aristotle's Major Works was designed in Arno by Kachergis Book Design of Pittsboro, North Carolina. It was printed on 55-pound Maple Antique Cream and bound by Maple Press of York, Pennsylvania.